MW00334699

19th EDITION

Law *for* Business

John D. Ashcroft, J.D., Distinguished Professor,
Regent University, Member of the Missouri and District of Columbia Bars

Katherine M. Ashcroft, J.D.,
Member of the Missouri Bar

Martha A. Patterson, J.D., Member of the Missouri,
Kansas, and Texas Bars

2493

CENGAGE
Learning·

Australia · Brazil · Mexico · Singapore · United Kingdom · United States

CENGAGE
Learning®

Law for Business, 19e
John D. Ashcroft,
Katherine M. Ashcroft,
and Martha A. Patterson

Vice President, General Manager, Social
Science & Qualitative Business: Erin Joyner
Product Director: Michael Worls
Senior Product Manager: Vicky True-Baker
Content Developer: Sarah Blasco
Product Assistant: Ryan McAndrews
Marketing Director: Kristen Hurd
Marketing Manager: Katie Jergens
Marketing Coordinator: Christopher Walz
Production Management, and Composition:
Lumina Datamatics Inc.
IP Analyst: Jennifer Nonenmacher
IP Project Manager: Betsy Hathaway
Manufacturing Planner: Kevin Kluck
Art Director: Michelle Kunkler
Cover and Internal Designer: Jennifer Wahi
Cover Image(s): © Nigel Sandor/Illustration
Works/Corbis

Library of Congress Control Number: 2015954156

ISBN: 978-1-305-65492-1

Cengage Learning
20 Channel Center Street
Boston, MA 02210
USA

Unless otherwise noted all items © Cengage Learning

Cengage Learning is a leading provider of customized learning solutions with employees residing in nearly 40 different countries and sales in more than 125 countries around the world. Find your local representative at www.**cengage.com**

Cengage Learning products are represented in Canada by Nelson Education, Ltd.

To learn more about Cengage Learning Solutions, visit www.**cengage.com**

Purchase any of our products at your local college store or at our preferred online store www.**cengagebrain.com**

Printed at CLDPC, USA, 08-22

Brief Contents

PART 1 The Legal System and the Legal Environment of Business   1

1 Introduction to Law 2
2 Courts and Court Procedure 11
3 Business Torts and Crimes 21
4 Government Regulation of Business 38

PART 2 Contracts   47

5 Nature and Classes of Contracts 48
6 Offer and Acceptance 57
7 Capacity to Contract 68
8 Consideration 77
9 Defective Agreements 86
10 Illegal Agreements 99
11 Written Contracts 110
12 Third Parties and Contracts 120
13 Termination of Contracts 131

Part 2 Summary Cases   145

PART 3 Personal Property   149

14 Nature of Personal Property 150
15 Special Bailments 163

Part 3 Summary Cases   178

PART 4 Sales   181

16 Sales of Personal Property 182
17 Formalities of a Sale 190
18 Transfer of Title and Risk in Sales Contracts 198
19 Warranties, Product Liability, and Consumer Protection 212

Part 4 Summary Cases   233

PART 5 Negotiable Instruments   237

20 Nature of Negotiable Instruments 238
21 Essentials of Negotiability 248
22 Promissory Notes and Drafts 257

23 Negotiation and Discharge 271
24 Liabilities and Defenses Specific to Negotiable Instruments 279

Part 5 Summary Cases   295

PART 6 Agency and Employment   299

25 Nature and Creation of an Agency 300
26 Operation and Termination of an Agency 311
27 Employer and Employee Relations 322
28 Employees' Rights 334

Part 6 Summary Cases   353

PART 7 Business Organization   357

29 Introduction to Business Organization 358
30 Creation and Operation of a Partnership 370
31 Dissolution of a Partnership 383
32 Nature of a Corporation 392
33 Ownership of a Corporation 401
34 Management and Dissolution of a Corporation 412

Part 7 Summary Cases   425

PART 8 Risk-Bearing Devices   429

35 Principles of Insurance 430
36 Types of Insurance 440
37 Security Devices 455
38 Bankruptcy 467

Part 8 Summary Cases   477

PART 9 Real Property   481

39 Nature of Real Property 482
40 Transfer of Real Property 492
41 Real Estate Mortgages 501
42 Landlord and Tenant 512
43 Wills, Inheritances, and Trusts 525

Part 9 Summary Cases   541

Contents

Preface   viii

PART 1
The Legal System and the Legal Environment of Business   1

CHAPTER 1: **Introduction to Law   2**
Objectives of Law 3 • Roots of Our Legal System 3 • The Common Law 3 • Equity 3 • Sources of Law 4 • Civil Versus Criminal Law 6 • Ethics 8

CHAPTER 2: **Courts and Court Procedure   11**
Function of the Courts 11 • Jurisdiction of Courts 12 • Classification of Courts 13 • Court Officers 17 • Procedure in Courts of Record 18 • Procedure in Small Claims Court 20

CHAPTER 3: **Business Torts and Crimes   21**
Torts 21 • Business Crimes 27

CHAPTER 4: **Government Regulation of Business   38**
Purpose of Regulation 39 • Administrative Agencies 39 • Antitrust 41 • Environmental Protection 43

PART 2
Contracts   47

CHAPTER 5: **Nature and Classes of Contracts   48**
Requirements for a Contract 49 • Contracts Contrasted with Agreements 49 • Classification of Contracts 49

CHAPTER 6: **Offer and Acceptance   57**
Requirements of a Valid Offer 57 • Invitations to Make Offers 60 • Duration of the Offer 61 • The Acceptance 63 • Counteroffers 64 • Inquiries Not Constituting Rejection 64 • Manner of Acceptance 65

CHAPTER 7: **Capacity to Contract   68**
Minors 69 • Mentally Incompetent People 73 • Intoxicated People 74 • Convicts 74

CHAPTER 8: **Consideration   77**
Nature of Consideration 77 • Adequacy of Consideration 78 • Exceptions to Requirement of Consideration 82

CHAPTER 9: **Defective Agreements   86**
Mistakes 86 • Mistakes That Invalidate Contracts 87 • Mistakes That Do Not Invalidate Contracts 89 • Fraud 90 • Duress 93 • Undue Influence 94 • Remedies for Breach of Contract Because of Fraud, Duress, or Undue Influence 95

CHAPTER 10: **Illegal Agreements   99**
Contracts Prohibited by Statute 101 • Contracts Contrary to Public Policy 106

CHAPTER 11: **Written Contracts   110**
Reasons for Written Contracts 110 • Statute of Frauds 111 • Note or Memorandum 115 • Other Written Contracts 116 • Parol Evidence Rule 116

CHAPTER 12: **Third Parties and Contracts   120**
Involving a Third Party 120 • Technicalities of an Assignment 124 • Joint, Several, and Joint and Several Contracts 127

CHAPTER 13: **Termination of Contracts   131**
Methods by Which Contracts Are Terminated 131 • Remedies for Breach of Contract 138 • Malpractice 141

Part 2 Summary Cases   145

PART 3
Personal Property   149

CHAPTER 14: **Nature of Personal Property   150**
Personal Property 150 • Methods of Acquiring Personal Property 151 • Bailments 156 • The Bailment Agreement 156 • Delivery and Acceptance 156 • Return of the Bailed Property 157 • Types of Bailments 157 • Conversion of Bailed Property by the Bailee 160

CHAPTER 15: **Special Bailments 163**
Carriers 163 • Liability of Common Carriers of Goods
165 • Hotelkeepers 171

Part 3 Summary Cases   178

PART 4
Sales   181

CHAPTER 16: **Sales of Personal Property 182**
Property Subject to Sale 182 • Sales and Contracts
to Sell 183 • Sales of Goods and Contracts
for Services 184 • Price 184 • Existing Goods
185 • Future Goods 185 • Bill of Sale 186 •
Illegal Sales 187 • International Sales Contracts 187

CHAPTER 17: **Formalities of a Sale 190**
Multiple Purchases and the Statute of Frauds 191
• When Proof of Oral Contract Is Permitted 191 •
Nature of the Writing Required 194

CHAPTER 18: **Transfer of Title and Risk in Sales
Contracts 198**
Potential Problems in Sales Transactions 199 •
Classification of Sales Transactions 200 • Ownership,
Insurable Interests, and Risk of Loss in Particular
Transactions 200 • Damage to, or Destruction of,
Goods 203 • Sales on Approval and with Right
to Return 205 • Special Rules on Transfer of
Title 206

CHAPTER 19: **Warranties, Product Liability, and
Consumer Protection 212**
Express Warranties 212 • Implied Warranties 214
• Full or Limited Warranties 214 • Warranties of All
Sellers 214 • Additional Warranties of Merchant 217
• Warranties in Particular Sales 218 • Exclusion and
Surrender of Warranties 219 • Product Liability 221
• Identity of Parties 222 • Nature and Cause of
Harm 223 • Consumer Protection 224

Part 4 Summary Cases 233

PART 5
Negotiable Instruments   237

CHAPTER 20: **Nature of Negotiable Instruments 238**
History and Development 238 • Negotiation 239 •
Order Paper and Bearer Paper 239 • Classification
of Commercial Paper 240 • Parties to Negotiable

Instruments 241 • Negotiation and Assignment
243 • Credit and Collection 244 • Electronic
Fund Transfers 244

CHAPTER 21: **Essentials of Negotiability 248**
Requirements 248 • Issue and Delivery 253 •
Delivery of an Incomplete Instrument 254 • Date and
Place 254

CHAPTER 22: **Promissory Notes and Drafts 257**
Notes 257 • Drafts 260 • Checks 262

CHAPTER 23: **Negotiation and Discharge 271**
Place of Indorsement 272 • Multiple Payees 273
• Kinds of Indorsements 274 • Liability of Indorser
276 • Obligation of Negotiator of Bearer Paper 276
• Discharge of the Obligation 277

CHAPTER 24: **Liabilities and Defenses Specific to
Negotiable Instruments 279**
Liability for the Face of the Paper 280 • Liability for
Warranties 283 • Liability of Agents 283 • Holders
in Due Course 284 • Holder Through a Holder in Due
Course 285 • Holders of Consumer Paper 286
• Defenses 287 • Miscellaneous Matters 291

Part 5 Summary Cases   295

PART 6
Agency and Employment   299

CHAPTER 25: **Nature and Creation of an Agency 300**
Importance of Agency 301 • What Powers May Be
Delegated to an Agent? 301 • Who May Appoint an
Agent? 301 • Who May Act as an Agent? 302 •
Classification of Agents 302 • Additional Types of Agents
303 • Extent of Authority 304 • Creation of an Agency
306 • Other Employment Relationships 307

CHAPTER 26: **Operation and Termination of an
Agency 311**
Agent's Duties to Principal 312 • Principal's Duties
to Agent 314 • Agent's Liabilities to Third Parties
315 • Principal's Duties and Liabilities to Third Parties
316 • Termination of an Agency by Acts of the Parties
316 • Termination by Operation of Law 318 •
Notice of Termination 319

CHAPTER 27: **Employer and Employee Relations 322**
Creation of Employer and Employee Relationship
323 • Duties and Liabilities of the Employer 324

- Common Law Defenses of the Employer 325
- Statutory Modification of Common Law 326 •
Liabilities of the Employer to Third Parties 327 •
Employee's Duties to the Employer 328 • Federal
Social Security Act 329 • Patient Protection and
Affordable Care Act 331

CHAPTER 28: **Employees' Rights 334**
Union Representation 335 • Discrimination 336 •
Testing 343 • Protections 346 • Other Sources of
Rights 349

Part 6 Summary Cases 353

PART 7
Business Organization 357

CHAPTER 29: **Introduction to Business
Organization 358**
Sole Proprietorship 359 • Partnership 361

CHAPTER 30: **Creation and Operation of a
Partnership 370**
Partnership Agreements 370 • Partnership Firm
Name 372 • Partner's Interest in Partnership Property
373 • Duties of Partners 373 • Rights of Partners
375 • Liabilities of Partners 377 • Nature of
Partnership Liabilities 378 • Authority of a Partner
379 • Sharing of Profits and Losses 380

CHAPTER 31: **Dissolution of a Partnership 383**
Dissolution by Acts of the Parties 384 • Dissolution
by Court Decree 385 • Dissolution by Operation of
Law 387 • Effects of Dissolution 388 • Notice of
Dissolution 388 • Distribution of Assets 389

CHAPTER 32: **Nature of a Corporation 392**
Classification by Purpose 392 • Classification
by State of Incorporation 394 • Formation of a
Corporation 394 • Liability on Promoter's Contracts
and Expenses 395 • Issuance of Stock 395
• Articles of Incorporation 396 • Powers of a
Corporation 397 • *Ultra Vires* Contracts 398

CHAPTER 33: **Ownership of a Corporation 401**
Ownership 402 • Stock Certificate 402 • Transfer
of Stock 402 • Classes of Stock 403 • Kinds of
Stock 405 • Stock Options 406 • Dividends 406
• Laws Regulating Stock Sales 407

CHAPTER 34: **Management and Dissolution of a
Corporation 412**
Stockholders' Meetings 413 • Rights of Stockholders
417 • Directors 418 • Officers 418 • Liabilities
of Directors and Officers 419 • Corporate
Combinations 421 • Dissolution 421

Part 7 Summary Cases 425

PART 8
Risk-Bearing Devices 429

CHAPTER 35: **Principles of Insurance 430**
Terms Used in Insurance 431 • Types of Insurance
Companies 432 • Who May Be Insured 432 •
Some Legal Aspects of the Insurance Contract 434

CHAPTER 36: **Types of Insurance 440**
Life Insurance 440 • Property Insurance 444 •
Description of the Property 446 • Coinsurance 446
• Repairs and Replacements 447 • Defense and
Notice of Lawsuits 447 • Automobile Insurance 448

CHAPTER 37: **Security Devices 455**
Guaranty and Suretyship 455 • Secured Credit Sales
460 • Effect of Default 463

CHAPTER 38: **Bankruptcy 467**
Who Can File a Petition of Bankruptcy? 468 • Kinds
of Debtors 468 • Required Counseling 469 •
Procedure in a Chapter 7 Case 469 • Nonliquidation
Plans 469 • Eligibility Restrictions for Chapter 7 470
• Exempt Property 471 • Included Property 471
• Debtor's Duties during Bankruptcy 472 • Proof
of Claims 472 • Reclamations 472 • Types of
Claims 472 • Priority of Claims 473 • Discharge
of Indebtedness 473 • Debts Not Discharged 474

Part 8 Summary Cases 477

PART 9
Real Property 481

CHAPTER 39: **Nature of Real Property 482**
Distinguishing Real Property 482 • Multiple
Ownership 484 • Estates in Property 487 • Other
Interests in Real Property 488 • Acquiring Real
Property 489

CHAPTER 40: **Transfer of Real Property** 492
Deeds 492 • Provisions in a Deed 495 • Delivery
497 • Recording 498 • Abstract of Title 498 •
Title Insurance 498

CHAPTER 41: **Real Estate Mortgages** 501
The Mortgage Contract 502 • Recording 503
• Duties of the Mortgagor 504 • Rights of the
Mortgagor 505 • Foreclosure 507 • Assignment
of the Mortgage 508 • Deed of Trust 508 •
Mortgage Insurance 509

CHAPTER 42: **Landlord and Tenant** 512
The Lease 513 • Types of Tenancies 515 •
Rights of the Tenant 516 • Duties of the Tenant
518 • Rights of the Landlord 519 • Duties of the
Landlord 519 • Termination of the Lease 521 •
Improvements 523 • Discrimination 523

CHAPTER 43: **Wills, Inheritances, and Trusts** 525
Limitations on Disposition of Property 526 • Terms
Common to Wills 527 • Distinguishing Characteristics
of a Will 527 • Formalities 527 • Special Types
of Wills 528 • The Wording of a Will 529 •
Codicils 529 • Revocation 530 • Abatement and
Ademption 531 • Probate of a Will 532 • When
Administration Is Unnecessary 533 • Title by Descent
533 • *Per Capita* and *Per Stirpes* Distribution 533 •
Administrators 534 • Trusts 535

Part 9 Summary Cases   541

Glossary   543

Index   555

Preface

WHY STUDY BUSINESS LAW?

Newspapers, magazines, television, radio—and even our computers—constantly relate business information to us. Behind the scenes of business activity—from startups of new businesses to corporate mergers, marketing, advertising, technology, and employment—laws governing business play a vital role. The study of business law is necessary to provide students with an overview of the law of commercial transactions and other business legal issues. *Law for Business*, nineteenth edition, focuses on these laws to prepare students to conduct business in our dynamic world marketplace.

PURPOSE OF THE TEXT

Law for Business, nineteenth edition, is a practical approach to law that emphasizes current, relevant topics involving business transactions and issues, such as contracts, property, employer–employee relations, and insurance. The basic concepts of business law are covered without the excessive theory that often makes law seem incomprehensible. Practical coverage of the law pertaining to business, without the detailed treatment found in other law school material, is the hallmark of this text. The substantial breadth of this text, complete with examples and cases, is an effective introduction to a variety of legal topics.

TEXT FEATURES

Integrated Learning Objectives. Each chapter begins with learning objectives that outline what the students will accomplish after reading the chapter. Margin icons indicate where learning objectives are first discussed in the text. Each objective is briefly restated as reinforcement, so students need not refer to the beginning of each chapter. These learning objective icons create a natural outline to help students easily comprehend the information.

Actual U.S. Court Cases with Citations. This book contains no make-believe cases. Every case example, problem, and summary is an actual U.S. court case, transferring theory into reality. These exciting actual cases help students relate to the subject as they learn about real-world legal situations that can occur in business. Case citations are included in the text for each case example, to further clarify these resources and inspire additional research and reading.

Ethical Points. In order to give greater focus to ethical considerations in various business situations, the text contains ethical point questions and comments interspersed in the margins. These questions highlight pertinent ethical issues, show the relationships between law and ethics, and serve as a basis for class discussion.

Ethics in Practice. The Ethics in Practice features appear at the end of each Part, just before the Part Summary Cases. Ethics in Practice poses a hypothetical business situation and asks students to consider the ethical implications. In conjunction with the Ethical Points scattered throughout the chapters, the Ethics in Practice feature reinforces the importance of ethical responsibility in today's climate of corporate scandal and recrimination.

Enhanced Content and Other Important Features. In the nineteenth edition, the format of the previous edition has been largely retained, but of course, the content has been updated as needed throughout. In response to high-profile instances of computer hacking and growing privacy concerns, this edition includes an expansive discussion on privacy and data security laws applicable to businesses' collecting and storing customers' personal information. This topic is of particular importance given the online presence most businesses have. The nineteenth edition also includes an expanded discussion on the Office of Foreign Assets Control (OFAC), a powerful federal agency that enforces economic and trade sanctions imposed by the United States. OFAC regulations are especially significant to businesses operating in the global market. This edition has been shortened by two chapters in response to feedback from faculty and to better accommodate their use of the text. The part on Negotiable Instruments has combined two smaller chapters so that defenses are now included in Chapter 24 Liabilities and Defenses Specific to Negotiable Instruments. Important materials from the previous stand-alone chapter on labor legislation have been integrated and combined with material in the other chapters within the Agency and Employment part.

In addition, this edition contains many new cases, some of which are:

- *Michigan v. Bay Mills Indian Community,* 134 S.Ct. 2024 (U.S.)
- *Macy's Inc. v. Martha Stewart Living Omnimedia, Inc.,* 127 A.D.3d 48 (N.Y.A.D.)
- *U.S. v. Steele,* 595 Fed.Appx. 208 (4th Cir.)
- *Steinhausen v. Home Services of Nebraska, Inc.,* 289 Neb. 927 (Neb.)
- *SEC v. E-Smart Technologies, Inc.,* 2104 WL6612422 (D.D.C.)
- *Nichols v. Zurich American Ins. Co.,* 423 S.W.3d 698 (Ky.)

Ample Questions and Cases. The end-of-chapter materials include questions and case problems. This gives the teacher and the student the opportunity to check how well students understand the material.

Key Terms and Definitions. Key terms and their definitions, critical to students' understanding of business law, are printed in the margins for easy identification and mastery. The terms are also compiled into a glossary at the end of the text.

Improved Readability. In *Law for Business*, special attention has been given to improving the readability of the text and cases by using such techniques as shortened sentences, active voice, and information presented in lists rather than in paragraph form.

Short Chapters. Long chapters tend to dilute the critical points and confuse the reader. *Law for Business* is set up in short, easy-to-understand chapters so that critical points stand out.

Chapter Opening Preview Case and Preview Case Revisited. After two introductory chapters, each chapter begins with a Preview Case segment to involve students in the issues that will be discussed in the chapter. Each Preview Case ends with a question that is answered by the court's decision in the Preview Case Revisited.

DIGITAL COMPONENTS

MindTap. New for *Law for Business*, nineteenth edition, MindTap is a personalized teaching experience with relevant assignments that guide students to analyze, apply, and improve thinking, allowing you to measure skills and outcomes with ease. Personalized teaching becomes yours through a pre-built Learning Path designed with key student objectives and your syllabus in mind. The customizable online course allows you to control what students see and when they see it. Relevant readings, multimedia, and activities within the learning path intuitively guide students up the levels of learning to (1) Prepare, (2) Engage, (3) Apply and (4) Analyze business law content. These activities are organized in a logical progression to help elevate learning, promote critical thinking skills and produce better outcomes. Analytics and reports provide a snapshot of class progress, time in course, engagement and completion rates.

Instructors can personalize the experience by customizing authoritative Cengage Learning content and learning tools. MindTap offers instructors the ability to add their own content in the Learning Path with apps that integrate into the MindTap framework seamlessly with Learning Management Systems (LMS).

Instructor's Manual. The Instructor's Manual, written by the authors, acts as a guide to the text and course, providing teaching suggestions, lesson outlines, explanations, and citations for the example cases, as well as answers to the problems contained in the text. It also adds a suggestion for group projects at the beginning of each part.

Test Bank. This supplement provides more than 700 test questions. Each chapter includes true/false questions, multiple-choice questions, and a short essay question, giving the instructor additional assignments and questions for student testing. The test bank is available through Cognero.

Cengage Learning Testing Powered by Cognero is a flexible, online system that allows you to:

- author, edit, and manage test bank content from multiple Cengage Learning solutions
- create multiple test versions in an instant
- deliver tests from your LMS, your classroom or wherever you want

PowerPoint Presentation Slides. A PowerPoint presentation package provides enhanced lecture materials for the instructor, as well as study aids for students.

ACKNOWLEDGMENTS

We would like to thank the following reviewers who helped with the revision of this and other editions of the text, as well as the many reviewers whose assistance was invaluable throughout numerous past editions. It is your suggestions and comments that have helped make this text what it is today.

Kristel Baranko, Albany Technical College; Harry Cooper, Columbia College; Brenda Cornelius, University of Arkansas Community College; Regina Davenport, Pearl River Community College; Paul Howe, Caldwell Community College;

Denise Lefort, Arapahoe Community College; Darlene Ratte, Kennebec Valley College; and Connie Strain, Arapahoe Community College.

John D. Ashcroft
Katherine M. Ashcroft
Martha A. Patterson

ABOUT THE AUTHORS

John Ashcroft served as the seventy-ninth attorney general of the United States from February 2001 to February 2005. He served in the United States Senate from 1995 to 2001, and previously served as governor of Missouri for two terms. In addition he served as state auditor of Missouri and eight years as attorney general of Missouri.

Fortune magazine rated Ashcroft one of the top ten education governors. In the Senate, he took a leading role on key issues such as welfare reform, juvenile crime, and reform of the civil justice system, while authoring significant changes to federal law. He served on the Judiciary, the Commerce, Science, and Transportation, and the Foreign Relations Committees and was also the chairman of subcommittees on the Constitution, consumer affairs, and Africa, respectively.

Ashcroft, widely recognized for his innovative use of technology and the Internet, has taught students in Missouri and across the country about using the Internet and online information as a tool of citizenship.

Prior to entering public service, Ashcroft taught business law at what is now Missouri State University in Springfield. He graduated with honors from Yale University and met his wife, Janet, at the Law School of the University of Chicago where they received their law degrees. They later co-authored two college textbooks together.

Ashcroft currently is distinguished professor of law and government at Regent University in Virginia Beach, Virginia. He leads a strategic corporate consulting firm and a law firm focusing on compliance issues.

Katherine Ashcroft served as in-house counsel for a private holding company, advising senior management on legal matters, including regulatory compliance, contract negotiation, and business organization.

Having graduated from the University of Missouri–Columbia with a Bachelor of Science degree in business and a Bachelor of Arts degree in international studies, Katherine Ashcroft received a master's degree in public administration from the Monterey Institute of International Studies. She earned her law degree from the Saint Louis University School of Law.

Martha Ashcroft Patterson began her legal career handling complex matters of estate planning and administration in an international law firm. She has had considerable experience in state and federal tax law matters. Small business organization; the legal issues attending the startup, financing, maintenance, and sale of companies; and advising entrepreneurs constitutes the bulk of her current practice. A graduate of Wheaton College, Wheaton, Illinois, with a mathematics major, and the University of Virginia School of Law, Patterson also serves on the board of Rescue: Freedom International, an organization dedicated to providing aftercare for survivors of human trafficking.

The Legal System and the Legal Environment of Business

1 Introduction to Law

2 Courts and Court Procedure

3 Business Torts and Crimes

4 Government Regulation of Business

The court system involves much more than just the various types of courts and the judges who preside over them. You can learn more about the entire system, its administration, and its functioning at the U.S. Courts website, www.uscourts.gov. To find federal regulations and comment on them, visit www.regulations.gov.

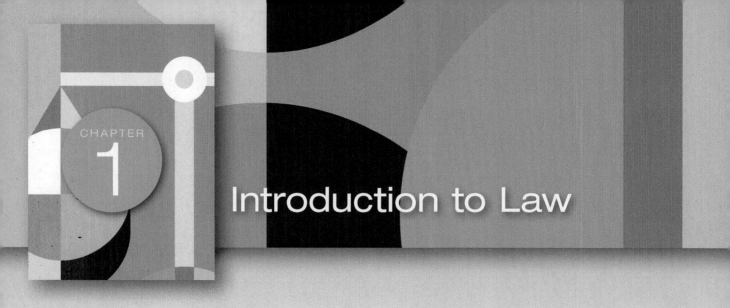

Introduction to Law

LEARNING OBJECTIVES

1. Define law.
2. Explain why we have laws.
3. List four sources of law.
4. Distinguish among crimes, torts, and ethics.

LO ①
Define law

law
governmental rule
prescribing conduct and
carrying a penalty for
violation

damages
a sum of money a
wrongdoer must pay to an
injured party

business law
rules of conduct for the
performance of business
transactions

The famed jurist William Blackstone defined law by pronouncing: "**Law** is a rule of civil conduct, commanding what is right and prohibiting what is wrong." Many rules of civil conduct commend what is right and condemn what is wrong, but rules are not necessarily laws. Only when a sovereign state issues rules prescribing what is right and what is wrong can a rule be called a law. Even then, rules are not effective unless penalties are applied when the rules are broken. Thus, a law is a rule that prescribes certain conduct and is enacted and enforced by a government.

Religious teachings, social mores, habits, and peer pressure all contribute to social control of conduct by various people, but only the rules of law apply with equal force to every member of society. A breach of some of these rules is a crime for which the penalty is a fine, a jail sentence, or both. A breach of other rules is a civil wrong for which the penalty most often is the payment of a sum of money called **damages**.

Business law is that class of laws that are concerned primarily with rules of conduct prescribed by government for the performance of business transactions. The laws governing business transactions in the United States did not come into existence overnight. Laws result from society's changing concepts of what is right and what is wrong. They may be created or modified to deal with new technology or circumstances. For example, for several centuries in England and America, an individual who owned land owned the soil and minerals below the topsoil and the air above the land "all the way to heaven." The law prohibited trespassing on a person's land or air. A telephone company that wanted to string a telephone wire through the air had to buy a right of way. When airplanes were invented, this law became a millstone around society's neck. Under this law, a transcontinental airline would have to buy a right of way through the air of every property owner in its path from New York to San Francisco. The modification of this rule by judicial decree shows how the law changes when circumstances change.

1-1 Objectives of Law

LO ②
Why we have laws

We live in a complex society. Every time we have business dealings with others—working, making a purchase, starting a business, traveling, renting an apartment, or trying to insure against loss—we have the potential for a dispute. The law seeks to establish rules so that we will be able to peacefully resolve those disputes that arise.

The law also sets the rules of conduct for many transactions so that we will know how to avoid disputes. The law thus tries to establish a stable framework to keep society operating as smoothly as possible.

1-2 Roots of Our Legal System

When European colonists settled in this country, they instituted legal systems similar to what they had in their native lands. Therefore, English, French, and Spanish colonists set up legal systems that resembled those in England, France, and Spain. The thirteen colonies that later became the United States were all English colonies, so they adopted a legal system like England's. Although additional territory was added, and other legal systems have influenced our laws, the system we have today is still based heavily on the English legal system of common law and equity.

1-3 The Common Law

Common law is a custom that came to be recognized by the courts as binding on the community and therefore law. In medieval England, there were no laws prescribing the proper rule of conduct in hundreds of situations. When a dispute came before a judge, the court prescribed a rule of its own based on the customs of the time. Over a period of several centuries, these court decisions developed into a body of law. The colonists brought this body of law from England to America. After the United States became a sovereign nation, most of these common laws, including legal maxims developed here, were either enacted as statutory laws or continued as judge-made laws. Much of our current law is based on this common law.

common law
English custom recognized
by courts as binding

COURT CASE

FACTS: William Egan was charged with the common law offense of nonfeasance (the failure to perform a required duty). State law provided that, in relation to crimes, the common law of England was in full force and effect where there was no statute on the subject. Egan said the law was vague and that there was no need for it.

OUTCOME: The court said it was clear that the legislature intended the common law of England to apply. Because the common law provided for the offense of nonfeasance, the prosecution of Egan could continue.

—State v. Egan, 287 So.2d 1 (Fla.)

1-4 Equity

Uniformity in the common law spread throughout England because judges tended to decide cases the same way other judges had decided them. But some wrongs occurred for which the law provided no remedy except for money damages.

In some cases, money was not an appropriate remedy. To obtain suitable relief, people began to petition the king for justice. The king delegated these matters to the chancellor, who did not decide the cases on the basis of recognized legal principles, but rather on the basis of *equity*—what in good conscience ought to be done. Eventually, an additional system of justice evolved that granted judicial relief when no adequate remedy at law existed. This system is called **equity**.

Courts of equity, although they sometimes recognized legal rights, also provided new types of relief. For example, instead of merely ordering a person who had breached a contract agreeing to sell real estate to pay money damages, courts would order "specific performance"—that is, require the seller to comply with the terms of the contract and sell the real estate. They also provided for preventive action to protect individuals from likely harm. In that type of case, a court with equity powers might initially issue a **restraining order**, a temporary order forbidding a certain action. Upon a complete hearing, the court might issue an **injunction**, a permanent order forbidding activities that would be detrimental to others. In most states, courts apply legal and equitable principles to each case as the facts justify, without making any formal distinction between law and equity.

equity
justice system based on fairness; provides relief other than merely money damages

restraining order
court's temporary order forbidding an action

injunction
court's permanent order forbidding an action

1-5 Sources of Law

LO ③
Sources of law

Our laws come from several sources. They include federal and state constitutions, statutes, judges' decisions, and administrative agency orders.

1-5a CONSTITUTIONS

constitution
document that contains fundamental principles of a government

A **constitution** is the document that defines the relationships of the parts of the government to each other and the relationship of the government to its citizens or subjects. The U.S. Constitution is the supreme law of the land. State constitutions, as well as all other laws, must agree with the U.S. Constitution. The Supreme Court of the United States is the final arbiter in disputes about whether a state or federal law violates the U.S. Constitution. A state supreme court is the final authority as to whether a state law violates the constitution of that state.

The section of the U.S. Constitution that is the basis for most laws regulating business is called the Commerce Clause. That section gives Congress the power to regulate commerce "among the several States."

In 1791, after the U.S. Constitution had been adopted, it was amended by the addition of the Bill of Rights. The Constitution contained no specific guarantees of individual liberty. The **Bill of Rights** consists of ten amendments specifically designed to protect the civil rights and liberties of citizens and the states. It is a part of the U.S. Constitution. Rights protected by the Bill of Rights are frequently referred to by the number of the amendment in which they can be found. Most people have heard of First Amendment rights to free speech or Fifth Amendment rights against self-incrimination.

Bill of Rights
first ten amendments to the U.S. Constitution

1-5b STATUTES

statute
law enacted by legislative bodies

ordinance
law enacted by cities

Statutes are laws enacted by legislative bodies. The federal Congress, state legislatures, and city councils, all composed of people that voters elect, comprise the three chief classes of legislative bodies in the United States. Cities and other municipalities make laws usually called **ordinances**, a specific type of statutory law. Sometimes a systematic collection of the laws, rules, or regulations of a government body or authority is called a **code**.

Sometimes, statutes enacted by one legislative body conflict with statutes enacted by another legislative body. Statutes enacted by a higher legislative body prevail over those of lower legislative bodies. Thus, a state law prevails over conflicting county or municipal legislation. A constitutional federal statute prevails over a conflicting state statute.

Unlike constitutions, which are difficult to amend and are designed to be general rather than specific, statutes may be enacted, repealed, or amended at any regular or special session of the lawmaking body. Thus, statutes normally respond more to the changing demands of the people.

In the field of business law, the most important statute is the Uniform Commercial Code (UCC).[1] The UCC regulates sales and leases of goods; negotiable instruments, such as checks; secured transactions; and particular aspects of banking and fund transfers, letters of credit, warehouse receipts, bills of lading, and investment securities. Although all fifty states have enacted at least some portions of the UCC, individual states have made changes. Therefore, variations in the UCC exist from state to state.

code
collection of laws, rules, or regulations

1-5c JUDICIAL DECISIONS

Judicial interpretation is an important element of the legal process. Because courts can interpret laws differently, the same law might have somewhat different consequences in different states. Interpretations by the highest courts have the effect of setting **precedents**. A precedent is a decided case or court decision that determines the decision in a subsequent case because the cases are so similar. Under the doctrine of *stare decisis* (stand by the decision), these precedents bind the lower courts. These interpretations may concern a situation not previously brought before the court, or the court may decide to reverse a previous decision.

precedent
court decision that determines the decision in a subsequent, similar case

stare decisis
principle that a court decision controls the decision of a similar future case

COURT CASE

FACTS: The State of Michigan agreed to allow Bay Mills Indian Community, a federally recognized Indian Tribe, to operate a casino on reservation lands within Michigan. Bay Mills later bought additional land beyond the reservation with proceeds from a congressional land trust and built a second casino on the newly purchased land. Michigan sued to stop the gaming activity of the second casino. Bay Mills claimed that under common law, it was considered a sovereign authority and thus immune from lawsuits.

OUTCOME: The court held that a previous case had established that sovereign authorities were entitled to immunity from suit, and the doctrine of *stare decisis* compelled the court to adhere to the precedent case in the interest of promoting "consistent development of legal principles." Bay Mills was immune from the suit.

—*Michigan v. Bay Mills Indian Community*,
134 S.Ct. 2024 (U.S.)

---

[1] The UCC has been adopted at least in part in every state. The UCC also has been adopted in the U.S. Virgin Islands and the District of Columbia.

Any state supreme court or the Supreme Court of the United States can reverse a decision of a lower court. For legal stability and so that we can know our rights before we undertake a transaction, courts must generally adhere to the judicial precedents set by earlier decisions. However, changing situations or practices sometimes result in the previous case law being overturned, and a new rule or practice being established.

1-5d ADMINISTRATIVE AGENCY ORDERS

administrative agency
governmental board or commission with authority to regulate matters or implement laws

Administrative agencies set up by legislative bodies carry on many governmental functions today. **Administrative agencies** are commissions or boards that have the power to regulate particular matters or implement laws. At the federal level alone, there are dozens of agencies that are involved in regulatory activity. The legislative branch of government enacts laws that prescribe the powers that administrative agencies may exercise, the principles that guide the agencies in exercising those powers, and the legal remedies available to those who want to question the legality of some administrative action.

Administrative agencies may be given practically the same power to make law as the legislature and almost the same power to decide cases as the courts. However, agencies are created by laws and have the power to enact law only if the legislature has delegated them that power.

COURT CASE

FACTS: When the Department of Citywide Administrative Services (DCAS) denied Thomas Auringer's application for a hoisting machine operator's license, Auringer asked a court to vacate and annul the denial. The law required two years of "appropriate experience" for a person who wanted such a license. The DCAS interpreted the law to mean two years of "full-time experience."

OUTCOME: The requirement of two years of full-time experience as a condition for the issuance of a hoisting machine operator's license was not rational. The court advised Auringer to resubmit his application and the DCAS to reconsider its interpretation of the law.

—*Auringer v. Department of Bldgs. of City of New York*, 805 N.Y.S.2d 344 (N.Y.)

The president of the United States, with the consent of the Senate, appoints the heads of federal administrative agencies. The governor normally appoints heads of state administrative agencies. Administrative agencies are given wide latitude in setting up rules of procedure. They issue orders and decrees that have the force of law unless set aside by the courts after being challenged. If an agency rule or decision conflicts with a statute, the statute takes precedence.

LO
Distinguish among crimes, torts, and ethics

1-6 Civil Versus Criminal Law

civil law
law dealing with enforcement or protection of private rights

Law may be classified as either civil or criminal. A person may file a lawsuit in order to enforce or protect a private right by requesting compensation for damage suffered or other action for restoration of his or her property. This action in **civil law** is concerned with private or purely personal rights.

Criminal law is that branch of the law dealing with crimes and the punishment of wrongdoers. A **crime** is an offense that tends to injure society as a whole. Therefore, an employee of the government—usually called the **prosecutor** or **district attorney**—institutes and pursues criminal actions. A criminal action differs from a civil action in other respects. The standard of proof required is greater than in a civil case. A person can be convicted of a crime only if proven guilty "beyond a reasonable doubt." If a person accused of a crime is subject to the penalty of imprisonment, the accused has a right to an attorney even if he or she cannot pay for one. In addition, the constitutional prohibition against double jeopardy means that a person can only be tried for a particular crime once. This protection is not absolute, because it allows for retrial, for example, if a conviction is overturned or if there is no decision in a first trial.

criminal law
law dealing with offenses against society

crime
offense against society

prosecutor or district attorney
government employee who brings criminal actions

Historically, crimes are usually classified, according to the nature of the punishment provided, as felonies or misdemeanors. Generally speaking, **felonies** are the more serious crimes and are usually punishable by death or by imprisonment in a penitentiary or state prison for more than one year. **Misdemeanors** are offenses of a less serious character and are punishable by a fine or imprisonment in a county or local jail. Forgery is a felony, but disorderly conduct and unauthorized entry of a dwelling are misdemeanors.

felony
a more serious crime

misdemeanor
a less serious crime

COURT CASE

FACTS: Roosevelt Terry reached into a car and stole a purse. This petty theft was normally a misdemeanor punishable by a fine and/or imprisonment in the county jail for, at most, six months. However, Terry had two prior felony convictions. In that case, state law provided that the penalty for petty theft was one year in the county jail or the state prison. The judge sentenced Terry to the state prison. The state had a "three strikes" sentencing law. Terry was sentenced to twenty-five years to life for the petty theft as if it were a third felony. Terry argued he should not get such a severe penalty.

OUTCOME: The punishment imposed determines whether an offense is a felony or a misdemeanor. Because Terry had been sentenced to state prison for the petty theft, that offense was a felony, making it his third felony under the "three strikes" law.

—*People v. Terry*, 54 Cal.Rptr.2d 769 (Cal.)

Some offenses carry penalties that can be either misdemeanor penalties or felony penalties. These offenses are called **wobblers**. In the case of wobblers, if the punishment imposed is more than a year of imprisonment, the offense is a felony. If the punishment is less than a year of imprisonment, the offense is a misdemeanor.

wobbler
an offense that can be either a felony or a misdemeanor

Because there are some offenses punished by government that are not considered serious offenses and therefore do not carry severe penalties, a number of states have established a third level of offense. These offenses are at a level below than that of misdemeanors and might be called violations or infractions. An infraction could be speeding or making an illegal U-turn while driving. In some states, **violations** or **infractions** might not even be considered criminal offenses. They would carry penalties of a fine or imprisonment, but only in a local jail for a few days. Obviously, criminal statutes vary somewhat from state to state.

violation or infraction
offense less serious than a misdemeanor

COURT CASE

FACTS: Laurie Ann Benoit was arrested as part of the "Occupy" movement and jailed with other protesters. The state charged Benoit with a criminal trespass misdemeanor. As permitted under state law, prosecutors opted to prosecute the charge as a violation, which meant that if convicted, Benoit could face a maximum fine of $1,250 and risked no incarceration. Benoit moved for a trial by jury, arguing that a violation was still considered a crime and that she was entitled to protections afforded other criminal defendants.

OUTCOME: The court held that in all criminal prosecutions, the state constitution required the defendant be entitled to a jury trial. Because the court deemed the violation was still a criminal proceeding in nature, Benoit could not be deprived of a jury trial.

—*State v. Benoit*, 311 P.3d 874 (Or.)

1-7 Ethics

This chapter has discussed the basis for laws. One of the most important ideas mentioned is that "laws are the result of society's changing concepts of what is right and what is wrong." That means laws are based on our judgment regarding what human conduct is right and therefore should be encouraged, and what conduct is wrong and therefore should be discouraged. We thus base our laws on our morals. Those principles that help a person determine the morality of conduct, its motives, and its duties are called our **ethics**.

ethics
principles that determine the morality of conduct, its motives, and its duties

1-7a BASES FOR ETHICAL JUDGMENT

Everyone has opinions on what behavior and thinking is right and what is wrong, basing these ethical judgments on personal values. We develop our values from our religious beliefs, our experience, our cultural background, and our scientific knowledge. Because people have differing backgrounds, our judgments as to what is right and wrong vary somewhat.

1-7b ETHICAL PRINCIPLES

In considering how ethics relates to the law, several principles regarding the application of ethics emerge. These principles include:

1. Seriousness of consequences
2. Consensus of the majority
3. Change in ethical standards

Seriousness of Consequences. Although law is based on what we believe to be right and wrong, our laws do not reflect everything that we believe is right or wrong. Our laws set a minimum standard for behavior. Ethics sets a higher standard of behavior.

When unethical behavior can harm others—when the matter is of serious consequence to people—laws are usually enacted to regulate that behavior. Less serious matters can be considered wrong, but laws do not address them. For example, rules of etiquette frequently reflect our ethical judgments about behavior, but they do not have serious enough consequences that we pass laws to enforce them.

Consensus of the Majority. Our laws cannot express every individual's ethical principles because individuals do not agree on what is moral. There may be no law reflecting a judgment on a particular matter, or the laws might reflect the judgment of some. For example, vegetarians and nondrinkers may not believe laws permitting the eating of meat or the consumption of alcoholic beverages are ethical. Their morality may not be reflected in law. In a democratic society such as the United States, the laws are designed to reflect the ethical view of the majority.

Change in Ethical Standards. Ethical standards change over time. Behavior once believed ethical can become unethical, and behavior previously viewed as immoral can become acceptable. Consider the matter of cigarette smoking on airplanes.

Many years ago, airline passengers could smoke no matter where they were seated. Then the law mandated smoking and nonsmoking sections on planes. Now, all commercial airlines in the United States prohibit smoking in all sections, and the federal government uses the force of law to enforce this rule.

This change in government rules reflects most people's change in the view about the harmful effects of cigarette smoking. Our ethical standards have changed, and this is reflected in the law.

1-7c BUSINESS ETHICS

Our ethical standards apply to every aspect of life. For businesspeople, this means that ethical standards help determine their business practices. In our competitive economic system, the standard that people in business have been expected to follow in determining behavior is "the bottom line." Is the behavior something that will help the business financially? When studying ethics as applied to business, we ask whether a business has obligations other than simply to make a profit or maximize "the bottom line."

Many types of businesses and professional organizations have adopted codes of ethics to guide the behavior of their members. Variety exists not only in the types of businesses that have adopted such codes, but also in the impact of the codes on business. Some codes are legally enforceable, technically making them laws, not ethical rules. Other codes are strictly voluntary and are thus truly rules of ethics.

Legally Enforceable. A number of professions have codes of ethics, usually called *codes of professional responsibility*, which when violated provide the basis for penalties against members of the profession. For example, the American Bar Association has produced a model code and model rules for ethical behavior by lawyers. Although these particular models have not been adopted by every state, each state has adopted an ethical code for lawyers. A violation of the ethical code subjects a lawyer to discipline, including suspension from practicing law or even disbarment.

Voluntary. Some businesses have adopted codes of ethics as guides for individuals employed in these businesses. Because government has not imposed the codes, they do not carry legal penalties for violation. However, employees who violate ethical codes subject themselves to discipline by their employers. The codes recognize that ethical business conduct is a higher standard than that required by law and encourage behavior that is fair, honest, and, if disclosed, not embarrassing to the individual or the business.

The need for ethical practices, particularly in business, is greater than ever. The demand for such ethical behavior is so great that we often see it reflected in new legislation. If the public is not confident that businesses will comply with their ethical responsibilities, we will undoubtedly see more and more legislation asking business to rise to ethical, rather than just the previously legal, standards. Chapter 34 discusses some requirements for ethical behavior by corporate officers.

1-7d ETHICS IN PRACTICE

The law seeks to make business behavior conform to society's standards of what is appropriate behavior by punishing those who do not live up to the standards. In reality, businesspeople find that there is a positive incentive to be ethical in business. In the long run, it is a good business practice to be ethical. Businesses find that customers are more likely to want to do business with ethical establishments.

Customers who deal with unethical businesses are much more likely to have problems with the business, causing additional time and expense.

QUESTIONS

1. What is business law?

2. What is the normal penalty for breach of a civil wrong?

3. What kind of relief were courts of equity designed to give?

4. Explain what the roots of our legal system are.

5. Why do courts generally adhere to the judicial precedents set by earlier decisions?

6. Why was the Bill of Rights enacted?

7. Explain the difference between actions in civil and criminal law.

8. What section of the Constitution is the basis for most laws governing business transactions, and what does it provide?

9. What determines whether an offense is a felony or a misdemeanor? Are there offenses less serious than misdemeanors?

10. List some guiding principles that determine how ethics relates to the enactment of laws.

Courts and Court Procedure

CHAPTER 2

LEARNING OBJECTIVES

① Explain the function of the courts.

② Explain the relationships of the various courts in our society.

③ Describe the procedure for filing a lawsuit.

④ Describe the basic procedure for a jury trial.

Each state has two distinct court systems—federal and state. Federal courts are part of the federal government headquartered in Washington, D.C. There are fifty different state court systems, each being part of a state government headquartered at its state capital. Although the federal and state court systems are largely independent of each other, they have similar functions.

2-1 Function of the Courts

LO ①
Function of courts

A court declares and applies judicial precedents, or case law, and applies laws passed by the legislative arm of government. However, this is not the whole story. Constitutions, by their very nature, must be couched in generalities. Statutes are less general than constitutions, but they could not possibly be worded to apply to every situation that may arise. Thus, the chief function of the courts is to interpret and apply the law from whatever source to a given situation. For example, the U.S. Constitution gives Congress power to regulate commerce "among the several States." This is the power to regulate interstate commerce. Under this power, Congress passes a law requiring safety devices on trains. If the law is challenged on constitutional grounds, the court must decide whether this is a regulation of interstate commerce.

Similarly, an act of Congress regulates the minimum wage for the vast majority of workers. A question may arise as to whether this applies to the wages paid in a sawmill located in a rural section of the country. The court must decide whether or not the sawmill owner engages in interstate commerce. The court's decision may become a judicial precedent that will be followed in the future unless the court changes its decision in a subsequent case.

2-2 Jurisdiction of Courts

jurisdiction
authority of a court to hear a case

The power or authority of a court to hear cases is called its **jurisdiction**. Before any court can try a case, it must be established that the court has jurisdiction over the subject matter of the case, the persons involved, and the geographic area where the events in controversy occurred.

Subject-matter jurisdiction is the authority to hear a particular type of case or relating to a specific subject matter. If a claim is made for damages as a result of an automobile accident, a probate court does not have jurisdiction over the subject matter, because a probate court deals with the distribution of deceased persons' property. The damage action would have to be brought in a court of general jurisdiction.

A court may have jurisdiction over the subject matter but not over the person. If a resident of Ohio is charged with trespassing on a neighbor's property in that state, the courts in Indiana do not have personal jurisdiction over the accused. Nor does the Ohio court system have jurisdiction over the person of the accused if the accused has not been properly served with notice of the trial.

COURT CASE

FACTS: Cheap Escape Co. published a magazine and in Summit County, Ohio, entered into contracts to sell ads in the magazine to Haddox LLC. The contracts stated that any legal action based on them "will be in the Franklin County Municipal Court or Franklin County Common Pleas." Haddox allegedly defaulted on the contracts, so Cheap Escape sued in Franklin County Municipal Court and got a judgment. Subject matter jurisdiction of municipal courts in Ohio is set by statute as "original jurisdiction within its territory." Haddox argued this meant a municipal court only had jurisdiction over events having a territorial connection to the court.

OUTCOME: The court reasoned that the logical way to read the phrase "original jurisdiction within its territory" was that a municipal court could only hear cases that had a territorial connection to it. The judgment was reversed and the case dismissed.

—*Cheap Escape Co. Inc. v. Haddox LLC*, 900 N.E.2d 601 (Ohio)

long-arm statute
law allowing a state to have jurisdiction over nonresidents

Because Americans travel so much, and because businesses frequently operate in more than just one state, laws have been enacted that in specified cases allow the courts of one state to have jurisdiction over residents of another state. These laws are called **long-arm statutes** and normally are based on some action in the state where suit is brought. The party being sued must have had minimum contacts in that state. A court may try a case and enter an enforceable judgment even against a nonresident when the minimum contacts exist. If you drive a car in another state and are involved in an accident, a long-arm statute would allow a person injured in the accident to sue you in the state where the accident occurred after you return to your home state.

2-2a VENUE

Once it is determined which court system has jurisdiction to decide a case, it must be decided at what location the case should be tried. Determining the location where a case is to be tried means determining the proper venue. Each state has trial courts throughout the state. Proper venue requires choosing the proper one of these courts. For example, if two citizens of San Diego have a controversy, proper **venue** would be in San Diego, not Sacramento. However, the right to a particular venue can be surrendered. In criminal cases, the court frequently changes venue to try to give the defendant a fairer trial.

venue
location where a case is to be tried

2-3 Classification of Courts

Courts are classified for the purpose of determining their jurisdiction. This classification can be made in a variety of ways. One classification can be made according to the governmental unit setting up the court. Under this classification system, courts are divided into (1) federal courts, (2) state courts, and (3) municipal courts.

The same courts may be classified according to the method of hearing cases. Under this system, they are classified as trial courts and appellate courts. **Trial courts** conduct the original trial of cases. **Appellate courts** review cases appealed from the decisions of lower courts. A losing party appeals to the higher court to review the lower court's decision by claiming the lower court made a mistake that caused the party to lose. Appellate courts include courts of appeals and supreme courts. Appellate courts exercise considerable authority over the courts under them. Lower courts are bound by the decisions of their appellate courts.

LO ②
Relationships of various courts

trial court
court that conducts original trial of a case

appellate court
court that reviews the decision of another court

2-3a FEDERAL COURTS

The federal courts have exclusive jurisdiction over such matters as bankruptcy, claims against the United States, and patent and copyright cases. Federal courts (see Illustration 2-1) include:

1. Special federal courts
2. Federal district courts
3. Federal courts of appeals
4. The United States Supreme Court

Special Federal Courts. The special federal courts are limited in their jurisdiction by the laws of Congress creating them. For example, the Court of International Trade hears cases involving the rates of duty on various classes of imported goods, the collection of the revenues, and similar controversies. The U.S. Court of Federal Claims hears cases involving claims against the U.S. government. The U.S. Tax Court hears only cases involving tax controversies. Bankruptcy courts decide bankruptcy cases. Most bankruptcy appeals are to a three-judge appellate panel of bankruptcy judges.

special federal court
federal trial court with limited jurisdiction

Federal District Courts. By far, the largest class of federal courts consists of the almost one hundred **federal district courts**. There is at least one district court in each state, and in some states there are as many as four. These courts are trial courts in which criminal cases involving a violation of the federal law are tried. The district courts also have jurisdiction over civil suits that: (1) are brought by the United States; (2) arise under the U.S. Constitution, federal laws, or treaties; or (3) are brought by citizens of different states—called **diversity jurisdiction**—or between citizens of one state and a foreign nation or one of its citizens in which the amount in controversy is more than $75,000.

federal district court
trial court of federal court system

diversity jurisdiction
federal jurisdiction based on parties being from different states

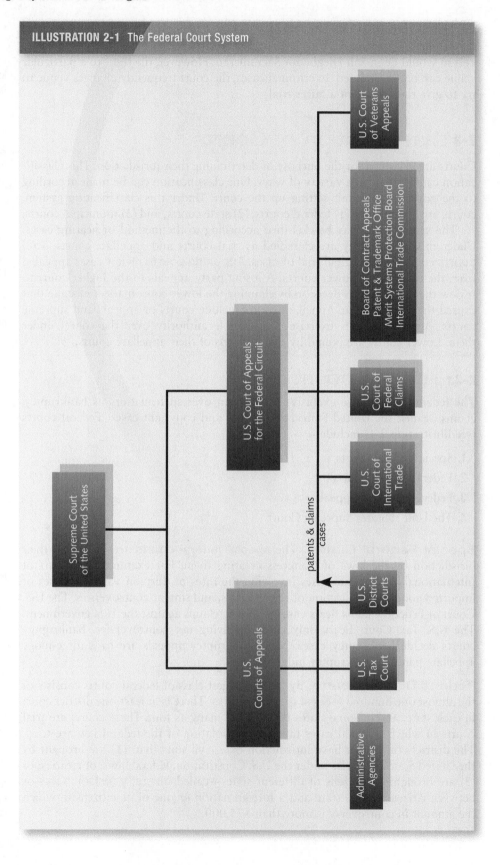

ILLUSTRATION 2-1 The Federal Court System

COURT CASE

FACTS: Acorne Productions, LLC contracted with filmmakers Zareh and Alina Tjeknavorian to produce a documentary film on the Armenian Genocide. The parties agreed that Acorne would pay the Tjeknavorians a monthly fee and provide film-making equipment. The parties also agreed to a funding limit and deadline for the project. After the Tjeknavorian's failed to meet the deadline and went over budget, Acorne filed a lawsuit in a New York state court for breach of contract and other state-law claims. The Tjeknavorians moved the case to federal court, because, they argued, the claims arose under the Copyright Act—a federal law.

OUTCOME: The federal court held that Acorne's claims did not arise out of the Copyright Act and thus the court lacked jurisdiction over the claims. The case was sent back to the state court to be decided.

—Acorne Productions, LLC v. Tjeknavorian, 33 F.Supp.3d 175 (E.D.N.Y.)

Federal Courts of Appeals. The United States is divided geographically into twelve federal judicial circuits. Each circuit has a court of appeals, which hears appeals from cases arising in its circuit. The **federal courts of appeals** hear appeals from federal district courts and from federal administrative agencies and departments. A decision of a federal court of appeals is binding on all lower courts within the jurisdiction of that circuit.

It is possible that one court of appeals could decide an issue one way and another court of appeals could decide it another way. Because the lower courts within each court of appeals' jurisdiction must follow the decision of its court of appeals, courts in different circuits might decide similar cases differently. When this occurs, there is a conflict between the circuits. The conflict lasts until one circuit changes its decision or the U.S. Supreme Court rules on the issue.

There is also another court of appeals called the Court of Appeals for the Federal Circuit. It reviews decisions of special federal courts (such as the Court of International Trade and the U.S. Court of Federal Claims), decisions of four administrative agencies, and appeals from district courts in patent and claims cases.

federal court of appeals
court that hears appeals in federal court system

United States Supreme Court. The **Supreme Court of the United States** has original jurisdiction in cases affecting ambassadors, public ministers, and consuls, and in cases in which a state is a party. It has appellate jurisdiction in cases based on the U.S. Constitution, a federal law, or a treaty.

The majority of cases heard by the U.S. Supreme Court are cases appealed from the federal courts of appeals. Under certain circumstances, a decision of a federal district court may be appealed directly to the Supreme Court. A state supreme court decision also may be reviewed by the U.S. Supreme Court if the case involves a federal constitutional question or if a federal law or treaty has been held invalid by the state court. Unlike the courts of appeals, the Supreme Court does not have to take all cases appealed. It chooses which appealed cases it will hear.

The normal way a case gets to the Supreme Court is by application for a **writ of certiorari**. The party asking for the Supreme Court review of a case asks the court to issue a writ of *certiorari*, which requires the lower court that has decided the case to produce the record of the case for the Supreme Court's review. The Court issues a writ for only a small number of requests.

Supreme Court of the United States
the highest court in the United States

writ of *certiorari*
order to produce record of a case

The U.S. Supreme Court is the highest tribunal in the land, and its decisions are binding on all other courts. Its decisions are final until the court reverses its own decision or until the effect of a given decision is changed by a constitutional amendment or an enactment by Congress. The Constitution created the Supreme Court and gave Congress the power to establish inferior courts.

2-3b STATE COURTS

State courts (see Illustration 2-2) can best be classified into the following groups:

1. Inferior courts
2. Courts of original general jurisdiction
3. Appellate courts
4. Special courts

inferior court
trial court that hears only cases involving minor offenses and disputes

Inferior Courts. Most states have **inferior courts** that hear cases involving minor criminal offenses and minor disputes between citizens. The names of inferior courts vary greatly from state to state. These courts are most frequently called district, magistrate, county, municipal, small claims, justice, or even taxi courts.

Some states have more than one of these named courts. Civil jurisdiction is limited to controversies involving a maximum amount of money, which generally varies from $1,000 to $25,000, or to a particular type of controversy. In addition, these courts may try all criminal cases involving misdemeanors. The loser in any of these courts may normally appeal to a court of original general jurisdiction.

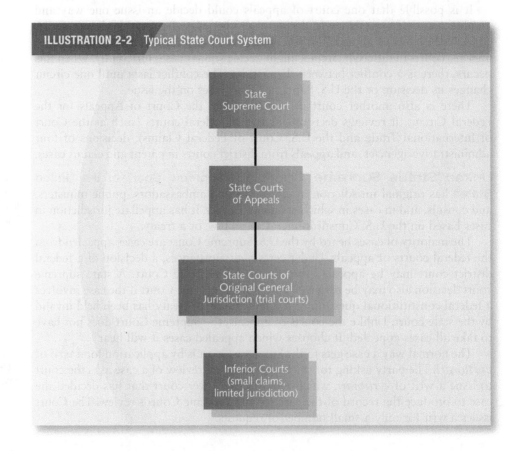

ILLUSTRATION 2-2 Typical State Court System

State Supreme Court

State Courts of Appeals

State Courts of Original General Jurisdiction (trial courts)

Inferior Courts (small claims, limited jurisdiction)

Courts of Original General Jurisdiction. The most important courts of a state for the average citizen are called courts of original general jurisdiction. These courts have broad jurisdiction over disputes between two or more parties as well as criminal offenses against the state. They are called courts of original general jurisdiction because the case is first instituted in them. On occasion, they hear appeals from inferior courts, but this does not make them true appellate bodies, because the entire case is retried at this level. Thus, such an appeal is actually treated as a case of original jurisdiction. These courts are also called trial courts because they hear witnesses, receive evidence, and try the case.

An official, permanent record is kept of the trial showing the testimony, evidence, statements of counsel and the judge, the judgment, and the findings of the court. For this reason, these courts are referred to as courts of record. The official name of such a court of original general jurisdiction varies from state to state but in almost every state it is one of the following: circuit court, district court, or superior court.[1]

Appellate Courts. All states provide for an appeal to an appellate court by the party dissatisfied with the final judgment of the trial court or any of its rulings and instructions. Most states have a system of intermediate appellate courts, usually called state courts of appeals, as well as one final appellate court. Decisions of the appellate courts bind lower courts. The state supreme court is usually the title of the highest appellate court of a state.

Special Courts. Many states have additional special courts, such as probate courts that handle wills and estates; juvenile courts that are concerned with delinquent, dependent, and neglected children; and domestic relations courts that handle divorce and child custody cases. These are not courts of general jurisdiction but of special jurisdiction. In some states, these courts are on the same level as the trial courts. When this is the case, they are properly called *trial courts* and are courts of record. In other states, they are on the same level as the inferior courts and are not courts of record.

2-4 Court Officers

The chief officer of an inferior court is the judge, justice of the peace, magistrate, trial justice, or similar officer. The executive officer is the constable or bailiff. In a state court of record, the chief officer is the judge, the executive officer is the sheriff, and the recorder is the clerk of the court. These titles are the same in the federal courts, except that the executive officer is called a marshal.

Persons educated in the profession of the law and licensed to practice law, which means they may represent others in legal matters, are known as lawyers or attorneys. They are officers of the court and are subject to punishment for a breach of duty. Lawyers ordinarily represent the parties in a civil or a criminal action, although many states permit the parties to represent themselves. The practice of presenting one's own case, however, is usually not advisable, because a disinterested person is normally better able to assess and present the case rationally.

---

court of original general jurisdiction
court of record in which case is first tried

court of record
court in which an official record of the proceedings is kept

state courts of appeals
intermediate appellate court

state supreme court
highest court in most states

probate court
court that handles estates

juvenile court
court that handles delinquent, dependent, and neglected children

domestic relations court
court that handles divorce and related cases

judge, justice of the peace, magistrate, or trial justice
chief officer of court

sheriff
court of record executive officer

marshal
executive officer of federal court

lawyer or attorney
person licensed to represent others in court

---

[1] In New York, this court is known as a supreme court, and in Ohio it is known as a court of common pleas.

2-5 Procedure in Courts of Record

LO ③
Lawsuit procedure

procedural law
law specifying how actions are filed and what trial procedure to follow

Procedural laws specify how parties are to go forward with filing civil actions and how these actions are to be tried. They are a method of enforcing rights or getting compensation for violation of rights and must be followed if the parties wish to have the case settled by a court. If they are not followed, the case can be lost, and the decision will be as final as if it was decided on the merits of the case.

COURT CASE

FACTS: Brian Guyer was convicted of sexual assault. As a result, he was required to, and did, register as a sex offender stating his place of employment. Ten years later, the registration law was amended to require sex offenders to inform the police within three days if they changed jobs. Guyer changed jobs but did not notify the police. He alleged that the amended law could not be applied retrospectively to him.

OUTCOME: The court held that the amended law was just a procedural device to make sure the information Guyer was required to give, following his conviction, was accurate. It did not impose any new substantive obligation on him. As a procedural law, it could constitutionally be applied to him.

—*State v. Guyer*, 353 S.W.3d 458 (Mo. Ct. App.)

2-5a FILING SUIT IN A CIVIL ACTION

complaint or petition
written request to a court to settle a dispute

plaintiff
person who begins a civil lawsuit

defendant
person against whom a case is filed

summons or process
notice of suit

answer or motion
response of defendant to a complaint

discovery
means of obtaining information from other party before a trial

With few exceptions, courts are powerless to settle disputes between individuals unless one of the parties so requests the court. The written request, called a **complaint** or **petition**, begins a civil suit. The individual who institutes a civil action is called the **plaintiff**, and the individual against whom action is brought is called the **defendant**. The order of events in bringing an action is generally as follows:

1. *Filing suit.* The first step in a lawsuit is the filing of the complaint or petition with the clerk of the court by the plaintiff. This petition sets forth the jurisdiction of the court, the nature of the claim, and the remedy sought.

2. *Notice of suit.* As soon as the petition is filed, the clerk issues a **summons** or, as it is sometimes called, a **process**. This gives the defendant notice of the complaint and informs the defendant of the time in which to respond.

3. *Response.* The defendant has a specified number of days available in which to file an **answer** or a **motion**. The answer admits or denies the facts alleged in the complaint. A motion is an application to the judge for an order requiring an act be done in favor of the moving party. The complaint and answer constitute the first pleadings.

4. *Discovery.* To obtain information relevant to the subject matter of the action, the parties may request unprivileged information from another party in a number of ways, called **discovery**, including:

   a. Interrogatories: Written questions to be answered in writing

   b. Depositions: Examination of a party or potential witness outside court and under oath

c. Admissions: Requests to agree that a certain fact is true or a matter of law is decided

d. Medical examination by a physician

e. Access to real and personal property

If a court issues an order compelling discovery, failure to comply can result in punishment. The party who does not comply may be found in contempt of court, or the judge may dismiss the case.

The parties may take other actions after a case has been instituted and before it goes to trial. A party may file a wide variety of motions, including a motion to dismiss the case, a motion for a judgment based solely on the pleadings, and a motion to obtain a ruling on the admissibility of certain evidence or to suppress evidence prior to trial.

5. *Fact finding.* If disagreements occur about facts of the case, a jury may be impaneled to decide these facts. If neither party requests a jury, the case may be tried before a judge alone, who would act as both judge and jury.

2-5b TRIAL PROCEDURE

A typical jury trial proceeds in the following order:

LO ④
Jury trial procedure

1. The jury is selected and sworn in.

2. The attorney for the plaintiff makes an opening statement to the jury indicating the nature of the action and what the plaintiff expects to prove. This is usually followed by the defendant's attorney's opening statement.

3. The plaintiff presents evidence in the form of testimony of witnesses and exhibits designed to prove the allegations made in the plaintiff's petition. The plaintiff has the burden of proving facts adequate to support the petition's allegations. If this burden is not met, the case can be dismissed, and the lawsuit ends. The plaintiff's evidence is followed by the defendant's evidence. The defendant tries to disprove the plaintiff's allegations. The defendant also may present evidence excusing the behavior complained of by the plaintiff.

4. The attorneys for each side summarize the evidence and argue their points in an attempt to win the jury to their version of the case.

5. The judge instructs the jury as to the points of law that govern the case. The judge has the sole power to determine the points of law, and the jury decides what weight is to be given to each point of evidence.

6. The jury adjourns to the jury room and in secret arrives at its decision, called the **verdict**. The judge may set aside this verdict if it is contrary to the law and the evidence. Unless this is done, the judge enters a judgment in accordance with the verdict.

verdict
decision of a jury

2-5c APPEALS

If either the plaintiff or the defendant is dissatisfied with the judgment and can cite an error of law by the court, an appeal generally may be taken to a higher court. The procedure by which the court learns about the case is very different when an appeal is taken than when the trial court hears a case. A complete transcript or written record of the trial court proceedings is given to the appellate court. Rather than hear testimony from witnesses, the appellate court reviews the proceedings from the transcript. The attorneys for each side file a written brief, setting forth their arguments as to why the appellate court should either affirm or reverse the judgment of the lower court. In some cases, the attorneys also make oral arguments before the appellate court. The decision of the appellate court becomes judicial precedent and is binding on lower courts. The appellate court may, however, reverse itself in a future case, although this seldom occurs.

2-6 Procedure in Small Claims Court

Filing and trying a suit in an inferior court like a small claims court is a much simpler matter than filing and trying a suit in a court of record. A form for the complaint may be obtained from the court and filled out by the plaintiff without help from a lawyer. Frequently, court employees will assist in filling out the forms. The defendant is then served with the complaint.

When the case is tried, the procedure is much more informal than in a court of record. A judge tries the case, so there is no jury. Because neither party has to be represented by an attorney, and in some courts may not be so represented, the judge asks the parties to state their positions. Witnesses and evidence may be presented, but the questioning is more informal. The judge is likely to ask questions in order to assist in ascertaining the facts. The judge then renders the verdict and judgment of the court. Normally, either party may appeal the judgment to a court of record, in which case the matter is retried there.

QUESTIONS

1. What is the chief function of the courts?
2. Over what must a court have jurisdiction before it can try a case?
3. How does a party get a case to the U.S. Supreme Court?
4. Name the court in which the following disputes would be settled:
   a. A claim for an unpaid bill of $100
   b. A dispute over the amount of income taxed owed
   c. An allegation that a lower court made a mistake
   d. A controversy among cousins regarding their share of a deceased grandparent's estate
   e. A divorce case
   f. A damage suit for $7,500
5. Must a party to a lawsuit be represented by a lawyer? Explain.
6. Why are courts of original general jurisdiction referred to as courts of record?
7. Who are the officers of
   a. An inferior court?
   b. A state court of record?
   c. A federal court?
8. Why is it important to comply with procedural laws?
9. List the ordered events that occur when a civil action is brought.
10. What is the procedure by which an appellate court learns about a case?

Business Torts and Crimes

LEARNING OBJECTIVES

① Discuss the basis for intentional and negligent tort liability.
② List and explain the generally recognized business torts.
③ Explain what business crimes are.
④ Describe what computer crimes are and the three types that affect business.

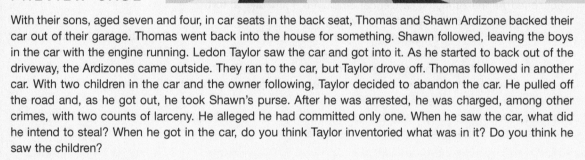

PREVIEW CASE

With their sons, aged seven and four, in car seats in the back seat, Thomas and Shawn Ardizone backed their car out of their garage. Thomas went back into the house for something. Shawn followed, leaving the boys in the car with the engine running. Ledon Taylor saw the car and got into it. As he started to back out of the driveway, the Ardizones came outside. They ran to the car, but Taylor drove off. Thomas followed in another car. With two children in the car and the owner following, Taylor decided to abandon the car. He pulled off the road and, as he got out, he took Shawn's purse. After he was arrested, he was charged, among other crimes, with two counts of larceny. He alleged he had committed only one. When he saw the car, what did he intend to steal? When he got in the car, do you think Taylor inventoried what was in it? Do you think he saw the children?

How do businesses relate to society and to other businesses? Can the activity of a business unfairly damage another business or even violate a criminal law? With some variations among the states, courts have found some activities by businesses, and some activities against businesses, to be actionable.

LO ①
Basis for tort liability

3-1 Torts

A **tort** is a private or civil wrong or injury for which there may be an action for damages. A tort may be intentional, or it may be caused by negligence. **Negligence** is the failure to exercise reasonable care toward someone. It is tort law that allows a person injured by a product to sue the manufacturer for damages. Injured persons

tort
private wrong for which damages may be recovered

negligence
failure to exercise reasonable care

tortfeasor
person whose action causes injury

themselves must sue for any injuries caused by the intentional or negligent acts of others. The person who causes the injury is called a **tortfeasor**.

3-1a INTENTIONAL TORTS

To recover for an intentional tort, the injured person must show three things:

1. An act by the defendant
2. An intention to cause the consequences of the act
3. Causation—the injury was caused by the defendant's act or something set in motion by the act

Intentional torts include such actions as assault (putting a person in fear of a wrongful touching), battery (a wrongful touching), trespass (invading someone's property), and false imprisonment (improperly confining a person). Although a business could be involved in these torts, the parties could be anyone.

COURT CASE

FACTS: Security personnel of Liz Claiborne, Inc. questioned Andria Arrington, a clerical employee, about her time sheet. She admitted in writing that she had falsified it. After being fired, Arrington sued Liz Claiborne for false imprisonment. She alleged that she "thought" the door to the office in which she had been questioned was locked. She also did not "feel" free to leave because she had been told that if she did not cooperate, the police would be called. Questioning Arrington was clearly an intentional act, so she claimed there had been an intentional tort.

OUTCOME: To find the intentional tort of false imprisonment, the court said Arrington had to prove that the Claiborne personnel intended to confine her, not just question her. She did not do this.

—*Arrington v. Liz Claiborne, Inc.*, 688 N.Y.S.2d 544 (N.Y. App. Div.)

3-1b NEGLIGENCE TORTS

To recover for a tort based on negligence, the plaintiff (the injured party) must show:

1. A duty of the tortfeasor to the injured party
2. Breach of that duty
3. That the breach was the actual and a proximate cause of the injury, and
4. Injury or damage

One common type of tort lawsuit based on negligence is one resulting from an automobile accident. The duty of a driver is to operate a vehicle in a safe and prudent manner. A breach of that duty occurs if the driver operates the vehicle in an unsafe manner. If operating the vehicle in an unsafe manner causes someone injury, the breach of the duty would be a proximate cause of the injury. Proximate cause requires that the plaintiff shows injury and that the injury was a foreseeable result of the defendant's action. Finally, the plaintiff would have to prove the amount of the damage. If more than one person's action is a proximate cause of a plaintiff's injuries, everyone whose breach of duty contributed to the plaintiff's injuries could be liable.

In some states, in order for an injured party to recover anything in a negligence action, the injured party cannot have been negligent. Negligence on the part of the injured party is called **contributory negligence**. However, other states allow injured parties to recover even when they have been partially at fault. The doctrine of **comparative negligence** allows courts to reduce damage awards to plaintiffs by the percentage of the damage attributable to the plaintiffs' negligence. For example, if a plaintiff's total damages are $100,000, and the plaintiff was 20 percent at fault, the award would be $80,000.

contributory negligence
negligence of the injured party

comparative negligence
contributory negligence that reduces but does not bar recovery

3-1c BUSINESS TORTS

The type of tort caused by a business or involving a business is a **business tort**. Businesses become involved in a tort action in several common ways.

LO ②
General business torts

business tort
tort caused by or involving a business

Product Liability. Manufacturers, dealers, suppliers, and rental companies incur potential liability in tort for injuries caused by products they have provided. Liability can be based on two theories:

1. Negligence
2. Strict liability

Negligence. The suppliers of products are potentially liable for negligence as a result of one of the following three reasons:

1. The use or condition of the product
2. A design defect
3. Failure to warn

A person injured through the use or condition of a product could sue on the basis of the manufacturer's negligence in the preparation or manufacture of the article. In that case, the plaintiff must learn how the article was made and prove negligence. Unless the plaintiff can show negligence in the design of the manufacturer's product, the general method of manufacture, or a failure to warn, it is unlikely that the plaintiff will be able to prove negligence.

Whenever a manufacturer, as a reasonable person, should foresee that a particular class of people would be injured by the product, the manufacturer is liable to an injured member of that class without regard to whether such member purchased from the manufacturer or from anyone else.

Strict Liability. Because of the difficulty of proving negligence, courts have expanded a doctrine called **strict liability**. This doctrine makes entities in the chain of manufacture of a product—manufacturer, wholesaler, or retailer—liable without proof of negligence. It applies to anyone injured because of a defect in the manufacture of a product when such defect makes the use of the product dangerous to the user or people in the vicinity of the product.

strict liability
manufacturer of product liable without proof of negligence for dangerous product

COURT CASE

FACTS: While "Great Balls of Fire" played on the jukebox, the bartender at Brother Jimmy's BBQ poured 151 proof Bacardi rum onto the bar and then lit it. Unfortunately the flame blew back into the bottle, and the burning contents shot out. Lauren Sclafani, a patron, was severely burned and sued the restaurant and Bacardi claiming strict liability. Bacardi had included warning labels and installed a removable flame arrester.

OUTCOME: The court held that Sclafani had a viable claim for strict liability against Bacardi.

—*Sclafani v. Brother Jimmy's BBQ, Inc.*, 930 N.Y.S.2d 566 (N.Y. App. Div.)

Business Activity. Other business activities have been widely recognized as intentional torts. Although state laws vary, an injured party may recover damages on the basis of conduct that causes:

1. Interference with a contract or economic advantage
2. Confusion about a product

3-1d INTERFERENCE WITH A CONTRACT OR ECONOMIC ADVANTAGE

The tort of interference with a contract or economic advantage occurs when a business relationship has been formed, and in some way a third party intentionally causes one party to end the relationship. If injured, the other party to the business relationship may have a cause of action against the party causing the breakup.

Many states require that the intentional interference be improper. Improper interference can occur because of an improper motive or an improper means, or

COURT CASE

FACTS: Macy's, Inc. and Martha Stewart Living Omnimedia, Inc. entered a licensing agreement that granted Macy's exclusive rights to certain products designed by Martha Stewart and branded with her mark. The contract provided that Macy's would manufacture the products, which included bedding, housewares, and cookware, and sell them exclusively in Macy's stores. Martha Stewart promised not to enter into any new agreement with another department store that would provide for the sale of the same branded products that Macy's was licensed to sell. JCPenney executives began to negotiate a retail partnership with Martha Stewart, despite their knowledge of the Macy's licensing agreement and its exclusivity provision. As a result of the negotiations, Martha Stewart entered into an agreement with JCPenney permitting the department store to manufacture products under the Martha Stewart brand and to have them retailed within JCPenney stores. Macy's sued JCPenney for tortuous interference with a contract, arguing that JCPenney intentionally caused Martha Stewart to breach the exclusivity provision of the Macy's agreement.

OUTCOME: The court found that JCPenney's efforts to engage Martha Stewart "exceeded the minimal level of ethical behavior in the marketplace" and wrongfully caused Martha Stewart to breach the contract with Macy's.

—*Macy's Inc. v. Martha Stewart Living Omnimedia, Inc.*, 127 A.D.3d 48 (N.Y.A.D.)

by acting other than in the legitimate exercise of the defendant's own rights. It is not improper to protect one's economic or safety interests or assert honest claims. Interference with leasing opportunities, with the opportunity of buying and selling goods, and with hiring employees are interferences that can be actionable.

3-1e CONFUSION ABOUT A PRODUCT

Intentionally causing confusion about another's product can be a tort. This can be done by making false statements about another's product or by representing goods or services as being the goods or services of someone else.

Injurious Falsehood. When a person makes false statements of fact that degrade the quality of another's goods or services, the tort of **injurious falsehood** occurs. Some courts call this tort **commercial disparagement** or **trade libel**. The false statement must be made to a third person. This is **communication**. The hearer must understand the statement to refer to the plaintiff's goods or services and to degrade their quality. An injured party must show the statement was a substantial element in causing damage. In some states, the plaintiff must identify specific customers lost as a result of the statement.

The false statement normally must have been made maliciously. Malice can be shown by proving that the statement was made as a result of ill will, spite, or hostility with the intention of causing the plaintiff harm. In some jurisdictions, the plaintiff need only show that the defendant knew the statement was false or had a reckless disregard as to its truth or falsity.

injurious falsehood, commercial disparagement, or trade libel
false statement of fact that degrades quality of another's goods or services

communication
telling a third person

COURT CASE

FACTS: Brook Mays Music Co., a retail seller of band instruments, published a document titled "ISO Alert." The ISO Alert was headed, "Instrument Shaped Object; Attention: Music Supervisors, Bank Directors. . . ." It stated that stores were selling beginner "instruments" or "Instrument Shaped Objects under the name brands of First Act" and others. It further stated, "we have determined that they will not play for the long term (if even the short term)! The ISO's break and parts are NOT available. . . . [S]tudents that will be playing these instruments will likely not survive the first few months of band because of the design and quality." First Act sued Brook Mays for injurious falsehood. Brook Mays said First Act had to prove malice.

OUTCOME: The court stated that Brook Mays either intended or reasonably should have recognized that the ISO Alert would cause First Act pecuniary loss. First Act was awarded damages.

—*First Act Inc. v. Brook Mays Music Co.*, 429 F.Supp.2d 429 (D. Mass.)

Confusion of Source. The tort that occurs when a person attempts to represent goods or services as being the goods or services of someone else is **confusion of source**. The law assumes customers would be confused as to the source of the goods or services. Actual confusion need not be shown. This tort occurs from trademark or trade name infringement or unfair competition.

Trademarks. A **trademark** is a word, name, symbol, device, or any combination thereof adopted and used to identify and distinguish one's goods from another's goods and to indicate the source of the goods. A trademark or trade name gives

confusion of source
representing goods or services as those of another

trademark
word, symbol, device, or combination of them used to identify and distinguish goods

the owner the exclusive right to use a word or device to distinguish a product or a service. As a type of property, trademarks are discussed in Chapter 14.

Only those marks used by a business in a way that identifies its goods or services and differentiates them from others are entitled to trademark protection. The mark normally must be inherently distinctive, which means unique, arbitrary, and nondescriptive.

Marks that are fanciful or subtly suggest something about the product can be protected. They include words such as *Ivory* for soap, abbreviations and nicknames such as *Coke*, made-up words such as *Exxon* and *Rolex*, and the shapes of packages and products.

secondary meaning
special meaning of a mark
that distinguishes goods

A mark that is not distinctive may be a trademark if it has acquired **secondary meaning**. Secondary meaning is a special or trade meaning developed by usage that distinguishes the goods or services so as to warrant trademark protection.

A trademark may be registered or unregistered. A trademark registered under the federal trademark law gives the holder the rights and remedies of that law. The holder of an unregistered trademark has some rights under the federal law and rights provided by the common law. Many states also have trademark laws that vary greatly.

**trademark or trade
name infringement**
unauthorized use or
imitation of another's mark
or name

Trademark or **trade name infringement** is unauthorized use or confusingly similar imitation of another's mark or name. A trademark owner may get a court to halt anyone's commercial use of the mark. Courts will halt imitation if it is likely to cause confusion, mistake, or deception. Factors that commonly indicate a likelihood of confusion include:

1. The similarity of the two marks
2. The similarity of the products represented by the marks
3. The similarity of marketing and customers
4. The similarity and amount of advertising used
5. The area of overlapping use
6. The intent of the parties in adopting the marks
7. The strength of the marks
8. Actual confusion by the public

COURT CASE

FACTS: Janet Travis, Inc. had operated family-owned restaurants under the trademark "TRAVIS" since 1944 and registered the mark in the 1960's. Preka Holdings, LLC purchased a restaurant that was licensed to use the "TRAVIS" trademark. However, Preka bought only the restaurant and did not discuss rights to retain the license to use the "TRAVIS" mark. Nonetheless, Preka continued using the "TRAVIS" mark by calling the restaurant Travis Grill, using the trademark on advertisements, and including the "famous Travis burger" on its menu. Janet Travis sued Preka for trademark infringement and presented affidavits from customers stating that

they mistakenly believed the Travis Grill was affiliated with Janet Travis. Preka argued that "TRAVIS" was not a valid trademark, because it was merely a surname and not distinctive.

OUTCOME: The court held that Janet Travis' decades long use of the "TRAVIS" mark had caused the mark to attain a secondary meaning that distinguished their restaurant business to customers. Preka's use of the mark was trademark infringement.

—*Janet Travis, Inc. v. Preka Holdings, LLC,* 856 N.W.2d 206 (Mich. App.)

Where the imitation of another's mark is for the purpose of jest or commentary, the parody is successful when there is no confusion and therefore no infringement.

Trademarks identify and distinguish tangible goods; service marks identify and distinguish services. The same legal principles govern trademark and service mark infringement.

Trademark or **trade name dilution** reduces the capacity of a mark to identify and distinguish goods or services. This could be done by *blurring* a trademark. Blurring diminishes the selling power of a trademark by unauthorized use on noncompeting products. Blurring would be making McDonald's light bulbs or Chrysler tires, for example. Dilution can also *tarnish* a trademark by using the mark in a disparaging manner or on low-quality goods.

The federal Anticybersquatting Consumer Protection Act (ACPA) gives trademark owners the right to sue people who register Internet domain names of trademarks and then try to profit from them. The trademark owner needs to show ownership of the mark, that the defendant registered or trafficked in identical or confusingly similar domain names, and that the defendant in bad faith intended to profit from the mark.

> **trademark or trade name dilution**
> lessening the capacity of a famous mark to identify and distinguish goods

COURT CASE

FACTS: Webadviso, owned by J. Taikwok Yung, acquired 180 domain names and parked them with providers of domain parking services in order to produce pay-per-click revenue. The domain names included well-known trademarks of Merrill Lynch (ML) and Bank of America (B of A), and the websites at times displayed information relating to financial services. When ML and B of A found out about the websites, Yung offered to sell the sites to them. A lawsuit resulted.

OUTCOME: In seeking to produce pay-per-click revenue, the court said Yung clearly intended to profit from the goodwill associated with the trademarks. Since he wanted to divert Internet users to his website, which had content that could tarnish the infringed marks, he had registered the names in bad faith and violated the ACPA.

—*Webadviso v. Bank of America Corp.*, 448 Fed. Appx. 95 (2d Cir.)

Unfair Competition. **Unfair competition** exists when the total impression a product gives to the consumer results in confusion as to the origin of the product. When unfair competition is claimed, the total physical image conveyed by the product and its name are considered together.

> **Unfair competition**
> total impression of product results in confusion as to its origin

3-2 Business Crimes

Crimes committed against a business or in which the perpetrator uses a business to commit a crime are **business crimes**. Some criminal offenses, such as forgery, fraudulent conveyances, shoplifting, and embezzlement, closely relate to business activities.

> **LO** ③
> What business crimes are
>
> **business crime**
> crime against a business or committed by using a business

3-2a TYPES OF BUSINESS CRIMES

In this age of computers, electronic transfers, and organized crime, the range of crimes against businesses has been growing. There are also laws which can have a serious impact on businesses and make some seemingly innocuous business transaction criminal. Businesses should be aware of:

1. Theft
2. RICO cases
3. Computer crimes
4. Privacy and data security laws
5. The Foreign Corrupt Practices Act

theft
taking another's property
without consent

Theft. Theft is the crime of stealing. It involves taking or appropriating another's property without the owner's consent and with the intention to deprive the owner of it. This includes when a thief initially obtains the property lawfully.

Theft includes shoplifting, embezzlement, and larceny. The crimes generally consist of the following:

shoplifting
taking unpurchased goods
from a store

1. **Shoplifting**: Taking possession of goods in a store with the intent to use them as the taker's own without paying the purchase price. Concealing unpurchased goods while in a store can constitute shoplifting.

embezzlement
fraudulent conversion of
property lawfully possessed

2. **Embezzlement**: Fraudulent conversion of another's property by someone in lawful possession of the property with the intent to defraud the owner of the property. Conversion means handling the property inconsistently with the arrangement by which the defendant has possession of it. Because businesses rely on employees to receive payments and make disbursements, embezzlement is often a crime against a business.

COURT CASE

FACTS: Kriemhilde Bixby had deteriorating health, so Heidi Hemmingway and Beverly Cogswell took care of her and handled all household tasks for her. Hemmingway persuaded Bixby to execute a living will and contacted attorney Sheri Paige. Paige told Hemmingway and Cogswell that Bixby's assets should be sold to avoid estate taxes. Bixby purportedly signed a document allowing Hemmingway to sell her house. Paige held the proceeds of the sale in her attorney's account. On September 19, she issued two checks from the account for $15,000 each, to herself and her husband. By then, Bixby was suffering from severe dementia and died eight days later. When charged with embezzlement, Paige produced a document supposedly signed by Bixby, dated September 19, authorizing the checks. Paige alleged that Bixby had authorized the checks.

OUTCOME: It was reasonable to conclude that with severe dementia, Bixby could not have known she was authorizing the sale. Since Bixby had not consented, as trustee of the proceeds of the house sale, Paige had embezzled $30,000.

—*State v. Paige*, 40 A.3d 279 (Conn.)

larceny
taking and carrying away of
property without consent

3. **Larceny**: Taking the property of another without the consent of the person in possession, with the intent of depriving the possessor of the property. The intent to deprive the possessor of the property must exist when the property is taken. The taker need not take the property from the owner. Whenever someone takes any business property, whether inventory, tools, or even office supplies, larceny occurs.

PREVIEW CASE REVISITED

FACTS: With their sons, aged seven and four, in car seats in the back seat, Thomas and Shawn Ardizone backed their car out of their garage. Thomas went back into the house for something. Shawn followed, leaving the boys in the car with the engine running. Ledon Taylor saw the car and got into it. As he started to back out the driveway, the Ardizones came outside. They ran to the car, but Taylor drove off. Thomas followed in another car. With two children in the car and the owner following, Taylor decided to abandon the car. He pulled off the road, and, as he got, out he took Shawn's purse. After he was arrested, he was charged, among other crimes, with two counts of larceny. He alleged he had committed only one.

OUTCOME: The court said that, although the purse was in the car when Taylor stole the car, when he decided it was not worthwhile to keep a car with two children in it, he made an independent decision to steal the purse. He had committed two larcenies.

—*Taylor v. State*, 879 N.E.2d 1198 (Ind. Ct. App.)

RICO Cases. The Racketeer Influenced and Corrupt Organizations Act, also called RICO, is a federal law designed to prevent the infiltration of legitimate businesses by organized crime. It prohibits investing income from racketeering to obtain a business, using racketeering to obtain a business (through, for example, conspiracy, and extortion), using a business to conduct racketeering, and conspiring to do any of these.

RICO includes civil sanctions as well as criminal ones. As a result, it has been used by one business against another in cases not involving organized crime. The injured party brings the action under RICO based on the perpetration of criminal activity and requests damages. In criminal cases, the government brings the action. To prove a business violation of RICO, a plaintiff must show:

1. Conduct
2. Of an enterprise (at least two people)
3. Through a pattern (at least two related acts within ten years)
4. Of racketeering activity

Racketeering activity means acts specified in the law that are labeled criminal under state or federal laws. Examples of the specified crimes include murder, kidnapping, arson, robbery, bribery, distribution of illegal narcotics, obstruction of justice, mail or wire fraud, money laundering, forgery, and securities fraud. The defendant does not have to have been convicted; it is enough to have engaged in activity for which a conviction could be obtained. This makes it easier to win a civil RICO case than a criminal one.

Civil suits under RICO have been popular because RICO provides recovery of three times the damages suffered as a result of the RICO violation. It also allows the recovery of attorneys' fees, which can be a very substantial sum.

Computer Crimes. Crimes committed with the aid of a computer or because computers are involved are called **computer crimes**. Computers can be involved in crimes in various ways:

1. They can be the objects of crime—such as when a computer is stolen or damaged.
2. They can be the method of committing a crime—such as when a computer is used to take money from an account.

LO ④
What computer crimes are

computer crime
crime that is committed with the aid of computers or because computers are involved

3. They can represent where the crime is committed—such as when copyrights are infringed on the Internet.

Sometimes prosecutors can successfully prosecute computer offenses by using existing criminal laws prohibiting theft, mail fraud, wire fraud, and the transportation of stolen property. However, both the federal government and the states have enacted specific computer crime legislation.

COURT CASE

FACTS: Seikaly & Stewart, P.C., a small law firm, contracted with The Rainmaker Institute, LLC to provide Internet marketing services and create new business for the law firm. Rainmaker promised to improve the firm's ranking and visibility in search engine results through an optimization process that involved Internet link building and the creation of blogs. Despite a lack of results, Rainmaker persuaded the firm to renew its marketing contract and continued marketing the same services to other small law firms. After several years of seeing no additional Internet business, Seikaly & Stewart claimed that Rainmaker had fraudulently marketed a search engine optimization process that it knew violated major search engine's guidelines, causing the firm's website to be downgraded and ineffective for search engine purposes. The firm sued Rainmaker under RICO, citing repeated instances where Rainmaker used the Internet, telephones, and U.S. Mail to advance the fraudulent scheme to the Seikaly law firm and other small law firms.

OUTCOME: The court held that Seikaly had sufficiently alleged a pattern of at least two related acts of racketeering in the form of mail fraud and wire fraud. The firm successfully stated a cause of action against Rainmaker under RICO.

—*Seikaly & Stewart, P.C. v. Fairley*, 18 F.Supp.3d 989 (D. Ariz.)

The federal government has enacted the Electronic Communications Privacy Act. The law prohibits the interception of computer communications, such as e-mail, or obtaining and divulging without permission data stored electronically.

State laws generally prohibit alteration of a computer program or intentional, unauthorized access to a computer regardless of the reason for the access and the disclosure of any information gained by such access.

Criminal activity relating to computers can be classified as three types: trespass, fraud, and criminal copyright infringement.

computer trespass
unauthorized use of, or access to, a computer

Trespass. Computer trespass means unauthorized use of, or access to, a computer. Using a business computer to play games or prepare personal documents may constitute computer trespass. More serious trespasses include learning trade secrets, gaining customer lists, and obtaining classified defense information. Because computer trespass involves the use of computer time without permission, all trespass is theft of computer time.

Computer trespass has been the focus of state computer crime laws. Most jurisdictions protect the confidentiality of all information stored in computers.

Unauthorized access might be by:

1. An employee not authorized to use a computer in the business

2. An employee authorized to use a computer who uses it for nonbusiness purposes

3. An unauthorized outsider who gains access to the business's computer system—called a **hacker**

One method of trespass involves the use of **rogue programs**. A rogue program is a set of software instructions that produces abnormal or unexpected behavior in a computer. Rogue programs have such colorful names as "viruses," "bacteria, "worms," "Trojan horses," and "time bombs." They may cause computer users difficulty or inhibit normal use by altering the operations of a program, or impose injury by destroying data or screen displays, creating false information, or damaging the computer. The programs can infect a computer by being attached to a useful program or e-mail; they spread to other computers through modems, removable storage, or network connections. Rogue programs might not show up for some time, so they can spread and damage all files in a computer system.

Fraud. As applied to computer crime, fraud encompasses larceny and embezzlement. It includes causing bank deposits to be credited to one individual's account. Such action might be prosecuted under traditional crime statutes or new computer crime statutes.

hacker
unauthorized outsider who gains access to another's computer system

rogue program
set of software instructions that produces abnormal computer behavior; see www.copyright.gov

COURT CASE

FACTS: S&M Brands made a $6,500 loan to its director of human resources, Jeremy DiMaio. DiMaio agreed to pay back the loan by having money withheld from his paycheck starting six months later. Three months after the withholdings were to have started, DiMaio quit. S&M found out he had asked a payroll employee not to make the withholdings and that she had complied. William Snell, DiMaio's replacement, found that hundreds of valuable documents and computer files were missing from S&M's personnel records. DiMaio agreed to return the missing items if S&M would forgive the loan. DiMaio was then arrested and charged with computer fraud. Snell and S&M's lawyer testified that the value of the more than 800 personnel files DiMaio had taken was more than $10,000.

OUTCOME: The court found that the testimony of Snell and the lawyer about the value of the files taken was adequate to prove their value. The charge of computer fraud was proven.

—*DiMaio v. Com.*, 636 S.E.2d 456 (Va.)

The federal Computer Fraud and Abuse Act makes it an offense to, without authorization, access a computer or exceed authorized access of a computer used by or for the U.S. government or a financial institution and to (1) fraudulently obtain anything of value; (2) intentionally and without authorization obtain or destroy information; (3) affect the use of the computer; or (4) intentionally cause damage. It is also an offense to (1) deal in computer passwords and thereby affect interstate commerce; (2) knowingly access a computer, obtain national defense information, and disclose, attempt to disclose, or retain that information; or (3) transmit a threat to damage a U.S. government or financial institution computer in order to extort money.

COURT CASE

FACTS: Robert Steele worked for a company that provided contract IT services to governmental agencies. Through his job duties, Steele had access to the company's server and other employees' email accounts. Several years later, Steele resigned from SRA International, Inc. and took a job with a competing company that also provided IT services to government agencies. Upon his resignation, SRA took back Steele's company-issued computer, denied him access to the office building, and terminated his access to the main computer system. The company, however, neglected to change the password on a backdoor account to the server that Steele had created. In the nine months following his departure, Steele secretly logged into the email server of his former employer over 80,000 times and downloaded emails and documents related to the company's bids for government contracts. Steele was convicted of violating the Computer Fraud and Abuse Act. He argued that the evidence did not support the charge that his access to SRA's server was "without authorization," because the company never changed the password on his backdoor account.

OUTCOME: The court noted that SRA took steps to deny Steele access to company property and systems after his departure, and it was logical to conclude that Steele was not authorized to access to the computer system after leaving the company. His conviction was upheld.

—*U.S. v. Steele*, 595 Fed. Appx. 208 (4th Cir.)

A wide variety of frauds have been perpetrated on unsuspecting businesses and individuals via the Internet. These have included a long-distance telephone company employee selling more than 50,000 calling card numbers. That employee was sent to prison. Businesses frequently suffer losses quietly in preference to advertising to customers, stockholders, and clients that they are vulnerable to hackers, so it is impossible to measure accurately the dollar amount of loss to business from computer fraud.

Criminal Copyright Infringement. The crime of criminal copyright infringement has been estimated to cost copyright holders billions of dollars each year. In order to establish the offense, a prosecutor needs to prove (1) there has been copyright infringement, (2) the infringement was willful, and (3) the infringement was done for business advantage or financial gain.

A particularly serious type of copyright infringement for business occurs when software is copied. Software that is copied illegally is called **pirated software**. Pirating software is a worldwide industry because the Internet links people everywhere. Software can be copied, and within a relatively short time, people all over the world can make numerous illegal copies.

pirated software
software copied illegally

Privacy and Data Security Laws. In response to computer hacking and growing privacy concerns, state and federal laws now require businesses which collect and store personal data to do so in a secure manner. Personal data may include information such as a person's birthdate, Social Security Number, e-mail and physical addresses, credit card number, and health records. At the federal level, several laws regulate businesses in specific industries, but there is no single, comprehensive privacy framework to govern the collection and storage of personal information. Under the Health Insurance Portability and Accountability Act (HIPAA), for example, health-care providers and plans, as well as the directors, officers, and employees of these entities, can be held criminally liable for knowingly obtaining and disclosing an individual's personal health information in violation of HIPAA rules. In addition to criminal prosecution, businesses may be subject to civil

COURT CASE

FACTS: Robin Rothberg, Christian Morley, and perhaps hundreds of others were members of a computer software piracy group called "Pirates with Attitudes." The group stored huge numbers of pirated software programs at file transfer protocol (called FTP) sites. Members of the group could download the pirated software to their own computers. When the FBI seized computer hardware at the University of Sherbrooke in Canada, there were still 5,000 programs on it; however, at trial, an FBI computer specialist testified that more than 54,000 programs had been uploaded to the hardware. Rothberg, Morley, and others were charged with conspiracy to commit copyright infringement.

OUTCOME: All the defendants either pled guilty or were found guilty after trial of the conspiracy charge. The pirated software was clearly on the computer hardware and available for downloading.

—*United States v. Rothberg,* 2002 WL 171963 (N.D. Ill.)

penalties for their failure to protect customers' personal information. The Federal Trade Commission (FTC) is a leading agency that enforces laws against companies for failing to implement adequate safeguards to secure customers' personal data.

Even with safeguards in place, businesses may still experience security breaches. Many laws require businesses to notify customers of a security breach within a specified time of the company's discovery of the breach, so that customers can monitor their personal and financial records for fraudulent activity. Businesses are also often required to notify state attorneys general of security breaches.

The Children's Online Privacy Protection Act (COPPA) is a far-reaching law enforced by the FTC that applies to businesses operating websites and online services directed to children under the age of 13. The FTC considers factors such as the use of animated characters, subject matter content, and the age of models to determine whether children are a website's target audience. COPPA also covers businesses operating general audience websites that knowingly collect information from children under the age of 13. COPPA requires businesses to provide notice on the website of what information the website is collecting on children and how the data is used. Businesses must also obtain parental consent prior to collecting and using personal information from children, and the law gives parents the right to review and prevent the retention of the information.

Foreign Corrupt Practices Act. After more than 400 companies admitted making hundreds of millions of dollars in questionable or illegal payments to foreign government officials, politicians, and political parties, Congress enacted the Foreign Corrupt Practices Act (FCPA). It prohibits corrupt payments (bribes) to foreign officials, politicians, and political parties in order to get or keep business and mandates record-keeping requirements by companies.

The anti-bribery sections apply to any U.S. person (including a business) who bribes a foreign official and also to foreign businesses and persons who act in the United States in furtherance of such a bribe. The record-keeping requirements apply to publicly held corporations, domestic or foreign, whose securities are listed on U.S. stock exchanges.

In most of the recent FCPA cases, liability resulted from misconduct by foreign third persons such as agents, suppliers, distributors, and consultants. Businesses are responsible for the acts of foreign subsidiaries when they have authorized, directed, or controlled the acts.

Understanding the breadth of this law can be difficult. This is true with respect to knowing who a "foreign official" is, what outlays constitute a bribe, and what the standard for knowledge of a questionable activity is.

Foreign Officials. In addition to individuals employed in running the government, employees of businesses controlled by foreign governments are considered to be foreign officials. In countries with national health-care systems, for example, doctors would be considered foreign officials.

COURT CASE

FACTS: Lindsey Manufacturing Company (LMC) made payments to Grupo International (Grupo) ostensibly as commissions for services of Enrique Aguilar, LMC's sales representative in Mexico. Large portions of the payments were used to bribe Nestor Moreno and Arturo Hernandez, high-ranking employees of the Comisión Federal de Electricidad (CFE). CFE was an electric utility wholly owned by the government of Mexico. LMC was charged with violating the FCPA. LMC alleged that Moreno and Hernandez were not "foreign officials" because a state-owned corporation could not be a department, agency, or instrumentality of a foreign government.

OUTCOME: The court held that a state-owned corporation could be an instrumentality of a foreign government and that officers of such a corporation may be "foreign officials" for purposes of the FCPA.

—*U.S. v. Aguilar*, 783 F.Supp.2d 1108 (C.D. Cal.)

While in the Aguilar case the government totally owned the electric utility for which the bribed individuals worked, an entity need not be wholly owned or even majority owned by a government in order for its employees to be considered foreign officials under the FCPA.

Bribes. The mere offer or promise of a corrupt payment can constitute a bribe in violation of the act. The payment can be money or anything of value, including entertainment.

Standard for Knowledge. Managers and executives may be held strictly liable for company books and records that do not honestly account for corrupt payments, even if they have no knowledge of the payments. They may not knowingly avoid or fail to implement proper accounting controls or knowingly falsify records. But "knowing" can mean a person is merely aware of a high likelihood that a forbidden situation exists. A business cannot avoid the impact of the FCPA by being purposely blind or intentionally avoiding learning whether a bribe is likely to be paid.

Consequences of Violation. The potential consequences for violation of the law include heavy fines, imprisonment of individuals, and debarment as well as the potential of civil suits by stockholders.

Fines. Companies, and individuals who are not allowed to be reimbursed by their companies, have had to pay criminal penalties—from tens of thousands to hundreds of millions of dollars. Companies also frequently must pay back any profits received as a result of corrupt payments. This is called **disgorgement of profits**.

disgorgement of profits
having to pay back profits received illegally

Imprisonment. Individuals found in violation of the FCPA have been sentenced to prison for terms ranging from months to several years.

Debarment. **Debarment** means a firm is prohibited from doing business with the government. When a company does a lot of business with the government, debarment is a severe penalty. Corporations or individuals in violation of the FCPA may be subject to debarment. In fact, a corporation guilty of a felony is subject to debarment.

debarment
prohibition on doing business with government

The FCPA does except from the bribery provisions payments made to speed up performance of a "routine governmental action." This includes such things as obtaining a permit, water, mail or phone service, or police protection.

QUESTIONS

1. a. What must an injured party show in order to recover for an intentional tort?

   b. What must be shown for a negligence tort?

2. Is it always a tort when competitors intentionally injure one another? Explain.

3. Explain the benefit to plaintiffs of the doctrine of strict tort liability.

4. What marks are entitled to trademark protection?

5. How does the Anticybersquatting Consumer Protection Act (ACPA) protect trademark owners from trademark infringement and dilution?

6. What rights do parents have under the Children's Online Privacy Protection Act (COPPA)?

7. Why have civil RICO cases been so popular?

8. What are the three elements of criminal copyright infringement?

9. To whom does the FCPA apply?

10. For what companies is debarment a serious penalty and why?

CASE PROBLEMS

When the concluding question in a case problem can be answered simply yes or no, state the legal principle or rule of law that supports your answer.

1. Frank Martini and Satanand Sharma hired James Little to represent them when sued by Amber Hotel Company. Little agreed to be paid $100 an hour less than his normal fee, provided that he would have a lien against any attorney fee award. In December, the court entered judgment against Amber. Amber appealed. The court then amended the judgment to award Martini and Sharma $152,700 in attorney's fees, and Amber did not appeal this. Martini, Sharma, and Amber negotiated about a settlement, and Little advised them of his right to the attorney's fee award. Martini and Sharma signed a settlement agreement by which Amber agreed to dismiss its appeal, and the plaintiffs agreed to abandon the fee award. The parties did not inform Little. He sued Amber for intentionally interfering with the performance of a contract. Should he recover? **LO ②**

2. Teleline, Inc. ran a telephone gambling game called "Let's Make a Deal" (LMD) using a 900 phone number. Playing the game cost $3.88 a minute. People who called were not charged for the phone **LO ③**

CASE PROBLEMS (CONTINUED)

calls, but only for the ability to gamble provided by Teleline. AT&T carried the calls over its long-distance lines, and Teleline paid AT&T for the cost of the calls. Felix Kemp's grandson called the 900 number. AT&T listed Teleline's charges under the heading "direct-dialed calls," as long-distance charges mixed in with charges for long-distance calls on phone bills mailed to Kemp. AT&T's name and logo were displayed on the pages showing the LMD charges. The LMD charges were illegal gambling debts not collectable under state law. Kemp's local phone company told him he had to pay the charges, or his phone would be disconnected. He paid the phone bill and sued AT&T for violating RICO, claiming mail fraud. Were the bills so misleading that they constituted fraud?

LO ①, ②   3. Shelly Nitz, a real estate agent affiliated with Home Services of Nebraska, Inc., represented the seller of a home. The home purchaser hired Matthew Steinhausen, sole member of Steinhausen Home Inspections, LLC, to perform an inspection prior to closing the home sale. Nitz considered some of the items in Steinhausen's report to be beyond the scope of a typical home inspection and felt his comments were detrimental to the home seller. Some time later, Nitz responded to a question regarding Steinhausen's services via an e-mail forum for Home Services agents. Nitz stated that Steinhausen had done an inspection for one of her listings and that she "would never let him near one of [her] listings ever again!!! Total idiot." Steinhausen sued Nitz and Home Services, alleging libel. Was Nitz's description of Steinhausen as a "total idiot" fact or opinion? Should she be liable?

LO ②   4. Universal Furniture International, Inc. held copyrights on the designs of two furniture lines it sold. The designer had started with public domain sources, but blended elements from different historical periods and created changes until he found the designs aesthetically pleasing. He had blended the elements to create a different look. A major buyer of the lines asked Collezione Europa USA, Inc. to produce a cheaper version. Collezione did not know of the copyrights, but thought the designs were not entitled to copyright protection and could be imitated. It produced furniture so similar that when Universal's senior vice president saw the pieces, he thought they actually were Universal pieces. Universal sued Collezione for infringement. Did Collezione have the right to imitate the designs?

LO ③, ④   5. The Los Angeles Police Department charged police officer Kelly Chrisman with misuse of department computers. He accessed the police department's computer system for nonduty-related activities—specifically to search about people such as celebrities, his girlfriend, her friends, and himself. The relevant statute made it a crime to access any computer knowingly and without permission. Did Chrisman violate the statute?

LO ④   6. When Emeka Uyamadu tried to check his luggage at an airport, seven laptop computers in it set off an alarm. Since he did not have required export documents, customs officials kept the computers. When Uyamadu returned to the United States, he told police and signed a statement saying he had bought the computers at Internet auctions in May, even though he was told they were stolen June 6. He was charged with their theft. Should he be found guilty of computer theft?

LO ②   7. Haydel Enterprises owned and operated a bakery in New Orleans, Louisiana, selling pastries such as Mardi Gras king cakes. Haydel asked an artist to design a "bead dog" to replicate the dogs made out of beads thrown at Mardi Gras celebrations. Haydel registered the words "MARDI GRAS BEAD DOG" and the bead dog design as trademarks covering items such as king cake pastries, jewelry, and clothing. Over a six-year period, Haydel sold about 80 clothing items and 300 jewelry items featuring bead dogs, plus an unidentified number of king cakes with bead dogs. One magazine article featuring Haydel's products called bead dogs "an iconic Mardi Gras symbol." Three years after Haydel registered the bead dog trademarks, Raquel Duarte began selling jewelry featuring bead dogs. Duarte filed a lawsuit against Haydel in which she asked the court to declare that she was not breaking any trademark law by selling the bead dog jewelry and requested Haydel's trademarks be canceled. Duarte argued that Haydel's trademarks were descriptive in nature and had not acquired distinctiveness whereby customers associated the trademarks with Haydel's goods. Was Duarte correct?

CASE PROBLEMS (CONTINUED)

8. While they were dating, Heather Borrack and her boyfriend, Charles Reed, spent a day with his family on a lake swimming. Reed led Borrack up a steep path to a cliff above the lake. Once at the top of the cliff, Borrack told Reed that she wanted to return to the lake, but he refused to go back down the path with her and she was too frightened to return on the steep path by herself. Reed then tricked Borrack into jumping off the cliff by jumping himself and leaving her alone at the top. Borrack jumped off the cliff and was severely injured when she hit the water. She sued Reed for negligence, arguing that his conduct created a significant risk for her due to the terrain and that he had a duty to lessen the risk or take precautions so that Borrack did not harm herself. Did Reed's actions create a duty to Borrack? **LO ①**

9. Charles Ndhlovu regularly purchased large quantities of materials used in counterfeit manufacturing, such as blank CDs and DVDs, cases, and labeling paper. A store run by Ndhlovu did not display a business license and offered no signage or advertisement to indicate he sold CDs and DVDs. Law enforcement authorities sent a confidential informant to Ndhlovu's store to purchase CDs and DVDs. With $180, the informant bought 80 counterfeit discs labeled with well-known movie and music titles. Police raided Ndhlovu's store and seized over 6,500 counterfeit CDs and DVDs. Ndhlovu was charged and convicted of criminal copyright infringement. He argued on appeal that the government had failed to prove that his copyright infringement was committed for purposes of commercial gain. Should Ndhlovu's conviction be upheld? **LO ②**

10. A shipment of computers arrived at a freight-moving facility and was moved to a trailer. At night, employees in the warehouse at the facility heard suspicious noises outside and called the police. Upon arriving, an officer saw a man carrying a box and stepping down from a trailer. The officers approached but could not find the man. They looked under the trailers and found five unopened computer boxes hidden behind the wheels of a trailer. The officers finally spotted the legs of two people under another trailer. Adolph Spears, Jr., was one of the men. A hand truck was found near a hole in the fence enclosing the facility. Was there evidence of any computer crime? **LO ③**

Government Regulation of Business

LEARNING OBJECTIVES

1. Explain why government regulates business.
2. Discuss the types and powers of administrative agencies.
3. List the major antitrust laws.
4. Summarize the areas in which the federal government has enacted legislation for environmental protection.

PREVIEW CASE

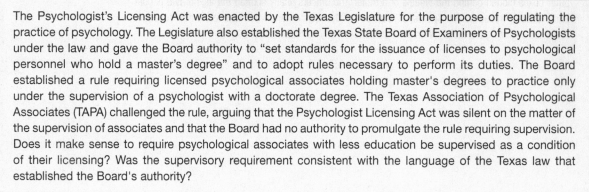

The Psychologist's Licensing Act was enacted by the Texas Legislature for the purpose of regulating the practice of psychology. The Legislature also established the Texas State Board of Examiners of Psychologists under the law and gave the Board authority to "set standards for the issuance of licenses to psychological personnel who hold a master's degree" and to adopt rules necessary to perform its duties. The Board established a rule requiring licensed psychological associates holding master's degrees to practice only under the supervision of a psychologist with a doctorate degree. The Texas Association of Psychological Associates (TAPA) challenged the rule, arguing that the Psychologist Licensing Act was silent on the matter of the supervision of associates and that the Board had no authority to promulgate the rule requiring supervision. Does it make sense to require psychological associates with less education be supervised as a condition of their licensing? Was the supervisory requirement consistent with the language of the Texas law that established the Board's authority?

Government rules and regulations affect the operation of every business, no matter what type. Government regulations, both state and federal, affect areas of business operation ranging from prices and product safety to the relationship of the business to its employees. This chapter discusses some ways in which government regulates the operation of business. Some other aspects of governmental regulation of business are discussed in Chapter 19 (consumer protection) and in Chapters 28 and 29 (employers and employees).

4-1 Purpose of Regulation

Government regulates business in order to eliminate abuses and to control conduct considered to be unreasonable. The goal is to enhance the quality of life for society as a whole by setting the rules under which all businesses compete.

4-2 Administrative Agencies

Chapter 1 defined administrative agencies as governmental boards or commissions with the authority to regulate or implement laws. Most governmental regulation of business is done by administrative agencies.

Most administrative agency regulation occurs because of the complex nature of the area of regulation. Each administrative agency can become a specialist in its particular area of regulation. Agencies can hire scientists and researchers to study industries or problems and set standards which businesses must follow. Agencies conduct research on proposed drugs (the Food and Drug Administration), examine the safety of nuclear power facilities (the Nuclear Regulatory Commission), certify the wholesomeness of meat and poultry (the Food Safety and Inspection Service), and set standards for aircraft maintenance (the Federal Aviation Administration). In all these areas, research has been necessary to determine a safe level for the public.

Some agencies investigate industries and propose rules designed to promote fairness to the businesses involved and the public. This occurs in the area of trading in stocks (the Securities and Exchange Commission), the granting of radio and television licenses (the Federal Communications Commission), and the regulation of banks (the Federal Deposit Insurance Corporation). The legislature thus can set up the guidelines and specify the research to be done by specialists in the field.

4-2a STRUCTURE OF ADMINISTRATIVE AGENCIES

Agencies may be run by a single administrator who serves at the pleasure of the executive, either the president of the United States in the case of federal agencies or the governor in the case of state agencies. Alternatively, a commission, the members of which are appointed for staggered terms, frequently of five years, may run agencies.

4-2b TYPES OF AGENCIES

The two types of administrative agencies are usually referred to as regulatory and nonregulatory. Regulatory agencies govern the economic activity of businesses by prescribing rules stating what should or should not be done in particular situations. They decide whether a law has been violated and then proceed against those violating the law by imposing fines and, in some cases, ordering that the activity be stopped. Regulatory-type agencies include agencies such as the Environmental Protection Agency, the Securities and Exchange Commission, and the Federal Trade Commission.

Regulatory agencies also regulate a wide variety of professions that serve the public. Those supervised by governmental agencies in an effort to protect the interests of consumers include barbers, doctors, insurance agents, morticians, cosmetologists, fitters of hearing aids, and restaurateurs. In order to be licensed to practice a regulated profession, an individual must meet the requirements set by the appropriate regulatory agency.

Public utility companies, which are granted monopoly status, are regulated to ensure that they charge fair rates and render adequate service. Such businesses include natural gas, electric, and water companies. A public service commission or public utilities commission regulates these companies in most states.

Nonregulatory agencies, also called social regulatory agencies, dispense benefits for social and economic welfare and issue regulations governing the distribution of benefits. Such agencies include the Railroad Retirement Board, the Farm Credit Administration, and the Department of Health and Human Services.

4-2c OFFICE OF FOREIGN ASSETS CONTROL

Office of Foreign Assets Control (OFAC)
federal agency that enforces economic and trade sanctions

Agencies are also used by the government to carry out foreign policy objectives and enhance national security. The **Office of Foreign Assets Control (OFAC)** is a powerful agency that enforces economic and trade sanctions imposed by the United States against foreign countries, terrorists, drug dealers, and other individuals and organizations deemed a threat to national security. OFAC regularly publishes lists naming thousands of individuals and organizations with whom American companies are prohibited from conducting business. Many businesses screen their customers against the names on OFAC lists to ensure they do not process transactions for prohibited individuals and entities. OFAC also administers sanction programs against foreign governments, such as those in North Korea and Sudan. In special cases, companies may apply for a license granting them permission to do business with individuals and entities named on OFAC lists. Violations of OFAC regulations may result in civil and criminal penalties.

4-2d POWERS OF AGENCIES

Different regulatory agencies have different powers. However, the three major areas of regulations include:

1. Licensing power—Allowing a business to enter the field being regulated
2. Rate-making power—Fixing the prices that a business may charge
3. Power over business practices—Determining whether the activity of the entity regulated is acceptable or not

Agencies such as the Federal Communications Commission, the Nuclear Regulatory Commission, and the Securities and Exchange Commission have licensing power. The Civil Aeronautics Board, the Federal Power Commission, and the Interstate Commerce Commission all have rate-making power. The primary powers of the Federal Trade Commission and the National Labor Relations Board are to control business practices.

4-2e RULE MAKING

Administrative agencies primarily set policy through the issuance of rules and regulations. When an agency's rule is challenged, courts primarily focus on the procedures followed by the agency in exercising its rule-making power. The rule-making procedure followed by state agencies resembles that which federal agencies must use.

After investigating a problem, an agency will develop a proposed rule. A federal agency must publish a notice of the proposed rule in the *Federal Register*. This allows interested parties the opportunity to comment on the proposed rule.

The agency might hold formal hearings, but informal **notice and comment rule making** has become more and more common. When an agency uses notice and comment rule making, it publishes a proposed rule but does not hold formal hearings. After allowing time for comments from the public, the proposed rule could be published as proposed, changed, or entirely abandoned by the agency. Once a rule or regulation is adopted, it has the force of a statute; however, people affected by it may challenge it in court.

notice and comment rule making
enacting administrative rules by publishing the proposed rule and then the final rule without holding formal hearings

4-2f STATE AGENCIES

Whereas federal administrative agencies affect businesses throughout the country, state administrative agencies affect businesses operated in their states. The most common state agencies include public service commissions, state labor relations boards or commissions, and workers' compensation boards.

PREVIEW CASE REVISITED

FACTS: The Psychologist's Licensing Act was enacted by the Texas Legislature for the purpose of regulating the practice of psychology. The Legislature also established the Texas State Board of Examiners of Psychologists under the law and gave the Board authority to "set standards for the issuance of licenses to psychological personnel who hold a master's degree" and to adopt rules necessary to perform its duties. The Board established a rule requiring licensed psychological associates holding master's degrees to practice only under the supervision of a psychologist with a doctorate degree. The Texas Association of Psychological Associates (TAPA) challenged the rule, arguing that the Psychologist Licensing Act was silent on the matter of the supervision of associates and that the Board had no authority to promulgate the rule requiring supervision.

OUTCOME: The court held that the plain language of the Psychologist's Licensing Act gave the Board broad discretion in setting licensing standards for psychological associates. The Board had authority to issue the rule requiring supervision of associates, because the rule did not impose conditions in excess of the Act and was consistent with the Act.

—*Texas Ass'n of Psychological Associates v. Texas State Bd. of Examiners of Psychologists,*
439 S.W.3d 597 (Tex. App.)

4-3 Antitrust

Government also regulates business by means of **antitrust laws** that seek to promote competition among businesses.

The most important antitrust law, the federal Sherman Antitrust Act, declares, "Every contract, combination in the form of trust or otherwise, or conspiracy, in restraint of trade or commerce among the several states, or with foreign nations is . . . illegal."[1] It further provides that anyone who monopolizes or tries to obtain a monopoly in interstate commerce is guilty of a felony.

The Sherman Act applies to commerce or trade between two or more states and to buyers and sellers. Most states also have antitrust laws, very similar to the Sherman Act, which prohibit restraint of trade within their states.

In interpreting the Sherman Act, the federal courts have said it prohibits only those activities that *unreasonably* restrain trade. The *rule of reason* approach means

LO ③
Major antitrust laws

antitrust law
statute that seeks to promote competition among businesses

---

[1] 15 U.S.C. § 1.

that the courts examine and rule on the anticompetitive effect of a particular activity on a case-by-case basis. The effect of the activity, not the activity itself, is the most important element in deciding whether the Sherman Act has been violated.

However, some activities are illegal under the Sherman Act without regard to their effect. Called *per se* violations, they include price fixing, group boycotts, and horizontal territorial restraints.

Many activities may lessen competition. Obviously, every business firm seeks to have cooperation within its firm. This is the basis of economic productivity, and this is lawful under the antitrust laws. Only when separate businesses make a commitment to a common plan or some type of joint action to restrain trade does an antitrust violation occur.

In addition to the Sherman Act, the federal government has enacted other important antitrust laws. These include the Clayton Act, the Robinson–Patman Act, and the Federal Trade Commission Act.

The Clayton Act amends the Sherman Act by prohibiting certain practices if their effect may be to substantially lessen competition or to tend to create a monopoly. The Clayton Act prohibits price discrimination to different purchasers when price difference does not result from differences in selling or transportation costs. The Clayton Act also prohibits agreements to sell on the condition that the purchaser shall not use goods of the seller's competitors, ownership of stock or assets in a competing business where the effect may be to substantially lessen competition, and interlocking directorates between boards of directors of competing firms.

per se violation
activity that is illegal regardless of its effect

COURT CASE

FACTS: Chicago Bridge and Iron Co. (CB&I) obtained all the assets for the design, engineering, and building of field-erected cryogenic storage tanks from Pitt–Des Moines Inc. (PDM). CB&I and PDM were the dominant suppliers of the tanks in the United States. The Federal Trade Commission (FTC) ordered CB&I to dispose of the assets, charging that the acquisition would likely substantially lessen competition or tend to create a monopoly in violation of the Clayton Act. CB&I alleged there were new companies that could compete; however, because none had won a bid to construct a tank since CB&I's acquisition, customers were not aware of the new companies, and CB&I continued to get contracts without bidding.

OUTCOME: The court required CB&I to dispose of the assets. The fact that no other company had been able to win a bid to construct a tank, and customers were not aware of any new companies, showed that there had been a lessening of competition.

—*Chicago Bridge and Iron Co. NV v. F.T.C.*, 534 F.3d 410 (5th Cir.)

The Robinson–Patman Act, an amendment to the Clayton Act, prohibits price discrimination generally and geographically for the purpose of eliminating competition. It also prohibits sales at unreasonably low prices in order to eliminate competition.

The Federal Trade Commission Act prohibits "unfair methods of competition in commerce and unfair or deceptive acts or practices in commerce."[2] In addition, this law prohibits false advertising. To prevent these unfair and deceptive practices, a federal administrative agency, the Federal Trade Commission, was established.

---

[2] 15 U.S.C. § 45(a)(1).

4-4 Environmental Protection

LO ④
Federal environmental
protection legislation

Recognizing that the environment is the property of everyone, the federal government and many states have enacted a number of laws to protect our environment. A federal agency, the Environmental Protection Agency (EPA), administers many of these federal laws. The laws the EPA administers include the following:

1. The Clean Air Act
2. The Water Pollution and Control Act
3. The Resource Conservation and Recovery Act
4. The Comprehensive Environmental Response, Compensation, and Liability Act

4-4a CLEAN AIR ACT

The Clean Air Act was the first national environmental law. Under this law, the EPA sets minimum national standards for air quality and regulates hazardous air pollutants. These standards protect public health and welfare. The states apply and enforce these standards under EPA-approved state implementation plans setting limits on pollutants. The law provides civil and criminal penalties for its violation.

4-4b WATER POLLUTION AND CONTROL ACT

Congress enacted the Water Pollution and Control Act (also referred to simply as the Clean Water Act—or CWA) to restore and maintain the proper chemistry of U.S. waters, including adjacent wetlands. The law seeks to prevent the discharge of pollutants into interstate and navigable waters. The EPA has the primary administration and enforcement responsibility under the law. It sets limits on discharges, including pollutants into sewer systems; has the responsibility for wetlands protection; and can block or overrule the issuance of permits under the law. The EPA or private citizens may sue on the basis of the act, which even includes criminal liability for violation.

COURT CASE

FACTS: Braulio Agosto-Vega (Agosto) owned a real estate development company, Mansiones de Hacienda Jiménez Inc. (Mansiones). Mansiones built a housing project that abutted Jiménez Creek. The creek ran into a major river, the Espíritu Santo, which was subject to the ebb and flow of tides and navigable. Very shortly after occupancy of Mansiones, raw sewage repeatedly overflowed its septic tanks. Mansiones employees used a hose to suction sewage from the septic tanks. They discharged it into storm sewers that emptied into the creek or into a large tank truck and then into the storm sewers or directly into the creek. Agosto was charged with conspiracy to violate the CWA.

OUTCOME: Since the river was subject to the ebb and flow of tides and navigable, it was subject to the CWA. Having caused the discharge of pollutants into it, Agosto was guilty.

—*U.S. v. Agosto-Vega*, 617 F.3d 541 (1st Cir.)

4-4c RESOURCE CONSERVATION AND RECOVERY ACT

The Resource Conservation and Recovery Act regulates the generation, storage, transportation, treatment, and disposal of hazardous waste. The law lists certain wastes defined as hazardous, but the term includes ignitable, corrosive, reactive, or toxic waste.

The law gives the EPA the duty of setting standards for individuals who own or operate hazardous waste disposal facilities. Anyone who generates or transports hazardous waste, and owners and operators of facilities for the treatment, storage, or disposal of such waste, must obtain a permit and must comply with the requirements of the permit. The law requires individuals handling hazardous waste to keep extensive records in order to track it from generation to disposal. It provides large civil and criminal penalties for its violation. This law also permits suits by private citizens.

4-4d COMPREHENSIVE ENVIRONMENTAL RESPONSE, COMPENSATION, AND LIABILITY ACT

Perhaps the most discussed federal environmental legislation, the Comprehensive Environmental Response, Compensation, and Liability Act (CERCLA), also called the "Superfund" law, seeks the cleanup of waste from previous activities and requires notification of the release of hazardous substances. CERCLA imposes liability for cleanup on past and current owners or operators of facilities where hazardous substances have been released, on anyone who arranged for disposal of substances where released, and on anyone who transported them. CERCLA imposes liability retroactively—acts that occurred before enactment of this law and were not negligent or illegal then can be the basis of liability.

Multiple Party Liability. Because CERCLA imposes liability on four groups of people—owners, operators, disposers, and transporters—several parties could be liable for one site. A liable party may take legal action to require other responsible or potentially responsible parties to pay a share of cleanup costs. Courts have stated that when several defendants are responsible under CERCLA, liability should be apportioned according to their contribution to the problem. However, if liability cannot be apportioned, or only one liable party has any funds, one party could be liable for the entire cleanup cost. These costs can run into the millions of dollars.

Business Costs. These provisions of CERCLA concern businesses and potential business owners because of the possibility of courts imposing huge cleanup costs on them as new owners of facilities who never released hazardous wastes there. A past owner of a facility could have released a hazardous substance twenty years ago. There could have been a series of sales of the facility so that the current owner did not know about the release. Yet, the current owner might still have to pay for or help pay for the cleanup. Some courts have found everyone in the chain of ownership of contaminated property, from disposal of the substance to the current owner, liable for cleanup. Thus, anyone buying contaminated land is potentially liable for cleanup costs. This can have serious repercussions for all landowners but particularly for businesses, as business or manufacturing sites are the most likely to have been the sites of a release of hazardous substances.

Business costs could include not only large cleanup costs but also legal fees. Litigation under the Superfund law can be extremely expensive. A party responsible for cleanup costs can sue to require other "potentially" liable parties to share in the costs. Just the cost of defending against such a lawsuit can be very expensive. Legal fees have been reported to be 30 percent to 60 percent of Superfund costs.

In addition to owners of facilities, courts have imposed CERCLA liability on business employees who had control over disposal decisions. Even lenders have been found liable for cleanup costs if the court found them adequately involved in running the business.

4-4e STATE LAWS

A number of states have enacted state Superfund laws. They also impose liability for cleanup costs and may require notification of release of hazardous substances to state environmental agencies.

4-4f PROTECTION FROM LIABILITY

A person can take some steps to help reduce the potential of liability under CERCLA and state Superfund statutes. Banks and other lending institutions should require environmental assessments of properties before making a loan and before foreclosing on property. Before anyone buys or invests in property, an investigation should be made to identify any environmental risks and determine expected cleanup costs. Cleanup costs that run into the millions of dollars can be much greater than the value of the property involved.

QUESTIONS

1. Why does government regulate business?
2. By whom are administrative agencies run? How long do these individuals serve?
3. What is the difference between regulatory and nonregulatory agencies?
4. How does the Office of Foreign Assets Control (OFAC) enforce economic and trade sanctions imposed by the U.S. government?
5. What is the procedure a federal agency must follow to develop a new rule?
6. Why was the Federal Trade Commission (FTC) established? pg 42
7. What is the rule of reason approach used by courts in antitrust cases?
8. What is the purpose of the Water Pollution and Control Act?
9. How can a potential buyer of property take steps to help reduce the potential of liability under CERCLA and state Superfund statutes?
10. On whom does CERCLA impose liability for cleanup of waste?

ETHICS IN PRACTICE

Is it ethical for the law to impose liability retroactively? Should government force a person to pay for doing something that was legal and carried no penalty at the time it was done?

PART

2

5 Nature
and Classes
of Contracts

6 Offer and
Acceptance

7 Capacity
to Contract

8 Consideration

Defective
Agreements

Illegal
Agreements

Written
Contracts

Third Parties
and Contracts

13 Termination
of Contracts

Contracts

Businesses can be the targets of scams as easily as the average consumer. Educate your employees on what to watch out for, and before you sign on the dotted line, get all of the loan terms in writing, including the payment schedule and interest rate. If the lender is not familiar to you, contact your state banking department and ask how to confirm that the lender is licensed and operating properly. More information on fraud can be found at the website www.fraud.org, a project of the National Consumers League.

Nature and Classes of Contracts

LEARNING OBJECTIVES

① State the five requirements for a valid contract.

② Describe the types of contracts and how they differ from agreements.

③ Explain the difference between a contract and a *quasi* contract.

PREVIEW CASE

Brooklyn Union Gas Co. (BUG) discovered that gas was being consumed at 369 Euclid Avenue although there was no record of an account or meter at that address. The last account at that address had been closed fourteen years earlier. John Diggs was in possession of the premises at 369 Euclid. BUG sued him for the gas consumed at that location on the basis of a *quasi* contract for his unjust enrichment. Had BUG suffered any detriment? Had Diggs received any benefit for which he had not paid? Do you think it was ethical for Diggs to use the gas when there was no account for his address?

contract
legally enforceable
agreement

A **contract** can be defined as a legally enforceable agreement between two or more competent people. At first glance, this seems like a very simple definition. Notice that this definition does not even require a written document. Chapters 5 through 13 are devoted exclusively to explaining and clarifying this definition.

Making contracts is such an everyday occurrence that we often overlook their importance, except when the contracts are of a substantial nature. When one buys a cup of coffee during a coffee break, a contract has been made. When the purchaser agrees to pay $2 for the coffee, the seller agrees not only to supply one cup of coffee but also agrees by implication of law that it is safe to drink. If the coffee contains a harmful substance that makes the purchaser ill, a breach of contract has occurred that may call for the payment of damages. A **breach of contract** is the failure of one of the parties to perform the obligations assumed under the contract.

breach of contract
failure to perform
contractual obligations

Business transactions result from agreements. Every time a person makes a purchase, buys a theater ticket, or boards a bus, an agreement is made. Each party to the agreement obtains certain rights and assumes certain duties and obligations. When such an agreement meets all the legal requirements of a contract, the law recognizes it as binding on all parties. If one of the parties to the contract fails or refuses to perform, the law allows the other party an appropriate action for obtaining damages or enforcing performance by the party breaking the contract.

Contracts are extremely important in business because they form the very foundation upon which all modern business rests. Business consists almost entirely of the making and performing of contracts. A contract that is a sale of goods is governed by the Uniform Commercial Code (see Chapter 16).

5-1 Requirements for a Contract

LO ①
Requirements for contract

A contract is an agreement that courts will enforce against the parties to the agreement. It is sometimes referred to as a valid contract to distinguish from unenforceable arrangements. A contract must fulfill the following definite requirements:

1. It must be based on a mutual agreement by the parties to do or not to do a specific thing.
2. It must be made by parties who are competent to enter into a contract that will be enforceable against both parties.
3. The promise or obligation of each party must be supported by consideration (such as the payment of money, the delivery of goods, or the promise to do or refrain from doing some lawful future act) given by each party to the contract.
4. It must be for a lawful purpose; that is, the purpose of the contract must not be illegal, such as the unauthorized buying and selling of narcotics.
5. In some cases, the contract must meet certain formal requirements, such as being in writing or under seal.

You may test the validity of any alleged contract using these five requirements.

5-2 Contracts Contrasted with Agreements

LO ②
Types of contracts and differences from agreements

A contract must be an agreement, but an agreement need not be a contract. An agreement results whenever two or more people's minds meet on any subject, no matter how trivial. Only when the parties intend to be legally obligated by the terms of the agreement will a contract come into existence. Chapter 6 explains how such agreements are formed. Ordinarily, the subject matter of the contract must involve a business transaction as distinguished from a purely social transaction.

If Mary and John promise to meet at a certain place at 6 P.M. and have dinner together, this is an agreement, not a contract, as neither intends to be legally bound to carry out the terms of the agreement.

If Alice says to David, "I will pay you $25 to be my escort for the Spring Ball," and David replies, "I accept your offer," the agreement results in a contract. David is legally obligated to provide escort service, and Alice is legally bound to pay him $25.

5-3 Classification of Contracts

Contracts are classified by many names or terms. Unless you understand these terms, you cannot understand the law of contracts. For example, the law may state that executory contracts made on Sunday are void. You cannot understand this law unless you understand the words *executory* and *void*. Every contract may be placed in one of the following classifications:

1. Contracts, void agreements, and voidable contracts
2. Express and implied contracts
3. Formal and simple contracts
4. Executory and executed contracts
5. Unilateral and bilateral contracts

5-3a CONTRACTS, VOID AGREEMENTS, AND VOIDABLE CONTRACTS

Agreements classified according to their enforceability include contracts (defined earlier), **void** agreements, and voidable contracts.

An agreement with no legal effect is void. An agreement not enforceable in a court of law does not come within the definition of a contract. A void agreement (sometimes referred to as a "void contract") must be distinguished from an **unenforceable contract**. If the law requires a certain contract to be in a particular form, such as a deed to be in writing, and it is not in that form, it is merely unenforceable, not void. It can be made enforceable by changing the form to meet the requirements of the law. An agreement between two parties to perform an illegal act is void. Nothing the parties can do will make this agreement an enforceable contract.

A **voidable contract** would be an enforceable agreement but, because of circumstances or the capacity of a party, one or both of the parties may set it aside. The distinguishing factor of a voidable contract is the existence of a choice by one party to abide by or to reject the contract. A contract made by an adult with a person not of lawful age (legally known as a "minor" or "infant") is often voidable by the minor. Such a contract is enforceable against the adult but not against the minor. If both parties to an agreement are minors, either one may avoid the agreement. Until the party having the choice to avoid the contract exercises the right to set the contract aside, the contract remains in full force and effect. An agreement that does not meet all five of the requirements for a valid contract might be void, or it might be a voidable contract.

5-3b EXPRESS AND IMPLIED CONTRACTS

Contracts classified according to the manner of their formation fall into two groups: express and implied contracts. In an **express contract**, the parties express their intentions by words, whether in writing or orally, at the time they make the agreement. Both their intention to contract and the terms of the agreement are expressly stated or written. Customary business terms, however, do not need to be stated in an express contract in order to be binding.

An **implied contract** (also called an **implied in fact contract**) is one in which the duties and the obligations that the parties assume are not expressed but are implied by their acts or conduct. The adage "Actions speak louder than words" very appropriately describes this class of contracts. The facts of a situation imply that a contract exists. The parties indicate that they have a mutual agreement so clearly by their conduct and what they intend to do that there is no need to express the agreement in words to make it binding.

---

void
of no legal effect

unenforceable contract
agreement that is not currently binding

voidable contract
enforceable agreement that may be set aside by one party

express contract
contract with the terms of the agreement specified in words

implied contract or implied in fact contract
contract with major terms implied by the parties' conduct

COURT CASE

FACTS: The City of Dillon, Montana, agreed to allow Robert and Patricia McNeill to connect "one water service" to the city water main. Years later, the McNeills asked the city to approve a second water service. It did not approve, because of a "lack of information." Three years later, the McNeills sold a parcel of property. The city installed a water meter on a second tap on the McNeills' line and started billing the owner of the parcel for water. Justin and Susan Conner later bought the parcel and received and paid the city's monthly water bills. Four years later, the creek that supplied the water and the water main froze. The Conners were without water for several weeks. They sued the city, alleging an implied contract to supply them with water.

OUTCOME: The court held that the conduct of the city in installing a water meter and billing and collecting for the water supplied manifested the existence of a contract.

—*Conner v. City of Dillon*, 270 P.3d 75 (Mont.)

COURT CASE

FACTS: Double Knobs Mountain Ranch purchased real estate from Susan Chacon. The sale was accomplished through a note, a deed of trust, and a warranty deed with a vendor's lien. The note provided that payments to Chacon were due the first of every month, but would not be considered late until after the tenth of the month. The note did not define the term "default." For 22 of the 24 payments, Chacon accepted payments made after the first, but before the tenth of the month. Chacon then sold the note to Schuhardt Consulting Profit Sharing Plan, but Double Knobs was unaware of the transfer. For its upcoming September payment, Double Knobs sent a check to Chacon's agent, who cashed the check and then sent payment to Schuhardt. Chacon's agent sent Double Knobs a letter at the end of September stating that Chacon wanted payments to be made by the first of the month from that point forward. Chacon did not make its next payment by October 1st. On October 3rd, Schuhardt notified Double Knobs that it was the owner of the note and that Double Knobs was in default of the terms of the note, because it had not made payment by the first of the month. Double Knobs delivered payment on October 5th. Schuhardt rejected that payment, accelerated payment for the outstanding balance, and began foreclosure proceedings. Double Knobs sued Schuhardt to obtain a declaratory judgment that under an implied agreement, its October 5th payment was not in default.

OUTCOME: The court found that the regular conduct of the Double Knobs and Chacon created an implied agreement that payments made after the first of the month were not in default of the terms of the note.

—*Schuhardt Consulting Profit Sharing Plan v. Double Knobs Mountain Ranch, Inc.*, 2014 WL 7185081 (Tex. Ct. App.)

5-3c FORMAL AND SIMPLE CONTRACTS

A **formal contract** must be in a special form or be created in a certain way. Formal contracts include contracts under seal, recognizances, and negotiable instruments.

When very few people could write, contracts were signed by means of an impression in wax attached to the paper. As time passed, a small wafer pasted on

formal contract
contract with special form or manner of creation

the contract replaced the use of wax. The wafer seal was used in addition to the written signature.

This practice is still used occasionally, but the more common practice is to sign formal contracts using the word "Seal" or the letters "L.S." after the signatures:

Jane Doe (Seal); Jane Doe [L.S.]

Today, it is immaterial whether these substitutes for a seal are printed on the document, or typewritten before signing, or the people signing write them after their respective names. However, in some states, the document itself also must recite that it is under seal. In jurisdictions where the use of the seal has not been abolished, the seal implies consideration.

In some states, the presence of a seal on a contract allows a party a longer time in which to bring suit if the contract is broken. Other states make no distinction between contracts under seal and other written contracts. The Uniform Commercial Code abolishes the distinction with respect to contracts for the sale of goods.

COURT CASE

FACTS: Columbia, Maryland, and Aileen Ames executed a declaration by which Columbia conveyed real property to Ames subject to certain charges and liens. The declaration provided for an annual assessment and lien against the property. It stated that by accepting a deed to a lot in the property, each owner would be subject to the annual assessment. At the end the declaration stated: "the parties. . . have set their. . . seals" and the word "seal" was printed after Ames's signature. Joseph Poteet and his wife, Shirley, obtained a lot in the property by a deed, which recited it was subject to the charges and liens in the declaration. Columbia billed the Poteets for the annual assessment, but for 30 years

they did not pay. The statute of limitations was 12 years for documents under seal and only 3 years for other documents. When sued, the Poteets argued the declaration was not under seal.

OUTCOME: The court held that the word "seal" after Ames's name made the declaration under seal as to her. It also held that the words "the parties . . . have set their . . . seals" were conclusive evidence of an intent by both parties to create a sealed document.

—*Columbia Ass'n Inc. v. Poteet*, 23 A.3d 308 (Md. Ct. Spec. App.)

recognizance
obligation entered into before a court to do an act required by law

Recognizances, a second type of formal contract, are obligations entered into before a court whereby people acknowledge that they will do a specified act that is required by law. By these obligations, people agree to be indebted for a specific amount if they do not perform as they agreed, such as the obligation a criminal defendant undertakes to appear in court on a particular day.

negotiable instrument
document of payment, such as a check

Negotiable instruments, discussed in later chapters, are a third type of formal contract. They include checks, notes, drafts, and certificates of deposit.

simple contract
contract that is not formal

All contracts other than formal contracts are informal and are called **simple contracts**. A few of these, such as an agreement to sell land or to be responsible for the debt of another, must be in writing in order to be enforceable; otherwise, they need not be prepared in any particular form. Generally speaking, informal or simple contracts may be in writing, oral, or implied from the conduct of the parties.

A **written contract** is one in which the terms are set forth in writing rather than expressed orally. An **oral contract** is one in which the terms are stated in spoken, not written, words. Such a contract is usually enforceable; however, when a contract is oral, disputes may arise between the parties as to the terms of the agreement. No such disputes need arise about the terms of a written contract if the wording is clear, explicit, and complete. For this reason, most businesspeople avoid making oral contracts involving matters of great importance. Some types of contracts are required to be in writing and are discussed in Chapter 11.

written contract
contract with terms in writing

oral contract
contract with terms spoken

5-3d EXECUTORY AND EXECUTED CONTRACTS

Contracts are classified by the stage of performance as executory contracts and executed contracts. An **executory contract** is one in which the terms have not been fully carried out by all parties. If a person agrees to work for another for one year in return for a salary of $3,500 per month, the contract is executory from the time it is made until the twelve months expire. Even if the employer should prepay the salary, it would still be an executory contract because the other party has not yet worked the entire year; that is, executed that part of the contract.

executory contract
contract not fully carried out

An **executed contract** is one that has been fully performed by all parties to the contract. The Collegiate Shop sells and delivers a dress to Benson for $105, and Benson pays the purchase price at the time of the sale. This is an executed contract because nothing remains to be done on either side; that is, each party has completed performance of each part of the contract.

executed contract
fully performed contract

COURT CASE

FACTS: Lila Clavin and Robert Gilbert formed Pastimes, LLC as equal owners and signed an operating agreement that provided the company would terminate upon the death of either member, unless two remaining members should agree to continue operating the company. Lila died and her son, Tim, became the personal representative for her estate. Gilbert and Tim orally contracted not to terminate Pastimes and to continue operating the company until it attained a profit. Under the oral contract, Lila's estate paid half of Pastimes's annual tax liability and received a half interest in the company's liquor license, whereas Gilbert continued to manage the company. Sometime later, after a disagreement, Gilbert sued to obtain a declaratory judgment that the valuation of Lila's portion should be controlled by the operating agreement in place at the time of her death, without regard to the oral contract between Gilbert and Tim.

OUTCOME: The court stated that the oral contract between the parties to continue running the business was fully executed and eliminated the need to use the operating agreement to value the estate's portion of the company. The determination of value was made at the time of trial.

—*Pastimes, LLC v. Clavin*, 274 P.3d 714 (Mont.)

5-3e UNILATERAL AND BILATERAL CONTRACTS

When an act is done in consideration for a promise, the contract is a **unilateral contract**. If Smith offers to pay $100 to anyone who returns her missing dog, and Fink returns the dog, this would be a unilateral contract. It is unilateral (one-sided) in that only one promise is made. A promise is given in exchange for an act. Smith

unilateral contract
contract calling for an act in consideration for a promise

bilateral contract
contract consisting of mutual exchange of promises

quasi **contract or implied in law contract**
imposition of rights and obligations by law without a contract

unjust enrichment
one party benefiting unfairly at another's expense

LO ③
Difference between contract and *quasi* contract

ETHICAL POINT

Notice that *quasi* contracts arise because of strictly ethical considerations. It is unfair for one person to benefit at the expense of another.

made the only promise, which was to pay anyone for the act of returning the dog. Fink was not obligated to find and return the dog, so only one duty existed.

A **bilateral contract** consists of a mutual exchange of promises to perform some future acts. One promise is the consideration for the other promise. If Brown promises to sell a truck to Adams for $5,000, and Adams agrees to pay $5,000, then the parties have exchanged a promise for a promise—a bilateral contract. Most contracts are bilateral, because the law states that a bilateral contract can be formed when performance is started. This is true unless it is clear from the first promise or the situation that performance must be completed. The test is whether there is only one right and duty or two.

5-3f *QUASI*-CONTRACT

One may have rights and obligations imposed by law when no real contract exists. This imposition of rights and obligations is called a *quasi* **contract** or **implied in law contract**. It is not a true contract, because the parties have not made an agreement. Rights and obligations will be imposed only when a failure to do so would result in one person unfairly keeping money or otherwise benefiting at the expense of another. This is known as **unjust enrichment**. For example, suppose a tenant is obligated to pay rent of $300 per month but by mistake hands the landlord $400. The law requires the landlord to return the overpayment of $100. The law creates an agreement for repayment even though no actual agreement exists between the parties. For the landlord to keep the money would mean an unjust enrichment at the expense of the tenant. Courts will also invoke the principles of unjust enrichment when there is a contract, but there is no remedy provided under the contract. An unjust enrichment offends our ethical principles, so the law imposes a contractual obligation to right the situation.

PREVIEW CASE REVISITED

FACTS: Brooklyn Union Gas Co. (BUG) discovered that gas was being consumed at 369 Euclid Avenue although there was no record of an account or meter at that address. The last account at that address had been closed fourteen years earlier. John Diggs was in possession of the premises at 369 Euclid. BUG sued him for the gas consumed at that location on the basis of *quasi* contract for his unjust enrichment.

OUTCOME: The fact that Diggs knew he was receiving gas and BUG was not paid for it established his *quasi*-contractual liability.

—*Brooklyn Union Gas Co. v. Diggs*, 2003 WL 42106 (N.Y. City Civ. Ct.)

QUESTIONS

1. What provision does the law allow if a party to a contract fails or refuses to perform it?

2. What is a contract?

3. How does a contract differ from an agreement?

4. Would an agreement to launder money be considered an unenforceable contract or void? Why?

QUESTIONS (CONTINUED)

5. What two items must be expressed in order to have an express contract?

6. How must a sealed contract be executed?

7. What is a recognizance?

8. Why are most business contracts written rather than oral?

9. When does an executory contract become an executed contract?

10. Why do courts sometimes impose a *quasi* contract on parties?

CASE PROBLEMS

When the concluding question in a case problem can be answered simply yes or no, state the legal principle or rule of law that supports your answer.

1. While shopping at Home Depot (HD), Carl Murphy cut his thumb, requiring 12 stitches. HD paid this medical bill, but the cut developed a staph infection, and Murphy claimed he lost $3,500 in medical bills and lost wages. Murphy sued HD. His lawyer wrote HD and offered to settle for $7,500. HD's lawyer offered $7,247 representing $7,500 minus HD's previous medical payment. Murphy's lawyer sent a proposed release to HD's lawyer covering "all losses . . . directly resulting from this incident. My release does not include any other claims." HD's lawyer sent back a new release with much broader language which Murphy's lawyer refused. No settlement was signed, and Murphy received no further payment. HD then asked the court to enforce the settlement agreement it said Murphy's lawyer had agreed to in the correspondence with HD's lawyer. Had a binding agreement been made? **LO ①**

2. By letters, the Twin Buttes School District had hired Cheryle Good Bird to be the elementary school head cook for two different school years. Each letter specifically set the term of employment as one school year. Before the first contract had expired, Good Bird had received a letter telling her she had been chosen to be the head cook specifically for the next school year. During the second contract period, the principal, by letter, told Good Bird the head cook position for the next school year was going to be advertised, but that she could apply for it. Good Bird reapplied but was not hired. Good Bird sued the school district, claiming it had breached an implied contract. Did Good Bird have an implied contract to continue to be the head cook? **LO ②**

3. ICG Link Inc. (ICG) maintained and serviced the website needs of TN Sports, LLC (TN). Greg Jones, ICG's developer and programmer who serviced TN's website, recommended a new website be built. He e-mailed a price quote for a new website to Philip Steen, who managed TN. The "quote" listed about 30 features to be included, the hours for each, and an hourly rate of $85. The total cost was $12,622. Steen liked the quote, and Jones started working on the new site. Although not finished, five months later the site was launched. Immediately there were problems with it. Four months later, TN stopped working with ICG. TN had not paid ICG for the new site or maintenance for seven months, so ICG sued alleging a *quasi* contract. Was there a *quasi* contract? **LO ③**

4. Uhrhahn Construction prepared proposals for work on construction projects for Lamar and Joan Hopkins. The Hopkinses signed the proposals for each project under sections titled "Acceptance of Proposal." The proposals stated that any changes to the written estimates and specifications had to be in writing. During the construction, the Hopkinses made several oral requests for additional work not included in the proposals. They paid for some of them after receiving invoices labeled "change orders" for such work. When they did not pay for the rest, Uhrhahn sued, alleging there was an implied contract to make oral changes. Was there such an implied contract? **LO ②**

CASE PROBLEMS (CONTINUED)

LO ③   5. Wendell Lund worked on his parents' farm, maintaining equipment, providing labor and supplies, and paying a portion of real estate taxes on the property. His parents, Orville and Betty Lund, let Wendell live on the farm and provided meals to him free of charge. The Lunds also provided Wendell assistance with the yard work. Wendell Lund's siblings helped the Lunds with farm work as well. After Orville and Betty Lund divorced and divided their property, Wendell claimed that his parents had been unjustly enriched by his years of labor. He sued his mother for $545,000 and his father for ownership of the family farm. Was there an implied in law contract between Wendell and his parents?

LO ①   6. Nina Parkhurst owned a ranch and asked her son, Doug Boykin, to move to it and manage it for her. Boykin and his wife moved to the ranch and managed it for several years. They talked with Parkhurst many times, urging her to transfer 49 percent of the ranch to them. Parkhurst said she had thought and talked about possibly transferring the ranch but had made no decision. The Boykins claimed they were on the ranch under an oral contract with Parkhurst and that the oral contract also entitled them to a 49 percent interest in the ranch. She sued them and asked the court to declare that there was no contract. Was there a contract?

LO ②   7. Attorney Mark Davis sought the services of a professional translator to translate an audio recording of his client as part of a divorce proceeding. Davis's office contacted Norma Chaparro and asked her to perform the services. Chaparro had previously translated documents for Davis, and her typical arrangement was to invoice and be paid by Davis for the services. Chaparro told Davis's office she could translate the tape but could not provide a quote for the services until she had examined the tape. After Chaparro assessed the tape, Davis's office was informed that the transcription would exceed 50 pages. The staff instructed Chaparro to do whatever necessary to finish the transcription. After delivering the completed transcription to Davis, Chaparro presented an invoice of $1,500 for her services. Davis refused to pay, stating that he had never promised to pay Chaparro and that she should seek payment from his client instead. Chaparro sued Davis, claiming that she had contracted with him, not his client, and that he had breached their contract by refusing to pay her. Did Davis breach an implied in fact contract with Chaparro?

Offer and Acceptance

CHAPTER 6

LEARNING OBJECTIVES

1. Discuss the requirements for a valid contract.
2. Explain the difference between an offer and an invitation to make an offer.
3. Summarize the rules affecting the duration of an offer.
4. Define a counteroffer.
5. State the way to accept an offer made by mail.

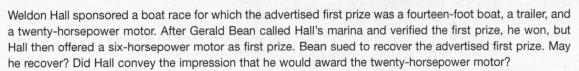

PREVIEW CASE

Weldon Hall sponsored a boat race for which the advertised first prize was a fourteen-foot boat, a trailer, and a twenty-horsepower motor. After Gerald Bean called Hall's marina and verified the first prize, he won, but Hall then offered a six-horsepower motor as first prize. Bean sued to recover the advertised first prize. May he recover? Did Hall convey the impression that he would award the twenty-horsepower motor?

LO ①
Valid contracts

A valid contract is created by the agreement of the parties. This agreement, vital to the formation of a contract, is frequently called "a meeting of the minds" of the parties. The agreement exists when one party makes an offer, and the other party accepts the offer.

The parties may expressly state, either orally or in writing, what they agree to do, or they may indicate their intentions by their actions. If A's conduct reasonably leads B to believe that A intends to enter into a binding contract, then A is bound as effectively as if the contract had been expressed. However, in business, a person seldom indicates every intention solely by acts. In most cases, only a part of the contract is expressed, and the other part is implied.

Two essential elements of a contract are: (1) an offer, either expressed or implied; and (2) an acceptance, either expressed or implied.

6-1 Requirements of a Valid Offer

The proposal to make a contract is the **offer**. The **offeror** is the person who makes the offer; the **offeree** is the person to whom the offer is made. An offer expresses the willingness of the offeror to enter into a contractual agreement. The

offer
proposal to make a contract

offeror
person who makes an offer

offeree
to whom an offer is made

mutual agreement required for a contract is composed of an offer and an acceptance. A valid offer includes three requirements:

1. It must be definite.
2. It must appear to be seriously intended.
3. It must be communicated to the offeree.

6-1a THE OFFER MUST BE DEFINITE

A contract will not be enforced unless the court can determine what the parties agreed to. The offeror's intentions are ascertained from the offer, and these intentions cannot be ascertained unless the offer is definite. Terms usually required to be stated would include the identity of the offeree; the subject matter of the offer; and the price, quantity, and time of performance.

COURT CASE

FACTS: Gaylord Smelser bought a Dodge 4WD diesel truck from a dealer. He immediately had trouble with the transmission and repeatedly took the truck in for repair, but the problem persisted. He sued DaimlerChrysler, the manufacturer. Smelser instructed Price, his attorney, to negotiate a settlement that contained a "lifetime warranty" for the truck. DaimlerChrysler's attorney believed the attorneys had reached a settlement and sent Price a letter with settlement terms. They did not include a "lifetime warranty." Price never communicated with Smelser about the letter. DaimlerChrysler moved to enforce the settlement. Smelser argued there was no contract to settle the case.

OUTCOME: The court found that Smelser had never agreed to the alleged settlement terms, so there was no settlement contract.

—*DaimlerChrysler Corp. v. Smelser*, 375 Ark. 216 (Ark.)

The Uniform Commercial Code modifies this strict rule somewhat as to contracts for the sale of goods. It is not always practical for a businessperson to make an offer for the sale of merchandise that is definite as to price. The offeror may state that the price will be determined by the market price at a future date or by a third party. If the contract does not specify the price, the buyer must ordinarily pay the reasonable value of the goods.

6-1b THE OFFER MUST APPEAR TO BE SERIOUSLY INTENDED

One may make an offer in jest, banter, fear, or extreme anger, and if this fact is known or should be known by the offeree because of the surrounding circumstances, no contract is formed. A business transaction is ordinarily not entered into in jest or because of extreme fear or anger, and the offeree has no right to think that the offer is seriously intended when it is made under these circumstances.

COURT CASE

FACTS: James Mason, a defense attorney, represented a client charged with murder. In a highly publicized television interview, Mason discussed his client's alibi and the implausible time line for the murder set forth by the prosecutor. Mason stated that he would pay a million dollars to anyone who could make it off a flight in Atlanta's busy airport and travel to a specific hotel several miles away within twenty-eight minutes. Dustin Kolodziej watched an edited version of the interview, and, being a law student, interpreted Mason's challenge as a serious offer. Kolodziej recorded himself retracing the defendant's route and making it to the specified hotel in less than twenty-eight minutes. Kolodziej then sent Mason a copy of the recording as proof that he had accepted Mason's offer and requested payment of one million dollars. Mason refused, stating that the challenge was not seriously made. Kolodziej sued for breach of contract.

OUTCOME: The court held that given the context of the interview and the exaggerated amount, a reasonable person would not find Mason's statement to be a serious offer. There was no contract.

—*Kolodziej v. Mason*, 774 F.3d 736 (11th Cir.)

There are times when the offer is not seriously intended, but the offeree has no way of knowing this. In that event, if the offer is accepted, a binding contract results.

6-1c THE OFFER MUST BE COMMUNICATED TO THE OFFEREE

Until the offeror makes the offer known to the offeree, it is not certain that it is intended that the offeree may accept and thereby impose a binding contract. Accordingly, the offeree cannot accept an offer until the offeror has communicated the offer to the offeree. If one writes out an offer, and it falls into the hands of the offeree without the knowledge or consent of the offeror, it cannot be accepted. Furthermore, an offer directed to a specific individual or firm cannot be accepted by anyone else. This is because people have a right to choose the parties with whom they deal.

COURT CASE

FACTS: Injured when her car collided with a vehicle driven by Shawn Dale, Sheila McEvoy sued Dale and his employer, Aerotek Inc. McEvoy settled with Dale for $100,000. Believing that her damages were greater, McEvoy proceeded to trial against Aerotek. Prior to judgment, Aerotek had mailed an offer of judgment of $100,001, but neither McEvoy nor her attorney received it. The jury awarded McEvoy $75,000. In this state, there were sanctions against a party who did not accept an offer of judgment when the result of the trial was more favorable to the opposing party than the offer of settlement. Aerotek argued that McEvoy should be sanctioned.

OUTCOME: While Aerotek had mailed the offer of settlement, since McEvoy had not received it, she could not have accepted it. No sanctions were imposed.

—*McEvoy v. Aerotek Inc.*, 34 P.3d 979 (Ariz. Ct. App.)

LO
Offer versus invitation
to make offer

6-2 Invitations to Make Offers

In business, many apparent offers are not true offers. Instead, they are treated as invitations to the public to make offers at certain terms and prices. If a member of the public accepts the invitation, and an offer is submitted embodying all the terms set out in the invitation, the inviter may refuse to accept the offer. Ordinarily, however, as a practical matter and in the interest of maintaining goodwill, such an offer will be accepted. The most common types of general invitations are advertisements, window displays, catalogs, price lists, and circulars. If a merchant displays a coat for $95 in a store window, there is no binding requirement to sell at this price. Most businesspeople would consider refusing to sell to be a very poor business policy, but nevertheless merchants may legally do so. Considering advertisements and window displays as invitations to make offers rather than offers provides protection to businesspeople. Otherwise, they might find that they were subjected to many suits for breach of contract if they oversold their stock of goods.

COURT CASE

FACTS: Audio Visual Associates Inc. sued Sharp Electronics Corp. for, among other things, breach of contract. In its complaint, Audio alleged that it had contacted Sharp about purchasing 1,400 Sharp graphing calculators and that Sharp had first quoted a price of $71 per calculator, but later orally quoted Audio a price of $31. Audio faxed a purchase order to Sharp for 1,400 calculators at $31 each. When Audio inquired about its order, a Sharp employee told it the calculators were "sold out." Audio alleged that Sharp had more than 30,000 in stock. Sharp did refer Audio to a Sharp distributor, from whom Audio purchased the calculators.

OUTCOME: The court stated that buyers and sellers may exchange price quotations, purchase orders, telephone calls, and faxes concerning a proposed transaction without incurring contractual obligations until there is an offer by one party, followed by an acceptance by the other. Unless there is more, a price quote is simply an invitation to negotiate. There was no contract in this case.

—Audio Visual Associates Inc. v. Sharp Electronics Corp., 210 F.3d 254 (4th Cir.)

The general rule is that circulars are not offers but invitations to the recipients to make an offer. However, it is often difficult to distinguish between a general sales letter and a personal sales letter. The fact that the letter is addressed to a particular individual does not necessarily make it a personal sales letter containing an offer. If the wording indicates that the writer is merely trying to evoke an offer on certain terms, it is an invitation to the other party to make an offer.

An advertisement, however, may be an offer when it clearly shows it is intended as an offer. This is primarily true with advertisements that offer rewards.

PREVIEW CASE REVISITED

FACTS: Weldon Hall sponsored a boat race for which the advertised first prize was a fourteen-foot boat, a trailer, and a twenty-horsepower motor. After Gerald Bean called Hall's marina and verified the first prize, he won, but Hall then offered a six-horsepower motor as first prize. Bean sued to recover the advertised first prize.

OUTCOME: The court found that Hall had made an offer to the public, which Bean accepted by winning the race.

—Hall v. Bean, 582 S.W.2d 263 (Tex. Civ. App.)

6-3 Duration of the Offer

Several rules affect the duration of an offer:

LO ③
Rules on duration of offers

1. The offeror may revoke an offer at any time before its acceptance. If it has been revoked, the offeree can no longer accept it and create a contract. Normally, the offer can be revoked even if the offeror has promised to keep it open.

COURT CASE

FACTS: Joe Trejo was charged with several counts of second degree robbery and, prior to his trial, engaged in plea bargain negotiations with the prosecution. One day while in the courtroom, the defense counsel mistakenly represented to Trejo that an offer of 20 years was made in exchange for a guilty plea. A member of the prosecution team did not correct the defense counsel's assertion regarding the offer. The defendant declined the 20 year offer. The next day, a dispute arose between the defense counsel and the lead prosecutor, who had not been present in the courtroom when the discussion regarding the 20 year plea deal occurred. The prosecutor contended that the offer was for 28 years, and that an offer for

20 years was never made. After Trejo was convicted of all counts, he claimed that the prosecution's conduct had negatively impacted the integrity of the plea bargain process and asked the appellate court to remand the case so that he could accept the 20 year settlement offer.

OUTCOME: Despite the confusion over the 20 year offer, the prosecution clearly withdrew the 20 year offer, before Trejo accepted it. Trejo's conviction was upheld.

—People v. Trejo, 199 Cal. App. 4th 646 (Cal. App.)

2. An option cannot be revoked at will. If the offeror receives something of value in return for a promise to hold the offer open, it is said to be an **option**, and this type of offer cannot be revoked.

option
binding promise to hold an offer open

If the offer relates to the sale or purchase of goods by a merchant, a signed written offer to purchase or sell that states that it will be held open cannot be revoked

firm offer
merchant's signed, written offer to sell or purchase goods, saying it will be held open

during the time stated. If no time is stated, it cannot be revoked for a reasonable time, not to exceed three months. This type of offer is called a **firm offer**. It is valid even though no payment is made to the offeror.

COURT CASE

FACTS: Tenants Glen and Dale Phillips's lease stated: "Tenant shall have the right of first refusal to match any . . . [genuine] offer to purchase. . . . In the event Tenant fails to exercise his option within thirty days following presentment of said . . . offer . . . the option herein granted shall terminate." The owner notified them of an offer to buy the property and prior to the expiration of thirty days attempted to revoke the option. The Phillipses sued to require sale of the property to them.

OUTCOME: The court stated that the option was irrevocable for thirty days. The seller could not revoke it.

—*In re Smith Trust*, 731 N.W.2d 810 (Mich. Ct. App.)

In states in which the seal has its common law effect, an offer cannot be revoked when it is contained in a sealed writing that states that it will not be revoked.

3. A revocation of an offer must be communicated to the offeree prior to the acceptance. Mere intention to revoke is not sufficient. This is true even though the intent is clearly shown to people other than the offeree, as when the offeror dictates a letter of revocation.

Notice to the offeree that the offeror has behaved in a way that indicates the offer is revoked, such as selling the subject matter of the offer to another party, revokes the offer.

COURT CASE

FACTS: Conference America (CA) contracted to provide telephone and Internet conferencing services to Conexant Systems. The contract terminated fifteen days after notice of termination by a party and did not mention deactivation fees. Conexant eventually established 1,778 accounts with CA. No fee was charged to deactivate accounts during the term of the contract. CA terminated the contract effective July 10, stating, "[S]ervices used by Conexant after termination will be made available only on and subject to Conference America's standard terms, conditions, and prices effective at the time." On July 20, Conexant e-mailed CA, "requesting that all Conexant conferencing accounts be disconnected" by July 31. CA replied that deactivating all Conexant conferencing accounts effective August 1 was a service it offered and that it would comply. In a letter received by CA on August 1, Conexant responded that "Conexant . . . does not agree to any new terms governing our relationship. We continue to operate under . . . terms and conditions in the [original contract]." CA deactivated the accounts July 31; its standard terms included deactivation fees of $74.95 for each account amounting to $146,453. Conexant alleged that its letter saying that it did not agree to new terms constituted a revocation of its request of July 20 to disconnect all conferencing accounts.

OUTCOME: The court stated that in order to have an effective revocation, Conexant would have had to communicate it to CA before CA performed the requested service. This, Conexant had not done. The judgment was in favor of CA.

—*Conference America Inc. v. Conexant Systems Inc.*, 508 F.Supp.2d 1005 (M.D. Ala.)

4. An offer is terminated by the lapse of the time specified in the offer. If no time is specified in the offer, it is terminated by a lapse of a reasonable time after being communicated to the offeree. A reasonable length of time varies with each case, depending on the circumstances. It may be ten minutes in one case, and sixty days in another. Important circumstances are whether the price of the goods or services involved is fluctuating rapidly, whether perishable goods are involved, and whether there is keen competition with respect to the subject matter of the contract.

5. Death or insanity of the offeror automatically terminates the offer. This applies even though the offeree is not aware of the death or the insanity of the offeror and communicates an acceptance of the offer. Both parties must be alive and competent to contract at the moment the acceptance is properly communicated to the offeror.

6. Rejection of the offer by the offeree and communication of the rejection to the offeror terminates the offer.

7. If, after an offer has been made, the performance of the contract becomes illegal, the offer is terminated.

6-4 The Acceptance

When an offer has been properly communicated to the party for whom it is intended, and that party or an authorized agent accepts, a binding contract is formed. The offer then can no longer be revoked. **Acceptance** is the assent to an offer that results in a contract. The acceptance must be communicated to the offeror, but no particular procedure is required. A mere mental intention to accept is not sufficient for an acceptance. The acceptance may be made by words—oral or written—or by some act that clearly shows an intention to accept.

acceptance
assent to an offer resulting in a contract

COURT CASE

FACTS: When Dorothy Drury, who suffered from dementia and could not manage her affairs, was admitted to an assisted-living facility, her son, Eddie, signed the residency agreement. Eddie had no authority to sign on Dorothy's behalf. A year later, Dorothy died from injuries suffered in a fall, and the personal representative of her estate sued the assisted-living facility. The Residency Agreement provided that binding arbitration would be used to settle any disputes, so the facility asked the court to require arbitration.

OUTCOME: Because Dorothy suffered from dementia, she had not knowingly accepted the benefits of the agreement, so arbitration was not required.

—*Drury v. Assisted Living Concepts Inc.*, 262 P.3d 1162 (Or. Ct. App.)

Only in rare cases does silence constitute an acceptance. Those instances include:

1. When the offeree accepts the benefit of offered services with reasonable opportunity to reject them, knowing compensation is expected

2. When the offeree has given the offeror reason to know that assent might be shown by silence, and in remaining silent the offeree intends to accept the offer

3. When, because of previous dealings, it is reasonable for the offeree to notify the offeror of non-acceptance

If the offer stipulates a particular mode of acceptance, the offeree must meet those standards in order for a contract to be formed.

LO ④
Define counteroffer

counteroffer
offeree's response that rejects offer by varying its terms

6-5 Counteroffers

An offer must be accepted without any deviation in its terms. If the intended acceptance varies or qualifies the offer, this **counteroffer** rejects the original offer. This rejection terminates the offer. This rule is changed to some extent when the offer relates to the sale or purchase of goods. In any case, a counteroffer may be accepted or rejected by the original offeror.

COURT CASE

FACTS: Johnny Thompson's son was a passenger in a car accident in which everyone in the car was killed. Thompson, as personal representative for his son's estate, sent a settlement offer to the insurance company. Thompson's letter listed four conditions for acceptance. The insurance company responded with a letter stating that the company accepted the terms and conditions of Thompson's settlement offer and mirrored the four conditions set forth in Thompson's letter. However, the insurance company's letter went on to state that prior to issuing a settlement check, the insurance company wanted Thompson to sign a release of all claims against Geico's insureds, Christice Guillaume and Patricia Guillaume, who were also involved in the car crash. Thompson declined to sign the release and

sued Christice and Patricia. Christice and Patricia argued that Thompson was barred from filing suit by the settlement contract between Thompson and the insurance company.

OUTCOME: The insurance company's letter did not constitute acceptance of Thompson's settlement offer, because the indemnification language in the release significantly changed the terms of the contract. The insurance company's letter was a counteroffer, which Thompson did not accept. Hence, there was no settlement contract.

—*Thompson v. Estate of Maurice*, 150 So.3d 1183
(Fla. Dist. App.)

6-6 Inquiries Not Constituting Rejection

The offeree may make an inquiry about terms that differ from the offer's terms without rejecting the offer. For example, if the offer is for 1,000 shares of stock for $20,000 cash, the offeree may ask, "Would you be willing to wait thirty days for $10,000 and hold the stock as collateral security?" This mere inquiry about changed terms does not reject the offer. If the offeror says no, the original offer may still be accepted if it has not been revoked in the meantime.

6-7 Manner of Acceptance

LO ⑤
Acceptance by mail

An offer that does not specify a particular manner of acceptance may be accepted in any manner reasonable under the circumstances. However, the offeror may stipulate that the acceptance must be written and received by the offeror in order to be effective. If there is no requirement of delivery, a properly mailed acceptance is effective when it is posted. This rule is called the "mailbox rule," and it applies even though the offeror never receives the acceptance. In former years, the courts held that an offer could be accepted only by the same means by which the offer was communicated to the offeree, called the "mirror-image rule," but this view is being abandoned in favor of the provision of the Uniform Commercial Code, Sec. 2-206(1)(a), relating to sales of goods: "Unless otherwise unambiguously indicated by the language or circumstances, an offer to make a [sales] contract shall be construed as inviting acceptance in any manner and by any medium reasonable in the circumstances." Under this principle, an acceptance can be made by telephone, by fax, or in some jurisdictions by e-mail. The contract is made on the date and at the place the fax acceptance is sent.

COURT CASE

FACTS: The City of El Paso condemned the vacant house of Corral Lerma and ordered the structure be demolished in the interest of public safety. Corral's husband, Eddie Lerma, contacted Border Demolition & Environmental to discuss the project. Border Demolition offered to demolish the house for $11,000 and sent Eddie a written contract with the terms. After several telephone conversations, Eddie called Border Demolition's president and said "I need you to get started" on the project. Border Demolition requested a signed contract, but Eddie stated that he had already sent that to the company. Border Demolition proceeded to demolish Corral's house. Border Demolition sent Eddie an invoice and when he refused to pay, the company filed suit for breach of contract. Eddie argued no contract was formed, because he had not signed the written contract from Border Demolition.

OUTCOME: The court held that the terms of the written contract did not preclude oral acceptance and that Eddie's request for performance constituted acceptance of the contract. Thus, a valid contract existed between the parties.

—*Lerma v. Border Demolition & Environmental Inc.*,
459 S.W.3d 695 (Tex. Ct. App.)

Careful and prudent people can avoid many difficulties by stipulating in the offer how it must be accepted and when the acceptance is to become effective. For example, the offer could state, "The acceptance must be sent by letter and be received by me in Chicago by noon on June 15 before the contract is complete." The acceptance would not be effective unless it was sent by letter and actually received by the offeror in Chicago by the time specified.

QUESTIONS

1. What does it mean for parties to have "a meeting of the minds"?
2. Explain the two essential elements of a contract.
3. List the three requirements for a valid offer.
4. What are common types of invitations to make an offer?
5. When may an offeree accept an offer?
6. a. When may an offer be revoked?

   b. What is the effect of death or insanity of the offeror on an offer?
7. How long is an offer open for acceptance?
8. Does a mere inquiry about the terms of an offer cause the offer to be rejected? Why or why not?
9. Explain the consequences when an intended acceptance varies or qualifies the offer.
10. What is the "mailbox rule"?

CASE PROBLEMS

LO ⑤

1. Larry Horton negotiated with Commercial Recovery Systems Inc. to settle a debt. Commercial sent Horton a letter saying that $1,000 would be accepted as full and final settlement of the $25,038 owed. The letter continued, "This offer will be extended through June 30 . . . after which time the full balance will be due. In addition, all derogatory credit information regarding the account to be settled. . . . Terms: $500.00 due 6/15 . . . & $500 due 6/30. . . ." On June 18, Commercial received a $500 check from Horton dated June 14. On July 2, it received a second $500 check dated July 27. Two years later, Horton learned that his credit report still contained adverse information concerning the account. Horton sued, saying that Commercial had not complied with its contract. Commercial argued that its letter offer had not been accepted because the only way Horton could have accepted was by making full payment on or before June 30. Had Horton accepted the letter offer?

LO ②

2. A group of plaintiffs alleged that a gas station ran a promotion with an advertisement stating that if individuals purchased ten gallons of gas, they would get a free ski lift ticket voucher upon presentation of their gas receipt. However, when individuals attempted to obtain their ski lift ticket vouchers, the gas station gave them a "buy one get one free" coupon that required them to purchase one lift ticket at full price from the ski lodge in order to get a free ski lift ticket. The individuals who purchased ten gallons of gas alleged that a contract existed between the gas station and themselves, because the gas station's advertisement was an offer that they had accepted. Were they correct?

LO ①

3. After the borrower defaulted on a $16.8 million note, Principal Life Insurance Co. (Principal), who owned the note, asked its employee, Michael Logsdon, to sell it. Paul Cheng agreed to buy the note for $14.3 million. Logsdon sent Cheng a blank purchase and sale agreement (PSA). Logsdon phoned Cheng and told him that Principal's Investment Committee had approved the sale and asked for a written PSA. Cheng said, "I agree to it. . . . I accept it." He sent Logsdon a PSA with changes, including altering: the buyer from Cheng to Revalen Development, the price from $14.3 million to $14.299 million, and the earnest money from $71,500 to $100. The defaulting borrower and Principal agreed to refinance the note so it was no longer for sale. Revalen sued, alleging breach of an oral contract. Principal claimed there had been no offer. Had there been an offer?

CASE PROBLEMS (CONTINUED)

4. Zalman Silber, an insurance agent for New York Life Insurance Co. (NY), had another business that the company prohibited its agents from undertaking. NY's senior vice president wrote Silber, ". . . you agreed . . . [to] resign as an agent of New York Life and that once your . . . business was sold you would apply for reinstatement. . . . I agreed that we would review your application for reinstatement . . . and so long as . . . your other outside business activities were acceptable to the Company, and there were no intervening compliance issues, we would reinstate your contract. . . . If you are in agreement . . . sign below and return a copy of this letter." Silber did not sign the letter, return it, or resign. NY then sent Silber a letter saying that since he had not responded and could not be reached, he was suspended, and that unless it heard from him by June 16, it would terminate his agency. Silber wrote there would be no point in "moving forward" unless one term were resolved and that they should discuss credit of his service time upon reinstatement, the sale of his prohibited business, and other matters. NY terminated him. He later applied for reinstatement, but NY denied his application. Silber sued, claiming he had an oral agreement confirmed by the letter from the senior vice president. Did he have a contract with NY? **LO ①**

5. Cherokee Rose Design & Build LLC hired Muilenburg Inc. to install underground utilities in a subdivision. After the work was done, Muilenburg sued Cherokee, alleging it had not been paid. Cherokee's lawyer sent a proposed settlement to Muilenburg. It stated: Cherokee would sell three lots to Muilenburg for $75,000; the parties would fully release each other; Muilenburg would dismiss the lawsuit; each party would bear its own costs. Muilenburg's lawyer responded, writing, "My client has authorized me to convey its acceptance of the settlement offer," but Cherokee would have to "convey marketable title by way of a warranty deed," and Muilenburg would like Cherokee to provide a title insurance commitment. After Rose's lawyer prepared releases, Muilenburg realized it had to pay $75,000 for the lots and alleged it had not made an unconditional acceptance because of the requirement of marketable title and request for a title insurance commitment. Was Muilenburg's response a counteroffer? **LO ④**

6. MLS Construction LLC asked MD Drilling and Blasting Inc. to do rock drilling and blasting work required for an excavation project. MD had previously done work for MLS but had not been fully paid. MD agreed to do the new work if MLS made a significant payment on the balance due. MLS agreed and gave MD a check for $15,000. MD began work and the same day faxed an unsigned written agreement to MLS. Two weeks later, MD learned that MLS had stopped payment on the check. MD stopped work on the project and sued MLS for breach of contract. MLS argued that the unsigned agreement that MD faxed revoked the original offer, and therefore there was no contract. Did it? **LO ③**

7. Yolanda Mulato had a mortgage on her home through Wells Fargo Bank and made timely mortgage payments for several years. After retiring from her job, Mulato's monthly income fell, and she began to experience financial difficulty. Mulatto sought to reduce her monthly mortgage payment by requesting a loan modification from Wells Fargo. The bank's home preservation specialist acknowledged Mulato's request and sent her a stack of forms to complete. Upon returning the completed forms to the bank, Mulato received a letter from the Wells Fargo stating, in part: "Now that we've received your documents (applying for mortgage assistance), our home preservation team will carefully review what you've submitted to determine if you are eligible for mortgage assistance. . . . *If you are eligible and your modification does not require a trial period plan, you will receive a final loan modification agreement adjusting the terms of your mortgage.*" Sometime later, the bank notified Mulato that she was ineligible for mortgage assistance, because she had other assets that could be used to pay the mortgage. Mulato claimed that the italicized language of the bank's letter constituted a promise to provide a loan modification plan and that a contract had been formed. Was she correct? **LO ①**

CHAPTER 7

Capacity to Contract

LEARNING OBJECTIVES

① Identify classifications of individuals who may not have the capacity to contract.

② Define disaffirmance.

③ Explain how a minor's contract can be ratified.

④ Discuss reasons other than age that may impair a person's ability to contract.

PREVIEW CASE

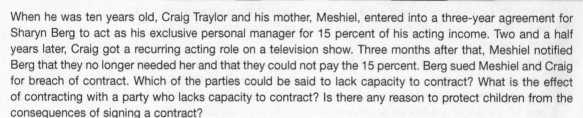

When he was ten years old, Craig Traylor and his mother, Meshiel, entered into a three-year agreement for Sharyn Berg to act as his exclusive personal manager for 15 percent of his acting income. Two and a half years later, Craig got a recurring acting role on a television show. Three months after that, Meshiel notified Berg that they no longer needed her and that they could not pay the 15 percent. Berg sued Meshiel and Craig for breach of contract. Which of the parties could be said to lack capacity to contract? What is the effect of contracting with a party who lacks capacity to contract? Is there any reason to protect children from the consequences of signing a contract?

LO ①
Those lacking capacity

For an agreement to be enforceable at law, all parties must have the legal and mental capacity to contract. This means that the parties must have the ability to understand that a contract is being made, have the ability to understand its general nature, and have the legal competence to contract. The general rule is that the law presumes that all parties have this capacity. This means that anyone alleging incapacity must offer proof of incapacity to overcome that presumption.

However, in the eyes of the law, some parties lack such capacity because of age, physical condition, or public policy. Among those whom the law considers to be incompetent, at least to some degree, are minors, mentally incompetent people, intoxicated people, and convicts.

7-1 Minors

The common-law rule that people under twenty-one years of age are **minors** has been abolished. Most states have enacted statutes making individuals competent to contract at eighteen years of age, and a few set the age at nineteen. In some states, all married minors are fully competent to contract. In still other states, minors in business for themselves are bound on all their business contracts.

minor
person under the legal age to contract

7-1a CONTRACTS OF MINORS

Almost all of a minor's contracts are voidable at the minor's option. That is, if a minor so desires, the minor can avoid or repudiate the contract. If a minor wishes to treat a contract made with an adult as valid, the adult is bound by it. An adult cannot avoid a contract on the ground that the minor might avoid it. If a contract is between two minors, each has the right to avoid it. Should the minor die, the personal representative of the minor's estate may avoid the contract that the minor could have avoided.

PREVIEW CASE REVISITED

FACTS: When he was ten years old, Craig Traylor and his mother, Meshiel, entered into a three-year agreement for Sharyn Berg to act as his exclusive personal manager for 15 percent of his acting income. Two and a half years later, Craig got a recurring acting role on a television show. Three months after that, Meshiel notified Berg they no longer needed her and that they could not pay the 15 percent. Berg sued Meshiel and Craig for breach of contract.

OUTCOME: Because he was a minor at the time of the agreement, the court said Craig was eligible to avoid it, which he clearly did.

—*Berg v. Traylor*, 56 Cal.Rptr.3d 140 (Cal. App.)

Firms that carry on business transactions in all the states must know the law dealing with minors in each state. Internet businesses and correspondence schools are susceptible to losses when dealing with minors. The significance of the law is that, with but few exceptions, people deal with minors at their own risk. The purpose of the law is to protect minors from unscrupulous adults, but in general the law affords the other party no more rights in scrupulous contracts than in unscrupulous ones. The minor is the sole judge as to whether a voidable contract will be binding.

7-1b CONTRACTS THAT CANNOT BE AVOIDED

Although most contracts made by minors are voidable, a few are not. These include contracts for necessaries, business contracts, and other specially enforced contracts, such as student loan agreements.

Contracts of Minors for Necessaries. If a minor contracts for **necessaries**, the contract is voidable, but the minor is liable for the reasonable value of whatever has been received. Necessaries include items required for a minor to have a reasonable standard of living that are not provided by the minor's parents or guardian. The dividing line between necessaries and luxuries is often a fine one. Historically, necessaries included food, clothes, and shelter. With the raising of standards of living, courts now hold that necessaries also include medical services such as surgery, dental work, and other medical care; education through high school or trade school, or even through college; working tools for a trade; and

necessaries
items required for living at a reasonable standard

other goods that are luxuries to some people but necessaries to others because of the particular circumstances.

The minor's liability is quasi-contractual in nature. The reasonable value of what is actually received must be paid in order to prevent the minor from being unjustly enriched. The minor is not, however, required to pay the contract price.

COURT CASE

FACTS: When Daphne Williams was a minor, she was admitted to Birmingham Baptist Medical Center Princeton. She was hospitalized for various tests and received several units of blood by transfusion. The services were reasonable, necessary, and professionally performed. At the time, Daphne did not work, had no income, and was dependent on her mother for support. Daphne's mother did not pay the hospital bill and in fact obtained bankruptcy relief, which prevented the hospital from recovering from the mother. The hospital sued Daphne.

OUTCOME: Judgment was for the hospital. The court stated that when a parent has failed or refused to provide necessary medical care for a child, the provider of services may enforce liability for payment of the reasonable cost on the minor.

—*Williams v. Baptist Health Systems Inc.*, 857 So.2d 149 (Ala. Civ. App.)

Minors' Business Contracts. Many states, either by special statutory provision or by court decisions, have made a minor's business contracts fully binding. If a minor engages in a business or employment in the same manner as a person who has legal capacity, contracts that arise from such business or employment cannot be set aside.

Other Enforceable Contracts. A number of states prevent a minor from avoiding certain specified contracts. These contracts include educational loan agreements, contracts for medical care, contracts made with court approval or in performance of a legal duty, and contracts involving bank accounts. Some states find that contracts may be enforced against a married minor. In some states, minors also may not use the defense of infancy to avoid contractual obligations when they have accepted the benefits of a contract.

COURT CASE

FACTS: Turnitin, owned by iParadigms, is a technology system that compares work submitted by students to material available on the Internet, previously submitted student works, and databases of journals and periodicals. It then supplies teachers with a report indicating whether the submission was original. Turnitin archives the works submitted to enlarge its database of student works. In order to submit a paper, a student must create a profile and click "I agree" to the terms of the user agreement. Four high-school students who were required by their schools to use Turnitin did not want their works

archived and sued iParadigms. Asserting their infancy, the students said the user agreements were void.

OUTCOME: The court pointed out that the students had obtained benefits from their agreement such as a grade on their works, which allowed them to maintain good standing in their classes. Having received benefits, they could not now assert that the agreements were void.

—*A.V. ex rel. Vanderhye v. iParadigms, LLC*, 562 F.3d 630 (4th Cir.)

Disaffirmance. The term **disaffirmance** means the repudiation of a contract; that is, the election to avoid it or set it aside. A minor has the legal right to disaffirm a voidable contract at any time during minority or within a reasonable time after becoming of age. In some states, if the minor has received no benefits under the contract, disaffirmance does not have to be within a reasonable time. If the contract is wholly executory, a disaffirmance completely nullifies the contract.

LO ② Define disaffirmance

disaffirmance
repudiation of a voidable contract

COURT CASE

FACTS: Julie began dating Jay Fetters when she was 14 and he was 29. At the age of 16, Julie agreed to marry Jay. He persuaded Julie to sign a premarital agreement prepared by his attorney. The agreement provided that the parties would keep their own separate property if they divorced at a future date. Julie signed the agreement, despite the fact that she could not read well and had no legal counsel. Over 15 years later, Julie filed for divorce and sought to disaffirm the premarital agreement. Jay argued that Julie was precluded from disaffirming the contract, because over a decade had passed since she became of age.

OUTCOME: Because Jay provided no proof that he detrimentally relied on Julie's failure to disavow the agreement, Julie was allowed to do so.

—*Ferris v. Fetters*, 26 N.E.3d 1016 (Ind. Ct. App.)

On electing to disaffirm contracts, minors must return whatever they may have received under the contracts, provided they still have possession of it. The fact that the minor does not have possession of the property, however, regardless of the reason, does not prevent the exercise of the right to disaffirm the contract. In most jurisdictions, an adult may not recover compensation from a minor who returns the property in damaged condition.

If an adult purchases personal property from a minor, the adult has only a voidable title to the property. If the property is sold to an innocent third party before the minor disaffirms the contract, the innocent third party obtains good title to the property. However, the minor may recover from the adult the money or the value of property received from the third party. Statutes in some states make minors' contracts void, not merely voidable. In these states, disaffirmance is not necessary.

Ratification. A minor may ratify a voidable contract only after attaining majority. **Ratification** means indicating one's willingness to be bound by promises made during minority. It is in substance a new promise and may be oral, written, or merely implied by conduct; however, some states require it to be in writing. After majority is reached, silence ratifies an executed contract.

A minor cannot ratify part of a contract and disaffirm another part; all or none of it must be ratified. Ratification must be made within a reasonable time after reaching majority. A reasonable time is a question of fact to be determined in light of all surrounding circumstances.

LO ③ Minor's ratification

ratification
indication by adult that a contract made while a minor is binding

COURT CASE

FACTS: While a minor and a passenger in a car, Holly Parsons was seriously injured in a crash. Brett Klug, a front-seat passenger, arguably contributed to the crash. Parsons filed suit, and a guardian was appointed to represent her interests in the suit. Klug's insurer, General Casualty Co. (General), sent the guardian an offer of judgment for $100,000. The guardian accepted and received a check made out to Parsons and the guardian. The check recited that it was in full settlement of claims against General and the Klug family. Parsons cashed the check. She then added Klug's parents to her lawsuit as defendants. Shortly thereafter, she attained majority. During the litigation, General argued that since three years had passed since Parsons got and kept the $100,000, she had ratified the release on the check.

OUTCOME: The court said that keeping the $100,000 was an implied ratification of the release of the Klug family.

—*Parsons ex rel. Cabaniss v. American Family Ins. Co.,*
740 N.W.2d 399 (Wis. Ct. App.)

7-1c CONTRACTING SAFELY WITH MINORS

Because in general it is risky to deal with minors, every businessperson must know how to be protected when contracting with them. The safest way is to have an adult (usually a parent or guardian) join in the contract as a cosigner with the minor. This gives the other party to the contract the right to sue the adult who cosigned. A merchant must run some risk when dealing with minors. If a sale is made to a minor, the minor may avoid the contract and demand a refund of the purchase price years later. Because few minors exercise this right, businesspeople often run the risk of contracting with minors rather than seeking absolute protection against loss.

7-1d MINORS' TORTS

As a general rule, a minor is liable for torts as fully as an adult is. If minors misrepresent their age, and the adults with whom they contract rely on the misrepresentation to their detriment, the minors have committed a tort. The law is not uniform throughout the United States as to whether or not minors are bound on contracts induced by misrepresenting their age. In some states, when sued, they cannot avoid their contracts if they fraudulently misrepresented their age. In some states, they may be held liable for any damage to or deterioration of the property they received under the contract. If minors sue on the contracts to recover what they paid, they may be denied recovery if they misrepresented their age.

COURT CASE

FACTS: The Manasquan Savings & Loan Association loaned Lynn Mayer, a minor, and her husband $22,000 based on her sworn statement that she was of age. Mayer and her husband later separated and defaulted on the loan. When Manasquan sued to recover the collateral, Mayer asserted her minority and demanded that Manasquan return all her funds used to make payments on the note.

OUTCOME: The court held that minority was no defense to Manasquan's action because Mayer had misrepresented her age.

—*Manasquan Savings & Loan Assn. v. Mayer,*
236 A.2d 407 (Super. Ct. of N.J.)

7-2 Mentally Incompetent People

LO ④
Impairment other than
by reason of age

A number of reasons beyond a person's control can result in mental incompetence. These include insanity or incompetence as a result of stroke, senile dementia, and other diminished mental capacity. In determining a mentally incompetent person's capacity to contract, the intensity and duration of the incompetency must be determined. In most states, if a person has been formally adjudicated incompetent, contracts made by the person are void without regard to whether they are reasonable or for necessaries. Such a person is considered incapable of making a valid acceptance of an offer, no matter how fair the offer is. When a person has been judicially declared insane, and sanity is later regained, and a court officially declares the person to be competent, the capacity to contract is the same as that of any other sane person.

COURT CASE

FACTS: A neighbor, James Nichols, looked after Ernest Tyler, 76, who had an extensive history of mental illness. Tyler asked Nichols to help him deal with the bank after he lost $10,000 in a check fraud scam. He signed a revocable living trust with Nichols as trustee. Tyler transferred his farm valued at $1.5 million to the trust. Three years later, Tyler signed a document directing Nichols, as trustee, to sell the farm to Nichols. Tyler kept a life estate, and Nichols was required to pay $200 a month while Tyler lived, plus taxes, assessments, and insurance. Five months later, Tyler's sister went to see him, but the house was locked. Nichols had left with the only key. The sheriff got Nichols to return. Tyler was filthy and had eye and ear infections, and there was so much trash on the floor that some rooms could not be entered. Two weeks later, Tyler's relatives took him to a physician, who found he was mentally and physically incapacitated by Alzheimer's disease. It was the doctor's opinion Tyler had been incapacitated for about a year. Five months later, Tyler died. His personal representative challenged the sale of the farm to Nichols.

OUTCOME: The court held that the opinion of the doctor who examined Tyler and the conditions in which he lived indicated that he did not have adequate mental capacity at the time the farm was sold to Nichols.

—*Nichols v. Estate of Tyler*, 910 N.E.2d 221
(Ind. Ct. App.)

If a person is incompetent but has not been so declared by the court, then the person's contracts are voidable, not void. Like a minor, the person must pay the reasonable value of necessaries that have been supplied. On disaffirmance, anything of value received under the contracts that the person still has must be returned.

A person who has not been declared by a court to be insane and has only intervals of insanity or delusions can make a contract fully as binding as that of a normal person if it is made during a sane or lucid interval. The person must be capable of understanding that a contract is being made at the time the contract is entered into.

COURT CASE

FACTS: A dispute arose between Legacy Hall of Fame Inc. and Transport Trailer Service Inc., in which Legacy Hall alleged that Transport Trailer failed to deliver a tour bus that had been used by Elvis Presley. In an effort to resolve the dispute, the parties entered a settlement agreement on September 12. Bill Kinard, a director of Legacy Hall, signed the agreement on behalf of the company. Kinard later testified that he recalled signing the agreement. A court reporter present during the signing stated that she spoke at length with Kinard and that he was "very calm." Kinard's physician said he appeared "intact" the day after the agreement was signed. After Legacy Hall lost rights to the bus, the directors sought to invalidate the settlement agreement on the grounds that Bill Kinard was mentally incompetent when he signed the settlement agreement.

OUTCOME: The court held that the contract was binding, because Legacy Hall failed to provide clear and convincing evidence that Kinard lacked the mental capacity to sign the settlement agreement.

—*Legacy Hall of Fame Inc. v. Transport Trailer Service Inc.*, 139 So.3d 105 (Miss. App.)

7-3 Intoxicated People

People also may put themselves in a condition that destroys contractual capacity. Contracts made by people who have become so intoxicated that they cannot understand the meaning of their acts are voidable. On becoming sober, such persons may affirm or disaffirm contracts they made when drunk. If one delays unreasonably in disaffirming a contract made while intoxicated, however, the right to have the contract set aside may be lost.

That a contract is foolish and would not have been entered into if the party had been sober does not make the contract voidable.

A person who has been legally declared to be a habitual drunkard cannot make a valid contract but is liable for the reasonable value of necessaries furnished. If a person is purposely caused to become drunk in order to be induced to contract, the agreement will be held invalid.

The rule regarding the capacity of an intoxicated person also applies to people using drugs.

7-4 Convicts

convict
person found guilty by court of a major criminal offense

Although many states have repealed their former laws restricting the capacity of a **convict** (one convicted of a major criminal offense, namely, a felony or treason) to contract, some jurisdictions still have limitations. These range from depriving convicts of rights as needed to provide for the security of the penal institutions in which they are confined and for reasonable protection of the public, to classifying convicts as under a disability, as are minors and insane persons. In these instances, the disability lasts only as long as the person is imprisoned or supervised by parole authorities.

QUESTIONS

1. Generally, what presumption does the law make regarding parties' legal and mental capacity to contract?

2. When a contract is made between an adult and a minor, how enforceable is it against each of the parties?

3. What types of contracts cannot be avoided by a minor?

4. If a minor contracts for necessaries, to what extent is the minor liable?

5. How much of a voidable contract may a minor ratify?

6. What is the obligation of a minor on disaffirming a contract?

7. What is the safest way for an adult to be protected when contracting with minors?

8. If Gordon, a minor, lies about his age to induce an adult to enter a contract, is he guilty of a tort? Can any resulting contract be enforced?

9. Does an intoxicated person have the capacity to contract? Why or why not?

10. Can a person who has not been judicially declared insane and has only intervals of insanity or delusions make a binding contract?

CASE PROBLEMS

1. To settle a lawsuit concerning ownership of their childhood home, sisters Frances Sparrow and Susan Demonico engaged in voluntary mediation. During mediation, Demonico slurred her words and cried much of the day. Before leaving the mediation, she authorized her attorney to execute a settlement agreement. The agreement required sale of the property, and Demonico to pay Sparrow $100,000. When Sparrow asked the court to enforce the agreement, Demonico claimed she had lacked the capacity to contract at the time of the agreement. However, she testified that she had known she was participating in mediation to negotiate settlement of the lawsuit and that the subject of the mediation had been the childhood home. She had participated in the mediation and listened to the lawyers' arguments, and "couldn't believe how things [were] turning out." Did Demonico lack capacity to contract? **LO ④**

2. Kristina Bishop was charged with a third offense of driving under the influence (DUI), a felony. She had twice previously entered into diversion agreements when charged with DUI. A diversion agreement is a contract with the state providing conditions the defendant must fulfill. When entered to avoid criminal prosecution for DUI, a diversion agreement is considered a prior conviction. Bishop had signed the first diversion agreement a year and a half before she became 18. She argued that it was voidable, that she was disaffirming, and therefore the first diversion agreement could not count as a prior conviction. Was she correct? **LO ②**

3. Tina Muller applied for a loan with CES Credit Union so that she could buy a car from her brother, Joseph Muller. They both signed the loan contract, with Joseph signing as a cosigner. It was two months before Joseph's eighteenth birthday. The loan was approved, so Joseph transferred the car to Tina. When she defaulted on the loan, CES repossessed the car and sold it for less than the loan amount. More than ten years after Joseph cosigned the note, CES sued him for the deficiency. He tried to disaffirm the contract. Could he? **LO ③**

4. J.T., Jr., a minor and competitive motocross rider, traveled to Monster Mountain MX park with his coach and friends to ride around the track. J.T.'s parents authorized the coach to sign a release and waiver of liability agreement at Monster Mountain, which released the track operator and owner **LO ①**

CASE PROBLEMS (CONTINUED)

from liability caused by their negligence. Prior to entering the parkway, J.T.'s coach executed the release on J.T.'s behalf. While riding around the track, J.T. became airborne and crashed into a tractor. He sued Monster Mountain, alleging the racetrack was liable to him on the basis of negligence. Monster Mountain claimed that J.T. was bound by the release agreement and barred from bringing a negligence claim against the parkway. Was the release binding on J.T.?

LO ②   5. When fifteen, Hilda Villalobos suffered cuts to her head and face when the car in which she was riding collided with another vehicle. The vehicles were insured, but a year after the accident, Shirley Smith, an insurance adjuster, discovered that Hilda's claims had not been finally resolved. Smith phoned Hilda's father, Antonio, and told him that Hilda was entitled to compensation. Antonio described Hilda's scars but was in a hurry to leave for Mexico. Hilda was already there for the next year. Smith explained that without seeing Hilda's scars, her estimate of the value of Hilda's claim could be inaccurate, but offered $3,000. Antonio wanted the money for Hilda right away. Smith paid him $3,000, and he and Hilda's mother, as Hilda's parents, signed releases for Hilda's injuries. Eight months later, when Hilda was seventeen, Antonio sued on behalf of Hilda. Did the suit constitute disaffirmance by Hilda?

LO ①, ④   6. Robert Thomas entered into an agreement with License Realty Corp. to lease a building for 20 years. The lease also included an option to purchase the property. Richard DeSouza, an alcoholic undergoing treatment, signed the lease on behalf of License Realty. Eleven years later, Thomas exercised his option to purchase the property. The owner refused to sell and stated that DeSouza lacked the capacity to sign the contract due to his alcoholism. Was the contract voidable?

LO ③   7. Howard Wilcox was the president of Superior Automation Co. On behalf of Superior, Wilcox signed a lease with Marketing Services of Indiana Inc., which included a personal guarantee from Wilcox. Superior made payments for about two and a half years after executing the lease. Six months before executing the lease, Wilcox complained that he had problems with concentration and functioning at work. His psychiatrist said he had lithium toxicity, which lasted at most ten months after execution of the lease. During this time, he had impaired cognitive function that limited his ability to appreciate and understand the nature and quality of his actions and judgments. Superior stopped making payments, and MSI sued. Is the lease enforceable?

LO ②, ③   8. S.L. began working at a fast-food restaurant when she was 16 years old. At the beginning of her employment, she signed a mandatory arbitration agreement, promising to resolve any and all claims with her employer through an arbitration process. S.L. was injured on the job, and her mother filed suit against the restaurant to recover medical expenses related to the injury. The mother argued that S.L. disaffirmed the arbitration agreement by terminating her employment and filing suit against the company while still a minor. The restaurant company argued that S.L.'s minority did not prohibit enforcement of the arbitration agreement, because the lawsuit was for necessaries. Which party was correct?

Consideration

LEARNING OBJECTIVES

1. Define consideration.
2. Explain when part payment constitutes consideration.
3. Give three examples of insufficient or invalid consideration.
4. Recognize when consideration is not required.

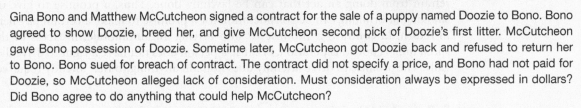

PREVIEW CASE

Gina Bono and Matthew McCutcheon signed a contract for the sale of a puppy named Doozie to Bono. Bono agreed to show Doozie, breed her, and give McCutcheon second pick of Doozie's first litter. McCutcheon gave Bono possession of Doozie. Sometime later, McCutcheon got Doozie back and refused to return her to Bono. Bono sued for breach of contract. The contract did not specify a price, and Bono had not paid for Doozie, so McCutcheon alleged lack of consideration. Must consideration always be expressed in dollars? Did Bono agree to do anything that could help McCutcheon?

LO ①
Define consideration

Courts will compel compliance with an agreement only when it is supported by consideration. Consideration distinguishes mere agreements from legally enforceable obligations. **Consideration** is whatever the promisor demands and receives as the price for a promise. This could be money, personal or real property, a service, a promise regarding behavior, or another item.

consideration
what promisor requires as the price for a promise

8-1 Nature of Consideration

In most contracts, the parties require and are content with a promise by the other party as the price for their own promises. For example, a homeowner may promise to pay a painter $4,000 in return for the promise of the painter to paint the house. Correspondingly, the painter makes the promise to paint in return for the promise of the homeowner to make such payment. By its nature, this exchange of a promise for a promise occurs at the same time creates a contract.

For a promise to constitute consideration, the promise must impose an obligation on the person making it. If a merchant promises to sell a businessperson all of the computer paper ordered at a specific price in return for the businessperson's promise to pay that price for any computer paper ordered, there is no contract. There is no certainty that any computer paper will be needed.

COURT CASE

FACTS: Zoltek Corp. contracted to manufacture and sell to Structural Polymer Group (SP), all of SP's requirements for "Large Filament Count Carbon Fibers" for ten years at "then-current market price." SP agreed to "obtain their total requirements for suitable quality . . . Carbon Fibers from [Zoltek]." In the fifth and sixth years of the agreement, SP placed orders that Zoltek never filled. SP sued Zoltek for breach of contract. Zoltek argued the contract lacked consideration since it did not require SP to order any carbon fibers.

OUTCOME: The court stated that Zoltek's right to exclusively supply SP, so long as it matched a market price offered by another supplier, was adequate to create mutuality of obligation and consideration. It was a valid requirements contract.

—*Structural Polymer Group, Ltd. v. Zoltek Corp.*,
543 F.3d 987 (8th Cir.)

A promise that is conditional can still be consideration for a contract. Such a promise is consideration even if the condition is unlikely to occur. If *A* promises to sell *B* paint if the paint shipment arrives, the promise is consideration.

Consideration may also be the doing of an act or the making of a promise to refrain from doing an act that can be lawfully done. Thus, a promise to give up smoking or drinking can be consideration for a promise to make a certain payment in return. In contrast, a promise to stop driving an automobile in excess of the speed limit is not consideration, because a person does not have a right to drive illegally. The promise to drive lawfully does not add anything to that already required.

8-2 Adequacy of Consideration

As a general rule, the adequacy of the consideration is irrelevant because the law does not prohibit bargains. Except in cases in which the contract calls for a performance or the sale of goods that have a standard or recognized market value, it is impossible to fix the money value of each promise. If the consideration given by one party is grossly inadequate, this is a relevant fact in proving fraud, undue influence, duress, or mistake.

PREVIEW CASE REVISITED

FACTS: Gina Bono and Matthew McCutcheon signed a contract for the sale of a puppy named Doozie to Bono. Bono agreed to show Doozie, breed her, and give McCutcheon second pick of Doozie's first litter. McCutcheon gave Bono possession of Doozie. Sometime later, McCutcheon got Doozie back and refused to return her to Bono. Bono sued for breach of contract. The contract did not specify a price, and Bono had not paid for Doozie, so McCutcheon alleged lack of consideration.

OUTCOME: Bono, the court held, had given consideration when she had agreed to give McCutcheon the second pick of Doozie's first litter. The agreement to provide a puppy to McCutcheon resulted in a benefit to him, so there had been consideration.

—*Bono v. McCutcheon*, 824 N.E.2d 1013 (Ohio Ct. App.)

8-2a PART PAYMENT

LO ②
Part payment as consideration

A part payment of a past-due debt is not consideration to support the creditor's promise to cancel the balance of the debt. The creditor is already entitled to the part payment. Promising to give something to which the other party is already entitled is not consideration.

Several exceptions apply to this rule:

1. If the amount of the debt is in dispute, the debt is canceled if a lesser sum than that claimed is accepted in full settlement.

2. If there is more than one creditor, and each one agrees, in consideration of the others' agreement, to accept in full settlement a percentage of the amount due, this agreement will cancel the unpaid balance due these creditors. This arrangement is known as a **composition of creditors**.

composition of creditors when all of multiple creditors settle in full for a fraction of the amount owed

3. If the debt is evidenced by a note or other written evidence, cancellation and return of the written evidence cancels the debt.

4. If the payment of the lesser sum is accompanied by a receipt in full and some indication that a gift is made of the balance, the debt may be cancelled.

5. If a secured note for a lesser amount is given and accepted in discharge of an unsecured note for a greater amount, the difference between the two notes is discharged. The security is the consideration to support the contract to settle for a lesser sum.

COURT CASE

FACTS: Woodrow Wilson Construction Co. Inc. contracted to remodel a building. Wilson awarded the drywall and painting portion of the job to Precision Drywall & Painting Inc. Wilson alleged that it had problems with Precision's performance and logged the expenses Precision had caused. Wilson deducted the expenses from its final check to Precision and indicated that it was full payment for the job. Precision's lawyer informed Wilson that Precision rejected the final check but offered to settle. Then Precision deposited the check. Precision then sued Wilson for the expenses deducted from the payment.

OUTCOME: The court stated that because the amount of the debt was in dispute, and a lesser sum than that claimed by Precision was accepted by Precision, it could not now sue for more.

—*Precision Drywall & Painting Inc. v. Woodrow Wilson Constr. Co. Inc.*, 843 So.2d 1286 (La. Ct. App.)

8-2b INSUFFICIENT OR INVALID CONSIDERATION

LO ③
Insufficient and invalid consideration

Many apparent considerations lack the full force and effect necessary to make enforceable agreements. Consideration of the following classes is either insufficient or invalid:

1. Performing or promising to perform what one is already obligated to do

2. Refraining or promising to refrain from doing what one has no right to do

3. Past performance

Performing or Promising to Perform What One Is Already Obligated to Do. If the supposed consideration consists merely of a promise to do what one is already legally obligated to do, consideration is invalid. If the consideration is invalid, the contract is invalid. In such case, the promise gives nothing new to the other contracting party.

COURT CASE

FACTS: The judgment dissolving the marriage of Greg Dombek and Jaime Collins included a parenting plan that granted Collins sole legal and physical custody of their son. Dombek was awarded specific visitation rights on December 25 under the dissolution judgment. After Collins learned of an assault charge filed against Dombek, she hired an attorney to draft a child visitation contract and required Dombek to sign the contract before allowing him to pick up their son for court-ordered visitation on December 25. The contract provided in part that Dombek agreed not to keep their son past 7 P.M. "in consideration of Jaime allowing supervised visits of [their son] in lieu of allowing no visitation at all." The contract also stated

that if Dombek breached the child visitation contract, that he would owe Collins' attorney $2,500. Dombek did not return the boy before the time specified in the contract, and Collins' attorney filed suit for breach of contract to recover the $2,500 fee.

OUTCOME: Collins' promise to allow visitation on December 25 was insufficient consideration, because under the court-ordered parenting plan, Collins was legally obligated to allow Dombek that visitation right. The child custody contract was not a valid contract.

—*Miller v. Dombek*, 390 S.W.3d 204 (Mo. App.)

Parties to a contract may at any time mutually agree to cancel an old contract and replace it with a new one. For this new contract to be enforceable, there must be some added features that benefit both parties, although not necessarily to an equal extent. If a contractor agrees to build a house of certain specifications for $150,000, a contract of the homeowner to pay an additional $10,000 is not binding unless the contractor concurrently agrees to do something the original contract did not require as a consideration for the $10,000. The value of the additional act by the contractor need not be $10,000. It merely must have a monetary value.

If unforeseen difficulties arise that make it impossible for the contractor to complete the house for $150,000, completing construction may, in rare cases, constitute additional consideration. Unforeseen difficulties include underground rock formations or a change in the law relative to the building codes and zoning laws. The homeowner is not bound to agree to pay more because of unforeseen difficulties, but if such an agreement is made, these difficulties will constitute a consideration even though the contractor does not agree to do anything additional. Strikes, bad weather, and a change in prices are examples of foreseeable difficulties, which would not be consideration.

Refraining or Promising to Refrain from Doing What One Has No Right to Do. When one refrains or promises to refrain from doing something, this conduct is called **forbearance**. If the promisor had a right to do the act, forbearance is a valid consideration. Consideration is invalid when it consists of a promise to forbear doing something that one has no right to do, such as to commit an unlawful act.

forbearance
refraining from doing something

Often, the forbearance consists of promising to refrain from suing the other party. Promising to refrain from suing another constitutes consideration if the promisor has a reasonable right to demand damages and intends to file a suit. Such a promise is even valid when a suit lacks merit if the promisor mistakenly, but honestly and reasonably, believes a suit would be valid.

COURT CASE

FACTS: Aspen Specialty Insurance Company issued a homeowners insurance policy to Crystal Colony Condominium Association to protect their condominiums in Miami. After the property was damaged by a hurricane, Crystal Colony filed a claim with the insurance company. Aspen Specialty Insurance adjusted the claim and agreed to pay $1,071,349.52 to cover damages in exchange for a release whereby Crystal Colony promised to forebear pursuing legal action against the insurance company related to the claim. Nearly six years after the release was executed, Crystal Colony informed the insurance company that it disagreed with the loss evaluation and sued Aspen Specialty Insurance for breach of the insurance policy. Crystal Colony argued that the release was invalid, because it was not supported by consideration. According to Crystal Colony, the $1,071,349.52 was a partial payment under the policy and not consideration for Crystal Colony's promise not to file future lawsuits against the insurance company.

OUTCOME: Crystal Colony's promise to forebear legal action against Aspen Specialty Insurance related to the claims was adequate consideration to make the release an enforceable contract.

—*Crystal Colony Condominium Ass'n Inc. v. Aspen Specialty Ins. Co.*, 6 F.Supp.3d 1295 (S.D. Fla.)

Past Performance. An act performed prior to the promise does not constitute valid consideration. If a carpenter gratuitously helps a neighbor build a house with no promise of pay, a promise to pay made after the house is completed cannot be enforced. The promise to pay must induce the carpenter to do the work, and this cannot be done if the promise is made after the work is completed.

COURT CASE

FACTS: Timothy Barton was contacted by Edward Brooks about purchasing 2,000 square acres of land. Barton signed an agreement making Brooks his broker for the purchase. At a second meeting of them, Salvatore Sclafani, a business acquaintance of Barton's, was present and encouraged Barton to buy the property. Barton asked Sclafani to prepare a letter to the owner showing his interest in buying it, which Sclafani did. Two months later, a sales contract was signed by the owner, Barton, Brooks, and Sclafani. The contract called for a brokerage commission of 3 percent to the owner's broker, 2 percent to Brooks, and 2 percent to Sclafani. Sclafani prepared a feasibility study. Barton and Sclafani's relationship went bad, and Barton told him he was removing Sclafani as payee of any commission. Sclafani sued Barton a month before the sale closed. Barton claimed that any consideration of Sclafani's was past consideration, since any brokerage services he performed had been done before the contract providing the commission was signed.

OUTCOME: While Sclafani did the feasibility study after the contract was signed, the court stated that work was not brokerage work. All brokerage work, including writing the letter to the property owner and encouraging Barton to buy the property, was done prior to any agreement for payment.

—*Barton v. Sclafani Investments Inc.*, 320 S.W.3d 453 (Tex. Ct. App.)

A debt that is discharged by bankruptcy may be revived under certain circumstances, usually by the debtor's agreeing, with approval from the bankruptcy court, to pay it. Such promises are enforceable even though the creditor, the promisee, gives no new consideration to support the promise. The debtor is said to have waived the defense of discharge in bankruptcy; the original debt, therefore, is deemed to remain in force.

8-3 Exceptions to Requirement of Consideration

LO ④
When consideration is not required

As a general rule, a promise must be supported by consideration. Certain exceptions to the rule involve voluntary subscriptions, debts of record, *promissory estoppel*, and modification of sales contracts.

8-3a VOLUNTARY SUBSCRIPTIONS

When charitable enterprises are financed by voluntary subscriptions of many people, the promise of each person is generally held to be enforceable. When a number of people make pledges to or subscribe to a charitable association or to a church, for example, the pledges or subscriptions are binding. One theory for enforcing the promise is that each subscriber's promise is supported by the promises of other subscribers. Another theory is that a subscription is an offer of a unilateral contract that is accepted by the charity creating liabilities or making expenditures—by relying on the promise. Despite the fact that such promises lack the technical requirements of ordinary contracts, the courts in most states will enforce the promises as a matter of public policy.

COURT CASE

FACTS: Reinhard Schmidt told his church pastor he wanted to fund the remodeling of the parsonage, church basement, and cemetery. He also told Loren Milligan, who helped him with his finances. Milligan got estimates and told Schmidt it would cost $115,000 to $150,000. In reliance on Schmidt's promise of payment, work was begun on a bathroom in the parsonage, flooring in the basement, and landscaping of the cemetery. Then, Schmidt died. Milligan was executor of his will. The will left nothing to the church, but Milligan paid $135,410 in estate funds for church projects. Ilse Mueller, a beneficiary under Schmidt's will, objected.

OUTCOME: The court held that the church had clearly accepted Schmidt's offer before his death, so the voluntary subscription was enforceable.

—*In re Estate of Schmidt*, 723 N.W.2d 454 (Iowa Ct. App.)

8-3b DEBTS OF RECORD

Consideration is not necessary to support an obligation of record, such as a judgment, on the basis that such an obligation is enforceable as a matter of public policy.

8-3c *PROMISSORY ESTOPPEL*

Although not supported by considerations, courts enforce some promises on the basis of *promissory estoppel*. According to this doctrine, if one person makes a promise to another, and that other person acts in reliance on the promise, the promisor will not be permitted to claim lack of consideration. Enforcement is held to be proper when the promisor should reasonably expect to cause, and does cause, action by the promisee, and the promisee would be harmed substantially if the promise were not enforced. The theory has gained support as a means of realizing justice. The elements of *promissory estoppel* include:

promissory estoppel
substitute for consideration
when another acts in reliance
on a promisor's promise

1. A promise is made.
2. The promisor reasonably expects the promise to induce action by the promisee.
3. The promisee does act.
4. Justice requires enforcement of the promise.

Courts will find that justice requires enforcement of the promise when the promisee would be substantially harmed if it were not enforced.

COURT CASE

FACTS: Because he did not have adequate funds, Frank Perry asked Jan Marquardt whether she wanted to invest $200,000 in a trade that promised a 40 percent return. To do so in time, Marquardt would have to wire-transfer the funds. She contacted Perry's stockbroker and got wire-transfer instructions. Several hours later, Perry e-mailed Marquardt, saying that she would make $80,000 from the trade and "[i]n the interest of you sleeping better, given that the trade is through my account, I'll guarantee your $200,000." An hour later, Marquardt wired the funds. The trade was a fraud, and the $200,000 was lost. Marquardt sued Perry, alleging *promissory estoppel*.

OUTCOME: The court held that there was *promissory estoppel* because Marquardt had relied on Perry's promise. Marquardt could recover.

—*Marquardt v. Perry*, 200 P.3d 1126 (Co. Ct. App.)

8-3d MODIFICATION OF SALES CONTRACTS

The Uniform Commercial Code (see Chapter 16) regulates sales of goods. The code provides that when a contract for the sale of goods is modified by agreement of the parties, no consideration is necessary to make it enforceable.

QUESTIONS

1. What is consideration? Explain.
2. When does a promise constitute consideration?
3. Generally, why is the law not concerned with the adequacy of consideration?
4. George agrees to remodel a kitchen for Harry for $30,000, but after beginning work he asks Harry to pay $34,000. Can George enforce Harry's new promise to pay $34,000?

QUESTIONS (CONTINUED)

5. When can partial payment of a past-due debt constitute consideration to support the creditor's promise to cancel the balance of the debt?

6. If a friend gratuitously helps do yard work one weekend with no promise to pay, can he then enforce a promise to pay made the following week after the work is done?

7. When does forbearance not constitute valid consideration?

8. Why are courts willing to enforce a promise to pay a voluntary subscription that lacks consideration?

9. Why is consideration unnecessary to support an obligation of record?

10. When will courts apply the doctrine of *promissory estoppel*?

CASE PROBLEMS

LO ③   1. Willamette Management Associates Inc. contracted to perform extensive accounting services involving Kimberly Palczynski's husband's business interests in connection with a marital case between the couple. The contract required Palczynski to pay any outstanding fees to Willamette before its principal, Alan Schachter, would be asked to testify in court. Right before trial, Palczynski owed Willamette $67,000. Schachter urged Palczynski to make a payment arrangement because he thought his testimony would be very helpful to her. The parties signed a second agreement requiring Willamette to continue to perform the same work for $57,000, to be paid in monthly installments by Palczynski. She made no payments, so Willamette sued her. Willamette argued that the second agreement was unsupported by consideration and thus the court should enforce the first agreement. Should it?

LO ②   2. Success Management Team Inc. (Success) and Town & Country Real Estate Inc. (Town) agreed that Success would sell stock and a Coldwell Banker franchise to Town for $40,000. Town paid Success $20,000 with the agreement and signed a note for $20,000. Success later sued Town on the note. Town's lawyer sent Success's lawyer a check for $18,500 with a letter saying that Town had incurred $1,500 in attorney's fees because of Success's failure to transfer the Coldwell franchise timely. The check was deposited in Success's attorney's escrow account. Success's attorney replied that Town could not set off disputed damages (the attorney's fees) against the promised amount ($20,000). He continued that Town owed interest and attorney's fees for breaching the note and contract, but Success would accept $25,000. Town argued that by keeping the money, Success had cancelled the debt. Had it?

LO ①, ③   3. John and Lori Finstad granted Ransom-Sargent Water Users an option to purchase their farmland and drill water wells. The option also permitted the Finstad's to lease the property for up to ten years, provided they only use the land for pasture purposes. Four years later, Ransom-Sargent terminated the Finstad's lease rights, because the Finstad's had tilled up some of the land. In order to continue receiving government farm payments, the Finstad's signed a new contract with Ransom-Sargent permitting the Finstad's to lease the land for one year and to collect government payments for that year. By signing the contract, they also avoided a lawsuit with Ransom-Sargent. The contract included a release of all rights the Finstad's had to lease the property under the original option agreement. The following year, Ransom-Sargent accepted bids to lease the land. After they were not awarded the lease, the Finstad's sued Ramson-Sargent, alleging that their second contract was not supported by consideration and that their original option to lease should be upheld. Were they correct?

LO ④   4. Brian Center Nursing Care/Austell Inc. leased five nursing homes from William Foster. The leases expired, and Brian kept possession of the nursing homes while it negotiated a new lease with Foster. No new lease was agreed upon, and Foster leased the homes to another company. Brian would not give up possession, so Foster sued. Brian alleged Foster had promised that the terms of the lease

CASE PROBLEMS (CONTINUED)

would continue as long as Brian paid the rent and continued to negotiate. Brian claimed it had been injured by relying on this promise, because it had continued to occupy the premises, pay the rent, and negotiate for a new lease. Did *promissory estoppel* apply to these facts?

5. Star Valley Ranch Association managed a subdivision. When Vince Zimmer resigned as general manager, he requested payment for unpaid overtime. The board of the association denied the request. The board later discovered that through clerical error, Zimmer had been overpaid and demanded he repay $1,380. Zimmer responded by demanding $2,483 for unpaid overtime. Because the legal costs of pursuing collection were not worth the amount in dispute, Zimmer and the association signed a settlement mutually releasing each other from the claims. Ronald Mueller owned a lot in the subdivision and sued, alleging that Zimmer's claim for overtime was without merit so that by settling the former directors and general managers deprived the association of funds to which it was entitled. Was the settlement agreement valid?

LO ②

6. R. Gary Schreiber and Robert Schreiber signed a bill of sale for the intellectual property rights in the recorded media of Robert Knievel's stunt performances. The Schreibers stated that they paid off Knievel's motor bus in exchange for the film rights. However, the payoff for the bus occurred weeks before the bill of sale was executed, and Knievel already had the bus in his possession. Twenty-five years after the bill of sale was executed and after Knievel's death, the Schreibers sued Kneivel's estate to obtain a declaration of the ownership rights in the intellectual property. Was there sufficient consideration to support the contract?

LO ③

7. Anthony and Philip Conway were the founders of a publicly traded medical device company called Rochester Medical Corporation (RMC). C.R. Bard Inc. negotiated to purchase RMC, but prior to closing the transaction, C.R. Bard's board required the Conways to each sign a separate five-year non-compete agreement. After the Conways executed the non-compete agreements, C.R. Bard paid shareholders a significant premium for their shares of RMC. The Conways received close to $40 million from the sale. However, shortly after the sale, the Conways regretted signing the non-compete agreements and filed a lawsuit stating that the agreements were invalid for lack of consideration. Were they correct?

LO ①

8. The Orleans Parish School Board employed Mary Ellen Carter as a Secretary I. Later, Carter performed the responsibilities of an Executive Secretary, then an Administrative Assistant, and finally a Software Resources Coordinator without a change in title or increase in pay. Her supervisors continuously assured her that her position and pay grade would be reclassified and that she would be paid retroactively for her greater duties. The request was submitted to the budget committee. For five years, she performed the duties and responsibilities of higher levels than her pay grade. When she was not compensated for the higher-level duties, she sued the school board. Did Carter demonstrate a case of *promissory estoppel*?

LO ④

Defective Agreements

LEARNING OBJECTIVES

1. Describe the mistakes that invalidate a contract.
2. State what types of mistakes normally do not invalidate contracts.
3. Identify the situations in which fraud, duress, or undue influence is present.

PREVIEW CASE

Miller Pipeline Corporation signed a contract with Zurich American Insurance Company to purchase automobile insurance, including uninsured motorist coverage. While negotiating the contract, Miller Pipeline informed Kathy Kebo, an insurance broker, that they did not want uninsured motorist coverage in states that did not legally require that coverage. Kebo failed to communicate that to Zurich Insurance. The final contract thus promised uninsured motor coverage in Kentucky, even though that state did not legally require it. An employee of Miller Pipeline was injured in a car accident in Kentucky and sought to recover damages under the uninsured motorist coverage provision in Miller Pipeline's insurance policy. Zurich was informed after the accident of Miller Pipeline's original intent to exclude uninsured motorist coverage in some states. Zurich denied the employee's claim on the basis that there was mutual mistake between Miller Pipeline and Zurich in drafting the contract, which invalidated the uninsured motorist coverage. Were both parties mistaken as to whether they intended the contract to include uninsured motor coverage? What do you think the intention of Zurich was at the time the policy was issued?

Even when an offer and an acceptance have been made, situations exist in which the resulting contract is defective. Some mistakes make contracts defective. In addition, fraud, duress, or undue influence makes contracts voidable because they are defective. A victim of an act rendering a contract defective has a choice of remedies.

unilateral mistake
mistake by one party to a contract

mutual mistake
mistake by both parties to a contract

9-1 Mistakes

Whether a mistake affects the validity of a contract normally depends on whether just one of the parties or both parties have made a mistake. A **unilateral mistake** occurs when only one party makes a mistake regarding the contract. When both parties to a contract make the same mistake, a **mutual mistake** occurs.

9-2 Mistakes That Invalidate Contracts

LO 1
Invalidating mistakes

For a mistake to invalidate a contract, the mistake ordinarily must be a mutual one about a material fact. However, there are some very limited cases in which a unilateral mistake will invalidate a contract.

9-2a MUTUAL MISTAKES

When a mutual mistake concerns a material fact, some courts say such a contract is void, because no genuine assent by the parties existed. Other courts say the contract is voidable. Some courts are not precise about whether the contract is void or voidable. However they classify a mutual-mistake contract, courts do not find them enforceable.

COURT CASE

FACTS: Harold and Ann White arranged a horse-trade between Laura Lane-Lott and Gerald Gambrel. The trade contract provided that Lane-Lott would exchange her mare, Ima Slow Lopin Dream, for Gambrel's pregnant mare, Kcees Time To Skeik. Lane-Lott had researched Kcees's bloodline and found it to be of value. After the exchange and the mare Lane-Lott received gave birth to a foal, it was discovered through DNA testing that the foal's mother was actually Miss Savannah Steel. The parties were mistaken as to the identity of the pregnant mare, because several months prior to the exchange, Gambrel had inadvertently picked up Miss Savannah Steel at the White's farm, believing it to be Kcees, and had returned Miss Savannah Steel to the Whites to be bred. Lane-Lott sued Gambrel and the Whites for fraud.

OUTCOME: The court held that the parties were mutually mistaken regarding the identity of the pregnant mare. The contract was void, because neither party realized at the time of formation that a pregnant Kcees did not exist.

—*Lane-Lott v. White*, 126 So.3d 1016
(Miss. Ct. App.)

The area of mistake is one in which significant variations exist among the states and also where exceptions to the general rules have been established by courts in order to avoid harsh results. In some states, it is much easier than in others to get the courts to agree with a party that a contract should not be enforced when there has been a mistake.

9-2b UNILATERAL MISTAKES

As a general rule, a unilateral mistake made at the time of contracting has no effect on the validity of a contract. However, when there has been a unilateral mistake of a fact, the mistaken party sometimes receives relief. Courts will generally allow a unilateral mistake of fact to impair the enforceability of a contract if the nonmistaken party caused the mistake or knew or should have known of the other party's mistake, and the mistaken party exercised ordinary care. Courts show extreme unwillingness to allow one party to hold the other to a contract if the first party knows that the other one has made a mistake.

FACTS: The deed by which Betty Long and Nancy Vonada obtained title to a house granted William and Bonnie Vonada a right of first refusal to buy the house. Before Betty and Nancy could sell to someone other than a relative, they had to offer the property to William and Bonnie on the same terms. Betty and Nancy got an offer to buy the house for $145,000. They had an attorney notify William and Bonnie of the offer and remind them they had 30 days to exercise their right of first refusal. Six days later, William and Bonnie wrote a letter accepting the offer to buy the house. Six days after that, Betty and Nancy wrote saying they had not known the offeror was Betty's son, so "the right of first refusal . . . would not come into play" and they would sell to him. William and Bonnie sued. Betty and Nancy alleged there was a mutual mistake that allowed them to rescind the agreement with William and Bonnie.

OUTCOME: The court held that the mistake that had occurred was unilateral by Betty and Nancy and not the fault of William and Bonnie, who were unaware of it.

—*Vonada v. Long*, 852 A.2d 331 (Pa. Super.)

A small number of states allow a party who has made a unilateral mistake of fact to raise the mistake as a defense when sued on the contract. This is allowed when the party has not been inexcusably negligent in making the mistake, and the other, nonmistaken, party has not taken actions in reliance on the contract so that failure to enforce it would be unconscionable.

To entitle a party to relief, the mistake must be one of fact, not mere opinion. If A buys a painting from B for $10, but it is actually worth $5,000, even if A knows B is mistaken as to its value, there is a valid contract. B's opinion as to its value is erroneous, but there is no mistake as to a fact.

Because there are few exceptions to the rule that a unilateral mistake does not affect a contract, it is clear that the law does not save us from the consequences of all mistakes. The exceptions cover a very small percentage of mistakes made in business transactions. Knowledge and diligence, not law, protect businesses against losses caused by mistakes.

9-2c CONTRACT TERMS GOVERN

It is important to remember that no matter what the law provides when a mistake occurs, the parties may specify a different outcome in their contract. And when the contract specifies what is to happen in the case of a mistake, the contract provision will apply even if the law would be otherwise. The contract also could indicate which party assumes the risk that the facts are not as believed. The law as to mistake applies only in the absence of a governing provision in the contract, as long as that governing provision is not unconscionable.

A contract could specify that it will be void if a specified fact is not as believed. A, owning a stone, could believe it to be worth very little money. However, if A wants to sell the stone to B for $100, the contract could recite that it is void if the stone is found to be actually a valuable diamond. This applies in spite of the general rule, outlined previously, that a unilateral mistake does not invalidate a contract.

The contract also could make the realization of certain expectations a condition of the contract. If those expectations were not realized, even if only one party were mistaken about them, the contract would not be binding.

Frequently, contracts are entered into orally and then reduced to writing. If, through an error in keyboarding, the written form does not conform to the oral form, the written form does not bind the parties. The contract is what the parties agreed to orally.

9-3 Mistakes That Do Not Invalidate Contracts

LO ② Noninvalidating mistakes

It is said that every rule has an exception, and the rules regarding the impact of mistake on contract validity also have exceptions. Most states recognize the exceptions to the rule on mutual mistake; however, significant variation occurs among the states regarding whether exceptions to the unilateral-mistake rule are recognized.

9-3a UNILATERAL MISTAKES

The rule is that a unilateral mistake has no effect on a contract. Such a mistake will not, for example, invalidate a contract if a unilateral mistake occurs as to price or quantity. Even if the unilateral mistake as to price results from an error in keyboarding or in misunderstanding an oral quotation of the price, the contract is valid.

PREVIEW CASE REVISITED

FACTS: Miller Pipeline Corporation signed a contract with Zurich American Insurance Company to purchase automobile insurance, including uninsured motorist coverage. While negotiating the contract, Miller Pipeline informed Kathy Kebo, an insurance broker, that they did not want uninsured motorist coverage in states that did not legally require that coverage. Kebo failed to communicate that to Zurich Insurance. The final contract thus promised uninsured motor coverage in Kentucky, even though that state did not legally require it. An employee of Miller Pipeline was injured in a car accident in Kentucky and sought to recover damages under the uninsured motorist coverage provision in Miller Pipeline's insurance policy. Zurich was informed after the accident of Miller Pipeline's original intent to exclude uninsured motorist coverage in some states. Zurich denied the employee's claim on the basis that there was mutual mistake between Miller Pipeline and Zurich in drafting the contract, which invalidated the uninsured motorist coverage.

OUTCOME: The court held that the mistake was a unilateral mistake by Miller Pipeline in believing the coverage excluded certain states. Zurich was not mistaken as to the terms of the contract, because they did not learn of Miller Pipeline's desire to omit coverage in certain states until after the employee's accident. Zurich could not disclaim coverage under the contract to Miller's employee.

—*Nichols v. Zurich American Ins. Co.*, 423 S.W.3d 698 (Ky.)

9-3b MUTUAL MISTAKES

The rule given previously is that a mutual mistake will normally make a contract defective. However, this is not true in the case of mistake as to:

1. Value, quality, or price
2. The terms of the contract

3. The law

4. Expectations

Mistakes as to Value, Quality, or Price. A contract is not affected by the fact that the parties made mistaken assumptions as to the value, quality, or price of the subject matter of the contract. Normally, the parties assume the risk that their assumptions regarding these matters can be incorrect. If buyers do not trust their judgment, they could require a warranty from the seller as to the quality or value of the articles they are buying. Their ability to contract wisely is their chief protection against a bad bargain. If Snead sells Robinson a television set for $350, Robinson cannot rescind the contract merely because the set proved to be worth only $150. This is a mistake as to value and quality. As a part of the contract, Robinson should obtain an express warranty as to the set's quality. Conversely, if the seller parts with a jewel for $50, thinking it is a cheap stone, a complaint cannot be made later if the jewel proves to be worth $2,500.

Mistakes as to the Terms of the Contract. A mistake as to the terms of the contract usually results from failure to understand a contract's meaning or significance or from failure to read a written contract. Such mistakes in both written and oral contracts do not affect their validity; otherwise, anyone could avoid a contract merely by claiming a mistake as to its terms.

Mistakes of Law. Ordinarily, when the parties make a mutual mistake of law, the contract is fully binding. The parties are expected to have knowledge of the law when making a contract.

COURT CASE

FACTS: Arthur Ward, Sr., executed a deed conveying real estate to his son, Arthur Ward, Jr. The deed retained a life estate for the father. After Arthur, Sr.'s, two daughters learned of the conveyance, Arthur, Sr., asked his son to deed the property back to him. Arthur, Jr., refused. Arthur, Sr., then sued his son for rescission and reformation of the deed, claiming he thought he could change the deed after he signed it.

OUTCOME: The court declared that Arthur, Sr., could not have the deed set aside on the grounds that he had not understood the legal consequences of executing it. Relief would not be granted merely on the grounds of mistake of law.

—*Ward v. Ward*, 874 N.E.2d 433 (Mass. App. Ct)

Mistakes as to Expectations. When the parties to a contract are mutually mistaken as to their expectations, the contract is binding.

LO ③
Situations of fraud, duress, or undue influence

fraud
inducing another to contract as a result of an intentionally or recklessly false statement of a material fact

9-4 Fraud

One who intends to, and does, induce another to enter into a contract as a result of an intentionally or recklessly false statement of a material fact commits **fraud**. The courts recognize two kinds of fraud relating to contracts. These are fraud in the inducement and fraud in the execution.

9-4a FRAUD IN THE INDUCEMENT

When the party defrauded intended to make the contract, **fraud in the inducement** occurs. Fraud in the inducement involves a false statement regarding the terms or obligations of the transaction between the parties and not the nature of the document signed. The false statement might relate to the terms of the agreement, the quality of the goods sold, or the seller's intention to deliver goods. A contract so induced is voidable.

fraud in the inducement
party intended to make a contract based on false statement of terms or obligations of transaction

COURT CASE

FACTS: When Geraldine McKenney died, her son, Joseph, was a banquet steward with no real estate experience who lived in a shelter at a hospital. Her only asset was her home. For ten years, property taxes were not paid. Khalid Eltayeb asked Joseph whether he knew that taxes of $100,000 were owed and whether he "was in any position to do anything about the property." Joseph thought he had already lost the house due to unpaid taxes. Without disclosing its value or the right to redeem the house, Eltayeb offered to buy Joseph's interest for $1,200 and introduced him to a man he said had a contract for demolition of the house. The next day, Eltayeb pressed Joseph for a decision, and Joseph accepted. Eltayeb paid Joseph $1,200 and took him to his attorney's office. He had Joseph sign an assignment that showed no value for the property.

Eltayeb showed Joseph only pages one, two, and four of a probate petition of Geraldine's estate requesting Eltayeb be appointed personal representative. Page three, which he did not disclose, listed the home's value at $150,000. Eltayeb was appointed and deeded the property to himself. Two months later, someone told Joseph the property's value, so he sued to rescind the assignment, claiming fraud in the inducement.

OUTCOME: The court found that Eltayeb knowingly made false representations in order to get Joseph to make the assignment and that Joseph reasonably relied on the false statements. The assignment was rescinded.

—*In re Estate of McKenney*, 953 A.2d 336 (D.C.)

9-4b FRAUD IN THE EXECUTION

The defrauded party might also be tricked into signing a contract under circumstances in which the nature of the writing could not be understood. The law calls this **fraud in the execution** or fraud in the *factum*. In this case, the victim unknowingly signs a contract. A person who cannot read or who cannot read the language in which the contract is written could be a victim of this type of fraud. When fraud in the execution occurs, the contract is void.

Fraud also may be classified according to whether a party engages in some activity that causes the fraud, or does nothing. A party who actually does something or takes steps to cause a fraud commits **active fraud**. Sometimes a party may be guilty of fraud without engaging in any activity at all. **Passive fraud** results from the failure to disclose information when there is a party guilty of fraud without engaging in any activity at all. Passive fraud results from the failure to disclose information when there is a duty to do so.

fraud in the execution
defrauded party did not intend to sign a contract when nature of writing could not be understood

active fraud
party engages in action that causes the fraud

passive fraud
failure to disclose information when there is duty to do so

9-4c ACTIVE FRAUD

Active fraud may occur either by express misrepresentation or by concealment of material facts.

Express Misrepresentation. Fraud, as a result of express misrepresentation, consists of four elements, each of which must be present to constitute fraud:

misrepresentation
false statement of a
material fact

1. **Misrepresentation:** a false statement of a material fact.
2. Must be made by one who knew it to be false or made it in reckless disregard of its truth or falsity.
3. Must be made with intent to induce the innocent party to act.
4. The innocent party justifiably relies on the false statement and makes a contract.

If these four elements are present, a party who has been harmed is entitled to relief in court.

Concealment of Material Facts. If one actively conceals material facts for the purpose of preventing the other contracting party from discovering them, such concealment results in fraud even without false statements.

COURT CASE

FACTS: Before contracting to sell their home, Eric and Joyce Jensen filled out a disclosure statement. A question asked whether they were aware "of any improvements . . . constructed in violation of building codes or without necessary permits." The Jensens checked the "NO" box. After Gene and Cynthia Bailey purchased the house, they sued the Jensens for fraudulent concealment because there were unpermitted changes to the house not in conformity with building codes. The Jensens had hired contractors and were not aware permits had been required but not obtained.

OUTCOME: Since the Jensens had not had actual knowledge of any problem, they did not have a duty to disclose anything to the Baileys.

—*Jensen v. Bailey*, 76 So.3d 980 (Fla. App.)

ETHICAL POINT

Refraining from disclosing pertinent facts might not be fraud, but is it ethical behavior?

Merely refraining from disclosing pertinent facts unknown to the other party is not fraud in some states. In those states, there must be an active concealment. However, in other states, refraining from disclosing relevant facts does constitute fraud.

9-4d PASSIVE FRAUD

If one's relationship with another relies on trust and confidence, then silence may constitute passive fraud. Such a relationship exists between partners in a business firm, an agent and principal, a lawyer and client, a guardian and ward, a physician and patient, and in many other trust relationships. In the case of an attorney–client relationship, for example, the attorney has a duty to reveal anything material to the client's interests, and silence has the same effect as making a false statement that there was no material fact to be told to the client. In such a case, the client could avoid the contract.

Silence, when one has no duty to speak, is not fraud. If Lawrence offers to sell Marconi, a diamond merchant, a gem for $500 that is actually worth $15,000, Marconi's superior knowledge of value does not, in itself, impose a duty to speak.

9-4e INNOCENT MISREPRESENTATION

When a contract is being negotiated, one party could easily make a statement believing it to be true when it is in fact false. Such a statement, made in the belief that it is true, is called an **innocent misrepresentation**. Courts generally hold that if it was reasonable for the misled party to have relied on the innocent misrepresentation, the contract is voidable.

innocent misrepresentation
false statement made in belief it is true

9-4f STATEMENTS OF OPINION

Statements of opinion, as contrasted with statements of fact, do not, as a rule, constitute fraud. The person hearing the statement realizes, or ought to realize, that the other party is merely stating a view and not a fact. But if the speaker is an expert or has special knowledge not available to the other party and should realize that the other party relies on this expert opinion, then a misstatement of opinion or value, intentionally made, would amount to fraud.

Such expressions as "This is the best buy in town," "The price of this stock will double in the next twelve months," and "This business will net you $25,000 a year" are all statements of opinion, not statements of fact. However, the statement "This business has netted the owner $25,000" is presented not as an opinion or a prophecy but a historical fact.

9-5 Duress

For a contract to be valid, all parties must enter into it of their own free will. **Duress** is a means of destroying another person's free will by one party obtaining consent to a contract as a result of a wrongful threat to do the other person or family members some harm. Duress causes a person to agree to a contract he or she would not otherwise agree to. Normally, to constitute duress, the threat must be made by the other party and must be illegal or wrongful. A contract made because of duress is voidable.

duress
obtaining consent by means of a threat

COURT CASE

FACTS: Amy Maida was employed by RLS Legal Solutions, LLC. RLS told her to sign an employment agreement containing an arbitration provision. Maida initially refused to sign the agreement because she did not agree to the arbitration provision. RLS withheld her pay for work already performed because she had not signed the agreement. Maida was afraid she would not be able to pay her mortgage, car loan, and insurance without her compensation. She finally signed the agreement but told RLS she was signing under duress. Maida sued RLS.

OUTCOME: RLS was not entitled to withhold pay to which Maida was entitled on condition that she sign an agreement to arbitrate. This was duress.

—*In re RLS Legal Solutions, LLC*, 156 S.W.3d 160 (Tex. App.)

Duress is classified according to the nature of the threat as physical, emotional, or economic.

9-5a PHYSICAL DURESS

When one party makes a threat of violence to another person who then agrees to a contract to avoid injury, physical duress occurs. Holding a gun to another's head, or threatening to beat a person, clearly risks injury to a human being and is unlawful.

9-5b EMOTIONAL DURESS

Emotional duress occurs when one party's threats of something less than physical violence result in such psychological pressure that the victim does not act under free will. Courts will consider the age, health, and experience of the victim in determining whether emotional duress occurred.

COURT CASE

FACTS: John Hollett was thirty years older than Erin and a successful businessman. Two days before their scheduled wedding, Erin learned that he wanted her to sign a prenuptial agreement. John's lawyers had hired a recent law school graduate to counsel Erin, who had not finished high school. The lawyer arranged to meet Erin at John's lawyers' office the next day, one day before the scheduled wedding. All the arrangements for an elaborate 200-guest wedding had been made and paid for, and Erin's parents had flown in from Thailand. During the meeting with the lawyer and negotiations with John's lawyers, Erin sobbed for three or four hours and was frequently unable to speak with her lawyer. Her lawyer got some provisions of the agreement changed in her favor, but she remembered almost nothing about the conference. The agreement was signed the morning of the wedding. Erin and John were married until John died eleven years later. Erin asked the court to invalidate the agreement on the basis of emotional duress.

OUTCOME: The court found that Erin's signing of the prenuptial agreement was involuntary as a result of duress. It was invalid.

—*In re Estate of Hollett*, 834 A.2d 348 (N.H.)

9-5c ECONOMIC DURESS

When one party wrongly threatens to injure another person financially in order to get agreement to a contract, economic duress occurs. However, duress does not occur when a person agrees to a contract merely because of difficult financial circumstances that are not the fault of the other party. Duress also does not occur when a person drives a hard bargain and takes advantage of the other's urgent need to make the contract.

9-6 Undue Influence

One person may exercise such influence over the mind of another that the latter does not exercise free will. Although there is no force or threat of harm (which would be duress), a contract between two such people is nevertheless regarded as voidable. If a party in a confidential or fiduciary relationship to another induces the execution of a contract against the other person's free will, the agreement is voidable because of <u>undue influence.</u> If, under any relationship, one is in a position to take undue advantage of another, undue influence may render the contract voidable. Relationships that may result in undue influence are family relationships, a guardian and ward, an attorney and client, a physician and patient, and any other relationship in which confidence reposed on one side results in domination by the other. Undue influence may result also from sickness, infirmity, or serious distress.

In undue influence, there are no threats to harm the person or property of another as in duress. The relationship of the two parties must be such that one relies on the other so much that he or she yields because it is not possible to hold out against the superior position, intelligence, or personality of the other party. Whether undue influence occurred is a question for the court (usually the jury) to determine. Not every influence is regarded as undue; for example, a nagging spouse is ordinarily not regarded as exercising undue influence. In addition, persuasion and argument are not per se undue influence. The key element is that the dominated party is helpless in the hands of the other.

undue influence
person in special relationship causes another's action contrary to free will

COURT CASE

FACTS: Charles and Liddia Porter owned a house, which their daughter Brenda Mays and her husband desired to own. Throughout their marriage, the Porters had a history of Liddia complying with Charles's business decisions, despite her personal misgivings. The Mayses asked the Porters to deed the house to them, because they argued Brenda would better care for her parents than her siblings. During their discussion with the attorney drafting the deed, Charles did not permit Liddia to ask questions about the deed. When Liddia informed Charles she would not sign the deed, he said "Oh, yes you are."

Charles had become increasingly belligerent, so Liddia signed the deed "to avoid an argument." After Charles's death, Liddia sought to set aside the deed, stating she never would have signed it if Charles had not required her to do so.

OUTCOME: Charles's dominance of Liddia was such that she did not act voluntarily and with free agency when executing the deed. The deed was set aside because of Charles's undue influence over Liddia.

—*Mays v. Porter*, 398 S.W.3d 454 (Ky. App.)

9-7 Remedies for Breach of Contract Because of Fraud, Duress, or Undue Influence

Because some mistakes, such as fraud in the inducement, duress, and undue influence, render contracts voidable, not void, you must know what to do if you are a victim of one of these acts. If you do not take steps to protect your rights, your right to avoid the contract's provisions may be lost. Furthermore, you may ratify the contract by some act or word indicating an intention to be bound. After you affirm or ratify the contract, you are as fully bound by it as if there had been no mistake, fraud, duress, or undue influence. But still you may sue for whatever damages you have sustained.

rescind
to set a contract aside

If the contract is voidable, you might elect to **rescind** it or set it aside. Rescission seeks to put the parties in the position they were in before the contract was made. In order to rescind, you must first return, or offer to return, what you received under the contract. After this is done, you are in a position to take one of four actions, depending on the circumstances:

1. You may bring a suit to recover any money, goods, or other things of value given up, plus damages.

2. If the contract is executory on your part, you may refuse to perform. If the other party sues, you can plead mistake, fraud, duress, or undue influence as a complete defense.

3. You may bring a suit to have the contract judicially declared void.

4. If a written contract does not accurately express the parties' agreement, you may sue for **reformation**, or correction, of the contract.

reformation
judicial correction of a
contract

In no case can the wrongdoer set the contract aside and thus profit from the wrong. If the agreement is void, neither party may enforce it, so no special act is required for setting the agreement aside.

QUESTIONS

1. What does the determination of whether a mistake affects the validity of a contract normally depend on?

2. When will courts allow a unilateral mistake of fact to impair the enforceability of a contract?

3. What is the effect when a contract specifies what is to happen in the case of a mistake?

4. How can buyers protect themselves from a mistake as to value or quality?

5. Explain the difference between fraud in the inducement and fraud in the execution of a contract.

6. Under what circumstances will an innocent misrepresentation by a party cause a contract to be voidable?

7. When can a statement of opinion constitute fraud?

8. When does emotional duress occur?

9. When is a contract voidable because of undue influence?

10. Why should the victims of acts that make contracts voidable, such as duress or undue influence, take steps to protect their rights?

CASE PROBLEMS

 LO ②

1. Elizabeth Young, an employee of Paper Converting Machine Company (PCMC), was severely injured while working on a machine made by PCMC, and PCMC learned about the accident. At the time, PCMC was self-insured. Several months later, PCMC was purchased by another company, and it bought a $2 million policy from Admiral Insurance Co. (Admiral). In applying for the policy, PCMC disclosed the Young accident to Admiral's underwriting department. When Young sued PCMC, the company notified Admiral's claims department. Thinking the policy might cover Young's injuries, Admiral participated in settlement negotiations and agreed to pay $2 million. Before sending the money, Admiral decided the policy did not cover that claim, because its policy excluded known claims, and the Young accident occurred prior to the policy being issued. Admiral said it would not pay unless

CASE PROBLEMS (CONTINUED)

PCMC reimbursed it. PCMC alleged that Admiral was bound by the settlement agreement. In the resulting lawsuit, Admiral claimed it was not bound by the agreement because of mistake of fact or mistake of law. Decide the case.

2. Randall Shanks was a successful attorney, and Teresa, his fiancée, was a secretary and office manager in his office. To preserve his assets for his children from a prior marriage, Randall suggested they sign a premarital agreement, and Teresa agreed. Randall drafted an agreement and gave it to Teresa ten days before their wedding. He responded to Teresa's questions about it, but he told her to get independent legal advice. Teresa consulted an attorney licensed in another state, who concluded the agreement would force Teresa to waive all rights as a spouse. She told Teresa to get advice from an attorney licensed in Teresa's state. Teresa returned the agreement to Randall and asked him to make some changes the attorney had suggested. Randall gave a revised agreement to Teresa and told her to review it with her attorney. Teresa did not seek further legal advice. Randall and Teresa signed the agreement and were married. The marriage failed, and when Randall asked for enforcement of the premarital agreement, Teresa alleged undue influence. Was there undue influence? **LO ③**

3. While working, an ore bucket hit Henry Kruzich on the side of his face, causing a severe head injury. Old Republic Insurance Co. insured his employer's workers' compensation plan. It paid Kruzich total disability and medical benefits. Kruzich ultimately needed domiciliary care, so Old Republic started paying Henry's wife, Kathy, to stay at home and care for him. Six years after the accident, Henry and Old Republic signed a settlement agreement for $132,701 that ended "fully and forever . . . all present and future domiciliary care" benefits. Ten years later, Henry was diagnosed with Parkinson's disease, most likely from the accident. Henry sought rescission of the settlement agreement on the basis of mutual mistake of fact saying that at the time of the settlement, neither party knew there was any connection between head injuries and Parkinson's disease. Was the agreement rescinded? **LO ①**

4. Paul Lietz worked for Hansen Law Offices. Hansen terminated Lietz, who then sued for breach of employment contract and unpaid wages. He asked for economic damages, double damages, costs, and attorney's fees. Hansen submitted an offer of judgment, saying it offered "to settle the claim against defendants at the present time in the amount of $7,500." Lietz responded by saying he "accepts Defendants' offer of judgment . . . in the amount of seven thousand five hundred dollars ($7,500)." Neither writing mentioned attorney's fees. Hansen sent Lietz a check for $7,500. He returned the check, saying he would seek attorney's fees since the law allowed such fees when an offer of judgment is made. Hansen said her attorney had made a mistake in drafting the offer of judgment. Should the court find the entry of judgment valid? **LO ②**

5. State police suspected David Miller and Miller's Auto Body, Inc. of enhancing damages to vehicles and billing for damages not sustained in an attempt to get more money from insurance companies. The state Attorney General brought charges against Miller, but agreed to dismiss charges on the condition that Miller sign a settlement agreement; pay restitution to insurance carriers; and release the carriers from all claims, demands, and actions that Miller might have. With the counsel of an attorney, who drafted the release, Miller signed the settlement agreement. Fifteen months later, Miller filed suit against the insurance carriers named in the agreement. Miller claimed he was experiencing "severe financial and emotional distress" at the time he signed the agreement and felt he had "no other choice" but to sign. He argued it was signed under duress and voidable. Was he correct? **LO ③**

6. Glen and Marlene Spitznogle purchased a parcel of land from Kevin and Krista Durbin. The land contract described the 138-acre property and excepted a small lot and house trailer from the purchase. At the time the parties executed the contract, the Durbins' interest in the land was subject to a reservation of oil and gas rights for the lifetime of each of the prior owners, the Scherichs. The Durbins owned a vested remainder interest in the oil and gas rights, which meant the oil and gas rights would be theirs after the Scherichs died. However, in the land sale contract to the Spitznogles, the **LO ②**

CASE PROBLEMS (CONTINUED)

Durbins did not except their remainder interest in the oil and gas rights. After the land contract was fully consummated, the Durbins attempted to except their interest to gas and oil rights in the land. They claimed they did not initially except their rights, because they had been confused about the nature of their interest to the oil and gas rights in the land. Could they set the contract aside?

LO ① 7. Orange County, New York, deeded two lots to Josclynne and Harriet Grier. At the time of the execution of the deeds, all the parties believed that Orange County owned the property. When it later turned out that the county did not own the lots, the county asked the court to vacate the deeds. How should the court rule on the case?

LO ③ 8. Kenneth Smith obtained a second home equity line of credit and forged the signature of his wife, Sue-Anna Smith, on the loan documents submitted to the bank. Several years later, Sue-Anna filed for divorce and alleged that the home equity loan was obtained through fraud. To resolve the divorce litigation, the state court entered a series of orders dividing the property and obligations of each party. The order included a provision that after 12 months, it would be Sue-Anna's responsibility to make payments on the home equity loan and sell the property, from which she would receive the proceeds. Sue-Anna made payments on the home equity loan after the 12-month period. She then contacted the bank and told them that the loan had been fraudulently obtained. The bank was unable to complete a fraud investigation, because Sue-Anna failed to provide a copy of the police report. The bank then offered Sue-Anna the opportunity to modify the terms of the loan, which she accepted. Despite her knowledge of the forgery, Sue-Anna signed the modification agreement and continued making payments as modified by the agreement. The modification agreement also listed Sue-Anna as the sole borrower. After declaring bankruptcy, Sue-Anna sought to invalidate the home equity loan contract on the grounds that her signature was fraudulently obtained. How should the court rule on this case?

LO ② 9. A month before they were divorced, Margaret Janusz and Francis Gilliam entered into a property settlement agreement. The agreement provided that Gilliam would continue funding and maintain in effect his survivor's annuity through the federal Civil Service Retirement System. The annuity would pay a monthly amount to Janusz after Gilliam's death. Several years after the divorce, the federal Office of Personnel Management told Janusz that pursuant to federal law, she was not eligible for Gilliam's survivor benefits. Janusz sued to rescind the settlement agreement on the basis of mutual mistake of fact. Was the agreement rescinded?

Illegal Agreements

LEARNING OBJECTIVES

1. Explain the consequences of a contract for an unlawful purpose or a purpose achieved illegally.
2. Explain what types of contracts are void for illegality.
3. Identify the types of contracts that are contrary to public policy.

PREVIEW CASE

Rainbow International Marriage Services Inc. advertised as a convenient way for people to meet their marriage partner. Rainbow contracted with Ping Cui to introduce her to suitable prospective marriage partners until she was married. Ping Cui paid a registration fee of $700 and agreed to pay $7,500 following her marriage to a person introduced by Rainbow. She was listed and profiled on Rainbow's website. John Choma expressed an interest in her. Rainbow relayed information Choma had given about himself to Ping Cui, and they corresponded. She and Choma were later married, but she did not pay the $7,500 fee. Rainbow sued her for breach of contract. Was the agreement to pay someone to find a spouse valid? Is it consistent with public policy to treat marriage like a business? Are there possibilities for deception and exploitation associated with matchmaking over the Internet?

A contract must be for a lawful purpose, which must be achieved in a lawful manner. Otherwise, the contract is void. If this were not true, the court might force one party to a contract to commit a crime. If the act itself is legal, but the manner of committing the act that is called for in the contract is illegal, the contract is void.

LO ①
Unlawful contracts

If the parties are not equally guilty, courts may assist the less guilty party. However, courts will not allow a wrongdoer to enforce a contract against an innocent party.

A contract that is void because of illegality does not necessarily involve the commission of a crime. It may consist merely of a private wrong—the commission of a tort—such as an agreement by two people to slander a third. A contract contrary to public policy is also illegal.

COURT CASE

FACTS: As a physician with a law degree, Jeannette Martello reviewed medical malpractice cases for attorney Joshua Santana. Martello did not practice law, because she had not passed the bar exam. For three cases, Santana agreed to pay Martello a percentage of his fees if the cases settled in exchange for Martello referring the clients to him. The Kentucky Rules of Professional Conduct prohibited payment of Martello, who was not an attorney, on a contingency basis in this manner. Despite this, Martello received a percentage of Santana's settlement fees for each of the three cases. Later, Martello discovered that Santana had misled her as to the settlement amount of two of the cases. She sued Santana for breach of contract.

OUTCOME: The court held that Martello's contracts were void as against public policy, because the fee-sharing arrangement violated Kentucky ethics rules.

—*Martello v. Santana*, 713 F.3d 309 (6th Cir.)

If the contract is indivisible, that is, it cannot be performed except as an entity, then the illegality of one part renders the whole contract invalid. If the contract is divisible, so that the legal parts can be performed separately, the legal parts of the contract are enforceable. For example, when one purchases several articles, each priced separately, and the sale of one article is illegal because the price was illegally set by price-fixing, the whole contract will not fall because of the one article.

COURT CASE

FACTS: Akbar Ali owed a debt to Hanif Roshan. Ali, Roshan, and Madatali Unami entered into an agreement by which Ali agreed to pay Roshan $75,000 and Unami guaranteed the payment. The agreement contained a confidentiality provision providing it would not be disclosed to anyone. Roshan encountered Arif Merchant and happened to mention that Ali owed him money. Merchant funded a business run by Ali and Unami contingent upon them disclosing all their debts and not incurring further debts. He withdrew his funding. The business suffered financially. Ali stopped payment on a check he had given Roshan under their agreement, so Roshan sued. Unami alleged that Roshan had breached the agreement by disclosing the debt to Merchant.

OUTCOME: Ali and Unami were required to disclose to Merchant their indebtedness to Roshan. They sought to conceal the indebtedness via the confidentiality provision. That provision was thus void as against public policy, so Unami could not use enforcement of it to avoid payment to Roshan. However, that provision could be separated from the remaining terms, which were enforceable. Unami had to pay.

—*Unami v. Roshan*, 659 S.E.2d 724 (Ga. App.)

10-1 Contracts Prohibited by Statute

LO ②
Contracts void for illegality

There are many types of contracts declared illegal by statute. Some common ones include:

1. Gambling contracts
2. Sunday contracts
3. Usurious contracts
4. Contracts of an unlicensed operator
5. Contracts for the sale of prohibited articles
6. Contracts in unreasonable restraint of trade

10-1a GAMBLING CONTRACTS

A **gambling contract** is a transaction wherein the parties stand to win or to lose based on pure chance. What one gains, the other must lose. Under the early common law, private wagering contracts were enforceable, but they are now generally prohibited in all states by statute. In recent years, certain classes of gambling contracts regulated by the state, such as state lotteries and pari-mutuel systems of betting on horse races and dog races, have been legalized in many states.

gambling contract
agreement in which parties win or lose by chance

In general, the courts will leave the parties to a private gambling contract where it finds them and will not allow one party to recover damages from the other for the breach of a gambling debt. If two parties to a gambling contract give money to a stakeholder with instructions to pay the money to the winner, the parties can demand a return of their money. If the stakeholder pays the money to the winner, then the loser may sue either the winner or the stakeholder for reimbursement. No state will permit the stakeholder, who is considered merely a trustee of the funds, to keep the money. The court in this event requires the stakeholder to return each wagerer's deposit.

COURT CASE

FACTS: After borrowing $50,000 from Carnival Leisure Industries, Ltd., with which to gamble legally at Carnival's casino in the Bahamas, Phil Froug lost it all. He did not repay the loan. Carnival sued him to collect in a Florida court. Froug argued that recovery was barred by law. Florida law provided that "all promises . . . for the repayment of money lent . . . for the purpose of being . . . wagered, are void. . . ."

OUTCOME: Although the gambling debt may have been legally incurred in the Bahamas, the court said Florida law prohibited recovering it there.

—*Froug v. Carnival Leisure Industries, Ltd.*, 627 So.2d 538 (Fla. Ct. App.)

Closely akin to gambling debts are loans made to enable one to gamble. If *A* loans *B* $100 and then wins it back in a poker game, is this a gambling debt? Most courts hold that it is not. If *A* and *B* bet $100 on a football game, and *B* wins, and if *A* pays *B* by giving a promissory note for the $100, such a note may be declared void.

Trading on the stock exchange or the grain market represents legitimate business transactions. But the distinction between such trading and gambling contracts is sometimes very fine. Alewine and Goodnoe could form a contract whereby Alewine agrees to sell Goodnoe 10,000 shares of stock one month from the date, at $42 a share. If they do not actually intend to buy and sell the stock, but agree to settle for the difference between $42 a share and the closing price on the date fixed in the contract, this is a gambling contract.

However, Ripetto could agree to sell Bolde 10,000 bushels of wheat to be delivered six months later at $1.70 a bushel. Ripetto does not own any wheat, but he intends to buy it for delivery in six months. They agree that at the end of the six-month period, the seller does not actually have to deliver the wheat. If the price of wheat has gone up, the seller may pay the buyer the difference between the current price and the contract price. If the price of wheat has gone down, the buyer may pay the seller the difference. Such a contract is legal because the intention was to deliver. The primary difference between the Alewine case and the Ripetto case is the intention to deliver. In the case of trading, the seller (Ripetto) intended at the time of the contract to deliver the wheat, and the buyer to accept it. In the gambling case, the seller (Alewine) did not intend to deliver.

10-1b SUNDAY CONTRACTS

The laws pertaining to Sunday contracts resulted from statutes and judicial interpretation. They vary considerably from state to state. Most states have repealed their statutes that made Sunday contracts illegal. Some states prohibit the sale of particular items on Sunday such as liquor. The violators of Sunday acts are seldom prosecuted. For this reason, the types of transactions one observes being undertaken on Sunday do not necessarily indicate restrictions imposed by these laws.

10-1c USURIOUS CONTRACTS

usury
charging higher rate of interest than the law allows

maximum contract rate
highest legal rate of interest

legal rate
interest rate applied when no rate is specified

State laws that limit the rate of interest that may be charged for the use of money are called **usury** laws. Frequently, there are two rates: the maximum contract rate and the legal rate. The **maximum contract rate** is the highest rate that may be charged; any rate above that is usurious. In some states, this rate fluctuates, depending on the prime rate. The **legal rate**, which is a rate somewhat lower than the contract rate, applies to all situations in which interest may be charged but in which the parties were silent as to the rate. If merchandise is sold on thirty days' credit, the seller may collect interest from the time the thirty days expire until the debt is paid. If no rate is agreed on in a situation of this kind, the legal rate may be charged.

The courts will treat transactions as usurious when there is in fact a lending of money at a usurious rate even though disguised. Such activities as requiring the borrower to execute a note for an amount in excess of the actual loan and requiring the borrower to antedate the note so as to charge interest for a longer period than that agreed on could make a loan usurious.

The penalty for usury varies from state to state. In most states, the only penalty might prohibit the lender from collecting the excess interest. In other states, the entire contract is void, and in still others, the borrower need not pay any interest but must repay the principal. If the borrower has already paid the usurious interest, the court will require the lender to refund to the borrower any money collected in excess of the contract rate.

In all states, special statutes govern consumer loans by pawnbrokers, small loan companies, and finance companies. In some states, these firms may charge much higher rates of interest. In addition, loans of very large amounts of money or business loans are frequently not covered by usury laws.

COURT CASE

FACTS: Royal Links USA Inc. (Royal) told Lake McBride Golf Course (Lake) it could acquire a snack and beverage cart at no cost for displaying advertising on the cart. Lake executed an agreement allowing Royal to display advertising on the cart in exchange for 60 monthly payments of $299. Lake also executed a lease of a beverage cart from C&J Vantage Leasing Co. (C&J) that stated the equipment supplier was not an agent of C&J and called for 60 monthly lease payments of $299 from Lake. It recited in bold capital letters, "THIS LEASE IS NONCANCELLABLE." C&J bought a beverage cart from Royal for $12,500 and shipped it to Lake.

A year later, Royal told Lake it would no longer pay the $299 per month for advertising, so Lake stopped making the $299 lease payments. C&J sued Lake for breach of the lease. Lake complained the lease payments were usurious.

OUTCOME: Since the cart was used to sell refreshments to customers at the golf course, it was used for a business purpose. State law had an exception in the usury statute for loans for a business purpose.

—C&J Vantage Leasing Co. v. Wolfe, 795 N.W.2d 65 (Iowa)

10-1d CONTRACTS OF AN UNLICENSED OPERATOR

Statutes make it illegal to operate certain types of businesses or professions without a license. Most of these statutes are enacted to protect the public from incompetent operators. The most common types of professional people who must be licensed to operate include doctors, lawyers, certified and licensed public accountants, dentists, and insurance and real estate salespeople. A person who performs these services without a license not only cannot sue to collect for the services but also may be guilty of a crime.

A licensing law may be designed solely as a revenue measure by requiring payment of a fee for a license. Contracts made by an unlicensed person operating in one of the fields or businesses covered by such a law are normally held valid. However, the unlicensed operator may still be subject to fine or imprisonment for violating the law.

COURT CASE

FACTS: Meteor Motors Inc. owned Palm Beach Acura, an auto dealership in Florida. It agreed to pay Thompson Halbach & Associates a commission of 5 percent of the sales price if Thompson found a buyer for the stock of the dealership. Neither Halbach nor any of its principals was a licensed broker in Florida. Halbach gave Craig Zinn Automotive Group, a Florida-based automotive group, information about Meteor so that Zinn could evaluate the possibility of purchasing Meteor. Halbach did not participate in negotiations between Meteor and Zinn. Zinn purchased Meteor's stock for $5,000,000, and Halbach was not paid a commission. Halbach sued Meteor for breach of contract.

OUTCOME: As Halbach was not registered in Florida, the court held that the contract was invalid.

—*Meteor Motors Inc. v. Thompson Halbach & Associates*, 914 So.2d 479 (Fla. App.)

10-1e CONTRACTS FOR THE SALE OF PROHIBITED ARTICLES

If a pharmacist sells morphine or a similar drug to one who does not have a prescription, a suit to collect the price would not be successful. One who sells cigarettes or alcoholic beverages to a minor when such a sale is prohibited cannot recover on the contract. In such cases, the court will not interfere to protect either party.

10-1f CONTRACTS IN UNREASONABLE RESTRAINT OF TRADE

Government policy encourages competition. Any contract, therefore, intended to restrain trade unreasonably is null and void. The dividing line between reasonable and unreasonable restraint of trade is often dim, but certain acts have become well established by judicial decision as being unreasonable restraints of trade. The most common acts in this class include:

1. Contracts not to compete
2. Contracts to limit competition
3. Contracts to fix the resale price
4. Unfair competitive practices

Contracts Not to Compete. Normally, a contract not to compete is illegal; however, it can be valid when buying a business or making an employment contract. When one buys a going business, not only are the physical assets acquired but also the goodwill, which is often the most valuable asset of the firm. In the absence of a contract prohibiting the seller from attempting to retake the goodwill, the seller may engage in the same business again and seek to retain former customers. It is customary and highly desirable when purchasing a business to include in the contract a provision prohibiting the seller from entering the same business again in the trade territory for a specified length of time. Such a contract not to compete is legal if the restriction is reasonable as to both time and place.

The restriction as to territory should not go beyond the trade area of the business. Because the restriction is sustained to protect the buyer of the business from competition of the seller, it follows that the restriction should not reach out into areas where the buyer's reputation has not reached, nor should the seller be subjected to the restriction longer than is reasonably necessary for the buyer to become established in the new business. When the restriction goes further or longer than necessary to protect the buyer of the business, it is unlawful not only because it burdens the seller but also because it deprives the business community and society in general of the benefit of the activities of the seller.

COURT CASE

FACTS: Jani-King of Omaha was a franchisor of professional cleaning services. The company secured clients and then connected them with franchisees, who provided janitorial services. The franchise agreement included a noncompete clause, which prohibited franchisees from owning or operating any business with services similar to Jani-King's during the term of the agreement and for a one-year period after the agreement terminated in any territory where Jani-King operated. Jani-King operated in almost every state and in numerous foreign countries. Anthony Waadah was a Jani-King franchisee,

who began recruiting clients for his own cleaning company. Jani-King sued Waadah for breach of noncompete clause in the franchise agreement.

OUTCOME: The court held that the one-year restriction was reasonable, but the territory covered was unreasonable, because Jani-King operated in so many places. The noncompete agreement was unenforceable.

—*Unlimited Opportunity, Inc. v. Waadah*, 290 Neb. 629 (Neb.)

Closely allied to this type of contract is one whereby an employee, as a part of the employment contract, agrees not to work for a competing firm for a certain period of time after terminating employment. These contracts must be reasonable as to time and place.

Contracts to Restrain Trade. Contracts to fix prices, divide up the trade territory, limit production so as to reduce the supply, or otherwise limit competition are void. The Sherman Antitrust Act and the Clayton Act specifically declare illegal such contracts that affect interstate commerce and are therefore subject to regulation by the federal government. Most of the states have similar laws applicable to intrastate commerce.

Contracts to Fix the Resale Price. An agreement between a seller and a buyer that the buyer shall not resell below a stated price is generally illegal as a price-fixing agreement. The original seller (manufacturer) can, of course, control the price by selling directly to the public through outlet stores.

Unfair Competitive Practices. The Robinson–Patman Act attempted to eliminate certain unfair competitive practices in interstate commerce. Under this act, it is unlawful to discriminate in price between competing buyers if the goods are of like grade, quantity, and quality. Most states have passed similar laws for intrastate commerce. Some state statutes go further and prohibit the resale of goods at a loss or below cost for the purpose of harming competition.

10-1g ADMINISTRATIVE AGENCY ORDERS

As was mentioned in Chapter 4, many government administrative agencies have the authority to issue rules and regulations that have the force of law. A contract that violates such a rule is illegal.

LO ③
Contracts against public policy

10-2 Contracts Contrary to Public Policy

Contracts contrary to public policy are unenforceable. The courts must determine from the nature of the contract whether it is contrary to public policy or not. One court, in attempting to classify contracts contrary to public policy, defined them thus: "Whatever tends to injustice, restraint of liberty, restraint of a legal right, whatever tends to the obstruction of justice, a violation of a statute, or the obstruction or perversion of the administration of the law as to executive, legislative, or other official action, whenever embodied in and made the subject of a contract, the contract is against public policy and therefore void and not susceptible to enforcement." (*Brooks v. Cooper*, 50 N.J. Eq. 761, 26 A. 978)

The most common types of contracts contrary to public policy include:

1. Contracts limiting the freedom of marriage
2. Contracts obstructing the administration of justice
3. Contracts injuring the public service

10-2a CONTRACTS LIMITING THE FREEDOM OF MARRIAGE

It is contrary to public policy to enter into any contract the effect of which is to limit freedom of marriage. Such contracts are void. The following provisions in contracts have been held to render the contract a nullity: (1) an agreement whereby one party promises never to marry; (2) an agreement to refrain from marrying for a definite period of time (an agreement not to marry during minority, however, is valid); and (3) an agreement not to marry certain named individuals.

Similarly, marriage brokerage contracts are unenforceable as against public policy. A marriage brokerage contract is one in which a person agrees to pay another for negotiating, procuring, or bringing about a marriage.

Also, in order to preserve and protect marriages, it is held that an agreement to seek a divorce for a consideration is void as against public policy. However, property settlement agreements made in contemplation of divorces are valid.

PREVIEW CASE REVISITED

FACTS: Rainbow International Marriage Services Inc. advertised as a convenient way for people to meet their marriage partner. Rainbow contracted with Ping Cui to introduce her to suitable prospective marriage partners until she was married. Ping Cui paid a registration fee of $700 and agreed to pay $7,500 following her marriage to a person introduced by Rainbow. She was listed and profiled on Rainbow's website. John Choma expressed an interest in her. Rainbow relayed information Choma had given about himself to Ping Cui, and they corresponded. She and Choma were later married, but she did not pay the $7,500 fee. Rainbow sued her for breach of contract.

OUTCOME: The court found that the contract was clearly a marriage brokerage contract and void as against public policy.

—*Ureneck v. Cui*, 798 N.E.2d 305 (Mass. App. Ct.)

10-2b CONTRACTS OBSTRUCTING THE ADMINISTRATION OF JUSTICE

Any contract that may obstruct our legal processes is null and void. It is not necessary that justice actually be obstructed. If the contract has the tendency to do so, the courts will not enforce it.

The following provisions have been held to render contracts void: (1) an agreement to pay a witness a larger fee than that allowed by law, provided the promisor wins the case; (2) an agreement by a candidate for sheriff that a certain individual will be appointed deputy sheriff in return for aid in bringing about the promisor's election; (3) an agreement to pay a prospective witness a sum of money to leave the state until the trial is over; and (4) an agreement not to prosecute a thief if the stolen goods are returned.

10-2c CONTRACTS INJURING THE PUBLIC SERVICE

Any contract that may, from its very nature, injure public service is void. A person may contract as an attorney to appear before any public authority to encourage or oppose the passage of any bill. But a contract to use improper influence such as bribery to obtain the desired results is void.

Contracts to use one's influence in obtaining a public contract that by statute must be let to the lowest responsible bidder, to obtain pardons and paroles, or to pay a public official more or less than the statutory salary are also void.

COURT CASE

FACTS: George Ventura had worked for Chiquita Brands International Inc. Ventura learned that Michael Gallagher, a reporter for the *Cincinnati Enquirer*, was investigating Chiquita, and Ventura volunteered to help as a confidential source. He had broken Chiquita's password system, getting unauthorized access to individual voicemail messages. He provided the passwords so that Gallagher could listen to these messages and use them in articles. A grand jury subpoenaed Gallagher and his materials so Ventura's identity was disclosed. He was charged with attempted unauthorized access to a computer system. Ventura sued the *Enquirer* for breaching its promise to protect his identity.

OUTCOME: The court said it was against public policy to enforce an agreement to conceal a crime. The *Enquirer* was not liable.

—*Ventura v. The Cincinnati Enquirer*, 396 F.3d 784 (6th Cir.)

QUESTIONS

1. Does a contract that is void for illegality necessarily involve the commission of a crime?
2. With regard to illegality of a contract, what is the difference between a divisible and an indivisible contract?
3. What constitutes a usurious contract?
4. Why is it that the types of transactions one observes being undertaken on Sunday do not necessarily indicate restrictions imposed by Sunday acts?

QUESTIONS (CONTINUED)

5. Why are noncompete contracts that have restrictions that go further or longer than necessary to protect the buyer of the business unlawful?

6. Why are most statutes making it illegal to operate certain types of businesses or professions without a license enacted?

7. If Tom contracts to sell cigarettes to Mary and her friends, who are minors, can he recover on the contract? Why not?

8. Can a contract provision in which a party promises to never marry be enforced?

9. Under what circumstances will a contract that may obstruct our legal processes be void?

10. Give three examples of contracts that injure public service.

CASE PROBLEMS

LO ②

1. Yancey Brothers Co. (Yancey) employed Edward Murphree as a heavy equipment salesman. His employment contract prohibited him from attempting to solicit any customers procured or serviced by him for two years after leaving Yancey. Murphree used a thumb drive to copy company files from his company laptop. He resigned and took a job with Flint Equipment Co. (Flint), a competitor selling the same equipment in the same territory. Murphree contacted his former Yancey clients and submitted heavy equipment bids to some. Yancey sued Murphree and Flint, alleging Murphree was in violation of his employment contract. Should the contract's nonsolicitation provision be enforced?

LO ③

2. Julianna Robertson's will set up a trust that left her home to her husband, Lynn, for his lifetime or until he remarried or allowed "any female companion to live with him who is not a blood relative." During the probate of the will, the court held that Lynn had a life estate in the property and that the provision regarding his remarriage was an invalid restraint on marriage. James Nye, Julianna's son and the executor, appealed. Was the provision invalid?

LO ②

3. Pines Grazing Association Inc. (Pines) contracted to sell a ranch to J. C. Investments (JC). Before the sale, the parties discovered that 80 acres they thought had been included in the ranch were not. They went ahead with the sale while Pines tried to buy the 80 acres from Lemhi County. The county had to sell the property at public auction. Pines sent Fred Snook, and JC sent Scott Karterman to the auction to buy the acreage. They met at the auction, and JC agreed to pay Pines $20,000 if it would not bid on the property so they would not bid against each other and drive up the price. Pines did not bid, and JC bought the property for much less than it would have had to pay Pines. JC did not pay Pines the $20,000, and in the resulting lawsuit JC argued that the agreement not to bid was illegal and therefore unenforceable. Should the court enforce the agreement to pay Pines $20,000?

LO ①

4. Youcheng Wu, a married man, entered into a relationship with Jian Xu, a single woman. Xu claimed that Wu promised to divorce his wife and marry her. Wu denied this, but did sign a letter drafted by Xu's attorney in which he apologized for hurting her and promised to pay $500,000 if Xu would refrain from disclosing the relationship to Wu's wife. After paying approximately $47,000, Wu stopped making payments. Xu threatened to sue for the remaining amount. Wu responded by filing suit for a declaratory judgment that the letter was an unenforceable contract and against public policy. How should the court rule in this case?

LO ②

5. Chuck Denson owned a car dealership, ABCD Auto Inc. that was licensed to sell cars in Tarrant and Wood counties but not in Dallas County. Through its agent, Otis Chapman, Dallas County Credit Union and Denson agreed that Denson would find cars for the credit union's customers that the credit union would finance. The activities were all conducted in Dallas County. The profits would be split

CASE PROBLEMS (CONTINUED)

one-third among each of ABCD, Denson, and Chapman. After making sales, Denson sued, alleging that Chapman had understated the sale prices reducing the share paid to ABCD and Denson. The credit union said the agreement was void for illegality because ABCD was not licensed. Was the agreement void?

6. Seven valuable paintings were stolen from the home of Michael Bakwin, including a still life by Paul Cezanne. Sometime later, while cleaning out the loft where a client had been living, attorney Robert Mardirosian found the paintings. Instead of reporting his discovery to the police, Mardirosian shipped the paintings out of the country and sought to have the Cezanne insured in London through a third party. The insurer contacted authorities, who enabled Bakwin to contact Mardirosian's agent. Bakwin reluctantly agreed to convey six of the paintings to the anonymous holder in exchange for the return of the Cezanne. The agreement was executed and the Cezanne was returned. Mardirosian was later discovered and apprehended when he attempted to sell the remaining six paintings. He was convicted of possessing stolen paintings. On appeal, Mardirosian argued that in light of his contract with Bakwin to exchange the paintings, the government could not prove the paintings were "stolen" after a certain date. Did the contract extinguish Mardirosian's offense of possessing stolen paintings? **LO ①**

7. CIBER was competing on a bid to provide software services to the District of Columbia government and retained the services of CapitalKeys to help win the contract. CIBER and CapitalKeys entered an agreement that stipulated, among other things, that in the event CIBER was awarded the contract, CapitalKeys would be paid a 3 percent commission on the value of the contract. CIBER procured the contract worth $17,000,000, and CapitalKeys invoiced CIBER for $323,785 pursuant to their agreement. After CIBER refused to pay, CapitalKeys sued for breach of contract. CIBER responded that because the 3 percent fee was a contingent fee for the purpose of securing a public contract, that the clause was void and in violation of public policy. Were they correct? **LO ③**

8. The town of Lunenburg asked for bids on a multimillion-dollar construction project to be financed by the state. State law required the town to publish a notice for bids in a newspaper of general circulation in the locality. Lunenburg failed to advertise for bids in a local newspaper. Baltazar Contractors Inc. was the low bidder, and Lunenburg signed a contract with the company. The state Department of Environmental Protection questioned the bid award and told Lunenburg its state financing was in jeopardy. Lunenburg told Baltazar it was ending the contract. It re-advertised for bids, this time publishing a notice in the local newspaper. Baltazar bid again, but MDR Construction Co. Inc., who had not bid the first time, was the low bidder and got the contract. Baltazar sued Lunenburg for damages. Should Baltazar recover? **LO ②**

11

Written Contracts

LEARNING OBJECTIVES

① Identify which contracts the Statute of Frauds requires to be in writing.
② Distinguish adequate from inadequate writings when a written contract is required.
③ Explain the parol evidence rule.

PREVIEW CASE

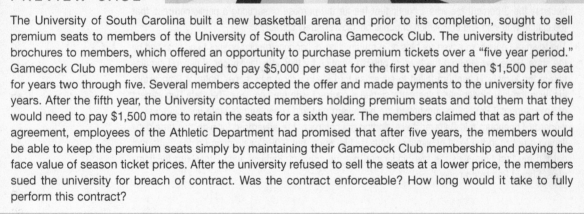

The University of South Carolina built a new basketball arena and prior to its completion, sought to sell premium seats to members of the University of South Carolina Gamecock Club. The university distributed brochures to members, which offered an opportunity to purchase premium tickets over a "five year period." Gamecock Club members were required to pay $5,000 per seat for the first year and then $1,500 per seat for years two through five. Several members accepted the offer and made payments to the university for five years. After the fifth year, the University contacted members holding premium seats and told them that they would need to pay $1,500 more to retain the seats for a sixth year. The members claimed that as part of the agreement, employees of the Athletic Department had promised that after five years, the members would be able to keep the premium seats simply by maintaining their Gamecock Club membership and paying the face value of season ticket prices. After the university refused to sell the seats at a lower price, the members sued the university for breach of contract. Was the contract enforceable? How long would it take to fully perform this contract?

LO ①
Requirement of writing

Contracts may be in written or oral form. All contracts of importance ought to be in writing, but only a few must be written in order to be enforceable. An oral contract is just as effective and enforceable as a written contract unless it is one of the few types specifically required by statute to be in writing.

11-1 Reasons for Written Contracts

A written contract has advantages over an oral contract, provided it includes all the terms and provisions of the agreement. The existence of a contract cannot be denied if it is in writing. If there were no witnesses when an oral contract was formed, one of the parties might successfully deny that any contract was made. In addition, the terms of the contract can be ascertained. One of the parties to an oral contract might die or become incompetent and, therefore, be unable to testify as to the terms of an oral contract. The administrator or executor of an estate in case of death or the committee or guardian in case of incapacity is tremendously handicapped in enforcing an oral agreement that the deceased or incompetent person made. Even when there are witnesses present at the time an oral contract is formed, their testimony may vary considerably as to the actual terms of the contract. Written evidence, composed in clear and unambiguous language, is more reliable than oral evidence.

For these reasons, most businesspeople prefer to have contracts pertaining to matters of importance put in writing, even when the law does not require them to do so.

11-2 Statute of Frauds

In 1677, the English Parliament enacted a law known as the **Statute of Frauds**. This statute listed certain classes of contracts that could not be enforced unless their terms were evidenced by a written document. Most of our states have adopted this list but with slight variations.

Statute of Frauds law requiring certain contracts to be in writing

The Statute of Frauds applies only to executory contracts. If two parties enter into an oral contract that falls under the Statute of Frauds, and both parties have fully performed according to its terms, neither party can seek to set aside the transaction on the ground that there was no writing.

The Statute of Frauds provides that the following types of agreements must be in writing:

1. An agreement to sell land or any interest in or concerning land
2. An agreement the terms of which cannot be performed within one year from the time it is made
3. An agreement to become responsible for the debts or default of another
4. An agreement of an executor or administrator to pay the debts of the estate from the executor's or the administrator's personal funds
5. An agreement containing a promise in consideration of marriage
6. An agreement to sell goods for $500 or more (discussed in detail in Chapter 17)

However, if one has paid money or performed a service under an oral contract required by the Statute of Frauds to be in writing, the money or the value of the service may be recovered even though the executory part of the contract cannot be enforced. If one party has made part performance of an oral contract and would be hurt if the contract were not enforced, courts will allow enforcement of it. These outcomes are based on equitable principles of preventing the unjust enrichment of one party.

11-2a AN AGREEMENT TO SELL LAND OR ANY INTEREST IN OR CONCERNING LAND

An agreement to sell any interest in land comes under the Statute of Frauds. The required writing differs from the deed, which will be executed later and by which the seller makes the actual transfer of title to the buyer.

One may wish to sell not the land itself, but only an interest in the land. This type of contract also must be in writing. These sales usually involve rights of way, joint use of driveways, mineral rights, or timber. A lease of real property for more than one year must be in writing in order to be binding.

Frequently, oral contracts relative to land are performed before any question of their validity is raised. For example, one leases a building by oral contract for two years. The building is occupied for that period, and then the rent is not paid on the ground that the oral contract is invalid. The law will compel payment of the rent orally agreed to for the time that the premises were occupied.

COURT CASE

FACTS: Abraham Lorenz orally agreed to sell his ranch to Deward Miller so he could subdivide it. Because of financing problems, the ranch was conveyed to Miller in two parcels at different times. After buying the first parcel, Miller filed a preliminary plat covering the whole ranch. He applied with the county to subdivide the entire tract called Granite Springs Retreat and indicated it had sixty lots. Miller filed a declaration of protective covenants for Granite Springs Retreat without a legal description. He then took legal title to the second parcel. Years later, owners of lots in the second parcel claimed the covenants did not apply to their property. They argued that when the covenants were recorded,

Miller only had an oral agreement to buy the property and that the agreement was void under the Statute of Frauds.

OUTCOME: The court held that Lorenz and Miller had an agreement covering the entire Granite Springs Retreat property. When Miller filed the Declaration, both parties had partially performed the oral agreement by completing the transaction involving the first parcel, and therefore the agreement fell into the exception of the requirement of a written contract.

—*Cash v. Granite Springs Retreat Ass'n Inc.*, 248 P.3d 614 (Wyo.)

11-2b AN AGREEMENT THE TERMS OF WHICH CANNOT BE PERFORMED WITHIN ONE YEAR FROM THE TIME IT IS MADE

The terms of a contract that cannot be performed in one year might easily be forgotten before the contract is completed. To minimize the need to resort to the courts because the parties do not remember the terms of a contract, the law requires all contracts that cannot be performed within one year to be in writing.

This provision of the Statute of Frauds means that if the terms of the contract are such that, by their nature, they cannot be performed within one year from the date of formation, then the contract must be in writing. The contract can be so worded that it may not be completed for fifty years, yet if it is physically possible to complete it within one year, it need not be in writing. If John agrees in consideration of $50,000 to care for Chen for "as long as he (Chen) lives," this contract need not be in writing because there is no certainty Chen will live one year. But an agreement to manage a motel for five years will, by its terms, require more than one year for performance; therefore, it comes under the Statute of Frauds.

PREVIEW CASE REVISITED

FACTS: The University of South Carolina built a new basketball arena and prior to its completion, sought to sell premium seats to members of the University of South Carolina Gamecock Club. The university distributed brochures to members, which offered an opportunity to purchase premium tickets over a "five year period." Gamecock Club members were required to pay $5,000 per seat for the first year and then $1,500 per seat for years two through five. Several members accepted the offer and made payments to the university for five years. After the fifth year, the University contacted members holding premium seats and told them that they would need to pay $1,500 more to retain the seats for a sixth year. The members claimed that as part of the agreement, employees of the Athletic Department had promised that after five years, the members would be able to keep the premium seats simply by maintaining their Gamecock Club membership and paying the face value of season ticket prices. After the university refused to sell the seats at a lower price, the members sued the university for breach of contract.

OUTCOME: Since the agreement to sell premium tickets to Gamecock Club members could not be fully performed within a year, the Statute of Frauds required the agreement to be in writing. The oral contract was unenforceable.

—*Springob v. University of South Carolina*, 757 S.E.2d 384 (S.C.)

11-2c AN AGREEMENT TO BECOME RESPONSIBLE FOR THE DEBTS OR DEFAULT OF ANOTHER

The term **debt** refers to an obligation to pay money; **default** refers to a breach of any contractual obligation including the payment of money, but also other obligations such as the failure to build a house. An agreement to be responsible for the debts or default of another occurs when the promisor undertakes to make good the loss that the promisee would sustain if another person does not pay the promisee a debt owed or fails to perform a duty imposed by contract or by law. If Allen promises Charlotte to pay Betty's debt to Charlotte if Betty fails to pay, the Statute of Frauds requires Allen's promise to be in writing. Allen's promise is to be responsible for the debt of another. This provision of the Statute of Frauds was designed especially for those situations in which one promises to answer for the debt of another person purely as an accommodation to that person.

debt
obligation to pay money

default
breach of contractual obligation

An exception to the Statute of Frauds occurs if in fact a promise is an original promise by the promisor rather than a promise to pay the debt of another. For example, if Andy buys goods on credit from Betsy and tells Betsy to deliver the goods to Cindy, Andy is not promising to pay the debt of another; the promise is to pay Andy's own debt. Andy's promise does not have to be in writing.

COURT CASE

FACTS: When the commonwealth of Pennsylvania contracted with A&L Inc. to resurface a road, A&L got a bond from Safeco Insurance and retained Boss Construction Inc. as a subcontractor. Boss bought material from Trumbull Corp. but failed to pay the bill. At a meeting of A&L and Trumbull, Louis Ruscitto, president of A&L, promised that A&L would pay the bill at the end of the fiscal year if Trumbull would not pursue a claim on the bond. Trumbull did not proceed on the bond claim until after the end of A&L's fiscal year, when the bill was still unpaid. Ruscitto and his wife, who was a co-owner of Boss, had personally guaranteed the bond. A&L alleged that its oral promise to pay another's debt was unenforceable.

OUTCOME: The facts that Ruscitto and his wife had guaranteed the bond and that she was a co-owner of Boss meant that Ruscitto's oral promise was for his financial advantage. The oral promise was enforceable.

—*Trumbull Corp. v. Boss Constr. Inc.*, 801 A.2d 1289 (Pa. Commw. Ct.)

The Statute of Frauds requirement of writing does not apply if the main purpose of the promise is to gain some advantage for the promisor. Sometimes one person promises to answer for the debt or default of another because it is in the promisor's personal financial interest to do so. In such a case, the promise does not need to be in writing.

The Statute of Frauds does not apply when the promisor promises the debtor that the promisor will pay the debt owed to the third person.

COURT CASE

FACTS: Sharon Steinberger sued her husband, Chaim, for divorce. Chaim sued his father-in-law, Marton Grossman, seeking a declaration that Grossman was primarily liable for payment of the mortgage on the Steinbergers' house. The oral promise allegedly made by Grossman to be primarily liable on the mortgage was made to Chaim. Grossman alleged that such a promise was not enforceable under the Statute of Frauds.

OUTCOME: Because the promise was made to Chaim and not to the lender bank, it did not fall under the prohibitions of the Statute of Frauds.

—*Steinberger v. Steinberger*, 676 N.Y.S.2d 210 (N.Y. App. Div.)

11-2d AN AGREEMENT OF AN EXECUTOR OR ADMINISTRATOR TO PERSONALLY PAY THE DEBTS OF THE ESTATE

When a person dies, an executor or administrator takes over all of the deceased's assets. From these assets, the executor or administrator pays all the debts of the deceased before distributing the remainder according to the terms of the decedent's will or, in the absence of a will, to the decedent's heirs. The executor or the administrator is not obligated to pay the debts of the deceased out of the executor's personal funds. For this reason, an executor's or administrator's promise to pay the debts of the estate from personal funds is, in reality, a contract to become responsible for the debts of another and must be in writing to be enforceable.

11-2e AN AGREEMENT CONTAINING A PROMISE IN CONSIDERATION OF MARRIAGE

An agreement by which one person promises to pay a sum of money or to transfer property to another in consideration of marriage or a promise to marry must be in writing. However, this requirement of the Statute of Frauds does not apply to mutual promises to marry.

COURT CASE

FACTS: When Michael Curtis and Michelle Anderson became engaged, Curtis gave Anderson a diamond ring. At the time of the engagement, they agreed that if their wedding were called off, Anderson would return the ring. Several weeks later, the engagement ended, and Anderson refused to return the ring. Curtis sued Anderson, who argued that the agreement to return the ring was oral and that the Statute of Frauds prohibited the enforcement of an oral agreement made in consideration of marriage.

OUTCOME: The court said that an engagement ring is a symbol of a couple's mutual agreement to marry and is traditionally given in contemplation of marriage. Because the agreement to return the ring was not in writing, it was not enforceable.

—*Curtis v. Anderson*, 106 S.W.3d 251 (Tex. App.)

11-3 Note or Memorandum

LO ②

When a party sues to enforce an alleged contract, the Statute of Frauds requires that the contract be evidenced by a writing signed by both parties or that there be a note or memorandum in writing signed by the party against whom the claim for breach of contract is made. With the enactment of the federal Electronic Signatures in Global and National Commerce Act, that signature no longer has to be on paper. This law makes electronic signatures legally enforceable.

Adequacy of written contract

With the exception of the case of the sale of goods (Chapter 17), the contract and the note or memorandum required by the Statute of Frauds must set forth all the material terms of the transaction. For example, in the case of the sale of an interest in real estate, the memorandum must contain the names of the parties, the subject matter of the contract, and the basic terms of the contract, including the price and the manner of delivery, and it must be signed by the party against whom it is being enforced.

The law states that the memorandum must contain all the essential terms of the contract, yet the memorandum differs materially from a written contract. Probably the chief difference is that one may introduce oral testimony to explain or complete the memorandum. A court held that the following receipt was an adequate memorandum: "Received of Sholowitz $25 to bind the bargain for the sale of Moorigan's brick store and land at 46 Blackstone Street to Sholowitz. Balance due $1,975."

COURT CASE

FACTS: Lawson's Home Center, Inc. completed a credit application with House Hasson Hardware Co., Inc., which named Lawson's Home Center as the "Applicant." A paragraph at the bottom of the form stated that the undersigned would guarantee all debts of "the above Applicant" to House Hasson Hardware, whether current or incurred at a later date. Scott and Richard Lawson signed under the paragraph as guarantors of Lawson's Home Center's debt. Several years later, Lawson's Home Center executed a promissory note, promising to pay House Hasson Hardware $64,814.40 at a future date. After Lawson's Home Center defaulted on the note, House Hasson Hardware sued both Lawson's Home Center and Scott and Richard Lawson, as guarantors, to recover the amount due. Scott and Richard Lawson argued that the credit application they signed did not satisfy the Statute of Frauds, because the guarantee paragraph at the bottom of the form referred only to "the above Applicant" and did not specifically identify the name of the principal debtor.

OUTCOME: The court held that the guaranty language was on the same page as the credit application, and when read together, the guaranty made Lawson's Home Center the "Applicant" or principal debtor. The guaranty on the credit application satisfied the Statute of Frauds.

—*House Hasson Hardware Co., Inc. v. Lawson's Home Center, Inc.*, 772 S.E.2d 389 (Ga. App.)

The memorandum need not be made at the time the contract is executed. It only needs to be in existence at the time suit is brought, so it must have been executed by then. The one who signs the memorandum need not sign with the intention of being bound. If Jones writes to Smith, "My agreement to pay you the $500 Jacobson owes you was oral, so I am not bound by it," there is a sufficient memorandum that removes the objection based on the Statute of Frauds.

While the Statute requires a written memorandum, it is not necessary that all the information required is on one piece of paper. As long as a group of papers together include all the information required, there will be an adequate "memorandum."

11-4 Other Written Contracts

The five classes of contracts listed by the Statute of Frauds are not the only contracts required by law to be in writing in order to be enforceable. Every state has a few additional types of contracts that must be in writing to be enforceable. The more common ones are contracts for the sale of securities, agreements to pay a commission to a real estate broker, and a new promise to extend the statute of limitations.

LO ③
Parol evidence rule

parol evidence
oral testimony

parol evidence rule
complete, written contract may not be modified by oral testimony unless evidence of fraud, accident, or mistake exists

11-5 Parol Evidence Rule

Spoken words, or **parol evidence**, will not be permitted to add to, modify, or contradict the terms of a written contract that appears to be complete unless evidence of fraud, accident, or mistake exists so that the writing is in fact not a contract or is incomplete. This is known as the **parol evidence rule**.

If a written contract appears to be complete, the parol evidence rule will not permit modification by oral testimony or other writing made before or at the time of executing the agreement. However, an exception is made when the contract refers to other writings and indicates they are considered as incorporated into the contract.

The parol evidence rule assumes that a written contract represents the complete agreement. If, however, the contract is not complete, the courts will admit parol evidence to clear up ambiguity or to show the existence of trade customs that are to be regarded as forming part of the contract. If the contract is ambiguous and there is no oral evidence that can clear up the ambiguity, the contract is construed against the party who wrote it.

COURT CASE

FACTS: Maureen Hemond signed a written agreement to sell three lots of real estate to Brown Development Corporation. Sale of just two of the lots was closed because Hemond thought there were legal difficulties in selling three lots within five years. After five years had passed, Brown requested transfer of the third lot. Hemond refused, saying there was an oral condition on the transfer of the third lot, requiring Brown to acquire another lot from a third party (the Davidson lot). Brown sued Hemond to require her to transfer the third lot, arguing that extrinsic evidence could not be used to contradict the terms of the written agreement.

OUTCOME: The court said that the agreement was clearly not complete, because the parties agreed there was to be a five-year delay in conveying the third lot, and that was not reflected in the written agreement. As the requirement of acquiring the Davidson lot did not contradict the written agreement, the parol evidence rule did not preclude consideration of it.

—*Brown Development Corp. v. Hemond*, 956 A.2d 104 (Me.)

A contract that appears to be complete may, in fact, have omitted a provision that ought to have been included. If the omission is due to fraud, alteration, typographical errors, duress, or other similar conduct, oral testimony may be produced to show such conduct.

QUESTIONS

1. What advantages does a written contract have over an oral contract?
2. Under what circumstances will the courts allow enforcement of an oral contract required by the Statute of Frauds to be in writing?
3. Give three examples of contracts not involving the sale of land, but only an interest in the land, that the Statute of Frauds requires to be in writing.
4. If David agrees in consideration of $1,000 to mow his elderly neighbor's lawn "for as long as she lives next door to him," does the contract have to be in writing? Why or why not?
5. Under what circumstances is the Statute of Frauds requirement of a writing unnecessary when a person agrees to be responsible for the debt of another?
6. When a party sues to enforce an alleged contract, what is the requirement of the Statute of Frauds regarding the evidence of an agreement of the parties to an alleged contract?
7. What must be included in a note or memorandum required by the Statute of Frauds?
8. How does a memorandum differ from a written contract?

QUESTIONS (CONTINUED)

9. When will the parol evidence rule permit modification of a written contract that appears to be complete, by another writing made before or at the time of executing the contract?

10. Under what circumstances will courts admit oral evidence to add to or modify a written contract?

CASE PROBLEMS

LO ②

1. Preston Exploration Co. (Preston) entered into purchase and sale agreements (PSAs) to sell certain oil and gas leases to Chesapeake Energy Corp. and GSF, LLC (Chesapeake). The PSAs stated that the leases to be conveyed were the ones that had marketable title and would continue for at least one year. Exhibits were attached to the PSAs and specifically referenced in them. The PSAs provided that Preston was to convey "[a]ll of Seller's right, title and interest in . . . oil and gas leases" as defined in Exhibit A. Among other items, the exhibit referenced the county, lease ID, lease name, lessee, effective date, gross acres, and net acres. The day before the sales were to close, Chesapeake said it would not close. Preston sued. Chesapeake claimed enforcement was barred by the Statute of Frauds. Was it?

LO ③

2. Nodak Mutual Insurance Co. (Nodak) terminated Barry Myaer's contract as an insurance agent. The most recent contract Myaer had signed provided a 10 percent commission on gross premiums for sales of insurance, with a 1 percent bonus if notes for insurance were paid by a set date. However, the contract allowed Nodak to "modify . . . any bonuses that might apply." A subsequent contract, sent by e-mail, provided for a reduction of 1 percent in commissions if all submissions and loss reports were not submitted online, and another 1 percent if all notes for insurance were not paid and received by the home office by a specified date. When Nodak failed to pay Myaer deferred commissions on the policies he had sold, Myaer sued. He stated in an affidavit that if he did his reports via the Internet and all notes were paid, his total commission would be 12 percent. Nodak argued Myaer's claim to a 12 percent commission was barred by the parol evidence rule. Was it?

LO ①

3. Michael Kalmus entered an oral employment contract with Financial Necessities Network, Inc. The contract provided that Kalmus would work as a commissioned salesman, with a starting salary and a 25–70 percent commission rate. After an initial period, Kalmus' salary would decrease to zero while his commission rate increased to a maximum of 50–70 percent. The contract also provided that Kalmus would receive "any and all commissions" regarding his insurance sales as long as they were being generated, regardless of whether Kalmus was still employed with the company. The parties never specified the duration of the employment agreement. After Kalmus was terminated from the company, the management told him it would only pay a 25–50 commission rate for a limited period of time. Kalmus sued for breach of contract. Financial Necessities Network asserted that the oral contract was unenforceable, because it was intended to be a "lifetime contract or contract until the age of retirement" and was required to be in writing under the Statute of Frauds. Was the contract barred by the Statute of Frauds?

LO ③

4. To organize West Valley Surgical Center (WVSC), Welden Daines and Richard Vincent signed a memorandum of understanding (MOU) giving Daines $150,000 plus expenses to provide Ambulatory Surgical Centers Group (ASC) a list of physicians from West Valley City. A founder of ASC, Vincent signed under the heading "ASC." Daines supplied a list of physicians and negotiated with ASC on behalf of physicians, but felt he was also negotiating on behalf of ASC. He told Vincent he was uncomfortable, and they orally agreed he would forego the $150,000 in exchange for eight Class II shares of WVSC. WVSC was formed with ASC as a member. The Boyer Company orally agreed to pay Daines $50,000 if its site were chosen for WVSC. That site was chosen, and Daines requested $50,000 from Boyer. Boyer said it would pay when WVSC leased the premises. ASC agreed to pay Boyer $6,000 in expenses if Daines signed a release. It stated that Daines released WVSC and its members "from any

CASE PROBLEMS (CONTINUED)

and all liabilities and or claims . . . [for] services rendered to . . . Valley West Surgical Center or on behalf of its members . . . for any services connected with the organization, development and operation" of WVSC. The release said, "it encompasses . . . any prior agreements or discussions whether written or verbal." Daines signed the release and received $6,000. After Boyer paid $50,000, Daines asked Vincent for eight shares of WVSC. Vincent refused, so Daines sued ASC and Vincent for breach of an oral contract for the shares. Should he succeed?

5. Glenn Page began borrowing money from Gulf Coast Motors. He had a gambling problem. One of the owners of Gulf Coast, Jerry Sellers, became concerned about Page's debt to Gulf Coast. He testified that he had phoned Page's wife, Mary, who orally promised to pay the debt. There was no evidence that Mary had received any benefit from the money Glenn borrowed. Gulf Coast sued both Glenn and Mary for the debt. Must Mary pay it?   **LO** ①

6. Don Wang and Royal Investment Group, LLC signed a contract of sale of Wang's house. Sean Shahparast was the sole member of Royal. The parties signed an addendum obligating Wang to remove all trash by January 21 and permitting Royal to do "any repair/construction at buyer's risk and expense." The trash was not removed, and additional addenda were signed obligating Royal to remove the trash, and Wang to remove a derelict car. On June 16, the car was still in the way, so Wang's real estate agent phoned Shahparast. They agreed to reduce the sale price to $600,000, set August 31 as the closing date, and require Wang to remove the car in two days. Wang signed the addendum and had the car towed that day. Royal then asked to extend the closing date to December. Negotiations followed without agreement. The closing was not held on August 31, so Wang's lawyer wrote Shahparast, saying it was clear he was not going to settle under the terms of the contract, and asking for release of the earnest money to Wang. Letters went back and forth. In October, after Royal had the house demolished, it unilaterally set a new closing date. The June 16 addendum, signed but undated by Shahparast, was sent to the closing company. Royal applied for and received a building permit saying that Wang authorized the work. Royal built a house on the property. Royal sued Wang to execute the sale of the property, alleging the June 16 addendum did not satisfy the Statute of Frauds memorandum requirement because it was signed after the August 31 settlement date, thus after a breach of contract. Was the June 16 addendum enforceable?   **LO** ②

7. Lang Industries, Inc. negotiated and entered into a business loan agreement with Bank of America, N.A. The written contract clearly stated the terms of the loan, including the principal amount, interest rate, and the repayment schedule to be paid in 120 monthly payments. The loan agreement stated that the final monthly payment would be a larger "balloon" payment for all remaining principal and accrued interest due on the loan. After Lang Industries failed to make the final payment, the bank sued to recover the interest and fees associated with the loan. Lang Industries argued that the contract was ambiguous and that when negotiating the loan, David Lang and a bank employee had agreed that there would be no balloon payment at the end of the loan. Should the court allow oral evidence to be admitted in interpreting the contract?   **LO** ③

8. As the operator of a baseball stadium, Metropolitan Entertainment & Convention Authority (MECA) entered negotiations with Fall Ball Sports, LLC to bring a baseball team to the stadium. An officer of MECA sent Fall Ball Sports a draft lease agreement with blue editing marks which stated that MECA would lease the stadium to Fall Ball Sports for five years for the purpose of "presenting Northern League baseball games." Fall Ball Sports paid Northern League franchise and applications fees. However, the draft agreement between MECA and Fall Ball Sports was never signed by MECA. After Northern League ceased operations, MECA informed Fall Ball Sports that it was no longer interested in leasing the stadium. Fall Ball Sports argued that MECA had represented that the lease was a "done deal" and sued MECA for breach of contract. Was an oral lease agreement sufficient to bind MECA?   **LO** ①

Third Parties and Contracts

LEARNING OBJECTIVES

① Discuss the difference between a third-party beneficiary contract and a novation.

② Explain the difference between assignment of a contract and delegation of duties under it.

③ Describe the different types of contracts involving more than two parties.

PREVIEW CASE

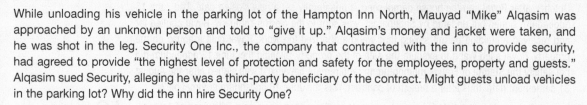

While unloading his vehicle in the parking lot of the Hampton Inn North, Mauyad "Mike" Alqasim was approached by an unknown person and told to "give it up." Alqasim's money and jacket were taken, and he was shot in the leg. Security One Inc., the company that contracted with the inn to provide security, had agreed to provide "the highest level of protection and safety for the employees, property and guests." Alqasim sued Security, alleging he was a third-party beneficiary of the contract. Might guests unload vehicles in the parking lot? Why did the inn hire Security One?

A contract creates both rights and obligations. Ordinarily, one who is not a signer of the contract has no right to the benefits to be derived from the contract or responsibility for any of the duties or obligations. However, parties may intend to benefit a third person when they make a contract. Third parties may also acquire rights or assume duties.

LO ①
Third-party beneficiary versus novation

12-1 Involving a Third Party

A third party can become involved in a contract in several common ways. These include as a third-party beneficiary, by novation, by assignment, and by delegation.

12-1a THIRD-PARTY BENEFICIARY

At common law, only the parties to a contract could sue upon or seek to enforce the contract. Courts held that strangers to a contract had no rights under it. But courts began to make exceptions to the rule when it seemed evident that the contracting parties intended to benefit a third person, called a **third-party beneficiary**.

The rule today specifies that a third person expressly benefited by the performance of a contract may enforce it against the promisor if the contracting parties intended to benefit the third party. The third person may be either a creditor beneficiary or a donee beneficiary. A **creditor beneficiary** is a person to whom the promisee owes an obligation or duty that will be discharged to the extent that the promisor performs the promise. If *A* makes a contract to pay *B*'s debt to *C*, *C* is the creditor beneficiary of the contract between *A* and *B*. A **donee beneficiary** is one to whom the promisee owes no legal duty but to whom performance is a gift, such as the beneficiary named in a life insurance contract. When an event must occur before the donee beneficiary is benefited, the contracting parties may change the beneficiary.

third-party beneficiary
person not party to contract but whom parties intended to benefit

creditor beneficiary
person to whom promisee owes obligation, which is discharged if promisor performs

donee beneficiary
third-party beneficiary for whom performance is a gift

PREVIEW CASE REVISITED

FACTS: While unloading his vehicle in the parking lot of the Hampton Inn North, Mauyad "Mike" Alqasim was approached by an unknown person and told to "give it up." Alqasim's money and jacket were taken, and he was shot in the leg. Security One Inc., the company that contracted with the inn to provide security, had agreed to provide "the highest level of protection and safety for the employees, property and guests." Alqasim sued Security, alleging he was a third-party beneficiary of the contract.

OUTCOME: The court said that, because one of Security's duties was to protect guests at the inn, Alqasim was a third-party beneficiary of the contract between the inn and Security One.

—*Alqasim v. Capitol City Hotel Investors*, 989 So.2d 488 (Miss. Ct. App)

Not everyone who benefits by the performance of a contract between others is properly considered a third-party beneficiary with rights under the contract. If a person merely incidentally benefits by the performance of a contract, suit for breach or for performance will not be successful. For example, a town contracts with a contractor for the paving of a certain street, and the contractor fails to perform. The property owners whose property would have been improved by the paving are not entitled to sue for damages for nonperformance because they were to be only incidentally benefited. The contract for the paving of the street was designed essentially to further the public interest, not to benefit individual property owners. The property owners are merely **incidental beneficiaries**.

incidental beneficiary
person who unintentionally benefits from performance of contract

12-1b NOVATION

The party entitled to receive performance under a contract may agree to release the party who is bound to perform and to permit another party to render performance. When this occurs, it is not just a matter of delegating the duties under the contract; rather, it is a matter of abandoning the old contract and substituting a new one in its place. The change of contract and parties is called a **novation**. To be more precise, a novation substitutes a new party for one of the original parties in an existing contract at the mutual agreement of the original parties, such that

novation
termination of a contract and substitution of a new one with same terms but a new party

the prior contract terminates, and a new one substitutes for it. The terms of the contract remain the same but with different parties. For example, if Koslov and Burnham have a contract, they, together with Caldwell, may agree that Caldwell shall take Koslov's place, and a novation occurs. Koslov is discharged from the contract, and Burnham and Caldwell are bound. It must be shown that a novation was intended. However, a novation does not need to be in writing, nor must it be expressed. It can be implied from the parties' actions. When a novation occurs, the original obligor drops out of the picture. The new party takes the original obligor's place and is solely liable for the performance.

COURT CASE

FACTS: Cincinnati Insurance Co. issued a bond for payment of motor fuel taxes by Dixie Management Group Inc. Dixie officers Timothy Leighton and Mark and Kathy Beeler signed the bond application as guarantors. Leighton was fired, and a year later Cincinnati requested execution of a new bond application. Cincinnati insisted on updated financial information from the Beelers because it knew that Leighton no longer worked at Dixie, and it had relied on his personal financial statement when issuing the initial bond. The Beelers executed a new bond application and guarantee. The state asked Cincinnati to pay the amount of the bond to cover unpaid taxes. Cincinnati demanded that Dixie and the Beelers create a cash reserve to cover its loss under their guarantee. Two years later, Dixie and the Beelers declared bankruptcy, and Cincinnati paid the amount of the bond to the state. Cincinnati then sued Leighton. He argued that the second bond application was a novation of the first and released him from his guarantee.

OUTCOME: The court found a novation. Leighton was released as a guarantor by the creation of the substitute agreement.

—*Cincinnati Ins. Co. v. Leighton*, 403 F.3d 879 (7th Cir.)

LO ②
Assignment versus delegation

assignment
conveyance of rights in a contract to a person not a party

assignor
person making an assignment

assignee
person to whom a contract right is assigned

12-1c ASSIGNMENT

An **assignment** means that one party conveys rights in a contract to another who is not a party to the original undertaking.

As a general rule, a party's rights under a contract may be assigned. One's rights under a contract may be transferred almost as freely as property. The party making the assignment is known as the **assignor**; the one to whom the right is transferred is known as the **assignee**.

Statutes may impose some restrictions on the assignment of rights. Statutes in a number of states prohibit employees from assigning their wages. Statutes also prohibit the assignment of future pay by soldiers, sailors, and marines. Many states and cities also prohibit the assignment of the pay of public officials. In many states, the law prohibits public works employees from assigning more than a specified maximum percentage of their wages. This protects wage earners and their families from hard-pressing creditors.

Often, one's right under a contract is to receive the services of the other party, such as a bookkeeper, salesperson, or other employee. A right to personal services cannot be assigned, because an employee cannot be required to work for a new employer without the employee's consent.

The parties may include in the original contract a prohibition of the assignment of rights thereunder. Such a prohibition, however, is not effective in some states when only the right to money has been assigned.

Thus, whether rights may be assigned depends on their nature and the terms of the contract.

COURT CASE

FACTS: Robin Sims stopped working at J. H. Renarde Inc.'s beauty shop and two weeks later opened a shop three miles away. Renarde was the assignee of an employment contract Sims had signed with Renarde's predecessor. The contract prohibited a former employee from competing within nine miles of Renarde's business for nine months. When Renarde sued to enforce the contract, Sims claimed that enforcing it would be compelling specific performance of a personal services contract against an employee in violation of the Thirteenth Amendment.

OUTCOME: The court stated that Renarde was not asking for the enforcement of a personal services contract. It was not asking Sims to continue working for it. Renarde was simply asking to enforce rights under an assignment.

—*J. H. Renarde Inc. v. Sims*, 711 A.2d 410 (N.J. Super. Ct. Ch. Div.)

12-1d DELEGATION

The term **delegation** describes a transfer of the duties alone without a transfer of rights. Neither party can delegate the duties under a contract as readily as the rights can be assigned because a "personal" element more frequently exists in the performance aspect of a contract. It would change the obligation thereof if another were to perform it. If Allen retains Bentley, an attorney, to obtain a divorce for a fee of $350, Bentley can assign to anyone the right to receive the $350, and Allen must pay. The duty to represent Allen in the divorce proceeding, however, may not be delegated. In those contracts that involve trust and confidence, one may not delegate the duties. If one employs the Local Wonder Band to play at a dance, the contract cannot be delegated, even to a nationally known band. Taste, confidence, and trust cannot be scientifically measured. It is not material that a reasonable person would be satisfied or contented with the substitution.

> **delegation**
> transfer of duties

But if one hires Horne to paint a house for $900, whether the house has been painted properly or not can readily be determined by recognized standards in the trade. Therefore, this task could be delegated.

Only when the performance is standardized may one delegate its performance to another. In the construction industry, for example, many instances of delegation of duties occur because the correct performance can be easily ascertained. Contracts calling for unskilled work or labor may, in most instances, be delegated.

In all cases of delegation, the delegating party remains fully liable under the contract. Suit may be brought for any breach of contract even though another party actually performed. In such an event, the delegating party may in turn sue the party who performed inadequately. The parties to the original contract may expressly prohibit the delegation of duties thereunder.

COURT CASE

FACTS: Robert and Joanie Emerson hired Martin Winters to replace the roof on their home. Winters' company was not capable of replacing an entire roof, so without telling the Emersons, he subcontracted the job to Terry Monk. When the Emersons told Winters the roof leaked, he agreed to repair the roof, but subcontracted the repair to Bruce Jacobs. Jacobs used a propane torch in repairing the roof, causing a fire and $871,000 in damage to the house. The Emersons' insurance company had paid the claim, so it sued Winters, who claimed he was not liable because he had delegated the job to Jacobs.

OUTCOME: The court said that the delegation of performance under the contract did not relieve Winters from the duties of the original contract. Since he remained liable on the contract, he was liable for the damages.

—*Federal Ins. Co. v. Winters*, 354 S.W.3d 287 (Tenn.)

The assignment or transfer cannot modify rights transferred by assignment or duties transferred by delegation. They remain the same as though only the original parties to the contract were involved.

A party to a contract may wish to assign the rights and delegate the duties under the contract. If one party transfers the contract in its entirety, it is "an assignment of rights and a delegation of duties."

12-2 Technicalities of an Assignment

Even if a contract may be assigned, there may be some technical requirements that must be met to make sure the assignment is effective. It is also important to understand the legal positions of the three parties involved as a result of the assignment.

12-2a NOTICE OF AN ASSIGNMENT

Notice need not be given to the other party in order to make the assignment effective as between the assignor and the assignee. Business prudence demands that the original promisor be notified, however. The assignee may not receive payment if notification of the assignment is not given to the original promisor. The promisor has a right to assume that the claim has not been assigned unless otherwise notified. For example, Gonzales promised to pay Hodges $500 in thirty days. When the account came due, as no notice of assignment had been given, Gonzales was safe in paying Hodges. But if Hodges had assigned the account to Wilson, and Wilson had not given Gonzales notice, Wilson would not have been able to collect from Gonzales.

In most jurisdictions, if a party to a contract makes more than one assignment, and the assignees all give notice, the law gives priority in the order in which the assignments were made.

In the event the assignor assigns a larger sum than the debtor owes, the debtor has no obligation to pay the entire assignment. When the creditor assigns only part of a claim, the debtor has no obligation to make payment thereof to the assignee, although such payment may be made, and it reduces the debtor's liability to the creditor to the extent of such payment.

12-2b FORM OF THE ASSIGNMENT

An assignment may be made either by operation of law or by the act of the parties. In the event of death, the law assigns the rights and duties (except for personal services) of the deceased to the executor or administrator of the estate. In the event of bankruptcy, the law assigns the rights and duties of the debtor to the trustee in bankruptcy. These two types of assignments are effective without any act of the parties.

When the assignment is made by the act of the parties, it may be either written or oral; however, it must be clear that a present assignment of an interest held by the assignor is intended. If the original contract must be in writing, the assignment must be in writing; otherwise, it may be made orally.

COURT CASE

FACTS: Brand Jackman hired attorney Stephen Winship to represent him in a suit against Wyoming Technical Institute (WTI) for personal injuries. Gem City Bone and Joint, P.C. (Gem) had treated Jackman. To obtain his medical records, he and Winship signed Gem's release. The release granted Gem a lien for its charges on any "claims for liability or indemnity for damages." Another attorney, Jeremy Michaels, negotiated a settlement with WTI and prepared a statement of distribution of the proceeds. That statement indicated that the proceeds were distributed to Jackman, his family, and his lawyers.

It also stated, "CLIENT IS SOLELY RESPONSIBLE FOR PAYMENT OF ALL MEDICAL BILLS/LIENS." Jackman did not pay Gem, so it sued Winship.

OUTCOME: The court held that Jackman clearly assigned his interest in the proceeds of the personal injury action to Gem in order to pay his medical bills. Since Winship had notice of the assignment, he had to honor it.

—*Winship v. Gem City Bone and Joint, P.C.*, 185 P.3d 1252 (Wyo.)

It is always preferable to make an assignment in writing. This may be done in the case of written contracts by writing the terms of the assignment on the back of the written contract. Any contract may be assigned by executing an informal written assignment. The following written assignment is adequate in most cases:

In consideration of the Local Finance Company's canceling my debt of $500 to it, I hereby assign to the Local Finance Company $500 owed to me by the Dale Sand and Gravel Company.

Signed at noon, Friday, December 16, 20--, at Benson, Iowa.

(Signed) Harold Locke

Although an assignment may be made for consideration, consideration is not necessary.

12-2c EFFECT OF AN ASSIGNMENT

An assignment transfers to the assignee all the rights, title, or interest held by the assignor in whatever is being assigned. The assignee does not receive any greater right or interest than the assignor held.

The nonassigning party retains all rights and defenses as though there had never been an assignment. For example, if the nonassigning party lacked competence to contract or entered into the contract under duress, undue influence, fraud, or misrepresentation, the nonassigning party may raise these defenses against the assignee as effectively as they could have been raised against the assignor.

12-2d WARRANTIES OF THE ASSIGNOR

When one assigns rights under a contract to an assignee for value, the assignor makes three implied warranties:

1. That the assignor is the true owner of the right
2. That the right is valid and subsisting at the time the assignment is made
3. That there are no defenses available to the debtor that have not been disclosed to the assignee

If the assignor commits a breach of warranty, the assignee may seek to recover any loss from the assignor.

COURT CASE

FACTS: Constellation Energy Commodities Group ("Constellation") agreed to buy coal from Black Diamond Mining Company. Their contract allowed each party to "net" offsetting payment obligations to avoid making extra payments to one another. Black Diamond then assigned to CIT Group its right to receive payments for coal delivered to Constellation. After Black Diamond declared bankruptcy, Constellation refused to pay CIT Group for $10 million in coal that had been received. Constellation stated that Black Diamond owed Constellation $90 million and argued that under the netting provision of their contract, Constellation could offset its $10 million debt against the $90 million and pay nothing to CIT Group.

OUTCOME: Because CIT Group was the assignee of Black Diamond, Constellation could assert the netting defense against CIT Group just as it would have done against Black Diamond. Constellation owed nothing to CIT Group.

—*In re Black Diamond Min. Co., LLC*, 596 Fed. Appx. 477 (6th Cir.)

Most assignments involve claims for money. The Fair Deal Grocery Company assigned $10,000 worth of its accounts receivable to the First National Bank. The assignor warranted that the accounts were genuine. If a customer, therefore, were to refuse to pay the bank and prove that no money were owed, the grocery company would be liable. If payment were not made merely because of insolvency, most courts would hold that the assignor was not liable.

In the absence of an express guarantee, an assignor does not warrant that the other party will perform the duties under the contract, that the other party will make payment, or that the other party is solvent.

If the Harbottle Distributing Company were to owe the Norfolk Brewery $10,000, it could assign $10,000 of its accounts receivable to the Norfolk Brewery in full satisfaction of the debt. If the assignee were able to collect only $7,000 of these accounts because the debtors were insolvent, the brewery would have no recourse against Harbottle. If the $3,000 were uncollectible because the debtors had valid defenses to the claims, the Harbottle Distributing Company would have to make good the loss.

The Norfolk Brewery Company should not take these accounts receivable by assignment. An assignment allows Harbottle Distributing Company to pay its debt, not with cash but by a transfer of title to its accounts receivable. From the brewery company's standpoint, the same result can be obtained not by taking title to these accounts but by taking them merely as collateral security for the debt with a provision that the brewery is to collect the accounts and apply the proceeds to the $10,000. Under this arrangement, the brewery can look to the distributing company for the balance of $3,000.

12-3 Joint, Several, and Joint and Several Contracts

LO ③
Contracts with more than two people

When two or more people enter into a contract with one or more other parties, the contract may be joint, several, or joint and several. The intention of the parties determines the type of contract.

12-3a JOINT CONTRACTS

A **joint contract** is a contract in which two or more parties have all promised the entire performance, which is the subject of the contract. Each obligor is bound for the performance of the entire obligation. A joint contract is also a contract in which two or more parties are jointly entitled to the performance of another party or parties. If Sands and Cole sign a contract stating, "We jointly promise . . .," the obligation is the joint obligation of Sands and Cole. If the promise is not carried out, both Sands and Cole must be joined in any lawsuit. The aggrieved party may not sue just one of them. Unless otherwise expressed, a promise by two or more parties is generally presumed to be joint and not several.

joint contract
contract obligating or entitling two or more people together to performance

12-3b SEVERAL CONTRACTS

A **several contract** arises when two or more people individually agree to perform the same obligation even though the individual agreements are contained in the same document. Express words must be used to show that a several contract is intended.

If Anne and Cathy sign a contract stating, "We severally promise" or "Each of us promises" to do a particular thing, the two signers are individually bound to perform. If the contract is not performed, either Anne or Cathy may be sued alone for the obligation she assumed.

several contract
two or more people individually agree to perform obligation

COURT CASE

FACTS: The City of Alexandria hired Craig Davidson and John Sharp to pursue claims that energy companies had over-charged the city for services. Although Davidson and Sharp worked for separate law firms, the city signed a single contract with them. The contract referred to both attorneys as the "Attorney" and assigned a single task of controlling proceedings related to the city's legal claims. The contract also promised a joint contingency fee of 20 percent, with no indication of how the fee would be split between Davidson and Sharp. Midway through the case, the Louisiana Bar Disciplinary Counsel recommended the disbarment of Sharp for unethical conduct, and he was removed from the case. Davidson was side-lined and new attorneys were brought in to negotiate a final settlement. After the case settled, Davidson sued the city for legal fees. Davidson claimed that the intent of the contract was to hire Sharp and himself separately, each at a 10 percent fee. The city countered that Davidson's obligation was joint with Sharp's to provide two attorneys in exchange for a 20 percent contingency fee.

OUTCOME: The court held the agreement was a joint contract, with Davidson and Sharp promising the services of two attorneys in exchange for a 20 percent contingency fee. Sharp's disbarment rendered performance impossible. They were thus in breach of their joint obligation, and Davidson could not collect a contingency fee under the contract.

—*City of Alexandria v. Brown*, 740 F.3d 339 (5th Cir.)

12-3c JOINT AND SEVERAL CONTRACTS

joint and several contract
two or more people bound jointly and individually

A **joint and several contract** is one in which two or more people are bound both jointly and severally. If Sands and Cole sign a contract stating, "We, and each of us, promise" or "I promise" to perform a particular act, they are jointly and severally obligated.

The other party to the contract may treat the obligation as either a joint obligation or a group of individual obligations and may bring suit against all or any one or more of them at one time. Statutes in some states interpret a joint contract to be a joint and several contract.

QUESTIONS

1. What is the rule regarding the ability of a person who is not a party to a contract to enforce a contract?
2. What is the difference between a creditor beneficiary and a donee beneficiary?
3. May everyone who benefits by the performance of a contract between others successfully sue for breach or performance of the contract?
4. When a novation occurs, who is liable for performance under the contract?
5. Why is a right to personal services nonassignable?
6. What is the difference between an assignment of a contract and the delegation of duties under it?
7. In what way does an assignment or transfer modify rights or duties transferred?
8. While not required, why is it a prudent business practice to give the original promisor notice of an assignment?

QUESTIONS (CONTINUED)

9. What is it called when one party to a contract transfers the contract in its entirety to another?

10. If Rich jointly promises to pay $10,000 with Sharon, and Andrew severally promises to pay $10,000, who will have to pay more?

CASE PROBLEMS

1. An ordinance of the City of Miami authorized the city attorney to take any action to collect on municipal liens and to delegate this authority to holders of municipal liens. Joel Israel purchased lien certificates from the city on property on which assessments were outstanding, including on parcel 9, owned by Manuel Ismael. The city attorney assigned to Israel the city's right to take any action to collect on the lien certificates. He followed the legal procedure to foreclose on and sell the property, including notifying Ismael, who did not respond. A foreclosure sale was held. A year and a half later, Ismael asked the court to void the sale, arguing that Israel had no standing to foreclose. If the city had the right to foreclose, did Israel also have that right? **LO** ②

2. AutoLife Acquisition Corp. engaged in transactions that left it owing secured creditors about $5.5 million due in two months. It contracted with Kann Capital, Ltd. to seek $9 million in financing and "advise and assist AutoLife in devising and executing a program to secure" the financing. The agreement had an arbitration clause for any controversy arising out the agreement or breach, termination, interpretation, or validity of it. The financing did not materialize, but the secured creditors did not foreclose because the owners of AutoLife and Kann repeatedly represented that financing would soon be obtained. AutoLife went into bankruptcy, and the secured creditors sued Kann. Kann alleged that the creditors were third-party beneficiaries of its contract with AutoLife and therefore that the arbitration clause governed. Were the creditors third-party beneficiaries of the contract between AutoLife and Kann? **LO** ①

3. Former asbestos companies signed an agreement forming the Center for Claims Resolution (CCR) to administer and resolve asbestos-related claims. The agreement included a formula for calculating the share of liability payments of each member. The CCR negotiated a settlement agreement for nineteen member companies with the law firm of Kelley & Ferraro, LLP, resolving 15,000 claims. The settlement was to be paid to Kelley in biannual installments. The agreement stated that "each CCR member shall be liable . . . only for its individual share." An installment was $1 million short because GAF Corp. disputed CCR's calculation of its share. Kelley sued, alleging the agreement was joint and several so that the other companies had to make up the full installment even if one company were to withhold its contribution. Was the agreement joint and several or merely several? **LO** ③

4. New Century Financial Services, Inc. purchased charged-off credit card debt from credit card issuers and attempted to collect the debt from card holders. New Century sued two debtors, Ahlam Oughla and Azeem Zaidi, and claimed that as the assignee of their debt, Oughla and Zaidi owed New Century the amount of the charged-off credit card debt. Oughla and Zaidi argued, among other things, that the assignment of their debt to New Century was invalid, because New Century failed to notify them of the assignment. Was New Century required to give notice of the assignment to the debtors? **LO** ②

5. Van Cleef Asset Management, Inc. contracted to sublease office space from NCS Healthcare, Inc. for a five year term. After two years, NCS Healthcare directed Van Cleef to mail checks to a different location. Van Cleef complied, but for a thirteen-month period, the checks were never endorsed or deposited by NCS Healthcare. Around this time, NCS Healthcare was acquired by Omnicare, Inc., which contacted Van Cleef to inform them that recent rent payments to NCS Healthcare had not been received. An Omnicare representative directed Van Cleef to send future rent payments to Omnicare **LO** ①

CASE PROBLEMS (CONTINUED)

for the remaining term of the lease and that "if those payments were made . . . all obligations of Van Cleef under the sublease would be duly performed and satisfied." Van Cleef sent remaining rent payments to Omnicare and after the sublease terminated, Van Cleef vacated the premises. An affiliate of NCS Healthcare later argued that it was the assignee of rent payments owed to NCS Healthcare under the sublease agreement and sued Van Cleef for the thirteen months worth of rent that it alleged had not been received. Van Cleef argued that the negotiated agreement with Omnicare for the sublease payments was a novation of the original sublease agreement. Who was correct?

LO ③ 6. Ti-Well International Corp. contracted with Qingdao First Textile Co. to import corduroy fabric. Wujin Nanxiashu Secant Factory contracted to supply the fabric to Qingdao. Wujin delivered the fabric to Ti-Well through Qingdao, but Ti-Well did not pay Qingdao, which did not pay Wujin. After negotiations, Juntai Li, the sole shareholder, director, officer, and employee of Ti-Well, executed a note agreeing to make payments to Wujin. The note did not mention Ti-Well. Li also signed an agreement stating that Ti-Well and Li would assume responsibility for Qingdao's debt to Wujin. When the debt was not paid, Wujin sued Li. Was his obligation joint with Ti-Well's?

LO ① 7. Charles Daley slipped on snow and ice while walking on a sidewalk outside Canal Pharmacy. Daley was paralyzed as a result of his injuries. He sued Canal Pharmacy and Eileen Fryer, the pharmacy's landlady, arguing that the parties breached their lease agreement by failing to keep the sidewalks free of snow and ice. Daley claimed that as a customer of Canal Pharmacy, he was a third-party beneficiary of the landlord–tenant lease contract. Was he?

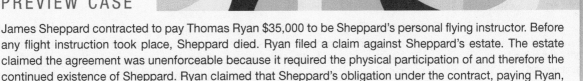

Termination of Contracts

CHAPTER 13

LEARNING OBJECTIVES

1. Describe the requirements for terminating a contract by performance.
2. Recognize the circumstances that discharge a contract by operation of law.
3. Explain what breach of contract is and the potential remedies for breach.

PREVIEW CASE

James Sheppard contracted to pay Thomas Ryan $35,000 to be Sheppard's personal flying instructor. Before any flight instruction took place, Sheppard died. Ryan filed a claim against Sheppard's estate. The estate claimed the agreement was unenforceable because it required the physical participation of and therefore the continued existence of Sheppard. Ryan claimed that Sheppard's obligation under the contract, paying Ryan, was not personal to him and could be assumed by the estate. What was Sheppard's total obligation under the contract? What was Ryan's obligation under the contract?

Although it is important to know how a contract is formed and who is bound on it, it is also important to know when it is ended, or terminated, and when the parties are no longer bound.

13-1 Methods by Which Contracts Are Terminated

Five common methods by which contracts may be terminated include: (1) by performance of the contract, (2) by operation of law, (3) by voluntary agreement of the parties, (4) by impossibility of performance, and (5) by acceptance of a breach of contract.

13-1a PERFORMANCE

When all the terms of a contract have been fulfilled, the contract is discharged by performance. Not all the parties need to perform simultaneously, however. Parties are discharged from further liability as soon as they have done all that they have

LO 1
Terminating contract
by performance

agreed to do. The other party or parties are not discharged, nor is the contract, if any material thing remains to be done by them.

Several factors determine whether there has been performance:

1. Time of performance
2. Tender of performance
3. Tender of payment
4. Satisfactory performance
5. Substantial performance

Time of Performance. If the contract states when performance is to be rendered, the contract provisions must be followed unless under all the circumstances, performance on the exact date specified is not vital. When performance on the exact date is deemed vital, it is said that "time is of the essence." If the contract states no time for performance, then performance must ordinarily be rendered within a reasonable time.

tender of performance
offer to perform in satisfaction of terms of contract

Tender of Performance. An offer to perform an obligation in satisfaction of the terms of a contract is called a **tender of performance**. If a contract calls for the performance of an act at a specified time, a tender of performance will discharge the obligation of the one making the tender so long as the tender conforms to the agreement.

tender of payment
offer and ability to pay money owed

Tender of Payment. An offer to pay money in satisfaction of a debt or claim when one has the ability to pay is a **tender of payment**. The debtor must offer the exact amount due, including interest, costs, and attorneys' fees, if any are required. If the debtor says, "I am now ready to pay you," a sufficient tender has not been made. The debtor must pay or offer the creditor the amount due.

legal tender
any form of lawful money

A tender in the form of a check is not a proper tender. The payment must be made in **legal tender**. With but few minor exceptions, this is any form of U.S. money. If a check is accepted, the contract is performed as soon as the bank on which it is drawn honors the check.

If the tender is refused, the debt is not discharged. However, proper tender does stop the running of interest. In addition, if the creditor should bring suit, the person who has tendered the correct amount is not liable for court costs after the date of the tender. The debtor must, however, be in readiness to pay at any time. If a tender is made after a suit, the debtor frequently pays the money over to the court.

Satisfactory Performance. Contracts often specifically state that the performance must be "satisfactory to" or "to the satisfaction of" a certain person. What constitutes satisfactory performance is frequently a disputed question. The courts generally have adopted the rule—especially when a definite, objective measure of satisfaction exists—that if the contract is performed in a manner that would satisfy an ordinary, reasonable person, the terms of the contract have been met sufficiently to discharge it. If the performance is clearly intended to be subject to the personal taste or judgment of one of the parties, however, it may be rejected on the ground that it is not satisfactory to that particular party.

COURT CASE

FACTS: The contract under which Optus Software hired Michael Silvestri to supervise the support services staff gave Optus the right to fire him for failure to perform to Optus's satisfaction. Nine months later, Optus had received numerous complaints from clients and other employees about the performance and attitude of the support services staff. A major customer complained about Silvestri's lack of cooperation and dour, condescending attitude. Optus fired him. Silvestri sued for breach of contract.

OUTCOME: The court said that, as long as Optus's dissatisfaction was genuine, the satisfaction clause in the contract gave the company the right to fire Silvestri. The complaints made Optus's dissatisfaction genuine.

—*Silvestri v. Optus Software Inc.*, 814 A.2d 602 (N.J.)

Substantial Performance. Under the early common law, each party to a contract had to perform to the last letter of the contract before a demand for the party's rights under the contract could be made. Such a rule was often extremely inequitable. If a contractor were to build a $50 million office building, it might be grossly unfair to say that none of the $50 million could be collected because of a relatively minor breach.

The law today can be stated as follows: If a construction contract is substantially performed, the party performing may demand the full price under the contract less the damages suffered by the other party. In the case of the office building, if the contract price is $50 million, and the damages are $5,000, the contractor will be allowed to collect $49,995,000. Suppose, however, that the contractor completed the excavation and then quit. The contractor would be entitled to collect nothing.

Just how far the contractor must proceed toward full performance before there has been substantial performance is often difficult to determine. The performance must be so nearly complete that it would be a great injustice to deny the contractor any compensation for the work, and there must have been an honest attempt to perform. A court will weigh all the circumstances surrounding the deviation, including the significance and reasons for it, the ease of correction, the extent to which the purpose of the contract is defeated, and the use or benefit to the owners of the work completed. For construction contracts, some statutes prescribe substantial performance as being that stage of progress of the project at which the project is sufficiently complete in accordance with the contract that the owner can occupy or utilize the project for its intended use.

COURT CASE

FACTS: General contractor Bobb Fostveit was hired by James and Debra Poplin to build self-storage units on their property. Their contract provided that Fostveit would build 35 storage units in exchange for a per-unit fee and a 12 percent overhead fee of the total project cost. To help lower costs, Fostveit agreed to let the Poplins install the roofing, siding, and insulation of the units and do the paving around the buildings. Fostveit and his subcontractor excavated the site, did the concrete and electrical work, and built a retaining wall and storage units. Some minor work, such as repair of poorly-installed thresholds, remained for Fostveit to finish. The Poplins installed the roofing, but did not include gutters. The Poplins also altered the grade of the driveway such that it sloped downward toward the storage units. Shortly after the final inspection of the building, the Poplins discovered water leakage in some of the newly constructed storage units. The Poplins refused to pay Fostveit for the balance due under the contract, arguing that construction was flawed and that Fostveit had breached the contract. Fostveit countered that he had substantially completed the project and that the water leakage was due to deficiencies in the Poplins' work on the roof and driveway. Fostveit sued the Poplins for the unpaid balance.

OUTCOME: The court held that Fostveit substantially performed under the contract and the water leakage was due to the Poplins' faulty work. The Poplins were required to pay the balance due under the contract, less the cost of repairing minor deficiencies in Fostveit's work.

—*Fostveit v. Poplin*, 301 P.3d 915 (Or. App)

13-1b DISCHARGE BY OPERATION OF LAW

Under certain circumstances, the law will cause a discharge of the contract, or at least the law will bar all right of action. The most common conditions under which the law operates to discharge contracts include:

1. Discharge in bankruptcy
2. Running of the statute of limitations
3. Alteration of written contract

Bankruptcy. Individuals and business firms overwhelmed with financial obligations may petition the court for a decree of voluntary bankruptcy. Creditors may, under certain circumstances, force one into involuntary bankruptcy. In either event, after a discharge in bankruptcy, creditors' rights of action to enforce most of the contracts of the debtor are barred.

statute of limitations
time within which the right
to sue must be exercised
or lost

Statute of Limitations. A person's right to sue must be exercised within the time fixed by a statute called the **statute of limitations**. This time varies from state to state, for different types of suits and for different types of debts. For open accounts, accounts receivable, and ordinary loans, the time varies from two to eight years, whereas for notes it varies from four to twenty years.

After a person has brought suit and obtained judgment, the judgment must be enforced by having the property of the debtor levied upon and sold. If this is not done, in some states a statute of limitations operates even against judgments. If a payment is made on a judgment, the payment constitutes an acknowledgment of the debt, and the statute starts to run again from the date of payment.

The time is calculated from the date the obligation is due. In the case of running accounts, such as purchases from department stores, the time starts from the date of the last purchase. If a part payment is made, the statute begins to run again from the date of such payment. If the promisor leaves the state, the statute ceases to run while the promisor is beyond the jurisdiction of the court. In the law, the suspension of the statute of limitations means the statute is tolled.

A debt that has been outlawed by a statute of limitations may be revived. Some states do this by a written acknowledgment of—or a promise to pay—the debt, others by part payment after the debt has been outlawed, and still others by the mere payment of the interest. After the debt is revived, the period of the statute of limitations begins to run again from the time of the revival.

COURT CASE

FACTS: Ecoair Corporation (Ecoair) executed a promissory note to Globe Scott Motors Private Limited (Globe) for $125,000. Six years later, Kirtida Zatakia bought the note for 25,000 Indian rupees and four months after that demanded payment from Ecoair. Seven years after buying the note, Zatakia sued Ecoair, who claimed the suit was barred by the statute of limitations. Zatakia produced a letter on Ecoair's letterhead, signed by Ecoair's president, stating the terms and unpaid amounts of the note.

Sent by Ecoair's auditors, the letter referred to "our note payable to you" and asked for confirmation. Zatakia argued that the letter tolled the statute of limitations.

OUTCOME: The court found the letter was a clear acknowledgement of the debt sufficient to toll the statute of limitations.

—*Zatakia v. Ecoair Corp.*, 18 A.3d 604 (Conn. App. Ct.)

Alteration of Written Contract. If one of the parties intentionally and without the consent of the other party alters the written contract, the other innocent party is discharged. However, the altering party can be held to either the original contract terms or the terms as altered. In most states, the alteration must also be material or important. If a contractor who has undertaken to build a house by January 15 realizes that because of winter conditions it cannot be finished by that date erases and changes the date to March 15, there is a material alteration that will discharge the other party to the contract.

13-1c VOLUNTARY AGREEMENT OF THE PARTIES

A contract is a mutual agreement. The parties are as free to change their minds by mutual agreement as they are to agree in the first place. Consequently, whenever the parties to a contract agree not to carry out its terms, the contract is discharged.

The contract itself may recite events or circumstances that will automatically terminate the agreement. The release of one party to the contract constitutes the consideration for the release of the other.

13-1d IMPOSSIBILITY OF PERFORMANCE

If the act called for in an alleged contract is impossible to perform at the time the contract is made, no contract ever comes into existence. However, impossibility of performance frequently arises after a valid contract is formed. This type of impossibility discharges the contract under certain circumstances. The fact that performance has merely become more difficult does not automatically discharge the contract. Yet, if, in a practical sense, the contract is impossible to perform, it is discharged.

In some states, a contract is discharged by impracticability of performance rather than strict impossibility. In such states, extreme and unreasonable difficulty, expense, injury, or loss would discharge a contract.

COURT CASE

FACTS: While a District of Columbia (DC) public school student receiving special education services, seventeen-year-old Antonio Hester was convicted of criminal offenses and sentenced to time in a Maryland prison. Federal law required school districts to provide the special education services, so Hester and DC agreed that DC would provide special education services in the prison. However, the employees of the private organization DC hired to provide the services were not allowed in the prison. Maryland provided its own special education services to Hester. Hester sued DC, requesting special education services from DC to make up for the time he spent in the Maryland prison without receiving services from DC.

OUTCOME: The court stated that because Maryland made it impracticable for DC to provide special education services in the prison, DC had not breached its agreement with Hester.

—*Hester v. District of Columbia*, 505 F.3d 1283
(D.C. Cir.)

The most common causes of discharge by impossibility of performance occurring after the contract is made include:

1. Destruction of the subject matter
2. New laws making the contract illegal
3. Death or physical incapacity of a person to render personal services
4. Act of the other party

Destruction of the Subject Matter. If the contract involves specific subject matter, the destruction of this specific subject matter without the fault of the parties discharges the contract because of impossibility of performance. This rule applies only when the performance of the contract depends on the continued existence of a specified person, animal, or thing. The contract is not discharged if an event occurs that it is reasonable to anticipate. Any payment made in advance must be returned when performance of the contract is excused.

PREVIEW CASE REVISITED

FACTS: James Sheppard contracted to pay Thomas Ryan $35,000 to be Sheppard's personal flying instructor. Before any flight instruction took place, Sheppard died. Ryan filed a claim against Sheppard's estate. The estate claimed the agreement was unenforceable because it required the physical participation, and therefore the continued existence, of Sheppard. Ryan claimed that Sheppard's obligation under the contract, paying Ryan, was not personal to him and could be assumed by the estate.

OUTCOME: Since the contract required Ryan to act as Sheppard's personal instructor, and he could not do that, Ryan's promised services were impossible to perform.

—*In re Estate of Sheppard*, 789 N.W.2d 616 (Wis. Ct. App.)

New Laws Making the Contract Illegal. If an act is legal at the time of the contract but is subsequently made illegal, the contract is discharged. However, if one of the parties takes deliberate action to render the contract illegal, that party will be liable in damages.

Death or Physical Incapacity. If the contract calls for personal services, death or physical incapacity of the person to perform such services discharges the contract. The personal services must be such that they cannot readily be performed by another or by the personal representative of the promisor.

Death or incapacity discharges such acts as painting a portrait, representing a client in a legal proceeding, and other services of a highly personal nature. In general, if the performance is too personal to be delegated, the death or disability of the party bound to perform will discharge the contract.

Act of Other Party. When performance of a contract by a party is made impossible by the wrongful act of the other party, the performance is excused. The party who cannot perform has not breached the contract by the failure to perform.

***Force Majeure* Clauses.** Similar to impossibility of performance, but resulting from agreement of the parties, is release from performance because of a *force majeure* clause in the contract. Many contracts commonly contain such a clause that excuses performance by a party when an extraordinary event outside the party's control occurs that prevents the party's performance of the contract. Such extraordinary events are usually limited to natural disasters, war, or failure by a third party to perform to one of the contracting parties.

***force majeure* clause** contract provision excusing performance when extraordinary event occurs

COURT CASE

FACTS: Allegiance Hillview, L.P. (Allegiance) owned the surface of a tract of land. Rayzor Investments, Ltd. (Rayzor) owned the mineral interest, and Range Texas Production, LLC was Rayzor's oil and gas lessee. Allegiance and Rayzor had a surface use agreement (SUA) that terminated if Range did not begin drilling by July 11. The SUA also provided that the deadline could be extended if Range were prevented from drilling by an event of *force majeure*, which included the city's failure to issue the necessary permits. The city council did not vote on Range's permit application by July 11. Range sued when Allegiance threatened to terminate the SUA.

OUTCOME: Failure of the city to issue the necessary permits was a *force majeure* event that excused Range's failure to begin drilling by July 11.

—*Allegiance Hillview, L.P. v. Range Texas Production LLC*, 347 S.W.3d 855 (Tex. Ct. App.)

13-1e ACCEPTANCE OF BREACH OF THE CONTRACT BY ONE OF THE PARTIES

breach
failure or refusal to perform contractual obligations

When one of the parties fails or refuses to perform the obligations assumed under the contract, there is a **breach** of the contract. This does not terminate the contract. Only if the innocent party accepts the breach of the contract is the contract discharged.

anticipatory breach
one party announces intention not to perform prior to time to perform

If one party, prior to the time the other party is entitled to performance, announces an intention not to perform, **anticipatory breach** occurs. When there has been anticipatory breach, the innocent party may sue immediately for breach of contract and be released from any obligations under the contract.

LO ③
Breach of contract and remedies

13-2 Remedies for Breach of Contract

If a breach of contract occurs, the innocent party has three courses of action that may be followed:

1. Sue for damages

2. Rescind the contract

3. Sue for specific performance

13-2a SUE FOR DAMAGES

damages
sum of money awarded to injured party

The usual remedy for breach of contract is to sue for **damages** or a sum of money to compensate for the breach. A suit for damages really consists of two suits in one. The first requires proving breach of contract. The second requires proving damages. Four kinds of damages include: (1) nominal, (2) compensatory, (3) punitive, and (4) liquidated.

nominal damages
small amount is awarded when there is technical breach but no injury

Nominal Damages. If the plaintiff in a breach-of-contract suit can prove that the defendant broke the contract, but cannot prove any loss was sustained because of the breach, then the court will award **nominal damages**, generally one dollar, to symbolize vindication of the wrong done to the plaintiff. Although very low damages are frequently awarded, the award also can be substantial.

COURT CASE

FACTS: MTW Investment Co. was a limited partner in Regency Forrest Association. Regency sold some land to Alcovy Properties Inc. MTW sued Alcovy, alleging that Regency did not have authority to sell the land. Alcovy alleged that MTW's action clouded the title to the land and that it had lost a substantial profit it could have made by subdividing the land. When MTW alleged that the loss of profits was too speculative, the jury awarded Alcovy $625,000 in nominal damages. MTW appealed, saying the amount was excessive.

OUTCOME: The court held that although nominal damages are normally a trivial amount when no serious loss is shown, they are not restricted to a very small amount. The award was not excessive.

—*MTW Inv. Co. v. Alcovy Properties Inc.*, 616 S.E.2d 166 (Ga. Ct. App.)

Compensatory Damages. The theory of the law of damages is that an injured party should be compensated for any loss that may have been sustained but should not be permitted to profit from the other party's wrongdoing. When a breach of contract occurs, the law entitles the injured party to compensation for the exact amount of loss, but no more. Such damages are called **compensatory damages**. Sometimes the actual loss is easily determined, but at other times it is very difficult to determine. As a general rule, the amount of damages is a question for the jury to decide.

> **compensatory damages**
> amount equal to the loss sustained

Punitive, or Exemplary, Damages. In most breach-of-contract cases, the awarding of compensatory damages fully meets the ends of justice. Cases occur, however, in which compensatory damages are not adequate. In these instances, the law may permit the plaintiff to receive **punitive damages**. Punitive damages are damages paid to the plaintiff in order to punish the defendant, not to compensate the plaintiff. Punitive damages are more common in tort than contract actions. For example, if a tenant maliciously damages rented property, the landlord may frequently recover as damages the actual cost of repairs plus additional damages as punitive damages.

> **punitive damages**
> amount paid to one party to punish the other

Liquidated Damages. When two parties enter into a contract, in order to avoid the problems involved in proving actual damages, they may include a provision fixing the amount of damages to be paid in the event one party breaches the contract. Such a provision is called **liquidated damages**. Such a clause in the contract specifies recoverable damages in the event that one party establishes a breach by the other. The parties must intend to establish liquidated damages in advance of any breach. Liquidated damages must be reasonable and should be provided only in those cases in which actual damages are difficult or impossible to prove. If the amount of damages fixed by the contract is unreasonable, and in effect the damages are punitive, the court will not enforce this provision of the contract.

> **liquidated damages**
> sum fixed by contract for breach where actual damages are difficult to measure

COURT CASE

FACTS: A subsidiary of Hilton Worldwide, Inc. ("Hilton") entered a franchise agreement with Worcester Hospitality Group ("WHG"), allowing WHG to be the franchisee of a Hampton Inn hotel. The agreement provided that Hilton would routinely inspect WHG's hotel and review customer surveys to ensure the hotel met Hilton's quality standards. In the event of repeated non-compliance, Hilton reserved the right to terminate the franchise agreement and was entitled to liquidated damages under the agreement. After numerous failed evaluations, Hilton terminated the franchise agreement with WHG and

sued for damages as provided for by the contract. WHG claimed the liquidated damages were an unenforceable remedy.

OUTCOME: The court enforced the liquidated damages provision because WHG gave no proof that actual damages were readily ascertainable at the time the franchise contract was signed.

—HLT Existing Franchise Holding, LLC v. Worcester Hospitality Group, LLC, 994 F.Supp.2d 520 (S.D. N.Y)

13-2b RESCIND THE CONTRACT

rescind
set aside or cancel

When a contract is breached, the aggrieved party may elect to **rescind** the contract, which releases this party from all obligations not yet performed. If this party has executed the contract, the remedy is to sue for recovery of what was parted with. If the aggrieved party rescinds a contract for the sale of goods, damages for the breach also may be requested.

13-2c SUE FOR SPECIFIC PERFORMANCE

specific performance
carrying out the terms
of contract

In some cases, neither a suit for damages nor for rescission will constitute an adequate remedy. The injured party's remedy under these circumstances is a suit in equity to compel **specific performance**; that is, the carrying out of the specific terms of the contract.

COURT CASE

FACTS: Grady Reed was a shareholder and employee of Triton Services, Inc. As a condition of employment, Reed was required to sign a shareholders' agreement, which provided that upon termination of his employment with Triton, Reed would sell all of his stock in the company. In such an event, Triton would be given the option to purchase the stock first, and if it failed to do so within 120 days, the remaining stockholders would purchase the stock. Reed's employment was later terminated with Triton and when both Triton and its other stockholders failed to purchase Reed's shares of stock, he sued them for breach of contract. In his

suit, Reed requested compensatory damages in the amount of the contract price of the stock.

OUTCOME: The court held compensatory damages were the wrong remedy, because that would allow Reed to receive payment for the value of the stock while retaining ownership of the stock, rendering him in a better position than if the contract had been fully performed. The proper remedy was specific performance requiring Triton to purchase the stock back from Reed.

—Reed v. Triton Servs., Inc., 15 N.E.3d 936 (Ohio Ct. App.)

This remedy is available in limited cases. This includes most contracts for the sale of real estate or any interest in real estate and for the sale of rare articles of personal property, such as a painting or an heirloom, the value of which cannot readily be determined. There is no way to measure sentimental value attached to a relic. Under such circumstances, mere money damages may be inadequate to compensate the injured party. The court may compel specific performance under such circumstances.

As a general rule, contracts for the performance of personal services will not be specifically ordered. This is both because of the difficulty of supervision by the courts and because of the Constitution's prohibition of involuntary servitude except as a criminal punishment.

13-3 Malpractice

A professional person, such as a lawyer, accountant, or doctor, who makes a contract to perform professional services has a duty to perform with the ability and care normally exercised by others in the profession. A contract not so performed is breached because of **malpractice**. An accountant is liable to a client who suffers a loss because the accountant has not complied with accepted accounting practices.

In some cases, a person other than a party to the contract may sue a professional person for malpractice. In the case of a contract for accounting services, a third party may, under certain circumstances, recover when the negligence or fraud by the accountant causes a loss to that party.

malpractice
failure to perform with ability and care normally exercised by people in a profession

QUESTIONS

1. When are parties to a contract discharged by performance? Are all parties discharged simultaneously?

2. If a contract states "time is of the essence," when must it be performed?

3. What rule do courts generally apply when determining whether satisfactory performance has occurred to discharge the terms of a contract?

4. What circumstances surrounding a deviation from a contract will a court weigh in determining whether there has been substantial performance of a contract?

5. How free are the parties to a contract to change their minds, and what is the result?

6. May a debt that has been outlawed by the statute of limitations ever be revived?

7. If a singer contracts to sing at a party, is the contract released if the singer develops laryngitis just before the party starts?

8. What is the effect of a *force majeure* clause?

9. Does a breach of a contract terminate the contract? Explain.

10. What is the purpose of punitive damages in a breach-of-contract suit?

11. Under what circumstances is a court likely to compel specific performance of a contract?

12. Explain who might breach a contract because of malpractice.

CASE PROBLEMS

LO ② 1. Brothers Tom and John Silbernagel sued their brother Steven and his wife, Jane, over a parcel of real estate. They reached a settlement agreement by which Steven and Jane agreed to pay Tom and John $150,000 for their interests in the real estate. Steven and Jane would have a reasonable time to secure financing to raise the money. It was later determined that Betty Jo Elliot, a cousin of the brothers, owned a 1/12 interest in the real estate. As a result, Steven and Jane were unable to borrow $150,000 on their interest in the real estate. When Tom and John sued them for the $150,000, Steven and Jane claimed the agreement was discharged because the purpose could not be achieved. They could not borrow the $150,000, and they did not get title to 100 percent of the real estate. Was the contract discharged by impossibility of performance?

LO ③ 2. William and Karen McCoy contracted to buy James and Nancy Brown's house and made a deposit of $127,000. The contract stated the sale was conditioned upon the McCoys getting a commitment for a mortgage "with interest at the prevailing rate." The McCoys agreed to "pursue [a mortgage commitment] diligently." If the McCoys could not obtain the mortgage and "demonstrated due diligence," they could terminate the contract, and their deposit would be returned to them. The McCoys submitted a mortgage application to one bank, which issued a commitment letter conditioned on William, who was unemployed, obtaining full-time, salaried employment. McCoy sought such a position from one employer and did not obtain it. The McCoys then notified the Browns they were unable to obtain a mortgage commitment and requested return of their deposit. The Browns refused, and the McCoys sued them. Did the McCoys breach the contract, and if so, what should the damages be?

LO ① 3. MH Metropolitan (MH) hired Weitz Co. LLC (Weitz) to construct a multibuilding apartment complex. The construction became delayed. MH withheld two payments to Weitz, which then stopped construction. MH terminated Weitz for cause and completed the project without it. Weitz sued for the unpaid amount of the contract. The evidence at trial was that Weitz failed to provide proper lien waivers, allowed liens to be filed against the job, falsified a pay application, caused substantial delays, and did poor quality construction. It could not properly prepare, update, or follow its schedules, which contributed to delay. To recover, Weitz had to have substantially performed the contract. Had it?

LO ③ 4. A & B Industries of Morgan City, Inc., a shipbuilder, contracted to build two tug boats for Odyssea Vessels, Inc. in consideration of $3,752,000 per boat. Under the contract, A & B was responsible for securing materials, fabrication, and general outfitting of the vessels. Odyssea agreed to provide design drawings through an engineering firm. The agreement also provided that A & B would not be liable for liquidated damages or penalties for failure to complete their work within the specified time. After signing the contract, Odyssea delayed in sending necessary design drawings to A & B. Over several months, the shipbuilder repeatedly requested the design package and warned Odyssea that it would be impossible to continue the project without the drawings. The delay caused A & B extensive loss, due to the rise in building materials and labor costs. Odyssea filed suit against A & B for breach of contract, because A & B failed to finish the vessels on time. A jury found that Odyssea breached the contract and awarded A & B $393,527 in damages. Odyssea argued that the court erred in awarding damages and the remedy for the breach should have been an extension of time for A & B to complete the work. Would simply granting an extension of time to finish the project fully compensate A & B for its loss?

LO ① 5. Brothers Edward, Robert, and William Radkiewicz were the beneficiaries of a trust that owned a twenty-seven-acre tract. Edward and Robert contracted with Olympia Investments to convey clear title to the land to Olympia and it put up $55,000 in earnest money. The contract contemplated that the balance of the purchase price and the deed of sale would be exchanged at closing. The closing was to be within fifteen days of March 1. Alleging he needed to approve a sale, William sued his brothers and Olympia. He filed a notice of the suit to secure his claim on the property, called a *lis pendens*. The brothers and Olympia exchanged many notices regarding the cloud on title to the

CASE PROBLEMS (CONTINUED)

property the *lis pendens* created and whether it could be removed. The brothers did not possess all of the required closing documents by March 1, and the *lis pendens* was not lifted. No date was set for closing, but on March 11 the brothers told Olympia it was in default, and the contract was terminated. When Olympia did not release the earnest money, the brothers sued. Olympia alleged that the brothers had never tendered their required performance and thus it did not have to comply with the contract. Had the brothers tendered performance?

6. Turbines, Ltd. provided helicopter support services to customers. Monarch Aviation, an Asian company, contacted Turbines and sought to buy a turbine nozzle for shipment to Malaysia. Turbines did not have the part in stock and contacted Transupport, Inc. to purchase the part. Turbines purchased the nozzle from Transupport and tendered payment of $30,000. Transupport shipped the nozzle to Turbines, but when Turbines attempted to forward the piece to Malaysia, the shipment was intercepted by U.S. Customs. While the part was in the custody of U.S. Customs, Turbines learned that a person associated with Monarch Aviation was subject to a federal indictment and that Monarch was redirecting goods to Iran. Federal law thus prohibited Turbines from shipping the nozzle to Monarch Aviation. Turbines attempted to return the nozzle to Transupport, which refused to accept the part and refund Turbines's payment. Turbines sued Transupport to rescind the sales contract, arguing that federal law made it illegal for Turbines to ship the part to Malaysia. Should the contract between Turbines and Transupport be rescinded? **LO ②, ③**

7. Yakima Compost Company, Inc. entered into a twenty-five year agreement with La Paz County, Arizona to receive and process sewage sludge from treatment facilities inside and outside of Arizona through a solar drying process on county land. After executing agreement, the county decided it no longer wanted to do business with Yakima and terminated the contract. The termination caused Yakima to lose millions of dollars in business from other governmental entities that had committed to sending Yakima their sewage for treatment. A jury awarded Yakima $9.2 million in compensatory damages for lost profits as a result of the terminated contract. Yakima appealed, arguing that in addition to compensatory damages, the court should have awarded specific performance that would require La Paz County to complete its twenty-five year agreement with Yakima. Was specific performance an appropriate remedy in this case? **LO ③**

8. Mills Construction Inc. contracted with Double Diamond Construction to erect a steel arena. Mills was to provide the parts for the building, and Double Diamond was to provide the labor and equipment. Double Diamond began construction, the materials were delivered late, and many of the steel components did not fit together properly. Some of the mainframes were twisted, and other parts were missing or the wrong length. Double Diamond reported the problems to Mills and its supplier, but nothing was done. Double Diamond stopped work on the project, and three days later the structure collapsed. Double Diamond billed Mills for the work it had completed up to the collapse and said it would not continue work until the bill was paid. When it was not paid, Double Diamond sued Mills. Had Mills made it impossible for Double Diamond to complete the contract? **LO ②**

9. Jack Shewmake and Jim Kelly contracted to add a playroom, hobby room, and concrete deck to Al and Lisa DelGreco's home. After the new concrete deck was poured, rain leaked into the new playroom and hobby room. Shewmake and Kelly tried to correct this, but after three months the leak had still not been corrected. Al told Shewmake and Kelly he would not make any more payments until the leak was corrected. They did not perform any more work on the house, so the DelGrecos paid an architect $1,500 to determine what needed to be done to correct the defects in the work. They paid another contractor $18,500 to correct the job. To eliminate the leak, the second contractor demolished the concrete deck Shewmake and Kelly had installed. The DelGrecos sued Shewmake and Kelly for breach of contract. They claimed they had spent $19,100 in labor and materials to work on the house, for which they had not been paid. What, if anything, should the DelGrecos recover? **LO ①**

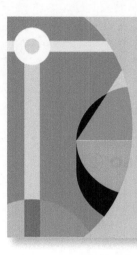

ETHICS IN PRACTICE

You have learned what a contract is and the consequences for failing to live up to the provisions of a contract. The usual remedy for breach of contract is money damages. But can money truly compensate the nonbreaching party for all the loss suffered? How accurately can loss of potential profit be estimated? What about the stress and inconvenience caused the nonbreaching party by the breach? Would this be difficult to measure in monetary terms? What example does failing to live up to a promise set? If an employee finds out that the company is manufacturing appliances with substandard parts so that the appliances will fail much sooner, does the employee have an ethical obligation to do anything?

PART 2 SUMMARY CASES

CONTRACTS

1. Cornerstone Jeffrey Wilson, L.L.C. (Wilson) contracted with B&R Construction Management Inc. (B&R) for B&R to demolish a Portsmouth Redevelopment and Housing Authority (PRHA) facility. The contract required B&R to provide performance and payment bonds. The contract also provided: "All rights under this Contract Agreement shall be for the benefit of [WILSON] and its successors and assigns, including PRHA" and that nothing in the contract shall be construed "to give any third party any claim or right of action against PRHA or HUD." B&R subcontracted some work to Beamon Enterprises Inc. (Beamon) who subcontracted to Environmental Staffing Acquisition Corp. (En-Staff). Beamon did not pay En-Staff, who discovered B&R's bonding company was not licensed in the state and was out of business. En-Staff sued B&R for breach of contract, claiming it was a third-party beneficiary of the contract between Wilson and B&R. Should En-Staff succeed? [*Environmental Staffing Acquisition Corp. v. B&R Const. Management Inc.*, 725 S.E.2d 550 (Va.)]

2. Robert and Deborah Philabaun owned Philabaun's Hidden Cove Resort. When about to undergo surgery for lung cancer, Robert handwrote a document titled "Agreement," which only he signed. The document stated that in case he did not survive his surgery, Robert wanted it to be known that he wished to sell the resort to Danny Gajovski for $900,000. Robert survived the surgery but died ten months later. Deborah would not sell the resort, so Gajovski sued for breach of contract. Did he have an enforceable contract to buy the resort? [*Gajovski v. Estate of Philabaun*, 950 N.E.2d 595 (Ohio Ct. App.)]

3. FCI Group Inc. was a building contractor hired by the City of New York. FCI's work was substantially completed when two Department of Citywide Administrative Services (DCAS) employees who oversaw FCI's work reported that envelopes containing $3,000 had been left on their desks. One envelope contained a change order request amounting to $101,708, which awaited the employee's approval. FCI's president and secretary, Choon Won Lee, admitted to leaving the envelopes, and he pled guilty to attempted giving of unlawful gratuities. DCAS cancelled the contract after Lee's misconduct and told FCI it would make no more payments on the construction work. FCI sued the city for the unpaid balance on the contract, $260,928. Should it recover? [*FCI Group Inc. v. City of New York*, 862 N.Y.S.2d 352 (N.Y. App. Div.)]

4. Tim Beverick, an attorney for Koch Power Inc. was negotiating a contract for the purchase of electricity over a ten-year period. He alleged that Koch orally had promised that he and another attorney would split a bonus of 10 to 15 percent of the expected savings when the contract was executed. It took Beverick two years to get the contract signed. Koch did not pay the bonus, and Beverick sued for breach of contract and *promissory estoppel*. He testified

there would have had to be a lot of things fall in place to get the contract signed within one year. Did the Statute of Frauds ban the suit based on an oral promise that could not be completed within one year? [*Beverick v. Koch Power Inc.*, 186 S.W.3d 145 (Tex. Ct. App.)]

5. Martin Marietta Materials wanted to mine minerals from some land. Martin sent the landowner's attorney, Michael Antrim, a proposed lease that provided a 4 percent royalty on materials mined. Antrim contacted William Karns, an expert, for help in determining the proper royalty. Antrim and Karns had not agreed on a fee for Karns's services. With Karns's advice, Antrim negotiated and signed a contract paying a 6 to 6.5 percent royalty. Karns then sent a letter stating that his fee was one cent ($0.01) for every ton of materials extracted as long as extraction continued, with a minimum annual fee of $7,500. Over twenty years, this would amount to about $771,000. Antrim testified he had told Karns by phone the fee proposal had been rejected. Six months later, Antrim sent Karns a check for $25,000 that Karns did not cash. Four years later, in legal proceedings, Karns alleged his letter had constituted a binding contract because Antrim had not rejected it. Was Karns correct that his offer had been accepted? [*Mueller v. Kerns*, 873 N.E.2d 652 (Ind. Ct. App.)]

6. Velma Lee Robinson executed a will by which she left most of her property to the Velma Lee and John Harvey Robinson Charitable Foundation. Twelve years later, she executed new estate planning documents that left her estate to her nieces and nephews. Nine months after executing the later will, she suffered the first of a series of strokes. After she died, there was a contest between the two wills. Friends and caregivers testified that Robinson would have been unable to read the later documents and would not have understood them at the time she signed them. She was unable to handle her business and became confused. A physician testified from her medical records that there was a progression of pathological disease processes that was causing her to lose brain cells. Did Robinson have the necessary capacity to execute the later will? [*In re Estate of Robinson*, 140 S.W.3d 782 (Tex. Ct. App.)]

7. Michael Hall was incarcerated eight months after he married Susan Hall. Susan told Michael she planned to dissolve the marriage due to his untruthfulness about his criminal history and hired counsel to accomplish a dissolution. Michael did not want a dissolution, said he would do anything to "make her more comfortable with him," and proposed that they enter into an agreement that would protect Susan financially in the event of a future divorce. Susan consented to not seek a dissolution in exchange for such an agreement. Both parties signed the postnuptial agreement and complied with its terms for eight years. At that point, Susan filed to dissolve the marriage and moved to enforce the postnuptial agreement. Michael argued that the agreement lacked adequate consideration. Was he correct? [*Hall v. Hall*, 27 N.E.3d 281 (Ind. Ct. App.)]

8. Jerry Worley worked for Wyoming Bottling. He wanted to get a loan to buy a new car and appliances for his home. He asked Joe DeCora, the company president, about job security. DeCora told him his job was secure and to take out the loan. Worley checked with his supervisor, Butch Gibson, to make sure his job performance was satisfactory. Gibson told him everything was fine and "to go on about [his] affairs." Worley took out the loan, and the next month

Wyoming demoted Worley, so he lost the use of a company car and $11,000 in annual pay. Worley sued, alleging *promissory estoppel*. Did these facts state a case for it? [*Worley v. Wyoming Bottling Co. Inc.*, 1 P.3d 615 (Wyo.)]

9. General Tire decided to terminate Horst Mehlfeldt's employment and through its vice president of human relations, Ross Bailey, made several proposals to Mehlfeldt in lieu of the benefits provided in his employment contract. Bailey thought Mehlfeldt had accepted a proposal, while Mehlfeldt expected a larger final figure. In drafting a separation agreement, Bailey made a mistake so that General Tire had to pay $494,000—the total Bailey had offered—plus what the employment contract specified. Mehlfeldt thought the larger amount was a result of his request for more money and signed the agreement. General Tire paid him $494,000. When Mehlfeldt asked when he would get the rest, General Tire realized the mistake. It sued, alleging mutual mistake. Was it? [*Gen. Tire Inc. v. Mehlfeldt*, 691 N.E.2d 1132 (Ohio Ct. App.)]

10. Two Russian boxing promoters doing business under the name World of Boxing ("WOB") signed a contract with Don King, an American boxing promoter, in which King promised to produce Guillermo Jones for a match against Denis Lebedev. Jones and Lebedev had been scheduled to fight the previous year, but the match was canceled due to Jones' positive drug tests. In his contract with WOB, King promised to produce Jones for a fight, but the contract required Jones to take drug tests before and after the match. On the day of the fight, Jones tested positive once again for performance enhancing drugs and was disqualified from the match. WOB sued King, claiming that King breached their contract by failing to produce Jones for the fight. King argued that his breach was excused, because Jones' performance was impossible due to his disqualification. Was King right? [*World of Boxing, LLC v. King*, 56 F.Supp.3d 507 (S.D. N.Y.)]

11. LexisNexis provided e-filing services to litigators in certain county courts in Texas. In exchange for its filing services, LexisNexis charged a fee for filing documents with the court. Karen McPeters sued LexisNexis, alleging among other things that the fees were illegal, because they obstructed the administration of justice and violated the Texas constitution's open-courts provision. McPeters argued that the filing fee restricted litigants' access to the courts, but she failed to show the filing fees prevented or even delayed her and other litigants in filing claims. Should LexisNexis' e-filing fees be prohibited? [*McPeters v. LexisNexis*, 11 F.Supp.3d 789 (S.D. Tex.)]

12. Siblings Cynthia Easterling and Rhett Russell were the sole members of a limited liability company formed to purchase real estate. After several years in business, the two began discussing the idea of dissolving the company and distributing its properties. Easterling proposed a division of property in a letter to Russell, the text of which consistently referred to its contents as a settlement "offer." In her letter, she divided the property into two parts, labeled Exhibit A and Exhibit B, and gave Russell the choice of either property. Russell responded in writing that he accepted Easterling's offer and chose Exhibit A as his property distribution. He then proceeded to have deeds to the property recorded in the chancery clerk's office. Easterling sued to set aside the deeds, claiming there was no binding contract, because Russell had not specifically addressed all of the terms of her offer. Was their contract valid? [*Easterling v. Russell*, 2015 WL 1198651 (Miss. Ct. App.)]

PART 3

14 Nature of Personal Property

15 Special Bailments

Personal Property

Personal property encompasses a wide variety of things. Intangible personal property is covered in Chapter 14. The most personal kind of intangible personal property is your identity, and its theft, through use of your Social Security number, bank account, or credit card numbers, not only is frightening but also could pose difficult problems to solve. Federal and state governments continue to address the problem through various laws and regulations. For information on this particular issue, visit the Federal Trade Commission's website on Consumer Information and Identify Theft at www.idtheft.gov.

Nature of Personal Property

LEARNING OBJECTIVES

① Discuss the types of personal property and how it can be acquired.
② Explain the difference between lost and abandoned property.
③ Define and give examples of a bailment.
④ Distinguish the three types of bailments.

PREVIEW CASE

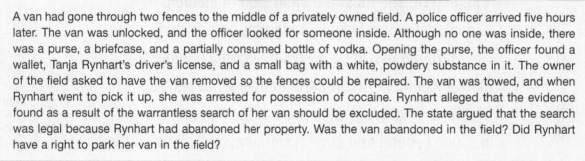

A van had gone through two fences to the middle of a privately owned field. A police officer arrived five hours later. The van was unlocked, and the officer looked for someone inside. Although no one was inside, there was a purse, a briefcase, and a partially consumed bottle of vodka. Opening the purse, the officer found a wallet, Tanja Rynhart's driver's license, and a small bag with a white, powdery substance in it. The owner of the field asked to have the van removed so the fences could be repaired. The van was towed, and when Rynhart went to pick it up, she was arrested for possession of cocaine. Rynhart alleged that the evidence found as a result of the warrantless search of her van should be excluded. The state argued that the search was legal because Rynhart had abandoned her property. Was the van abandoned in the field? Did Rynhart have a right to park her van in the field?

property
anything that may be owned

Anything that may be owned is **property**. The law protects not only the right to own property but also the right to use it. A person may enter into a contract with the owner to use property without becoming the owner of the property. Property includes not only physical things but also such things as bank deposits, notes, and bonds that give the right to acquire physical property or to use such property.

LO ①
Types of personal property

14-1 Personal Property

personal property
movable property; interests less than complete ownership in land or rights to money

Property is frequently classified according to its movability. If it is movable property, it is **personal property**. Thus, clothing, food, TVs, theater tickets, and even house trailers are personal property.

COURT CASE

FACTS: Ted Oldja decided to ride on a zip line operated by Warm Beach Christian Camp and Conference Center. The zip line carried riders in a harness along a cable. The harness was supported by two ropes—a white rope, which bore the rider's weight, and a black rope, which acted as a secondary connection and safety feature. Instead of holding onto the rope, Oldja wrapped his fingers in the white rope, and when he sat in the harness, his body weight caused the rope to crush his fingers. At trial, Oldja claimed that Warm Beach had a duty to protect Oldja from known or obvious dangers on the land.

OUTCOME: The court held that the zip line was not part of the land; rather, it was personal property. As a result, in order to recover Oldja had to show that he had no reason to believe the zip line might be dangerous. The court held that common sense was sufficient to show the zip line could be dangerous.

—Oldja v. Warm Beach Christian Camp and Conference Center, 793 F.Supp.2d 1208 (E.D. Wash.)

Land is not personal property, but an interest in land less than complete ownership, such as a leasehold, is normally classified as personal property.

In addition to movable physical property, personal property includes rights to money such as notes, bonds, and all written evidences of debt. Personal property is divided into two classes:

1. Tangible
2. Intangible

14-1a TANGIBLE PERSONAL PROPERTY

Tangible personal property is personal property that can be seen, touched, and possessed. Tangible personal property includes animals, merchandise, furniture, annual growing crops, clothing, jewelry, and similar items.

tangible personal property
personal property that can be seen, touched, and possessed

14-1b INTANGIBLE PERSONAL PROPERTY

Intangible personal property consists of evidences of ownership of rights or value. The property itself cannot be touched or seen. Some common forms of intangible personal property include checks, stocks, contracts, copyrights, and savings account certificates.

intangible personal property
evidences of ownership of rights or value

14-2 Methods of Acquiring Personal Property

The title to personal property may be acquired by purchase, possession, will, descent, gift, accession, confusion, and creation.

14-2a PURCHASE

Ownership most commonly occurs through **purchase**. The buyer pays the seller, and the seller transfers the property to the buyer.

purchase
ownership by payment

14-2b WILL

The owner of property may convey title to another by will. Title does not transfer by will until the person who made the will dies and appropriate judicial proceedings have taken place.

14-2c DESCENT

intestate
a person who dies without leaving a will

When a person dies without leaving a will, that person dies **intestate**. The person's heirs acquire title to the personal property according to the laws existing in the decedent's state of residence.

gift
transfer without consideration

14-2d GIFT

donor
person who makes a gift

A **gift** is a transfer made without consideration in return. The person making a gift is called the **donor**. The person receiving the gift is called the **donee**. In order to have a valid gift, the donor must have the intention to make the gift, and there must be a delivery of the property being given to the donee.

donee
person who receives a gift

COURT CASE

FACTS: After their marriage, William and Peggy Brackin kept their individual property separately titled. They had signed a premarital agreement that said either could make any gift to his or her respective spouse and that the gift would become the separate property of the donee spouse. William told Peggy to give her car to her grandson and that William would buy her a car. After Peggy gave away her car, and prior to the marriage, William purchased a Pontiac, telling Peggy that it was her car. William titled the Pontiac in his name only. After their marriage, William traded in the Pontiac and purchased a Buick. William paid for the Buick with his own funds but titled the vehicle in both his and Peggy's names. William drove the Buick home and said, "Peggy, come out and see the car I bought you." Peggy primarily drove the car. Later, during an argument with Peggy, William took a hammer and repeatedly struck the door handle of the Buick until the handle fell off. In divorce proceedings, Peggy claimed that William had made a gift to her of the Buick.

OUTCOME: The court found that William's statement indicated his intention to make the Buick a gift to Peggy and that her driving it showed delivery and acceptance of the gift.

—*Brackin v. Brackin*, 894 N.E.2d 206 (Ind. Ct. App.)

14-2e ACCESSION

accession
adding property of another

Accession is the acquiring of property by means of the addition of personal property of another. If materials owned by two people are combined to form one product, the person who owned the major part of the materials owns the product.

14-2f CONFUSION

confusion
inseparable mixing of goods of different owners

Confusion is the mixing of the personal property of different owners so that the parts belonging to each owner cannot be identified and separated. Grain, lumber, oil, and coal are examples of the kinds of property susceptible to confusion. The property, belonging to different owners, may be mixed by common consent, by accident, or by the willful act of some wrongdoer.

When confusion of the property occurs by common consent or by accident, each party will be deemed the owner of a proportionate part of the mass. If the confusion is willful, the title to the total mass passes to the innocent party, unless it can be clearly proven how much of the property of the one causing the confusion was mingled with that of the other person.

ETHICAL POINT

Why do you suppose a willful confusion results in title passing to the innocent party? Is this result based on the principles of ethics?

COURT CASE

FACTS: Mr. and Mrs. Strange owned a property and leased the rights to extract oil to W.R. Lindeman Operating Company, Inc. (Lindeman). After Mr. Strange's death, while visiting the property and oil operations, Mrs. Strange discovered that a separator intended to separate oil from wastewater was mis-set, allowing oil to flow in with the water. The mixed water flowed into operations on another property operated by Lindeman. Strange argued that Lindeman intentionally mis-set the separator so that more oil would be produced on the other property (at a presumably better fee for Lindeman) and in turn reducing the amount of funds due Strange. Strange argued that Lindeman was responsible for lost oil revenues because Lindeman willfully mixed Strange's oil with other oil.

OUTCOME: The court did not find willful misconduct, in part due to the fact that any oil misdirected into the wastewater would not have been produced or sold at all. It was unlikely Lindeman would intentionally divert oil to achieve zero profit, when it would otherwise have been produced through Strange's well, with a share of profit to Lindeman.

—*W.L. Lindeman Operating Company, Inc. v. Strange*, 256 S.W.3d 766 (Tex. App.)

14-2g CREATION

One may acquire personal property by **creation**. This applies to inventions, paintings, musical compositions, books, artwork, trade secrets, and other intellectual productions. This unique intangible personal property is called **intellectual property** because it is produced by human innovation and creativity. The law recognizes the value of this type of property and gives its creator title for a period of years through patents and copyrights. This property also can be protected by trademark and trade secret protection.

creation
bringing property into being

intellectual property
property produced by human innovation and creativity

Patents. The one who first applies for and obtains a **patent** gets title to the invention. Creation does not give absolute title; it gives only the right to obtain absolute title by means of a patent. Patents are granted for a term of 14 or 20 years from the date the patent is granted, depending on the type of patent. This means that no one else may use the invention for that time without the patent owner's permission.

patent
absolute title to invention for fourteen or twenty years

Copyrights. Songs, books, and other compositions fixed in any tangible medium of expression are protected by **copyright** from their creation. A copyright gives the owner the exclusive right to reproduce, copy, perform publicly, or display publicly the work or to authorize another to do so. Exceptions include for teaching,

copyright
exclusive rights given to author of songs, books, and compositions

research, or scholarship. Although the copyright provides protection from the time of creation of the work, the copyright must be registered for the owner to sue for infringement. Copyrights protect authors for their lifetime plus seventy years, as of January 1, 1978.

Trademarks. Symbols, names, and images such as logos that identify products or services can be protected by means of trademarks or trade names. A trademark can be established either by use or by registration with the federal government. Chapter 3 discusses when a trademark owner can protect use of the mark by legal action. Normally, trademarks are protected in the jurisdiction in which they are used; however, there are international trademark laws that try to protect marks in more than one jurisdiction.

trademark
word, symbol, device, or combination of them used to identify and distinguish the source of goods

Trade Secrets. Trade secrets are:

a. information
b. with economic value
c. not generally known, and
d. the subject of efforts to keep them secret.

trade secret
secret, economically valuable information

Trade secrets can be a wide variety of information such as formulas, plans, and customer and financial information. They differ from patents, copyrights, and trademarks because they are not known outside the business entity. One may not misappropriate the trade secrets of another. This means wrongfully acquiring, using, or disclosing them. Independently developing or discovering them is not misappropriation and is legal. The owner of a trade secret may sue to protect it under state law; however, theft or misappropriation of a trade secret is a federal crime.

The Internet has allowed the sharing of huge amounts of information, but it also allows individuals to violate laws protecting intellectual property by quickly and easily copying and distributing enormous amounts of intellectual property illegally. This is a serious problem for owners of intellectual property as billions of computer files are shared each month, and many of these are copyrighted files. Record companies and artists as well as movie studios have sued to try to stop the illegal sharing of copyrighted material, but the problem is a global one.

COURT CASE

FACTS: Grokster, Ltd. and StreamCast Networks Inc. distributed free software that allowed computer users to share files by means of peer-to-peer networks allowing users' computers to communicate directly with each other. Because almost 90 percent of the files available for sharing were copyrighted, software users mainly employed it to share copyrighted music and video files without permission of the copyright owners. Grokster and StreamCast knew their software was used to download copyrighted material and encouraged that use. The companies sold advertising that appeared on the computer screens of users of the software while downloading. Thus, the more downloading that occurred, the greater the companies' revenue. A group of movie studios and other copyright holders sued them.

OUTCOME: Grokster and StreamCast aimed to cause third-party copyright infringement and profit from it by distributing their software. The court held they could be held liable for the infringement of third parties.

—*Metro-Goldwyn-Mayer Studios Inc. v. Grokster, Ltd.*, 545 U.S. 913

14-2h LOST AND ABANDONED PROPERTY

The difference between **abandoned** and lost property lies in the intention of the owner to part with title to it. Property becomes abandoned when the owner actually discards it with no intention of reclaiming it.

A person who discovers and takes possession of property that has been abandoned and that has never been reclaimed by the owner acquires a right thereto. The finder of abandoned goods has title to them and thus has an absolute right to possession. To be abandoned, the property must be personal property. The prior owner must have relinquished ownership completely.

LO ②
Lost versus abandoned property

abandoned property
property discarded with no intention to reclaim

PREVIEW CASE REVISITED

FACTS: A van had gone through two fences to the middle of a privately owned field. A police officer arrived five hours later. The van was unlocked, and the officer looked for someone inside. Although no one was inside, there was a purse, briefcase, and partially consumed bottle of vodka. Opening the purse, the officer found a wallet, Tanja Rynhart's driver's license, and a small bag with a white, powdery substance in it. The owner of the field asked to have the van removed so the fences could be repaired. The van was towed, and when Rynhart went to pick it up, she was arrested for possession of cocaine. Rynhart alleged the evidence found as a result of the warrantless search of her van should be excluded. The state argued the search was legal because Rynhart had abandoned her property.

OUTCOME: By leaving her van and purse at an accident scene without any indication she intended to return, Rynhart had abandoned them, and the search was legal.

—*State v. Rynhart*, 125 P.3d 938 (Utah)

A number of states have enacted the Uniform Disposition of Unclaimed Property Act. This law provides that holders of property that the law presumes is abandoned must turn the property over to the state.

Property is considered to be lost when the owner, through negligence or accident, unintentionally leaves it somewhere. The finder of **lost property** has a right of possession against all but the true owner as long as the finder has not committed a wrong of some kind. No right of possession exists against the true owner except in instances when the owner cannot be found through reasonable diligence on the part of the finder, and certain statutory requirements are fulfilled.

lost property
property unintentionally left, with no intention to discard

In a few cases, the courts have held that if any employee finds property in the course of employment, the property belongs to the employer. Also, if property is mislaid, not lost, then the owner of the premises has first claim against all but the true owner. This especially applies to property left on trains and airplanes or in restaurants and hotels.

COURT CASE

FACTS: Thinking a house was abandoned, Steven Ingram entered it without permission. He found some personal property and took it. He was convicted of burglarizing a home. He appealed, claiming he had made a mistake thinking the house was no longer a home and that he could take the personal property.

OUTCOME: The court said that because real estate could not be abandoned, Ingram's entry was illegal. Taking any personal property was wrongful, so he could not be the owner of it.

—*Ingram v. State*, 261 S.W.3d 749 (Tex. Ct. App.)

LO ③
Nature and examples of bailment

bailment
transfer of possession of personal property on condition that property will be returned

bailor
person who gives up possession of bailed property

bailee
person in possession of bailed property

14-3 Bailments

The transfer of possession, but not the title, of personal property by one party, usually the owner, to another party is called a **bailment**. The transfer is on condition that the same property will be returned or appropriately accounted for, either to the owner or to a designated person at a future date. The person who gives up possession, the **bailor**, is usually the owner of the property. The **bailee** accepts possession of the property but not the title.

Some typical transactions resulting in a bailment include:

1. A motorist leaving a car with the garage for repairs
2. A family storing its furniture in a warehouse
3. A student borrowing a tuxedo to wear to a formal dance
4. A neighbor leaving a pet with a friend for safekeeping while going on vacation

14-4 The Bailment Agreement

A true bailment is based on, and governed by, a contract—express or implied—between the bailor and the bailee. When a person checks a coat upon entering a restaurant, nothing might be said, but the bailment is implied by the acts of the two parties. A bailment can be created by the conduct of the parties, whether spoken or written.

COURT CASE

FACTS: Computer hackers stole credit and debit card information from Target. A group of customers brought suit against Target claiming, among other things, that Target's receipt of the information from the customers was a form of bailment.

OUTCOME: The customers could not allege that they intended that their property be returned to them. There was no bailment.

—*In re Target Corp. Data Sec. Breach Litigation,*
2014 WL 7192478 (D. Minn.)

14-5 Delivery and Acceptance

A bailment can be established only if delivery occurs accompanied by acceptance of personal property. The delivery and acceptance may be actual or constructive. Actual delivery and acceptance results when the goods themselves are delivered and accepted. When no physical delivery of the goods occurs, constructive delivery and acceptance results when control over the goods is delivered and accepted.

constructive bailment
bailment imposed when a person controls lost property

A **constructive bailment** arises when someone finds and takes possession of lost property. The owner does not actually deliver the property to the finder, but the law holds this to be a bailment. A constructive bailment also can occur when property of one person is washed ashore. The finder becomes a bailee if some overt act of control over the property occurs.

14-6 Return of the Bailed Property

In some cases, a bailment may exist when the recipient does not return the actual goods. In the case of fungible goods, such as wheat, a bailment exists if the owner expects to receive a like quantity and quality of goods. If the goods are to be processed in some way, a bailment arises if the product made from the original goods is to be returned.

When a consignment exists, the property may be sold by the holder and not returned to the original owner. Finally, when property is left for repair, the property returned should be repaired and therefore not be identical to the property left. In each case, a bailment arises although the identical property is not returned.

COURT CASE

FACTS: FVTS was an authorized dealer of GMC trucks, and Wolverine sold customized fire trucks and other utility vehicles. Wolverine contracted to purchase a truck from FVTS, but delivery was delayed, and Wolverine later informed FVTS it was no longer able to pay for the truck. When the truck was later available, FVTS and Wolverine agreed that Wolverine would take possession of the truck as a demonstrator. No payment was made, and no paper title was issued to Wolverine. In Wolverine's later bankruptcy, the trustee claimed that the truck was an asset of Wolverine under the contract.

OUTCOME: The court found that the contract between FVTS and Wolverine had been abandoned. Instead, since both FVTS and Wolverine anticipated a sale to a third party, a consignment existed.

—*In re Wolverine Fire Apparatus Co. of Sherwood Michigan*, 465 B.R. 808 (E.D. Wisc.)

14-7 Types of Bailments

LO ④
Types of bailments

The three types of bailments include:

1. Bailments for the sole benefit of the bailor
2. Bailments for the sole benefit of the bailee
3. Mutual-benefit bailments

14-7a BAILMENTS FOR THE SOLE BENEFIT OF THE BAILOR

If one holds another's personal property only for the benefit of the owner, a bailment for the sole benefit of the bailor exists. This occurs when a person takes care of a pet for a vacationing friend, for example. The bailee receives no benefits or compensation.

Such a bailment also arises when a person asks a friend to store some personal property. For example, a friend may keep a piano until the owner finds a larger apartment. The friend may not play the piano or otherwise receive any benefits of ownership during the bailment. The bailee may only use the property if the use will benefit or preserve it.

A constructive bailment is a bailment for the sole benefit of the bailor. The loser is the bailor, and the finder is the bailee. In a bailment for the sole benefit of the bailor, most states hold that the bailee need exercise slight care and is liable only for gross negligence with respect to the property.

COURT CASE

FACTS: Edward Robinson was employed by National Autotech and was required to provide his own tools. He took a leave of absence for a work-related injury and was allowed to leave his toolbox containing his tools at Autotech. About a year later, while Robinson was still on leave, a person claiming to be Robinson went to Autotech and said he was there to pick up his tools. The man knew which toolbox was Robinson's without assistance, acted like he knew what he was doing, and did nothing to raise suspicions. The man had a set of keys to open the toolbox. Finding that his toolbox had been removed from Autotech without his permission, Robinson sued.

OUTCOME: Because Autotech derived no benefit from the tools being left, the arrangement was a bailment for the sole benefit of the bailor. The fact that the man knew which toolbox was Robinson's and had keys for it justified Autotech in allowing him to take it.

—*Robinson v. National Autotech Inc.*, 117 S.W.3d 37 (Tex. Ct. App.)

14-7b BAILMENTS FOR THE SOLE BENEFIT OF THE BAILEE

If the bailee holds and uses another's personal property, and the owner of the property receives no benefit or compensation, a bailment for the sole benefit of the bailee exists. This type of bailment arises when someone's personal property is borrowed.

The bailee must exercise great care over the property. However, any loss or damage due to no fault of the bailee falls on the owner. If Petras borrows Walker's diamond ring to wear to a dance and is robbed on the way to the dance, the loss falls on Walker, the owner, as long as Petras was not negligent.

The bailee must be informed of any known defects in the bailed property. If the bailee is injured by reason of such a defect, the bailor who failed to inform the bailee is liable for damages.

COURT CASE

FACTS: Garofoli contracted with Whiskey Island Partners for storage of his sailboat. Garofoli docked the sailboat next to Whiskey Island's lift equipment, but due to mechanical problems and the ensuing backup, Garofoli's boat was not moved to storage by the time Superstorm Sandy moved through a few days later. Garofoli sued Whiskey Island for the damage on a bailment cause of action.

OUTCOME: A bailee promises to return bailed property undamaged at the termination of the bailment. Whiskey Island failed to exercise the ordinary care it was required to provide.

—*Garofoli v. Whiskey Island Partners, Ltd.*, 25 N.E.3d 400 (Ohio App.)

14-7c MUTUAL-BENEFIT BAILMENTS

Most bailments exist for the mutual benefit of both the bailor and the bailee. Some common bailments of this type include a TV left to be repaired; laundry and dry cleaning contracts; and the rental of personal property, such as an automobile or furniture. The bailor of rented property must furnish safe property, not just inform the bailee of known defects.

In mutual-benefit bailments, the bailee renders a service and charges for the service. This applies to all repair jobs, laundry, dry cleaning, and storage bailments. The bailee has a lien against the bailed property for the charges. If these charges are not paid after a reasonable time, the bailee may advertise and sell the property for the charges. Any money remaining after paying expenses and the charges must be turned over to the bailor.

A bailee rendering services may receive a benefit other than a fee or monetary payment. For example, a skating rink may offer to check shoes for its customers without charging for the service. A mutual-benefit bailment exists. The customer (bailor) receives storage service, and the skating rink (bailee) gains the benefit of a neater, safer customer area.

In mutual-benefit bailments, the standard of care required of the bailee for the property is reasonable care under the circumstances. Such care means the degree of care that a reasonable person would exercise in order to protect the property from harm. The bailee is liable for negligence.

COURT CASE

FACTS: Felice Jasphy took three fur coats to Cedar Lane Furs for cleaning and storage. Three years earlier, the coats had been appraised at $18,995. Above the signature line on the receipt that Jasphy signed was the statement, "I . . . agree that Cedar Lane Furs liability for loss or damage from any cause whatsoever, including their own negligence . . . is limited to the declared valuation." Jasphy was not told of the limitation, asked for a value for the furs, or given room on the receipt to indicate a valuation.

The next day, a fire caused by an iron left plugged in overnight at Cedar destroyed all the coats that had not been put in the vault. When she was not reimbursed for her loss, Jasphy sued.

OUTCOME: The court said Cedar was liable for its negligence in failing to put the coats in the vault and unplug the iron.

—*Jasphy v. Osinsky*, 834 A.2d 426 (N.J. Super. Ct. App. Div.)

14-7d SPECIAL MUTUAL-BENEFIT BAILMENTS

A mutual-benefit bailment includes the deposit of personal property as security for some debt or obligation. Tangible property left as security, such as livestock, a radio, or an automobile, is a **pawn**. Intangible property left as security, such as notes, bonds, or stock certificates, is a **pledge**.

pawn
tangible personal property left as security for a debt

pledge
intangible property serving as security for a debt

14-8 Conversion of Bailed Property by the Bailee

conversion
unauthorized exercise of ownership rights

Not being the owner of the property, a bailee normally has no right to convert the property. **Conversion** is the unauthorized exercise of ownership rights over another's property. Thus, the bailee may not sell, lease, or even use the bailed property as security for a loan, and one who purchases such property from a bailee ordinarily does not get good title to it.

However, when the purpose of the bailment is to have the property sold, and the proceeds remitted to the bailor, the bailee has the power to sell all goods regardless of any restriction on the right to sell, unless the buyer knows of the restriction.

A bailor may mislead an innocent third person into believing that the bailee owns the bailed property. In this situation, the bailee may convey good title.

QUESTIONS

1. a. What is property?

   b. May only the owner use property?

2. What is the most common method of acquiring personal property? What other methods are there?

3. Can personal property be created? If so how?

4. How may trade secrets be misappropriated, and how may a business legally acquire them?

5. What difference does it make whether confusion of property is willful or by accident?

6. What is the key factor in determining whether property is lost or abandoned?

7. If the owner of a car has it in B's garage for protection from the weather, and then later gives the keys to C with instructions to get the car, is there a bailment?

8. Give an example of a bailment where the bailee is not expected to return the bailed property in its original condition.

9. What standard of care is required of a bailee in a bailment for the sole benefit of the bailor?

10. What is conversion?

CASE PROBLEMS

LO ③

1. Charlie operated a restaurant and pub, offering the customary variety of fried, greasy foods. From time to time, Charlie (or his employee) took the accumulated dirty bar rags down the street to Egypt Laundromat to wash and dry them. On one occasion, an employee washed the rags, started them in the dryer, and then left the Laundromat. Some minutes later, the rags began to smolder and eventually burst into flames, causing damage not only to the rags, but to the dryer and the Laundromat. Egypt Laundromat argued the relationship was a bailment for mutual benefit, and as a result, the restaurant, as bailee, owed a duty of ordinary care to Egypt Laundromat, as bailor, to ensure its laundry did not spontaneously combust in the dryer. Was Charlie liable for the cost of the fire?

LO ①

2. During her life, Bernice David purchased several subordinated certificates of indebtedness through West Baton Rouge Credit. Some were purchased in her name alone, some jointly with her daughter, Veronica, or son, Donald. In every case, Bernice supplied all the purchase funds. After Bernice's death, Donald consolidated seven certificates which had been titled in both his and Bernice's names,

CASE PROBLEMS (CONTINUED)

with a total principal sum of $97,749.20, into one new certificate in his name only. Veronica claimed that the certificates were property of Bernice's estate, and that Donald did not have authority to convert them to his own name because ownership had not legally transferred to him. Were the certificates registered in Bernice and Donald's name a gift to Donald?

3. Johnson-Schmitt gave several dogs to Dispenza to find good homes for them. Dispenza did not find good homes for them, but rather kept them on his property in such deplorable conditions that they were eventually seized by the sheriff, turned over to the local SPCA, and adopted out to other families. Johnson-Schmitt later sued the county claiming an unlawful conversion of her property (the dogs). Did Johnson-Schmitt have any property right in the dogs at the time they were seized? **LO** ④

4. Starko was one of many pharmacists providing prescription drugs to Medicare patients. New Mexico law provided that pharmacists would be reimbursed "the wholesale cost of the lesser expensive therapeutic equivalent drug generally available in New Mexico plus a reasonable dispensing fee of at least three dollars [and] sixty-five cents." As time passed, New Mexico, like virtually every other state, transitioned to a managed care program for pharmacy services. Starko claimed that the managed care program paid significantly less than the statutory minimum. Was the right to receive $3.65 per prescription property of the pharmacists? **LO** ②

5. Foster owned a prize-winning stallion and entered into an agreement with Colorado State University's Equine Reproduction Laboratory (Lab) to provide certain reproductive treatments. The Lab collected several "straws" of semen and stored them in its specialized facility, pursuant to a fee paid by Foster. The Lab and most of its contents were later destroyed by fire, and Foster sued the Lab for failure to exercise reasonable care. The Lab argued that there was no contract. Was the Lab liable for the lost straws? **LO** ③, ④

6. High Mountain, LLC managed condominium units owned by John and Diane Mullin. It would collect and deposit rental income and send the Mullins the net rental income after High Mountain's fees and expenses were deducted. The Mullins sued High Mountain for failure to forward $32,989.36 in rental income and obtained a judgment, but High Mountain declared bankruptcy. Travelers Indemnity Company of Connecticut insured High Mountain, so the Mullins sued Travelers for the amount of the judgment. Travelers argued that it was not obligated to pay the default judgment because the policy covered only money High Mountain was legally obligated to pay because of property damage to which the policy applied. The policy defined "property damage" as loss of use of tangible property that is not physically injured. Did the Mullins suffer a loss of use of tangible property that was not physically injured when High Mountain did not forward the rental payments to them? **LO** ①

7. Michael LaPlace owned a horse named Park Me In First. He entered into a verbal agreement with Pierre Briere Quarter Horses for the care, maintenance, and training of his horses, which, two years later, included Park Me In First. Briere stable was responsible for providing shelter, food, water, training, and grooming to the horses when they were there. Briere stable would also arrange for shoeing and veterinary care for horses at the stable. LaPlace would from time to time remove the horse from the stable in order to ride it and take it to horse shows. While LaPlace was at a horse show, Park Me In First died while being exercised at Briere stable. LaPlace sued the stable, asserting breach of a bailment agreement. Briere said there was no bailment because he did not have complete and exclusive control over the horse. Briere argued that LaPlace had complete access and control over the horse; he would ride it and transport it to shows at his discretion at any time. Briere said at most there was joint control of the horse between the stable and LaPlace, hence no bailment. Was there a bailment? **LO** ③

CASE PROBLEMS (CONTINUED)

LO ②   8. While Tait and her boyfriend were spending the day at Chincoteague National Wildlife Refuge, they came upon a large fishing boat that had run aground, half in the water, half in the sand. There were already a number of people playing on and around the boat. Tait decided to cut a length of rope from a line, one end of which was in the sand and the other in the water. She then noticed a buoy floating in the water, not attached to the boat, but bearing the same name as the boat. She also picked up the buoy before driving away. A National Park Service Ranger later asked Tait whether he could look into the bed of her truck. The Ranger seized the rope and buoy and cited Tait for removal of private property in violation of federal law. Was Tait entitled to cut the rope and pick up the buoy?

LO ①   9. Patricia Amich and John Adiutori were married in February. In May, Patricia petitioned for a declaration of the invalidity of the marriage. She had left their home but failed to remove her jewelry, which was in a jewelry box in the home. John still lived in the home. On May 11, Patricia went to the home to remove her personal belongings, but she did not remove the jewelry box. That was the last time she saw the box. While living there, John had last seen it on June 14, before he was removed from the property. After he was removed, Patricia obtained a key, but the jewelry box could not be found. Was John a bailee of the jewelry, and, if so, what kind of bailment was it?

LO ③   10. Rimma Vaks and her husband arranged for a consignment sale of their furniture with Denise Ryan. The six-page agreement included descriptions of the items to be sold, the commission, and a statement that "after thirty days, any unsold or unclaimed items would become the property of Ryan without notice or payment." Approximately seventy-five percent of the items were sold on six auction days. After Vaks failed to pick up the remaining items within thirty days of the final auction date, Ryan donated them to charity. Vaks claimed breach of bailment contract with respect to the donated items. Was there really a bailment, a consignment, or a contract for sale?

Special Bailments

CHAPTER 15

LEARNING OBJECTIVES

① Explain what a carrier does, and name the two categories of carriers.

② Identify the exceptions to the normal rule of a common carrier being an insurer of the safety of goods.

③ Discuss the difference between hotelkeepers and boardinghouse keepers, explaining the special duties and liabilities of hotelkeepers.

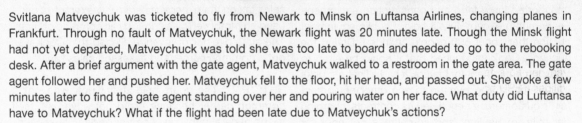

PREVIEW CASE

Svitlana Matveychuk was ticketed to fly from Newark to Minsk on Luftansa Airlines, changing planes in Frankfurt. Through no fault of Matveychuk, the Newark flight was 20 minutes late. Though the Minsk flight had not yet departed, Matveychuck was told she was too late to board and needed to go to the rebooking desk. After a brief argument with the gate agent, Matveychuk walked to a restroom in the gate area. The gate agent followed her and pushed her. Matveychuk fell to the floor, hit her head, and passed out. She woke a few minutes later to find the gate agent standing over her and pouring water on her face. What duty did Luftansa have to Matveychuk? What if the flight had been late due to Matveychuk's actions?

There are several types of mutual-benefit bailments in which the bailee, under the common law, is held to a higher-than-normal standard of care for the bailed property. These bailments, sometimes called *extraordinary bailments*, include common carriers and hotelkeepers.

15-1 Carriers

LO ①
Categories of carriers

A **carrier** engages in the business of transporting either goods or persons, or both. A carrier of goods is a bailee. Because a carrier charges a fee for such service, the bailment exists for the mutual benefit of both parties.

carrier
transporter of goods, people, or both

15-1a CLASSIFICATION OF CARRIERS

Carriers are usually classified into two groups:

1. Private carriers

2. Common carriers

15-1b PRIVATE CARRIERS

private carrier
carrier that transports under special arrangements for a fee

A **private carrier**, for a fee, undertakes to transport goods or persons. It transports only under special instances and special arrangements and may refuse service that is unprofitable. The usual types of private carriers are trucks, moving vans, ships, and delivery services. A carrier owned by the shipper, such as a truck from a fleet owned and operated by an industrial firm for transporting its own products, is a private carrier.

common carrier
one that undertakes to transport without discrimination for all who apply for service

Private carriers' contracts for transporting goods are mutual-benefit bailments, and the general law of bailments governs them. They are liable only for loss from the failure to exercise ordinary care. By contract, a private carrier may further limit liability for loss to the goods.

COURT CASE

FACTS: Cook Tractor Co. Inc. bought, sold, and transported large farm and construction equipment. Every month except July, it held a public equipment auction that about 500 people attended. During the auctions, Cook announced that it could be hired to transport equipment for buyers. It had a fleet of trucks it used for hauling purchased and other equipment for its customers. It negotiated its contracts, charging per mile for hauling, and sometimes per hour for loading. It had no hauling income in July. It did not advertise as a hauler of goods, but its employees regularly hauled equipment, using trucks with the company's name and phone number on the side.

Cook bought motor vehicle parts and did not pay sales tax on them, because state law exempted parts used on motor vehicles engaged as common carriers. The state director of revenue alleged that Cook was not a common carrier and assessed sales tax.

OUTCOME: The court held that Cook was not a common carrier because it did not advertise itself to the general public as a carrier or offer its services without discrimination at an approved rate.

—*Cook Tractor Co. Inc. v. Director of Revenue*, 187 S.W.3d 870 (Mo.)

15-1c COMMON CARRIERS

consignor
one who ships by common carrier

consignee
one to whom goods are shipped

bill of lading
receipt and contract between a consignor and a carrier

A **common carrier** undertakes to transport goods or people, without discrimination, for all who apply for that service. The goods to be transported must be proper, and facilities must be available for transport. One who ships goods by a common carrier is called the **consignor**; the one to whom the goods are shipped is called the **consignee**; and the receipt and contract between the carrier and the consignor is called a **bill of lading**.

A common carrier must serve, without discrimination, all who apply. If it fails to do so, it is liable for any damages resulting from such a refusal. A common carrier may, however, refuse service because the service is not one for which it is properly equipped. For example, an express company does not have to accept lumber for transportation. A common carrier also may refuse service if its equipment is inadequate to accommodate customers in excess of the normal demands. A common carrier of people is not required to transport (1) any person who requires unusual attention, such as an invalid, unless that person is accompanied by an attendant; (2) any person who intends or is likely to cause harm to the carrier or the passengers; or (3) any person who is likely to be offensive to passengers, such as an intoxicated person.

The usual types of common carriers of people are trains, buses, airplanes, ships, and subways. Common carriers are public monopolies and are subject to regulations as to their prices, services, equipment, and other operational policies. This public regulation is in lieu of competition as a determinant of their prices and services.

15-2 Liability of Common Carriers of Goods

LO ②
When a common carrier is not an insurer

Although common carriers of goods and common carriers of people are alike in that they must serve all who apply, they differ sharply in their liability for loss. Common carriers of goods are insurers of the safety of the transported goods and are liable for loss or damage regardless of fault, unless the carrier can prove the loss arises from:

1. Acts of God
2. Acts of a public authority
3. Inherent nature of the goods
4. Acts of the shipper
5. Acts of a public enemy

These exceptions do not excuse the carrier if the carrier failed to safeguard the goods from harm.

15-2a ACTS OF GOD

The carrier is not liable for unusual natural occurrences such as floods, snowstorms, tornadoes, lightning, or fire caused by lightning, as these are considered acts of God. Normal weather, such as a rainstorm, is not.

15-2b ACTS OF A PUBLIC AUTHORITY

An act of a public authority occurs if public officials seize illicit goods, or if health officials seize goods that are a menace to health. The carrier is not liable for such loss.

15-2c INHERENT NATURE OF THE GOODS

The carrier is not liable for damage due to the inherent nature of the goods, such as decay of vegetables, fermentation or evaporation of liquids, and death of livestock as a result of natural causes or the fault of other animals.

15-2d ACTS OF THE SHIPPER

Acts of the shipper that can cause loss include misdirection of the merchandise, failure to indicate fragile contents, and improper packing. If improper packing is noticeable, the carrier should refuse to accept the goods because it is still liable for damage. If improper packing is latent and cannot be noticed on ordinary observation, the shipper, not the carrier, will be liable because of the improper packing.

15-2e ACTS OF A PUBLIC ENEMY

Organized warfare or border excursions of foreign bandits constitute acts of a public enemy. Mobs, strikers, and rioters are not classified as public enemies in interpreting this exclusion.

COURT CASE

FACTS: Kraze Trucking, LLC (Kraze) delivered a truckload of kosher cheddar cheese to Oshkosh Storage Co. (Oshkosh). When the driver arrived at Oshkosh, the receptionist gave him an instruction sheet noting that Oshkosh reserved the right to reject a load of food products for which the seal had been broken. In addition, signs in the check-in area instructed drivers NOT to break the seal before it was verified by Oshkosh staff. Kraze's driver admitted that he broke the seal and opened the trailer doors after he arrived at the storage facility, but before it could be inspected by Oshkosh. Oshkosh rejected the load. Oshkosh claimed the value of the cheese was reduced 25 percent due to the absence of a verified seal.

OUTCOME: The court listed the five exceptions to a common carrier's liability for damage to goods and found none of them applied. Kraze was liable for the lost value.

—*Oshkosh Storage Co. v. Kraze Trucking, LLC,*
2014 WL 7011850 (E.D. Wisc.)

15-2f CONTRACTUAL LIMITATIONS ON LIABILITY

A common carrier may attempt to limit or escape the extraordinary liability imposed on it by law, often by a contract between the shipper and the carrier. As the written evidence of the contract, the bill of lading sets out the limitations on the carriers' liability. Because the shipper does not have any direct voice in the preparation of the bill of lading, the law requires every carrier to have its printed bill of lading form approved by a government agency before adoption. This restricts the way in which liability can be limited by the bill of lading.

In addition to uniform limitations set out in the printed form of a bill of lading, additional limitations may be added that the shipper and the carrier may agree on. The Federal Bills of Lading Act governs this matter as to interstate shipments, and the Uniform Commercial Code controls with respect to intrastate shipments. In general, the limitations on the carrier's liability permitted by these acts fall into the following classes:

1. A carrier may limit its loss by agreement to a specified sum or to a specified percentage of the value of the goods. However, a carrier must give the shipper the choice of shipping at lower rates subject to the limited liability or at a higher rate without limitation of liability.

COURT CASE

FACTS: Seagate Technology, LLC, contracted with UPS Supply Chain Solutions Inc. (UPS) for global transportation services on air, land, and sea. The Global Logistics Service Provider Agreement limited UPS's liability to $100,000, except in the case of gross negligence. A truck with nearly $500,000 worth of disk drives was subsequently stolen in transit. For what amount of damages was UPS liable?

OUTCOME: The court confirmed that a carrier may limit its liability to a specified sum, and UPS's liability was limited.

—*UPS Supply Chain Solutions, Inc. v. Megatrux Transport, Inc.*, 750 F.3d 1282 (11th Cir.)

2. Most states permit carriers to exempt themselves from liability because of certain named hazards. The most common named hazards include fire, leakage, breakage, spoilage, and losses due to riots, strikes, mobs, and robbers. Some states specifically prohibit an exemption for loss by fire. These exemptions must be specifically enumerated in the bill of lading or shipper's receipt. The exemptions are not effective if the loss is due to carrier negligence.

3. Delay in transportation of livestock may result in serious losses or extra expense for feed. Most states allow some form of limitation on the carrier's liability if the loss is due to a delay over which the carrier has no control.

In those cases in which the carrier is held liable only for loss due to negligence, the Uniform Commercial Code provides for liability only for ordinary negligence.

15-2g DURATION OF THE SPECIAL LIABILITY

The carrier's high degree of liability lasts only during transportation. If the goods are delivered to the carrier ready for shipment and are received from the carrier promptly on arrival, the goods are regarded as being transported during the entire transaction.

15-2h CARRIER AS BAILEE BEFORE TRANSPORTATION

Frequently, goods are delivered to the carrier before they are ready for transportation. The carrier is liable only as a mutual-benefit bailee until the goods are ready for transportation.

15-2i CARRIER AS BAILEE AFTER TRANSPORTATION

When the goods arrive at their destination, the consignee has a reasonable time to accept delivery of the goods. Railroads need only place the goods in the freight depot, or, in the case of car lots, set the car on a siding where the consignee can unload the goods. If the consignee does not call for the goods within a reasonable time after being notified by the carrier that the goods have arrived, the carrier is liable only as a mutual-benefit bailee.

15-2j CONNECTING CARRIERS

The initial carrier and the final, or terminal, carrier are each liable for a common carrier loss occurring on the line of a connecting carrier. Whichever of these carriers has been held liable may then compel the connecting carrier to reimburse it.

15-2k BILLS OF LADING

The bill of lading not only sets forth the contract between the shipper and the carrier but also is a document of title. Transferring a bill of lading may transfer title to the goods described in it to the purchaser. There are two types of bills of lading:

1. Straight, or nonnegotiable, bills of lading
2. Order, or negotiable, bills of lading

straight bill of lading contract requiring delivery of shipped goods to consignee only

Straight Bills of Lading. Under a **straight bill of lading** (see Illustration 15-1), the consignee alone is designated as the one to whom the goods are to be delivered.

ILLUSTRATION 15-1 Bill of Lading

21040

ALWAYS LIST HAZARDOUS MATERIALS FIRST IN DESCRIPTION OF ARTICLES COLUMN.

STRAIGHT BILL OF LADING - SHORT FORM - Original-Not Negotiable

RECEIVED, subject to the classification and tariffs in effect on the date of issue of this Original Bill of Lading

NOT to be used for ORDER NOTIFY SHIPMENTS. DATE

BIG BEAR Transfer Company

BIG BEAR TRANSFER COMPANY

NOTE: DRIVER AFIX PRO NUMBER LABEL HERE

(NAME OF CARRIER) (SCAC)

CUSTOMER P.O. NO. ROUTE SHIPPER'S NUMBER

TO: CONSIGNEE on COD shipments the letters 'COD' must appear before consignee's name. | FROM: SHIPPER

STREET | STREET

(DESTINATION) CITY, STATE, ZIP | (ORIGIN) CITY, STATE, ZIP

C.O.D. AMT $ ________ FEE PPD ☐ COL ☐ IS CUSTOMER'S CHECK ACCEPTABLE FOR C.O.D? YES ☐ NO ☐

NO.SHIPPING UNITS	(X) HM	RATE AND CLASS	KIND OF PACKAGING, DESCRIPTION OF ARTICLES, SPECIAL MARKS AND EXPECTIONS (LIST HAZARDOUS MATERIALS FIRST)	WEIGHT LBS (Subject to Corrections)	NOTE: Where the rate is dependent on value, shippers are required to state specifically in writing the agreed or declared value of the property. The agreed or declared value of the property is hereby specifically stated by the shipper to be no: exceeding $ ______ per ______
					Subject to Section 7 of the conditions, if this shipment is to be delivered to the consignee without recourse on the consignor, the consignor shall sign the following statement: The carrier shall not make delivery of this shipment without payment of freight and all other lawful charges. ______ (Signature of Consignor)
	◄ TOTAL		TOTAL ►		FREIGHT CHARGES WRITE IN PREPAID OR COLLECT

RECEIVED, subject to the classifications and tariffs in effect on the date of the issue of this Bill of Lading, the property described above in apparent good order, except as noted (contents and condition of contents of packages unknown), marked, consigned and destined as indicated above which said carried (the word carrier being understood throughout this contract as meaning any person or corporation in possession of the property under the contract) agrees to carry to its usual place of delivery at said destination, if on its route, otherwise to deliver to another carrier on the route to said destination. It is mutally agreed as to each carrier of all or any of, said property over all or any to all the bill of lading terms and conditions in the governing classification on the date of shipment.

Shipper hereby certifies that he is familier with all the bill of lading terms and conditions in the governing classification and the said terms and conditions are hereby agreed to by the shipper and accepted for himself and his assigns.

This is to certify that the above-named materials are properly classified, described, packaged, marked and labeled, and are in proper condition for transportation according to the applicable regulations of the department of Transportation	SHIPPER:	**BIG BEAR TRANSFER COMPANY**	
	PER:	DRIVER	TRAILER
		PIECES	DATE

MARK "X" IN "HM" COLUMN FOR HAZARDOUS MATERIALS.

The consignee's rights may be transferred to another, but the third party normally obtains no greater rights than the shipper or the consignee had. However, if the bill of lading contains a recital as to the contents, quantity, or weight of the goods, the carrier is bound to a bona fide transferee as to the accuracy of these descriptions unless the bill of lading itself indicates that the contents of packages are unknown to the carrier.

The assignee should notify the carrier of the assignment when the original consignee sells the goods before receipt. The carrier is justified in delivering goods to the consignee if it has not received notice of assignment.

COURT CASE

FACTS: Regal-Beloit Corporation (RBC) delivered goods to Kawasaki, in China, for shipment. The bills of lading covered transport through the entire course of shipment, both over the ocean and to several inland U.S. destinations. The bills each included a clause stating that Japanese courts had jurisdiction over the shipment. The cargo was allegedly destroyed while being transported by Union Pacific inside the U.S., near Tyrone, Oklahoma. RBC sued Union Pacific, in the United States, for damages.

OUTCOME: Even though Union Pacific did not itself issue a bill of lading, the terms of the shipment were covered in the through bill of lading issued by Kawasaki. The court found that parties could use terms in a bill of lading to determine jurisdiction over any disputes.

—*Kawasaki Kisen Kaisha Ltd. v. Regal-Beloit Corporation*, 130 S.Ct. 2433

Order Bills of Lading. The **bill of lading** may set forth that the goods are shipped to a designated consignee or order, or merely "to the bearer" of the bill of lading. In such case, the bill of lading is an **order**, or negotiable, **bill of lading** and must be presented to the carrier before the carrier can safely deliver the goods. If the goods are delivered to the named consignee, and later a bona fide innocent purchaser of the order bill of lading demands the goods, the carrier is liable to the holder of the bill of lading.

bill of lading
receipt and contract between a consignor and a carrier

order bill of lading
contract allowing delivery of shipped goods to bearer

15-2l COMMON CARRIERS OF PEOPLE

Common carriers of people have the right to prescribe the place and time of the payment of fares, usually before boarding the plane, train, bus, or other vehicle. They also have the right to prescribe reasonable rules of conduct for transporting passengers. They may stop the vehicle and remove any passenger who refuses to pay the fare or whose conduct offends the other passengers. They also have the right to reserve certain coaches, seats, or space for special classes of passengers, as in the case of first-class seats in the forward cabin of aircraft.

15-2m LIABILITY OF COMMON CARRIERS OF PEOPLE

The liability of a carrier for the passengers' safety begins as soon as passengers enter the terminal or waiting platform and does not end until they have left the terminal at the end of the journey. Unlike a common carrier of goods, a common carrier of people is not an insurer. In most states, a carrier must provide only ordinary care while passengers are in the terminal; however, some states have modified this rule. When passengers board the bus, train, plane, or other vehicle, the highest degree of care consistent with practical operation is required. Once a passenger disembarks, the carrier must exercise ordinary care to see that the passenger is not endangered by the carrier starting up again. However, even when the highest degree of care is required, a carrier of people is only liable if it has been negligent.

COURT CASE

FACTS: While a passenger in a city bus in Shreveport, Roger Lewis was injured when the bus left the road and struck a steel utility pole. He sued the city, which argued it was not liable because the bus driver had suddenly and unexpectedly lost consciousness, causing the bus to swerve.

OUTCOME: The court held that although not an insurer of its passengers' safety, the city was liable for the slightest negligence. Lewis was able to recover.

—*Lewis v. City of Shreveport*, 985 So.2d 1249
(La. Ct. App.)

15-2n DUTIES OF COMMON CARRIERS OF PEOPLE

A carrier's duties to its passengers consist of:

1. Duty to provide reasonable accommodations and services
2. Duty to provide reasonable protection to its passengers

Duty to Provide Reasonable Accommodations and Services.
A carrier is required to furnish adequate and reasonable service. A passenger is not necessarily entitled to a seat; however, the carrier must make a reasonable effort to provide sufficient facilities so that the public can be accommodated, which may be merely standing room. A passenger may make an express reservation that requires the carrier to provide a seat. The carrier must notify the passenger of the arrival of the train, bus, or airplane at the destination and stop long enough to permit the passenger to disembark.

Duty to Provide Reasonable Protection to Its Passengers.
Common carriers of passengers need not insure the absolute safety of passengers but must exercise extraordinary care to protect them. Any injury to the passenger by an employee or fellow passengers subjects the carrier to liability for damages, provided the injured passenger is without blame. The vehicle must stop at a safe place for alighting, and passengers must be assisted when necessary for alighting.

PREVIEW CASE REVISITED

FACTS: Svitlana Matveychuk was ticketed to fly from Newark to Minsk, on Luftansa Airlines, changing planes in Frankfurt. Through no fault of Matveychuk, the Newark flight was 20 minutes late. Though the Minsk flight had not yet departed, Matveychuck was told she was too late to board and needed to go to the rebooking desk. After a brief argument with the gate agent, Matveychuck walked to a restroom in the gate area. The gate agent followed her and pushed her. Matveychuck fell to the floor, hit her head, and passed out. She woke a few minutes later to find the gate agent standing over her and pouring water on her face.

OUTCOME: The court affirmed that the common carrier is liable for bodily injury that takes "place on board the aircraft, or in the course of any of the operations of embarking or disembarking." Matveychuck had not missed her connection through her own fault, she was still in the secure area reserved for international travelers, and at a restroom in the gate area.

—*Matveychuk v. Deutsche Lufthansa, AG,* 2010 WL 3540921 (E.D. N.Y.)

15-2o BAGGAGE

Baggage consists of those articles of personal convenience or necessity usually carried by passengers for their personal use at some time during the trip. Articles carried by travelers on similar missions and destinations constitute the test. For example, fishing paraphernalia is baggage for a person who expects to go fishing while away, but not for the ordinary traveler. Any article carried for one who is not a passenger is not baggage. A reasonable amount of baggage may be carried as a part of the cost of the passenger's fare. The carrier may charge extra for baggage in excess of a reasonable amount.

Historically, the liability of a common carrier for checked baggage was the same as that of a common carrier of goods—an insurer of the baggage with the five exceptions previously mentioned. The liability for baggage retained in the possession of the traveler was only for lack of reasonable care or for willful misconduct of its agents or employees. However, today federal law allows carriers to limit their liability for loss of baggage to a fixed maximum amount. This amount will be stated on the ticket. Such limitations are binding on passengers.

baggage
articles necessary for personal convenience while traveling

15-3 Hotelkeepers

A **hotelkeeper** regularly engages in the business of offering lodging to all transient people. The hotelkeeper also may supply food or entertainment, but providing lodging to transients is the primary business.

A person who provides rooms or room and board to permanent lodgers, but does not behave as able and willing to accommodate transients, is not a hotelkeeper. Such people are **boardinghouse keepers**, and the laws of hotelkeepers do not apply to them. The owner of a tourist home is not a hotelkeeper if the establishment does not advertise as willing to accommodate all transients who apply. Most people who run hotels and motels are hotelkeepers. A hotel that caters to both permanent residents and transients is a hotelkeeper only with respect to the transients.

LO ③
Boardinghouse keeper versus hotelkeeper and special duties of hotelkeeper

hotelkeeper
one engaged in business of offering lodging to transients

boardinghouse keeper
person in business to supply accommodations to permanent lodgers

15-3a WHO ARE GUESTS?

guest
transient received by hotel
for accommodations

To be a **guest**, one must be a transient obtaining lodging, not a permanent resident or visitor. One who enters the hotel to attend a ball or other social function, to visit a guest, or to eat dinner is not a guest. A guest need not be a traveler nor come from a distance. A guest might be a person living within a short distance of the hotel who rents a room and remains there overnight.

The relationship of guest and hotelkeeper does not begin until the hotelkeeper receives the person seeking lodging as a guest. The relationship terminates when the guest leaves or makes arrangements for permanent residence at the hotel.

15-3b DUTIES OF A HOTELKEEPER

The duties of a hotelkeeper include:

1. To serve all who apply
2. To protect a guest's person
3. To care for the guest's property

COURT CASE

FACTS: Drake walked her dogs along an icy walkway at the Sagamore Resort. She fell, and sued the resort for negligent maintenance of the premises. The resort disclaimed liability, in part, on the basis that Drake was not a guest, and so the hotel owed her no particular duty.

OUTCOME: The court noted that the outdoor walkways were accessible to the public, and

there was no gate, barrier, or sign indicating only hotel guests were permitted. The hotel may not have owed her a particular duty, but it did owe a duty to the public in such a generally accessible area.

—*Drake v. Sagbolt, LLC*, 112 A.D.3d 1132
(N.Y.A.D.)

15-3c DUTY TO SERVE ALL WHO APPLY

The basic test of hotelkeepers is that they hold themselves out as willing to serve, without discrimination, all who request lodging. However, this does not require hotelkeepers to serve someone who is drunk, someone who is criminally violent, or someone who is not dressed in a manner required by reasonable hotel regulations applied to all, or to serve someone when no rooms are available. If a hotel refuses lodging for an improper reason, it is liable for damages, including exemplary damages, to the person rejected.

In addition, a hotel may be liable for discrimination under a civil rights or similar statutory provision and may also be guilty of a crime if a court has issued an injunction prohibiting such discrimination. By virtue of the Federal Civil Rights Act of 1964, neither a hotel nor its concessionaire can discriminate against patrons nor segregate them on the basis of race, color, religion, or national origin. When there has been improper discrimination or segregation, or it is reasonably believed that such action may occur, the federal act authorizes the institution of proceedings in the federal courts for an order to stop such practices.

15-3d DUTY TO PROTECT A GUEST'S PERSON

A hotelkeeper must use reasonable care for the guests' personal safety. The same standard applies to the personal safety of a visitor or a patron of a newsstand or lunchroom.

Reasonable care requires that a hotelkeeper provide fire escapes and also have conspicuous notices indicating directions to the fire escapes. If a fire starts due to no negligence of the hotelkeeper or employees, there is no liability to the guests for their personal injuries unless they can show that the fire was not contained because of a failure to install required fire safety features. In one case, the court held that the hotelkeeper was not liable for the loss of life on the floor where the fire started but was liable for all personal injuries on the four floors to which the fire spread because of the negligence of the hotel.

If a hotelkeeper knows of prior criminal acts on or near the hotel premises, additional security measures may be required. However, the hotelkeeper is not liable if the guest's behavior increases the risk of criminal attack.

COURT CASE

FACTS: While attending a fraternity reunion, Bradley Smith stayed at Del Lago resort. While at the bar, a wedding party group came in. A fraternity brother "hit on" a woman in the wedding party group. A verbal altercation ensued. The conflict between the two groups lasted an hour and a half. At closing, another verbal confrontation erupted between a fraternity brother and wedding party member. The two sides "bunched up" against each other, shoving, jabbing, and arguing. Punches were thrown, and Spencer Forsythe, who was in poor health, was pushed against a wall and shoved to the floor. Smith, who had not previously been involved, saw Forsythe being kicked and entered the melee to pick him up. Smith was hit on the back and head. As he and Forsythe were moving out, someone put Smith in a headlock. Smith and his assailant went across the floor with their and the crowd's momentum, and Smith's face hit the wall. A waitress finally called Del Lago security, but the fight was over when security arrived. Smith sued Del Lago. In the three-and-one-half years before Smith's injuries, there were fourteen documented assaultive crimes, eight involving the bar or intoxication, and Del Lago security responded to forty-five similar, undocumented altercations.

OUTCOME: The court held that because of the prior incidents, it was foreseeable that an assault might occur in Del Lago's bar. Smith recovered $1.5 million.

—*Del Lago Partners Inc. v. Smith*, 206 S.W.3d 146
(Tex. Ct. App.)

15-3e DUTY TO CARE FOR THE GUEST'S PROPERTY

Traditionally, the hotelkeeper had a very high duty and was an insurer of the guest's property except for losses occurring from:

1. An act of God
2. An act of a public enemy

3. An act of a public authority

4. An act of the guest

5. The inherent nature of the property

In every state, this liability has been modified to some extent. The statutes vary greatly, but most limit a hotel's liability to a designated sum or simply declare that the law of mutual-benefit bailments applies.

Some states permit the hotelkeeper to limit liability by posting a notice in the guest's room. Some of the statutes require that the hotelkeeper, in order to escape full liability, provide a vault or other safe place of deposit for valuables such as furs and jewelry. If a guest fails to deposit valuable articles when proper notice required by state law, such as the availability of a safe, has been posted, the hotelkeeper is released from liability as an insurer.

COURT CASE

FACTS: Peter Schaufler and Christiane Schaufler-Muench rented a room at the Ritz-Carlton hotel in Chicago. While they went sightseeing, they left jewelry and cash in a wall safe in their room. When they returned, the valuables were missing. Zurich Insurance Company claimed that the property was not in the "care, custody or control" of the hotel since the Schauflers also had access to the safe.

OUTCOME: The court held that the hotel had a duty to safeguard the property of its guests. The hotel fully controlled the security arrangements for property left in the room as well as access to the guests' rooms.

—*Liberty Mutual Insurance Company v. Zurich Insurance Company*, 402 Ill. App. 3d 37 (Ill. App. Ct.)

15-3f HOTELKEEPER'S LIEN

A hotelkeeper has a lien on the baggage of guests for the value of the services rendered. This lien extends to all wearing apparel not actually being worn, such as an overcoat or an extra suit.

If hotel charges are not paid within a reasonable time, the hotelkeeper may sell the baggage to pay the charges. Any residue must be returned to the guest. The lien terminates if the property is returned to the guest, even though the charges are unpaid.

The lien usually attaches only to baggage. It does not apply to an automobile, for example, in most states. If a hotelkeeper charges separately for car storage, this charge (but not the room charge) must be paid before the car can be removed.

QUESTIONS

1. Why are some bailments called extraordinary bailments?
2. What is the difference between a private carrier and a common carrier?
3. Why are common carriers regulated by the government as to their prices, services, equipment, and other operational policies?
4. When does the liability of a common carrier of goods begin?

QUESTIONS (CONTINUED)

5. Why does the law require every carrier to have its printed bill of lading form approved by a government agency before adoption?

6. How long does a carrier's high degree of liability last?

7. What are the different types of bills of lading, and what makes them different?

8. When does the liability of a carrier of people for the passengers' safety begin and end?

9. Is a common carrier liable for injuries to a passenger caused by fellow travelers?

10. How may a carrier of people limit its liability for the loss of baggage?

11. What are the duties and liabilities of a hotelkeeper to guests?

12. If a guest refuses to pay for services rendered, may a hotel sell any possessions left behind to pay the charges?

CASE PROBLEMS

1. Marcos Arguello left his car with the valet at Sunset Station Hotel and Casinos. When he returned a few hours later for the car, it had apparently been stolen from the valet parking lot. It was found "stripped" the next day. Nevada statutes limited liability for hotelkeepers from damage due to theft of property "left in a motor vehicle upon the premises." Was the casino liable for the damage to the stolen car? **LO ③**

2. First State Depository, LLC (First State), contracted with United Parcel Service (UPS) for shipments of coins and special metals. In an eight-week period, 27 packages were lost or stolen by UPS or its employees. First State argued that it was unfair to allow UPS to limit its liability for lost or stolen shipments when UPS (or its employees) was doing the stealing. Should UPS be liable for the full amount? **LO ②**

3. Raineri contracted with North American Van Lines (NAVL) to both pack up and move her belongings from New Jersey to California. NAVL delayed the start of packing by a few days, and subsequent loading and delivery dates were also delayed. Raineri also claimed NAVL damaged the New Jersey home and several items of property during the move. Raineri signed NAVL's bill of lading, which included specific terms for filing a claim. However, Raineri determined that it would be too cumbersome for her to comply with the claims process, compared it to a full-time job, and declared it to be a waste of her time. Instead, Raineri sued. Was NAVL entitled to require Raineri to comply with the claim terms in the bill of lading before she could prevail in her lawsuit? **LO ①**

4. While traveling, Joseph and Marie Ippolito checked in to a Holiday Inn. The registration card Joseph signed and the pouch enclosing his key-card stated that the hotel was not responsible for valuables outside the hotel's safe deposit boxes. The Ippolitos put their luggage containing jewelry and cash worth $500,000 in their room and left for forty minutes. They did not see a notice on the back of their room door stating that safe deposit boxes were available. When the Ippolitos returned, the jewelry and money were gone. State law excused innkeepers from liability for loss of money and jewels if they posted notice in a conspicuous manner requiring guests to leave such items in the innkeeper's safe deposit box. Had the hotel complied with the law and thus limited its liability for the loss? **LO ③**

5. Eastman sold a diamond ring to Roberts and arranged for FedEx to ship the ring from Beachwood, Ohio, to Roberts in Houston, Texas. Eastman contracted for FedEx's "collect on delivery" (COD) service for a cashier's check in the amount of $6,850. The COD airbill listed various terms and conditions for COD service, including that "[a]ll checks and money orders are collected at your risk." A **LO ①, ②**

CASE PROBLEMS (CONTINUED)

cashier's check was delivered to FedEx in Houston, who released the ring. Eastman later learned from her bank that the check was invalid and sued FedEx. Is FedEx liable for the fraudulent check?

LO ③ 6. Irving Roth, seventy-five years old and using a walker, was a guest at the New Hotel Monteleone. Arriving at the hotel via its main Royal Street entrance, Roth received assistance from the bellhop to climb the steps in the foyer to the lobby. During Roth's stay, he exited and entered the hotel through the Royal Street entrance approximately twice a day with the assistance of hotel personnel. On the third day, Roth fell while attempting to descend the lobby steps. He had decided to descend the steps alone because the hotel staff were busy assisting other guests. Roth sued the Monteleone, alleging it was liable for the injury he sustained. He testified, "I didn't wait long at all. I waited a few minutes, there was nobody there, and I started down." He said the Monteleone staff did not advise him that there was a handicapped entrance and there were no signs at the main entrance to indicate that a handicapped entrance existed; however, he knew about the handicapped entrance but opted not to use it. Should the hotel be liable?

LO ①, ② 7. Two passengers on a county bus got into a noisy argument. To quiet them, the bus driver pulled the bus to the curb and ordered everyone off. All but three passengers, Courvoisier Carpenter and the two involved in the argument, complied. The driver exited the bus, leaving the engine running. The two involved in the argument eventually left the bus. The driver then re-entered the bus and again ordered Carpenter to disembark. Carpenter began exhibiting bizarre behavior, including acting as if he were talking to somebody outside the vehicle, although nobody was there, yelling unintelligibly, and striking the windows of the bus with his fists. After watching for several minutes, the driver exited the bus again, leaving the engine running and Carpenter on board. Carpenter got in the driver's seat of the fourteen-ton bus and drove it down the street and into several vehicles, including that of Elea and Roy Parrilla. The Parrillas sued the county, alleging that it owed them a duty of care by virtue of its status as a common carrier of passengers. For whom should the court find on this issue?

LO ② 8. Denbury Resources Inc. was engaged in collecting oil through a process that injects CO_2 into the ground. It wanted to build a pipeline from its CO_2 reserves in Mississippi to Texas oil wells. Under Texas law, a "common carrier" has the power of eminent domain to build pipeline over private land. Denbury filed the appropriate paperwork with the State of Texas and sent its employees out to survey land for a pipeline. Part of the path would cross land owned by Texas Rice Land Partners (Rice). When the Rice farmers refused to let the Denbury employees onto their land, Denbury sued. Was the proposed pipeline running from Denbury CO_2 reserves to the Denbury oil wells properly characterized as a common carrier?

LO ① 9. An industrial lathe manufactured in Japan was shipped to Rockford, Illinois. Various companies took part in the transportation by ship, rail, and truck. SLT Express Way provided motor carrier transportation. Initially, the SLT trucker refused to accept the shipment because it was improperly tarped. After some negotiation, SLT received a release stating that the tarp on the lathe was adequate and that SLT would not be responsible for a loss from not re-tarping. Within 50 miles of driving, the tarp was destroyed, and the lathe allegedly suffered damage. Is SLT responsible?

LO ①, ② 10. E. O. B. was a patient at a rehabilitation facility owned by Total Rehabilitation & Medical Centers Inc. She needed to be transported to Ft. Lauderdale to another of Total's facilities for an MRI. Jose Luis Laverde, a Total Rehab employee, was assigned to transport her in a company-owned van. Laverde attacked E. O. B. in the van on the return trip. She sued Total Rehab, alleging it was liable as a common carrier for the intentional tort of its employee. Should she recover on this basis?

ETHICS IN PRACTICE

Because a hotelkeeper has a higher degree of liability to guests if there has been criminal activity on the hotel's premises or even in the area of the hotel, would it be ethical for a hotel owner to instruct employees not to report crimes such a car break-ins or assaults committed at the hotel? What would be the likely result of such failure to report crime?

PART 3 SUMMARY CASES

PERSONAL PROPERTY

1. Maria Munar was a passenger on a city bus and rang the bell to exit. Instead of stopping at the bus stop at the intersection, the driver drove past it and stopped in the middle of the next block. Munar got off the bus; the bus pulled away, and Munar began walking the 150 feet back to the intersection. She stopped there for thirty seconds to check for traffic. She saw Kurt Schmersahl's car approaching but felt she had time to get across the intersection. As she stepped into the street, she was bumped by Schmersahl's vehicle. Munar fell, injuring her leg and wrist. She sued the city, alleging it had breached its duty to her as a passenger by dropping her off at a spot other than a designated bus stop. Had the city breached its duty to her as a passenger? [*Munar v. State Farm Ins. Co.*, 972 So.2d 1273 (La. Ct. App.)]

2. Hornbeck engaged R&R to repair its ship, the *Erie Service*. The *Erie Service* was delivered to R&R's shipyards on Lake Sabine in Port Arthur, Texas, for several months of repairs. During that time, Hornbeck retained access to the ship for inspection by its two on-site project managers. Four months into the repairs, R&R sent its workers home one day due to inclement weather. A tropical depression had formed which was headed toward Port Arthur. R&R informed Hornbeck of the weather by e-mail and asked for an extension of time to make the repairs. The *Erie Service* sank due to rainfall and waves. R&R claimed that only a limited bailment had been created, since Hornbeck's representatives were on site, inspecting the repairs as they were being made. Did R&R still have the liability of a bailee? [*National Liability & Fire Ins. Co. v. R&R Marine Inc.*, 756 F.3d 825 (5th Cir.)]

3. Robert Kulovany was injured while working when he fell through the floor of a trailer. Kulovany's employer leased the trailer from Cerco Products Inc. and had had the trailer in its possession for twenty months. At the time of the injury, there was a visible defect in the floor of the trailer. Under the lease agreement, Kulovany's employer had a duty to inspect the trailer for defects. Kulovany sued Cerco. As the bailor in a mutual-benefit bailment, was Cerco liable for Kulovany's injuries? [*Kulovany v. Cerco Products Inc.*, 809 N.Y.S.2d 48 (N.Y. App. Div.)]

4. DeMott purchased a ticket from Old Town Trolley Tours of Savannah Inc. (Old Town), and she began walking across the parking lot to the designated boarding place. On the way, she fell as a result of stepping in a pothole. Because the statute of limitations had passed for DeMott to sue under a premises liability theory, DeMott claimed that Old Town was liable to her under contract as a common carrier. Is a common carrier liable to a passenger for allowing its parking lot to remain in a hazardous condition? [*DeMott v. Old Town Trolley Tours of Savannah Inc.*, 760 S.E.2d 703 (Ga. App.)]

5. Viola Waterton rented a room at Linden Motor Inn. She had parked her car in the below-ground garage on the inn's premises. There was no separate charge for parking the car, and Waterton did not register it with the inn. There was nothing to control entry or exit from the garage and no attendant in it. The next morning, Waterton discovered that the car had been vandalized and that several items had been stolen from it. Waterton sued Linden for the loss. Was the inn the bailee of the car? [*Waterton v. Linden Motor Inc.*, 810 N.Y.S.2d 319 (N.Y. Civ. Ct.)]

6. Devos, Ltd. acted as a "reverse distributor" of pharmaceutical products: It collected pharmaceuticals from parties wishing to receive credit for returns and consolidated returns to the producer. Rebel shipped products for return to Devos, who forwarded the products to Stericycle. Stericycle processed the return, but the return credit was refused. Rebel then sued Devos as bailee for failure to return to Rebel the bailed pharmaceutical products. Did Devos have a continuing responsibility to Rebel after delivering the product to Stericycle? [*Rebel Distributors Corp. v. Devos, Ltd.*, 376 Fed. Appx. 772 (9th Cir.)]

7. Plano Molding Co. (Plano) contracted with a Chinese company to manufacture molds for the plastic storage boxes it produced. The terms of the contract included that the molds were to be delivered to the Plano's Illinois facility, with delivery, customs, and other similar costs included in the total price. The manufacturer contracted with THI Group, Ltd. (THI) to ship the molds from China to Plano's plant. A train carrying the molds derailed near Tyrone, Oklahoma, causing damage to the goods and personal injuries. Under THI's bill of lading for shipping, the "Merchant" warranted safe packaging for the molds. THI's insurer sued Plano for injuries caused by the train derailment. Had liability actually shifted to Plano under the bill of lading? [*Kawasaki Kisen Kaisha, Ltd. v. Plano Molding Co.*, 696 F.3d 647 (7th Cir.)]

8. Jan Greer purchased real property owned by Vincent and Shirley Arroz at a foreclosure sale on the property. Two years after the sale, the Arrozes sued Greer for wrongful possession of several items left on the property, including miscellaneous furniture, rolls of carpet, Christmas decorations, and ceramic accessories. Was the property abandoned when the Arrozes left it behind at the foreclosure sale? [*Greer v. Arroz*, 330 S.W.3d 763 (Ky. Ct. App.)]

Sales

Part 4 covers topics in sales, including what is required for a sale, warranties, product liability, and consumer protection. If you buy a used computer through a newspaper ad, will you have a warranty with it? If you purchase used goods over the Internet—for example, through an auction site such as eBay—you may or may not have protection for some aspects of your purchase. As recourse to fraud, trading offenses, illegally auctioned items, and other Internet sales offenses, the Internet Crime Complaint Center (IC3), through the FBI and the National White Collar Crime Center, acts on complaints. Visit eBay (www.ebay.com) to examine its safety measures, and then visit IC3 (www.ic3.gov) to see how complaints are handled.

16 Sales of Personal Property

17 Formalities of a Sale

18 Transfer of Title and Risk in Sales Contracts

19 Warranties, Product Liability, and Consumer Protection

Sales of Personal Property

LEARNING OBJECTIVES

1. Define goods.
2. Define a sale of goods, and distinguish it from a contract to sell.
3. Distinguish between existing and future goods.

PREVIEW CASE

Frank Sabia agreed to purchase a boat from Mattituck Inlet Marina & Shipyard, Inc. Although Mattituck was the true seller, title was transferred to Sabia through R. Gil Liepold & Associates in a scheme to avoid $23,000 in sales tax. Sabia alleged that the boat was defective and sued Mattituck for breach of contract and fraud. Would a court consider a scheme to avoid sales tax an appropriate activity and one that should be encouraged? Do you think it would be legal to engage in such a scheme?

LO 1
Define goods

goods
movable personal property

In terms of the number of contracts as well as the dollar volume, contracts for the sale of **goods**—movable personal property—constitute the largest class of contracts in our economic system. Every time one purchases an ice cream bar, one makes a sales contract. If the ice cream bar contained some harmful substance, the sale could be the basis of a suit for thousands of dollars in damages. Article 2 of the Uniform Commercial Code (UCC), effective in all states except Louisiana, governs sales of movable personal property.

A sales contract that does not meet the requirements of the UCC is unenforceable. However, if both parties—the buyer and the seller—choose to abide by its terms even if they are not legally bound to do so, neither one can later avoid the contract. Both parties must honor the contract.

16-1 Property Subject to Sale

movable personal property
all physical items except real estate

As used in the UCC and in these chapters, sale applies only to the sale of movable personal property (discussed in Chapter 14). Thus, it does not apply to (1) real property or (2) intangible personal property. **Movable personal property** consists of all physical items that are not real estate. Examples include food, vehicles, clothing, and furniture. **Real property** is land, interests in land, and things permanently attached to land. **Intangible personal property** consists of evidences of ownership of personal property, such as contracts, copyrights, certificates of stock accounts receivable, notes receivable, and similar assets.

Sales contracts must have all the essentials of any other contract, but they also have some additional features. Many rules pertaining to sales of personal property have no significance to any other type of contract, such as a contract of employment.

real property
land and things permanently attached to land

intangible personal property
evidences of ownership of personal property

16-2 Sales and Contracts to Sell

A sale differs from a contract to sell, and it is important to know the differences.

A **sale** of goods involves the transfer of title, or ownership, to identified goods from the seller to the buyer for a consideration called the price. The ownership changes from the seller to the buyer at the moment the bargain is made, regardless of who has possession of the goods. Even if the parties call a transaction something other than a sale, courts will find that a sale has occurred when the circumstances fit.

A **contract to sell** goods is a contract whereby the seller agrees to transfer ownership of goods to the buyer in the future for a consideration called the *price*. In this type of contract, individuals promise to buy and to sell in the future. The party seeking to purchase the goods does not have the right to possess the goods unless the contract specifically so provides.

LO ②
Sale versus contract to sell

sale
transfer of title to goods for a price

contract to sell
agreement to transfer title to goods for a price

COURT CASE

FACTS: Jeffrey Crutchfield drove his car to Guthrie Motors, where he contracted to trade the car for a pickup truck. Because the car was worth more than the pickup, Guthrie gave Crutchfield a check for $1,690 with a written understanding that it would pay an additional $500.00 once Crutchfield produced clear title to the car. Crutchfield took the pickup and later that day was involved in a collision in which Holliann Nelson was seriously injured. Unknown to Guthrie, there was a lien on the car Crutchfield had traded. When Guthrie discovered the lien, it told Crutchfield "the deal was off" and demanded return of the pickup and $1,690. By then, the pickup

had been wrecked. Crutchfield returned $700 of the $1,690 that Guthrie Motors had paid him. Six months later, Guthrie was able to clear title to the car and sell it. Nelson sued Guthrie. Guthrie's insurance company was liable if Guthrie still owned the pickup at the time of the accident.

OUTCOME: The court held that there had been a sale of the pickup to Crutchfield, so Guthrie's insurance company was not liable.

—*Farmers Ins. Exch. v. Crutchfield*, 113 P.3d 972
(Or. Ct. App.)

An important distinction exists between a sale and a contract to sell. In a sale, the actual **title**, or the ownership of the subject matter, is transferred at once. Title can be transferred as soon as there is agreement on the goods, and the price is fixed. The goods need not be delivered, nor the price paid. In a contract to sell, the title will be transferred at a later time. A contract to sell is not, in the true sense of the word, a sale; it is merely an agreement to sell.

title
ownership

In order to determine who owns goods, a sale must be distinguished from a contract to sell. Ownership always rests with either the seller or the buyer. Because the owner normally bears the risk of loss, the question of whether the seller or buyer has ownership must be answered. Also, any increase in the value of the property belongs to the one who owns it. It is essential, therefore, to have definite rules to aid the courts in determining when ownership and risk of loss pass from one party to another if the parties to the contract have not specified these matters. If the parties specify when title or risk of loss passes, the courts will enforce that agreement.

16-3 Sales of Goods and Contracts for Services

An agreement to perform some type of service must be distinguished from a sale of goods because Article 2 of the UCC governs sales of goods but not agreements to perform services. When a contract includes the supplying of both services and articles of movable personal property, the contract is not necessarily considered a contract for the sale of goods. Whether it is a sale or service is determined by which factor is predominant. If the predominant factor is supplying a service, with the goods being incidental, the contract is considered a service contract and is not covered by Article 2. For example, the repair of a television set is not a sale, even though new parts are supplied.

COURT CASE

FACTS: Timothy Grebing was a member of 24 Hour Fitness USA, Inc. (24 Hour), and a regular user of its facilities near his home. While using a "low row machine," he was injured when a clip or snap hook which connected the handlebar to a cable running through the machine snapped and struck him in the forehead. Grebing sued 24 Hour, alleging that 24 Hour's sale to him of goods was the cause of his injury.

OUTCOME: 24 Hour did not manufacture exercise machines, it purchased or leased them for the use of its members. As a result, 24 Hour was providing a service and not selling a good.

—*Grebing v. 24 Hour Fitness USA, Inc.*, 184 Cal.Rptr.3d 155 (Cal. App.)

16-4 Price

price
consideration in a sales contract

The consideration in a sales contract is generally expressed in terms of money or money's worth and is known as the **price**. The price may be payable in money, goods, or services.

The chapters on contracts explained that an express contract is one in which all the terms are stated in words, either orally or in writing. An implied contract is one in which some of the terms are understood without being stated. A sales contract is ordinarily an express contract, but some of its terms may be implied. If the sales contract does not state the price, it will be held to be the reasonable price for the same goods in the market. For goods sold on a regulated market, such as a commodity exchange, the price on that market will be deemed the reasonable price. If the parties indicate that the price must be fixed by them or by a third person at a later date, no binding contract arises if the price is not thus fixed. If the price can be computed from the terms of the contract, the contract is valid.

COURT CASE

FACTS: Six L's Packing Co. (Six L's) bought and sold fresh produce. James R. Beale operated Sunfresh Farms (Sunfresh), and would order tomatoes from Six L's. The orders included a quantity of tomatoes and a pick-up date. The price would be the market value of the produce on the date it was picked up. When a disproportionate number of tomatoes proved to be damaged, Sunfresh declined to pay, and disputed the existence of a contract based on the fact that no price had been set.

OUTCOME: The court held that a sales contract may be enforceable even though it lacks a price term. In this case, the parties agreed to use the price set by the market.

—*Six L's Packing Co., Inc. v. Beale*, 524 Fed. Appx. 148 (6th Cir.)

16-5 Existing Goods

In order to be the subject of a sale, the goods must be existing. **Existing goods** are those both in existence (as contrasted with goods not yet manufactured) and then owned by the seller. If these conditions are not met, the goods are not existing, and the only transaction that can be made between the seller and the buyer will be a contract to sell goods.

Identified goods are a type of existing goods. They are goods that the seller and buyer have agreed are to be received by the buyer or have been picked out by the seller. When the seller specially manufactures the goods to the buyer's order, identification occurs at the time when manufacture begins.

LO ③
Existing versus future goods

existing goods
goods that are in being and owned by the seller

identified goods
goods picked to be delivered to the buyer

16-6 Future Goods

Goods that are not existing goods are **future goods**. The seller expects to acquire the goods in the future either by purchase or by manufacture. For example, if Arnold contracts to buy an antique dresser, he might then contract to sell the dresser to Biff. As Arnold does not yet own the dresser, he cannot now sell the dresser to Biff. He can only make a contract to sell it in the future, after he acquires title to it. Any contract purporting to sell future goods is a contract to sell and not a sale, because the seller does not have title to the goods. Thus, future goods are goods that are not yet owned by the seller or not yet in physical existence. However, title to future goods does not pass immediately to the buyer when the goods come into existence. The seller must first take some further action, such as shipment or delivery.

future goods
goods not both existing and identified

COURT CASE

FACTS: McConnell Hall Manufacturing, LLC (MHM) retained Curtis 1000 Inc. (Curtis) to produce "product kits" for obtaining a personalized photo tapestry. The kits contained instructions and also a plain white envelope in which customers could mail their photos and order forms to MHM. A large number of the kits were sold, and tapestries produced, before MHM found that the venture had become unprofitable. It discovered that Curtis was packaging UPS overnight shipping envelopes with the kits instead of plain white envelopes. The UPS overnight shipping charges ate up MHM's profit.

MHM asked Curtis to correct the error, and Curtis refused. A lawsuit ensued. Curtis claimed that the venture was a transaction in goods and thus the UCC governed the suit.

OUTCOME: The court held that the parties had entered into the transaction for the sale of a future good—the photo tapestry. Thus, the suit was governed by the UCC.

—*Agri-Sales Associates Inc. v. McConnell*, 75 UCC Rep.Serv.2d 24 (Tenn.)

16-7 Bill of Sale

bill of sale
written evidence of title to tangible personal property

A **bill of sale** provides written evidence of one's title to tangible personal property (see Illustration 16-1). No particular form is required for a bill of sale. It can simply state that title to the described property has been transferred to the buyer.

ILLUSTRATION 16-1 Bill of Sale

BILL OF SALE OF CATTLE

Purchaser Mickey Bedrosian
Address Bedrosian Farms
Rt. 3 Box 1246-A
Miller, KS

Date March 26 20—

Animals	Tattoo#	Sex	Price
Simmental cow with heifer by side	6783	F	$950
Simmental heavy heifer	17302	F	$725

By receipt of above, which is hereby acknowledged, the undersigned grants, bargains, sells and assigns all its rights, title and interest in and to the cattle described above; if check or draft is given in full or part payment of said described animal(s), title and ownership shall remain with Seller until check is cleared by the bank on which drawn.

Seller Cadaret & Co.
Address Rt. 1 Box 1793-C
Wichita, KS
Signed Curt McCaskill

Generally, a buyer does not need a bill of sale as evidence of ownership, but if a person's title is questioned, such evidence is highly desirable. If an individual buys a stock of merchandise in bulk, livestock, jewelry, furs, or any other relatively expensive items, the buyer should demand a bill of sale from the seller. The bill of sale serves two purposes:

1. If the buyer wishes to resell the goods, and the prospective buyer demands proof of ownership, the bill of sale can be produced.

2. If any question arises as to whether the buyer came into possession of the goods legally, the bill of sale is proof.

16-8 Illegal Sales

Many difficulties arise over illegal sales; that is, the sale of goods prohibited by law, such as stolen property. If the sale is fully executed, the court will not normally intervene to aid either party. However, if one party is completely innocent and enters into an illegal sale, the court will compel a restoration of any goods or money the innocent party has transferred.

If the illegal sale is wholly executory, that is, has not yet been completed, the transaction is a contract to sell and will not be enforced. If it is only partially executory, the court will leave the parties where it finds them, unless the one who has fulfilled his or her part of the contract is an innocent victim of a fraud.

If the sale is divisible with a legal part and an illegal part, the court will enforce the legal part. If the individual goods are separately priced, the sale is divisible. If the sale involves several separate and independent items but is a lump-sum sale, then the sale is indivisible. An indivisible sale with an illegal part makes the entire sale illegal.

PREVIEW CASE REVISITED

FACTS: Frank Sabia agreed to purchase a boat from Mattituck Inlet Marina & Shipyard, Inc. Although Mattituck was the true seller, title was transferred to Sabia through R. Gil Liepold & Associates in a scheme to avoid $23,000 in sales tax. Sabia alleged that the boat was defective and sued Mattituck for breach of contract and fraud.

OUTCOME: Because the arrangement was for the purpose of improper tax avoidance, the contract for the purchase of the boat was illegal. Sabia was barred from suing on the contract.

—*Sabia v. Mattituck Inlet Marina & Shipyard*, 805 N.Y.S.2d 346 (N.Y. App. Div.)

16-9 International Sales Contracts

Questions may arise about what law governs an international contract for the sale of goods. These questions could present major problems to the parties if any litigation arises on the contract. Of course, the parties may specify in the contract what law governs. However, many international sales contracts are made without such a specification. To help in this type of situation, the United States has ratified the United Nations Convention on Contracts for the International Sale of Goods (CISG). This convention, or agreement, applies to contracts for the sale of goods if the buyer and seller have places of business in different countries that agree to the convention. Several dozen countries have ratified or acceded to the convention.

Businesses may choose to indicate in their international contracts that they will not be governed by the convention. However, unless the parties state that the contract will not be governed by the convention, it will be. The convention does not cover contracts between two parties unless their places of business are in countries that have adopted the convention. It also does not cover personal consumer transactions but is intended to apply in business-to-business situations. Some provisions of the CISG are similar to the UCC, but many are not.

QUESTIONS

1. In terms of the number of contracts as well as the dollar volume, what kind of contract constitutes the largest class of contracts in our economic system?

2. Under what circumstances may a party to a sales contract that does not meet the requirements of the UCC be unable to avoid the contract?

3. To what kind of property does the term "sale," as used in the UCC, apply? Give two examples of that kind of property.

4. a. What is the difference between a sale and a contract to sell?

   b. Why is it important to make a distinction between a sale and a contract to sell?

5. What is the difference between an agreement to perform services and a sale of goods?

6. Is an offer to sell a specified amount of wheat at the Chicago market closing price on July 7 an acceptable offer?

7. Is a bill of sale necessary to pass title?

8. To what contracts does the United Nations Convention on Contracts for the International Sale of Goods apply?

CASE PROBLEMS

LO ③

1. Simulados Software, Ltd. (Simulados) developed PC software to prepare teachers for the Texas Examinations of Educator Standards. In order to serve the Apple Macintosh computer community, Simulados contracted with Photon Infotech Private, Ltd. (Photon) to develop a version compatible with Macintosh computers. Simulados and Photon entered into a detailed contract regarding the specific steps which needed to be taken, a time frame for completion, installment payments as various benchmarks were reached, and final delivery of a workable product. However, Photon never provided Simulados with a fully functioning application. Photon defended Simulados's subsequent lawsuit by claiming, among other things, that the UCC did not apply because the contract did not involve a sale of goods. Did it?

LO ②

2. Bruel & Kjaer (B&K) contracted to upgrade noise-monitoring and radar systems and provide an annual servicing agreement to the village of Bensenville. It agreed to deliver, assemble, install, test, and make fully operational the equipment and system. The contract referred to the parties as "buyer" and "seller" and stated, "Upon final payment [B&K] shall deliver to [Bensenville] a Bill of Sale for

CASE PROBLEMS (CONTINUED)

the Equipment and System free and clear of any and all liens and encumbrances." An annual servicing agreement was required so B&K would "provide all software adjustments necessary." B&K developed custom software and provided site visits and engineering support during installation of the systems. After B&K repeatedly billed Bensenville the $227,000 contract price, the village paid only $50,000. B&K sued for breach of contract. Bensenville argued that the applicable statute of limitations was the four-year sale of goods statute and that time had run. B&K argued that the contract was not for the sale of goods but the provision of services and thus a ten-year statute of limitations, which had not yet run, applied. Was the contract for the sale of goods or the provision of services

3. Steve Atwell purchased the shell of a 1965 Dodge racecar specially manufactured for legendary drag racer Dave Strickler. Even though the car had been transferred through many owners, and substantial modifications had been made, Atwell received significant documentation regarding the vehicle's history, ownership, and even the original certificate of title Dave Strickler's name and address. Atwell spent more than ten years restoring the car, using as many original 1965 parts as possible. Atwell then undertook to sell the car, while loaning it to the Chrysler Museum for display. Nicholas Smith, a collector of classic cars, entered into a contract with Atwell to purchase the restored Strickler car. Smith then further altered the car according to his own preferences. At a classic car event, a car historian claimed that the body had been replaced and it was not the "real" Strickler car. Smith sued under Article 2 of the UCC, among other claims. Was the car a "good"? **LO ①**

4. Dexter & Chaney Inc. (DCI) contracted to sell to Wachter Management Company an accounting and project-management software system. The contract included installation of the software, a full year of maintenance, and a training and consulting package. DCI shipped the software and assisted Wachter in installing it. After encountering problems with the software, Wachter sued DCI for breach of contract. Was the contract one for the sale of goods so that the UCC applied? **LO ②**

5. Jim and Kathy Shafer formed Sunbelt Grain WKS, LLC (Sunbelt), which operated grain storage facilities, purchased grain from local farmers and resold it, and stored grain for farmers for a fee. Sunbelt had executed promissory notes to Security State Bank (SSB) and had a line of credit loan with it. The indebtedness was secured by mortgages. Sunbelt contracted to sell Whitham Farms Feedyard L.P. (Whitham) 100,000 bushel lots of corn. They executed Confirmation of Sale and Purchase (CSP) forms, which stated that Whitham would prepay for the corn. There was no record of how much corn Sunbelt had at that time. Whitham received no bills of sale or warehouse receipts for the corn it paid for and neither charged nor paid any storage fees to Sunbelt for the corn to be sold. Sunbelt was in default of the terms of its loans, so SSB closed its line of credit. A week later, SSB began foreclosure on Sunbelt's grain inventory, so Sunbelt had to stop delivering corn to Whitham. Sunbelt went into bankruptcy, and the court ordered its grain inventory sold. There was $3.875 million for creditors and SSB claimed $3.2 million and Whitham claimed $2.2 million. Whitham claimed it had constructive possession of the corn thus it should be paid from the sale of it. To have constructive possession, the court said the goods had to be identified to the contract. Were they identified in this case? **LO ①**

6. Click2Boost Inc. (C2B) entered into an agreement with the New York Times Company (NYT) to solicit subscribers for home delivery of the New York Times newspaper by means of "pop up ads" at Internet websites with which C2B had an agreement. The agreement required NYT to pay C2B a commission for each home delivery subscription C2B submitted to NYT. NYT paid C2B more than $1.5 million in subscription submission fees and then terminated the agreement. In the lawsuit that followed, the court had to decide whether C2B's submissions were goods such that the UCC applied. Were the submissions goods? **LO ②**

17

Formalities of a Sale

LEARNING OBJECTIVES

① List the requirements of the Statute of Frauds for sales, and explain the exceptions to it.

② Define an auction sale, and describe its peculiarities compared to the law of sales.

③ Describe the nature of the writing required by the Statute of Frauds.

PREVIEW CASE

Fred Trost was the host and producer of the "Michigan Outdoors" and "Practical Sportsman" hunting and fishing shows on Michigan public television. Unfortunately, he incurred significant, multimillion-dollar debts in the process. After Fred's death, his widow, Sherry Trost, agreed to give Fred's son, Zachary Trost, the assets she owned related to the show—video tapes of episodes, raw footage, show memorabilia, hunting rifles, and other equipment—in exchange for Zachary's paying off the show's tax debts and outstanding loans. Zachary attempted to sell DVDs of old episodes over the Internet, but failed to pay the debts. Did Sherry and Zachary have a contract? What do you think Sherry believed when Zachary took the videos and memorabilia? What if Zachary returned the items? What are the exceptions to the Statute of Frauds' requirements of a written contract?

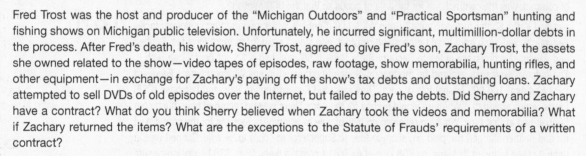

All contracts for the sale of goods must exist in writing when the sale price is $500 or more. This Statute of Frauds requirement has been included in the Uniform Commercial Code (UCC). If the sale price is less than $500, the contract may be oral, written, implied from conduct, or a combination of any of these.

FACTS: In one transaction, George Parrish bought land from TOCA Enterprises Inc. and a mobile home from Ideal Homes Inc. He obtained a loan from Hamilton Financial Services Inc. The law firm of Jackson W. Jones, P.C. prepared the closing documents. These documents showed a loan amount of $88,820 and a price for the mobile home of $58,500. Parrish signed the closing documents but did not read them until three weeks later. He sued the parties involved in the transaction for breach of contract. He alleged that prior to the transaction he was orally told the mobile home would cost $35,000, and the total loan would be $75,000.

OUTCOME: As there was no written agreement for the sale of the mobile home for $35,000, Parrish's claim was barred by the Statute of Frauds.

—*Parrish v. Jackson W. Jones, P.C.*, 629 S.E.2d 468
(Ga. Ct. App.)

17-1 Multiple Purchases and the Statute of Frauds

LO ①
Application of Statute of Frauds to sales

Frequently, one makes several purchases from the same seller on the same day. The question may then be raised whether there is one sale or several sales. If one contracts to purchase five items from the same seller in one day, each item having a sale price of less than $500 but, when combined, the total exceeds $500, must this contract meet the requirement of the Statute of Frauds? If the several items are part of the same sales transaction, it is one sale and must meet the requirement of the statute. If all the items are selected during the same shopping tour and with the same salesperson who merely adds up the different items and charges the customer with a grand total, the several items are considered to be part of the same transaction. However, if a separate sales slip is written for each purchase as an individual shops in a store, each transaction is a separate sale.

17-2 When Proof of Oral Contract Is Permitted

In some instances, the absence of a writing does not bar the proof of a sales contract for $500 or more.

17-2a RECEIPT AND ACCEPTANCE OF GOODS

An oral sales contract may be enforced if it can be shown that the goods were delivered by the seller and were received and accepted by the buyer. Both a receipt and an acceptance by the buyer must be shown. **Receipt** is taking possession of the goods. **Acceptance** is the assent of the buyer to become the owner of specific goods. The contract may be enforced only as it relates to the goods received and accepted.

receipt
taking possession of goods

acceptance
assent of buyer to become owner of goods

PREVIEW CASE REVISITED

FACTS: Fred Trost was the host and producer of the "Michigan Outdoors" and "Practical Sportsman" hunting and fishing shows on Michigan public television. Unfortunately, he incurred significant, multimillion-dollar debts in the process. After Fred's death, his widow, Sherry Trost, agreed to give Fred's son, Zachary Trost, the assets she owned related to the show—video tapes of episodes, raw footage, show memorabilia, hunting rifles, and other equipment—in exchange for Zachary's paying off the show's tax debts and outstanding loans. Zachary attempted to sell DVDs of old episodes over the Internet, but failed to pay the debts. When Zachary refused Sherry's requests to return the videos and other memorabilia, Sherry sued. Zachary claimed either there was no contract, or the contract could not be enforced due to the Statute of Frauds.

OUTCOME: Zachary accepted the goods and refused to return them when requested. Sherry's performance was sufficient to allow her to enforce the contract despite the lack of a writing.

—*Trost v. Trost*, 525 Fed. Appx. 335 (6th Cir.)

17-2b PAYMENT

An oral contract may be enforced if the buyer has made full payment on the contract. In the case of part payment, a contract may be enforced only with respect to goods for which payment has been made and accepted.

Some uncertainty occurs under this rule as to the effectiveness of payment by check or a promissory note executed by the buyer. Under the law of commercial paper, a check, draft, or note is a conditional payment when delivered. It does not become final and complete until a financial intermediary, such as a bank, pays the check, draft, or note. However, because businesspeople ordinarily regard the delivery of a check or note as payment, in most states the delivery of such an instrument is sufficient to make the oral contract enforceable. A check or promissory note tendered as payment, but refused by the seller, does not constitute a payment under the Statute of Frauds.

When the buyer has negotiated or assigned to the seller a negotiable instrument executed by a third person, and the seller has accepted the instrument, a payment has been made within the meaning of the Statute of Frauds.

COURT CASE

FACTS: Dumont Telephone Company (Dumont) contacted Power & Telephone Supply Company (Power) to purchase modernized telecommunications equipment. Negotiations between the parties continued for several months, but came to an oral agreement for equipment, installation, and software for just over $150,000. Dumont sent Power a check for 55 percent of the total price, and Power began shipping parts. Power also sent Dumont an invoice for an additional 35 percent of the price. Over the next two years, Dumont placed four additional orders, and Power accompanied each shipment with an invoice. When the invoices remained unpaid, Power sued for breach of contract.

OUTCOME: The court noted that an Article 2 contract can be formed simply by the conduct of both parties. In this case, goods were shipped, accepted, and paid for prior to any dispute arising.

—*Dumont Telephone Company v. Power & Telephone Supply Company*, 962 F.Supp.2d 1064 (N.D. Iowa)

17-2c JUDICIAL ADMISSION

When a person voluntarily acknowledges a fact during the course of some legal proceedings, this is a **judicial admission**. No writing is required when the person against whom enforcement of a sales contract is sought voluntarily admits, in the course of legal proceedings, to having made the sales contract.

judicial admission
fact acknowledged in the course of legal proceeding

17-2d NONRESELLABLE GOODS

Goods that are specifically made for the buyer and are of such an unusual nature that they are not suitable for sale in the ordinary course of the seller's business are called **nonresellable goods**. No writing is required in such cases. For this exception to apply, however, the seller must have made a substantial beginning in manufacturing the goods or, if an intermediary party, in procuring them before receiving notice of rejection by the buyer.

nonresellable goods
specially made goods not easily resellable

COURT CASE

FACTS: Comfort Keyboard Company Inc. (Comfort) orally ordered 4,000 printed circuit boards from ReMapp International Corporation (ReMapp) for a total price of $90,500. The boards were manufactured to fit Comfort's specific proprietary design and could not be used by another customer. ReMapp produced 1,000 boards and began billing Comfort for them. Comfort never paid for the boards. ReMapp had fabricated the remaining boards but the components were not on them. It

sued. Comfort argued the oral contract was not enforceable because it was a sale of goods for more than $500.

OUTCOME: Since the boards were specially manufactured to Comfort's design, the court held that the oral contract was enforceable.

—*ReMapp Intern. Corp. v. Comfort Keyboard Co. Inc.,*
560 F.3d 628 (7th Cir.)

17-2e AUCTION SALES

An **auction** is a sale in which a seller or an agent of the seller orally asks for bids on goods and orally accepts the highest bid. A sale by auction for any amount is valid even if it is oral. In most states, the auctioneer is the special agent for both the owner and the bidder. When the auctioneer, or the clerk of the auction, makes a memorandum of the sale and signs it, this binds both parties. The **bidder** is the one who makes the offer. There is no contract until the auctioneer accepts the offer, which may be done in several ways. The most common way is the fall of the hammer, with the auctioneer saying, "Sold" or "Sold to (a certain person)." In most auctions, several lower bids precede the final bid. When a person makes a bid to start the sale, the auctioneer may refuse to accept this as a starting bid. If the bid is accepted, and a higher bid is requested, the auctioneer can later refuse to accept this starting bid as the selling price.

If a bid is made while the hammer is falling in acceptance of a prior bid, the auctioneer has the choice of reopening the bid or declaring the goods sold. The auctioneer's decision is binding.

LO ②
Auctions and the law of sales

auction
sale of property to the highest bidder

bidder
person who makes the offer at an auction

without reserve
auction goods may not be
withdrawn after bidding
starts

with reserve
auction goods may be
withdrawn after bidding
starts

LO ③
Requirements of the
writing

Goods may be offered for sale with reserve or without reserve. If they are **without reserve**, then the goods cannot be withdrawn after the bidding starts, unless no bid is received within a reasonable time after the auctioneer calls for bids. It is presumed that goods are offered **with reserve**; that is, they may be withdrawn, unless the goods are explicitly put up without reserve.

17-3 Nature of the Writing Required

The UCC does not have stringent requirements that indicate what in a written contract or other writing is adequate to satisfy the Statute of Frauds for sales contracts.

17-3a TERMS

The writing need only give assurance that a transaction existed. Specifically, it must indicate that a sale or contract to sell has been made and state the quantity of goods involved. Any other missing terms may be shown by parol evidence in the event of a dispute.

17-3b SIGNATURE

When a suit is brought against an individual on the basis of a transaction, the terms of which must be in writing, either the person being sued or an authorized agent of that person must have signed the writing. The signature must be placed on the writing with the intention of authenticating the writing, or indicating an intent to form a contract. It may consist of initials; it may be printed, stamped, or typewritten, and the signature can be electronic as on an e-mail. The important thing is that it was made with the necessary intent.

COURT CASE

FACTS: Cloud Corporation supplied Hasbro Inc. with packets of powder for a toy. Hasbro would issue purchase orders to Cloud for a quantity of packets. Hasbro had sent Cloud a form stating that Cloud could not deviate from a purchase order without Hasbro's written consent. As requested, Cloud signed the form and sent it to Hasbro. Demand for the toy later decreased. With the supplies it had, Cloud figured it could fill Hasbro's existing purchase orders plus 1.8 million more packets. It sent an acknowledgment to purchase orders for this larger amount. Hasbro sent a number of e-mails to Cloud referencing quantities greater than in its purchase orders and consistent with Cloud's acknowledgment. When Hasbro did not purchase all of the packets, Cloud sued.

OUTCOME: The court found that the sender's name on an e-mail satisfied the signature requirement of the Statute of Frauds. Hasbro was liable for the purchase of all the packets.

—*Cloud Corp. v. Hasbro Inc.*, 314 F.3d 289 (7th Cir.)

The UCC makes an exception to the requirement of signing regarding a transaction between merchants. It provides that the failure of a merchant to refuse to accept within ten days a confirming letter sent by another merchant is binding just as though the letter or other writing had been signed. This ends the possibility of a situation under which the sender of the letter was bound, but the receiver could safely ignore the transaction or could hold the sender as desired, depending on which alternative gave the better financial advantage.

17-3c TIME OF EXECUTION

To satisfy the Statute of Frauds, a writing may be made at, or any time after, the making of the sale. It may even be made after the contract has been broken, or a suit brought on it. The essential element is the existence—at the time the trial is held—of written proof of the transaction.

17-3d PARTICULAR WRITINGS

The writing that satisfies the Statute of Frauds may be a single writing, or it may be several writings considered as a group. Formal contracts, bills of sale, letters, e-mails, and telegrams are common forms of writings that satisfy the Statute of Frauds.

Purchase orders, cash register receipts, sales tickets, invoices, and similar papers generally do not satisfy the requirements as to a signature, and sometimes they do not specify any quantity or commodity.

QUESTIONS

1. If a sale of goods is for less than $500, in what form may the contract be?
2. What facts would be relevant to determining whether the purchase of a number of items is one sale or many sales?
3. a. What is *receipt*?
   b. What is *acceptance*?
4. Is the delivery of a check of note as payment sufficient to make an oral contract enforceable? Why or why not?
5. What must have been done in order for the exception to the Statute of Frauds based on nonresellable goods to apply?
6. When is a contract of sale in an auction made?
7. What form of signature is acceptable to satisfy the Statute of Frauds?
8. What types of writings commonly satisfy the writing requirement of the Statute of Frauds?

CASE PROBLEMS

1. May Trucking Co. (May) negotiated orally and by e-mail with Volvo Trucks North America Inc. (VTNA), and its dealer, TEC Equipment Inc. (TEC), for the purchase of 499 tractor trucks for $89,000 each. TEC and VTNA exchanged e-mails in which VTNA instructed TEC that "VTNA's support for this transaction is to TEC Equipment not the customer. You will have to prepare your agreement with May Trucking based upon the support we are providing you." TEC and May exchanged drafts of a proposed contract. TEC prepared a final draft that listed three parties; TEC, May, and VTNA, with signature lines for each. This draft was e-mailed to various persons at VTNA. VTNA decided not to sign the agreement and May sued alleging breach of contract. May alleged the e-mails between VTNA and TEC with "To" and "From" heading and initials of the persons at the end and which summarized the points to which they agreed satisfied the writing requirement of the Statute of Frauds. Did they?

LO ③

CASE PROBLEMS (CONTINUED)

LO ①   2. After the Deepwater Horizon explosion and oil spill, BP Exploration, Inc. (BP), found itself in immediate need of oil containment boom. Packgen manufactured packaging products, and began constructing boom manufacturing equipment within days of the spill. Within a month, representatives of Packgen and BP had had several conversations, including an oral commitment from BP to purchase all of Packgen's present and future production of boom, subject to certain quality standards and testing. BP and Packgen went through several rounds of testing, field testing, and reengineering. By the time Packgen's final boom product was successfully field tested, the Deepwater Horizon well had been capped and BP began winding down its boom purchases. Ultimately, BP never paid Packgen for any boom, and Packgen was left with 60,000 feet of completed boom in its warehouse, which it could sell for only 10 percent of the price it had agreed to with BP. Packgen argued it was entitled to the specially manufactured goods exception to the Statute of Frauds and payment from BP for the boom. Was it?

LO ②   3. Brenda Darlene, Inc. (Brenda), operated a shrimp boat off the coast of Texas. Brenda entered into an agreement with Bon Secour Fisheries, Inc. (BSF), whereby BSF would purchase all of Brenda's shrimp. The price was determined by the market at the time of delivery to BSF. At the time the shrimp were delivered to BSF, Brenda's employee asked BSF's dock representative if he thought the previous week's market price for shrimp would hold, and BSF's representative responded that he "thought it would." BSF in fact paid a lower price than it had paid the previous week. Under either calculation, the value of shrimp was far in excess of $500. Brenda raised a judicial admission exception to the Statute of Frauds. How should the court rule?

LO ③   4. Under an oral contract, Scapa North America Inc. agreed to supply Eastern Adhesives Inc. with its requirements of a tape product for resale to a third party. Scapa also agreed not to supply the third party with that tape or a similar product directly. The contract was for more than $500. Scapa later began selling directly to the third party. Eastern sued for breach of contract and alleged that letters it had exchanged with Scapa satisfied the Statute of Frauds. Eastern argued that a letter it had sent Scapa that referred to an "account protection agreement" established the context for Scapa's signed, written responses. Scapa's letters did not refer to an account protection agreement. Because the letters failed to object to such an agreement, Eastern alleged that Scapa's letters admitted the agreement. Was there an enforceable contract?

LO ①   5. For years, under an oral agreement, Barbara Kalas printed and delivered written materials to Adelma Simmons. Simmons had designed the materials to sell at her herb farm, Caprilands, so they included that name. As Simmons had limited space, Kalas stored them until Simmons requested some. The town of Tolland, Connecticut, acquired the farm, and Simmons had to vacate by the end of the year. In December, Simmons died. Kalas made a $24,000 claim against Simmons's estate for unpaid deliveries of materials including two made after Simmons's death. The estate claimed the materials were goods printed under an oral contract in violation of the Statute of Frauds. Was the oral contract enforceable?

LO ①   6. Craig Robins collected paintings by Marlene Dumas. Dumas circulated to art galleries a list of people who were not allowed to buy her paintings. Because Robins had sold one of her paintings, his name was on the list. David Zwirner had told Dumas of the sale. Robins wanted to sue Zwirner, but the two orally agreed that instead Zwirner would give Robins "first choice, after museums, to purchase" Dumas's works whenever Dumas had an exhibition at his gallery and to remove Robins's name from Dumas's blacklist. Five years later, Zwirner had a Dumas exhibition but refused to sell to Robins three paintings he wanted to buy, each priced at more than $1 million. Robins sued for breach of contract. Can he recover?

CASE PROBLEMS (CONTINUED)

7. Charles Lohman wanted to convert his pig operation (raising them to fifty pounds) to a weaner pig facility (raising pigs only to seven to fourteen pounds). John Wagner was putting together a network of pork producers and buyers. Lohman began selling weaner pigs to Wagner although Lohman still needed a loan to remodel his building. Lohman asked Wagner for a sample of a weaner pig purchase agreement the pork network might use to show his banker. Wagner made one up and even signed it, although there were blanks including the quantity of pigs. He faxed it to Lohman, saying he hoped it would help Lohman get a loan. Lohman put in 300 per week for the quantity; he signed it but never sent it to Wagner. He supplied weaner pigs to Wagner at $28 per pig, consistent with the price in the sample agreement, until Wagner paid only $18 because the price of pork had dropped. Months later, Lohman sued Wagner for breach of contract. Was there an enforceable contract?

 LO ③

Transfer of Title and Risk in Sales Contracts

LEARNING OBJECTIVES

① Explain the importance of determining when ownership and risk of loss pass.

② Distinguish among a sale on approval, a sale or return, and a consignment.

③ Discuss the rule regarding attempted sales by people who do not have title to the goods, and list exceptions to the rule.

PREVIEW CASE

Brawn of California sold clothing by mail order. It required customers to pay a $1.48 "insurance fee" on all orders. This covered its costs to replace items lost or damaged in transit. Customers were entitled to return for a full refund any items with which they were not satisfied. Jacq Wilson bought items from Brawn and paid the insurance fee. He sued Brawn on behalf of himself and all other similarly situated people, claiming that Brawn's sales were sales on approval. Because they were this type of sale, he alleged that Brawn bore the risk of loss until buyers accepted the merchandise. What were the terms of the contracts between Brawn and Wilson? Can the parties to a sales contract determine when risk of loss passes?

title
evidence of ownership
of property

The right of ownership of property or evidence of ownership is called **title**. When a person owns a television set, for example, that owner holds all the power to control the set. If desired, the set may be kept or sold. When sold, title to—and, normally, physical possession of—the set passes to the buyer, who then has control over it. Normally, if the TV set is damaged or lost, the owner bears any loss. In business transactions, some problems may arise regarding title to goods and risk of loss. This is because businesses deal in large volumes of goods and often must arrange the sale of goods before they may even exist, both of which may make physical possession of the goods difficult or impossible.

18-1 Potential Problems in Sales Transactions

LO
When title and risk pass

In the vast majority of sales transactions, the buyer receives the proper goods and makes payment, which completes the transaction. However, several types of problems may arise that, for the most part, can be avoided if the parties expressly state their intentions in their sales contract.

COURT CASE

FACTS: AutoZone had a contract with American Remanufacturers Inc. (ARI) by which AutoZone purchased automotive parts from ARI and credited against its payments for purchases allowances for advertising, promotions, freight, and fees. The agreements also required ARI to credit AutoZone for returns, fill rate penalties, warranty claims of customers, and freight costs incurred by AutoZone. After operating under the contract for several years, ARI went into bankruptcy and stopped doing business. A trustee appointed for the bankruptcy estate sued AutoZone for $4.5 million for parts sold to it by ARI. AutoZone argued that ARI owed it credits for allowances, customer claims, for fill rate penalties, freight, and returns that were more than the amount due for parts it purchased.

OUTCOME: The court said that the contract language was clear and that when that is the case, the literal meaning of the contract terms governs. AutoZone was entitled to credit for the specified items.

—*In re American Remanufacturers Inc.*, 451 B.R. 349 (Bankr. D. Delaware)

When the parties have not specified the results they desire, however, the rules in this chapter apply. Some of the potential issues are ownership, insurance, and damage to goods.

18-1a OWNERSHIP

Creditors of the seller may seize the goods in the belief that the seller owns them, or the buyer's creditors may seize them on the theory that they belong to the buyer. In such a case, ownership of the goods must be determined. The question of ownership is also important in connection with resale by the buyer; liability for, or computation of, certain kinds of taxes; and liability under certain registration and criminal statutes.

18-1b INSURABLE INTEREST

Until the buyer has received the goods, and the seller has been paid, both the seller and buyer have an economic interest in the sales transaction. The question arises as to whether either or both have enough interest to entitle them to insure the property involved; that is, whether they have an insurable interest.

18-1c RISK OF LOSS

If the goods are damaged or totally destroyed through no fault of either the buyer or the seller, must the seller bear the loss and supply new goods to the buyer? Or must the buyer pay the seller the purchase price even though the buyer now has no goods or has only damaged goods? The essential element in determining who bears the risk of loss is identifying the party who has control over the goods.

18-2 Classification of Sales Transactions

The nature of the transaction between the seller and the buyer determines the answer to be given to each question in the preceding section. However, sales transactions may be classified according to

1. The nature of the goods; or
2. The terms of the transaction

18-2a NATURE OF THE GOODS

As explained in Chapter 16, goods may be existing goods, identified goods, or future goods. Goods are existing goods even if the sellers must do some act or complete the manufacture of the goods before they satisfy the terms of the contract.

18-2b TERMS OF THE TRANSACTION

The terms of the contract may require that the goods be sent or shipped to the buyer; that is, that the seller make shipment. In that case, the seller's part is performed when the goods are handed over to a carrier, such as a trucking line, for shipment.

Instead of calling for actual delivery of goods, the transaction may involve a transfer of the document of title representing the goods. For example, the goods may be stored in a warehouse with the seller and the buyer having no intention of moving the goods, but intending that there should be a sale and a delivery of the **warehouse receipt** that stands for the goods. In that case, the seller must produce the proper paper as distinguished from the goods themselves. The same is true when the goods are represented by a bill of lading issued by a carrier, or by any other document of title.

warehouse receipt
document of title issued by storage company for goods stored

18-3 Ownership, Insurable Interests, and Risk of Loss in Particular Transactions

The kinds of goods and transaction terms may be combined in a number of ways. Only the more common types of transactions will be considered here. The following rules of law apply only in the absence of a contrary agreement by the parties concerning these matters.

18-3a EXISTING GOODS IDENTIFIED AT TIME OF CONTRACTING

The title to existing goods, identified at the time of contracting and not to be transported, passes to the buyer at the time and place of contracting.

If existing goods require transporting, title to the goods passes to the buyer when the seller has completed delivery. If the seller is a merchant, the risk of loss passes to the buyer when the goods are received from the merchant. If the seller is a nonmerchant, the risk passes when the seller tenders or makes available the goods to the buyer. Thus, the risk of loss remains longer on the merchant seller on the ground that the merchant seller, being in the business, can more readily arrange to be protected against such continued risk.

COURT CASE

FACTS: Brett and Patricia Shulista were in the hog business and owned HighSide Pork, L.L.C. (HighSide), a company that produced special early wean pigs (SEW). Wells Fargo Bank, N.A. (Wells) was a creditor of both the Shulistas and HighSide. Veterinary Medical Center (VMC) was a creditor of HighSide. Both the Shulistas and HighSide filed for bankruptcy and there was a question about which one of them had title to 5,002 feeder pigs. The Shulistas said they had title to the pigs as a result of a sale from HighSide. HighSide sold SEW pigs to growers when the pigs weighed about 10–18 pounds. It utilized certain invoices showing delivery to document the sale of SEW pigs to parties. This type of sale invoice

was used to document the sale of the SEW pigs to the Shulistas. However, the Shulistas had not paid for the pigs. If the Shulistas owned the pigs before the bankruptcy, Wells would have a lien on them, but if HighSide owned them VMC would have a lien.

OUTCOME: The court said that title passes at the time the seller completes performance of physical delivery of the goods and that the seller did not have to be paid in order for title to pass. Since such delivery had taken place, the pigs were owned by the Shulistas.

—*In re HighSide Pork, L.L.C.*, 450 B.R. 173
(N.D. Iowa)

The buyer, who becomes the owner of the goods, has an insurable interest in them against risk of loss when title passes. Conversely, the seller no longer has an insurable interest unless by agreement a security interest has been reserved to protect the right to payment.

The buyer of a motor vehicle bears the risk of loss when the transaction between the buyer and seller is completed, even though the state may not yet have issued a new title in the buyer's name.

18-3b NEGOTIABLE DOCUMENTS REPRESENTING EXISTING GOODS IDENTIFIED AT TIME OF CONTRACTING

When documents that can transfer title, or ownership, represent existing, identified goods, the buyer has a property interest, but not title, and an insurable interest in such goods at the time and place of contracting for their sale. The buyer does not ordinarily acquire the title or become subject to the risk of loss until delivery of the documents is made. Conversely, the seller has an insurable interest and title up to that time.

18-3c FUTURE GOODS MARKING AND SHIPMENT

A buyer may send an order for goods to be manufactured by the seller or to be filled from inventory or by purchases from third persons. If so, one step in the process of filling the order is the seller's act of marking, tagging, labeling, or otherwise indicating to the shipping department or the seller that certain goods are the ones to be sent or delivered to the buyer under the contract. This act gives the buyer a property interest in the goods and the right to insure them. However, neither title nor risk of loss passes to the buyer until shipment or delivery occurs. The seller, as continuing owner, also has an insurable interest in the goods until shipment or delivery.

shipment contract
seller liable until goods delivered to carrier

When the contract is a **shipment contract**, the seller completes performance of the contract when the goods are delivered to a carrier for shipment to the buyer. Under such a contract, the title and risk of loss pass to the buyer when the goods are delivered to the carrier; that is, title and risk of loss pass to the buyer at the time and place of shipment.

destination contract
seller liable until goods delivered to destination

When the seller is required to deliver goods to a particular destination, the contract is a **destination contract**, and the seller's performance is not completed until the goods are delivered to the destination. Title and risk of loss do not pass to the buyer until such delivery is made.

COURT CASE

FACTS: After Payless Cashways filed for bankruptcy protection, its large supplier of wood products, Canfor Corp., received only Payless stock for its claim. Canfor continued to supply Payless with lumber but met with Payless to try to set up payment terms that would limit its risk of nonpayment. All the contracts were destination contracts to Payless facilities. Payless agreed to make all payments by electronic fund transfer (EFT) based on the average delivery time by rail or truck. After Payless again filed for bankruptcy protection, the bankruptcy trustee asked the court to order Canfor to return large payments. The outcome hinged on whether the sales were cash on delivery or credit transactions.

OUTCOME: Because the contracts were destination contracts, Canfor retained risk of loss, and title to, and control of, the lumber until it was delivered. Because Canfor retained title, they were not credit sales.

—*In re Payless Cashways*, 306 B.R. 243
(Bankr. 8th Cir.)

Normally, the contract will specify whether it is a shipment contract or a destination contract. If the contract does not expressly specify that the seller must deliver to a particular destination, the Uniform Commercial Code (UCC) presumes it is a shipment contract.

18-3d COD SHIPMENT

In the absence of an extension of credit, a seller has the right to keep the goods until the buyer pays for them. The seller loses this right if possession of the goods is delivered to anyone for the buyer. However, where the goods are delivered to a carrier, the seller may keep the right to possession by making the shipment cash on delivery (COD), or by the addition of any other terms indicating that the carrier is not to surrender the goods to the buyer until the buyer has paid for them. The COD provision does not affect when title or risk of loss passes.

18-3e AUCTION SALES

When goods are sold at an auction in separate lots, each lot is a separate transaction, and title to each passes independently of the other lots. Title to each lot passes when the auctioneer announces by the fall of the hammer or in any other customary manner completes the auction as to that lot.

18-3f FREE ON BOARD

A contract may call for goods to be sold **free on board (FOB)** a designated point. Goods may be sold FOB the seller's plant, the buyer's plant, an intermediate point, or a specified carrier. The seller bears the risk and expense until the goods are delivered at the FOB point designated.

free on board (FOB)
designated point to which seller bears risk and expense

18-3g INTERNATIONAL SALES TERMS

Sales in the United States are governed by the foregoing rules regarding commercial shipping terms and how they relate to when title and risk of loss pass. The situation can differ in the case of international sales. In Chapter 16, the Convention on Contracts for the International Sale of Goods (CISG) was mentioned because it could apply to parties whose countries have ratified it. The CISG incorporates thirteen International Commercial Terms, called **Incoterms**, to supply international rules to interpret sales terms widely used in international trade. For example, CFR, which is short for "Cost and Freight," when used in an international sales contract means the seller pays the costs and freight to the delivery port, but title and risk of loss pass to the buyer once the goods are on board the ship at the port of shipment. Because these Incoterms are incorporated into the CISG, parties whose contracts might be subject to the CISG should know what they mean before entering into an international sales contract.

Incoterms
international commercial terms

18-3h SALES OF FUNGIBLE GOODS

Fungible goods are goods of a homogeneous or like nature that may be sold by weight or measure. They include goods of which any unit is treated as the equivalent of any other unit, due to its nature or its commercial use. Fungible goods include wheat, oil, coal, and similar bulk commodities, as any one bushel or other unit of the whole will be the same as any other bushel or similar unit within the same grade.

fungible goods
goods of a homogeneous nature sold by weight or measure

The UCC provides that title to an undivided share or quantity of an identified mass of fungible goods may pass to the buyer at the time of the transaction. This makes the buyer an owner in common with the seller. For example, when one person sells to another 600 bushels of wheat from a bin that contains 1,000 bushels, title to 600 bushels passes to the buyer at the time of the transaction. This gives the buyer a six-tenths undivided interest in the mass as an owner in common with the seller. The courts in some states, however, have held that the title does not pass until a separation has been made.

The passage of title to a part of a larger mass of fungible goods differs from the passage of title of a fractional interest with no intent to make a later separation. In the former case, the buyer will become the exclusive owner of a separated portion, such as half a herd of cattle. In the latter case, the buyer will become a co-owner of the entire mass. Thus, there can be a sale of a part interest in a radio, an automobile, or a flock of sheep. The right to make a sale of a fractional interest is recognized by statute.

18-4 Damage to, or Destruction of, Goods

Damage to, or destruction of, goods affects the transaction.

18-4a DAMAGE TO IDENTIFIED GOODS BEFORE RISK OF LOSS PASSES

When goods identified at the time of contracting suffer some damage, or are destroyed through no fault of either party before the risk of loss has passed, the contract is avoided—or annulled—if the loss is total. If the loss is partial, or if the goods have so deteriorated that they do not conform to the contract, the buyer has the option, after inspecting the goods, (1) to treat the contract as avoided, or (2) to accept the goods subject to an allowance or deduction from the contract price. In either case, the buyer cannot assert any claims against the seller for breach of contract.

18-4b DAMAGE TO IDENTIFIED GOODS AFTER RISK OF LOSS PASSES

If partial damage or total destruction occurs after the risk of loss has passed, it is the buyer's loss. However, the buyer may be able to recover the amount of the damages from the person in possession of the goods or from a third person causing the loss. For example, in many instances, the risk of loss passes at the time of the transaction, even though the seller will deliver the goods later. During the period from the transfer of the risk of loss to the transfer of possession to the buyer, the seller has possession of the goods and is liable to the buyer for failure to exercise reasonable care.

18-4c DAMAGE TO UNIDENTIFIED GOODS

As long as the goods are unidentified, no risk of loss has passed to the buyer. If a buyer contracts, for example, to sell wheat without specifying whether it is growing, to be grown, or the land on which it is to be grown, the contract is for unidentified goods. If they are damaged or destroyed during this period, the seller bears the loss. The buyer may still enforce the contract and require the seller to deliver the goods according to the contract. A seller who fails to deliver the goods

COURT CASE

FACTS: Sunbelt Grain WKS, LLC (Sunbelt) operated six grain storage facilities where it purchased grain from farmers and resold it to buyers, as well as stored farmers' grain for a fee. Whitman Farms Feedyard L.P. (Whitman) contracted to purchase 580,000 bushel lots of corn from Sunbelt, with staggered deliveries scheduled to begin after six months and continue over a five-month period. Pursuant to the contract, Whitman prepaid for the corn approximately one month before deliveries were to commence. Whitman was neither charged with nor paid any storage fees for the corn. According to testimony, at that time Sunbelt had approximately 1.467 million bushels of corn. Prior to the first delivery to Whitman, Sunbelt's lender, Security State Bank (Bank), discovered that Sunbelt was in default on the terms and conditions

of its loan. Bank began foreclosure proceedings the following week, after Sunbelt had delivered only 57,000 bushels of the corn contracted for by Whitman. Bank claimed a higher priority interest in the remaining corn because it was collateral for Sunbelt's loan. Whitman responded that 483,000 bushels of the corn belonged to it, not Sunbelt, and as such could not be foreclosed by the Bank.

OUTCOME: The corn was not in existence at the time the contract was created. Because corn is fungible and was not identified to the contract, the Bank was able to foreclose.

—*In re Sunbelt Grain WKS, LLC*, 427 B.R. 896 (Kan.)

is liable to the buyer for breach of the contract. The only exceptions arise when the parties have specified in the contract that destruction of the seller's supply shall release the seller from liability, or when the parties clearly contracted for the purchase and sale of part of the seller's supply to the exclusion of any other possible source of such goods.

18-4d RESERVATION OF TITLE OR POSSESSION

When the seller reserves title or possession solely as security to make certain that payment will be made, the buyer bears the risk of loss if he or she would bear the loss without such a reservation.

18-5 Sales on Approval and with Right to Return

A sales transaction may give the buyer the privilege of returning the goods even though they conform to the contract. In a **sale on approval**, the sale is not complete until the buyer approves the goods. A **sale or return** is a completed sale with the right of the buyer to return the goods and thereby set aside the sale. The contract the parties have made determines whether the sale is a sale on approval or a sale or return. If the parties fail to indicate their intention, a returnable-goods transaction is deemed a sale on approval if a consumer purchases the goods for use. It is deemed a sale or return if a merchant purchases the goods for resale.

LO ②
Distinguish sale on approval, sale or return, consignment

sale on approval
sale that is not completed until buyer approves goods

sale or return
completed sale with right to return goods

PREVIEW CASE REVISITED

FACTS: Brawn of California sold clothing by mail order. It required customers to pay a $1.48 "insurance fee" on all orders. This covered its costs to replace items lost or damaged in transit. Customers were entitled to return any items with which they were not satisfied for a full refund. Jacq Wilson bought items from Brawn and paid the insurance fee. He sued Brawn on behalf of himself and all other similarly situated people, claiming that Brawn's sales were sales on approval. Because they were this type of sale, he alleged that Brawn bore the risk of loss until buyers accepted the merchandise.

OUTCOME: The court held that because Brawn's contracts required buyers to pay for insurance, the risk of loss in transit was on the buyers.

—*Wilson v. Brawn of California Inc.*, 33 Cal.Rptr.3d 7618 (Cal. Ct. App.)

18-5a CONSEQUENCE OF SALE ON APPROVAL

Unless agreed otherwise, title and risk of loss remain with the seller under a sale on approval. Use of the goods by the buyer for the purpose of trial does not mean approval. However, an approval occurs if the buyer acts in a manner inconsistent with a reasonable trial or if the buyer fails to express a choice within the time specified (or within a reasonable time if no time is specified). For example, a "ten-day home trial" of a set of encyclopedias allows a consumer to use the books for ten days. If the consumer does not return the encyclopedias by the tenth day, the books are considered approved. If the buyer returns the goods, the seller bears the risk and the expense involved. Because the buyer is not the "owner" of the goods while they are on approval, the buyer's creditors may not claim the goods.

18-5b CONSEQUENCE OF SALE OR RETURN

commercial unit
quantity regarded as
separate unit

In a sale or return, title and risk of loss pass to the buyer as in the case of an ordinary sale. In the absence of a contrary agreement, the buyer under a sale or return may return all of the goods or any commercial unit thereof. A **commercial unit** includes any article, group of articles, or quantity commercially regarded as a separate unit or item, such as a particular machine, a suite of furniture, or a carload lot. The goods must still be in substantially their original condition, and the option to return must be exercised within the time specified by the contract or within a reasonable time if not specified. The return under such a contract is at the buyer's risk and expense. As long as the goods are in the buyer's possession, the buyer's creditors may treat the goods as belonging to the buyer.

18-6 Special Rules on Transfer of Title

LO ③
Attempted sales without title

bailment
temporary transfer of possession of personal property

As a general rule, people can sell only such interest or title in goods as they possess. For example, if property is subject to a **bailment** (personal property temporarily in the custody of another person), a sale by the owner is subject to the bailment. Thus, if the owner of a rented car sells the car to another person, the person who has rented the car, the bailee, may still use the car according to the terms of the bailment. Similarly, bailees can only transfer their individual rights under the bailments, assuming that the bailment agreements permit the rights to be assigned or transferred.

A thief or finder generally cannot transfer legal title to property since the rights of the owner are superior. Only the actual property in possession (in the case of a thief or finder) can be passed. In fact, the purchaser from the thief not only fails to obtain title but also becomes liable to the owner as a converter of the property. Liability occurs even though the property may have been purchased in good faith.

Certain instances occur, however, when because of the conduct of the owner or the desire of society to protect the bona fide purchaser for value, the law permits a greater title to be transferred than the seller possesses. It is important to note that the purchaser must act in good faith, which means being unaware that the seller does not have title. These situations include:

1. A sale by an entrustee
2. A consignment sale
3. *Estoppel*
4. When documents of title transfer ownership
5. When documents must be recorded or filed
6. Voidable title

18-6a SALE BY ENTRUSTEE

If the owner entrusts goods to a merchant who deals in goods of that kind, the merchant has the power to transfer the entruster's title to anyone who buys in the ordinary course of business. This is true as long as the merchant is not doing business in the entrusting owner's name. Similarly, the goods are subject to the claims of the merchant's creditors.

It is immaterial why the goods were entrusted to the merchant. Hence, the leaving of a watch for repairs with a jeweler who sells new and secondhand watches would give the jeweler the power to pass the title to a buyer in the ordinary course of business. The entrustee is, of course, liable to the owner for damages caused by the sale of the goods and may be guilty of a statutory offense such as embezzlement.

COURT CASE

FACTS: Dimension Funding, LLC financed equipment for D.K. Associates Inc. (DK), a used car dealer. Under their agreement, Dimension remained the owner of a Volkswagen, but DK had possession of it for its business. Eight months later, Darrell Kempf, the owner of DK, said the car was part of DK's inventory and sold it to Edward Seabold. Kempf embezzled the proceeds from the sale and was believed to have gone to Bolivia. Dimension sued for return of the car.

OUTCOME: Dimension could not get the car back, because DK was a dealer in used cars.

—*Dimension Funding, LLC v. D.K. Associates Inc.*, 191 P.3d 923 (Wash. Ct. App.)

If the entrustee is not a merchant but merely a prospective customer, transfer of title may occur if the entrustee conveys the goods to a good faith purchaser for value. This is true whether the entrustee has obtained the goods by worthless check or fraud.

COURT CASE

FACTS: Nextday Network Hardware Corp. (Nextday) purchased information technology equipment listed on eBay from Christopher Brian Crowe, an employee of Vectren Corporation (Vectren). Unbeknownst to Nextday, Crowe had stolen the equipment from Vectren. Crow was arrested, and Nextday was informed by police that the equipment it purchased had been stolen. When Nextday refused to return the equipment, but instead sold it to Nextday's own customers, Vectren's insurer sued for conversion. Nextday argued that because Vectren and Nextday were both merchants who were in the business, the entrustment provision applied.

OUTCOME: In order for the entrustment provision to apply, the merchant and the buyer cannot be the same person. Furthermore, the entrustment provision only acts to protect the buyer. The merchant may still be liable.

—*Great American Insurance Company v. Nextday Network Hardware Corporation*, 2014 WL 7365805 (D. Md.)

18-6b CONSIGNMENT SALES

A manufacturer, distributor, or other person may send goods to a dealer for sale to the public with the understanding that the manufacturer, distributor, or other person is to remain the owner and that the dealer is, in effect, to act as an agent. This is a **consignment**. Title does not normally pass to the consignee. However, a

consignment
transfer of possession of goods for purpose of sale

dealer in goods of the kind consigned will pass good title to goods sold to a buyer in the ordinary course of business.

A consignment differs from a sale on approval or a sale with right to return. In the absence of any contrary provision, it is an agency and means that property is in the possession of the consignee for sale. Normally, the consignor may revoke the agency at will and retake possession of the property. Whether goods are sent to a person as buyer or on consignment to sell for the owner depends on the intention of the parties.

18-6c *ESTOPPEL*

ETHICAL POINT

How is the doctrine of estoppel based on ethical considerations?

The owner of property may be estopped (barred) from asserting ownership and denying the right of another person to sell the property to a good faith purchaser. A person may purchase a product and have the bill of sale made out in the name of a friend who receives possession of the product and the bill of sale. This might be done in order to deceive creditors or to keep other people from knowing that the purchase had been made. If the friend should sell the product to a bona fide purchaser who relies on the bill of sale, the true owner is estopped or barred from denying the friend's apparent ownership.

18-6d DOCUMENTS OF TITLE

document of title
document that shows ownership

Documents that show ownership are called **documents of title**. They include bills of lading and warehouse receipts. By statute, certain documents of title, when executed in the proper form, may transfer title. The holder of such a document may convey the title of the person who left the property with the issuer of the document if all of the following conditions are met:

1. The document indicates that it may be transferred.

2. The transferee does not know of any wrongdoing.

3. The transferee has purchased the document by giving up something of value.

In such cases, it is immaterial that the transferor had not acquired the documents in a lawful manner.

18-6e RECORDING OR FILING DOCUMENTS

In order to protect subsequent purchasers and creditors, statutes may require that certain transactions be recorded or filed. The statutes may provide that a transaction not recorded or filed has no effect against a purchaser who thereafter buys the goods in good faith from the person who appears to be the owner or against creditors who have lawfully seized the goods of such an apparent owner.

Suppose a seller makes a credit sale and wants to be able to seize and sell the goods if the buyer does not make payment. The UCC requires the seller to file certain papers. If they are not filed, the buyer will appear to own the goods free from any interest of the seller. Subsequent bona fide purchasers or creditors of the buyer can acquire title, and the seller will lose the right to repossess the goods.

18-6f VOIDABLE TITLE

If the buyer has a voidable title, as when the goods were obtained by fraud, the seller can rescind the sale while the buyer is still the owner. If, however, the buyer resells the property to a bona fide purchaser before the seller has rescinded the transaction, the subsequent purchaser acquires valid title. It is immaterial whether the buyer having the voidable title had obtained title by fraud as to identity, or by larceny by trick, or that payment for the goods had been made with a bad check, or that the transaction was a cash sale and the purchase price had not been paid.

QUESTIONS

1. What problems can arise when there is a question about who the owner of goods is?
2. If goods are to be sent to the buyer, when is the seller's performance completed?
3. When does title to existing and identified goods that are not to be transported pass?
4. Why does the risk of loss remain longer on a merchant seller when goods are existing and identified at the time of contracting?
5. What interest in the goods does a buyer have at the time and place of contracting when documents that can transfer title represent existing, identified goods?
6. a. When do title and risk of loss pass to the buyer of future goods?

   b. Does a buyer have any interest in future goods before title and risk of loss pass?
7. When goods are to be sold FOB, how long does the seller bear the risk of loss and expense of transportation?
8. If damage occurs to goods before risk of loss passes, what options does the buyer have?
9. What is the consequence if a transaction required to be recorded is not so recorded?

CASE PROBLEMS

1. Jackson Paper Manufacturing Company (Jackson) used recycled materials to make medium paper **LO ③** that was used to make cardboard. It supplied Stonewall Packaging, LLC (Stonewall) with paper, and Stonewall made cardboard. Stonewall did not buy paper from Jackson until it was actually used in making cardboard. Best Cartage Inc. (Best) was a trucking company that had an exclusive transportation contract with Stonewall. However, Jackson negotiated the terms of the contract and signed on behalf of Stonewall. It used the services of Jackson and its employees without reimbursement; Jackson bought the realty on which Stonewall was located; Jackson hired the employees and renovated the building in which Stonewall operated; and they shared common officers and directors. After Stonewall was put in receivership, Jackson retrieved paper from Stonewall since it had supplied it on consignment. Best sued both Stonewall and Jackson for breach of contract rather than making a claim in the receivership. It claimed that Jackson used Stonewall as a shell to insulate itself from potential claims of creditors and that the consignment arrangement constituted wrongdoing. Should Best prevail?

2. Automotive Finance Corporation (AFC) provided financing to R American Auto Inc. (R American) and **LO ①** got a security interest in all of R American's current and future inventory. R American bought a white Corvette. AFC took possession of the Corvette's certificate of title. Kip Rowley, the owner of R American, gave AFC a business check for $43,220 as payment in full for the Corvette, and on January 31, AFC gave Rowley the certificate of title. The check was dishonored, and AFC could not find the car. A year later, Steven Tolbert asked the court to release AFC's lien on the Corvette. He alleged that he was a bona fide purchaser of the Corvette. Tolbert testified he paid Kip Rowley $52,000 on November 2, and immediately took possession of the car. However, on December 12, an agent of AFC had

CASE PROBLEMS (CONTINUED)

physically inspected the Corvette on R American's lot. Tolbert had not received a bill of sale, a receipt for his payment, or the certificate of title. He testified that Rowley had given him a bill of sale and certificate of title the following January 21. Tolbert learned about AFC's lien when he attempted to have the Corvette titled in his name. Tolbert claimed he was a bona fide purchaser for value. Was he?

LO ②

3. Michelle Schneider and Michael Goldmuntz were close family friends, both involved in the jewelry business, although for different companies. Goldmuntz transferred to Schneider jewelry worth just over $200,000. They entered into a written contract, which they entitled "promissory note," calling for two separate payments from Schneider to Goldmuntz totaling the wholesale value of the jewelry. Schneider pledged some of her property as collateral in the agreement. The agreement made no mention of Schneider's ability to sell the jewelry, at what price it could be sold, or any commission to be paid to Goldmuntz. When Schneider failed to make the agreed payments, Goldmuntz sued. Schneider defended that their agreement was not sale or return, but rather a consignment, so that she was not liable to pay unless or until the jewelry had been sold. Was Goldmuntz entitled to be paid on the "promissory note"?

LO ①

4. Rad Source Technologies Inc. sold a blood irradiation machine to the University of Illinois. It was to be shipped FOB Atlanta. After arriving in Atlanta, the irradiation unit was damaged in transit, so the university sued Rad Source. Rad Source had a general liability insurance policy from Colony National Insurance Company. Colony refused to defend the lawsuit, because the policy excluded damage from assumption of liability in a contract. Rad Source asked the court to declare that Colony had a duty to defend the suit and indemnify it because Rad Source had not assumed liability for shipment of the unit. The lawsuit hinged on what Rad Source's responsibility for the machine was during shipment. What was Rad Source's responsibility?

LO ③

5. Robert Wilson gave Kenneth West a cashier's check, so West signed the title to his Corvette to Wilson and gave him the car. When West found out the cashier's check was a forgery, he filed a stolen-car report. Two years later, the police ran a check on the car's vehicle identification number and found that Tammy Roberts held the title to the car. Roberts had paid her brother for the car that he had bought in response to a newspaper ad Roberts did not know it was stolen. West sued Roberts for possession of the car. Should he be able to recover it?

LO ①

6. Steve Hammer and Ron Howe gave Kevin Thompson possession of 150 heifers for grazing. Thompson was an order buyer—he bought cattle for people who wanted to buy them and tried to help sell cattle for people who wanted to sell them. Thompson sold the 150 heifers to Roger Morris. Hammer and Howe sued. Thompson had purchased cattle in twenty-five transactions but made only six sales during the year prior to selling Hammer and Howe's heifers. During the five months after that sale, Thompson made many purchases but only one sale. Morris alleged the sale to him was by a merchant who dealt in goods of the kind. Was it?

LO ②

7. Italian Designer Import Outlet, Inc. d/b/a Casa Italia (Italia) sold men's clothing from several different suppliers, each with separate agreements regarding payments and returns. For example, with respect to one manufacturer, Cantoni I.T.C. USA, Inc. (Cantoni), approximately 70 percent of Italia's inventory was supplied directly from Cantoni's parent in Italy, with the balance from Uomonuovo, Gucci, and Xegna. For some transactions, payment was made "up front," for others, half payment "up front" with the balance due in 60 days, and for others, payment was not made until after both retail sale and the expiration of any time period for returns. A steam pipe burst in Italia's retail facility, and Italia made a claim for water damage to inventory to New York Central Mutual Fire Insurance Company (Mutual). Mutual declined coverage for certain items on the basis that Italia only held them for consignment purposes, and did not actually "own" those items. Italia claimed all the items had been sold to Italia on a "sale or return" basis. Was this situation best characterized as consignment or sale or return?

CASE PROBLEMS (CONTINUED)

8. A kiwi grower located in Italy, Martini E Ricci Iamino S.P.A. (Martini) contracted with Trinity Fruit Sales Company, Inc. (Trinity), a fruit wholesaler located in Fresno, California, to sell its crop of kiwifruit on an open consignment basis for the open market. There was no formalized written contract; there was an oral agreement followed by e-mails, transmitted accountings and, of course, net proceeds from Trinity back to Martini. After the success of the relationship in the first growing season, Martini contacted Trinity about the next season. Again, there were oral agreements, followed by e-mails covering particular issues as they arose. Trinity did not pay for boxes as they were shipped, but remitted a portion of the proceeds after Trinity sold the boxes on the open market. Martini alleged that there were minimum price expectations for each box shipped, and when Martini did not receive the expected proceeds back from Trinity, brought suit for breach of contract under the United Nations Convention for the International Sale of Goods (CISG). Martini alleged that the arrangement with Trinity was a sale, clearly covered and governed by the CISG. Trinity argued that the arrangement was in fact a consignment and, as a result, not covered by the CISG. Was it a sale or consignment?

LO ②

CHAPTER 19

Warranties, Product Liability, and Consumer Protection

LEARNING OBJECTIVES

1. Define a warranty, and distinguish between express and implied warranties.
2. Specify the warranties that apply to all sellers and those that apply only to merchants.
3. Explain how warranties may be excluded or surrendered.
4. Explain the various means the law uses to provide consumer protection.

PREVIEW CASE

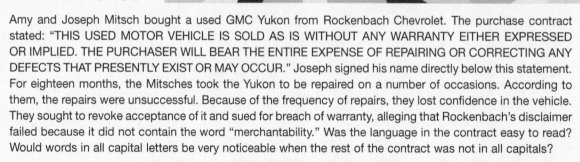

Amy and Joseph Mitsch bought a used GMC Yukon from Rockenbach Chevrolet. The purchase contract stated: "THIS USED MOTOR VEHICLE IS SOLD AS IS WITHOUT ANY WARRANTY EITHER EXPRESSED OR IMPLIED. THE PURCHASER WILL BEAR THE ENTIRE EXPENSE OF REPAIRING OR CORRECTING ANY DEFECTS THAT PRESENTLY EXIST OR MAY OCCUR." Joseph signed his name directly below this statement. For eighteen months, the Mitsches took the Yukon to be repaired on a number of occasions. According to them, the repairs were unsuccessful. Because of the frequency of repairs, they lost confidence in the vehicle. They sought to revoke acceptance of it and sued for breach of warranty, alleging that Rockenbach's disclaimer failed because it did not contain the word "merchantability." Was the language in the contract easy to read? Would words in all capital letters be very noticeable when the rest of the contract was not in all capitals?

warranty
assurance article conforms to a standard

In making a sale, a seller often makes a **warranty**. A warranty is an assurance that the article sold will conform to a certain standard or will operate in a certain manner. By the warranty, the seller agrees to make good any loss or damages that the purchaser may suffer if the goods are not as represented.

A warranty made at the time of the sale is considered to be a part of the contract and is therefore binding. A warranty made after a sale has been completed is binding even though not supported by any consideration; it is regarded as a modification of the sales contract.

LO ①
Warranties, express and implied

19-1 Express Warranties

express warranty
statement of guarantee by seller

The statement of the seller in which the article sold is warranted or guaranteed is known as an **express warranty**. The UCC specifically provides that any affirmation of fact or promise made by the seller to the buyer that relates to the goods and becomes part of the basis of the bargain creates an express warranty. The seller actually and definitely states an express warranty either orally or in writing. For example, the statement, "The whopper pizza contains one pound of cheese," is an express warranty as to the amount of cheese on the pizza.

However, the seller needs no particular words to constitute an express warranty. The words "warranty" or "guarantee" need not be used. If a reasonable interpretation of the language of a statement or a promise leads the buyer to believe a warranty exists, the courts will construe it as such. A seller is bound by the ordinary meaning of the words used, not by any unexpressed intentions.

The seller can use the word "warrant" or "guarantee" and still not be bound by it if an ordinary, prudent person would not interpret it to constitute a warranty. If the seller of a car says, "I will guarantee that you will not be sorry if you buy the car at this price," no warranty exists. This is mere sales talk, even though the seller used the word "garantee."

ETHICAL POINT

The law may not define statements of opinion as warranties, but is it ethical for a seller to make such statements when they are not true?

19-1a SELLER'S OPINION

Sellers may praise their wares, even extravagantly, without being obligated on their statements or representations. A person should not be misled by "puffing." Such borderline expressions as "Best on the market for the money," "These goods are worth $10 if they are worth a dime," "Experts have estimated that one ought to be able to sell a thousand a month of these," and many others, which sound very convincing, are mere expressions of opinion, not warranties.

ETHICAL POINT

Is it ethical for a seller to make extravagant claims about merchandise?

COURT CASE

FACTS: American Honda Motor Co. manufactured a motorcycle model known as GL 1800 for sale to the public. In marketing material, Honda described the GL 1800 as offering a ride that was "unbelievably smooth, quiet and vibration-free." Honda also stated that the motorcycle was "in a class of its own" and set the "touring motorcycle standard of the world." Thomas Aprigliano and Thomas Lucci purchased Honda GL 1800 motorcycles after the factory warranty on the vehicles had expired. Aprigliano and Lucci experienced difficulty shifting gears on their motorcycles and sued Honda, alleging breach of an express warranty. They claimed that Honda's marketing statements created an express warranty that the motorcycle would perform in a superior manner.

OUTCOME: The court held that Honda's statements were opinion and boastful sales talk and did not create an express warranty that the motorcycle would be completely free of vibration or set world standards for motorcycles.

—*Aprigliano v. American Honda Motor Co., Inc.,*
979 F.Supp.2d 1331 (S.D. Fla.)

Although an expression by the seller of what is clearly an opinion does not normally constitute either a warranty or a basis for fraud liability, the seller may be liable for fraud if, in fact, the seller does not believe the opinion. Also, a statement of opinion by the seller is a warranty if the seller asserts an opinion on a matter of which the buyer is ignorant so that the buyer has to rely on the seller for information on the matter. If the seller merely states an opinion on a matter of which the seller has no special knowledge and on which the buyer may be expected also to have an opinion and exercise judgment, it is not a warranty.

19-1b DEFECTIVE GOODS

If defects are actually known to the buyer, or defects are so apparent that no special skill or ability is required to detect them, an express warranty may not cover them. The determining factor is whether the statement becomes a part of the basis of the bargain. If it does, an express warranty results. This would not be true if the seller used any scheme or artifice to conceal the defect, such as covering the defect with an item of decoration.

19-2 Implied Warranties

implied warranty
warranty imposed by law

An **implied warranty** is one that the seller did not make but that is imposed by the law. The implied warranty arises automatically from the fact that a sale has been made. For example, every seller implies that he or she owns the goods being sold and has the right to sell them. Express warranties arise because they form part of the basis on which the sale has been made.

Express warranties do not exclude implied warranties. When both express and implied warranties exist, they should be construed as consistent with each other. When not construed as consistent, an express warranty prevails over an implied warranty as to the same subject matter, except in the case of an implied warranty of fitness for a particular purpose.

19-3 Full or Limited Warranties

full warranty
warranty with unlimited duration of implied warranties

limited warranty
written warranty, not a full warranty

A written warranty made for a consumer product may be either a **full warranty** or a **limited warranty**. The seller of a product with a full warranty must remedy any defects in the product in a reasonable time without charge, place no limit on the duration of implied warranties, not limit consequential damages for breach of warranty unless done conspicuously on the warranty's face, and permit the purchaser to choose a refund or replacement without charge if the product contains a defect after a reasonable number of attempts by the warrantor to remedy the defects. All other written warranties for consumer products are limited warranties (see Illustration 19-1).

19-4 Warranties of All Sellers

LO ②
Warranties of all sellers

The following warranties apply to all sellers.

19-4a WARRANTY OF TITLE

All sellers, by the mere act of selling, make a warranty that they have good title and make rightful transfers. This means that the seller is confirming ownership of the goods and that ownership is being transferred to the buyer.

A warranty of title may be excluded or modified by the specific language or the circumstances of the transaction. The latter situation occurs when the buyer has reason to know that the seller does not claim title or that the seller is purporting to sell only such right or title as the seller or a third person may have. For example, no warranty of title arises when the seller makes the sale in a representative capacity,

ONE-YEAR LIMITED WARRANTY

ABC Company warrants this product, to original owner, for one year from purchase date to be free of defects in material and workmanship.

Defective product may be brought or sent (freight prepaid) to an authorized service center listed in the phone book, or to Service Department, ABC Company, Main and First Streets, Riverdale, MO 65000, for free repair or replacement at our option.

Warranty does not include: cost of inconvenience, damage due to product failure, transportation damages, misuse, abuse, accident or the like, or commercial use. IN NO EVENT SHALL THE ABC COMPANY BE LIABLE FOR INCIDENTAL OR CONSEQUENTIAL DAMAGES. Some states do not allow exclusion or limitation of incidental or consequential damages, so above exclusion may not apply.

This warranty is the only written or express warranty given by The ABC Company. This warranty gives specific legal rights. You may have other rights which vary from state to state.

For information, write Consumer Claims Manager, at the Riverdale address. Send name, address, ZIP code, model, serial number, and purchase date.

Keep this booklet. Record the following for reference:

Date Purchased _____

Model Number _____

Serial Number _____

such as a sheriff or an administrator. In another example, there is no warranty of title when a governmental official sells a country singer's possessions to pay an income tax lien. Likewise, no warranty arises when the seller makes the sale by virtue of a power of sale possessed as a pledgee or mortgagee.

COURT CASE

FACTS: Rochester Equipment & Maintenance (Rochester) bought a used construction vehicle "as is" from Roxbury Mountain Service Inc. (Roxbury). There was no language in the sales agreement relating to the title of the vehicle. The vehicle, which turned out to have been stolen, was seized by the Department of Motor Vehicles. Rochester sued Roxbury for breach of the warranty of title.

OUTCOME: The court held that the warranty of title could be excluded only by specific language or a circumstance that let the buyer know the seller did not claim title. Selling a vehicle "as is" related to the condition and operability of the vehicle, not its title.

—*Rochester Equipment & Maintenance v. Roxbury Mountain Service Inc.*, 891 N.Y.S.2d 781 (N.Y. App. Div.)

19-4b WARRANTY AGAINST ENCUMBRANCES

Every seller also makes a warranty that the goods shall be delivered free from any security interest or any other lien or encumbrance of which the buyer at the time of making the sales contract had no knowledge. Thus, a breach of warranty exists when the automobile sold to the buyer is already subject to an outstanding claim that had been placed against it by the original owner and which was unknown to the buyer at the time of the sale.

The warranty against encumbrances applies to the goods only at the time they are delivered to the buyer. It is not concerned with an encumbrance that existed before or at the time the sale was made. For example, a seller may not have paid in full for the goods being resold, and the original supplier may have a lien on the goods. The seller may resell the goods while that lien is still on them. The seller's only duty is to pay off the lien before the goods are delivered to the buyer.

A warranty against encumbrances does not arise if the buyer knows of the existence of the encumbrance in question. Knowledge must be actual knowledge as contrasted with constructive notice. **Constructive notice** is information that the law presumes everyone knows by virtue of the fact that it is filed or recorded on the public record.

constructive notice
information or knowledge imputed by law

19-4c WARRANTY OF CONFORMITY TO DESCRIPTION, SAMPLE, OR MODEL

Any description of the goods, sample, or model made part of the basis of the sales contract creates an express warranty that the goods shall conform in kind and quality to the description, sample, or model. Ordinarily, a **sample** is a portion of a whole mass that is the subject of the transaction, whereas a **model** is a replica of the article in question. The mere fact that a sample is exhibited during negotiation of the contract does not make the sale a sale by sample. There must be an intent shown that the sample is part of the basis of contracting. For example, a sample may be exhibited not as a promise or warranty that the goods will conform to it but just to allow the buyer to make a judgment on its quality. A small piece of molded plastic shown to a boat buyer to illustrate the materials and methods used in the construction of boats does not create a sale by sample.

sample
portion of whole mass of transaction

model
replica of an article

19-4d WARRANTY OF FITNESS FOR A PARTICULAR PURPOSE

When the seller has reason to know at the time of contracting that the buyer intends to use the goods for a particular or unusual purpose, the seller may make an implied warranty that the goods will be fit for that purpose. Such an implied warranty arises when the buyer relies on the seller's skill or judgment to select or furnish suitable goods and when the seller has reason to know of the buyer's reliance. For example, where a government representative inquired of the seller whether the seller had a tape suitable for use on a particular government computer system, there arose an implied warranty, unless otherwise excluded, that the tape furnished by the seller was fit for that purpose. This warranty of fitness for a particular purpose does not arise when the goods are to be used for the purpose for which they are customarily sold or when the buyer orders goods on particular specifications and does not disclose the purpose.

The fact that a seller does not intend to make a warranty of fitness for a particular purpose is immaterial. Parol evidence is admissible to show that the seller had knowledge of the buyer's intended use.

19-5 Additional Warranties of Merchant

A seller who deals in goods of the kind involved in the sales contract, or who is considered because of occupation to have particular knowledge or skill regarding the goods involved, is a **merchant**. Such a seller makes additional implied warranties.

merchant
person who deals in goods of the kind or by occupation is considered to have particular knowledge or skill regarding goods involved

19-5a WARRANTY AGAINST INFRINGEMENT

Unless otherwise agreed, a merchant warrants that goods shall be delivered free of the rightful claim of any third person by way of patent or trademark infringement. However, this is not true when a buyer supplies the seller with exact specifications for the preparation or manufacture of goods. In such cases, the merchant seller makes no implied warranty against infringement. The buyer in substance makes a warranty to protect the seller from liability should the seller be held liable for patent violation by following the specifications of the buyer. For example, a business that orders the manufacture of a machine from blueprints and specifications supplied by the buyer must defend the manufacturer if it is later sued for patent infringement by someone holding a patent on a similar machine.

When the buyer furnishes the seller with specifications, the same warranties arise as in the case of any other sale of such goods by that seller. However, no warranty of fitness for a particular purpose can arise because the buyer is clearly purchasing on the basis of a decision made without relying on the seller's skill and judgment.

19-5b WARRANTY OF MERCHANTABILITY OR FITNESS FOR NORMAL USE

Unless excluded or modified, merchant sellers make an implied warranty of merchantability (or salability), which results in a group of warranties. The most important is that the goods are fit for the ordinary purposes for which they are sold.

The implied warranty of merchantability relates to the condition of the goods at the time the seller is to perform under the contract by selling the goods. Once the risk of loss has passed to the buyer, no warranty exists as to the continuing merchantability of the goods unless such subsequent deterioration or condition is proof that the goods were in fact not merchantable when the seller made delivery.

Warranty of merchantability relates only to the fitness of the product made or sold. It does not impose on the manufacturer or seller the duty to employ any particular design or to sell one product rather than another because another might be safer.

COURT CASE

FACTS: Garth Eggl bought a used John Deere tractor from Letvin Equipment Company for $47,500. He used it only for pulling a 26.5-foot cultivator. The tractor kept quitting in the field. Eggl took the tractor to Devils Lake Equipment Company, which discovered that defective o-rings had been installed. After the tractor was repaired, Eggl bought and used a 32-foot cultivator on the tractor, which was the type of work it was designed for. Eggl sued Letvin for breach of the warranty of merchantability, saying the tractor could not do the work it was designed for when he bought it and was therefore not fit for the purpose for which he purchased it.

OUTCOME: The court said that a farm tractor that cannot be used to pull an implement due to inoperable transmission was not fit for the ordinary purposes for which such goods are used. Eggl could recover.

—*Eggl v. Letvin Equipment Co.*, 632 N.W.2d 435 (N.D.)

19-6 Warranties in Particular Sales

As discussed in the following sections, particular types of sales may involve special considerations.

19-6a SALE OF FOOD OR DRINK

The sale of food or drink, whether to be consumed on or off the seller's premises, is a sale. When made by a merchant, the sale carries the implied warranty that the food is fit for its ordinary purpose of human consumption. Some courts find no breach of warranty when a harmful object found in food was natural to the particular kind of food, such as an oyster shell in oysters or a chicken bone in chicken.

Other courts regard the warranty as breached when the presence of the harm-causing substance in the food could not be reasonably expected, without regard to whether the substance was natural or foreign, as in the case of a nail or piece of glass. In these cases, a determination of fact must be made, ordinarily by the jury, to determine whether the buyer could reasonably expect the object in the food.

It is, of course, necessary to distinguish the foregoing situations from those in which the preparation of the foods involves the continued presence of some element such as prune pits in cooked prunes or shells of shellfish.

COURT CASE

FACTS: Before serving a beer to Christopher Daugherty at Allee's Sports Bar and Grill, bartender Jamie Yoder put a toothpick in the beer. Unaware of the toothpick, Daugherty drank the beer, swallowed the toothpick, and was injured as a result. He sued Allee's for breach of the implied warranty of fitness for human consumption. The trial court dismissed the complaint, and Daugherty appealed.

OUTCOME: The appellate court said that Allee's had sold Daugherty beer for human consumption, that he had drunk the beer, that when sold, the beer was not fit for human consumption, and that he was injured as a result. The case was reinstated.

—*Daugherty v. Allee's Sports Bar & Grill*, 260 S.W.3d 869 (Mo. Ct. App.)

19-6b SALE OF ARTICLE WITH PATENT OR TRADE NAME

The sale of a patented or trademarked article does not bar the existence of a warranty of fitness for a particular purpose, or of merchantability, when the circumstances giving rise to such a warranty otherwise exist. It is a question of fact whether the buyer relied on the seller's skill and judgment when making the purchase. If the buyer asked for a patented or trademarked article and insisted on it, the buyer clearly did not rely on the seller's skill and judgment. Therefore, the sale lacks the factual basis for an implied warranty of fitness for the particular purpose. If the necessary reliance on the seller's skill and judgment is shown, however, the warranty arises in that situation.

The seller of automobile parts, for example, is not liable for breach of the implied warranty of their fitness when the parts, for example, oil filters, were ordered by catalog number for use in a specified vehicle and the seller did not know that the lubrication system of the automobile had been changed so as to make the parts ordered unfit for use.

19-6c SALE OF SECONDHAND OR USED GOODS

No warranty arises as to fitness of used property for ordinary use from a sale made by a casual seller. If made by a merchant seller, such a warranty may exist. A number of states follow the rule that implied warranties apply in connection with the sale of used or secondhand goods, particularly automobiles and equipment.

19-6d LEASED GOODS

Rather than purchase expensive goods, many people and businesses lease them. The users of the goods could suffer personal injury or property damage from the use or condition of leased property. Most states have adopted Article 2A of the UCC, which applies to personal property leasing. Article 2A treats lease transactions similarly to the way Article 2 treats sales, which includes express and implied warranty provisions. However, a warranty of possession without interference replaces the warranty of title.

19-7 Exclusion and Surrender of Warranties

LO ③
Warranty exclusion and surrender

Warranties can be excluded or modified by the agreement of the parties, subject to the limitation that such a provision must not be unconscionable. If a warranty of fitness is to be excluded, the exclusion must be in writing and so conspicuous as to ensure that the buyer will be aware of its presence. Generally, if the implied warranty of merchantability is excluded or modified, the exclusion clause must expressly mention the word "merchantability" and, if in writing, must be conspicuous.

19-7a PARTICULAR PROVISIONS

A statement such as, "There are no warranties that extend beyond the description on the face hereof" excludes all implied warranties of fitness. Normally, implied warranties, including the warranty of merchantability, are excluded by the statements "as is" or "with all faults" or other language that in normal common speech calls attention to the warranty exclusion and makes it clear that no implied warranty exists. For example, an implied warranty that a steam heater would work properly in the buyer's dry cleaning plant is effectively excluded by provisions that "the warranties and guarantees herein set forth are made by us and accepted by you in lieu of all statutory or implied warranties or guarantees, other than title. . . . This contract contains all agreements between the parties, and there is no agreement, verbal or otherwise, that is not set down herein," and the contract has only a "one-year warranty on labor and material supplied by seller."

PREVIEW CASE REVISITED

FACTS: Amy and Joseph Mitsch bought a used GMC Yukon from Rockenbach Chevrolet. The purchase contract stated: "THIS USED MOTOR VEHICLE IS SOLD AS IS WITHOUT ANY WARRANTY EITHER EXPRESSED OR IMPLIED. THE PURCHASER WILL BEAR THE ENTIRE EXPENSE OF REPAIRING OR CORRECTING ANY DEFECTS THAT PRESENTLY EXIST OR MAY OCCUR." Joseph signed his name directly below this statement. For eighteen months, the Mitsches took the Yukon to be repaired on a number of occasions. According to them, the repairs were unsuccessful. Because of the frequency of repairs, they lost confidence in the vehicle. They sought to revoke acceptance of it and sued for breach of warranty, alleging that Rockenbach's disclaimer failed because it did not contain the word "merchantability."

OUTCOME: The court held that the words "as is" in the contract were sufficient to disclaim the implied warranty of merchantability. It found that the prominent placement and size of the disclaimer were effective to give notice of it.

—*Mitsch v. General Motors Corp.*, 833 N.E.2d 936 (Ill. Ct. App.)

In order for a disclaimer of warranties to be a binding part of an oral sales contract, the disclaimer must be called to the attention of the buyer. When the contract as made does not disclaim warranties, a disclaimer of warranties accompanying goods delivered later is not effective because it is a unilateral, or one-sided, attempt to modify the contract.

19-7b EXAMINATION BY THE BUYER

No implied warranty exists with respect to defects in goods that an examination should have revealed when, before making the final contract, the buyer has examined the goods, or a model or sample, as fully as desired. No implied warranty exists if the buyer has refused to make such examination.

19-7c DEALINGS AND CUSTOMS

An implied warranty can be excluded or modified by the course of dealings, the course of performance, or usage of trade. For example, if in the trade engaged in by the parties the words "no adjustment" meant "as is," the words "no adjustment" would exclude implied warranties.

19-7d *CAVEAT EMPTOR*

caveat emptor
let the buyer beware

In the absence of fraud on the part of the seller, or in circumstances in which the law imposes a warranty, the relationship of the seller and the buyer is described by the maxim **caveat emptor** (let the buyer beware). Common-law courts applied this rule, requiring purchasers in ordinary sales to act on their own judgment except when sellers gave express warranties. The trend of the earlier statutes, the UCC, and decisions of modern courts has been to soften this rule, primarily by establishing implied warranties for the protection of the buyer. Consumer protection statutes have also greatly softened this rule. The rule of *caveat emptor* still applies, however, when the buyer has full opportunity to make an examination of the goods that would disclose the existence of any defect, and the seller has not committed fraud.

19-8 Product Liability

When harm to person or property results from the use or condition of an article of personal property, the person injured may be entitled to recover damages. This right may be based on the theory of breach of warranty.

19-8a PRIVITY OF CONTRACT IN BREACH OF WARRANTY

In the past, in common law there could be no suit for breach of warranty unless **privity of contract** (a contract relationship) existed between the plaintiff and the defendant. Now, however, a "stranger," one who does not have a contractual relationship, can sue on the theory of breach of warranty. For example, it has been held that a mechanic injured because of a defect in an automobile being fixed may sue the manufacturer for breach of implied warranty of fitness.

privity of contract relationship between contracting parties

In most states, an exception to the privity rule allows members of the buyer's family and various other people not in privity of contract with the seller or manufacturer to sue for breach of warranty when injured by the harmful condition of food, beverages, or drugs.

The UCC expressly abolished the requirement of privity against the seller by members of the buyer's family, household, and guests in actions for personal injury. Apart from the express provision made by the UCC, a conflict of authority exists as to whether other cases require privity of contract. Some states lean toward the abolition of the privity requirement, while many states flatly reject the doctrine when a buyer sues the manufacturer or a prior seller. In many instances, recovery by the buyer against a remote manufacturer or seller is based on the fact that the defendant had advertised directly to the public and, therefore, made a warranty to the purchasing consumer of the truth of the advertising. Although advertising by the manufacturer to the consumer is a reason for not requiring privity when the consumer sues the manufacturer, the absence of advertising by the manufacturer frequently does not bar such action by the buyer. Although most jurisdictions have modified the privity requirement beyond the exceptions specified in the UCC, each state has retained limited applications of the doctrine.

Recovery also may be allowed when the consumer mails to the manufacturer a warranty registration card that the manufacturer had packed with the purchased article.

19-8b WARRANTY PROTECTION

The Magnuson–Moss Warranty and Federal Trade Commission Improvement Act requires that written warranties for consumer goods meet certain requirements. Clear disclosure of all warranty provisions and a statement of the legal remedies of the consumer, including informal dispute settlement, under the warranty must be a part of the warranty. According to the act, the consumer must be informed of the warranty prior to the sale. In order to satisfy the law, the language of warranties of goods costing more than $15 must not be misleading to a "reasonable, average consumer."

COURT CASE

FACTS: Arthur Glick Leasing Inc. bought a fifty-two-foot yacht, manufactured by Ocean Yachts Inc., from William J. Petzold Inc., a boat dealer. The yacht had Caterpillar motors. Immediately after delivery, Glick experienced problems with the boat, including alarms sounding that related to the boat's oil pressure and manifold inlet temperature without any discernable cause, rough running engines, acceleration problems, and a decrease of RPMs when the fuel reached a certain temperature. Caterpillar asserted that it had no privity of contract with Glick, rendering any claim of breach of implied warranties ineffective. Glick had followed Petzold's advice to purchase an Ocean Yachts boat with an upgrade to Caterpillar engines; Petzold had placed Glick's order with Ocean Yachts, which, in turn, ordered the Caterpillar engines for the boat's construction through Giles & Ransome Engine.

OUTCOME: There was no contract between Glick and Caterpillar. The extensive list of dealers separating Glick from Caterpillar rendered Glick a remote purchaser who was legally barred from claiming economic damages due to Caterpillar's alleged breach of implied warranties.

—*Arthur Glick Leasing, Inc., v. William J. Petzold, Inc.*, 858 N.Y.S.2d 405 (N.Y. App. Div.)

The warranty time can be extended if repairs require that the product be out of service for an unreasonable length of time. When this occurs, the consumer may recover incidental expenses. If, after a reasonable number of opportunities, the manufacturer is unable to remedy the defect in a product, the consumer must be permitted to elect to receive a refund or a replacement when the product has been sold with a full warranty.

A significant aspect of the act requires that no written warranty may waive the implied warranties of merchantability and fitness for a particular purpose during the term of the written warranty, or unreasonably soon thereafter. Thus, the previously common practice of replacing the implied warranties of fitness and merchantability with substandard written warranties has been significantly limited. The act also curtails the limitation of implied warranties on items for which a service or maintenance contract is offered within ninety days after the initial sale. In addition, the act extends the coverage of a warranty to those who purchase consumer goods secondhand during the term of the warranty.

19-8c EFFECT OF REPROCESSING BY DISTRIBUTOR

Frequently, a manufacturer produces a product, or a supplier distributes it, but believes or expects additional processing or changes by the ultimate distributor or retailer. Such a manufacturer or supplier is not liable to the ultimate consumer for breach of warranty or negligence if the retailer does not complete the additional processing. For example, a supplier of pork sausage to a delicatessen might advise the delicatessen it would no longer heat the sausage to destroy trichinae. If the delicatessen advises the supplier that it will heat the sausage and does not, a person who becomes ill from eating the sausage can sue the delicatessen but not the supplier.

19-9 Identity of Parties

The existence of product liability may be affected by the identity of the claimant or of the defendant.

19-9a THIRD PERSONS

Although the UCC permits recovery for breach of warranty by the guests of the buyer, it makes no provision for recovery by employees or strangers.

COURT CASE

FACTS: After J. C. Reed was arrested, he attempted suicide, so police officers removed his clothing and dressed him in a paper isolation gown. Reed's mother sued the manufacturer for breach of warranty when the gown did not tear away when he tried to hang himself.

OUTCOME: The court pointed out that the person who would benefit from any warranty by the manufacturer of the gown is a potentially suicidal prisoner such as Reed. The court allowed recovery by Reed's mother.

—*Reed v. City of Chicago*, 263 F.Supp.2d 1123 (N.D. Ill.)

A conflict of authority exists as to whether an employee of the buyer may sue the seller or manufacturer for breach of warranty. Some jurisdictions deny recovery on the ground that the employee is outside of the distributive chain, not being a buyer. Others allow recovery in such a case. By the latter view, an employee of a construction contractor may recover for breach of the implied warranty of fitness made by the manufacturer of the structural steel that proved defective and fell, injuring the employee. Because the UCC is a state law, some states have extended recovery in areas in which others have not.

19-9b MANUFACTURER OF COMPONENT PART

Many items of goods in today's marketplace were not made entirely by one manufacturer. Thus, the harm caused may result from a defect in a component part of the finished product. Because the manufacturer of the total article was the buyer from the component-part manufacturer, the privity rule barred suit against the component-part manufacturer for breach of warranty by anyone injured. In jurisdictions in which privity of contract is not recognized as a bar to recovery, it is not material that the defendant manufactured merely a component part. In these cases, the manufacturer of a component part cannot defend a lawsuit by the final purchaser on the ground of absence of privity. Thus, the purchasers of a tractor trailer may recover from the manufacturer of the brake system of the trailer for damages sustained when the brake system failed to work.

19-10 Nature and Cause of Harm

The law is more concerned in cases where the plaintiff has been personally injured rather than economically harmed. Thus, the law places protection of the person of the individual above protection of property rights. The harm sustained must have been "caused" by the defendant.

To prove a case for breach of warranty, only facts of which the plaintiff has direct knowledge, or about which information can readily be learned, need be proven. Thus, the plaintiff must only show that a sale and a warranty existed, that the goods did not conform to the warranty, and that injury resulted from the goods.

By the terms of a contract, a manufacturer or seller may always assume a liability broader than would arise from a mere warranty.

19-11 Consumer Protection

Consumer protection laws are designed to protect the parties to a contract from abuse, sharp dealing, and fraud. They also strengthen legitimate business interests. Laws requiring fairness and full disclosure of business dealings make it more difficult for unscrupulous businesspeople to operate and thus infringe on the trade of those with sound business practices.

19-11a PRODUCT SAFETY

The range of products affected by safety standards includes toys, television sets, insecticides, and drugs. The federal government has set safety standards for bumpers, tires, and glass. Substandard products are often subject to recall at the instigation of federal agencies. In some instances, fines and imprisonment may be imposed on corporate executives whose businesses have distributed clearly hazardous, substandard goods.

The federal government enacted the Consumer Product Safety Act, which established the Consumer Product Safety Commission (CPSC). The CPSC has broad power to promulgate safety standards for many products. Federal courts have the power to review these standards to make sure they are necessary to abolish or decrease the risk of injury and that they do so at a reasonable cost. The CPSC may order a halt to the manufacture of unsafe products. It may ban certain inherently dangerous or hazardous products, if there appears to be no way to make the product safe. The law requires manufacturers, distributors, and retailers of consumer products to immediately notify the CPSC if a product fails to comply with an applicable safety standard or contains a defect that creates a substantial risk of injury to the public.

COURT CASE

FACTS: Zen Magnets, LLC sold small magnets that were used as desk toys to make magnetic "sculptures." The Consumer Product Safety Commission (CPSC) received reports of serious gastrointestinal injuries to young children who had swallowed the magnets, leading it to file administrative complaints against Zen Magnets and a Zen competitor. The competitor sold much of its remaining magnet inventory to Zen Magnets and then settled with the CPSC, agreeing to stop selling the magnets and destroy remaining inventory. However, Zen Magnets continued selling the magnets and posted notice of the competitor's settlement on its website with the statement that Zen Magnets was the "last surviving magnet sphere company still

standing, selling, and fighting the United States." The CPSC filed suit against Zen Magnets, arguing that the company was violating the Consumer Product Safety Act by selling products that were subject to voluntary corrective action, and moved for a preliminary injunction to keep Zen from selling the magnets.

OUTCOME: The court granted the injunction against Zen Magnets, stating that there was substantial likelihood that Zen had sold the dangerous magnets and would continue doing so in the future.

—*United States v. Zen Magnets, LLC,* 2015
WL 2265385 (D. Colo.)

19-11b TRUTH IN ADVERTISING

The Federal Trade Commission (FTC) is charged with preventing "deceptive acts or practices in or affecting commerce." As a result, it has been active in demanding that advertisements be limited to statements about products that can be substantiated. The FTC may seek voluntary agreement from a business to stop false or deceptive advertising and, in some instances, to agree to corrective advertising. Such agreement is obtained by a business's signing a consent order. The FTC also has the power to order businesses to "cease and desist" from unfair trade practices. The business has the right to contest an FTC order in court.

COURT CASE

FACTS: The FTC filed a complaint against Publishers Business Services (PBS), alleging that it made material misrepresentations in telemarketing calls. It said that PBS failed to disclose the purpose of its calls to prospects, misrepresented the total cost of magazine subscriptions, and made false and misleading statements to induce payment for goods. PBS began calls by asking prospects to answer a few questions and offered a "small surprise, nothing big but it's nice," in return. The "surprise" was that the telemarketer was selling magazine subscriptions! PBS told prospects, "There is no catch involved" and that there was a "sound business reason" because the magazines' advertisers wanted to be assured their ads will be read, but PBS never provided any consumer information to any magazine advertisers. PBS's telemarketers said, "Now we're not going to ask you to buy any cash subscriptions or anything like that" but asked prospects to help defray the cost of the magazines. Although the total cost of the magazine subscriptions was $700, PBS initially represented it as only $2.76 a week. The telemarketers were instructed to speak rapidly so prospects could not ask questions or interrupt.

OUTCOME: The court said whether a misrepresentation, omission, or practice is likely to mislead, the court looks at the overall impression the representation creates. Here there was a misrepresentation as to the nature of the call and the price of the subscriptions.

—*F.T.C. v. Publishers Business Services Inc.*, 821 F.Supp.2d 1205 (D. Nevada)

The FTC has the authority to require that the name of a product be changed if it misleads or tends to mislead the public regarding the nature or quality of the product. If an advertisement actually misstates the quality of a product or makes the product appear to be what it is not, the FTC can prohibit the advertising.

19-11c PRODUCT UNIFORMITY

A number of required practices give consumers the ability to make intelligent choices when comparing competing products. For years, some states have required certain products to be packaged in specifically comparable quantities.

Some local governments require **unit pricing**. In unit pricing, the price for goods sold by weight is stated as the price per ounce or other unit of measurement of the product as well as a total price for the total weight. Thus, all products sold by the ounce would be marked with not only a total price but also a price per ounce that could be compared to competing products even if the competing products were not packaged in an equal number of ounces.

unit pricing
price stated per unit of measurement

19-11d USURY LAWS

Laws that fix the maximum rate of interest that may be charged on loans are called usury laws. They recognize that the borrower is frequently in a weak position and therefore unable to bargain effectively for the best possible rates of interest.

Most states provide for several rates of interest. The legal rate, which varies from state to state from about 5 percent to 15 percent, applies when interest must be paid but no rate has been specified. The maximum contract rate is the highest rate that can be demanded of a debtor. This rate varies from about 8 percent to as much as 45 percent. Some states allow the parties to set any rate of interest. A number of jurisdictions have recently adopted a fluctuating maximum rate of interest based on such rates as the Federal Reserve discount rate, the prime rate, or the rate on U.S. Treasury bills. Statutes usually permit a higher rate to be charged on small loans on the theory that the risks and costs per dollar loaned are greater in making small loans.

The laws vary regarding the damages awarded to a person charged a usurious rate of interest. Some laws allow recovery of the total interest charged and others allow recovery of several times the amount charged.

19-11e TRUTH IN LENDING

The federal Truth in Lending Act (TILA) requires lenders to make certain written disclosures to borrowers before extending credit. These disclosures include:

1. The finance charge
2. The annual percentage rate
3. The number, amount, and due dates of all payments, including any **balloon payments**—payments that are more than twice the normal installment payments

balloon payment
payment more than twice the normal one

finance charge
total amount paid for credit

annual percentage rate (APR)
amount charged for loan as percentage of loan

The **finance charge** is the total dollar amount the borrower will pay for the loan. The finance charge includes all interest and any other fees or charges the customer must pay to the creditor in order to get the loan.

The **annual percentage rate (APR)** is the amount charged for the loan, expressed as a percentage of the amount borrowed. The APR must be on a yearly rate. This helps a borrower "comparison shop" among different lenders when seeking credit.

The disclosures must be given before any fee is collected from the borrower except a fee for obtaining the borrower's credit report. A loan may not be closed until seven business days after the disclosures are made.

When a company solicits an application for a credit card, the required disclosures must be made in the solicitation literature. The company may not wait until the card is issued to make required TILA disclosures.

Advertisements indicating any credit terms also must meet substantially the same requirements regarding disclosure. The law provides that when a mortgage on the debtor's principal dwelling finances the purchase of consumer products, the debtor has three days in which to rescind the mortgage agreement. Both criminal penalties and civil recovery are available against those who fail to comply with the Truth in Lending Act.

19-11f STATUTES PROHIBITING UNCONSCIONABLE CONTRACTS

Section 2-302 of the UCC provides courts with authority to refuse to enforce a sales contract or a part of it because it is "unconscionable." If the terms of the contract are so harsh, or the price so unreasonably high, as to shock the conscience of the community, the courts may rule the contract to be unconscionable.

COURT CASE

FACTS: Michelle Cuello wanted to buy a car from Bengal Motor Company, Ltd. At the car dealership, she signed a Retail Sales Installment Contract (RSIC) containing the number of payments, payment amount, annual percentage rate, and other financing terms of the sale. The RSIC was to be submitted to the financing company for approval. Cuello also signed a Bailment Agreement, which stated that if the financing terms in the RSIC were not approved, Cuello could either sign another financing agreement with new terms or return the car. The financing company did not approve Cuello for financing under the terms of the RSIC.

Cuello refused to sign a new financing agreement with a higher annual percentage rate and declined to return the car. She sued Bengal Motors, claiming that the RISC violated the Truth in Lending Act, because the terms of the RSIC were negated by conditions in the Bailment Agreement.

OUTCOME: The court held that the RSIC violated the Truth in Lending Act, because it did not include the "final" financial terms of the car loan.

—*Bengal Motor Company, Ltd. v. Cuello*, 121 So.3d 57 (Fla. App)

19-11g FAIR CREDIT REPORTING

The Fair Credit Reporting Act requires creditors to notify a potential recipient of credit whenever any adverse action or denial of credit was based on a credit report. It permits the consumer about whom a credit report is written to obtain from a credit agency the substance of the credit report (see Illustrations 19-2 and 19-3 for sample forms). An incorrect credit report must be corrected by the credit agency. In some cases, if the consumer disagrees with a creditor about the report, the consumer may be permitted to add an explanation of the dispute to the report. Certain types of adverse information may not be maintained in the reports for more than seven years. The reports may only be used for legitimate business purposes such as for the extension of a firm offer of credit (an offer that may be conditioned on additional pre-existing internal criteria set by a lender), employment, to get insurance, or for the collection of an account. If the report is sought for debt collection purposes, it must be in connection with a credit transaction in which a consumer has participated directly and voluntarily.

COURT CASE

FACTS: Police officers found a vehicle belonging to Maria Pintos parked on the street. The vehicle's registration was expired. At police direction, P&S Towing towed the vehicle and obtained a lien on it for the cost of towing and impound. P&S transferred its claim to Pacific Creditor's Association (PCA). PCA obtained a credit report on Pintos in connection with its attempt to collect the towing and storing debt. Pintos claimed that PCA had violated the Fair Credit

Reporting Act (FCRA) by getting her credit report without having a FCRA-approved purpose.

OUTCOME: Because Pintos had not voluntarily sought credit, the court said that obtaining the credit report violated the FCRA.

—*Pintos v. Pacific Creditors Ass'n*, 605 F.3d 665 (9th Cir.)

ILLUSTRATION 19-2 Challenge to a Denial of Credit

S A M P L E

_____
_____
_____

December 05, 20--

_____
_____
_____   _____ _____

Dear Sir or Madam:

I applied for credit with you on _____ for _____.
I was notified on _____ that my application had been denied.

Please advise if the adverse action was based in whole or in part on information contained in a consumer credit report or on information obtained from a source other than a consumer reporting agency. If the adverse action was based on information from a source other than a consumer reporting agency, please indicate the nature of the adverse information, such as my credit worthiness, credit standing, credit capacity, character, general reputation, or personal characteristics.

If you have requested an investigative report, please provide me with a complete and accurate description of the nature and scope of the investigation.

Your review of this matter is greatly appreciated. Please respond as soon as possible regarding the results of your review.

Please contact me if you have any questions or need additional information.

Sincerely,

_____

ILLUSTRATION 19-3 Request for a Credit Report

S A M P L E

_____
_____
_____

December 05, 20--

_____
_____
_____

Re: Credit Report Request

Dear Sir or Madam:

I would like to request a copy of my credit report file. I am providing the following information to obtain the report.

Current address:

_____
_____ _____ _____

Previous name or address within the last five (5) years:

Other Information:
    Telephone number: _____

As proof of identity, enclosed _____.

Enclosed is a copy of a letter from _____, denying me credit within the last sixty (60) days. Therefore, the credit report should be provided to me free of charge.

Please contact me if you have any questions or need additional information.

Sincerely,

_____

Enclosure

Individuals whose rights under the act have been violated may sue and recover ordinary damages if the harm resulted from negligent noncompliance. If the injury resulted from willful noncompliance with the Fair Credit Reporting Act, the aggrieved party may seek punitive damages.

19-11h STATE CONSUMER PROTECTION AGENCIES

A number of states have enacted laws giving either the state attorney general or a special consumer affairs office the authority to compel fairness in advertising, sales presentations, and other consumer transactions. State officials will investigate complaints received from consumers. If the complaint appears valid, efforts will be made to secure voluntary corrective action by the seller. Frequently, these agencies have **injunctive powers**. That means they may issue cease-and-desist orders similar to those of the FTC. In a limited number of jurisdictions, the agencies may prosecute the offending business, and significant criminal penalties may be imposed that substantially augment the operation of these efforts.

injunctive powers
power to issue cease-and-desist orders

QUESTIONS

1. What is a warranty, and to what does a seller agree by making one?
2. How does a seller create an express warranty?
3. What are the warranties made by all sellers? Briefly explain each of them.
4. Do all merchant sellers make an implied warranty against infringement?
5. How does a merchant differ from a seller?
6. How does reprocessing of a product by a distributor or retailer affect a manufacturer's liability on a warranty?
7. What provision does the UCC make with regard to privity requirements in personal injury cases?
8. How may warranties be excluded or surrendered?
9. When does the rule of *caveat emptor* apply?
10. Give three examples of disclosures lenders are required to make to borrowers under the Truth in Lending Act.
11. For what may individuals whose rights under the Fair Credit Reporting Act have been violated sue?
12. According to the Magnuson–Moss Warranty and Federal Trade Commission Improvement Act, what must be included in a warranty?

CASE PROBLEMS

LO

1. Dentsply International Inc. (Dentsply) manufactured the Cavitron, commonly used to clean teeth but also used in treating periodontal disease. Their sale was restricted to dental professionals. Federal law required their labeling to have "information for use . . . under which practitioners . . . can use the device safely and for the purpose for which it is intended, including all purposes for which it is advertised or represented. . . ." Dentsply provided "Directions For Use" (Directions) included in the packaging of the device. Several dentists sued Dentsply for breach of express warranty because the Directions indicated Cavitrons could be used in oral surgery, but they were unsafe for such use because the Cavitron's inner tubing was not sterile and could not be sterilized so it could not deliver sterile output water for surgical applications. Did the statements included in the Directions constitute an express warranty?

CASE PROBLEMS (CONTINUED)

2. Sharron Poulin purchased a Saturn automobile from Balise Auto Sales Inc. (Balise) for $8,440. The NADA Official Used Car Guide, Eastern Edition (NADA Guide), listed the market value of this car as $3,900. Poulin executed a retail installment contract, which Balise subsequently assigned to Auto Credit Express Inc. (ACE). Balise had a policy that for a newer car, it advertised a retail price roughly the value in the NADA Guide. For an older car, however, Balise did not advertise a retail price. When prospective buyers with poor credit approached Balise, it steered them toward an older car and sold the older cars at prices substantially higher than the values in the NADA Guide. Poulin sued Balise, alleging violation of a TILA provision requiring a creditor to disclose any finance charge it imposed on a consumer. She alleged the amount in excess of the NADA Guide value Balise charged customers for older cars was a hidden finance charge buried in the price of the cars it sold to customers with poor credit. Did Balise's policy violate the TILA? **LO ④**

3. Green Tree Servicing, LLC (Green) agreed to sell a used mobile home located on Ben Gordon's property to Patrick Johnson, a mobile home dealer. Green told Johnson he might have trouble moving the home, since Gordon wanted payment for moving and storing it. Johnson had advertised the home and Nancy Henson agreed to buy it for $12,200 and move it off Gordon's property. Johnson told Green that Henson was buying the home. After Johnson paid for it, Green transferred the title to Henson. Henson paid $12,200 and received the title with no liens shown on it. Henson moved half the home off Gordon's property but could not move the rest, since Gordon parked his van in the way. Law enforcement officers confirmed that Henson had title to the home and the right to move it. The movers could have moved the van and taken the rest of the home, but Henson told them not to. For nine months, the half stayed on Gordon's property, where it deteriorated and was vandalized. Henson sued for breach of warranty of title. Did Green breach that warranty? **LO ②**

4. While visiting the Tractor Supply Company store, Melissa Leonard sat on a porch swing suspended by chains and was injured when the swing fell to the ground. Tractor Supply had not offered to sell Leonard the swing, nor was Leonard interested in buying the swing. However, Leonard sued Tractor Supply for breach of warranty, stating that Tractor Supply was a distributor of the swing, because Tractor Supply had assembled, displayed, and invited Leonard to sit on the swing as an initial step leading Leonard to use the swing. Was there privity of contract between Leonard and Tractor Supply to support a breach of warranty claim? **LO ③**

5. After having problems with her Mitsubishi car, Sandra Salazar had Santa Fe Mitsubishi install a used motor in it. When she picked up the car, a Mitsubishi employee told Salazar to bring the car back if she had any problems. The car was smoking when she drove it home, and two days later, after the car's oil light went on, a gas station attendant checked the oil and found that the car was totally out of oil. Salazar took the car back to Mitsubishi for repair. The car still smoked and lost oil quickly and finally would not run. When Mitsubishi would not replace the engine at no cost, Salazar sued Mitsubishi, alleging violation of an express warranty as a result of the employee's statement to bring the car back if she had any problems with it. Was the statement an express warranty? **LO ①**

6. Brian Dixon received a mailing from Shamrock Financial Corporation containing a personal invitation to Dixon to pay off his revolving debt and refinance his mortgage balance at a lower rate. It stated that the "prescreened" offer of credit was based on information in his credit report indicating that he met certain criteria. Dixon sued, claiming Shamrock violated the Fair Credit Reporting Act by accessing his consumer report without extending a "firm offer of credit" to him because Shamrock did not specify a set of terms that could be immediately accepted. Was there a violation of the act? **LO ④**

7. T&M Solar and Air Conditioning, Inc. was an air conditioning installation and maintenance company that purchased solar panels from Lennox International, Inc. The solar panels were marketed as being unique, because they were the only solar panels able to work directly through air conditioning systems. T&M purchased the solar panels for air conditioning systems to be installed in several clients' homes. **LO ②**

CASE PROBLEMS (CONTINUED)

However, for each of the clients, the air conditioning system did not work properly or the panels could not be installed, causing significant expense to the home owners and T&M Solar. T&M Solar sued Lennox, claiming, among other things that Lennox breached an implied warranty of fitness for a particular purpose, because the solar panels had not worked in air conditioning units. Did T&M sufficiently state a claim?

8. Cars 4 Causes was a nonprofit corporation that solicited donations of cars that it sold from its lot. It kept half the sales proceeds and after deducting towing costs, it distributed the remainder to charities. Cars 4 Causes advertised that it provided "free towing" of a vehicle from the donor's residence. Its advertising did not disclose that in fact it paid a fee to a towing company and deducted that fee from the portion of the sales proceeds it gave to charities. The state of California and its Department of Motor Vehicles sued Cars 4 Causes, alleging that it engaged in false advertising. Did it?

9. Omni USA, Inc. purchased industrial oil seals from Parker-Hannifin Corp. and installed the seals in gearboxes that were then used in agricultural irrigation systems. In the initial price quote Parker gave Omni, Parker included notice of terms and conditions of the sale in capital letters and an enlarged font. Warranty language was included in the sale terms in bold print, stating: "THE SELLER WARRANTS FOR A PERIOD OF ONE YEAR FROM THE DATE OF DELIVERY THAT THE PRODUCT IS FREE FROM DEFECTS IN MATERIALS AND WORKMANSHIP. THIS LIMITED WARRANTY IS YOUR EXCLUSIVE WARRANTY . . . THE PRODUCT IS NOT SOLD WITH ANY IMPLIED WARRANTIES. NOR ANY WARRANTY OF MERCHANTABILITY AND/OR OTHER WARRANTY FOR FITNESS FOR A PARTICULAR PURPOSE." More than a year later, Omni notified Parker that some of the gearboxes were leaking oil due to a manufacturing or design flaw with the oil seal. However, Omni discarded the deficient oil seals and was unable to present evidence that the deficient oil seals were from Parker, as compared to another vendor. Omni sued Parker for breach of express warranty. Parker argued that because Omni failed to give notice of a defective part within one year of the date of delivery and the disclaimer language was conspicuous, it were not liable for a breach of express warranty. Was Parker correct?

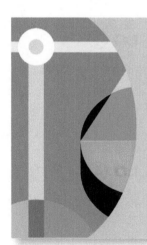

ETHICS IN PRACTICE

Consider the ethical implications of a seller who decides to make his product in a less expensive way. The less expensive way will shorten the life of the product. So, instead of giving a two-year written warranty that the seller has been giving, the seller no longer provides a warranty on the product. The seller cuts costs, reduces the likelihood of returns and lawsuits because of breached warranty, and is much happier. What about the consumer?

PART 4 SUMMARY CASES

SALES

1. VisionStream, Inc. (VisionStream), produced trade show displays and exhibits for a variety of clients across the country. Construction and production of the displays was done at the company's corporate headquarters in Missouri. While VisionStream's standard "Display Order" form listed the term "F.O.B. manufacturer," clients would often email orders, and generally did not include specific terms of title transfer. VisionStream shipped the displays to the trade show location by common carrier, where the client would first have the opportunity to inspect the finished product, and billed separately for shipping. VisionStream did not collect, or remit to the State of Missouri, sales tax on certain displays shipped to trade shows outside the state of Missouri. The Missouri Director of Revenue argued that the term "F.O.B. manufacturer" on the "Display Order" transferred title to the displays within the state, triggering state income tax liability on all VisionStream's sales. Was VisionStream liable to collect and pay the state sales tax? [*VisionStream, Inc. v. Director of Revenue*, 2015 WL 3978835 (Mo.)]

2. United Taconite, LLC (United) leased a 380,000-pound, diesel-powered drill called the PV–351, manufactured by Atlas Copco Drilling Solutions LLC (ACDS). After two six-month lease periods, United purchased the drill. Deane Driscoll, a United employee, was operating the drill on a steep slope at a mine when one of the drill's leveling jacks failed and the drill tipped over. Driscoll was thrown from the cab of the drill and killed. A lawsuit ensued. United argued that there was evidence that the drill jacks contained latent defects in the form of a tendency to crack at the bolt and flange level that could not have been discovered by routine examination. ACDS alleged that United had an ample opportunity to inspect the drill during its year-long lease, and therefore that any implied warranties were disclaimed and the suit should be dismissed. Was ACDS correct? [*Driscoll v. Standard Hardware Inc.*, 785 N.W.2d 805 (Minn. Ct. App.)]

3. Alan Vitt sued Apple Computer Co., alleging that its advertising of a laptop computer as "mobile," "durable," "portable," "rugged," "built to withstand reasonable shock," "reliable," "high performance," "high value," an "affordable choice," and an "ideal student laptop" was misleading. He alleged that one of the solder joints on the logic board of the computer degraded slightly each time the computer was turned on and off, eventually causing the joint to break, and the computer to stop working shortly after Apple's one-year express warranty expired. He claimed that Apple had misrepresented the durability, portability, and quality of the computer and not disclosed the alleged defect. Was Apple's advertising misleading? [*Vitt v. Apple Computer Inc.*, 469 Fed. Appx. 605 (9th Cir.)]

4. P&A Investments, Inc. d/b/a/ Andy's Mobile Home and Land Sales (Andy's), purchased for resale a mobile home which had been repossessed by Vanderbilt Mortgage and Finance, Inc. (Vanderbilt). Douglas Singletary then purchased

with cash the same mobile home from Andy's, "as is where is," rather than pay Andy's extra for delivery to another location. Andy's had not yet received all of the appropriate documentation from Vanderbilt to issue a certificate of title to Singletary. While Singletary was arranging the removal and delivery of the mobile home, it was destroyed by fire. Singletary demanded a return of the purchase price arguing that without the documents of title, neither ownership nor risk of loss had passed to him. Who bore the risk of loss? [*Singletary, III v. P&A Investments, Inc.*, 712 S.E.2d 681 (N.C. App.)]

5. Steve Morell sold a used tractor to James Tracy for $12,500, and Tracy signed a promissory note agreeing to make monthly payments. After Tracy heard that Morell had been arrested for receiving stolen farm equipment, he stopped making payments and asked the sheriff to find out whether the tractor he had bought was stolen. The tractor's identification number had been altered, so the only way to determine whether the tractor was stolen was to dismantle it to find the valid number in the engine. The prosecutor found the cost of doing so was prohibitive. A tractor with an altered identification number could not be knowingly or intentionally sold legally. Tracy sued Morell, and Morell counterclaimed for the balance due on the note. Should Tracy be able to rescind the sale? [*Tracy v. Morell*, 948 N.E.2d 855 (Ind. Ct. App.)]

6. Rodney Hale, who did business as RH Equipment, told Brad Lawson that he did not really know much about a tractor he had for sale except that it leaked oil and fuel. Lawson decided to buy the tractor and gave Hale $500 on the $8,500 purchase price. When Lawson returned to pay the remainder and pick up the tractor, he again asked Hale whether there was anything wrong with the tractor. Hale said it leaked oil and fuel. Lawson was given an invoice that said, "AS IS." Lawson signed the invoice and returned it to Hale. He drove the tractor to another implement dealer and found that oil was running out underneath the engine. The engine was cracked and had been welded. A few months before, someone else had purchased the tractor from Hale and after discovering the cracked engine had returned it when Hale said he could not satisfactorily fix it. Lawson sued, alleging that Hale had violated the warranty of merchantability. Had he? [*Lawson v. Hale*, 902 N.E.2d 267 (Ind. Ct. App.)]

7. Craig Robins is an art collector particularly interested in the works of Marlene Dumas, having amassed a substantial collection of her works. The time came when Robins wanted to sell one of the collected works. Dumas, however, opposed the sale of her works in the secondary market, and would refuse future sales to a collector who resold one of her paintings. After Robins nonetheless sold one painting, Dumas contacted her dealer and several galleries and "blacklisted" Robins from any future purchases. Robins threatened to sue a gallery owner, David Zwirner, for informing to Dumas regarding his sale, but Robins and Zwirner agreed to a "settlement." In exchange for Robins's promise not to sue, Zwirner agreed to give Robins "first choice, after museums, to purchase one or more" of Dumas' works when Dumas showed paintings in Zwirner's gallery. The settlement was not in writing, but sealed with a handshake. Five years later, Zwirner showed some of Dumas' works, and Robins contacted him about a purchase. At that time, Dumas' works were worth over $1 million each, and Zwirner refused to sell to Robins. Robins sought a restraining order against Zwirner to prevent Zwirner from selling to anyone else. Was Robins entitled to "first choice"? [*Robins v. Zwirner*, 713 F.Supp.2d 367 (S.D.N.Y.)]

8. Pamela Lee purchased a car from Mercedes-Benz USA, LLC (MBUSA). The car needed to be repaired an excessive number of times, so Lee lost the use of it. She also paid $7,300 for repairs not covered by the car's warranty. That warranty included the statement "NO PAYMENT OR OTHER COMPENSATION WILL BE MADE FOR INDIRECT OR CONSEQUENTIAL DAMAGE SUCH AS, DAMAGE OR INJURY TO . . . PROPERTY OR LOSS OF REVENUE." Lee sued, and at trial the judge instructed the jury that Lee could recover consequential damages even though MBUSA's warranty excluded them. Was the exclusion of consequential damages unconscionable? [*Lee v. Mercedes-Benz USA, LLC*, 622 S.E.2d 361 (Ga. Ct. App.)]

Negotiable Instruments

Information on bad checks and duties of a bank regarding negotiable instruments can be found in Chapter 22. Chapter 24 covers recourse, or defenses, to nonpayment of commercial paper. One recourse to checks not paid by a bank due to insufficient funds is a debt collection service. See the website of AllBusiness (www.allbusiness.com), a company dedicated to assisting small businesses with collections.

20 Nature of Negotiable Instruments

21 Essentials of Negotiability

22 Promissory Notes and Drafts

23 Negotiation and Discharge

24 Liabilities and Defenses Specific to Negotiable Instruments

CHAPTER 20

Nature of Negotiable Instruments

LEARNING OBJECTIVES

(1) Discuss how negotiable instruments are transferred.

(2) Differentiate between bearer paper and order paper.

(3) Describe an electronic fund transfer.

PREVIEW CASE

To purchase real property, Albert Austin executed a thirty-year promissory note for $65,913 payable to Harbor Financial Mortgage Corp. The note was reassigned several times, the last time to Countrywide Home Loans. After two years, Austin stopped making the monthly payments, and a lawsuit ensued. Austin alleged that Countrywide was not a valid assignee of the note, and thus it was unlawful for it to try to collect it. Kimberly Dawson, vice president of Countrywide, testified that the original note payable to Harbor was indorsed to Countrywide, which had possession of it and had not in any way transferred or pledged it or any interest in it. How may a note be transferred? What is the significance of an indorsement?

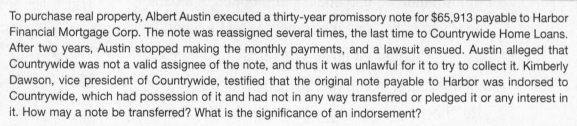

negotiable instrument or commercial paper
writing drawn in special form that can be transferred as substitute for money or as instrument of credit

Negotiable instruments or **commercial paper** are writings drawn in a special form that can be transferred from person to person as a substitute for money or as an instrument of credit. Such an instrument must meet certain definite requirements in regard to its form and the manner in which it is transferred. Two types of negotiable instruments include checks and notes. Since a negotiable instrument is not money, the law does not require a person to accept one in payment of a debt.

20-1 History and Development

The need for instruments of credit that would permit the settlement of claims between distant cities without the transfer of money has existed as long as trade has existed. Negotiable instruments were developed to meet that need. References to bills of exchange or instruments of credit appeared as early as 50 B.C. Their widespread usage, however, began about A.D. 1200 as international trade began to flourish in the wake of the Crusades. At first, these credit instruments were used only in international trade, but they gradually became common in domestic trade.

In England, before about A.D. 1400, special courts set up on the spot by the merchants settled all disputes between merchants. The rules applied by these courts became known as the **law merchant**. Later, the common law courts took over the adjudication of all disputes, including those between merchants. However, these courts retained most of the customs developed by the merchants and incorporated the law merchant into the common law. Most, but by no means all, of the law merchant dealt with bills of exchange or credit instruments.

law merchant
rules applied by courts set up by merchants in early England

In the United States, each state modified the common law dealing with credit instruments so that eventually the various states had different laws regarding them. The American Bar Association and the American Banks Association appointed a commission to draw up a Uniform Negotiable Instruments Law. In 1896, the commission proposed a uniform act. This act was adopted in all the states, but Article 3 of the Uniform Commercial Code (UCC) then displaced it.

In 1990, a commission that writes uniform laws issued a revised Article 3. This text explains the law according to the changes made by the 1990 revision. The revision uses the term *negotiable instruments*, whereas the original Article 3 uses the term *commercial paper*, and both terms remain in use. Although states adopt uniform laws, it is important to note that the states do not necessarily adopt the uniform laws exactly as written. Frequently they make minor changes that do not significantly affect the impact of the law. We say that a state has adopted a uniform law when it has adopted the law with but minor changes.

20-2 Negotiation

Negotiation is the act of transferring ownership of a negotiable instrument to another party. The owner may negotiate a negotiable instrument owned by, and payable to, such owner. The owner negotiates it by signing on the back of it and delivering it to another party. The signature of the owner made on the back of a negotiable instrument before delivery is called an *indorsement* (see Chapter 23).[1]

LO ①
Transfer of negotiable instruments

negotiation
act of transferring ownership of negotiable instrument

When a negotiable instrument is transferred by negotiation to one or more parties, these parties may acquire rights superior to those of the original owner. Parties who acquire rights superior to those of the original owner are known as **holders in due course**. It is mainly this feature of the transfer of superior rights that gives negotiable instruments a special classification all their own.

holder in due course
person who acquires rights superior to original owner

20-3 Order Paper and Bearer Paper

If commercial paper is made payable to the order of a named person, it is called **order paper**. If commercial paper is made payable to whoever has possession of it, the bearer, it is called **bearer paper**. Bearer paper may be made payable to bearer, cash, or any other indication that does not purport to designate a specific person. Order paper must use the word *order*, as in the phrase, "pay to the order of John Doe," or some other word to indicate it may be paid to a transferee. Order paper is negotiated only by indorsement of the person to whom it is then payable and by

LO ②
Bearer paper versus order paper

order paper
commercial paper payable to order

bearer paper
commercial paper payable to bearer

---

[1] "Indorsement" is the spelling used in the UCC, although "endorsement" is commonly used in business.

delivery of the paper to another person. In the case of bearer paper, merely handing the paper to another person may make the transfer.

Payment is made on a different basis with order paper than with bearer paper. Order paper may be paid only to the person to whom it is made payable on its face or the person to whom it has been properly indorsed. However, bearer paper may be paid to any person in possession of the paper.

COURT CASE

FACTS: Mark Stanley Miller and Jamileh Miller mortgaged their home and signed a note for $216,236 to IndyMac Bank, F.S.B. (Indy). The note stated that it could be sold one or more times without notice to the Millers. When the Millers defaulted, Deutsche Bank National Trust Company (Deutsche) claiming to be the holder of the note, began foreclosure proceedings. Deutsche attached a copy of the note to its papers showing it had been indorsed in blank. In a subsequent bankruptcy proceeding, the Millers alleged Deutsche could not foreclose because it did not produce the original note and therefore was not the holder.

OUTCOME: The court held that Deutsche had to prove it was the holder of the note, and in order to do that, it had to produce the original note.

—*In re Miller*, 666 F.3d 1255 (10th Cir.)

20-4 Classification of Commercial Paper

The basic negotiable instruments are:

1. Drafts

2. Promissory notes

20-4a DRAFTS

draft or bill of exchange
written order by one person directing another to pay a sum of money to a third person

A **draft** is also called a **bill of exchange**. It is a written order signed by one person requiring the person to whom it is addressed to pay on demand or at a particular time a fixed amount of money to order or to bearer. Checks and trade acceptances are special types of drafts. When you make out a check on your bank account, you are actually writing out a type of draft. (See Chapter 22.)

20-4b PROMISSORY NOTES

promissory note
unconditional written promise to pay sum of money to another

A **promissory note** is an unconditional promise in writing made by one person to another, signed by the promisor, engaging to pay on demand of the holder, or, at a definite time, a fixed amount of money to order or to bearer (see Illustration 20-1). If the note is a demand instrument, the holder may demand payment or sue for payment at any time and for any reason.

ILLUSTRATION 20-1 Promissory Note Parties: Maker, Jan L. Hendricks; Payee, Ana Nieves

---

NOTE

$ __7,000.00__   Greenfield, Missouri   __April 1,__ 20 __-___

____One (1) year____   after date, for value received ___I___   promise

to pay to the order of ____Ana Nieves____

the sum of ____Seven Thousand Dollars ($7,000.00)____

with interest thereon from date at the rate of ___fifteen percent (15%)___

per annum, interest payable _____semiannually_____ and if interest

is not paid ____semiannually____ to become as principal and bear

the same rate of interest.

Payable at __Northside Bank__

____Jan L. Hendricks____

20-5 Parties to Negotiable Instruments

Each party to a negotiable instrument is designated by a certain term, depending on the type of instrument. Some of these terms apply to all types of negotiable instruments, whereas others are restricted to one type. The same individual may be designated by one term at one stage and by another at a later stage through which the instrument passes before it is collected. These terms include *payee, drawer, drawee, acceptor, maker, bearer, holder, indorser,* and *indorsee.*

20-5a PAYEE

The person to whom any negotiable instrument is made payable is called the **payee**.

> **payee**
> party to whom instrument is payable

20-5b DRAWER

The person who executes or signs any draft is called the **drawer** (see Illustration 20-2).

> **drawer**
> person who executes a draft

20-5c DRAWEE

The person who is ordered to pay a draft is called the **drawee**.

> **drawee**
> person ordered to pay a draft

20-5d ACCEPTOR

A drawee who accepts a draft, thus indicating a willingness to assume responsibility for its payment, is called the **acceptor**. A person accepts drafts not immediately payable by writing on the face of the instruments these or similar words: *Accepted, Jane Daws.* This indicates that Jane Daws will perform the contract according to its terms.

> **acceptor**
> person who agrees to pay a draft

ILLUSTRATION 20-2 Draft Parties: Drawer, Lee W. Richardson; Drawee, Walter Evans; Payee, Community Bank

$ __450.00_____   __December 22,__ 20 ___--___

____Six months after date____   PAY TO THE

ORDER OF___Community Bank_____

__Four hundred fifty dollars and no/100_____

FOR CLASSROOM USE ONLY

VALUE RECEIVED AND CHARGE TO ACCOUNT OF   DOLLARS

TO __Walter Evans_____

No. __27 Walden, Virginia_____   __Lee W. Richardson__

20-5e MAKER

maker
person who executes a note

The person who executes a promissory note is called the **maker**. The maker contracts to pay the amount due on the note. This obligation resembles that of the acceptor of a draft.

20-5f BEARER

bearer
payee of instrument made payable to whomever is in possession

Any negotiable instrument may be made payable to whoever possesses it. The payee of such an instrument is the **bearer**. If the instrument is made payable to the order of *Myself*, *Cash*, or another similar name, it is payable to the bearer.

20-5g HOLDER

holder
person in possession of instrument payable to bearer or that person

Any person who possesses an instrument is the **holder** if it has been delivered to the person and it is either bearer paper or it is payable to that person as the payee or by indorsement. The payee is the original holder of an instrument.

PREVIEW CASE REVISITED

FACTS: To purchase real property, Albert Austin executed a thirty-year promissory note for $65,913 payable to Harbor Financial Mortgage Corp. The note was reassigned several times, the last time to Countrywide Home Loans. After two years, Austin stopped making the monthly payments, and a lawsuit ensued. Austin alleged that Countrywide was not a valid assignee of the note and thus that it was unlawful for it to try to collect it. Kimberly Dawson, vice president of Countrywide, testified that the original note payable to Harbor was indorsed to Countrywide, which had possession of it and had not in any way transferred or pledged it or any interest in it.

OUTCOME: The court found that Countrywide was the holder of the note, and Austin was obligated to pay it.

—*Austin v. Countrywide Home Loans*, 261 S.W.3d 68 (Tex. Ct. App.)

20-5h HOLDER IN DUE COURSE

A holder who takes a negotiable instrument in good faith and for value is a holder in due course.

20-5i INDORSER

When the payee of a draft or a note wishes to transfer the instrument to another party, it must be indorsed. The payee is then called the **indorser**. The payee makes the indorsement by signing on the back of the instrument.

indorser
payee or holder who signs back of instrument

20-5j INDORSEE

A person who becomes the holder of a negotiable instrument by an indorsement that names him or her as the person to whom the instrument is negotiated is called the **indorsee**.

indorsee
named holder of indorsed negotiable instrument

20-6 Negotiation and Assignment

The right to receive payment of instruments may be transferred by either negotiation or assignment. Nonnegotiable paper cannot be transferred by negotiation. The rights to it are transferred by assignment. Negotiable instruments may be transferred by negotiation or assignment. The rights given the original parties are alike in the cases of negotiation and assignment. In the case of a promissory note, for example, the original parties are the maker (the one who promises to pay) and the payee (the one to whom the money is to be paid). Between the original parties, both a nonnegotiable and a negotiable instrument are equally enforceable. The same defenses against fulfilling the terms of the instrument may be set up as well. For example, if one party to the instrument is a minor, the lack of capacity to contract may be set up as a defense against carrying out the agreement.

However, the rights given to subsequent parties differ, depending on whether an instrument is transferred by negotiation or assignment. When an instrument is transferred by assignment, the assignee receives only the rights of the assignor and no more. (See Chapter 12.) If one of the original parties to the instrument has a defense that is valid against the assignor, it is also valid against the assignee.

When an instrument is transferred by negotiation, however, the party who receives the instrument in good faith and for value may obtain rights that are superior to the rights of the original holder. Defenses that may be valid against the original holder may not be valid against a holder who has received an instrument by negotiation.

COURT CASE

FACTS: Syed Hussain gave Zakir Hussain two signed, but otherwise "blank" checks. Zakir filled in the blanks, making the checks payable to Patricia Malik in amounts Syed owed Malik. When Malik went to deposit the checks, they were returned by the bank for insufficient funds. Was Syed liable on the checks?

OUTCOME: The checks were negotiable instruments payable to bearer. By handing them over to a third party, Syed was subject to liability for them.

—*In re Hussain*, 508 B.R. 417 (9th Cir. BAP.)

20-7 Credit and Collection

Negotiable instruments are called *instruments of credit* and *instruments of collection*. If *A* sells *B* merchandise on sixty days' credit, the buyer may at the time of the sale execute a negotiable note or draft due in sixty days in payment of the merchandise. This note or draft then is an instrument of credit.

If the seller in the previous transaction will not extend the original credit to sixty days, a draft may be drawn on the buyer, who would be the drawee. In that case, the drawer may make a bank the payee, the bank being a mere agent of the drawer. Or one of the seller's creditors may be made the payee so that an account receivable will be collected, and an account payable will be paid all in one transaction. When the account receivable comes due, the buyer will mail a check to the seller. In this example, the draft is an instrument of collection.

20-8 Electronic Fund Transfers

LO ③
Electronic fund transfers

**electronic fund
transfer (EFT)**
fund transfer initiated
electronically, telephonically,
or by computer

More and more transfers of funds occur today in which a paper instrument is not actually transferred, and the parties do not have face-to-face, personal contact. An **electronic fund transfer (EFT)** is any transfer of funds initiated by means of an electronic terminal, telephonic instrument, or computer or magnetic tape that instructs or authorizes a financial institution to debit or credit an account. An EFT does not include a transfer of funds begun by a check, draft, or similar paper instrument.

EFTs are popular because they are faster and less expensive than the transfer of paper instruments. EFTs can reduce the risk of problems resulting from lost instruments. If a check, for example, does not have to make the entire trip from the payee to the drawee bank to the drawer customer, costs and delays can be reduced.

A federal law, the Electronic Fund Transfer Act (EFTA), regulates EFTs and defines them as carried out primarily by electronic means. A transfer initiated by a telephone call between a bank employee and a customer is not an EFT unless it is in accordance with a prearranged plan.

The EFTA requires disclosure of the terms and conditions of the EFTs involving a customer's account at the time the customer contracts for an EFT service. This notification must include:

1. What liability could be imposed for unauthorized EFTs

2. The type of EFTs the customer may make

3. The charges for EFTs

Under the EFTA, a customer's liability for an unauthorized EFT can be limited to $50; however, the customer must give the bank very prompt notice of circumstances that lead to the belief that an unauthorized EFT has been or may be made. Also, a bank does not need to reimburse a customer who fails to notify a bank of an unauthorized EFT within sixty days of receiving a bank statement on which the unauthorized EFT appears. Some states also have laws applying to EFTs that may give customers greater protection than the federal law.

Widely used types of EFTs include check truncation, preauthorized debits and credits, automated teller machines, and point-of-sale systems.

20-8a CHECK TRUNCATION

check truncation
shortening a check's trip
from payee to drawer

A system of shortening the trip a check makes from the payee to the drawee bank and then to the drawer is called **check truncation**. It used to be that all banks returned cancelled checks to customers with a monthly bank statement. However, most banks no longer return the actual cancelled checks to their customers with a monthly statement. Instead, statements to customers list the check numbers and the dollar amounts on the checks, and the transactions are printed in numerical order. The customer can easily reconcile the account without having the cancelled checks. Many banks do not mail monthly statements but send statements electronically. However, banks must be able to supply legible copies of checks at the customers' request for seven years. These are types of check truncation.

20-8b PREAUTHORIZED DEBITS AND CREDITS

Checking account customers may authorize that recurring bills, such as home mortgage payments, insurance premiums, or utility bills, be automatically deducted from their checking accounts each month. This is called a **preauthorized debit**. It allows a person to avoid the inconvenience and cost of writing out and mailing checks for these bills.

A **preauthorized credit** allows the amount of regular payments to be automatically deposited in the payee's account. This type of EFT is frequently used for depositing salaries and government benefits, such as Social Security payments. It benefits the payor, who does not have to issue and mail the checks. The payee does not have to bother depositing a check and normally has access to the funds sooner.

preauthorized debit automatic deduction of bill payment from checking account

preauthorized credit automatic deposit of funds to an account

20-8c AUTOMATED TELLER MACHINES

An **automated teller machine (ATM)** is an EFT terminal capable of performing routine banking services. Many thousands of such machines exist at locations designed to be accessible to customers. The capabilities of the machines vary; however, some ATMs do such things as dispense cash and account information and allow customers to make deposits, transfer funds between accounts, and pay bills. ATMs are conveniently found at many locations, even in foreign countries, and are open when banks are not.

automated teller machine (ATM) EFT terminal that performs routine banking services

20-8d POINT-OF-SALE SYSTEMS

Electronic fund transfers that begin at retailers when consumers want to pay for goods or services with debit cards are called **point-of-sale (POS) systems**. These transactions occur when the person operating the POS terminal enters information regarding the payment into a computer system. The entry debits the consumer's bank account and credits the retailer's account by the amount of the transaction.

point-of-sale (POS) system EFTs begun at retailers when customers pay for goods or services

QUESTIONS

1. What is a negotiable instrument?
2. Since all the states have adopted the Uniform Commercial Code, is the law the same in every state?
3. How does the owner negotiate a negotiable instrument?
4. What is the difference between order and bearer paper?
5. What is a demand instrument?
6. Who is a holder?

QUESTIONS (CONTINUED)

7. What rights are given to parties subsequent to the original payee when the instrument is transferred by assignment? What if the instrument is transferred by negotiation? Explain.

8. How does a customer limit liability for an unauthorized EFT?

9. What does it mean to a customer when a bank uses a system of check truncation?

10. What are the benefits of a preauthorized credit to both the payor and payee?

CASE PROBLEMS

LO ③

1. Jeremy Cobb submitted an apartment rental application to Common Properties Management Cooperative (Common) over the phone. Cobb authorized Common to debit his checking account for the $37.95 application fee. However, the debit was returned by Cobb's bank as unpaid, and Cobb was assessed a Non-Sufficient Funds (NSF) fee of $35.00 by Cobb's bank, along with a $25.00 "returned fee" by PayLease, LLC (PayLease), Common's financial institution. Cobb sued under the EFTA, alleging that the $25.00 "returned fee" had not been authorized. Was the $25.00 returned fee to PayLease covered by the EFTA?

LO ②

2. Bryce Erickson hired attorney William Bagley to represent him in a Chapter 11 bankruptcy. After the bankruptcy court dismissed his Chapter 11 proceeding, Erickson asked Bagley to represent him in a Chapter 12 bankruptcy. Bagley agreed, provided Erickson signed a promissory note payable to Sirius LC, a company co-owned by Bagley and his wife, in the amount of $29,173.38, secured by a mortgage on real property owned by Erickson. Erickson executed to Sirius a promissory note which stated, "For value received, the undersigned Bryce H. Erickson promises to pay to SIRIUS LC . . . the sum of Twenty-Nine Thousand One Hundred Seventy-Three Dollars and Thirty-Eight Cents ($29,173.38)" and executed the mortgage. Sirius sued to foreclose on Erickson's real estate after he refused to pay the note when due. The court had to decide whether the note was negotiable. Was it?

LO ①

3. Cynthia Dudley was a student at Southern Virginia University (SVU). Dudley obtained a loan from Nellie Mae, which included a note by which Dudley agreed to repay the money loaned to the order of Nellie Mae. SVU sued Dudley to collect on the note, but failed to produce the note in court, claiming that it had been lost or destroyed. Dudley responded that if SVU could not produce the note, it could not prove negotiation from Nellie Mae to SVU, and SVU could not collect. Could SVU simply claim the note had been lost or destroyed?

LO ③

4. By phone, Patricia Sanford bought fitness tapes. The call center operator read Sanford a script saying that for buying the tapes, MemberWorks Inc. (Member) was sending membership in a program called ESSENTIALS. The program had a thirty-day free trial and if not cancelled in that time, cost $6 per month, which was billed in advance to the credit card used to purchase the tapes. Sanford did not remember hearing the script, agreeing to the membership, or receiving a membership kit. She did not cancel, so her credit card was charged $72 the next month and $84 the next year. She sued, alleging, among other things, violation of the EFTA. Had the transaction violated that act?

LO ②

5. Gary and Clara Delffs signed a note to Joe Waldron that read " _____ after date _____ promise to pay to the order of." After the word *of* was a long blank line on which was handwritten, "one hundred and fifty-three thousand and four hundred and forty dollars." Following this was printed, "Dollars." The parties agreed the document was not order paper. A lawsuit ensued, and the court had to decide whether the note was bearer paper. Decide the case.

CASE PROBLEMS (CONTINUED)

6. Key Bank National Association operated ATMs that permitted bank customers and noncustomers to conduct transactions. Key Bank customers could use the ATMs without fees, but the bank assessed fees on most noncustomers. Noncustomers who were not charged fees included members of the military, customers of affiliated banks, and users of the Key Bank Cleveland Clinic ATM. When a noncustomer put a card in a Key Bank ATM and entered a personal identification number, the following message appeared on the screen:

   LO ③

   > This terminal may charge a fee of $2.00 for a cash withdrawal. This charge is in addition to any fees that may be assessed by your financial institution.
   >
   > Do you wish to continue this transaction?
   >
   > If yes press to accept fee.
   >
   > If no press to decline fee.

   Once a noncustomer accepted the fee, the bank would determine whether a fee would be charged. Michael Clemmer, not a Key Bank customer, made a withdrawal at a Key Bank ATM. When the screen had asked whether he accepted the fee, he selected "yes," and Key Bank had charged him $2. Clemmer sued the bank, alleging he did not receive adequate on-screen notice that he would be charged a fee. Had he received notice of the charge for using the ATM?

7. Dan Reade obtained a loan to purchase his home from ABN AMRO Mortgage Group, Inc. (AMRO). As part of the transaction, Reade executed a promissory note to AMRO. Over the course of time, AMRO merged with CitiMortgage, Inc. (CitiMortgage), with CitiMortgage as the surviving entity. Reade made some payments on the note, but he defaulted. When CitiMortgage tried to collect, Reade demanded that CitiMortgage produce evidence that the note had been negotiated to CitiMortgage. Did CitiMortgage have to show negotiation in order to collect on the note?

   LO ①

Essentials of Negotiability

LEARNING OBJECTIVES

① List the seven requirements of negotiability.

② Explain the requirements for issuance and delivery of a negotiable instrument.

③ State whether a negotiable instrument must be dated and whether the location of making payment must be indicated.

PREVIEW CASE

Soults Farms Inc. (SFI) was a family farming corporation, and Robert Soults, the president, was responsible for the day-to-day operations and maintenance of finances and was the majority stockholder. Charles Schafer and Soults entered into several short-term loans, which Soults told Schafer were for farm expenses. The loans were evidenced by promissory notes and checks. Soults mortgaged SFI real estate to secure the debt to Schafer, although the notes did not mention SFI, and the money was deposited into Soults's personal account. The loans totaled $440,000, but $359,000 was immediately transferred to SFI's account. Soults lost millions of dollars on an investment scheme and disappeared. SFI sued Schafer, asking the court to release the mortgage on its real estate, saying it was not liable on the loans. Who got the benefit of the loans? What did Soults say the loans were for?

One important characteristic of negotiable instruments is their transferability or negotiability. However, instruments must meet certain requirements in order to be negotiable.

LO ①
Requirements of negotiability

21-1 Requirements

An instrument must comply with seven requirements in order to be negotiable. If it lacks any of these requirements, the document is not negotiable. However, even though an instrument is not negotiable, it may be valid and enforceable between the original parties to it, and many are. The seven requirements are:

1. The instrument must be in writing and signed by the party executing it.

2. The instrument must contain either an order to pay or a promise to pay.

3. The order or the promise must be unconditional.

4. The instrument must provide for the payment of a fixed amount of money.

5. The instrument must be payable either on demand or at a fixed or definite time.

6. The instrument must be payable to the order of a payee or to bearer.

7. The payee (unless the instrument is payable to bearer) and the drawee must be designated with reasonable certainty.

21-1a A SIGNED WRITING

A negotiable instrument must be written. However, the law does not require that the writing be in any particular form. The instrument may be written with pen and ink or with pencil; it may be typed or printed; or it may be partly printed and partly typed or handwritten. An instrument executed with a lead pencil meets the legal requirements of **negotiability**. However, a person executing an instrument in pencil takes a risk because of the ease with which the instrument could be altered without detection.

negotiability
transferability

A signature must be placed on a negotiable instrument in order to indicate the intent of the promisor to be bound. The normal place for a signature is in the lower right-hand corner, but the location of the signature and its form are wholly immaterial if it is clear that a signature was intended. The signature may be handwritten, typed, printed, or stamped. It may consist of a name, a symbol, a mark, or a trade name. The signature, however, must be on the instrument. It cannot be on a separate paper attached to the instrument.

Some odd, but valid, signatures follow:

1. His
    Richard × Cooper
    Mark

    This type of signature might be made by a person who does not know how to write. The signer makes the × in the center. A witness writes the signer's name, Richard Cooper, and the words His Mark to indicate who signed the instrument and that it was intended as a signature.

2. "I, Tammy Morley," written by Morley in the body of the note but with her name typed in the usual place for the signature.

3. "Snowwhite Cleaner," the trade name under which Glendon Sutton operates his business.

The instrument may be signed by an agent, who is another person who has been given authority to perform this act.

PREVIEW CASE REVISITED

FACTS: Soults Farms Inc. (SFI) was a family farming corporation, and Robert Soults, the president, was responsible for the day-to-day operations and maintenance of finances and was the majority stockholder. Charles Schafer and Soults entered into several short-term loans which Soults told Schafer were for farm expenses. The loans were evidenced by promissory notes and checks. Soults mortgaged SFI real estate to secure the debt to Schafer, although the notes did not mention SFI, and the money was deposited into Soults's personal account. The loans totaled $440,000, but $359,000 was immediately transferred to SFI's account. Soults lost millions of dollars on an investment scheme and disappeared. SFI sued Schafer, asking the court to release the mortgage on its real estate, saying it was not liable on the loans.

OUTCOME: As president of SFI, the court held that Soults was the agent of SFI. Since SFI did benefit from the loans, the mortgage was not released.

—*Soults Farms Inc. v. Schafer*, 797 N.W.2d 92 (Iowa)

21-1b AN ORDER OR A PROMISE TO PAY

A draft, such as a trade acceptance or a check, must contain an order to pay. If the request is imperative and unequivocal, it is an order even though the word *order* is not used.

A promissory note must contain a promise to pay. The word *promise* need not be used—any equivalent words will answer the purpose—but the language used must show that a promise is intended. Thus, the words *I will pay, I guarantee to pay*, and *This is to certify that we are bound to pay* were held to be sufficient to constitute a promise. A mere acknowledgment of a debt does not suffice.

21-1c UNCONDITIONAL

The order or the promise must be absolute and unconditional. Neither must be contingent upon any other act or event. If Baron promises to pay Noffke $500 "in sixty days, or sooner if I sell my farm," the instrument is negotiable because the promise itself is unconditional. In any event, a promise to pay the $500 in sixty days exists. The contingency pertains only to the time of payment, and that time cannot exceed sixty days. If the words *or sooner* were omitted, the promise would be conditional, and the note would be nonnegotiable. As stated previously, however, an instrument may be binding on the parties even though nonnegotiable.

If the order to pay is out of a particular fund or account, the instrument is still negotiable. For example, "Pay to the order of Leonard Cohen $5,000 out of my share of my mother's estate" would not be a conditional order to pay. The order or the promise need not commit the entire credit of the one primarily liable for the payment of the instrument.

COURT CASE

FACTS: In order to buy a new Chevrolet Corvette, Cory Babcock and Honest Air Conditioning & Heating Inc. signed a retail installment sale contract (RISC) and made monthly payments to General Motors Acceptance Corp. (GMAC). In the RISC, Babcock and Honest agreed to buy the vehicle on credit, give GMAC a security interest in it, keep the Corvette in the United States, and reimburse GMAC for any advances for repairs or storage bills. A year later, Babcock and Honest Air traded the Corvette to Florida Auto Brokers for another vehicle. A few months later, Florida sent a check in the correct amount to GMAC, which released the lien on the Corvette and sent Florida the title. Florida's check bounced, so GMAC sued Babcock and Honest. They argued that the RISC was a negotiable instrument.

OUTCOME: The court stated that to be negotiable the RISC had to be an unconditional promise. It could not contain any other undertaking by the promisor other than the payment of money. The RISC was not negotiable.

—*General Motors Acceptance Corp. v. Honest Air Conditioning and Heating Inc.*, 933 So.2d 34 (Fla. Dist. Ct. App.)

A reference to the consideration in a note that does not condition the promise does not destroy negotiability. The clause "This note is given in consideration of a typewriter purchased today" does not condition the maker's promise to pay. If the clause were to read, "This note is given in consideration for a typewriter guaranteed for ninety days, breach of warranty to constitute cancellation of the note," the instrument would not be negotiable. This promise to pay is not absolute but conditional. Also, if the recital of the consideration is in such form as to make the instrument subject to another contract, the negotiability of the instrument is destroyed.

Thus, a mere reference to a separate agreement or a statement that the instrument arises out of a separate agreement does not make the promise or order conditional. However, if the promise or order states it is subject to, or governed by, another agreement, it is conditional because a right to payment of a negotiable instrument cannot be controlled by another document.

21-1d A FIXED AMOUNT OF MONEY

The instrument must call for the payment of money. It need not be American money, but it must be some national medium of exchange that is legal tender at the place payment is to be made. Thus, it could be payable in dollars, yen, euros, pounds, pesos, or rubles. It cannot be in scrip, gold bullion, bonds, or similar assets. However, the instrument may provide for the payment of either money or goods. If the choice lies with the holder, such a provision does not destroy its negotiability.

The sum payable must be a fixed amount, not dependent on other funds or on future profits.

COURT CASE

FACTS: Nancy Gardner took a loan from Flagstar Bank, FSB (Flagstar), to purchase a house, and signed a note secured by a mortgage on the property. Flagstar later assigned the mortgage to Quicken Loans, Inc. (Quicken). After a few years, Gardner fell behind in payments, and Quicken began foreclosure proceedings. Gardner opposed the foreclosure proceedings, claiming Quicken could not prove it was the holder of the mortgage, because the mortgage did not state a sum certain which Gardner was obliged to pay. Does Article 3 of the UCC apply?

OUTCOME: No. A mortgage is not a negotiable instrument, in part because it does not state a sum certain to be repaid. As a result, Quicken did not need to comply with Article 3.

—*Gardner v. Quicken Loans, Inc.*, 567 Fed. Appx. 362 (6th Cir.)

Not only must the contract be payable in money to be negotiable, but the amount must be determinable from the wording of the instrument itself. If a note for $5,000 provides that all taxes that may be levied on a certain piece of real estate will be paid, it is nonnegotiable. The amount to be paid cannot be determined from the note itself. A provision providing for the payment of interest or exchange charges, however, does not destroy negotiability. Other terms that have been held not to destroy negotiability are provisions for cost of collection, a 10 percent attorney's fee if placed in the hands of an attorney for collection, and installment payments.

A variable rate of interest does not destroy negotiability. Although the Uniform Commercial Code (UCC) requires the instrument to call for payment of a "fixed amount" of money, the fixed amount refers to principal. The UCC specifically permits the rate of interest to be a variable one without destroying negotiability.

Sometimes, through error of the party writing the negotiable instrument, the words on the instrument may call for the payment of one amount of money, while the figures call for the payment of another. The amount expressed in words prevails because one is less likely to err in writing this amount. Also, if anyone should attempt to raise the amount, it would be much simpler to alter the figures than the words. By the same token, handwriting prevails over conflicting typewriting, and typewriting prevails over conflicting printed amounts.

21-1e PAYABLE ON DEMAND OR AT A DEFINITE TIME

An instrument meets the test of negotiability as to time if it is payable on demand (as in a demand note) or at sight (as in a sight draft). If no time is specified (as in a check), the commercial paper is considered payable on demand.

COURT CASE

FACTS: Abby Novel signed a handwritten note which stated: "Glen Gallwitz . . . loaned me $5,000 at 6 percent interest a total of $10,000." When she did not pay the note, Gallwitz sued her for payment. She alleged that the note was not negotiable because it did not contain a certain or definite time for repayment.

OUTCOME: The court held that where no time for payment is stated on an instrument, the instrument is payable on demand. The note was a demand instrument.

—*Gallwitz v. Novel*, 2011 Ohio 297 (Ohio Ct. App.)

If the instrument provides for payment at a time in the future, the due date must be fixed.

Promissory notes often include either an acceleration clause or a prepayment clause. An acceleration clause protects the payee, and the prepayment clause benefits the party obligated to pay. A typical acceleration clause provides that in the event one installment is in default, the whole note shall become due and payable at once. This does not destroy its negotiability. Most prepayment clauses give the maker or the drawee the right to prepay the instrument in order to save interest. This also does not affect the negotiability of the instrument.

21-1f PAYABLE TO ORDER OR BEARER

The two most common words of negotiability are *order* and *bearer*. The instrument is payable to order when some person is made the payee, and the maker or drawer wishes to indicate that the instrument will be paid to the person designated or to anyone else to whom the payee may transfer the instrument by indorsement.

It is not necessary to use the word *order*, but it is strongly recommended. The law looks to the intention of the maker or the drawer. If the words used clearly show an intention to pay either the named payee or anyone else whom the payee designates, the contract is negotiable. A note payable to "Smith and assigns" was held to be nonnegotiable. If it had been payable to "Smith or assigns," it would have been negotiable.

However, there is an exception in the case of checks. Article 3 of the UCC provides that a check reading, "Pay to Smith" is negotiable. This applies only to checks and not to other drafts or notes.

The other words of negotiability, *payable to bearer*, indicate that the maker or the acceptor of a draft is willing to pay the person who possesses the instrument at maturity. The usual form in which these words appear is *Pay to bearer* or *Pay to Lydia Lester or bearer*. Other types of wording make an instrument a bearer instrument. For example, *Pay to the order of cash*, and *Pay to the order of bearer*, or any other designation that does not refer to a natural person or a corporation is regarded as payable to bearer.

21-1g PAYEE AND DRAWEE DESIGNATED WITH REASONABLE CERTAINTY

When a negotiable instrument is payable "to order," the payee must be so named that the specific party can be identified with reasonable certainty. For example, a check that reads, "Pay to the order of the Treasurer of the Virginia Educational Association" is not payable to a specific named individual, but that person can be ascertained with reasonable certainty. Therefore, the check is negotiable. However, if the check is payable "to the order of the Treasury of the YMCA," and the city has three such organizations, it would not be possible to ascertain the payee with reasonable certainty. This check would not be negotiable.

The drawee of a draft must likewise be named or described with reasonable certainty so that the holder will know who will accept or pay it.

21-2 Issue and Delivery

A negotiable instrument written by the drawer or maker does not have any effect until it is "issued." The UCC defines **issue** as "the first delivery of an instrument by the maker or drawer . . . for the purpose of giving rights on the instrument to any person." **Delivery** means the intentional transfer of possession and control of something. So, *issue* ordinarily means that the drawer or maker mails it or hands it over to the payee or does some other act that releases possession and control over it and sends it on its way to the payee. Whenever delivery is made in connection with either the original issue or a subsequent negotiation, the delivery must be absolute, not conditional. If it is conditional, the issuing of the instrument or the negotiation does not take effect until the condition is satisfied; however, as against a holder in due course, a defendant will be barred from showing that the condition was not satisfied.

LO ②
Issue and delivery requirements

issue
first delivery of negotiable instrument by maker or drawer to give rights to another

delivery
intentional transfer of possession and control of something

COURT CASE

FACTS: L.D.F. Family Farm, Inc. (Farm), obtained a loan from Charterbank to purchase and develop real property. At closing, the loan was smaller than the amount originally requested by Farm, leaving only enough money to purchase, but not develop the property. The Charterbank employee allegedly assured Farm that the bank would work with Farm to do what was needed to develop the property. Farm went ahead and purchased the property so it would not lose its earnest money. Farm defaulted on payments, and Charterbank sued on the note. Was delivery of the note conditional upon Charterbank's working with Farm to develop the property?

OUTCOME: The note could not be amended by conditions which were not expressed on the face of the note. Farm was still required to comply with the terms of the note.

—*L.D.F. Family Farm, Inc. v. Charterbank,*
756 S.E.2d 593 (Ga. App.)

To negotiate order paper, it must be both indorsed by the person to whom the paper is then payable and delivered to the new holder. Bearer payer requires no indorsement, and a physical transfer of the instrument alone effects negotiation.

21-3 Delivery of an Incomplete Instrument

If a negotiable instrument is only partially filled in and signed before delivery, the maker or drawer is liable if the blanks are filled in according to instructions. If the holder fills in the blanks contrary to authority, the maker or drawer is liable to the original payee or an ordinary holder for only the amount actually authorized. A holder in due course, however, can enforce the paper according to the filled-in terms even though they were not authorized.

21-4 Date and Place

Various matters not of commercial significance do not affect the negotiable character of a negotiable instrument.

COURT CASE

FACTS: Brian Bennett signed a two-year residential lease from Carole Broderick with monthly rental of $900. The lease recited that Bennett had on deposit with Broderick $900 as a security deposit and that any nonperformance or breach of a lease provision would constitute a material breach of the lease. It further provided that if Bennett were to commit a material breach, Broderick could terminate the lease. At the signing, Bennett gave Broderick a check for $1,800 to cover the security deposit and first month's rent. After Bennett left, Broderick noticed that the check was postdated. She took it to her bank, where a teller told her it could not be accepted, deposited, or cashed because it was postdated. She notified Bennett that she did not consider the lease valid since she had no security deposit. Bennett sued for breach of contract.

OUTCOME: The court held that Broderick had received the security deposit when she accepted Bennett's check, so the lease was binding.

—*Bennett v. Broderick*, 858 N.E.2d 1044
(Ind. Ct. App.)

1. The instrument need not be dated. The negotiability of the instrument is not affected by the fact that it is undated, antedated, or postdated. The omission of a date may cause considerable inconvenience, but the date is not essential. The holder may fill in the correct date if the space for the date is left blank. If an instrument is due thirty days after date and the date is omitted, the instrument is payable thirty days after it was issued or delivered. In case of dispute, the date of issue may be proved.

2. The name of the place where the instrument was drawn or where it is payable need not be specified. For contracts in general, the law where the contract is made or where it is to be performed governs one's rights. This rule makes it advisable for a negotiable instrument to stipulate the place where it is drawn and where it is payable, but neither is essential for its negotiability.

QUESTIONS

1. State the seven requirements of negotiability.

2. In what way may the signature on a negotiable instrument be placed on the instrument, and what may it consist of?

3. Must a draft contain the word "order" to be negotiable?

4. What does it mean for the order or promise in an instrument to be unconditional?

5. Does a reference in an instrument to a separate agreement make the order or promise conditional? Explain.

6. In order to be negotiable, must an instrument be payable in American money? Explain.

7. Give two examples of provisions in an instrument that do not destroy negotiability even though they would change the amount to be paid.

8. Explain the difference between negotiation of an instrument that is *payable to order* and one that is *payable to bearer*.

9. Give two examples of wording on a negotiable instrument that makes it a bearer instrument.

10. What are the consequences of blanks in a negotiable instrument?

CASE PROBLEMS

1. Mohammed Najar executed a note payable to Argent Mortgage Company, LLC (Argent), and secured the note with a mortgage on his house. The note included a provision that required Najar to give the Bank written notice if he wanted to prepay the loan, as well as a "safe harbor" provision stating that if the amount of interest listed were later determined by a court to be usurious, any excess interest collected would be applied to principal. Argent assigned the note to Deutsche Bank National Trust Co. (Bank). Najar failed to make payments on the note, and the Bank began foreclosure on the mortgage. Najar claimed in court that the prepayment and usury clauses on the note were "other undertakings" under the UCC, thus making the note nonnegotiable. Was the note a negotiable instrument? **LO ①**

2. Sondra and Neil Kumaraperu owned a private day-care center and preschool. The preschool maintained a checking account and an operating account, but only Neil and Ranjini Niyarapola (a former owner) were on the signature cards. After Neil's death, Sondra discovered that the school's director had inadvertently deposited a check for the operating account into the checking account. So she wrote a check out to herself, signed Niyarapola's name, and deposited it into the operating account. Was the check issued? **LO ②**

3. Lois and Jeffrey Arnold owned their home jointly. Jeffrey executed a promissory note for $128,000 to Advantage Bank (Advantage) using the home as collateral. Lois did not sign the note. Both Arnolds signed a mortgage of the home to Advantage. When Jeffrey died, title to the home immediately vested in Lois. There was default on the loan, and Advantage tried to foreclose on the mortgage. Lois asked the court to prevent the foreclosure arguing that Advantage could not enforce the note against her, so it could not enforce the mortgage. Was Lois liable on the note? **LO ①**

4. On a Thursday, Deborah Wallace went to Morris Murdock Travel to buy airline tickets. Because she did not have a credit card, Wallace had to pay cash. She told Murdock she did not have the money to cover the tickets in her account, but would have it the next Tuesday, and asked Murdock to take a postdated check. Wallace delivered to Murdock a check that was not postdated but dated the previous day. Murdock held the check until Tuesday, but it bounced, and Wallace was charged with issuing a bad check. Wallace argued the instrument was not a check. Did predating the check destroy negotiability? **LO ③**

CASE PROBLEMS (CONTINUED)

LO ① 5. Hartford Packing Company Inc. (Hartford) bought tomatoes from Luellen Farms Inc. (LFI). Hartford owed LFI $225,000 for tomatoes. John Jackson, the owner and president of Hartford, signed a note for the amount to memorialize the debt. A month later, Hartford went out of business, leaving $170,000 unpaid on the note. The note stated it was in renewal of a note described in a specific mortgage. It also said, "All covenants and agreements in said mortgage contained shall apply to this renewal note." There was no such mortgage. LFI sued Hartford and Jackson personally for payment of the note. For Jackson to have personal liability, the note had to be negotiable. Was it?

LO ② 6. Edward Saunders sold real property to 2107 Brandywine, LLC and 2109 Brandywine, LLC (Brandywine), and they executed a promissory note requiring monthly payments. Brandywine tendered payments to Saunders during his lifetime. Four years later, Saunders died. Brandywine knew of the death, and Saunders's girlfriend, Francina Mitchell, told Brandywine's principal, Frederic Harwood, that she was the personal representative of the estate, and the remaining note payments were to be delivered to her. Brandywine tendered twenty monthly payments on the note to Mitchell by checks payable to Saunders. Mitchell deposited them in an account at Provident Bank, which she and Saunders had held jointly. Calvin Jackson was appointed personal representative of Saunders's estate, and he claimed the estate never received payments due under the note. Brandywine filed a lawsuit to determine its liability under the note. Should the checks Brandywine issued after Saunders's death count as payments on the note?

LO ① 7. Gary Vaughn executed a document stating that Fred and Martha Smith were loaning him $9,900. With regard to when the loan was to be repaid, the document stated, "when you can." About eighteen months later, the Smiths sued Vaughn for the entire amount, contending that the document was a note payable on demand and that it was a negotiable instrument. Was the document a negotiable note?

Promissory Notes and Drafts

CHAPTER 22

LEARNING OBJECTIVES

1. State the accountability of the maker, and distinguish among the different types of notes.
2. Identify the two different kinds of drafts.
3. Explain how drafts are accepted and what admissions are made by acceptance.
4. Describe the characteristics of a check.

PREVIEW CASE

Robert Lanier managed REL Development Inc. (REL) and I–20 East Inc. (I-20). REL borrowed more than $4 million, and I-20 borrowed $120,000 from Branch Banking & Trust Company (Bank), all secured by different tracts of real estate and guaranteed personally by Lanier. There was default on the debts, so the Bank began foreclosure proceedings. Lanier asked the Bank to stop the foreclosure proceedings so the debtors could sell the property. No sales took place, and instead of resuming foreclosure proceedings, the Bank sued the companies and Lanier for the debts. Judgment was for the Bank. The debtors and Lanier appealed, arguing the real estate market declined greatly so the Bank should have reinstituted foreclosure proceedings in order to maximize the amount received from a sale of the properties. What is the obligation of the debtor for a real estate mortgage note? Why is there a mortgage as well as a note? If you were loaning money, would you want a note signed and a mortgage?

Notes and drafts are negotiable instruments widely used in commercial and personal transactions. Each has unique features.

22-1 Notes

LO ①
Types of notes

Any written promise to pay money at a specified time is a promissory note, but it might not be a negotiable instrument. To be negotiable, a note must contain the essential elements discussed in Chapter 21.

The two original parties to a promissory note are the maker, the one who signs the note and promises to pay, and the payee, the one to whom the promise is made.

22-1a ACCOUNTABILITY OF THE MAKER

The maker of a promissory note has accountability for (1) expressly agreeing to pay the note according to its terms, (2) admitting the existence of the payee, and (3) warranting that the payee is competent to transfer the instrument by indorsement.

COURT CASE

FACTS: Borley Storage sold its business to Borley Moving and Storage Inc., a new entity with no assets, formed by Dennis Bauder, and his wife, Wanda, the sole shareholders. Warren Whitted represented Borley Storage and prepared all the documents related to the sale. The purchase agreement recited: "The purchase price shall be represented by a promissory note executed by Buyers, Dennis Bauder and Wanda Bauder, husband and wife." Borley Moving agreed to pay $250,000, in monthly installments. A promissory note in that amount payable to Borley Storage was signed by Dennis Bauder, Wanda Bauder, and by Dennis Bauder as president of Borley Moving. The note provided that the parties "jointly and severally" promised to pay. Borley Moving granted Borley Storage a security interest in all the personal property of the business.

Whitted prepared and filed a financing statement to perfect the security interest. This security interest lapsed five years after filing because no continuation statement was filed timely. Eight years after the sale, Borley Moving defaulted. Borley Storage lost its priority with respect to the personal property and accounts receivable, so it sued Whitted for malpractice. Whitted alleged that the Bauders were personally liable on the note, so Borley Storage should have made a claim against them.

OUTCOME: The court found that the Bauders were principal obligors of the promissory note and therefore makers. They were personally liable on the note.

—*Borley Storage and Transfer Co. Inc. v. Whitted,*
710 N.W.2d 71 (Neb.)

22-1b TYPES OF NOTES

Types of notes known by special names include:

1. Bonds
2. Collateral notes
3. Real estate mortgage notes
4. Debentures
5. Certificates of deposit

bond
sealed, written contract obligation with essentials of note

Bonds. A **bond** is a written contract obligation, usually under seal, generally issued by a corporation, a municipality, or a government, that contains a promise to pay a fixed amount of money at a set or determinable future time. In addition to the promise to pay, it will generally contain certain other conditions and stipulations. A bond issued by a corporation is generally secured by a deed of trust on the property of the corporation. A bond may be a coupon bond or a registered bond.

coupon bond
bond with detachable individual coupons representing interest payments

A **coupon bond** is so called because the interest payments that will become due on the bond are represented by detachable individual coupons to be presented for payment when due. Coupon bonds and the individual coupons are usually payable to the bearer; as a result, they can be negotiated by delivery. There is no registration of the original purchaser or any subsequent holder of the bond.

A **registered bond** is a bond payable to a named person. The bond is recorded under that name by the organization issuing it to guard against its loss or destruction. When a registered bond is sold, a record of the transfer to the new bondholder must be made under the name of the new bondholder.

registered bond
bond payable to specific person, whose name is recorded by issuer

Collateral Notes. A **collateral note** is a note secured by personal property. The collateral usually consists of stock, bonds, or other written evidences of debt, or a security interest in tangible personal property given by the debtor to the payee-creditor.

collateral note
note secured by personal property

The transaction may vary in terms of whether the creditor keeps possession of the property as long as the debt is unpaid or whether the debtor may keep possession of the property until default. When the creditor receives possession of collateral, reasonable care of it must be taken, and the creditor is liable to the debtor for any loss resulting from lack of reasonable care. If the creditor receives any interest, dividend, or other income from the property while it is held as collateral, such amount must be credited against the debt or returned to the debtor.

Regardless of the form of the transaction, the property is freed from the claim of the creditor if the debt is paid. If not paid, the creditor may sell the property in the manner prescribed by law. The creditor must return to the debtor any excess of the sale proceeds above the debt, interest, and costs. If the sale of the collateral does not provide sufficient proceeds to pay the debt, the debtor is liable for any deficiency.

Real Estate Mortgage Notes. A **real estate mortgage note** is given to evidence a debt that the maker/debtor secures by giving to the payee a mortgage on real estate. As in the case of a real estate mortgage, generally the mortgagor/debtor retains possession of the property. If the real estate is not freed by payment of the debt, the holder may foreclose on the mortgage or sue the maker/mortgagor on the mortgage note to enforce liability.

real estate mortgage note
note secured by mortgage on real estate

Chapter 43 more thoroughly describes real estate mortgages.

COURT CASE

FACTS: Travis Ward created a trust for the benefit of his children. The trust loaned Ward a portion of the trust assets in exchange for a promissory note from Ward. Over time, the trust and Ward agreed to renew and extend the note, and signed a renewal note. The renewal note carried a principal amount of $2,000,000, payable to the trustees on or before January 31. It also contained a provision stating that it was given in renewal of the original note, and that all liens and security interests from the original note were renewed and extended in the renewal note. In a later dispute with the trustees, Ward's son Michael, a beneficiary of the trust, claimed the references to the original note in the renewal note made the renewal note nonnegotiable, delaying the statute of limitations and giving Michael more time to bring suit.

OUTCOME: While the renewal note expressly stated that it "amends and wholly restates" the original note, it also expressly states on its face the date, the amount due, and the payee. There was no requirement to refer to the original note, so the renewal note was negotiable.

—*Ward v. Stanford*, 443 S.W.3d 334 (Tex. App.)

debenture
unsecured bond issued by a business

Debentures. An unsecured bond or note issued by a business firm is called a debenture. A debenture, like any other bond, is nothing more or less than a promissory note, usually under seal. It may be embellished with gold-colored edges, but this does not in any way indicate its value. A debenture is usually negotiable in form.

certificate of deposit (CD)
acknowledgment by bank of receipt of money with engagement to repay it

Certificates of Deposit. The Uniform Commercial Code (UCC) defines a certificate of deposit (CD) as "an acknowledgment by a bank that a sum of money has been received by the bank and a promise by the bank to repay the sum of money." The bank repays the sum to the person designated on the CD. Normally, the money is repaid with interest. The UCC classifies a certificate of deposit as a note even though it does not contain the word. A CD is not a draft, because it does not contain an order to pay.

LO ②
Kinds of drafts

22-2 Drafts

The drawer draws or executes a draft in favor of the payee, who has the drawer's authority to collect the amount indicated on the instrument. It must be clear that the signature is intended to be that of a drawer; otherwise, the signature will be construed to be that of an indorser. A draft is addressed to the drawee, who is the person ordered by the drawer to pay the amount of the instrument. The drawee pays the amount to the payee or some other party to whom the payee has transferred the instrument by indorsement.

inland draft
draft drawn and payable in the United States

An inland, or domestic, draft is one that shows on its face that it is both drawn and payable within the United States. A foreign draft shows on its face that it is drawn or payable outside the United States.

22-2a FORMS OF DRAFTS

Two kinds of drafts exist to meet the different needs of business:

1. Sight drafts
2. Time drafts

sight draft
draft payable on presentation by holder

Sight Drafts. A sight draft is a draft payable at sight or on presentation by the payee or holder. By it, the drawer demands payment at once. Special types of sight drafts include money orders and checks.

time draft
draft payable specified number of days or months after date or presentation

acceptance
drawee's signed agreement to pay draft

Time Drafts. A time draft has the same form as a sight draft except with respect to the date of payment. The drawer orders the drawee to pay the money a certain number of days or months after the date on the instrument or a certain number of days or months after presenting it for acceptance. Acceptance is the drawee's signed agreement to pay a draft, delivered to the holder.

In the case of a time draft, the holder cannot require payment of the paper until it has matured. The holder normally presents the draft to the drawee for acceptance. However, whether or not the draft has been accepted does not affect the time when it matures if it is payable a certain length of time after its date.

A time draft payable a specified number of days after sight must be presented for acceptance. The due date is calculated from the date of the acceptance, not from the date of the draft.

22-2b TRADE ACCEPTANCE

A **trade acceptance** is a type of draft used in the sale of goods. It is a draft drawn by the seller on the purchaser of goods sold and accepted by such purchaser. The drawer draws a trade acceptance at the time goods are sold. The seller is the drawer, and the purchaser is the drawee. A trade acceptance orders the purchaser to pay the face of the bill to the order of the named payee, who is frequently the seller.

trade acceptance
draft drawn by seller on purchaser of goods

22-2c PRESENTMENT FOR ACCEPTANCE

All trade acceptances and all time drafts payable a specified time after sight must be presented for acceptance by the payee to the drawee. In case of other kinds of drafts, presentment for acceptance is optional and is made merely to determine the intention of the drawee and to give the paper the additional credit strength of the acceptance. A qualified acceptance destroys the negotiability of the instrument. An acceptance could be qualified by adding additional terms such as "if presented for payment within twenty-four hours" or "in ten days from date." The drawee, after accepting the instrument, that is, after agreeing to pay it, becomes the acceptor.

Place. The holder should present the instrument at the drawee's place of business. If there is no place of business, it may be presented at the drawee's home or wherever the drawee may be found.

Party. A draft must be presented to the drawee or to someone authorized either by law or by contract to accept it. If there are two or more drawees, the draft must be presented to all of them unless one has authority to act for them all.

22-2d FORM OF ACCEPTANCE

The usual method of accepting a draft is to write on the face:

LO ③
Acceptance procedure and admissions

> Accepted
> Jane Roe

The drawee's signature alone on the draft is sufficient to constitute a valid acceptance; however, adding the word is advisable to make clear that an acceptance is intended. If an acceptance on a sight draft does not include a date, the holder may supply the date. The drawee may use other words of acceptance, but the words used must indicate an intention to be bound by the terms of the instrument and must be written on the instrument. The instrument or notification of the acceptance must then be delivered to the holder for the purpose of giving rights on the acceptance to the holder.

If the drawee refuses to accept a draft or to accept it in a proper way, the holder of the draft has no claim against the drawee but can return the draft to the drawer. Any credit given the drawer by the delivery of the draft is thereby canceled. If the draft is a trade acceptance, the refusal of the drawee to accept means that the buyer refuses to go through with the financing terms of the transaction; unless some other means of financing or payment is agreed on, the transaction falls through.

22-2e ADMISSIONS OF THE ACCEPTOR

A draft presented to a drawee for acceptance must be either accepted or returned. If the draft is not returned, the drawee is treated as having accepted the paper from the holder. By accepting the instrument, the drawee assumes liability for the payment of the paper. This liability of the acceptor runs from the due date of the paper until the statute of limitations bars the claim.

When the drawee accepts a draft, two admissions concerning the drawer are made:

1. That the signature of the drawer is genuine
2. That the drawer has both the capacity and the authority to draw the draft

The drawee, by accepting a draft, also admits the payee's capacity to indorse, but not the genuineness of the payee's indorsement.

Having made these admissions, the acceptor cannot later deny them against a holder of the instrument.

22-2f MONEY ORDERS

money order
instrument issued by business indicating that payee may receive indicated amount

A **money order** is an instrument issued by a bank, post office, or express company indicating that the payee may request and receive the amount indicated on the instrument. When paid for, issued, and delivered to the payee, the issuer has made a contract to pay.

22-3 Checks

LO ④
Characteristics of checks

check
draft drawn on a bank and payable on demand

Chapter 20 mentioned that a **check** is a type of draft. To be a check, the draft must be drawn on a bank and payable on demand. It is a type of sight draft with the drawee, a bank, and the drawer, a depositor—a person who has funds deposited with a bank. Just like other drafts, a check is an order by the drawer, on the drawee, to pay a sum of money to the order of another person, the payee.

The numbers at the bottom of a check (see Illustration 22-1) are printed in magnetic ink. The numbers identify the specific account and the bank that holds the account. Because the numbers are printed in magnetic ink, the check may be sorted by electronic data processing equipment. The Federal Reserve System requires that all checks passing through its clearinghouses be imprinted with such

ILLUSTRATION 22-1 Check

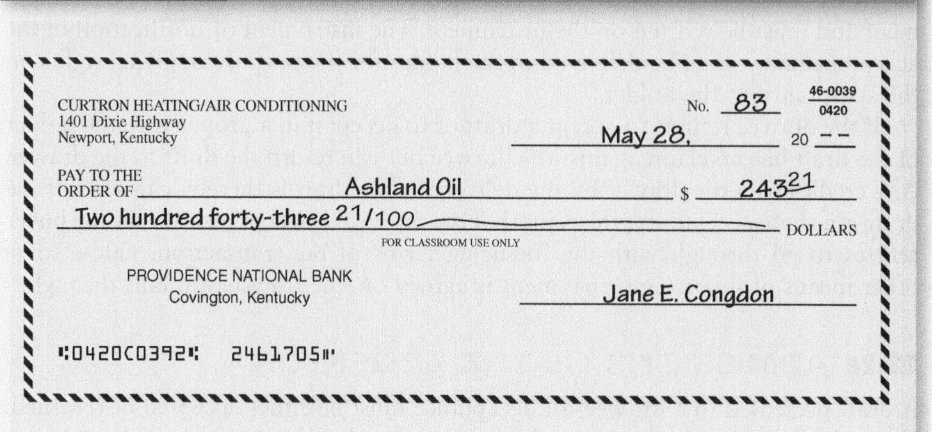
CURTRON HEATING/AIR CONDITIONING
1401 Dixie Highway
Newport, Kentucky

No. 83 46-0039/0420

May 28, 20 --

PAY TO THE ORDER OF Ashland Oil $ 243 21

Two hundred forty-three 21/100 DOLLARS

FOR CLASSROOM USE ONLY

PROVIDENCE NATIONAL BANK
Covington, Kentucky

Jane E. Congdon

⑆0420C0392⑆ 2461705⑈

identifying magnetic ink. In most cases, however, the drawee bank will accept checks that do not carry the magnetic ink coding. In fact, the material on which a check is written does not affect the validity of a check.

22-3a SPECIAL KINDS OF CHECKS

Five special types of checks include:

1. Certified checks

2. Cashier's checks

3. Bank drafts

4. Voucher checks

5. Traveler's checks

Certified Checks. A **certified check** is an ordinary check accepted by an official of the drawee bank. The official accepts it by writing across the face of the check the word *certified*, or some similar word, and signing it. Either the drawer or the holder may have a check certified. The certification of the check by the bank has the same effect as an acceptance. It makes the bank liable for the payment of the check and binds it by the warranties made by an acceptor. A certification obtained by a holder releases the drawer from liability.

> **certified check**
> check accepted by bank's writing certified on it

The drawer of a draft accepted by a bank is relieved of liability on the instrument. It does not matter when or by whom acceptance was obtained.

Cashier's Checks. A check that a bank draws on its own funds and that the cashier or some other responsible official of the bank signs is called a **cashier's check**. It is accepted for payment when issued and delivered. A bank in paying its own obligations may use such a check, or it may be used by anyone else who wishes to remit money in some form other than cash or a personal check.

> **cashier's check**
> check drawn by bank on its own funds

COURT CASE

FACTS: Citibank, N.A. (Citibank), issued a cashier's check to Richard Golden on behalf of a Citibank customer. Golden deposited the cashier's check into his account at JP Morgan Chase Bank (Chase). The customer later informed Citibank that she had arranged for alternate payment to Golden, and Citibank issued a stop payment order on the check. Golden sued Citibank to recover the funds.

OUTCOME: A bank may not stop payment on a cashier's check it has issued unless there is evidence of fraud or evidence the check was lost, stolen, or destroyed. Since none of these exceptions applied, Citibank was liable to Golden for the funds.

—*Golden v. Citibank, N.A.*, 853 N.Y.S.2d 261 (N.Y. App. Div.)

Bank Drafts. A **bank draft** or **teller's check** is a check drawn by one bank on another bank. Banks customarily keep a portion of their funds on deposit with other banks. A bank, then, may draw a check on these funds as freely as any corporation may draw checks. People purchase teller's checks because they rely on the bank's credit, not an individual's. Also, a purchaser of a teller's check has no right to insist that the issuing bank stop payment on a teller's check that is not payable

> **bank draft or teller's check**
> check drawn by one bank on another

to the purchaser. Thus, teller's checks are more readily accepted by payees than are personal checks. However, the issuing bank as the drawer may stop payment in proper circumstances.

COURT CASE

FACTS: Robert and Jolene Johnson got a $313,000 construction loan from First Midwest Bank and signed a promissory note, secured by a construction mortgage on the property. The note required an "interest reserve account" at the bank to pay the scheduled interest on the loan. The bank advanced the funds to set up the account. The note also said: "RIGHT OF SETOFF. To the extent permitted by applicable law, Lender reserves a right of setoff in all Borrower's accounts with Lender." The Johnsons became unable to keep up their end of the construction deal, and the bank would not advance more money. They conveyed the mortgaged real estate to the bank in return for a release. Their agreement with the bank said they would have no further obligation to it. Several months later, Robert went to the bank and asked that the interest reserve account be closed. A teller's check for the $10,000 balance was issued to him. The bank stopped payment on it, asserting its right of setoff. The Johnsons filed for bankruptcy, and the trustee charged that the bank had wrongfully dishonored the check.

OUTCOME: The bank, as the drawer, was allowed to stop payment.

—*In re Johnson*, 371 B.R. 336 (Bankr. C.D. Ill.)

voucher check
check with voucher attached

Voucher Checks. A **voucher check** is a check with a voucher attached. The voucher lists the items of an invoice for which the check is the means of payment. In business, the drawer of the check customarily writes on the check such words as "In full of account, For invoice No. 1622," or similar notations. These notations make the checks excellent receipts when returned to the drawer. A check on which additional space is provided for the drawer to make a notation for which the check is issued is sometimes referred to as a voucher check. A payee who indorses a check on which a notation has been made agrees to the terms of the check, which include the terms written in the notation by the drawer.

COURT CASE

FACTS: While Vice President of Finance of Koss Corporation (Koss), Sujata Sachdeva (Sachdeva) embezzled $16,000,000 via wire transfers, cashier's checks, and other checks drawn on Koss bank accounts in order to pay Sachdeva's personal American Express credit card bills. The embezzlements included over fifty separate transactions over almost two years. Koss sued American Express for its failure to act after its Financial Crimes Reporting Unit noticed the "clear case of embezzlement." With respect to the cashier's checks, American Express claimed that since Koss was a drawer of the checks, Koss could not sue for conversion.

OUTCOME: Sachdeva embezzled funds and then used those funds to purchase cashier's checks. As a result, Koss was not the drafter of any of the checks. The drawer of a cashier's check is the bank on which the checks are written.

—*Koss Corporation v. American Express Corporation*, 309 P.3d 898 (Ariz. App. Div.)

Traveler's Checks. A traveler's check is an instrument much like a cashier's check of the issuer except that it requires signature and countersignature by its purchaser. Traveler's checks, sold by banks and express companies, are pre-printed in a fixed amount and payable on demand. The purchaser of traveler's checks signs each check once at the time of purchase and then countersigns it and fills in the name of the payee when the check is to be used.

traveler's check pre-printed instrument in fixed amount requiring signature and countersignature

22-3b POSTDATED CHECKS

A check drawn before the time it is dated is a postdated check. If it is drawn on June 21, but dated July 1, it is, in effect, a ten-day draft. There is nothing unlawful about a postdated check as long as it was not postdated for an illegal or fraudulent purpose. A bank on which such a check is drawn may pay it before its date without liability unless the customer/drawer has properly notified the bank of the postdated check.

postdated check check drawn before its date

22-3c BAD CHECKS

If a check is drawn with intent to defraud the payee, the drawer is civilly liable as well as subject to criminal prosecution in most states under so-called bad check laws. A bad check is a check that the holder sends to the drawee bank and the bank refuses to pay, normally for insufficient funds. Usually, these statutes state that if the check is not made good within a specific period, such as ten days, a presumption arises that the drawer originally issued the check with the intent to defraud.

bad check check the drawee bank refuses to pay

22-3d DUTIES OF THE BANK

The bank owes several duties to its customer, the depositor/drawer. It must maintain secrecy regarding information acquired by it in connection with the depositor–bank relationship.

The bank also has the duty of comparing the signature on the depositor's checks with the signature of the depositor in the bank's files to make certain the signatures on the checks are valid. If the bank pays a check that does not have the drawer's signature, it is liable to the drawer for the loss.

Refusal of Bank to Pay. The bank is under a general contractual duty to its depositors to pay on demand all of their checks to the extent of the funds deposited to their credit. When the bank breaches this contract, it is liable to the drawer for damages. A bank may pay a properly payable check even when an overdraft will result, and it must pay checks that exceed the amount on deposit if there is an agreement that the bank will pay overdrafts. In the case of a draft other than a check, there is ordinarily no duty on the part of the drawee to accept the draft or to make payment if it has not been accepted. Therefore, the drawee is not liable to the drawer when an unaccepted draft is not paid.

COURT CASE

FACTS: William Elias had signatory authority over Direct Lending's (Direct) bank accounts at JP Morgan Chase Bank (Chase). He left Direct, and the signatory authority was revoked. Direct issued a check for $100,000 to EA Management (EA), an assumed name used by Elias. The check bounced. Direct then issued a check for $100,005 to EA. Elias deposited it in a new account at Chase and immediately withdrew $88,000. Three months later, Elias deposited the check that had earlier bounced and a starter check for $80,000 dated when Elias still worked for Direct. Elias had signed the check. That night, someone shifted funds among Direct's accounts at Chase resulting in the accounts on which the two checks were drawn having funds to cover them. The next morning, Elias went to a Chase branch and got three cashier's checks totaling $191,000. When Direct found that Elias had cashed the bounced and starter checks, it notified Chase that Elias was not authorized to cash them and that the overnight transfers were fraudulent, and to stop payment on the checks, which Chase did. Elias sued Chase, alleging that it had breached its account agreement with him by allowing Direct to stop payment on the cashier's checks.

OUTCOME: The court pointed out that Direct had not stopped payment on the cashier's checks. It had stopped payment on the bounced and starter checks. Elias's account agreement did not forbid Chase from complying with a stop payment order from another customer regarding checks drawn on that customer's account.

—*EA Management v. JP Morgan Chase Bank, N.A.*, 655 F.3d 573 (6th Cir.)

Even if the normal printed form supplied by the bank is not used, the bank must pay a proper order by a depositor. The bank must honor any written document that contains the substance of a normal printed check.

A divorced man making his last alimony payment wrote a check on a T-shirt to send a message to his ex-wife that she was taking "the shirt off his back." She did not care for the technique, but the T-shirt check was valid.

The liability of the drawee bank for improperly refusing to pay a check only runs in favor of the drawer. Even if the holder of the check or the payee may be harmed when the bank refuses to pay the check, a holder or payee has no right to sue the bank. However, the holder has a right of action against the person from whom the check was received. This right of action is based on the original obligation, which was not discharged because the check was not paid.

A check that is presented more than six months after its date is commonly called a **stale check**. A bank that acts in good faith may pay it. However, unless the check is certified, the bank is not required to pay it.

stale check
check presented more than six months after its date

Stopping Payment. Drawers have the power of stopping payment of checks. After a check is issued, a drawer can notify the drawee bank not to pay it when presented for payment. This is a useful procedure when a check is lost or mislaid. A duplicate check can be written, and to make sure that the payee does not receive payment twice or that an improper person does not receive payment on the first check, payment on the first check can be stopped. Likewise, if payment is made by check, and the payee defaults on the contract, payment on the check can be stopped, assuming that the payee has not cashed it.

A stop-payment order may be written or oral. The bank is bound by an oral stop-payment order only for fourteen calendar days unless confirmed in writing within that time. A written order is effective for no more than six months unless renewed in writing.

Unless a valid limitation exists on its liability, the bank is liable for the loss the depositor sustains when the bank makes payment on a check after receiving proper notice to stop payment. However, the depositor has the burden of proving the loss sustained.

PREVIEW CASE REVISITED

FACTS: Robert Lanier managed REL Development Inc. (REL) and I–20 East Inc. (I-20). REL borrowed more than $4 million, and I-20 borrowed $120,000 from Branch Banking & Trust Company (Bank), all secured by different tracts of real estate and guaranteed personally by Lanier. Upon default on the debts, the Bank began foreclosure proceedings. Lanier asked the Bank to stop the foreclosure so the debtors could sell the property. No sales took place, and instead of resuming foreclosure proceedings, the Bank sued the companies and Lanier for the debts. Judgment was for the Bank. The debtors and Lanier appealed, arguing that the real estate market had declined greatly, so the Bank should have reinstituted foreclosure proceedings in order to maximize the amount received from a sale of the properties.

OUTCOME: The court held that the Bank was not required to resume foreclosure proceedings and had the right to sue the debtors and Lanier.

—*REL Development Inc. v. Branch Banking and Trust Co.*, 699 S.E.2d 779 (Ga. Ct. App.)

A depositor who stops payment without a valid reason may be liable to the payee. Also, the depositor is liable for stopping payment with respect to any holder in due course or other party having the rights of a holder in due course unless payment is stopped for a reason that may be asserted against such a holder as a defense. The fact that the bank refuses to make payment because of the drawer's instruction does not make the case any different from any other instance in which the drawee refuses to pay, and the legal consequences of imposing liability on the drawer are the same.

When the depositor makes use of a means of communication such as the telegraph to give a stop-payment notice, the bank is not liable if the notice is delayed in reaching the bank, and the bank makes payment before receiving the notice. The depositor can, however, sue the telegraph company if negligence on its part can be shown.

A payee who wants to avoid the potential of payment being stopped may require a certified check of the buyer or a cashier's check from the buyer's bank because normally neither the buyer nor the buyer's bank can stop payment to the payee on such checks.

Payment after Depositor's Death. Usually, a check is ineffective after the drawer dies. However, until the bank knows of the death and has had a reasonable opportunity to act, the bank's agency is not revoked. A bank may even continue to pay or certify a depositor's checks for ten days unless a person claiming an interest in the estate orders it to stop.

22-3e BANK CUSTOMER'S RESPONSIBILITY

Although a bank has several duties to its customers, customers also have some important responsibilities. They must examine monthly bank statements and notify the bank "with reasonable promptness" of any forged signatures. If a customer fails to do this and the bank suffers loss as a result, the customer will be liable for the loss. "Reasonable promptness" is not defined, but the UCC provides that a customer who does not report an unauthorized signature or alteration within one year may not assert them against the bank. If there is a series of forgeries by the same person, the customer must discover and report the first forged check to the bank within the time prescribed by agreement between the customer and bank. If no such time is prescribed, it must be within thirty days of receiving the bank statement.

QUESTIONS

1. Who are the original parties to a promissory note? Explain.

2. What are the obligations of the maker of a promissory note?

3. What are the differences among a bond, a collateral note, a real estate mortgage note, a debenture, and a certificate of deposit?

4. What does the drawee of a draft do?

5. Why must a time draft payable a specified number of days after sight be presented for acceptance?

6. What is a trade acceptance?

7. How does a qualified acceptance affect the negotiability of an instrument?

8. In what way does a drawee accept a draft?

9. What kind of draft is a check?

10. What is the effect of the certification of a check?

11. How does a traveler's check differ from a cashier's check?

12. What is the duty and potential liability of a bank that refuses to pay a depositor's check?

CASE PROBLEMS

LO ④ 1. Skils'Kin was a community-based not-for-profit which provided services to adults with developmental, physical, and mental disabilities. One of the services provided included managing the monthly income and living expenses of clients, including acting as the "representative payee" for clients' Social Security checks. Over a four-year period, Shannon Patterson, while Director of Payee Services for Skils'Kin, presented checks made payable to Skils'Kin clients to Washington Trust Bank (Bank), signed them on the back in her own name, and embezzled the funds. The fraud was only detected after Patterson's suicide, when she disclosed the fraud in her suicide note. Skils'Kin sued the Bank for improper payment because Patterson's signature was not authorized. Was the Bank liable for payment on the checks?

LO ① 2. Gaby Gonzalez obtained two CDs at Second Federal Savings and Loan Association (Second) with her daughter, Juana Martinez, as beneficiary. Right before Gonzalez died, she told her cousin, Rafael Gonzalez, where to find her CDs. The CDs had a line through Martinez's name and Rafael Gonzalez's name added in the section for beneficiary with the notation, "REVISED BENEFICIARY . . . RC." After Gaby's death, Rafael withdrew some funds to pay funeral expenses and legal fees from one of the CDs. Several years later, Rafael discovered that Second had paid the CDs to Hector Gonzalez, who was the administrator of Martinez's estate. Rafael sued Second, claiming as the beneficiary that it should have paid him. Who was entitled to the proceeds of the CDs?

CASE PROBLEMS (CONTINUED)

3. Merri and Gary Brecher were president, vice president, and the sole owners of Contractors Source, Inc. (Source). Source opened a bank account with Amegy Bank National Association (Amegy) on which Merri and Gary were the only authorized signatories. Source hired Maria Straten, aka Maria Henry, as bookkeeper, and shortly thereafter Straten began using money from the Amegy account to pay her personal creditors. For the most part this was accomplished by providing the Amegy routing and checking account numbers to third-party websites, and continued for a period of about two years. Ultimately Straten forged Merri Brecher's name on two checks. Merri discovered the check forgeries upon examination of the monthly bank statement and notified Amegy within thirty days of receiving the monthly statement. Amegy refused to credit Source's account on the basis that the first misappropriation (via electronic transfer to a third-party website) had occurred more than one year ago. Was Amegy responsible to Source for the amount of the two forged checks? **LO ④**

4. M&O insulation was hired by Quality Insulation to install some insulation. Quality had a line of credit through a promissory note with Harris Bank Naperville. Quality had not complied with its payment schedule, so Harris declared the loan to be in default and immediately due and payable. On September 23, Quality paid M&O by check for $76,000 which M&O deposited in its bank. On September 24, Harris placed an administrative hold or "freeze" on Quality's account. The same day, M&O's $76,000 check was presented for payment. On the 25th, Quality's account had sufficient funds to pay the check, but Harris returned it for insufficient funds. Harris subsequently honored checks totaling $23,700 on the account. M&O sued Harris. Harris claimed it had never accepted the check. Had it? **LO ③**

5. James R. Sapp opened a checking account with Flagstar Bank, FSB (Flagstar) to facilitate his business. Sapp deposited a cashier's check for $125,000 into the account, and received a receipt from Flagstar. The receipt stated that "ALL DEPOSITS/PAYMENTS ARE SUBJECT TO PROOF." Flagstar lost the check, and contacted Sapp to try to identify the maker. In the meantime, about two weeks after opening the account, Sapp wrote a $100,000 check on the account to an investment company. Flagstar was ultimately unable to find the check or track down the maker to secure a replacement, and debited the $125,000 from Sapp's account. Had Flagstar accepted the check? **LO ③**

6. Diagnosed with terminal cancer, Ray Comeaux executed a handwritten will bequeathing five certificates of deposit (CDs) to four of his children and one grandchild. The CD bequeathed to his daughter, Louise, was payable to her on Ray's death. Three months later, he asked two of his sons, Michael and Rodney, to close out the CDs and put the proceeds in a checking account for the benefit of his wife, Betty. Michael and Rodney went to the bank, where they were told they could redeem their own CDs; however, Ray would have to sign the CDs made out in his name. Michael and Rodney gave Ray the CDs and told him they needed to be indorsed. Ray told Michael to have Betty sign his name, as he was physically unable to do so. Michael, Rodney, and Betty were all in the room when Ray made this request, and all were present when Betty signed the documents for Ray. Michael and Rodney returned to the bank, where all five CDs were redeemed, and the proceeds placed in a checking account. Ray died two months later. After Ray died, Louise went to the bank to redeem the CD. When she was unable, she sued the bank, alleging it should not have redeemed the CD. Was she correct? **LO ①**

7. Carter Petroleum Products Inc. sold fuel products to Highway 210, LLC. Brotherhood Bank & Trust Company issued a letter of credit, No. 2001-270, for $175,000 available by Carter's draft at "sight" on the account of Highway 210. It stated "all draft(s) drawn under and in compliance with the terms of this credit will be duly honored . . . if presented at this office in Shawnee, KS, no later than June 26." Hal O'Donnell, Carter's credit manager, delivered a sight draft to the bank for payment on June 26. The draft stated: "Pursuant to the terms stated in the Letter of Credit # 2001-270 . . . Carter, hereby exercises its option to draw against said Brotherhood Bank and Trust Company's Letter of Credit in the amount of $175,000 due to nonpayment of invoices." O'Donnell arrived at the bank just after 5 P.M., and the lobby was locked. After O'Donnell knocked on the door, he was admitted to the lobby. **LO ②**

CASE PROBLEMS (CONTINUED)

He indicated he was there to see Ward Kerby, the assistant vice president. O'Donnell handed Kerby the draft request, letter of credit, and unpaid Carter invoices to Highway 210. The draft request was stamped received on June 26. The drive-through window at the bank was still open. The bank dishonored Carter's draft request because it was presented after regular banking hours on the date the letter of credit expired. Carter sued the bank. Was the presentment proper?

LO ④ 8. After Mickey Marcus died, Melvyn Spillman presented fraudulent documents purporting to give him control of Marcus's estate to Jefferson State Bank, where Marcus had an account. Spillman withdrew most of the money in the account. More than three years after Marcus's death, the court appointed Christa Lenk, who knew of Spillman's fraud, to administer Marcus's estate. Presumably unaware of Lenk's appointment, the bank never informed her of Marcus's account or sent statements to her. Although she knew of the account at least five months after her appointment, she did not contact the bank for more than a year after that. When she demanded the amount Spillman had withdrawn, the bank refused, and she sued the bank. Should the bank have to pay?

Negotiation and Discharge

CHAPTER 23

LEARNING OBJECTIVES

1. Discuss how to negotiate by indorsement.
2. Identify the different types of indorsements and describe the liabilities of an indorser.
3. Explain how negotiable instruments may be discharged.

PREVIEW CASE

Summertime Development Corp. (Summertime) had Redondo Construction Corp. (Redondo) work on a beach resort financed by Bank & Trust of Puerto Rico (B&T). B&T issued checks paid to the order of Redondo, Summertime, & Lyon Builders Corp. (Lyon) in payment of work Redondo did on the resort. The checks were deposited in Lyon's account at Doral Bank without Redondo's indorsement. In Redondo's bankruptcy proceeding, it claimed the checks needed its indorsement to be validly negotiated. Why do you think there were three payees on the checks? When there are multiple payees on an instrument, who must indorse it?

Negotiation involves the transfer of a negotiable instrument in such a way that the transferee becomes the holder of the instrument. Bearer instruments may be negotiated by delivery. Delivery effectively vests ownership in the transferee. Thus, the transferee becomes the holder.

An instrument payable to "order" can be negotiated only by authorized indorsement and delivery. An **indorsement** is a signature on the back of an instrument (usually the holder's) along with any directions or limitations regarding use of or liability for the instrument. Indorsing or transferring a negotiable instrument creates certain liabilities, depending on the nature of the indorsement or transfer.

Although an indorsement is not required for negotiation of bearer paper, a transferee may require it because this adds the liability of the new indorser to the paper and thus makes it a better credit risk. It also preserves a written chronological record of all negotiations.

LO ①
Indorsements

indorsement
signature of holder on back of instrument with any directions or limitations

23-1 Place of Indorsement

trailing edge
left side of front of check

allonge
paper so firmly attached to instrument as to be part of it

Banks require that an indorsement on a check be on the back and within 1.5 inches of the trailing edge. The **trailing edge** is the left side of a check when looking at it from the front (see Illustration 23-1). If the indorser's signature appears elsewhere, and it cannot be determined in what capacity the signature was made, it will be considered an indorsement. In any event, an indorsement must be on the actual instrument to be indorsed or on a paper attached to the instrument. An **allonge** is a paper attached to an instrument. The Uniform Commercial Code (UCC) originally required it to be "securely attached," but revisions now only required it to be "attached." A paper stapled to an instrument is considered securely affixed. The UCC states that such a paper is part of the instrument. If a party wants to transfer an instrument but does not wish to be liable as an indorser, the instrument can be assigned by a written assignment on a separate piece of paper.

Occasionally, the name of the payee or indorsee of an instrument is misspelled. If a paycheck intended for, and delivered to, Janice F. Smith is made out to "Janice K. Smith" through clerical error, Janice F. Smith may ask her employer for a new check properly made out to her, or she may keep the check and indorse in any of the following ways:

1. Janice K. Smith

2. Janice F. Smith

3. Janice K. Smith, Janice F. Smith (If she intends to receive value for the check, the person to whom it is negotiated may require her to sign both names.)

However, if Janice F. Smith obtains a check made payable to, and intended for, Janice K. Smith, it would be illegal for Janice F. to indorse it and receive payment for it. Only when the check is actually intended for Janice F. Smith may she make a corrective indorsement.

It is not always necessary to correct an irregularity in the name of a party to an instrument. An irregularity does not necessarily destroy negotiability. Only if

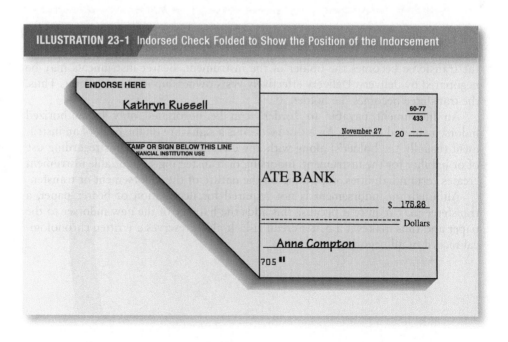

ILLUSTRATION 23-1 Indorsed Check Folded to Show the Position of the Indorsement

it is shown that different people were actually identified by the different names is the irregularity significant. If the different names stand for the same person, the irregularity does not matter. It has been held that a note was correctly negotiated when indorsed "Greenlaw & Sons by George M. Greenlaw," although it was payable to "Greenlaw & Sons Roofing & Siding Co." Nothing indicates that the two enterprises were not the same firm.

COURT CASE

FACTS: BNC Mortgage Inc. loaned Anthony Marcino $75,200, and he signed a note to BNC. He and his wife, Melissa Marcino, granted a mortgage on real estate to BNC. After the Marcinos defaulted on the note, U.S. Bank National Association sued them. Attached to the note was a separate document, titled "Allonge to Note," which read in its entirety, "PAY TO THE ORDER OF: ___ WITHOUT RECOURSE BNC MORTGAGE INC." The allonge was signed on behalf of BNC by "Dolores Martinez, Asst. Vice President." The Marcinos claimed that U.S. Bank was not the holder of the note, since they had executed the note in favor of BNC.

OUTCOME: The court said that the allonge, indorsed in blank, converted the note to bearer paper. U.S. Bank's possession of the original note was sufficient to establish that it was the real party in interest.

—*U.S. Bank Nat'l Assn. v. Marcino*, 908 N.E.2d 1032 (Ohio Ct. App.)

23-2 Multiple Payees

Frequently, negotiable instruments are made payable to more than one person. Whether the instrument must be indorsed by more than one of them depends on the exact language used in naming them on the instrument.

If the parties are named using the word *and* between their names, then it is payable jointly, and all of them must indorse the instrument in order to negotiate it. For example, if the instrument reads, "Pay to the order of Mary and John Doe," then both Mary and John must indorse the instrument. Neither can negotiate the instrument alone.

PREVIEW CASE REVISITED

FACTS: Summertime Development Corp. (Summertime) had Redondo Construction Corp. (Redondo) work on a beach resort financed by Bank & Trust of Puerto Rico (B&T). B&T issued checks paid to the order of Redondo, Summertime, & Lyon Builders Corp. (Lyon) in payment of work Redondo did on the resort. The checks were deposited in Lyon's account at Doral Bank without Redondo's indorsement. In Redondo's bankruptcy proceeding, it claimed the checks needed its indorsement to be validly negotiated.

OUTCOME: The court stated that when a check is payable to three parties jointly, it is payable to all of them and needs indorsement by all of them in order to be negotiated.

—*In re Redondo Construction Corp.*, 411 B.R. 114 (Bankr. D. Puerto Rico)

If the word *or* is used between the names of the parties, then the instrument is payable in the alternative, and only one needs to indorse the instrument in order to negotiate it. When an instrument reads, "Pay to the order of Hank or Nancy Florio," either Hank or Nancy can indorse and negotiate the instrument.

Normally, if the instrument is not clear as to whether it is payable jointly or alternatively, it will be construed to be payable in the alternative.

LO ②

Types of indorsements and liabilities of indorser

23-3 Kinds of Indorsements

Four types of indorsements include:

1. Blank indorsements
2. Special indorsements
3. Qualified indorsements
4. Restrictive indorsements

23-3a BLANK INDORSEMENTS

blank indorsement
indorsement consisting of signature of indorser

As the name indicates, a **blank indorsement** is one having no words other than the name of the indorser (see Illustration 23-2). If the instrument is bearer paper, it remains bearer paper when a blank indorsement is made. Thus, the new holder may pass good title to another holder without indorsing the instrument. The one primarily liable on the instrument is bound to pay the person who presents it for payment on the date due, even if the person is a thief or other unauthorized party.

If the instrument is order paper, a blank indorsement converts it to bearer paper; if thereafter indorsed to someone's order, it becomes order paper again. Converting the instruments to order paper can minimize risks involved in handling instruments originally payable to bearer or indorsed in blank.

23-3b SPECIAL INDORSEMENTS

special indorsement
indorsement that designates a particular person to whom payment is to be made

A **special indorsement** designates the particular person to whom payment should be made (see Illustration 23-2). After making such an indorsement, the paper is order paper, whether or not it was originally so payable or was originally payable to bearer. The holder must indorse it before it can be further negotiated. Of course, the holder may indorse the instrument in blank, which makes it bearer paper. Each holder has the power to decide to make either a blank or a special indorsement.

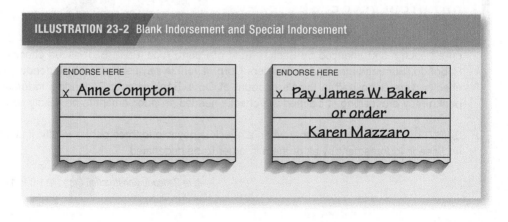

ILLUSTRATION 23-2 Blank Indorsement and Special Indorsement

ENDORSE HERE
x Anne Compton

ENDORSE HERE
x Pay James W. Baker
        or order
    Karen Mazzaro

An indorsee by a blank indorsement may convert it to a special indorsement by writing the words *pay to the order of [indorsee]* above the indorser's signature. Such an instrument cannot now be negotiated except by indorsement and delivery. This in no way alters the contract between the indorser and the indorsee.

23-3c QUALIFIED INDORSEMENTS

A **qualified indorsement** has the effect of qualifying, thus limiting, the liability of the indorser. This type of indorsement is usually used when the payee of an instrument is merely collecting the funds for another. For example, if an agent receives checks in payment of the principal's claims, but the checks are made payable to the agent personally, the agent can and should elect to use a qualified indorsement to protect from liability. There is no reason for the agent to risk personal liability when the checks are the principal's. The agent does this merely by adding to either a blank or special type of indorsement the words *without recourse* immediately before the signature (see Illustration 23-3). This releases the agent from liability for payment if the instrument remains unpaid because of insolvency or mere refusal to pay.

A qualified indorser still warrants that the signatures on the instrument are genuine, that the indorser has good title to the instrument, that the instrument has not been altered, that no defenses are good against the indorser, and that the indorser has no knowledge of insolvency proceedings with respect to the maker, acceptor, or drawer (as was mentioned in Chapter 22). An indorser may avoid these warranties as well by indorsing the instrument "without recourse or warranties."

qualified indorsement indorsement that limits liability of indorser

23-3d RESTRICTIVE INDORSEMENTS

A **restrictive indorsement** is an indorsement that attempts to prevent the use of the instrument for anything except the stated use (see Illustration 23-3). The indorsement may state that the indorsee holds the paper for a special purpose or as an agent or trustee for another, or it may impose a condition that must occur before payment. Such an indorsement does not prohibit further negotiation of the instrument.

Restrictive indorsements are ineffective with respect to anyone other than the indorser and indorsee. As against a holder in due course, it is immaterial whether the indorsee has in fact recognized the restrictions. A bank receiving a check for deposit is called a depository bank. A **depository bank** receiving a check with a restrictive indorsement, such as "for deposit" or "for collection," must honor the restriction.

restrictive indorsement indorsement that restricts use of instrument

depository bank bank receiving check for deposit

ILLUSTRATION 23-3 Qualified Indorsement and Restrictive Indorsement

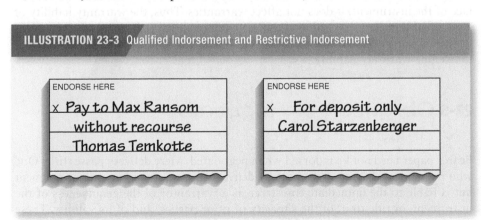

ENDORSE HERE

x Pay to Max Ransom
without recourse
Thomas Temkotte

ENDORSE HERE

x For deposit only
Carol Starzenberger

COURT CASE

FACTS: Mark Chartier and his wife, Lisa M. (Chartier) Heward opened a joint checking account with Gorham Savings Bank (Bank). Heward deposited a check for $100,000 made out to Chartier and marked "For Deposit Only," but not indorsed by Chartier, into their joint checking account. Two weeks later, Heward withdrew $40,000 from the same account and filed for divorce from Chartier. Chartier sued the Bank, claiming the $100,000 check was not properly negotiated because it had not been indorsed by him as the holder.

OUTCOME: The Bank had no liability to Chartier. As a depository bank, the Bank could receive the check for deposit only into an account on which Chartier was listed.

—*Chartier v. Farm Family Life Insurance Company,* 113 A.3d 234 (Me.)

23-4 Liability of Indorser

By indorsing a negotiable instrument, a person can become secondarily liable for payment of the face amount and responsible for certain warranties.

23-4a LIABILITIES FOR PAYMENT OF INSTRUMENT

By making an indorsement, an indorser, with the exception of a qualified indorser, agrees to pay any subsequent holder the face amount of the instrument if the holder presents the instrument to the primary party when due, and the primary party refuses to pay. The holder must then give the indorser in question notice of such default. This notice may be given orally, or it may be given by any other means, but it must be given before midnight of the third full business day after the day on which the default occurs.

23-4b WARRANTIES OF THE INDORSER

Chapter 24 lists the warranties of all transferors. They differ from liability for the face of the paper in that they are not subject to the requirements of presentment and notice. The distinction is also important for purposes of limiting liability; an indorsement "without recourse" destroys only the liability of the indorser for the face of the instrument. It does not affect warranties. Thus, the warranty liability of a qualified indorser is the same as that of an unqualified indorser. An indorsement "without warranties" or a combined "without recourse or warranties" is required to exclude warranty liability.

23-5 Obligation of Negotiator of Bearer Paper

Bearer paper need not be indorsed when negotiated. Mere delivery passes title. One who negotiates a bearer instrument by delivery alone does not guarantee payment but is liable to the immediate transferee as a warrantor of the genuineness of the instrument, of title to it, of the capacity of prior parties, and of its validity. These warranties are the same as those made by an unqualified indorser, except that the warranties of the unqualified indorser extend to all subsequent holders, not just to the immediate purchaser. But because negotiable instruments are not legal tender, no one is under any obligation to accept bearer paper without an indorsement. By requiring an indorsement even though it is not necessary to pass title, the holder is gaining protection by requiring the one who wishes to negotiate it to assume all the obligations of an indorser.

23-6 Discharge of the Obligation

Negotiable instruments may be discharged by payment, by cancellation, or by renunciation. Payment at or after the date of the maturity of the instrument by the party primarily liable constitutes proper payment. **Cancellation** consists of any act that indicates the intention to destroy the validity of the instrument. A cancellation made unintentionally, without authorization, or by mistake is not effective. A holder of several negotiable instruments might intend to cancel one on its payment and inadvertently cancel an unpaid one. This does not discharge the unpaid instrument. **Renunciation** is a unilateral act of a holder of an instrument, usually without consideration, whereby the holder gives up rights on the instrument or against one or more parties to the instrument.

The obligations of the parties may be discharged in other ways, just as in the case of a simple contract. For example, parties will no longer be held liable on instruments if their debts have been discharged in bankruptcy or if there has been the necessary lapse of time provided by a statute of limitations.

A negotiable instrument may be lost or accidentally destroyed. This does not discharge the obligation. A party obligated to pay an instrument has a right to demand its return if possible. If this cannot be done, then the payor has a right to demand adequate security from the holder to protect the payor from having to pay the instrument a second time. The holder usually posts an indemnity bond. This is an agreement by a bonding company to assume the risk of the payor's having to pay a second time.

LO ③
Discharge of negotiable instruments

cancellation
act that indicates intention to destroy validity of an instrument

renunciation
unilateral act of holder giving up rights in the instrument or against a party to it

QUESTIONS

1. What is an indorsement?

2. Why might a transferee require an indorsement on bearer paper?

3. If an instrument is to be indorsed, where must the indorsement be found?

4. Does an irregularity in the name of a party to an instrument destroy negotiability?

5. When there are multiple payees on an instrument, how can one know whether all must indorse or only one need indorse the instrument to negotiate it?

6. Name four kinds of indorsements, and give an example of the proper use of each one.

7. By making an indorsement what do all indorsers except qualified indorsers agree to?

8. How does an indorsement "without recourse" affect the indorser's warranty liability?

9. What does a person who negotiates a bearer instrument by delivery alone warrant?

10. How may a negotiable instrument be discharged?

CASE PROBLEMS

LO ①   1. Ronnie Gilley Properties, LLC (Gilley), wrote a check to Cile Way Properties, LLC (Cile), for $100,000. When Cile deposited the check in its bank, it was misencoded in the amount of $1,000. As a result, only $1,000 was credited to Cile's account and debited from Gilley's account. Was the obligation discharged?

LO ③   2. Daniel Manley executed a note for $420,000 secured by a mortgage to Independent National Bank (Independent). Manley's father, Thomas Manley, guaranteed payment of the note. Wachovia Small Business Capital (Wachovia) obtained the note as a result of a merger with Independent. There was default on the note. At trial, Thomas testified that he had taken $375,000 in $100 bills to Wachovia and requested a receipt. He said the Wachovia employee had told him a receipt would be mailed to him after the amount was verified, but he never received one. Three months later, Daniel received the original note in the mail in a Wachovia envelope. The note was stamped "Paid." Wachovia had no record of a $375,000 cash payment or of the normal audit procedures it followed when a note was paid. The Manleys argued that Wachovia's stamping "Paid" on the note and mailing it to Daniel discharged the note. Was it discharged?

LO ①   3. Howard Turner borrowed $85,000 from Fidelity Mortgage (Fidelity) and executed a mortgage to secure the loan. Turner died six months later, and the note went into default. HSBC Bank USA, N.A. (HSBC) sued Jamie Thompson, the daughter and administratrix of Turner's estate. HSBC produced copies of the note and mortgage and two separate, loose documents each titled "allonge." The first stated, "Pay to the order of ___" and was signed on behalf of Delta Funding Corp. The second stated, "Pay to the order of Delta Funding Corp." and was signed on behalf of Fidelity. Were the alleged allonges adequate to negotiate the note to Delta?

LO ②   4. Marian Gass executed a note and mortgage in favor of Option One Mortgage Corporation. The note was negotiated and ultimately EMC Mortgage Corporation (EMC) began foreclosure proceedings after Gass missed payments. Gass challenged EMC's standing to pursue foreclosure on the basis that the original note was "robo-signed" by individuals without authority, and that EMC never actually had possession of the note. Further, the evidence of indorsement consisted of an alleged allonge, which was obviously not proven to be attached to the note which was not produced in court. Did EMC have the right to enforce the note?

LO ③   5. Chester Crow signed a note for a loan from First National Bank (FNB). The note was due in ninety days, but Crow could not pay the full amount when due. Several years later, Premier Bank, the successor to FNB, returned three payments to Crow with a cover letter that called the payments "overpayments." It then issued an IRS Form 1099-C (Cancellation of Debt) to Crow, with these notations: "Date canceled: . . .; Amount of debt canceled: $7,991.00." The 1099-C resulted in a negative tax impact for Crow. At the same time, Premier sold the note and three dozen others having a total face value of $600,000 and indorsed: "without recourse, representation or warranty of any kind" to Credit Recoveries Inc. (CRI) for $1,500. Four months later, CRI demanded that Crow pay his note. Crow wrote CRI that Premier had "returned a refund check for the last payment." Four years later, after no contact, CRI again demanded that Crow pay the note. Crow replied that Premier had issued the 1099-C. CRI sued Crow. Had Premier cancelled the debt?

LO ①   6. Patricia Woodberry executed a promissory note to SouthStar Funding, LLC secured by a mortgage on her home. Two years later, she filed for bankruptcy and listed Structured Asset Investment Loan Trust, 2005-8 (ASC) as a creditor. In the bankruptcy proceedings, the court had to decide whether ASC was actually a party with an interest in the bankruptcy case. It was, if it was the holder of the note. ASC had possession of the note, and there was an attachment to the original note entitled "Allonge to Note," containing the statement: "Pay to the order of without recourse." Woodberry argued that ASC did not have an interest in the case. Was ASC the holder of the note?

Liabilities and Defenses Specific to Negotiable Instruments

LEARNING OBJECTIVES

① Summarize the rules for primary and secondary liability.

② Define holder in due course and holder through a holder in due course.

③ State the chief advantage of being a holder in due course of a negotiable instrument.

④ Distinguish between limited, universal, and hybrid defenses to holders.

PREVIEW CASE

James and Marie Estepp wanted to get a loan from United Bank & Trust Co. of Maryland. United required an additional signature by an owner of real estate. James brought Marvin Schaeffer to the bank, saying he needed Schaeffer, whose wife had died, to sign a character reference. Estepp supervised Schaeffer at work and had helped Schaeffer make funeral arrangements. Schaeffer had a learning disability and could not read or write. The bank officer handling the transaction did not explain to Schaeffer that he was assuming a financial responsibility. Schaeffer signed the note. The Estepps defaulted, so United sued Schaeffer. Did Schaeffer have an effective defense? What did the Estepps tell Schaeffer he needed to sign? Was this true?

The Uniform Commercial Code (UCC) imposes liability on parties to negotiable instruments depending on the nature of the paper; the role of the party as maker, acceptor, indorser, or transferor; and the satisfaction of certain requirements of conduct by the holder of the instrument. Two basic categories of liability incidental to negotiable instruments include (1) the liability created by what is written on the face of the paper (contractual liability), and (2) the liability for certain warranties regarding the instrument.

When the holder of commercial paper is refused payment, a lawsuit may be brought. Assuming that the court determines that the plaintiff is actually the holder of the paper and that the defendant is a person who would ordinarily have liability for payment of the face of the paper, what defenses can be raised successfully by a defendant being sued?

For example, assume that there are four successive indorsers, and that the holder who comes at the end of these four indorsers sues the first indorser. Can the first indorser raise against the holder a defense that the first indorser has against the second indorser? For example, can the defense be raised that the first indorser was induced by fraud to make the indorsement?

More commonly, the situation will arise in which the remote holder sues the drawer of a check. The drawer then defends on the ground that the check had been given in payment for goods or services that the drawer never got, did not work, or were not satisfactory. Can the drawer now raise against the remote holder the defense that the drawer has against the payee of the check, namely, the defense of failure of consideration? The answer to this depends on the nature of the drawer's defense against the person with whom the dealings were made and the character of the holder. If the defense is a **limited defense**, and the remote holder is a holder in due course, such a defense is not effective. This is the chief advantage of being a holder in due course of a negotiable instrument. If the defense is a **universal defense**, it is effective against all holders, including holders in due course.

limited defense
defense that cannot be used against a holder in due course

universal defense
defense against any holder

LO ①
Primary and secondary liability

24-1 Liability for the Face of the Paper

First the question of liability must be determined. Parties whose signatures do not appear on negotiable instruments are not normally liable for their payment. A signature can be any name, including a trade or assumed name, and may be handwritten, typed, or printed. It can even be a word or logo in place of an actual signature. For those whose signatures do appear, two types of contractual liability exist regarding the order or promise written on the face of the instrument: primary liability and secondary liability.

24-1a PRIMARY LIABILITY

primary liability
liability without conditions for commercial paper that is due

A person with **primary liability** may be called on to carry out the specific terms indicated on the paper. Of course, the paper must be due, but the holder of a negotiable instrument need meet no other conditions prior to the demand being made on one primarily liable. The two parties who ordinarily have the potential of primary liability on negotiable instruments include makers of notes and acceptors of drafts.

The maker of a note is primarily liable and may be called on for payment. The maker has intended this by the unconditional promise to pay. Such a promise to pay contrasts sharply with the terms used by drawers of drafts who order drawees to pay.

The drawer of a draft does not expect to be called on for payment; the drawer expects that payment will be made by the drawee. However, it would be unreasonable to expect that the drawee could be made liable by a mere order of another party, the drawer. Understandably then, the drawee of a draft who has not signed the instrument has no liability on it. Only when a drawee accepts a draft by writing "accepted" and signing it does the drawee have liability on the instrument. By acceptance the drawee in effect says, "I promise to pay . . ." This acceptance renders the drawee primarily liable just as the maker of a note is primarily liable.

24-1b SECONDARY LIABILITY

Indorsers and drawers are the parties whose liability on negotiable instruments is ordinarily secondary.

When the conditions of **secondary liability** have been met, a holder may require payment by any of the indorsers who have not limited their liability by the type of indorsement used or by the drawer. Except for drawers of checks or banks that have accepted a draft, who do not need notice of dishonor, three conditions must be met for a party to be held secondarily liable:

secondary liability
liability for a negotiable instrument that has been presented and dishonored, and for which notice of dishonor has been given

1. The instrument must be properly presented for payment.
2. The instrument must be dishonored.
3. Notice of the dishonor must be given to the party who is to be held secondarily liable.

Presentment. **Presentment** is the demand for acceptance or payment made on the maker, acceptor, drawee, or other payor of commercial paper. In order for indorsers to remain secondarily liable, the instrument must be properly presented. This means that the instrument should be presented to the correct person, in a proper and timely manner.

presentment
demand for acceptance or payment

Presentment of instruments that state a specified date for payment should be made on that date. Other instruments must be presented for payment within a reasonable time after a party becomes liable on the instrument. The nature of the instrument, existing commercial usage, and the facts of the case determine what length of time is reasonable. The UCC specifies that for drawers on uncertified checks, a presentment within thirty days after the date of the check or the date it was issued, whichever is later, is presumed to be reasonable. As to indorsers, the UCC specifies that presentment within seven days of the indorsement is presumed to be reasonable.

If presentment is delayed, drawers and makers of instruments payable at a bank may no longer have funds in the bank to cover the instruments if the bank fails. If the bank failure occurs, and the holder has delayed presentment for more than thirty days, drawers may be excused from liability on the basis that no proper presentment was made. To be so excused, the drawers must make a written assignment of their rights against the bank, to the extent of the funds lost, to the holders of the paper.

To reflect the fact that many banking transactions can be and are conducted by means of electronic devices, the UCC provides that presentment can be made electronically. The actual instrument need not be physically presented. Presentment takes place when a presentment notice is received. With electronic presentment, the banks involved have to have an agreement providing for presentment by electronic means. This agreement will specify what happens to the actual instrument—which bank holds it or whether it follows the presentment notice to the drawee bank.

Proper presentment is not a condition to secondary liability on a note when the maker has died or has been declared insolvent. A draft does not require presentment if the drawee or acceptor has died or gone into insolvency proceedings. Commercial paper may contain terms specifying that the indorsers and the drawer agree to waive their rights to the condition of presentment. Furthermore, the holder is excused from the requirement of presentment if, after diligent effort, the drawee of a draft or the maker of a note cannot be located.

Finally, if the secondary party knows that the draft or note will not be paid or has no reason to believe that the paper will be honored, presentment is excused.

Dishonor. The UCC states that **dishonor** occurs when a presentment is made and a due acceptance or payment is refused or cannot be obtained within the prescribed time. This occurs when, for example, a bank returns a check to the holder

dishonor
presentment made, but acceptance or payment not made

stamped "insufficient funds" or "account closed." Return of a check lacking a proper indorsement does not constitute dishonor.

Notice of Dishonor. A holder desiring to press secondary liability on an indorser or certain drawers must inform that party of the dishonor. Notice of dishonor must be conveyed promptly to these parties who are secondarily liable. The UCC requires that a bank give notice of dishonor to those it wishes to hold liable by midnight of the next banking day following the day on which it receives notice of dishonor. All other holders must give notice within thirty days following the day on which notice of dishonor is received. In order to avoid unduly burdening holders, the UCC provides that notice may be given by any commercially reasonable means. If by mail, proof of mailing conclusively satisfies the requirement of notice.

When a check is deposited into a bank account, the check can be from that bank or any other bank. When the drawee is a different bank, it needs to be returned to that bank for payment from the drawer's account. There is a system of clearing-houses that transfers checks from the banks in which they are deposited—depositary banks—to the drawee banks, called **payor banks**. Each bank in the clearinghouse system must give notice of dishonor in the prescribed time—by midnight of the next banking day following the day on which the check is received.

payor bank
the drawee bank

COURT CASE

FACTS: Agriprocessors, Inc. (Agriprocessors) operated a large kosher meatpacking and food-processing plant, and had a checking account with Luana Savings Bank (Luana). Luana operated under a "pay all" policy for check clearing. As checks were presented by the payee bank, Luana would "provisionally settle" on the checks. The next morning, Luana would review the details of the individual accounts, and if one of Agriprocessors's accounts appeared to be short, would call the company to be sure additional funds were coming in before the midnight deadline to cover them. After Agriprocessors's main facility was raided by U.S. Immigration and Customs Enforcement, 389 of its employees were arrested, and Agriprocessors declared bankruptcy. The bankruptcy trustee sued Luana for the value of the daily provisional

settlements, claiming they were actually short-term loans, and the prior-to-midnight payments were preferential transfers.

OUTCOME: The court found that under the UCC, final payment is made when an item is (1) paid in cash, or (2) a provisional settlement is not revoked in the time and manner provided by statute. During the provisional settlement, the bank is determining whether there are sufficient funds, and the final payment is not yet made. As a result, the court found that no debt, and therefore no loan, was created by the provisional settlement process.

—*In re Agriprocessors, Inc.*, 490 B.R. 852
(Bkrtcy. N.D. Iowa)

Delay or failure to give notice of dishonor is excused in most cases where timely presentment would not have been required. Basically, this occurs when notice has been waived; when notice was attempted with due diligence but was unsuccessful; or if the party to be notified had no reason to believe that the instrument would be honored, for example, because of death or insolvency.

24-1c UNAUTHORIZED SIGNATURES

Normally, an unauthorized signature does not bind the person whose name is used. The signature is a forgery. However, there are two exceptions: (1) when the person whose name is signed ratifies the signature, and (2) when the negligence of the person whose name is signed has contributed to the forgery.

When the forged signature is an indorsement, the loss usually falls on the first person to take the instrument after the forgery. That is one reason why banks ask for identification and even thumbprints before cashing a check for someone. Courts make the assumption that the person who deals with the forger is in the best position to prevent the loss.

24-2 Liability for Warranties

Contractual liability requires a signature on the paper. However, transferring negotiable instruments creates warranty liability. Unless specifically excluded, these warranties are automatically charged to every transferor of commercial paper. Note that a person can be liable as a warrantor even if the person's signature or name does not appear on the instrument, as, for example, when a person negotiates bearer paper by delivery alone.

The UCC specifies that each transferor who receives consideration and does not specifically limit liability makes a warranty that:

1. The transferor is entitled to enforce the instrument.
2. All signatures are genuine or authorized.
3. The instrument has not been altered.
4. The instrument is not subject to a defense or claim of any party that can be asserted against the transferor.
5. The transferor has no knowledge of any insolvency proceedings instituted with respect to the maker, acceptor, or drawer of an unaccepted draft.

24-3 Liability of Agents

An agent may sign a negotiable instrument, and the principal, not the agent, will be bound. If the agent (Jane Doe), authorized by the principal (John Smith), signs the instrument, "John Smith, Principal, by Jane Doe, Agent," or more simply, "John Smith by Jane Doe," the principal will be bound, but the agent will not be bound by the terms of the instrument.

Part 6 describes in further detail the responsibilities and liabilities of agents, but there is a special rule for checks signed by agents. If an agent signs a check in a representative capacity without indicating that capacity, but the check is on the principal's account, and the principal is identified, the agent is not liable. Almost all checks today are personalized to identify the individual on whose account the check is drawn. Therefore, the agent does not deceive anyone by signing such a check.

In the case of a corporation or other organization, the authorized agent should sign above or below the corporation or organization's name and indicate the position held after the signature. For example, Edward Rush, the president of Acme Industries, should sign:

ACME INDUSTRIES
By Edward Rush, President

If the instrument were signed this way, Acme Industries, not Edward Rush, would be bound.

If an individual signs an instrument as an agent, "John Smith, Principal, by Jane Doe, Agent," but the agent is not authorized to sign for the principal, the principal would not be bound. However, the agent who made the unauthorized signature would be bound. This protects innocent parties to the instrument who would not be able to enforce their rights against anyone if the unauthorized agent were not bound.

24-4 Holders in Due Course

LO ②
Holder in due course requirements

holder in due course
holder for value and in good faith with no knowledge of dishonor, defenses, or claims, or that paper is overdue

Negotiable instruments have an important advantage over ordinary contracts. Remote parties can be given immunity against many of the defenses available against simple contracts. To enjoy this immunity, the holder of a negotiable instrument must be a **holder in due course**, or an innocent purchaser. The terms *holder in due course* and *innocent purchaser* describe the holder of a negotiable instrument who has obtained it under these conditions:

1. The holder must take the instrument in good faith and for value.
2. The holder must have no notice the instrument is overdue or has been dishonored.
3. At the time the instrument is negotiated, the holder must have had no notice of any defense against or claim to the instrument.

24-4a FOR VALUE AND IN GOOD FAITH

To attain the specially favored status of being a holder in due course, the holder must give value for the paper. One who does not do so, such as a niece receiving a Christmas check from an uncle, cannot be a holder in due course. A mere promise does not constitute value.

The requirement that value be given in order to be a holder in due course does not mean that one must pay full value for a negotiable instrument. Thus, a person who purchases an instrument at a discount can qualify as a holder in due course. The law states that it must be taken "for value and in good faith." Good faith means honesty in fact and the observance of reasonable commercial standards of fair dealing.

COURT CASE

FACTS: Ron Scharf and Alexander Kogan entered into a series of complex business agreements. Later, Scharf sued Kogan, alleging breach of an agreement. They settled the suit with Kogan, agreeing to pay Scharf $1 million. Kogan tried to renegotiate the settlement and failed to meet his obligations under it. Rather than return to court, Scharf went to First Bank and opened a new account in the name of a Kogan company. He identified himself as a member of the company and said money was needed for a small closing. He then withdrew $650,000 from another Kogan account using documents obtained from prior dealings with Kogan. Scharf deposited the funds in the new account and obtained a cashier's check payable to his company, Transcontinental, using the funds from the new account. Scharf then went to another bank, where he opened an account for Transcontinental

and deposited the cashier's check. He asked that bank to wire $649,000 to a Transcontinental account in a third bank. The manager of First Bank inquired about the transactions and phoned Kogan, who told him that Scharf was not authorized to access Kogan's accounts. The bank stopped payment on the cashier's check. Transcontinental sued the bank and alleged that it was a holder in due course.

OUTCOME: The court found that Scharf had misled the bank when he stated he was a member of Kogan's company and needed the money for a small closing. Because he was not honest, he did not take the cashier's check in good faith.

—*Transcontinental Holding Ltd. v. First Banks Inc.,*
299 S.W.3d 629 (Mo. Ct. App.)

The test for good faith is: If the holder is notified of a problem with the instrument or a defect in the title of the transferor before the full purchase price has been paid, the holder will be a holder in due course to the extent of the amount paid before notification of the problem or defect.

24-4b NO KNOWLEDGE THAT INSTRUMENT IS PAST DUE OR DISHONORED

One who takes an instrument known to be past due cannot be an innocent purchaser. However, a purchaser of demand paper on which demand for payment has been made and refused is still a holder in due course if the purchaser had no notice of the demand. A purchaser who has reason to know that any part of the principal is overdue, that an **uncured default** exists in payment of an instrument in the same series, or that acceleration of the instrument has been made has notice that the instrument is overdue. A note dated and payable in a fixed number of days or months shows on its face whether it is past due or not.

> **uncured default**
> not all payments on instrument fully made and not all made by due date

An instrument transferred on the date of maturity is not past due but would be overdue on the next day. An instrument payable on demand is due within a reasonable time after issuance. For checks drawn and payable in the United States, thirty days is presumed to be a reasonable time.

24-4c NO KNOWLEDGE OF ANY DEFENSE OR CLAIM TO THE INSTRUMENT

When one takes a negotiable instrument by negotiation, to obtain the rights of an innocent purchaser there must be no knowledge of any defense against or claim adverse to the instrument. Knowledge of a claim may be inferred if, for example, the holder knows that a **fiduciary** has negotiated an instrument in payment of a personal debt. A fiduciary is a person in a relationship of trust and confidence such as a trustee. As between the original parties to a negotiable instrument, any act, such as fraud, duress, mistake, or illegality that would make a contract either void or voidable, will have the same effect on a negotiable instrument. However, as will be seen in the discussion of defenses below, many of these defenses are not effective if the instrument is negotiated to an innocent purchaser.

> **fiduciary**
> a person in relationship of trust and confidence

Knowledge of some potential irregularities does not destroy holder-in-due-course status. Knowing that an instrument has been antedated or postdated, was incomplete and has been completed, that default has been made in the payment of interest, or that it was issued or negotiated in return for an executory promise or accompanied by a separate agreement does not give a holder notice of a defense or claim.

24-5 Holder Through a Holder in Due Course

The first holder in due course brings into operation all the protections that the law has placed around negotiable instruments. These protections are not easily lost. A subsequent holder, known as a **holder through a holder in due course**, may benefit from them even though not a holder in due course itself. For example, Doerhoff, without consideration, gives Bryce a negotiable note due in sixty days. Before maturity, Bryce indorses it to Cordell under conditions that make Cordell a holder in due course. Thereafter, Cordell transfers the note to Otke for no consideration. Otke is not a holder in due course, as she did not give any consideration

> **holder through a holder in due course**
> holder subsequent to holder in due course

for the note. But if Otke is not a party to any wrongdoing or illegality affecting this instrument, she acquires all the rights of a holder in due course. This is true because Cordell had these rights, and when Cordell transferred the note to Otke, he transferred all of his rights, which included his holder-in-due-course rights. This rule allowing a person who would otherwise not be a holder in due course to have the rights of such a holder, if a holder in due course were a previous holder, is known as the **shelter principle**.

shelter principle
rule giving holder rights of holder in due course

COURT CASE

FACTS: To refinance their home, Hosea and Bernice Anderson signed a note agreeing to pay Wilmington Finance Inc. (Wilmington) the $227,000 they borrowed. Wilmington transferred the note to Morgan Stanley Mortgage Capital Holding Inc., which in turn transferred it to Morgan Stanley ABS Capital I Inc. This transferee sold and conveyed all its right, title, and interest in the note to Deutsche Bank Trust Company Americas (Deutsche). The Andersons defaulted, and foreclosure proceedings were brought. At trial, it was shown that Wilmington qualified as a holder in due course, but Duetsche,

in possession of the note, was a successor to the holder of the note and entitled to enforce it. There was no allegation that anyone in the chain of title had engaged in any fraud or illegality. The Andersons asked the court to prevent the foreclosure.

OUTCOME: The court held that as a successor to a holder in due course, Deutsche had the same rights and could enforce the note against the Andersons.

—*Anderson v. Burson*, 9 A.3d 870
(Md. Ct. Spec. App.)

24-6 Holders of Consumer Paper

consumer goods or services
goods or services primarily for personal, family, or household use

The UCC rules regarding holder in due course status have been modified for holders of negotiable instruments given for consumer goods or services. **Consumer goods or services** are defined as goods or services for use primarily for personal, family, or household purposes. The changes resulted from both amendment to the UCC by the states—which means that the rules vary somewhat from state to state—and the adoption of a Federal Trade Commission (FTC) rule.

setoff
a claim by the party being sued against the party suing

Generally, the rights of the holder of consumer paper are subject to all claims, defenses, and setoffs of the original purchaser or debtor arising from the consumer transaction. A **setoff** is a claim a party being sued makes against the party suing. In the case of consumer sales, the FTC rule requires that consumer credit contracts contain specified language in bold print indicating that holders of the contracts are subject to all claims and defenses the debtor could assert against the seller. No subsequent holder can be a holder in due course. The language is:

NOTICE
ANY HOLDER OF THIS CONSUMER CREDIT CONTRACT IS SUBJECT TO ALL CLAIMS AND DEFENSES WHICH THE DEBTOR COULD ASSERT AGAINST THE SELLER OF GOODS OR SERVICES OBTAINED PURSUANT HERETO OR WITH THE PROCEEDS HEREOF. RECOVERY HEREUNDER BY THE DEBTOR SHALL NOT EXCEED AMOUNTS PAID BY THE DEBTOR HEREUNDER.

State laws generally make holder in due course rules inapplicable to consumer sales or limit the cutoff of consumer rights to a specified number of days after notification of assignment.

Normally, these rights of the debtor are available only when the loan was arranged by the seller or lessor of the goods or was made directly by the seller or lessor. State laws do not apply to credit card sales on a credit card issued by someone other than the seller. However, federal law allows a credit card holder to refuse to pay credit card issuers in some cases when an earnest effort at returning the goods is made, or a chance to correct a problem is given the seller.

Modifying or abolishing the special status of a holder in due course for consumer goods prevents frauds frequently practiced on consumers by unscrupulous businesspeople. Such individuals would sell shoddy merchandise on credit and immediately negotiate the instrument of credit to a bank or finance company. When the consumer discovered the defects in the goods, payment could not be avoided, because the new holder of the instrument had purchased it without knowledge of the potential defenses and was therefore a holder in due course. Furthermore, the seller, who had frequently left the jurisdiction or gone bankrupt, was unavailable to be sued. Thus, the consumer would be unable to assert a defense or rescind the transaction against either the seller or the holder. The modifications based on changes to the UCC and adoption of the FTC rule were enacted to remedy this problem. A consumer who purchases goods that are not delivered or worthless can avoid paying any more and recover what has been paid.

COURT CASE

FACTS: Consumer's Choice Foods, Inc. (CCF), sold food service plans to consumers on installment contracts. Jayco Acceptance Corporation (Jayco) purchased several contracts from CCF, and received monthly payments due on the contracts. The State of Nebraska brought a complaint against CCF and Jayco alleging violations of several consumer protection acts, including representing that goods had characteristics they did not have, engaging in unconscionable sales practices, and unfair and deceptive acts. The State won verdicts against both CCF and Jayco. Jayco appealed.

OUTCOME: The court held that a consumer may assert against a creditor or its assignee any defenses the consumer could have asserted against the seller had the contract not been assigned.

—State ex rel. Stenberg v. Consumer's Choice Foods, Inc., 755 N.W.2d 583 (Neb.)

24-7 Defenses

Certain defenses are limited to being raised against ordinary holders and cannot be raised against holders in due course. They are called **limited** or **personal defenses** and include:

1. Ordinary contract defenses

2. Fraud that induced the execution of the instrument

3. Conditional delivery

4. Improper completion

LO ③
Advantage of being a holder in due course

limited or personal defense
defense that cannot be used against a holder in due course

5. Payment or part payment

6. Nondelivery

7. Theft

LO ④

Limited, universal, and hybrid defenses

24-7a LIMITED DEFENSES

Ordinary Contract Defenses. In general, the defenses available in a dispute over a contract may be raised only against holders who do not qualify as holders in due course. If a holder in due course holds an instrument, the defense of failure of consideration is not effective when raised by a maker who alleges that no consideration was received for the paper. In an action on an ordinary contract, the promisor may defend on the ground that no consideration existed for the promise; or that if consideration did exist in the form of a counterpromise, the promise was never performed; or that the consideration was illegal. Thus, if Smith agreed to paint Jones's house but did not do it properly, Jones would have a right of action against Smith for breach of contract, or Jones could refuse to pay Smith the price they agreed on. If Smith assigned the right to payment, Jones would be able to raise against the assignee the defenses available against Smith.

However, if Jones paid Smith by check before the work was completed, and the check was negotiated to a holder in due course, Jones could not defend on the ground of failure of consideration. Jones's only right of action would be against Smith for the loss.

Fraud That Induced the Execution of the Instrument. When a person knows commercial paper is being executed and knows its essential terms but is persuaded or induced to execute it because of false representations or statements, this is not a defense against a holder in due course. For example, if Randolph persuades Drucker to buy a car because of false statements Randolph made about the car, and Drucker gives Randolph a note for it that is later negotiated to a holder in due course, Drucker cannot defend on the ground that Randolph lied about the car. Drucker will have to pay the note and seek any recovery from Randolph.

COURT CASE

FACTS: Damion and Kiya Carmichael executed a promissory note secured by a mortgage on real property to Ameriquest Mortgage Co. (AMC). AMC sold the note to Ameriquest Mortgage Services (AMS), which transferred it to Deutsche Bank National Trust Company (Deutsche). The note went into default, and Deutsche sought to foreclose on the mortgage. Deutsche was a holder in due course of the note. The Carmichaels claimed that AMC had fraudulently persuaded them to refinance their mortgage based on assurances that if they were to need to refinance the note, the prepayment penalty in their note would be waived.

OUTCOME: Since Deutsche was a holder in due course, the defense of fraudulent inducement was not effective against it.

—*In re Carmichael*, 443 B.R. 698
(Bankr. E.D. Pennsylvania)

Conditional Delivery. As against a holder in due course, an individual who would be liable on the instrument cannot show that the instrument, absolute on its face, was delivered subject to an unperformed condition or that it was delivered for a specific purpose but was not used for it. If Sims makes out a check for Byers and delivers it to Richter with instructions not to deliver it until Byers delivers certain goods, but Richter delivers it to Byers, who then negotiates it to a holder in due course, Sims will have to pay on the check.

Improper Completion. If any term in a negotiable instrument is left blank (for example, the payee or the amount), and the drawer then delivers the instrument to another to complete it, the drawer cannot raise the defense of improper completion against a holder in due course. In this case, the holder in due course may require payment from the drawer.

Payment or Part Payment. On payment of a negotiable instrument, the party making the payment should demand the surrender of the instrument. If not surrendered, the instrument may be further negotiated, and a later holder in due course would be able to demand payment successfully. A receipt is not adequate as proof of payment because the subsequent holder in due course would have no notice of the receipt from the instrument, whereas surrender of the instrument would clearly prevent further negotiation.

If only partial payment is made, a holder would not, and should not, be expected to surrender the instrument. In such a case, the person making the payment should be sure the fact of the partial payment is recorded on the instrument, thereby giving notice of the partial payment to any subsequent transferee.

Nondelivery. Normally, a negotiable instrument fully or partially completed, but not delivered to the payee, is not collectible by the payee. However, if a holder in due course holds the instrument, payment of it may be required. For example, if one person makes out a note to another person, and that other person takes the note from the maker's desk without the maker's permission and negotiates it to an innocent purchaser, or holder in due course, the holder in due course would be entitled to recover the amount of the note against the maker. This applies in spite of the nondelivery of the note.

Theft. A thief may not normally pass good title; however, an exception occurs when the thief conveys an instrument to a holder in due course. Such a purchaser will be able to enforce the obligation in spite of the previous theft of the paper. The thief or any ordinary holder cannot require payment of stolen paper.

24-7b UNIVERSAL DEFENSES

Those defenses thought to be so important that they are preserved even against a holder in due course are called **universal** or **real defenses**. Universal defenses can be raised regardless of whom is being sued or who is suing. Thus, they can be raised against a holder in due course as well as an ordinary holder. The more common universal defenses include:

universal or real defense
defense against any holder

1. Minority
2. Forgery
3. Fraud as to the nature of the instrument or its essential terms
4. Discharge in bankruptcy proceedings

Minority. The fact that the defendant is a minor capable of avoiding agreements under contract laws is a defense that may be raised against any holder.

Forgery. Except in cases in which the defendant's negligence made the forgery possible, forgery may be raised successfully against any holder. However, a forged signature operates as the signature of the forger in favor of a holder in due course, so the forger is liable on such an instrument.

Fraud as to the Nature of the Instrument and Its Essential Terms. The defense that one was induced to sign an instrument when one did not know that it was in fact commercial paper is available against any holder. For example, an illiterate person who is told that a note is a receipt and is thereby induced to sign it may successfully raise this defense against any holder. The defense is not available, however, to competent individuals who negligently fail to read or give reasonable attention to the details of the documents they sign.

PREVIEW CASE REVISITED

FACTS: James and Marie Estepp wanted to get a loan from United Bank & Trust Co. of Maryland. United required an additional signature by an owner of real estate. James brought Marvin Schaeffer to the bank, saying he needed Schaeffer, whose wife had died, to sign a character reference. Estepp supervised Schaeffer at work and had helped Schaeffer make funeral arrangements. Schaeffer had a learning disability and could not read or write. The bank officer handling the transaction did not explain to Schaeffer that he was assuming a financial responsibility. Schaeffer signed the note. The Estepps defaulted, so United sued Schaeffer.

OUTCOME: The court found that fraud as to the nature and essential terms of the note had occurred.

—*Schaeffer v. United Bank & Trust Co. of Maryland*, 360 A.2d 461 (Md. Ct. Spec. App.)

Discharge in Bankruptcy Proceedings. Even holders in due course are subject to the defense that a discharge in bankruptcy has been granted.

24-7c HYBRID DEFENSES

Several defenses may be either universal or limited, depending on the circumstances of a case. These include:

1. Duress

2. Incapacity other than minority

3. Illegality

4. Alteration

Duress. Whether or not duress is a valid defense against a holder in due course depends on whether the effect of such duress under state law makes a contract void or voidable. When the duress nullifies a contract, the defense is universal. When the duress merely makes the contract voidable at the option of the victim of the duress, the defense is limited.

Incapacity Other Than Minority. In cases of incapacity other than minority, if the effect of the incapacity makes the instrument void, a nullity, the defense is universal. If the effect of the incapacity does not make the instrument a nullity, the defense is limited.

Illegality. The fact that the law makes certain transactions illegal gives rise to a defense against an ordinary holder. Such a defense would be unavailable against a holder in due course unless the law making the transaction illegal also specifies that instruments based on such transactions are unenforceable.

COURT CASE

FACTS: Cumberland Farms, Inc. (Cumberland), issued payroll checks to its employees, and provided Bank of America (Bank) a list of its employees so that the bank could verify each payroll check listed the proper employee. Four unidentified individuals presented Cumberland payroll checks to E&G Food Corp. (E&G), and E&G cashed them. When E&G presented the checks to Bank, it was discovered that they bore the same check numbers and amounts as four checks cashed by Bank two months previously. However, the names of the payees on the checks was different. Bank refused to honor the recent checks, and E&G sued,

claiming that its status as holder in due course entitled it to payment on the checks. State law stated that the right to enforce the obligation to pay an instrument was nullified by the illegality of the transaction.

OUTCOME: The court concluded that the creation of the checks and their presentment by third-party actors were criminal acts. Bank had established the defense of illegality.

—*E&G Food Corporation v. Cumberland Farms, Inc.,* 2011 Mass. App. Div. 204

Alteration. The UCC defines an **alteration** as "an unauthorized change in an instrument that purports to modify in any respect the obligation of a party, or . . . an unauthorized addition . . . to an incomplete instrument." When an alteration is fraudulently made, the party whose obligation is affected by the alteration is discharged. A payor bank or a drawee who pays a fraudulently altered instrument, or a person who takes it for value in good faith and with no notice of the alteration, may enforce the instrument according to its original terms or to its terms as completed.

alteration
unauthorized change or completion of negotiable instrument to modify obligation of a party

24-8 Miscellaneous Matters

In addition to the defenses described earlier, remember that every lawsuit presents certain standard problems. Any defendant may, under appropriate circumstances, raise the defense that the suit is not brought in the proper court, that no service of process existed, or that the statute of limitations has run and bars the suit. Any defendant in a suit on a negotiable instrument can claim that the instrument is not negotiable; that the plaintiff is not the holder; and that the defendant is not a party liable for payment of the paper. If the holder claims that the defendant is secondarily liable for the payment of the face of the paper, the defendant also may show that the paper had not been properly presented to the primary party and that proper notice of default had not been given to the secondary party.

QUESTIONS

1. Upon what does imposition of liability on parties to negotiable instruments under the UCC depend?

2. How does the drawee of a draft become liable on an instrument, and what kind of liability does such a drawee have?

3. What conditions must be met for a party to be held secondarily liable?

4. What are the two exceptions to the rule that an unauthorized signature does not bind the person whose name is used?

5. What are the three required conditions for a holder to be a holder in due course?

6. What is the shelter rule?

7. Explain the difference between a limited defense and a universal defense.

8. What should the party making payment of a negotiable instrument demand to ensure that the instrument is not further negotiated to a holder in due course who could require payment?

9. May a thief convey good title to an instrument?

10. Under what circumstances is the defense of fraud as to the nature of the instrument and its essential terms unavailable?

11. When is duress a universal defense?

12. May a person who takes a fraudulently altered instrument for value in good faith and with no notice of the alteration enforce the instrument? Explain.

CASE PROBLEMS

1. DDH Construction Inc. (DDH) hired Whooping Creek Construction, LLC (WCC) to work on a construction project. The general contractor had hired Gavin Garrett, LLC (Garrett), who had hired DDH. WCC submitted a payment request for its work. The general contractor issued payment to Garrett, who transferred payment to DDH. WCC received a check for $60,000, drawn on DDH's account at Bartow County Bank (Bank). Wednesday, WCC deposited the check in its account at McIntosh Bank. Friday, the Bank ordered a hold on DDH's account for the amount of the check, to prevent payment, and returned the check in its normal way to the Federal Reserve Bank (Fed) by means of a software program that sent an electronic file with an image of the check stamped "uncollected funds hold." The check was marked received by the Fed on Monday. WCC's account was reduced by the amount of the check, so it sued the Bank. It alleged that the Bank's dishonor was not timely, because the check had to be returned to the Fed by midnight Friday, but the notation on the check showed that it was not received by the Fed until Monday. Was the dishonor timely?

2. A person purporting to be Ronald Wilder phoned American General Financial Services (American) requesting a loan. Wilder's credit was excellent, so American said it needed his prior two years' tax returns and asked what he wanted to do with the loan proceeds. The person said he wanted to renovate property he owned and faxed the tax returns and loan application. An $18,000 loan was approved. At American's office the person presented a driver's license with the person's photo but with Wilder's information. After signing the loan documents, the person left with a check for $18,000. He went to State Security Check Cashing Inc. (State) and presented the same driver's license. Considering the amount of the check "large," State's employee phoned State's compliance officer. He told her to verify the date of the check, name of the payee, address of the licensee, loan paperwork, and whether the check matched other checks State had cashed from American. She confirmed these and cashed the check with the officer's approval. The next business day, American learned of the forgery and stopped payment on the check. State, claiming it was a holder in due course, sued American for payment. American argued that State had not taken the check in good faith. Who should win?

CASE PROBLEMS (CONTINUED)

3. Nelson and Martha Soto executed a promissory note and mortgage in favor of Parkway Bank and Trust Co. (Parkway) for the purchase of their apartment. The Sotos procured insurance for their home from State Farm Fire and Casualty Co. (State Farm). Their apartment was subsequently damaged by a fire. Brickman Companies LLC (Brickman) was hired to make repairs to the home, and the Sotos authorized State Farm to name Brickman as an additional payee in the settlement. State Farm issued checks payable to "NELSON SOTO & MARTHA I. SOTO & PARKWAY BANK & TRUST COMPANY ITS SUCCESSORS AND/OR ASSIGNS & BRICKMAN CONSTRUCTION INC." and delivered the checks to Brickman. Brickman forged Parkway's indorsement and cashed the checks at JP Morgan Chase Bank. Two months later Parkway discovered the forgery and demanded replacement checks from State Farm. Was Parkway entitled to receive new checks from State Farm?   **LO ①**

4. Cactus Roofing, LLC issued a check to "Espino Roofing and/or Tomas Hernandez" for $4,768.47 for roofing work that Hernandez had performed for Cactus. That morning, Hernandez cashed the check at Hurst Enterprises, LLC, d/b/a Mr. Payroll Check Cashing. Hernandez had previously cashed three other checks from Cactus at Mr. Payroll. All three checks had cleared without problems. Mr. Payroll paid Hernandez the amount of the check minus a 1 percent check-cashing fee and deposited the check in its account at Bank of the Panhandle. A day after issuing the check, Cactus discovered that Hernandez's work had not been adequately completed. After unsuccessfully trying to contact Hernandez, Cactus stopped payment on the check. Mr. Payroll received the check back from its bank with notice that a stop payment had been issued. The manager of Mr. Payroll discovered that the stop payment had been issued three days after Hernandez had cashed the check. Mr. Payroll sued Cactus, alleging it was a holder in due course. Was it?   **LO ②**

5. Kenneth Wulf's job for Auto-Owners Insurance Co. was to decide whether Auto-Owners would pursue a claim. If so, he was to put a note in the file. When a check was received, clerical staff attached it to the file and gave the file to Wulf. He was to note receipt of the check in the file, complete a transmittal form, and return the check to the clerical staff. No record was kept of checks received or of pending claims. Wulf opened an account at Bank One in the name, "Auto Owners Insurance." Wulf would work on a claim but not note anything in the file. When a check arrived, the clerical staff would attach it to the file and give it to Wulf. He would take the check, indorse it with a stamp he had made that said "Auto Owners Insurance Deposit Only," and deposit it in his Bank One account. The checks were payable to "Auto-Owners Insurance," "Auto-Owners Insurance Company," and "Auto-Owners Insurance Co." When the embezzlement was discovered, Auto-Owners sued Bank One. Was Bank One liable?   **LO ①**

6. Houston Gold Exchange (Houston) purchased a purported Rolex watch from Shelly McKee, paying with a postdated check drawn on its bank. McKee endorsed the check to RR Maloan Investments, Inc. (Maloan), which cashed it prior to the issue date. The next day, Houston issued a stop-payment order on the check when it discovered information indicating that the watch was counterfeit. Maloan presented the check to Houston's bank, which refused to honor it based upon the stop-payment order. Maloan sued Houston. Was Maloan entitled to collect on the check due to its status as a holder in due course?   **LO ④**

7. Gregory Erkins executed a promissory note to Ameriquest Mortgage Co. (Ameriquest), secured by a mortgage on his house. Ameriquest assigned the note and mortgage to New York Trust Co., N.A. (New York). Elkins made the payments for two years and then defaulted. He sued New York to stop foreclosure proceedings, alleging that Ameriquest had engaged in tortuous behavior when the loan was taken out. If New York paid value for the note and had no knowledge of any allegedly tortuous behavior, should this defense be successful?   **LO ④**

8. NorVergence Inc. resold telecommunications services. Customers had to lease a matrix box (the box), which NorVergence said enabled it to supply low-cost services. IFC Credit Corporation bought leases from NorVergence. When IFC was to receive payments from the first leases it bought, it got   **LO ③**

CASE PROBLEMS (CONTINUED)

complaints from NorVergence customers about not getting services or savings. NorVergence and IFC amended their agreement, allowing IFC to withhold 25 percent of payment for leases pending the lessees' performance. Specialty Optical Systems agreed to switch to NorVergence if its contract with another company could be cancelled. NorVergence said that Specialty had to sign an Equipment Rental Agreement (the lease) to facilitate the application process, but NorVergence would not sign the lease, and Specialty would not be obligated unless its current contract were cancelled. Specialty signed the lease requiring sixty monthly payments of $543.67 for box rental, believing the payments included the box and telephone and Internet service. The lease said any claims or defenses that Specialty had against NorVergence could not be asserted against a purchaser of the lease and, as long as the box were delivered in outwardly good condition, Specialty had to pay rent even if it never received telephone services. Specialty accepted the box. NorVergence and IFC amended their agreement again to allow IFC to buy leases at a discounted rate and excuse it from paying more unless NorVergence were to provide acceptable service. NorVergence signed the Specialty lease. IFC confirmed that Specialty had received the box and would begin making payments in sixty days, so it took assignment of that lease. Specialty never got telephone services, nor was its prior contract cancelled. NorVergence went into bankruptcy. Specialty returned the box to IFC. When IFC demanded lease payments, Specialty sued. State law afforded IFC protection similar to that of a holder in due course if the same conditions were met. Did it meet holder in due course conditions?

LO ③ 9. Ohio Savings Bank (OSB) bought first mortgage loans from a branch of Advantage Investors Mortgage (AIM). OSB wired funds to an escrow account of AIM's closing agent, First National Title (FNT). Borrowers signed notes and mortgages to AIM as lender; AIM assigned them to OSB; and FNT was to disburse the loan proceeds appropriately from its escrow account, primarily to pay off existing first mortgages. James Niblock, who secretly owned FNT and controlled the AIM branch, embezzled $1 million from the FNT escrow account after borrowers' notes and mortgages were executed and assigned to OSB. The prior loans were unpaid, so the borrowers refused to pay the mortgage loans assigned to OSB. It sued Progressive Casualty Insurance Co., which had issued a bond covering losses "resulting directly from the Insured's having, in good faith . . . accepted or received or acted upon the faith of any real property mortgages . . . which prove to have been defective by reason of the signature thereon of any person having been obtained through trick, artifice, fraud or false pretenses. . . ." Did the bond cover OSB's losses?

ETHICS IN PRACTICE

You have learned about the benefits the law gives to a holder in due course in order to promote business transactions. Such a holder is given immunity against many potential defenses. Consider the ethical implications of this. Is it ethical that the obligee on a negotiable instrument is unable to raise otherwise valid defenses simply because the holder meets the requirements of being a holder in due course?

PART 5 SUMMARY CASES

NEGOTIABLE INSTRUMENTS

1. Coastal Agricultural Supply, Inc. (Coastal), sold farm and ranch equipment. For 30 years it employed Jimmy Hollaway, including several years as its bookkeeper. Hollaway's duties included receiving checks from customers made payable to Coastal, indorsing them on Coastal's behalf "for deposit only," and depositing them into Coastal's account. Hollaway opened a checking account with JP Morgan Chase Bank, N.A. (Chase) in the name "Jimmy Hollaway DBA Coastal Agricultural Limestone Supply." Hollaway subsequently deposited 964 checks intended for Coastal into this new account. Coastal was only able to recover about 15 percent of the stolen money from Hollaway, so it also sued Chase. Was Chase liable to Coastal for accepting the checks indorsed by Hollaway? [*Coastal Agricultural Supply, Inc. v. JP Morgan Chase Bank, N.A.*, 759 F.3d 498 (5th Cir.)]

2. InterAmerican Car Rental, Inc. (InterAmerican), purchased its fleet of rental vehicles from Maroone Chevrolet, L.L.C. (Maroone), using financing from several local banks. InterAmerican would place an order for cars with Maroone, who would order the necessary vehicles from the manufacturer. The manufacturer would ship vehicles directly to InterAmerican and invoice Maroone. Maroone then invoiced InterAmerican. InterAmerican would then submit a draw request to its financing bank, which would issue a check for the purchase money loan. The checks were delivered to InterAmerican, but payable jointly to InterAmerican and Maroone. However, InterAmerican did not deliver checks to Maroone, but simply typed Maroone's name on the back and deposited the checks in InterAmerican's own account. InterAmerican then paid Maroone over time. Maroone was unaware that the financing checks were payable jointly to InterAmerican and Maroone. When InterAmerican went out of business, Maroone sued the depository and financing banks for accepting checks not properly indorsed by Maroone. Should Maroone recover from the banks? [*Regions Bank v. Maroone Chevrolet, L.L.C.*, 118 So.3d 251 (Fla. App.)]

3. Vincent Schettler executed a promissory note to Silver State Bank (Silver) as part of a revolving line of credit for Schettler's business, which provided for a period of interest only payments until the maturity date. The maturity date was renegotiated several times during the term of the business relationship. Silver ultimately went into receivership, and the Federal Deposit Insurance Corporation (FDIC) was appointed receiver. Schettler then did not pay the outstanding balance of the note on the maturity date. RalRon Capital Corporation (RalRon) purchased the note and demanded payment from Schettler. Was RalRon a holder in due course entitled to payment from Schettler? [*Schettler v. RalRon Capital Corporation*, 275 P.3d 933 (Nev.)]

4. While employed as the bookkeeper by City Rentals Inc. (City), Robin Bauer forged several checks on City's account and deposited them directly into

Rodney Kesler's bank account to repay money she had borrowed from him. Kesler never saw or indorsed the checks and had no idea the funds had been embezzled. City notified Kesler that Bauer had forged the checks, and demanded that he return the funds. Kesler refused, so City sued him. He argued that because he had received the checks as payment of debts, he was a holder in due course and did not have to return the money. Should City be able to recover the funds? [*City Rentals Inc. v. Kesler*, 946 N.E.2d 785 (Ohio Ct. App.)]

5. Martha Jenkins signed a promissory note and other documents relating to an $88,000 loan from First Horizon Home Loans. She alleged she had not intended to take out a loan but had been defrauded into signing the papers by her cousins, Courtney and Gail Brown, and the closing attorney, Brian Pierce. A loan proceeds check for $69,000, payable to Jenkins and drawn on Pierce's account at Wachovia Bank, National Association (Wachovia), was never received by Jenkins. Apparently Courtney Brown forged Jenkins' signature and deposited the funds into two accounts at Wachovia. Jenkins sued Wachovia. Should she recover? [*Jenkins v. Wachovia Bank, Nat. Ass'n*, 711 S.E.2d 80 (Ga. Ct. App.)]

6. Liccardi Ford Inc. (Liccardi) issued a check to an employee, Charles Stallone, but did not deliver the check to Stallone because he was suspected of embezzlement. The check disappeared from Liccardi's offices, and when that was discovered, Liccardi ordered payment stopped on it. JCNB Check Cashing Inc. (JCNB) cashed the check for Stallone before its issue date and deposited it in its own bank account. The issuing bank refused to honor the check. Two years later, Robert Triffin acquired the dishonored check from JCNB and sued Liccardi and Stallone for its amount. While Triffin could not have acquired the check as a holder in due course, since he knew of its dishonor, if JCNB was a holder in due course, Triffin could enforce JCNB's rights. Was JCNB a holder in due course? [*Triffin v. Liccardi Ford Inc.*, 10 A.3d 227 (N.J. Super. Ct. App. Div.)]

7. Magloire and Marie Isaac signed a note secured by a mortgage to Option One. In a subsequent lawsuit to foreclose on the mortgage, Deutsche Bank National Trust Co. (Deutsche) produced the original mortgage, note and an allonge. The allonge was signed by an assistant secretary of Option One, but it did not state a payee. The Isaacs claimed that Deutsche needed to prove that it had standing to assert its right to foreclose on the mortgage. What status did Deutsche have if any? [*Isaac v. Deutsche Bank Nat. Trust Co.*, 74 So.3d 495 (Fla. Dist. Ct. App.)]

8. Regent Title Insurance Agency, LLC (Regent), served as settlement agent for real estate closings, cutting checks to distribute funds to the appropriate parties. On several occasions, Charae Pearson brought Regent checks to New Randolph Halsted Currency Exchange, Inc. (Randolph), and Randolph cashed them. Pearson then brought a check to Randolph made payable to "CHAREA PAERSON" which was for ten times more than any other check Randolph had cashed for Pearson, and required manager approval. Randolph cashed the check after checking both Pearson's state identification and check cashing history with Randolph, and calling Regent to confirm the transaction. After Pearson was arrested for check fraud, Regent told its bank to stop payment. Randolph sued. Was Randolph a holder in due course entitled to payment? [*New Randolph Halsted Currency Exchange, Inc. v. Regent Title Insurance Agency, LLC*, 939 N.E.2d 1024 (Ill. App.)]

9. Two related businesses, Grassi Design Group Inc. (Grassi) and Beauchemin Grassi Interiors Inc. (Beauchemin), had checking accounts with Bank of America, N.A. and RBS Citizens, N.A. An employee common to both corporations forged and cashed numerous checks that the banks honored. Both banks had used fraud-detection computer software to identify possibly fraudulent checks, but the companies had failed to examine the monthly statements sent by the banks, so no fraudulent checks were reported within thirty days of appearing on a statement. Grassi and Beauchemin sued the banks. Were the banks liable? [*Grassi Design Group Inc. v. Bank of America, N.A.*, 908 N.E.2d 393 (Mass. App. Ct.)]

10. Marie Hunt signed a promissory note in the amount of $35,000, payable to Robert Rice and secured by a mortgage on real property. Rice had given her only $23,354.87, which, Hunt claimed, she had repaid in full. For $25,000, Rice had assigned the note to Invest Co., which for $27,182.41 had assigned it to Chrysler First Financial Services Corporation. NationsCredit Financial Services Corporation was the successor corporation to Chrysler First and was the assignee of the note and mortgage. It had declared Hunt in default, had foreclosed on the mortgage, and had sold her property. Hunt sought a judgment declaring the foreclosure sale invalid, asserting the defense of failure (or partial failure) of consideration because Rice had given her as consideration for the note only $23,354.87 rather than $35,000 recited in the note. Nations Credit argued that Hunt could not assert the defense against it because it was a holder in due course. Was the defense valid against NationsCredit? [*Hunt v. NationsCredit Financial Services Corp.*, 902 So.2d 75 (Ala. Civ. App.)]

11. GreenPoint Credit, LLC had a security interest in a mobile home owned by Rosetta Lunsford. The home was destroyed by fire, and Lunsford's insurer, Kentucky Farm Bureau Mutual Insurance Co., issued a check payable to Lunsford and GreenPoint. Lunsford indorsed the check and presented it to Tri-County National Bank for payment. Tri-County negotiated the check without GreenPoint's indorsement. GreenPoint sued Tri-County. Was Tri-County liable to GreenPoint? [*Tri-County Nat. Bank v. GreenPoint Credit, LLC*, 190 S.W.3d 360 (Ky. Ct. App.)]

Agency and Employment

Employees and employers have rights and duties to each other. Many of these are covered in the chapters in this part. There are many sources of information on, and assistance in, maintaining employee/employer rights, including the Department of Labor (DOL), and the U.S. Equal Employment Opportunity Office. In addition to state employment offices, the DOL's *America's Career InfoNet* is a resource for jobs, and its website is www.acinet.org.

25 Nature and Creation of an Agency

26 Operation and Termination of an Agency

27 Employer and Employee Relations

Employees' Rights

Nature and Creation of an Agency

LEARNING OBJECTIVES

1. Explain the nature of an agency and identify the parties involved in one.
2. Describe the different classifications of agents and the corresponding authority of each.
3. Discuss how an agency is usually created.
4. Distinguish between an agency and independent contractor or employer–employee relationships.

PREVIEW CASE

Brandon Ballantyne had Lennon Madzima, who was in the business of doing so, prepare and file his tax returns for three years. Ballantyne gave Madzima his W-2s for this purpose. Unknown to Ballantyne, each return claimed deductions and credits to which he was not entitled. The refunds were sent to a bank account he did not own. Madzima would give Ballantyne some cash that was allegedly the refund. The next year, Madzima asked Ballantyne whether he wanted him to file his return. Ballantyne said yes and told Madzima to come pick up his W-2s. On April 3 Madzima electronically filed a return for Ballantyne. The return claimed deductions, filing status, and credits to which he was not entitled. The Internal Revenue Service (IRS) determined that he owed $4,256. In the ensuing legal action, Ballantyne alleged that Madzima did not have the authority to file his return electronically. Had Ballantyne clearly answered when Madzima asked about filing the return? Could Ballantyne have answered more clearly?

LO ①
Nature of agency

principal
person who appoints another to contract with third parties

agent
person appointed to contract on behalf of another

When one party, known as a **principal**, appoints another party, known as an **agent**, to enter into contracts with third parties on behalf of the principal and subject to the principal's oversight, a contract of agency is formed. Thus every contract that an agent negotiates involves at least three parties—the principal, the agent, and the third party. It is the making of contracts with third persons on behalf of the principal that distinguishes an agency from other employment relationships. The principal, the agent, or the third party may be an individual, a partnership, or a corporation.

25-1 Importance of Agency

Because of the magnitude and complexity of industries, business owners must delegate many of the important details pertaining to business transactions to agents. The general principles of law pertaining to contracts govern the relation creating this delegation of powers.

Even in the performance of routine matters by individuals, agents are necessary in order to bring one person into a business contractual relationship with other people. Thus, a farmer who sends an employee to town to have a piece of machinery repaired gives the employee the authority to enter into a contract that binds the farmer to the agreement.

25-2 What Powers May Be Delegated to an Agent?

As a general rule, people may do through agents all of those things that they could otherwise do themselves. However, the courts will not permit certain acts of a personal nature to be delegated to others. Some of these acts that may not be performed by an agent include voting in a public election, executing a will, or serving on a jury.

What one may not lawfully do may not be done through another. Thus, no person can authorize an agent to commit a crime, to publish a libelous statement, to perpetrate a fraud, or to do any other act judged illegal, immoral, or opposed to the welfare of society.

ETHICAL POINT

Would it be ethical for a person to try to do something through an agent that could not be done personally?

COURT CASE

FACTS: Robert Miner, a prisoner serving a life sentence, applied to participate in a department of corrections family reunion program and claimed he was legally married. Under state law, a person serving a life sentence was considered civilly dead and could not lawfully marry. Miner had executed a document appointing Michael Foster his agent for the purpose of entering into a proxy marriage, which Foster had done.

OUTCOME: The court held that Miner was not legally married. As a civilly dead person, he could not lawfully marry. Because he could not marry, Miner could not appoint an agent to enter into that relationship on his behalf.

—*Miner v. New York State Dept. of Correctional Servs.*, 479 N.Y.S.2d 703 (N.Y. Sup. Ct.)

25-3 Who May Appoint an Agent?

All people legally competent to act for themselves may act through an agent. This rule is based on the principle that whatever a person may do may be done through another. Hence, corporations and partnerships, as well as individuals, may appoint agents.

The contract by which a minor appoints an agent to act for the minor is normally voidable. Some states, however, find such contracts void, not voidable.

25-4 Who May Act as an Agent?

Ordinarily, any person who has sufficient intelligence to carry out a principal's orders may be appointed to act as an agent. The law does not impose this requirement. It arises from the practical consideration of whether the principal wants to have the particular person act as agent. Corporations and partnerships may act as agents.

An agent cannot perform some types of transactions without meeting certain requirements. For example, in many states a real estate agent must possess certain definite qualifications and must, in addition, secure a license to act in this capacity. Failure to do this disqualifies a person to act as an agent in performing the duties of a real estate agent.

LO ②
Agent classification and authority

25-5 Classification of Agents

Agents may be classified as:

1. General agents

2. Special agents

25-5a GENERAL AGENTS

general agent
agent authorized to carry out particular kind of business or all business at a place

A **general agent** is one authorized to carry out all of the principal's business of a particular kind or all of the principal's business at a particular place even though not all of one kind. Examples of general agents who perform all of the principal's business of a particular kind include a purchasing agent and a bank cashier. A general agent who transacts all of the principal's business at a particular place includes a manager in full charge of one branch of a chain of shoe stores. Such an agent buys and sells merchandise, employs help, pays bills, collects accounts, and performs all other duties. This agent has a wide scope of authority and the power to act without express direction from the principal.

A general agent has considerable authority beyond that expressly stated in the contract of employment. In addition to express authority, a general agent has that authority that one in such a position customarily has.

25-5b SPECIAL AGENTS

special agent
agent authorized to transact specific act or acts

A **special agent** is one authorized by a principal to transact some specific act or acts. Such an agent has limited powers that may be used only for a specific purpose. The authorization may cover just one act, such as buying a house; or it may cover a series of merely repetitive acts, such as selling admission tickets to a movie.

COURT CASE

FACTS: S.N.R. Management Corporation contracted with Rosa Belvin Properties, LLC (RBP) to purchase real estate. Lee McGregor was S.N.R.'s real estate broker. S.N.R. was unable to close on the designated date, due to the possible existence of an endangered plant species on the property. RBP would not grant an extension beyond January 30. Their agreement stated that if the closing had not occurred by January 29, the contract would become null, void, and of no further effect, and the parties would be relieved of all obligations under it. RBP sold the property to Danube Partners 141, LLC on March 26. In February or March, McGregor had given information he received from S.N.R. to Danube in order to assist it in the purchase of the property. McGregor had failed to notify S.N.R. that Danube and RBP were negotiating the sale of the property. S.N.R. sued, alleging that McGregor had violated his duty as an agent.

OUTCOME: Because RBP had refused to extend the deadline for closing beyond January 30, McGregor no longer owed any fiduciary duty to S.N.R. regarding the sale of the property after January 30.

—S.N.R. Management Corp. v. Danube Partners 141, LLC, 659 S.E.2d 442 (N.C. Ct. App.)

25-6 Additional Types of Agents

There are several additional types of agents. Most of these are special agents, but because of the nature of their duties, their powers may exceed those of the ordinary special agent:

1. Factors
2. Factors *del credere*
3. Brokers
4. Attorneys in fact

25-6a FACTORS

A **factor** is one who receives possession of another's property for the purpose of sale on commission. Factors, also called **commission merchants**, may sell in the name of the principal, but normally they sell in their own name. When factors collect the sale price, they deduct the commission, or factorage, and remit the balance to the principal. The third party, as a rule, is aware that the dealings are with an agent by the nature of the business or by the name of the business. The term "commission merchant" usually appears on all stationery. Commission merchants have the power to bind the principal for the customary terms of sale for the types of business they are doing. In this regard, their powers are slightly greater than those of the ordinary special agent.

factor or commission merchant
bailee seeking to sell property on commission

25-6b FACTORS *DEL CREDERE*

A **factor** *del credere* is a commission merchant who sells on credit and guarantees to the principal that the purchase price will be paid by the purchaser or by the factor.

factor *del credere*
factor who sells on credit and guarantees price will be paid

This is a form of contract of guaranty, but the contract need not be in writing as required by the statute of frauds, as the agreement is a primary obligation of the factor.

25-6c BROKERS

broker
agent with job of bringing two contracting parties together

A **broker** is a special agent whose task is to bring two contracting parties together. Unlike a factor, a broker does not have possession of the merchandise. In real estate and insurance, a broker normally acts as the agent of the buyer rather than the seller. If the job merely consists of finding a buyer or, sometimes, a seller, the broker has no authority to bind the principal on any contract.

25-6d ATTORNEYS IN FACT

attorney in fact
general agent appointed by written authorization

An **attorney in fact** is a general agent who has been appointed by a written authorization. The writing, intended to be shown to third persons, manifests that the agent has authority.

25-7 Extent of Authority

As a rule, a general agent has authority to transact several classes of acts: (1) those clearly within the scope of the express authority, (2) those customarily within such an agent's authority, and (3) those outside of express authority but that appear to third parties to be within the scope of the agent's authority.

express authority
authority of agent stated in agreement creating agency

Express authority is the authority specifically delegated to the agent by the agreement creating the agency. It amounts to the power to do whatever the agent is appointed to do.

PREVIEW CASE REVISITED

FACTS: Brandon Ballantyne had Lennon Madzima, who was in the business of doing so, prepare and file his tax returns for three years. Ballantyne gave Madzima his W-2s for this purpose. Unknown to Ballantyne, each return claimed deductions and credits to which he was not entitled. The refunds were sent to a bank account he did not own. Madzima would give Ballantyne some cash that was allegedly the refund. The next year, Madzima asked Ballantyne whether he wanted him to file his return. Ballantyne said yes and told Madzima to come pick up his W-2s. On April 3, Madzima electronically filed a return for Ballantyne. The return claimed deductions, filing status, and credits to which he was not entitled. The Internal Revenue Service (IRS) determined that he owed $4,256. In the ensuing legal action, Ballantyne alleged that Madzima did not have the authority to file his return electronically.

OUTCOME: The court said that Ballantyne had wanted Madzima to file his return and that by telling him to do so and giving him the W-2s, Madzima had the express authority to file the return.

—*Ballantyne v. C.I.R.*, 99 T.C. Memo. 2010-125 (T.C.)

---

implied authority
agent's authority to do things in order to carry out express authority

Frequently, in order to carry out the purposes of the agency, the agent must have the authority to do things not specifically enumerated in the agreement. This authority is called **implied authority**. An agent appointed to manage a retail shoe store, for example, has implied authority to purchase shoes from wholesalers in order to have a stock to sell.

When a particular type of agent normally possesses certain powers to act for the principal, the agent's authority arises by custom rather than express statement. Such authority is sometimes called **customary authority**.

customary authority
authority an agent possesses by custom

COURT CASE

FACTS: A police officer for the Unified Government of Wyandotte County/Kansas City, Kansas (UGWC/KC), Ryan Fincher was injured when his police motorcycle collided with a car driven by Carl Anderson. Fincher obtained a $575,000 judgment against Anderson. His insurer paid Fincher the $50,000 liability insurance limit of the policy. UGWC/KC had auto liability insurance of $500,000 per occurrence and underinsured motorist (UIM) coverage limited to $50,000 with St. Paul Fire and Marine Insurance Company (St. Paul). Since the UIM coverage equaled Anderson's coverage, St. Paul denied coverage to Fincher. UIM coverage was the same as liability coverage unless the insured rejected it. David Coleman, the risk manager for

UGWC/KC, had signed the rejection form limiting UIM to $50,000. For years, his job was to procure and determine what insurance was needed and to sign forms. His supervisor testified that Coleman had the authority to limit UIM coverage. Fincher argued that Coleman did not have the authority to sign the rejection form.

OUTCOME: The court held that Coleman had the implied authority to sign the rejection form. As the agent of UGWC/KC, Coleman had validly rejected UIM above $50,000.

—Fincher v. St. Paul Fire & Marine Ins. Co.,
595 F.3d 820 (8th Cir.)

In addition, without regard to custom, the principal may have behaved in a way or made statements that caused the third person to believe that the agent has certain authority. This is called **apparent authority**. For example, the Pardalos Insurance Company might advertise, "For all your insurance problems, see your local Pardalos Insurance agent." This would give the local Pardalos Insurance Company agent apparent authority to arrange any insurance matters, even though the agents did not actually have such authority or had been told that certain kinds of cases had to be referred to the home office.

apparent authority
authority an agent is believed to have because of principal's behavior

As to innocent third parties, the powers of a general agent may be far more extensive than those actually granted by the principal. Limitations on an agent's authority do not bind a third party who has no knowledge of them, but they do bind a third party who knows of them.

In every case, the person who would benefit by the existence of authority on the part of the alleged agent has the burden of proving the existence of authority. If a person appears to be the agent of another for the purpose of selling the car of that other person, for example, the prospective purchaser must seek assurance from the principal as to the agent's authority. Once the third party has learned the actual scope of an agent's express authority from the principal, the agent has no greater authority than the principal's actions and statements indicate, together with such customary authority as would apply.

LO ③
How agency is created

agency
contract under which
one party is authorized to
contract for another

25-8 Creation of an Agency

Usually, any one of the following may create the relationship of **agency**:

1. Appointment
2. Ratification
3. *Estoppel*
4. Necessity

25-8a APPOINTMENT

The usual way of creating an agency is by the statement of the principal to the agent. In most cases, the contract may be oral or written, formal or informal. In some instances, however, the appointment must be made in a particular form. The contract appointing an agent must be in writing if the agency is created to transfer title to real estate. Also, to extend an agent's authority beyond one year from the date of the contract, the statute of frauds requires the contract to be in writing. The appointment of an agent to execute a formal contract, such as a bond, requires a formal contract of appointment.

power of attorney
written instrument
appointing an agent

A written instrument indicating the appointment of an agent is known as a **power of attorney**. To record a power of attorney, it must also be acknowledged before a notary public or other officer authorized to take acknowledgments. Illustration 25-1 shows an ordinary form of power of attorney.

ILLUSTRATION 25-1   Power of Attorney

Know All Men by These Presents:

That I, Amelia Clermont
                                    of Portland
County of **Multnomah**   *, State of* **Oregon**
have made, constituted and appointed, and by these presents do make, constitute and
appoint James Turner
                                    of Vancouver
County of Clark   *, State of* Washington
my true and lawful attorney   in fact, for me and in my name, place and stead,
to manage, operate, and let my rental properties in
the City of Vancouver, County of Clark, State of
Washington

giving and granting unto my said attorney full power and authority to do and perform all
and every act and thing whatsoever requisite and necessary to be done in and about the
premises, as fully to all intents and purposes as I might or could do, if personally present,
with full power of substitution and revocation; hereby ratifying and confirming all that my
said attorney——or his   *substitute——shall lawfully do, or cause to be done,*
by virtue hereof.

In Witness Whereof, I have hereunto set my hand this tenth *day*
of July   *, 20 --*
Signed and acknowledged in presence of: Amelia Clermont
Samuel Adamick
Teresa Romano

25-8b RATIFICATION

Ratification is the approval by one person of the unauthorized act of another done in the former's name. An assumed agent who purported to act as an agent without actual or apparent authority may have committed the unauthorized act, or it may have been done by a real agent who exceeded actual and apparent authority. Such an act does not bind the supposed principal in such a case unless and until it is ratified. Ratification relates back to the date of the act done by the assumed agent. Hence, ratifying the act puts the assumed agent in the same position as if there had been authority to do the act at the time the act was done.

ratification
approval of unauthorized act

The requirements for valid ratification are as follows:

1. The one who assumed the authority of an agent must have made it known to the third person that he or she was acting on behalf of the party who attempts to ratify the act.
2. The one attempting to ratify must have been capable of authorizing the act at the time the act was done. Some jurisdictions apply this rule to corporations so that a corporation formed subsequent to the time of the act cannot ratify an act of a promoter. Other states have ignored this requirement in regard to ratification of the acts of corporate promoters.
3. The one attempting to ratify must be capable of authorizing the act at the time approval of the act is given.
4. The one attempting to ratify must have knowledge of all material facts.
5. The one attempting to ratify must approve the entire act.
6. The ratified act must be legal, although a person whose name was forged may ratify a forgery on commercial paper.
7. The ratification must be made before the third party has withdrawn from the transaction.

25-8c ESTOPPEL

Agency by *estoppel* arises when a person, by words or conduct, leads another person to believe that a third party is an agent or has the authority to do particular acts. The principal who has made representations is bound to the extent of those representations for the purpose of preventing an injustice to parties who have relied on the acts or the conduct of the principal.

agency by *estoppel*
agency arising when one person leads another to believe third party is agent

25-8d NECESSITY

The relationship of agency may be created by necessity. Parents must support their minor children. If they fail to provide their children with necessaries, the parents' credit may be pledged for the children, even against the parents' will. Agency by necessity also may arise from some unforeseen emergency. Thus, the driver of a bus operating between distant cities may pledge the owner's credit in order to have needed repairs made and may have the cost charged to the owner.

25-9 Other Employment Relationships

Following are two types of relationships that differ from agency relationships:

LO ④
Distinguish independent contractor

1. Independent contractor
2. Employer and employee, originally referred to in law as "master and servant"

25-9a INDEPENDENT CONTRACTOR

independent contractor
one who contracts to do jobs and is controlled only by contract as to how performed

An **independent contractor** is one who contracts to perform some tasks for a fixed fee. The other contracting party does not control an independent contractor as to the means by which the contractor performs except to the extent that the contract sets forth requirements to be followed. The independent contractor is merely held responsible for the proper performance of the contract. Because one who contracts with an independent contractor has much less control over the performance of the work, the contract does not create either a principal–agent relationship or an employer–employee relationship. The most common type of independent contractor relationship is in the building trades.

COURT CASE

FACTS: At the Masquerade nightclub, employee Christopher Wynne played dance music while female impersonators lip-synced while dancing. Wynne hired the performers by oral contract, paid them in cash at the end of the evening, and told them approximately when they would perform. No one at Masquerade provided the music or exercised control over their routines. A performer, Shawn Hickum, sang and danced brandishing a whip. He cracked the whip in the direction of the audience and hit a customer, Daniel Orton, seriously injuring his eye. Orton sued Masquerade. Orton said since Masquerade could have stopped the show, Hickum

was not an independent contractor; therefore, Masquerade was liable for his actions.

OUTCOME: The court held that Masquerade merely told the performers when they would perform and how much they would be paid. The right to stop the performance did not establish that Masquerade exercised control over the manner in which Hickum performed. Hickum was an independent contractor.

—*Orton v. Masquerade Inc.*, 716 S.E.2d 764
(Ga. Ct. App.)

25-9b EMPLOYER AND EMPLOYEE

An employee performs work for an employer. The employer controls the employee both as to the work to be done and the manner in which it is done. One contracting with an independent contractor does not have such control. The degree of control that the employer or principal exercises over the employee or agent and the authority the agent has to bind the principal to contracts constitute the main differences between an employee and an agent.

There are many reasons why a contract of employment must not be confused with a contract of an independent contractor. An employer may be held liable for any injuries employees negligently cause to third parties. This is not true for injuries caused by independent contractors. Second, employers must comply with laws relative to their employees. Employers must, for example, withhold Social Security taxes on employees' wages, pay a payroll tax for unemployment compensation, withhold federal income taxes, and, when properly demanded, bargain with their employees collectively. None of these laws applies when one contracts with independent contractors. Independent contractors are the employers of those employed by them to perform the contract.

QUESTIONS

1. Why are there always three parties involved when an agent enters into a contract for the principal?
2. What law governs an agency relationship?
3. May all acts be delegated to an agent?
4. May a minor make a valid contract appointing an agent?
5. What authority does a general agent have in addition to express authority?
6. What authority does a principal give to a special agent?
7. What power do commission merchants have to bind a principal?
8. What classes of acts does a general agent normally have the authority to transact?
9. What does ratification of an unauthorized act done in someone else's name do for the assumed agent?
10. When does an agency by *estoppel* arise?

CASE PROBLEMS

1. Injured while using exercise equipment at AMTX Hotel Corporation's Holiday Inn in Texas, Cathy Trei sued AMTX in New Mexico, where she lived. AMTX was a franchisee of Intercontinental Hotels Group (IHG), the franchisor of Holiday Inns. AMTX did not have any facilities, employees, or agents in New Mexico, so it normally could not be sued in New Mexico courts. But Trei alleged that the national advertising of IHG, which she saw and heard, should be imputed to AMTX. She alleged that IHG acted as AMTX's agent by promoting Holiday Inn in New Mexico since AMTX benefitted from these promotional activities. Was IHG the agent of AMTX? **LO ②**

2. Dennis Vackar suffered severe spinal injuries, resulting in paralysis and the use of a ventilator when he fell eight feet from the bucket of a front-end loader. He was estranged from his wife, Betty, and son, Dustin. Hospital staff suggested Dennis execute a durable power of attorney, which he did naming his sister, Magdalen (Maggie) Marbry, to be his agent. The document stated, "I, Dennis Vackar, appoint Maggie Marbry as my agent (attorney-in-fact) to act for me. . . ." Dennis signed by placing his thumbprint on the document. Using the power of attorney and at Dennis' request, Marbry named herself the beneficiary of his life insurance policy. His health declined, and Dennis decided to discontinue treatment and all supportive care. He died shortly thereafter. In a court proceeding that followed, Betty argued that the durable power of attorney was not valid. Had Dennis executed a power of attorney? **LO ③**

3. Ash Grove Cement Company hired Electric Company of Omaha (ECO) to relocate a cable tray. ECO gained access to the tray from the flat roof of Ash Grove's building and controlled the work. While walking backward and carrying cable, Darryl Didier, an employee of ECO, fell twenty feet off the roof, onto a concrete surface. He sued Ash Grove. Should he recover? **LO ④**

4. The City of Lebanon was having a budget crisis and its agreement with a union was about to expire. City councilors would vote to approve any agreement, but none were on the city's team that negotiated an agreement. City councilor Margaret Campbell wrote a letter to the newspaper telling union members to find out how to decertify the union so they could keep their union dues. The letter recited that she wrote as an individual and that it did not reflect the opinion of the city council or the city. The union filed an unfair labor practice complaint against the city alleging that Campbell was the apparent agent of the city when she wrote the letter. Was Campbell exercising apparent authority in writing the letter? **LO ②**

CASE PROBLEMS (CONTINUED)

LO ① 5. Sharon Ellison entered a Burger King and waited to order. After some time passed, Ellison said, "Hi, is anybody going to welcome me to Burger King? Somebody going to please take my order?" An employee explained the staff was busy with other orders and offered to take her order. The manager then walked out from behind the counter and asked, "Why is it every time you come into the restaurant, you have to make a noise?" The manager "put her hands around my neck in a semi-head lock position . . . and start[ed] shaking like three times or whatever. Then [the manager] turned loose and said, 'Are you all right now?'" Ellison filed a complaint against BKC (the franchisor), SRH (the franchisee and restaurant operator), and the manager. The manager was an employee of SRH (franchisee) not BKC. SRH owned and operated the restaurant in accordance with a franchise agreement with BKC. The franchise agreement specified that SRH was an independent contractor and that BKC was not an employer of SRH. SRH had the sole authority over employee hiring, working hours, benefits, wages, and employment policies. Should Ellison recover against BKC?

LO ③ 6. Robin Broussard purchased what she believed was a San Juan Capistrano fiberglass swimming pool from Hamilton Pools Inc., an authorized dealer in such pools. Defects appeared after installation, and Broussard discovered that the product she purchased was a "knock-off" manufactured by another company. Broussard sued the manufacturer of genuine San Juan Capistrano swimming pools, American Environmental Container Corporation (AECC), and its licensor, San Juan Products Inc. (SJP), alleging they were liable for the conduct of Hamilton Pools. She argued that because AECC and SJP failed to repudiate the transaction, they therefore ratified it. AECC and SJP neither provided the product involved in the transaction nor accepted any benefit from the transaction. Should AECC and/or SJP be liable?

LO ② 7. The Willamette Spine Center, LLC (WSC) leased a medical office building and sublet space in the building to various medical providers. Signs on and near the building identified it as WSC, and one sign included a logo. David Eads sought treatment for back pain from chiropractor Michael Freeman, whose office was in the building. Another tenant, Dr. Frederick Tiley, shared space in the building and collected rent from Dr. Timothy Borman. Freeman referred Eads to Borman, who operated on Eads at a local hospital and injured his spinal cord, leaving him partially paralyzed. Some physicians from WSC had advertised in the yellow pages using the term "WSC providers" and the logo, but Borman was not one of them. Borman's charges were billed to his individual professional accounts. Eads sued WSC alleging that Borman was its apparent agent. Should the court find an agency?

LO ③ 8. North American Specialty Insurance Co. (NAS) underwrote construction bonds. Brunson Bonding and Insurance Agency was an agent for NAS, and Reid Methvin was an employee of Brunson. The agency agreement between NAS and Brunson required NAS to give prior approval before a construction bond was issued. Methvin issued bonds without prior approval from NAS. After NAS learned about the unauthorized bonds, it accepted and kept the premiums from Brunson. When a number of the unauthorized bonds resulted in defaults, causing NAS to pay out claims on them, NAS sued Methvin, Brunson, and Brunson's insurer. The defendants argued that acceptance of the premiums by NAS constituted ratification of Methvin's unauthorized acts. Did it?

Operation and Termination of an Agency

LEARNING OBJECTIVES

① Specify the duties an agent owes the principal, and the principal owes the agent.

② Describe an agent's and principal's liabilities to third parties.

③ State how an agency may be terminated, either by the parties or by operation of law.

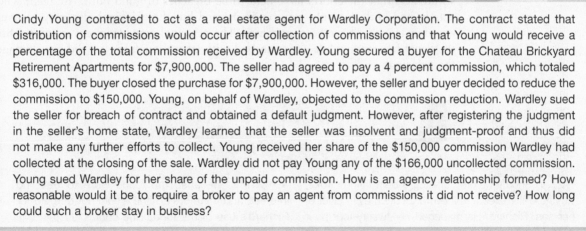

PREVIEW CASE

Cindy Young contracted to act as a real estate agent for Wardley Corporation. The contract stated that distribution of commissions would occur after collection of commissions and that Young would receive a percentage of the total commission received by Wardley. Young secured a buyer for the Chateau Brickyard Retirement Apartments for $7,900,000. The seller had agreed to pay a 4 percent commission, which totaled $316,000. The buyer closed the purchase for $7,900,000. However, the seller and buyer decided to reduce the commission to $150,000. Young, on behalf of Wardley, objected to the commission reduction. Wardley sued the seller for breach of contract and obtained a default judgment. However, after registering the judgment in the seller's home state, Wardley learned that the seller was insolvent and judgment-proof and thus did not make any further efforts to collect. Young received her share of the $150,000 commission Wardley had collected at the closing of the sale. Wardley did not pay Young any of the $166,000 uncollected commission. Young sued Wardley for her share of the unpaid commission. How is an agency relationship formed? How reasonable would it be to require a broker to pay an agent from commissions it did not receive? How long could such a broker stay in business?

When there is a contract of agency, the law imposes on the agent certain duties to the principal not set out in the contract. Likewise, the relationship of agency creates duties and obligations that the principal owes to an agent even though they are not specifically enumerated in the contract. In turn, the agency relationship imposes on both principal and agent certain duties and obligations to third parties. An examination of these duties and obligations will reveal the importance of the relationship of agent and principal as well as the necessity for each party in the relationship to be fully cognizant of the rights and duties that exist.

LO ①
Duties of agents and principals

26-1 Agent's Duties to Principal

An agent owes the following important duties to the principal:

1. Loyalty and good faith
2. Obedience
3. Reasonable skill and diligence
4. Accounting
5. Information

26-1a LOYALTY AND GOOD FAITH

The relationship of principal and agent is fiduciary in nature; thus, the principal must be able to trust the agent to perform the duties according to contract. The relationship of agent and principal calls for a higher degree of faith and trust than do most contractual relationships. For this reason, the law imposes on agents the duty of loyalty and good faith and deprives them of their right to compensation, reimbursement, and indemnification when they prove disloyal to their principal or act in bad faith. Agents must promote the interests of the principal to the utmost of their ability.

Loyalty and *good faith* are abstract terms. Thus, the courts have wide latitude in interpreting what acts constitute bad faith or a breach of loyalty. Such acts as secretly owning an interest in a firm that competes with the principal, disclosing confidential information, selling to or buying from the agent without the knowledge of the principal, and acting simultaneously as the agent of a competitor constitute acts that the courts have held to be breaches of good faith. An agent who acts in bad faith not only may be discharged but the principal also may recover any damages that have been sustained. The principal may also recover any profits the agent has made while acting in bad faith even though the act did not damage the principal.

COURT CASE

FACTS: Shortly before suffering a debilitating stroke, Edythe Miller executed a power of attorney in favor of her son, Richard. He managed her twenty-four hour care. He executed a document titled "Agreement for Reimbursement" on behalf of Edythe and himself which authorized the making of interest-free loans to each other in order to provide for the care of Edythe. After Edythe's death, Richard claimed $76,000 from her estate—the amount by which his loans to her exceeded her loans to him. Richard's brother and sister objected saying Richard had used his status as Edythe's agent to obtain a benefit to Edythe's detriment.

OUTCOME: Because the loans were to bear no interest, and therefore Edythe would not be paid for Richard's use of her funds, the court held that this provision benefited Richard at Edythe's expense. Since a fiduciary owes the principal the duty of good faith, fair dealing, honest performance, and strict accountability, the Agreement for Reimbursement was unenforceable.

—*In re Estate of Miller*, 446 S.W.3d 445
(Tex. Ct. App.)

26-1b OBEDIENCE

An agent may have two types of instructions from the principal: one routine, and the other discretionary. The agent must carry out all routine instructions to the letter as long as compliance would not defeat the purpose of the agency, be illegal, or perpetrate a fraud on others. An instruction not to accept any payments made by check illustrates a routine instruction. An agent incurs liability for any losses caused by disobeying these instructions. There is no justification for disobeying such instructions under any conditions.

Agents must use the best judgment of which they are capable regarding discretionary instructions. For example, an agent instructed to accept checks incurs no liability for a bad check when in the agent's judgment the drawer of the check is solvent and reliable. If an agent accepts a check that the agent has reason to believe is bad, the agent incurs liability for any loss that the principal sustains by reason of this act.

26-1c REASONABLE SKILL AND DILIGENCE

One who acts as an agent must possess the skill required to perform the duties and must be diligent in performing the skill. An implied warranty exists that the agent has such skill and will exercise such diligence. Any breach of this warranty subjects the agent to liability for damages for the loss by reason of the breach.

Because it is assumed that agents are appointed in reliance on their individual skills, talents, and judgment, agents may not generally appoint subagents. This, of course, is not true if the agency agreement provides for the appointment of subagents, if the work delegated is merely clerical, or if the type of agency is one in which it is customarily assumed that subagents would be appointed. Whenever appointing subagents, the agent must use skill and diligence in appointing competent subagents and remains liable to the principal for their breach of good faith or lack of skill.

26-1d ACCOUNTING

The duties of an agent include keeping a record of all money transactions pertaining to the agency. An accounting must be made to the principal for any of the principal's money and property that may come into the agent's possession. Money should be deposited in a bank in the name of the principal, preferably in a bank other than that in which the agent keeps personal funds. If the deposit is made in the name of the agent, any loss caused by the failure of the bank will fall on the agent. Personal property of the principal must be kept separate from property of the agent.

26-1e INFORMATION

Agents have a duty to keep principals informed of all facts pertinent to the agency that may enable the principals to protect their interests. In consequence, an agent cannot enforce a principal's promise to pay a bonus to the agent for information secured by the agent in the performance of agency duties because the principal was entitled to the information as a result of the agency. The promise was therefore not supported by consideration.

26-2 Principal's Duties to Agent

The principal has the following four important duties in respect to the agent:

1. Compensation
2. Reimbursement
3. Indemnification
4. Abidance by the terms of the contract

26-2a COMPENSATION

The contract of agency determines the compensation due an agent. As in most other contracts, this provision may be either express or implied. If the amount is clearly and expressly stated, disputes seldom arise. When an agency agreement does not state the amount of compensation, the agent may obtain reasonable or customary compensation for the services provided. In the absence of customary rates of compensation, the court will fix a reasonable rate according to the character of the services rendered. Frequently, the parties set the compensation on a contingent basis, such as a percentage of the selling price, provided a sale occurs. In such a case, the agent cannot collect compensation from the principal unless a sale actually occurs.

PREVIEW CASE REVISITED

FACTS: Cindy Young contracted to act as a real estate agent for Wardley Corporation. The contract stated that distribution of commissions would occur after collection of commissions and that Young would receive a percentage of the total commission received by Wardley. Young secured a buyer for the Chateau Brickyard Retirement Apartments for $7,900,000. The seller had agreed to pay a 4 percent commission, which totaled $316,000. The buyer closed the purchase for $7,900,000. However, the seller and buyer decided to reduce the commission to $150,000. Young, on behalf of Wardley, objected to the commission reduction. Wardley sued the seller for breach of contract and obtained a default judgment. However, after registering the judgment in the seller's home state, Wardley learned the seller was insolvent and judgment-proof and thus did not make any further efforts to collect. Young received her share of the $150,000 commission Wardley had collected at the closing of the sale. Wardley did not pay Young any of the $166,000 uncollected commission. Young sued Wardley for her share of the unpaid commission.

OUTCOME: Young's agreement with Wardley unambiguously provided that Wardley was obligated to pay Young her share only of commissions actually received by Wardley.

—*Young v. Wardley Corp.*, 182 P.3d 412 (Utah Ct. App.)

26-2b REIMBURSEMENT

The principal must reimburse an agent for any expenses incurred or disbursements the agent makes from personal funds as a necessary part of the agency. If, for example, an agent had to pay from personal funds a $500 truck repair bill before a trip on behalf of the principal could be continued, the agent would be entitled to reimbursement. If, however, the agent had to pay a $100 fine for speeding, the principal would not be required to reimburse this expense. Any expense incurred as a result of an agent's unlawful act must be borne by the agent.

26-2c INDEMNIFICATION

A contractual payment made by the agent for the principal is an expense of the principal. If the agent makes the payment not by reason of a contract but as a result of a loss or damage due to an accident, the principal must indemnify the agent. The principal must reimburse expenses and indemnify for losses and damages. If the principal directs the agent to sell goods in the stockroom that already belong to the principal's customer, that customer can sue both the principal and the agent. If the agent must pay the customer damages, the agent can, in turn, sue the principal for giving the instructions that caused the loss.

26-2d ABIDANCE BY THE TERMS OF THE CONTRACT

The principal must abide by the terms of the contract in all respects, including any implied compliance. Thus, the agent must be employed for the period stated in the contract unless justification exists for terminating the contract at an earlier date. If the cooperation or participation of the principal is required in order to enable the agent to perform duties under the agency agreement, the principal must cooperate or participate to the extent required by the contract. For example, if an agent sells by sample and receives a commission on all sales, the agent must be furnished samples, and the opportunity to earn the fee or commission must be given.

26-3 Agent's Liabilities to Third Parties

LO ②
Agent's and principal's liabilities to third parties

Ordinarily, whenever an agent performs duties, the principal is bound, but not the agent. In relations with third parties, however, an agent may be personally liable on contracts and for wrongs in several ways:

1. Agents who contract in their own names and do not disclose the name of the principal become liable to the same extent as though they were the principal. For this reason, agents who sign contracts in their own names will be held liable. The proper way for an agent to sign so as to bind only the principal is to sign "principal, by agent." A signing of the principal's name alone will likewise protect the agent, although the third person may require the placing of the agent's name under the name of the principal so that at a later date it can be determined which agent had obtained the contract.

2. Agents may make themselves personally liable to third parties by an express agreement to be responsible. This express agreement may be demonstrated if it is the only logical or legal interpretation of the contract.

3. People who presume to act for others, but actually have no authority, or who exceed or materially depart from the authority they are given, incur personal liability to those with whom they do business. The latter situation may arise when overzealous agents effect what they may think is a desirable contract.

4. An agent incurs personal liability for fraud or any other wrongdoing, whether caused by disobedience, carelessness, or malice, or whether committed on the order of the principal.

COURT CASE

FACTS: Michael and Lorie Bock had a physical damage insurance policy covering their home and debris removal issued by Travelers Property and Casualty Insurance Company (Travelers). A huge limb broke off an oak tree. It knocked down other large limbs, crashed into the front of the home, the chimney, and windows and significantly damaged them, a fence, and a car. That day the Bocks reported this to Travelers, which sent out Craig Hansen to adjust the loss. Hansen pushed branches out a window and removed branches from the chimney and fence before taking pictures of the damage. He wrote out a check for $675. When Mrs. Bock said that would not even pay for the cleanup, Hansen falsely said the policy did not cover cleanup. The second time Hansen came out, he again told the Bocks the policy did not cover cleanup. After Travelers denied coverage for some damage, the Bocks sued it and Hansen. Hansen claimed he could not be liable because he acted in the scope and course of his agency with Travelers.

OUTCOME: The court held that an agent acting in accordance with the principal's directions "is always liable for his or her own torts." Hansen was liable.

—*Bock v. Hansen*, 170 Cal.Rptr.3d 293
(Cal. Ct. App.)

26-4 Principal's Duties and Liabilities to Third Parties

The principal ordinarily has liability to third parties for contracts made within the actual or the apparent scope of an agent's authority.

When the agent enters into an unauthorized contract not within the apparent scope of authority, the principal is not bound unless the contract is subsequently ratified. The test of when an agent has apparent authority is whether, on the basis of the conduct of the principal, a reasonable person would believe that the agent had the authority to make the particular contract. If so, the contract binds the principal. For example, if the manager of a furniture store sells a suite of furniture on credit contrary to the authority granted, the principal must fulfill the contract with the third party, provided the third party did not know of the limitation on the agent's authority. The agent has liability to the principal for any loss sustained.

The principal, as well as the agent, has liability for an injury to the person or the property of a third party caused by the negligence or the wrongful act of the agent in the course of employment. When the agent steps aside from the business of the principal and commits a wrong or injury to another, the principal is not liable for an unratified act.

26-5 Termination of an Agency by Acts of the Parties

LO ③
How to terminate an agency

An agency may be terminated by acts of the parties by:

1. Original agreement
2. Subsequent agreement
3. Revocation
4. Renunciation by the agent

26-5a ORIGINAL AGREEMENT

The contract creating the agency may specify a date for the termination of the agency. In that event, the agency automatically terminates on that date. Most special agencies, such as a special agency to sell an automobile, terminate because their purpose has been accomplished.

26-5b SUBSEQUENT AGREEMENT

An agreement between the principal and the agent may terminate an agency at any time.

26-5c REVOCATION

The principal may revoke the agent's authority at any time, thereby terminating the agency. The principal may terminate the agency by notifying the agent of the termination or by taking actions that are inconsistent with the continuation of the agency.

One must distinguish between the right to terminate the agency and the power to do so. The principal has the right to terminate the agency any time the agent breaches any material part of the contract of employment. If the agent, for example, fails to account for all money collected for the principal, the agent may be discharged, and the principal incurs no liability for breach of contract. Conversely, the principal has the power, with one exception, to revoke the agent's authority at any time. Under these circumstances, however, the principal becomes liable to the agent for any damage sustained by reason of an unjustifiable discharge. This is the agent's sole remedy. The agent cannot insist on the right to continue to act as an agent, even though nothing has been done to justify a termination before the end of the contract period.

The only exception to this rule that the principal has the power to terminate the agency occurs in the case of an **agency coupled with an interest**. Interest may take one of two forms: (1) interest in the authority, and (2) interest in the subject matter. An agent has interest in the authority when authorized to act as an agent in collecting funds for the principal with an agreement not to remit the collections to the principal but to apply them on a pre-existing debt owed to the agent by the principal. In the second case, the agent has a lien on the property of the principal as security for a pre-existing debt and is appointed as agent to sell the property and apply the proceeds to the debt. Compensation merely for performing the agency is not considered such an interest.

agency coupled with an interest
agency in which agent has financial stake in performance of agency

COURT CASE

FACTS: After Tanya St. Felix's debts were paid through a bankruptcy proceeding, $6,338 remained. The trustee mailed a check to St. Felix that was returned, so the trustee sent the money to the court. St. Felix's bankruptcy attorney took no action with respect to it. Dale Kennedy of American Property Locators Inc. (APL) sent her a letter stating he had located $6,338 belonging to her. St. Felix executed a limited power of attorney to Kennedy to recover the money. Kennedy asked the court to refund the money to St. Felix by check to him. In the resulting court proceeding, the court had to decide whether St. Felix could revoke the power of attorney.

OUTCOME: The court pointed out that a principal may revoke an agent's authority at any time unless the agency were coupled with an interest. The court said an agent's right to compensation for performing the agency was not the grant of a power coupled with an interest.

—*In re St. Felix*, 436 B.R. 786 (E.D. Pennsylvania)

26-5d RENUNCIATION

Like the principal, the agent has the power to renounce the agency at any time. An agent who abandons the agency without cause before fulfillment of the contract incurs liability to the principal for all losses due to the unjustified abandonment.

26-6 Termination by Operation of Law

An agency also may be terminated by operation of law. This may occur because of:

1. Subsequent illegality
2. Death or incapacity
3. Destruction
4. Bankruptcy
5. Dissolution
6. War

26-6a SUBSEQUENT ILLEGALITY

Subsequent illegality of the subject matter of the agency terminates the agency.

26-6b DEATH OR INCAPACITY

Death or incapacity of either the principal or agent normally terminates the agency. For example, when the agent permanently loses the power of speech so that the principal's business cannot be performed, the agency automatically terminates.

durable power of attorney
appointment of agency that survives incapacity of principal

An exception to the rule of termination by incapacity has been enacted by states that provide for durable powers of attorney. A **durable power of attorney** is a written appointment of agency designed to be effective even though the principal is incapacitated. Such a power of attorney may allow an agent to make health care decisions for the principal such as admission to a hospital or nursing home, authorization of a medical procedure, or insertion of a feeding tube. It may also direct the attorney in fact to withhold certain, specified medical treatments or procedures.

26-6c DESTRUCTION

Destruction of the subject matter, such as the destruction by fire of a house to be sold by the agent, terminates the agency.

26-6d BANKRUPTCY

Bankruptcy of the principal terminates the agency. In most cases, bankruptcy of the agent does not terminate the agency.

26-6e DISSOLUTION

dissolution
termination of corporation's operation except activities needed for liquidation

Dissolution of a corporation terminates an agency in which the corporation is a party. This is similar to death, as dissolution of a corporation is a complete termination of operation except for the activities necessary for liquidation.

26-6f WAR

When the country of the principal and that of the agent are at war against each other, the agent's authority usually terminates or at least lapses until peace occurs. A war that makes performance impossible terminates the agency.

26-7 Notice of Termination

When principals terminate agencies, they must give notice to third parties with whom the agents have previously transacted business and who would be likely to deal with the agents as an agent. If such notice is not given, the principal might still be bound on any future contracts the agent negotiates. Notice can be given by sending written notice to the third parties in any way feasible. How the notice is given does not matter so long as the parties learn of the termination. Notice given to an agent constitutes notice to the principal.

When operation of law terminates an agency, notice need not be given either to the agent or to third parties.

COURT CASE

FACTS: Shortly after Science and Engineering Associates Inc. (SEA) employed Jerry Riehl as a part-time consultant for its clients, Stanton Keck and John Bevan asked him to supply consulting services for a venture, later incorporated as American Seamount Corp., involving incineration of hazardous wastes. He subsequently signed an agreement with Seamount not to disclose confidential information or to compete with the project. When SEA told Riehl to stop working with Seamount as SEA's agent, Riehl told Seamount but said he would work in his personal capacity. After Seamount laid Riehl off, he tried to sell the incineration project for himself. Seamount sued Riehl and SEA, alleging that Riehl was SEA's agent when he signed the agreement and then broke it.

OUTCOME: The court stated that once a third party has notice of the revocation of an agent's authority, the principal (SEA) was not liable for the agent's postrevocation acts.

—American Seamount Corp. v. Science and Engineering Assocs. Inc., 812 P.2d 505 (Wash. Ct. App.)

QUESTIONS

1) Why does the relationship of agent and principal call for a higher degree of faith and trust than do most contractual relationships?

2. What are the potential consequences to an agent for acting in bad faith?

3. How obedient must an agent be to routine instructions from the principal?

4. May agents appoint subagents? Why or why not?

5. What are the consequences if an agent deposits money of the principal in a bank in the agent's name?

6. May an agent enforce a principal's promise to pay a bonus to the agent for information secured by the agent in the performance of agency duties?

QUESTIONS (CONTINUED)

7. Must a principal reimburse an agent for all expenses incurred by the agent while carrying out the agency?

8. When are agents personally liable on contracts and for wrongs?

9. What is the test of when an agent has apparent authority?

10. How may a principal terminate an agency?

CASE PROBLEMS

LO ①

1. Having been diagnosed with Alzheimer's disease, Lorraine Batner executed a power of attorney to her son, David. She also executed a will leaving her property equally to David and his sister, Kimberly. About two years later, Lorraine moved in with Kimberly. Lorraine did not have her checkbook and her bank statements were mailed to David. After Lorraine's death, Kimberly sued David to require him to account for the funds in her mother's checking account during the time Lorraine lived with her, saying Lorraine had not gone shopping and did not know what was going on. Should David be required to account for Lorraine's funds?

LO ③

2. Astra Tech Inc. (Astra) purchased Atlantis Components Inc. (Atlantis). The parties put $6.3 million in an escrow fund to reimburse Astra if it had to pay claims against Atlantis. The parties chose a shareholders' agent to represent the stockholders and approve or challenge claims by Astra on the escrow. They set aside $100,000 for the agent's fees and expenses. The escrow was to be paid to the former Atlantis stockholders about a year later. Nobel Biocare USA, LLC (Nobel) claimed that Atlantis had infringed on its patents. Because it did not know the amount of Nobel's claim, Astra demanded the entire $6.3 million. Astra and Robert Stockard, the shareholders' agent, each claimed the escrow fund. Stockholders representing 39 percent of the shares agreed to settle with Astra by getting 39 percent of the escrow released and dividing it among them. Stockard claimed he had an agency coupled with an interest so the settlement should not be approved by the court. Did Stockard have an agency coupled with an interest?

LO ②

3. Lincoln Apartment Management Limited Partnership (Lincoln) was the property manager of Woodchase Village Apartments (Woodchase) for its owner, Terrell Mill Associates, LLC (Mill). Lincoln hired Grand Master Contracting, LLC (Grand) to renovate and repair Woodchase. Before Grand did any work, Lincoln had it sign an agreement that stated it "understands and agrees that the legal owner of the community is responsible for the payments of any services . . . performed . . . and not Lincoln, which is the property management company and Agent for the Owner." This agreement did not state that Mill owned Woodchase, but it required Grand to add the owner as an insured on all insurance policies. The liability insurance certificate issued to Grand included Mill as an insured. When Grand was not paid for all its work, it sued Lincoln, alleging that it had not made a valid disclosure of its principal. Should Lincoln be liable?

LO ①

4. State Farm Insurance hired James Falls as an agent trainee. After completing an internship phase, he was given an "agent start-up kit." He hired Michelle Quinlan, who had to pass online computer tests to be licensed to work for a State Farm agent. A problem with the Internet kept the tests from being marked as completed on her transcript. She told Falls, who contacted Yolanda Wilson, another State Farm employee, for help. They could not solve the problem. Since Quinlan was not working the next day, she gave Falls her coursework user name and password in case he needed to get into the online transcripts. The next day, Wilson told Falls that Quinlan's transcripts were still not showing up as completed. Falls logged onto Quinlan's account and completed coursework she had not completed. When State Farm later found out that Falls had completed the coursework, it terminated him. Falls sued State Farm for breach of contract. State Farm alleged that Falls had failed to act in good faith and thus it was justified in ending their agreement. Was State Farm so justified?

CASE PROBLEMS (CONTINUED)

5. Mission Energy, L.L.C. owned two mineral leases. Justin Sutton acted as Mission's sole manager. The estate of Lavinia Reott loaned Mission $160,000 that Mission did not repay, so Reott obtained a judgment against Mission. Sutton executed mineral lease assignment forms purporting to transfer all of Mission's leasehold rights to Wasatch Oil & Gas, L.L.C. The assignments were signed by Sutton on the line designated for "Lessee-Assignor" and did not identify Sutton as the manager of Mission or as a person authorized to act on Mission's behalf. On the back of the assignments, Wasatch agreed to accept the assignment from Mission. Reott purchased two other judgment interests against Mission and sought enforcement of all three judgments against Mission's leasehold interests. A sheriff's sale was held. As the only bidder, Reott obtained a certificate of sale for Mission's leases for a bid of $1.00. After learning of the sale, Wasatch filed a redemption notice, tendered a check in the amount of $1.06, and sued to quiet title in it to the leases. The trial court said Wasatch did not have title because the assignments failed to identify Sutton as a person authorized to execute assignments on Mission's behalf; therefore, they did not bind Mission. Could the assignment be binding on Mission?

LO ②

6. On September 21, under a power of attorney from Nell Pickett, Harold Johnson contracted for her to sell 181 acres of land to Bruce Kirkland. The sale was to close on December 15. Pickett died after the contract was executed but before the sale was completed. By the terms of her will, the land was to go to Kenneth and Betty Pearl Van Etten, while most of the rest of her estate went to nieces and nephews, including Johnson. Kirkland asked the court to require the executor to carry out the contract. Was the contract for sale voided by Pickett's death because the contract was executed under a power of attorney?

LO ③

7. Frank King had Alzheimer's disease, and his wife, Doris, was terminally ill with cancer. Her doctor, Phillip Sellers, pressed her to get in touch with someone to make arrangements for Frank's care after her death. Doris did not have a good relationship with Frank's daughter, Sherry Albert, and did not want her to get any of her money; however, under their wills, Albert would inherit from them. Doris said she trusted Kimzie Cowart, Frank's nephew. When Cowart visited, he found that Doris was in the hospital, and Sellers told him the Kings needed help. Doris asked Cowart to draw up a power of attorney, which she signed, authorizing Cowart to transact her banking business, including drawing checks, endorsing them, and making deposits. Doris signed a written request to open a joint checking account in Cowart's and her names to pay the Kings' medical bills. Cowart opened the account. They had previously signed an agreement to create a right of survivorship for any future joint accounts. At Doris' request, Cowart transferred half of the Kings' money, $460,000, into the account, leaving the other half for Frank's care. After Doris died, he paid her funeral expenses and then withdrew $450,000 from the new account. After Frank died, Albert sued Cowart alleging breach of his duty of loyalty and good faith because he made a gift to himself. Did Cowart breach his duty as an agent?

LO ①

8. Stephen Heintzelman contracted with Stanwade Metal Products Inc. to purchase a storage tank for $19,258.26. Stanwade sent the bill to Environmental Construction. As the sole shareholder and principal officer of Environmental Construction, Heintzelman had the tank delivered to Garner Transportation Group Inc. He issued an invoice to Garner under the trade name "All-American Construction dba The Home Medic." Garner paid Heintzelman $19,258.26. Heintzelman had three checks for $5,000 each bearing the trade name "The Home Medic" issued to Stanwade. The checks bounced. Stanwade sued Heintzelman and Environmental Construction, alleging that the company had sold the equipment to Environmental and that Heintzelman issued an invoice to Garner Trucking under the trade name of "All-American Construction dba The Home Medic." Heintzelman admitted these allegations and that All-American Environmental Inc. had received payment from Garner, that he was the sole shareholder and principal officer of All-American, and that "The Home Medic" was a trade name of All-American Environmental Inc. Should Heintzelman be personally liable?

LO ②

Employer and Employee Relations

LEARNING OBJECTIVES

① Recognize how the relationship of employer and employee arises.

② Identify the statutory modifications of an employer's defenses under the common law.

③ Describe the liability of an employer to third parties for acts of employees.

④ Name the duties an employee owes the employer.

PREVIEW CASE

While attending a contentious school board meeting as superintendent of schools, Nathan Chesler suffered a heart attack that resulted in his death. Chesler's contract had not been renewed, and the meeting was the night before his contract expired. The meeting concerned a personnel problem, and the board members directed angry questions to Chesler about the way he had handled it, and criticized his recommendation. The board asked Chesler to leave the room. When he returned, the chairman stated that the board would not take action on Chesler's recommendation. Chesler gasped, fell back in his chair, and died. His doctor said the stress at the meeting was a significant contributing factor to the attack. His widow sought workers' compensation. Was attendance at the board meeting part of Chesler's job? Was the stress that brought on the heart attack related to Chesler's job?

Over a period of many decades, the common law developed rules governing the relationship between an employer and employees. These rules have been greatly modified by statute. However, in every state, remnants of the common law still apply. Many of the common law rules concerning safe working conditions and other aspects of the employment contract have been retained in labor legislation. These laws do not cover all employees. In every state, a small number of employees still have their rights and duties determined largely by common law rules. This chapter addresses the common law and statutory modifications of it as they relate to employers and employees. However, the law regarding employers and employees varies significantly from state to state.

27-1 Creation of Employer and Employee Relationship

LO ①
Employer–employee relationship

The relationship of employer and employee arises only from a contract of employment, either express or implied. The common law allowed employers the right to hire whomever they wanted, and employees the right to choose their employers freely. The relationship of employer and employee could not be imposed on either the purported employer or employee without consent. One who voluntarily performs the duties of an employee cannot by that act subject the employer to the liability of an employer. But the relationship may be implied by conduct that demonstrates that the parties agree that one is the employer, and the other the employee.

27-1a LENGTH OF CONTRACT

An employee discharged without cause may recover wages due up to the end of the contract period from the employer. However, when creating an employer–employee relationship, seldom does either party mention the length of the contract period. In some jurisdictions, the terms of compensation determine the contract period. In such jurisdictions, the length of time used in specifying the compensation constitutes the employment period, and an employee may be discharged at the end of that time without further liability. For example, an employee paid by the hour may be discharged without liability at the end of any hour. An employee paid by the week or by the month, as are many office employees, has a term of employment of one week or one month, as the case may be. For monthly paid employees, the term of employment may depend on the way the employer specifies the compensation. A stated salary of $35,500 per year gives a one-year term of employment, even though the employer pays once per month. In other jurisdictions, employment at a set amount per week, month, or year does not constitute employment for any definite period but amounts to an indefinite hiring.

COURT CASE

FACTS: The Boeing Co. had a policy that the hiring, transfer, or placement of relatives of employees "must not result in actual or perceived preferential treatment, improper influence or other conflict." A Boeing investigation revealed that Reynold Quedado, a member of senior management, had improperly used his influence to get his nephew and second cousin hired. As a result, Quedado was demoted to a non-management position, which reduced his compensation. He sued, claiming the Boeing Code of Conduct and company policy documents provided enforceable promises about how employee conduct investigations would be made, and discipline imposed. The Code and the policy documents stated they did not constitute a contract or contractual obligation.

OUTCOME: The court held that Boeing's documents were guides regarding employment relationships and did not create a binding process or promise. As a result, Quedado was an at-will employee and could be demoted.

—*Quedado v. Boeing Co.*, 276 P.3d 365 (Wash. Ct. App.)

Many employer–employee situations have an indefinite length for the contract, and either the employer or the employee may terminate the employment for any reason or for no reason at any time. This situation is called **employment at will**.

However, as a result of labor legislation, union or other employment contracts, employee handbooks, or other exceptions that have developed to employment at will, many employees have significant job security. They may not be discharged except for good cause. As in the case of an employee discharged without cause who is employed for a specified period, such an employee may sue the employer for money damages. In some cases, the employee may also sue to be restored to the job.

27-1b DETERMINATION OF CONTRACT TERMS

Employer–employee contracts frequently do not state terms other than the compensation. Terms are determined by law, custom, employee handbooks, and, possibly, union contracts. If the employer publishes a handbook stating contract terms, the employer will usually be bound by those terms as long as the employee had a reasonable opportunity to learn them. In some cases, courts have held that statements in the employer's written policy manual constitute terms of employer–employee contracts.

27-1c UNION CONTRACTS

Formerly, the employer contracted individually with each employee. However, as the union movement developed, and collective bargaining became commonplace, employers began agreeing with unions to provisions of employment that applied to large numbers of employees. The signed contract between them embodied this agreement between the employer and the union. As an agent of the employees, the union speaks and contracts for all the employees collectively. As a general rule, the employer still makes a contract individually with each employee, but the union contract binds the employer to recognize certain scales of union wages, hours of work, job classifications, and related matters.

27-2 Duties and Liabilities of the Employer

Under the common law, the employer had the following five well-defined duties:

1. Duty to exercise care
2. Duty to provide a reasonably safe place to work
3. Duty to provide safe tools and appliances
4. Duty to provide competent and sufficient employees for the task
5. Duty to instruct employees with reference to the dangerous nature of employment

27-2a DUTY TO EXERCISE CARE

This rule imposes liability on employers if their negligence causes harm to an employee. Employers have exercised proper care when they have done what a reasonable person would have done under the circumstances to avoid harm.

27-2b DUTY TO PROVIDE A REASONABLY SAFE PLACE TO WORK

The employer must furnish every employee with a reasonably safe place to work. What constitutes a safe place depends on the nature of the work. Most states have statutes modifying the common law for hazardous industries.

27-2c DUTY TO PROVIDE SAFE TOOLS AND APPLIANCES

The tools an employer furnishes to employees must be safe. This rule also applies to machinery and appliances.

27-2d DUTY TO PROVIDE COMPETENT AND SUFFICIENT EMPLOYEES FOR THE TASK

Both the number of employees and their skill and experience affect the hazardous nature of many jobs. The employer has liability for all injuries to employees directly caused by either an insufficient number of workers or the lack of skill of some of the workers.

27-2e DUTY TO INSTRUCT EMPLOYEES

In all positions that use machinery, chemicals, electric appliances, and other production instruments, there are many hazards. The law requires the employer to give that degree of instruction to a new employee that a reasonable person would give under the circumstances to avoid reasonably foreseeable harm that could result from a failure to give such instructions.

27-3 Common Law Defenses of the Employer

Under the common law, when an injured employee sued the employer, the employer could raise the following defenses:

1. The employee's contributory negligence
2. The act of a fellow servant
3. A risk assumed by the employee

27-3a CONTRIBUTORY NEGLIGENCE RULE

The contributory negligence rule states that an employer can escape liability for breach of duty if it can be established that the employee's own negligence contributed to the accident. An employee who could have avoided the injury by the exercise of due diligence has no right to collect damages from the employer.

27-3b THE FELLOW-SERVANT RULE

The fellow-servant rule allows an employer to avoid liability by proving the injury was caused by a fellow servant. A **fellow servant** is an employee who has the

fellow servant
employee with same status and working with another worker

same status as another worker and works with that employee. This rule has been abrogated or so severely limited that it very rarely has any significance now.

27-3c ASSUMPTION-OF-RISK RULE

Every type of employment in industry has some normal risks. The assumption-of-risk rule states that employees assume these normal risks by voluntarily accepting employment. Therefore, if the injury results from the hazardous nature of the job, the employer cannot be held liable.

27-4 Statutory Modification of Common Law

LO ②
Statutory modification
of employer's defenses

The rules of the common law have been greatly altered by the enactment of laws modifying an employer's defenses when sued by an employee, laws providing for workers' compensation, and the Occupational Safety and Health Act.

27-4a MODIFICATION OF COMMON LAW DEFENSES

Statutes have modified the defenses that an employer may use when an employee sues for damages. For example, the Federal Employers' Liability Act and the Federal Safety Appliance Act apply to common carriers engaged in interstate commerce. A plaintiff suing under these laws must still bring an action in court and prove negligence by the employer or other employees. However, winning the case is easier because of limits on the employer's defenses. An employer has liability even if the employee is contributorily negligent. However, such negligence may reduce the amount of damages. Many states also have modified the common law defenses of employers of employees engaged in hazardous types of work.

27-4b WORKERS' COMPENSATION

Every state has adopted workers' compensation statutes that apply to certain industries or businesses. These statutes allow an employee, or certain relatives of a deceased employee, to recover damages for injury to, or death of, the employee. Recovery is allowed whenever the injury arose out of, and within, the course of the employee's work from a risk involved in that work. "In the course of employment" means the employee was on a mission for the employer.

An injured party receives compensation without regard to whether the employer or the employee was negligent. Generally, no compensation results for a willfully self-inflicted injury or an injury sustained while intoxicated. However, the employer has the burden of proving that the injury was intentional and self-inflicted. The law limits the amount of recovery and sets it in accordance with a prescribed schedule.

Workers' compensation laws generally allow recovery for accident-inflicted injuries and occupational diseases. Some states limit compensation for occupational diseases to those specified by name in the statute. These diseases include silicosis, lead poisoning, or injury to health from radioactivity. Other states compensate for any disease arising from the occupation.

Whether based on the common law or an employer's liability statute, damages actions are tried in court. Workers' compensation proceedings differ because a special administrative agency or workers' compensation board hears them. However, either party may appeal the agency or board decision to the appropriate court of law.

Workers' compensation statutes do not bar an employee from suing another employee for an injury.

PREVIEW CASE REVISITED

FACTS: While attending a contentious school board meeting as superintendent of schools, Nathan Chesler suffered a heart attack that resulted in his death. Chesler's contract had not been renewed, and the meeting was the night before his contract expired. The meeting concerned a personnel problem, and the board members directed angry questions to Chesler about the way he had handled it and criticized his recommendation. The board asked Chesler to leave the room. When he returned, the chairman stated that the board would not take action on Chesler's recommendation. Chesler gasped, fell back in his chair, and died. His doctor said the stress at the meeting was a significant contributing factor to the attack. His widow sought workers' compensation.

OUTCOME: The court held that a physical injury caused by work-related stress was a compensable injury. The widow was awarded death benefits.

—*Chesler v. City of Derby*, 899 A.2d 624 (Conn. App. Ct.)

27-4c OCCUPATIONAL SAFETY AND HEALTH ACT

The Williams–Steiger Occupational Safety and Health Act was designed to ensure safe and healthful working conditions. This federal law applies to every employer engaged in a business affecting interstate commerce except governments. The Occupational Safety and Health Administration (OSHA) administers the act and issues standards with which employers and employees must comply. In order to ensure compliance with the standards, OSHA carries out job-site inspections. Employers must maintain detailed records of work-related deaths, injuries, and illnesses. The act provides fines for violations, including penalties of up to $7,000 per day for failure to correct violations within the allotted time and imprisonment under certain circumstances.

27-5 Liabilities of the Employer to Third Parties

LO ③
Employer's liability

An employer has liability under certain circumstances for injuries that employees cause to third parties. The theory of *respondeat superior* imposes liability on an employer for torts caused by employees. The employer is liable for personal injury as well as property damage.

respondeat superior
theory imposing liability on employers for torts of employees

To be liable, the employee must have committed the injury in the course of employment. An employee, who, without any direction from the employer, injures a third party and causes injury not as a result of the employment, has personal liability, but the employer does not. The employer has liability, however, if it ordered the act that caused the injury or had knowledge of the act and assented to it. The employer also has liability for the torts of employees caused by the employer's negligence in not enforcing safe working procedures; not providing safe equipment, such as trucks; or not employing competent employees. In rare cases, the employer is liable for intentional torts when the conduct constitutes a risk attributable to the employer's business.

COURT CASE

FACTS: Rosemary O'Rourke hired McIlvaine Enterprises Inc., owned by Bruce McIlvaine, to replace insulation in the attic of her home. On the job, McIlvaine realized he needed more help to get it done in the time specified. An associate recommended laborer Santiago Waight. McIlvaine asked Waight to help and bring two more laborers. Waight brought Requena and Alan Romero. They finished the job in two days and then did not work for McIlvaine. Two months later O'Rourke found Requena had broken

into her home. He beat her and stole items from the house. O'Rourke sued McIlvaine under the theory of *respondeat superior*.

OUTCOME: The court found that the home invasion was neither at McIlvaine's job site nor did McIlvaine have a right to control Requena at the time. McIlvaine was not liable.

—*O'Rourke v. McIlvaine*, 19 N.E.3d 714 (Ill. App. Ct.)

LO ④
Duties of employee

27-6 Employee's Duties to the Employer

The employee owes certain duties to the employer. Failure to comply with these duties may result in discharge. An employee's duties include:

1. Job performance
2. Business confidentiality
3. Granting of right to use inventions

27-6a JOB PERFORMANCE

The duties required by the job must be performed faithfully and honestly and to advance the employer's interests. In skilled positions, the worker must perform the task with ordinary skill.

27-6b BUSINESS CONFIDENTIALITY

An employee has a duty of confidentiality regarding certain business matters. Trade secrets or other confidential business information must not be revealed.

27-6c INVENTIONS

In the absence of an express or implied agreement to the contrary, inventions belong to the employee who devised them, even though the time and property of the employer were used in their discovery, provided that the employee was not employed for the express purpose of inventing the things or the processes that were discovered.

If the invention is discovered during working hours and with the employer's material and equipment, the employer has the right to use the invention without charge in the operation of the business. If the employee has obtained a patent for the invention, the employer must be granted a nonexclusive license to use the invention without the payment of a royalty. This **shop right** of the employer does not give the right to make and sell machines that embody the employee's invention; it only entitles the employer to use the invention in the operation of the plant.

When an employer employs a person to secure certain results from experiments to be conducted by that employee, the courts hold that the inventions equitably belong to the employer. Courts base this result on a trust relation or an implied agreement to make an assignment.

In any case, an employee may expressly agree that inventions made during employment will be the property of the employer. Such contracts must be clear and specific, or else courts normally rule against the employer. The employee may also agree to assign to the employer inventions made after the term of employment.

shop right
employer's right to use employee's invention without royalty payment

COURT CASE

FACTS: While employed as field representatives by Service Employees International Union, Local 250, Torren Colcord and Stacy Rutherford secretly organized a campaign to decertify Local 250 as the collective bargaining agent for northern California's emergency medical technicians. They met with legal counsel to plan the decertification campaign, form the new union, and draft a constitution, by-laws, and decertification petition. They prepared a PowerPoint® presentation to introduce their new union to Local 250 members. The new union, the National Emergency Medical Services Association (NEMSA) and the decertification campaign were kicked off at a meeting of Local 250 shop stewards. Colcord represented that the meeting was an "extremely important" union meeting, i.e., a Local 250 meeting. Soon Colcord, Rutherford, and their supporters were able to gather the signatures required to force a decertification election. NEMSA won and became the authorized bargaining agent for the EMTs. Local 250 sued Colcord and Rutherford for breach of fiduciary duty and misappropriation of trade secrets. It sought to recover salaries paid to them while they were secretly organizing NEMSA.

OUTCOME: The court said had Colcord and Rutherford resigned when they began competing with Local 250 or honored their duty to it by disclosing their activities, the union would not have continued to pay them. Thus, the repayment of salary and benefits was an appropriate remedy.

—Service Employees Intern. Union, Local 250 v. Colcord, 72 Cal.Rptr.3d 763 (Cal. Ct. App.)

27-7 Federal Social Security Act

The federal Social Security Act has four major provisions:

1. Old-age and survivors' insurance
2. Assistance to persons in financial need
3. Unemployment compensation
4. Disability and Medicare benefits

27-7a OLD-AGE AND SURVIVORS' INSURANCE

The Social Security Act provides payments to the dependents of covered workers who die before the age of retirement. This part constitutes the survivors' benefits. If workers live to a specified age and retire, they and their spouses draw retirement benefits. This part constitutes the old-age benefits. Both parts are called insurance because they constitute risks that could be insured against by insurance companies. The survivors' insurance covers the risk of a breadwinner's dying and leaving dependents without a source of income. Old-age benefits cover the risk of outliving one's savings after retirement.

Who Is Covered? The old-age and survivors' insurance provisions of the Social Security Act cover almost everyone. Employees in state and local governments, including public school teachers, may be brought under the coverage of the act by means of agreements between the state and the federal government. This provision of the act also covers farmers, professional people (such as lawyers), and self-employed businesspeople. The act does not cover certain types of work of close relatives, such as a parent for a child, work by a child under twenty-one for parents, and employment of a spouse by a spouse.

Eligibility for Retirement Benefits. To be eligible for retirement benefits, one must meet certain requirements that involve working the mandated number of quarters of the year for a specified number of years. You must also be a minimum age—currently age sixty-two. However to be entitled to the maximum retirement benefits, one must wait until age sixty-five to age sixty-seven to apply for them.

Eligibility for Survivors' Benefits. The family of a worker who dies while fully insured or currently insured at the time of death has a right to survivors' benefits. Currently, if the deceased person had worked at least six quarters in the three years prior to death, survivors' benefits would be paid.

27-7b ASSISTANCE TO PEOPLE IN FINANCIAL NEED

People over sixty-five who have financial need may be eligible for federal supplemental security income payments. These monthly payments also go to blind or disabled people in financial need. No one contributes specifically to this system based only on need.

27-7c UNEMPLOYMENT COMPENSATION

In handling unemployment compensation, the federal government cooperates with the states, which set up their own rules, approved by the federal government, for the payment of unemployment benefits. The states, not the federal government, make payments of unemployment compensation.

The unemployment compensation laws of the various states differ, although they tend to follow a common pattern. They all provide for raising funds by levies on employers. The federal government pays the cost of running the programs.

State unemployment compensation laws apply in general to workers in commerce and industry. Agricultural workers, domestic servants, government employees, and employees of nonprofit organizations formed and operated exclusively for religious, charitable, literary, educational, scientific, or humane purposes may not be included.

To be eligible for benefits, a worker generally must meet the following requirements:

1. Be available for work and registered at an unemployment office
2. Have been employed for a certain length of time within a specified period in an employment covered by the law
3. Be capable of working
4. Not have refused reasonably suitable employment
5. Not be self-employed
6. Not be out of work because of a strike or a lockout still in progress or because of voluntarily leaving a job without cause
7. Have served the required waiting period

27-7d DISABILITY AND MEDICARE BENEFITS

The government makes monthly cash benefits, called *disability insurance benefits*, to disabled people under the age of sixty-five and their families. A disabled person is someone unable to engage in any substantial gainful activity because of a medically determinable physical or mental impairment expected to end in death or last continually for twelve months.

Medicare is insurance designed to help pay a large portion of personal health-care costs. Virtually everyone age sixty-five and over may be covered by this contributory hospital and medical insurance plan. The program covers only specified services. It has a number of parts, some of which individuals must voluntarily enroll in.

27-7e TAXATION TO FINANCE THE PLAN

To pay the life insurance and the annuity insurance benefits of the Social Security Act, both the employer and the employee pay a payroll tax (FICA) of an equal percentage of all income earned in any year, up to a specified maximum. The maximum income and the rate may be changed at any session of Congress. A payroll tax finances the unemployment compensation part of the act. In most states, the employer bears this entire tax. The assistance to people in need is paid for by general taxation. No specific tax is levied to meet these payments. Disability and Medicare benefits are funded from a combination of four sources: FICA, a Medicare tax on people who are not covered by the old-age and survivors' insurance, premiums paid by the people covered, and the general federal revenue.

27-8 Patient Protection and Affordable Care Act

The Patient Protection and Affordable Care Act, commonly nicknamed "Obamacare," requires employers with fifty or more full-time employees to provide health insurance to their employees. The insurance must provide a minimum value of coverage and the coverage cannot cost more than a fixed percentage of employee household income. If these requirements are not met, the employer must pay a tax.

QUESTIONS

1. Do common law rules determine the relationship between an employer and employees?
2. What recourse does a non-at-will employee have when discharged without good cause?
3. If an employment contract does not state any terms other than the compensation, how are the other terms determined?
4. If an employer who has a contract with a union still makes a contract individually with each employee, what meaning does the contract with the union have?
5. How has the statutory modification of an employer's common-law defenses made it easier for an employee to win a case?
6. When may an employee obtain recovery for damages for injury under workers' compensation?
7. When is an employer liable for injuries that employees cause to third parties?
8. When no contrary agreement has been made, to whom do inventions by employees belong?
9. How are the life and annuity insurance benefits of the Social Security Act funded?
10. What does the Patient Protection and Affordable Care Act require of employers?

CASE PROBLEMS

LO ①

1. NCR Corporation employed Mitch Tomlinson for ten years to service and repair ATMs at their locations. He was part of NCR's "core workforce." NCR fired him for failing to properly manage time reporting and call management procedures. NCR had issued corporate management policies that stated that its "tactical workforce"—temporary employees—were at-will employees. The policies were silent on the status of the core workforce. Tomlinson argued that since NCR's policies limited at-will employees to the tactical workforce, the core workforce were not at-will employees. Was Tomlinson an at-will employee?

LO ④

2. After Qosina Corp. sued C&N Packaging Inc. to recover some property it alleged C&N held, C&N countered that Qosina had interfered with its relationship with its employee, Doug Tichy. C&N also alleged that Tichy owed C&N a duty of good faith and loyalty. It claimed he had breached that duty by failing to disclose to C&N his relationship with Qosina and that he was acting for and on behalf of a competing business against C&N's interests. C&N further alleged that it had been damaged by Tichy's actions. Did these allegations by C&N state a basis for action against Tichy?

LO ①

3. After no current employees were interested in a job as benefits and special projects coordinator at Williamson Memorial Hospital, Crystal Hatfield applied. The employees had been told the pay would be less than what they made and that a two-year degree was required. Hatfield received a letter from the hospital, offering her the position. The letter was signed by the hospital's CEO, human resources director, and director of plant operations. The letter did not make any promise or representation concerning the duration of employment. Hatfield signed the letter and resigned from her current employment. Before beginning employment, Hatfield received a copy of the hospital's employee handbook and acknowledged, in writing, her status as an at-will employee. Individuals in charge of hospital operations began to receive complaints from other hospital employees about Hatfield's hiring because she did not have a two-year degree. They determined that firing Hatfield was the only way to appease the disgruntled hospital employees. At their direction, the human resources director terminated Hatfield's employment after four days. She sued the parent corporation of Williamson Memorial Hospital, alleging breach of contract. Did Hatfield have a viable complaint?

CASE PROBLEMS (CONTINUED)

4. Yzer Inc. (Yzer) asked for volunteers from its employees to help with yard work on its premises prior to a grand reopening. Barton Rodr, a salaried programmer who received no additional pay, suffered a heart attack while doing the lawn work. He sought workers' compensation benefits, but Yzer denied he was working as an employee at the time of the injury, claiming that it had not occurred during the course and scope of his employment. Should Rodr recover workers' compensation benefits?   **LO** ②

5. Heidi Haskell was the only sales assistant on duty at a model home owned by David Estes but leased to Comstock Homebuilding Companies Inc. It was Comstock's policy for a single sales assistant to remain on the premises of the model home except to show a property to a potential customer. Ms. Haskell went onto the attached deck of the home to smoke a cigarette. Hearing the telephone ring in the house, she attempted to put out her cigarette, went inside, and answered the phone. However, she failed to completely extinguish the cigarette, resulting in a fire and extensive damage to the home. Estes sued Comstock, alleging that Haskell had been negligent and an employee acting within the scope of her employment and thus Comstock was liable for the damage. Was Comstock liable?   **LO** ③

6. New York University (NYU) hired David O'Neill as a non-tenured, full-time faculty member. He was the assistant director of a medical laboratory. The NYU faculty handbook stated that appointment to a non-tenured faculty position was "for a definite period of time, not exceeding one academic year unless otherwise specified." Each year, NYU renewed his appointment for specific academic years. O'Neill believed that his supervisor engaged in research misconduct and reported his belief to her supervisor. He was fired the following April. O'Neill sued NYU. In the legal proceedings, O'Neill argued he was not an at-will employee but had been hired for a definite one-year period. Was O'Neill an at-will employee?   **LO** ①

7. ReadyLink Healthcare recruited and hired nurses and assigned them to its customer health-care providers who requested nurses. ReadyLink spent a great deal of time and money developing a database of nurses and its health-care providers. The information was used to hire nurses and service customers. ReadyLink hired Jerome Cotton as a nurse-recruiting agent but fired him for stealing confidential information. Police found confidential information in his possession, and videotapes showed him sneaking into the office at night and copying confidential information. ReadyLink sued Cotton. Does it have a cause of action against him?   **LO** ④

Employees' Rights

LEARNING OBJECTIVES

① Explain the rights of employees and employers under federal labor legislation.

② List the bases in federal law on which an employer may not discriminate against employees.

③ Describe the restrictions on employers in requiring invasive or offensive testing of employees and job applicants.

④ Discuss three significant protections given to employees by federal or state law, municipal ordinance, or employer regulation.

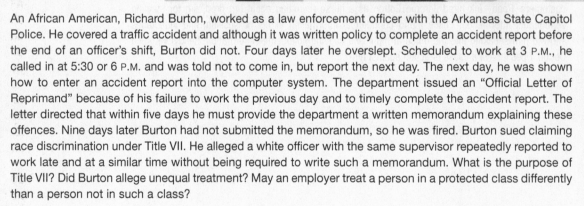

PREVIEW CASE

An African American, Richard Burton, worked as a law enforcement officer with the Arkansas State Capitol Police. He covered a traffic accident and although it was written policy to complete an accident report before the end of an officer's shift, Burton did not. Four days later he overslept. Scheduled to work at 3 P.M., he called in at 5:30 or 6 P.M. and was told not to come in, but report the next day. The next day, he was shown how to enter an accident report into the computer system. The department issued an "Official Letter of Reprimand" because of his failure to work the previous day and to timely complete the accident report. The letter directed that within five days he must provide the department a written memorandum explaining these offences. Nine days later Burton had not submitted the memorandum, so he was fired. Burton sued claiming race discrimination under Title VII. He alleged a white officer with the same supervisor repeatedly reported to work late and at a similar time without being required to write such a memorandum. What is the purpose of Title VII? Did Burton allege unequal treatment? May an employer treat a person in a protected class differently than a person not in such a class?

Many federal and state laws, municipal ordinances, and court decisions grant specific rights to employees. However, not all laws apply to all employees. State laws, court decisions, and ordinances vary. Some rights extend to all or most employees, whereas others may extend only to those in specified industries. The law is constantly extending rights to cover ever-larger numbers of workers. Some of these rights include the right to organize a union and have the union bargain for employees, rights against discrimination on specified bases, the right not to be subjected to certain invasive or offensive tests, and various protections such as for taking leave, receiving notification of plant closing, and being protected from secondhand smoke.

28-1 Union Representation

In order to create bargaining equality between employers and employees, federal labor law permits employees to organize a union to bargain for all employees. The process by which employers and employees' representatives negotiate and agree on the terms of employment for the employees is called **collective bargaining**. These terms are then spelled out in a written contract. Collective bargaining requires that the employer recognize and bargain with the representative the employees select. This representative is typically a union. Federal law also seeks to eliminate certain forms of conduct from the scene of labor negotiations and employment by condemning them as unfair labor practices. The law excludes agricultural laborers and domestic employees, individuals employed by a parent or spouse, and independent contractors from its definition of *employees*. Thus, they are not covered by laws requiring collective bargaining. Included are all employers engaged in interstate commerce except:

1. The railroad industry, covered by the Railway Labor Act of 1947
2. Supervisory employees—persons who can suspend, discharge, or discipline other employees
3. Governments or political subdivisions of governments

LO ①
Employers' and employees' labor rights

collective bargaining process by which employer and union negotiate and agree on terms of employment

COURT CASE

FACTS: Golden Living Center (Center) ran a nursing home whose registered nurses (RNs) reported directly to the Director of Nursing or her designee. The National Labor Relations Board (NLRB) certified the International Association of Machinists and Aerospace Workers, AFL–CIO (Union), to collectively bargain for the RNs. The Center, claiming the RNs supervised the certified nursing assistants (CNAs), refused to bargain with the Union and asked a court to agree. If a CNA misbehaved, RNs could elect to do nothing, give verbal counseling, or write a memorandum. If a memorandum was written, a written warning automatically resulted.

Four warnings led to a suspension. If investigation of the fourth warning showed misconduct occurred, the employee was fired.

OUTCOME: The court found that since the RNs had the authority to issue memoranda to CNAs, they had the authority to discipline. Because they had total freedom in deciding whether to issue a memorandum, they were supervisors.

—*GGNSC Springfield LLC v. N.L.R.B.*, 721 F.3d 403 (6th Cir.)

28-1a THE NATIONAL LABOR RELATIONS BOARD

To determine whether an unfair labor practice has been committed, federal law has created the National Labor and Relations Board (NLRB). The NLRB consists of five members appointed by the president and confirmed by the Senate. This board hears and, using subpoena power, conducts investigations of complaints of employer and union unfair labor practices. If the board finds that an unfair practice exists, it normally issues a "cease and desist order." If that does not prove effective, it has the power to seek an injunction to stop the practice. The NLRB supervises elections to determine the bargaining representative for the employees within each bargaining unit. In case of a dispute, the NLRB determines the size and nature of the bargaining unit.

28-1b PROHIBITION OF UNFAIR LABOR PRACTICES

Labor laws outlaw a number of actions by employers and unions by labeling them as unfair labor practices. Chief among the unfair practices of employers are as follows:

1. Interfering in the employees' exercise of the rights granted by law.
2. Refusing to bargain collectively with employees when they have legally selected a representative.
3. Dominating or interfering with the formation or administration of any labor organization or contributing financial support to it.
4. Discriminating against or favoring an employee in any way because of membership or lack of membership in the union. An employee may be fired for nonmembership in a union when the union has a valid union shop contract with the employer.
5. Discriminating against an employee who has filed charges against the employer under the act.

Unfair labor practices by unions and their leaders include:

1. Coercion or restraint of workers in the exercise of their rights under the law.
2. Picketing an employer to force bargaining with an uncertified union (one that has not been elected to represent the employees).
3. Refusal to bargain collectively with the employer.
4. Charging excessive initiation fees and discriminatory dues and fees of any kind.
5. Barring a worker from the union for any reason except the nonpayment of dues.
6. Secondary boycotts or strikes in violation of law or the contract, although certain exceptions are made in the construction and garment industries. A **secondary boycott** is an attempt by employees to cause a third party to stop dealing with the employer. The third party would normally be a customer or supplier of the employer. A strike and picketing are the most common ways to carry out a secondary boycott.
7. Attempts to exact payment from employers for services not rendered.

secondary boycott
attempt by employees to stop third party from dealing with employer

28-2 Discrimination

LO ②
Bases for protection from discrimination

Federal laws protect employees from discrimination on a number of grounds. Some laws prohibit discrimination on only one basis, whereas others protect on many bases. These laws include the Civil Rights Act of 1964, the Equal

Pay Act, the Age Discrimination in Employment Act, and the Americans with Disabilities Act.

28-2a CIVIL RIGHTS ACT OF 1964

The most important law governing employment discrimination and also harassment on the basis of race, color, religion, sex, and national origin is Title VII of the federal Civil Rights Act of 1964. The act applies to every employer who has fifteen or more employees and engages in an industry affecting interstate commerce and to labor unions with fifteen or more members. It does not apply to certain private membership clubs exempt from federal taxation.

This law makes it an unlawful employment practice for an employer to fail to hire, to discharge, or to discriminate in any way against anyone with respect to the terms, conditions, or privileges of employment because of the individual's race, color, religion, sex, or national origin. (Discrimination because of sex includes discrimination because of pregnancy, childbirth, or related medical conditions.) The employer also may not adversely affect an employee's status because of one of these factors. In addition, it is an unlawful employment practice for an employment agency or a labor organization to discriminate, classify, limit, or segregate individuals in any way on any one of these bases.

When a person sues under Title VII, the discrimination is usually claimed on either of two theories. These theories are disparate treatment and disparate impact.

Disparate Treatment. In a discrimination case on the ground of **disparate treatment** in employment, the plaintiff alleges that the discrimination was against the plaintiff alone and was because of the plaintiff's membership in a protected class. A **protected class** is any group given protection by antidiscrimination laws, such as groups based on race, color, religion, sex, or national origin and protected by Title VII. Disparate treatment is, basically, intentionally different treatment. That is, women being treated differently from men, blacks being treated differently from whites, and people of one religion being treated differently from people of another religion, solely because of their sex, race, or religion, respectively. The plaintiff must show that the employer acted with the intention of discriminating. Plaintiffs make a case by showing direct evidence of discrimination or by showing the following four essential elements:

disparate treatment intentional discrimination against a particular individual

protected class group protected by antidiscrimination laws

1. They belong to one of the protected classes.

2. They were qualified for the job or performed their job well.

3. They suffered an adverse employment action.

4. A person not in the protected class got the job or did not suffer the adverse action.

These elements vary slightly, depending on the plaintiff's situation—that is, whether the plaintiff applied for a job or had a job. But once plaintiffs prove the four elements, employers must offer a nondiscriminatory reason for their actions. If such reasons can be offered, plaintiffs must then show that the adverse treatment was because of their membership in one of the protected classes—that the employer intended to discriminate.

PREVIEW CASE REVISITED

FACTS: An African American, Richard Burton, worked as a law enforcement officer with the Arkansas State Capitol Police. He covered a traffic accident and although it was written policy to complete an accident report before the end of an officer's shift, Burton did not. Four days later he overslept. Scheduled to work at 3 P.M., he called in at 5:30 or 6 P.M. and was told not to come in, but report the next day. The next day, he was shown how to enter an accident report into the computer system. The department issued an "Official Letter of Reprimand" because of his failure to work the previous day and to timely complete the accident report. The letter directed that within five days he must provide the department a written memorandum explaining these offences. Nine days later Burton had not submitted the memorandum, so he was fired. Burton sued claiming race discrimination under Title VII. He alleged a white officer with the same supervisor repeatedly reported to work late and at a similar time without being required to write such a memorandum.

OUTCOME: The court found that the reasons the department gave for firing Burton were a pretext for race discrimination since the two officers' offenses were similar.

—*Burton v. Arkansas Secretary of State*, 737 F.3d 1219 (8th Cir.)

---

disparate impact
fair policy disproportionately affecting protected class

Disparate Impact. To prove a discrimination claim based on **disparate impact**, an employee must show that an action taken by the employer that appears fair nonetheless negatively and disproportionally affects a protected class of employees. An important difference between this theory and disparate treatment is that no intent to discriminate need be shown for disparate impact. The action complained of could be a testing policy, an application procedure, a job qualification, or any other employment practice whose adverse effect on employees is significantly greater on the members of a protected class than on employees who are not in that class.

hostile work environment
alteration of terms or conditions of employment by harassment

Sexual Harassment. Courts have held that the Title VII prohibition against discrimination on the basis of sex protects an employee against an employer who engages in or allows unwelcome sexual advances that create a **hostile work environment**. A hostile work environment exists when harassing conduct alters the terms or conditions of employment, creating an abusive work atmosphere, and it is based on the victim's membership in a protected class. Economic harm does not necessarily have to be proved. An employer can be liable for harassment by coworkers if the employer knows about the harassment and does not take prompt and appropriate corrective action. However, proper and corrective action by an employer after learning of harassment is an effective defense to a sexual harassment lawsuit.

In order to prove that the work environment was hostile, an alleged victim of sexual harassment must show that the environment was one that an objectively reasonable person would find abusive. This means that any reasonable employee would find the environment abusive. Such a requirement protects employers from overly sensitive employees who, for example, might feel that one isolated comment from a coworker created an abusive environment. In addition, victims themselves must find the environment abusive. A victim who is less sensitive than reasonable employees would probably have to have a more abusive work environment before a claim of sexual harassment would be upheld. If both of these requirements are met, the victim need not show psychological injury—the hostile work environment alone is actionable.

COURT CASE

FACTS: Police Sergeant Justo Cruz told Officer Blanca Valentín-Almeyda she had nice eyes, pretty hair, and great legs and that she looked beautiful in the morning. He drove by Valentín's house several times a day and honked his horn. Cruz became upset with her because she did not greet him with a kiss on the cheek. Valentín rebuffed Cruz and tried to complain to the police commissioner, but he had her meet with Lieutenant Juan Vélez, an investigator. Vélez told Valentín it was her fault because she had Cruz "bedazzled." She was assigned double shifts and given the worst job assignment. Cruz constantly tried to be near her at work and approached her at the mall. He left a note under her windshield wiper saying she was his. When she went to the station house to file a grievance, Cruz, Officer David Ferrer, and Vélez gave her three warning letters about her job performance. She transferred to the state police station, but the commissioner, Cruz, and Ferrer came once or twice a week and that the visits made her too uncomfortable to work. She sued for sexual harassment.

OUTCOME: The court found that there was ample evidence of a hostile work environment.

—*Valentín-Almeyda v. Municipality of Aguadilla,*
447 F.3d 85 (1st Cir.)

Although many types of actions are prohibited under Title VII, to be actionable, the victim must be affected because of membership in a protected class. Behavior could discriminate or create an abusive work atmosphere, but only that behavior based on the alleged victim's membership in a protected class is actionable. For example, a person could be teased about living in a high-rise apartment, having short hair, long hair, a pierced nose, driving a particular type of car, having freckles, or being tall. Even if they are insensitive or designed to humiliate, as long as a court does not find that the comments are based on membership in a protected class, they are not actionable under Title VII.

Successful plaintiffs in Title VII cases are entitled to a remedy that would put them in the same position they would have been in if the discrimination had not occurred. This might include some kind of corrective action by employers, posting of notices about sensitivity training, reinstatement, promotion, payment of lost benefits, and attorneys' fees. If the discrimination is intentional, the plaintiff may recover punitive damages.

The act established the Equal Employment Opportunity Commission (EEOC), which hears complaints alleging violations of this and other laws. Individuals may file the complaints, or the EEOC itself may issue charges. If the EEOC verifies the charge, it must seek by conference, conciliation, and persuasion to stop the violation. If this fails, the EEOC may bring an action in federal court. If the EEOC finds no basis for a violation, the employee may still sue the employer in court; however, the employee has the burden of hiring a lawyer and pursuing the case.

28-2b EQUAL PAY ACT

Recognizing that women were frequently discriminated against in the workplace by being paid less than men were paid for the same work, the federal government enacted the Equal Pay Act of 1963. The law applies to most large employers. The Equal Pay Act requires that employers pay men and women equally for equal work. The law prohibits employers from discriminating on the basis of sex by paying employees at a rate less than the rate at which employees of the opposite sex are paid for equal work. To be equal work, the jobs must be performed under similar working conditions and require equivalent skill, effort, and responsibility.

COURT CASE

FACTS: After working for Smarte Carte Inc. (Smarte) for a number of years, Jean Grover rose to the level of vice president of business development and operations for domestic locker and retail business. She complained repeatedly to the CEO that she received less compensation than males who were vice president of carts and lockers—international and vice president of business development and domestic airport operations. They were all vice presidents, reported to the CEO, and had similar job responsibilities. She received less guaranteed pay than one of them, and her base pay was substantially less than theirs. After she was fired, she sued Smarte, alleging violation of the Equal Pay Act. Smarte asked the court to find in its favor without holding a full trial.

OUTCOME: The court held that Grover had alleged facts showing that Smarte paid her less than similarly situated male employees for equal work in jobs that demanded equal skill, effort, and responsibility. The court denied Smarte's request.

—*Grover v. Smarte Carte Inc.*,
836 F.Supp.2d 860 (D. Minn.)

An employer is not required to pay employees at the same rate if the payments are made on the basis of:

1. A seniority system
2. A merit system
3. Quantity or quality of production
4. A differential resulting from any factor other than sex

In addition to its application to employers, the Equal Pay Act also prohibits labor unions from making or attempting to make employers discriminate against an employee on the basis of sex. Although the law was intended to help women, it is written in such a way that it requires equal pay for equal work and neither men nor women may be preferred.

28-2c AGE DISCRIMINATION IN EMPLOYMENT ACT

In order to protect people aged forty or over from employment discrimination, the federal government enacted the Age Discrimination in Employment Act (ADEA). This statute prohibits arbitrary age discrimination by employment agencies, employers, or labor unions against people aged forty or above. Employers are prohibited from firing or failing to hire people in this age group, and they may not limit, segregate, or classify their employees so as to discriminate against people in this age group solely because of their age. The firing can be an actual termination or a constructive discharge.

The ADEA does not prevent an employer from ever considering an employee's age or age-related criteria. It prohibits arbitrary discrimination, which occurs when age is considered despite its complete irrelevance to the decision being made. The law allows age discrimination when age is a true occupational qualification, such as the rule that commercial pilots cannot be more than sixty years old. In that case, the age limit is related to very significant safety considerations affecting the lives of millions of people. Company seniority systems are also permitted, even though they may have an impact on employees based on their ages.

COURT CASE

FACTS: Tommy Morgan, aged forty-five, was appointed managing partner of a New York Life Insurance Company (NYL) office. Morgan was given a series of performance benchmarks, but after the first year, the year-end evaluations showed that he had not met them. A series of events beyond Morgan's control plagued the office, lowering performance. When his performance did not improve after being on performance warning, he was put on final notice that stated he would be removed as managing partner if he did not meet specified goals, including a 5 percent growth in employees. It was determined on September 18 that 5 percent growth was not met. His employment was terminated the next day. Agents younger than Morgan had received lesser sanctions and, in some cases, even favorable treatment despite performance problems while other managing partners over age fifty had been eased out of the company. A NYL document dated September 2 listed replacements for Morgan. Claiming this proved that his forty-year-old successor had been chosen before it was determined that he had not met his goals, Morgan sued, alleging age discrimination.

OUTCOME: After a jury found in favor of Morgan, the appellate court ruled that there was a substantial amount of evidence tending to show that Morgan had been terminated because of his age. The jury verdict was upheld.

—*Morgan v. New York Life Ins. Co.,*
559 F.3d 425 (6th Cir.)

An employee who wishes to pursue an ADEA claim must file a claim with the EEOC within 180 days of the occurrence of the adverse employer action. If the EEOC does not find the claim valid, the employee may bring a court action against the employer. A successful employee could recover back pay, lost benefits, future pay (called *front pay*), and, at the discretion of the court, attorneys' fees. In addition, the court could order reinstatement, promotion, or, for an individual denied a job, hiring. If violation of the ADEA was willful, liquidated damages equal to the back-pay award are automatically awarded.

This law excludes from the definition of *employee* people elected to state or local office and people appointed at the policy-making level.

28-2d AMERICANS WITH DISABILITIES ACT

The Americans with Disabilities Act of 1990 (ADA), which applies to employers of fifteen or more employees, prohibits employment discrimination against qualified people with disabilities. An employer may not discriminate because of the disability in job application, hiring, advancement, or firing. For the purposes of the ADA, a disability requires two elements:

1. A physical or mental impairment
2. A substantial limitation of one or more major life activities

It is not enough simply to have an impairment and be unable to perform one specific job. The impairment must significantly limit a major life activity, such as being unable to perform a class or broad range of jobs. A "major life activity" includes such actions as caring for oneself, performing manual tasks, seeing, hearing, eating, sleeping, walking, standing, lifting, bending, speaking, breathing, learning, reading, concentrating, thinking, communicating, working, and the operation of major bodily functions, such as functions of the immune system, normal cell growth, and digestive, bowel, bladder, neurological, brain, respiratory, circulatory, endocrine, and reproductive functions. An impairment that is episodic or in remission is a disability if it would substantially limit a major life activity when active.

COURT CASE

FACTS: Jeffrey Willnerd was a bank loan officer/sales representative, meaning he solicited and prepared installment, consumer, and home-equity loan applications. He also sold credit cards and insurance products. Willnerd noticed a gradually worsening speech limitation. His voice would cut out and return, and it took considerable exertion for him to speak. The ailment baffled his doctors. Ultimately, his voice was basically limited to a whisper. His coworkers were aware of his speaking difficulty, and some had made fun of it. His position required substantial interaction with the public, and a supervisor worried about how customers perceived Willnerd. Based on a comparison of numerical rankings he received during performance reviews and on his loan productivity, his condition did not adversely affect his job performance. During the same general time frame as the onset and worsening of Willnerd's voice condition, overall performance at the bank was unacceptable. Supervisors met with

Willnerd and told him he had ninety days to increase production and improve his "overall proactive sales effort." Willnerd's loan production increased; however, he did not meet his production quota. The bank eliminated Willnerd's position, so he sued, alleging a violation of the ADA.

OUTCOME: Several coworkers joked or commented about Willnerd's voice, and a supervisor admitted worrying about how customers perceived Willnerd, so his speaking difficulty was open and obvious. Because performance reviews demonstrated that Willnerd performed the essential functions of his job, and it was clear that he suffered adverse employment action when the bank terminated him from his position, Willnerd had stated a case of ADA violation.

—*Willnerd v. First Nat. Nebraska Inc.,*
558 F.3d 770 (8th Cir.)

To determine whether other impairments constitute a major life activity, courts consider the type and severity of the impairment, the duration of the impairment, and any permanent or long-term impact of the impairment. Thus, temporary, short-term (with an actual or expected duration of six months or less), or nonchronic impairments with no long-term impact are not *disabilities*. Such impairments include broken bones, flu, sprains, appendicitis, and concussions. In addition, specifically excluded from the definition of a disability are compulsive gambling, kleptomania, pyromania, sexual behavior disorders, and current illegal drug use and alcoholism.

In addition, a person who has a history of an impairment that limits a major life activity, or is thought to have such a long-term impairment, is eligible for the benefits of the ADA. Thus, an employee can obtain the benefits of the ADA not because of actual impairment, but because the employee is treated by the employer as having a limiting impairment.

Once a job applicant or employee has been identified as disabled according to the law, it must be determined whether the individual with a disability is otherwise qualified for a particular job. If qualified, employers are required by the ADA to make "reasonable accommodations" to allow the disabled person to perform the essential functions of the job. The reasonable accommodations might include rescheduling employees, raising the height of desks to accommodate wheelchairs, acquiring equipment, or hiring a reader or sign language interpreter. An employer does not have to accommodate a disabled person if the accommodation would impose an undue hardship on the business. Violation of the ADA allows a qualified employee recovery, such as reinstatement, back pay, compensatory damages, punitive damages, and attorneys' fees.

28-3 Testing

LO ③
Restrictions on employee testing

In order to make sure businesses run properly, protect employees, protect company property from employee misuse, and weed out applicants for employment who might not be the best employees, many businesses have tried to institute various testing programs. These include polygraph testing, drug testing, and AIDS testing. The right of employers to use such tests, either on a pre-employment basis or on a random or mandatory basis after employment, has been limited by statute as well as by the courts.

28-3a POLYGRAPH TESTING

As lie detector tests appeared to become more reliable, increasing numbers of employers began using them, both as a tool to find out which employees had violated workplace rules and to screen applicants for employment. As a result of perceived injustices, both because of an intrusion on employees' rights and because of the debate about the reliability of such tests, the right to use these tests has been limited by statute. In 1988, the federal government enacted the Employee Polygraph Protection Act (EPPA). **Polygraph** is another word for lie detector.

polygraph
lie detector

The EPPA limits the use of lie detector devices for pre-employment screening or random testing of employees by employers engaged in interstate commerce. An employer may not retaliate against an employee who refuses to take a polygraph test and may not use the test results as the basis for an employment decision adverse to an employee who took such a test. Private employers may not use polygraphs unless:

1. The employer is investigating a specific incident of economic loss, such as theft or industrial espionage or sabotage.
2. The employer provides security services.
3. The employer manufactures, distributes, or dispenses drugs.

An employer may use a polygraph as part of an ongoing investigation if the employee tested had access to the subject of the investigation, and the employer has a reasonable suspicion of the employee's involvement. Before a polygraph test may be administered, the employee must be given written notice stating the specific economic loss, that the employee had access to the property that is the basis of the investigation, and giving a description of the employer's reasonable suspicion of the employee's involvement.

If an employer violates the EPPA, an employee or job applicant may sue the employer for the job, reinstatement, promotion, lost wages and benefits, or even punitive damages.

Except for the U.S. Congress, the law does not prohibit federal, state, and local governments from subjecting their employees to polygraphs.

28-3b AIDS TESTING

With the spread of the AIDS virus, employees have been concerned about contamination from afflicted coworkers. At the same time, workers with the virus have been concerned that they could be stigmatized and even lose their jobs. Because the test for AIDS is a blood test, the test is an invasive procedure, and there are some limits to what an employer can require on constitutional grounds. The Fourth Amendment to the Constitution prohibits "unreasonable search and seizure," and courts have held that requiring a blood test for AIDS is a search and seizure; therefore, it must be reasonable. To determine whether a search is reasonable, the court balances the intrusion the testing would cause on the constitutional rights of the person to be tested with the interests said to justify the intrusion.

28-3c DRUG TESTING

There has been concern about the ability of employees in certain jobs to do their jobs properly while under the influence of drugs. This concern has resulted in private employers and several federal administrative agencies requiring drug testing of employees or prospective employees. The U.S. Supreme Court has recognized three government interests that justify random drug testing: (1) maintaining the integrity of employees in their essential mission, (2) promoting public safety, and (3) protecting sensitive information. For example, Customs Service employees seeking transfers or promotions to sensitive positions, and railroad workers involved in major railroad accidents or who violate certain safety rules are tested for drug use. Courts have upheld random drug testing for employees in order to promote safety.

Of course, because at-will employees can be discharged at any time, employers are free to terminate such employees who refuse drug testing, even when their jobs cannot be held to involve public safety.

28-3d DNA TESTING

As DNA testing has become more reliable, it is possible that employers might require it of employees for the following two reasons:

1. To make employment decisions to exclude people with a genetic "defect"—a greater risk for certain diseases

2. For identification purposes

Many states have laws barring employers from discriminating against employees and prospective employees on the basis of their genetic makeup. These laws prohibit using genetic information when making hiring, promotion, or salary decisions. Victims of genetic discrimination normally can sue their employers for damages. It is likely that more states and the federal government will enact such legislation.

Employees in states that do not have such laws have sued employers for using DNA test results, alleging violation of the ADA, the constitutional prohibition on illegal searches and seizures, and Title VII of the Civil Rights Act. Employers should be very careful to ascertain their legal rights before using DNA tests in making hiring, promotion, or salary decisions.

As a reliable method of identifying people, DNA samples could be useful in a number of areas. The military (an employer) takes DNA samples of all personnel to use in identifying remains. The states and the federal government have passed laws setting up DNA databases to use in solving crimes. All states and the federal government require at least some convicted felons to submit DNA samples to their databases. The federal government has the authority to take DNA samples from some persons merely arrested or detained. The courts have almost uniformly upheld the legality of requiring DNA samples from criminals.

COURT CASE

FACTS: Martin Boroian was convicted of an offense and sentenced to one year of probation. The law provided that his conviction required him to give a DNA sample. The FBI keeps federal offenders' DNA profiles and samples after they have completed probation or supervised release. A month before Boroian's probation ended, he was ordered to submit a blood sample, which he did. He later sued the FBI, alleging that the government's retention and analysis of his DNA profile and sample after he completed his probation was an unreasonable search and seizure in violation of the Fourth Amendment. He asked the court to expunge his DNA profile and destroy the DNA sample.

OUTCOME: The court held that since the DNA profiles are limited by law to law enforcement identification purposes similar to fingerprint records, the retention was not violative of the Fourth Amendment.

—Boroian v. Mueller, 616 F.3d 60 (1st Cir.)

Many employers who need to be sure their employees are law abiding, such as those providing security services or dealing with large sums of cash, might want to have prospective employees provide a DNA sample to make sure they are not convicted felons. Just as the military wants to have DNA samples to help in identifying remains, employers of employees involved in hazardous occupations, such as firefighters, pilots, and demolition workers, would have an interest in having DNA samples for identification.

LO ④
Protections for employees

28-4 Protections

In addition to rights against discrimination on various bases and against certain kinds of invasive or offensive testing, employees have been accorded a variety of protections. These include protection of their jobs when a family necessity or medical condition requires a leave, notification of plant closings, and protection from secondhand cigarette smoke.

28-4a FAMILY AND MEDICAL LEAVE

In order to allow employees the right to take leaves when family circumstances or illnesses require it, the federal government enacted the Family and Medical Leave Act (FMLA). This law allows an employee to take an unpaid leave of up to twelve workweeks in a twelve-month period on the following occasions:

1. Because of the birth, adoption, or foster care of the employee's child
2. To care for the employee's spouse, child, or parent with a serious health condition
3. Because of a serious health condition that makes the employee unable to perform the job
4. Because of an emergency from an employee's spouse, child, or parent who is a military member on active duty
5. An employee may also take up to 26 weeks of leave in a twelve-month period to care for certain service members with a serious injury or illness.

COURT CASE

FACTS: Fincantieri Marine Group, LLC (FMG) gave points for unexcused work absences. An employee got one point for missing more than four hours of a scheduled workday. Any employee who accumulated ten points in a year could be fired. No points accrued for taking FMLA leave. James Hansen had accrued nine points. He was absent from work May 3–6 and May 9. But on May 3 he requested FMLA leave for a serious health condition—depression. On May 11 Hansen's physician certified his condition would cause episodic flare-ups preventing him from working. The condition would probably last months and he estimated Hansen would have four episodes lasting two to five days every six months. FMG granted FMLA leaves until he had requested leave

for a total of ten episodes by July 18. Because the frequency of absences was greater than the four in six months the doctor had estimated, Hansen incurred four points. These points made his total thirteen and Hansen was fired. He sued, claiming he was entitled to FMLA leave.

OUTCOME: While the court stated that Hansen's absences were greater than the doctor's estimated frequency and duration, it said estimated frequency and duration of intermittent leave were not complete limits on an employee's right to FMLA leave.

—Hansen v. Fincantieri Marine Group, LLC, 763 F.3d 832 (7th Cir.)

The law applies to public and private employers who have fifty or more full- or part-time employees for twenty weeks during the year. It gives leave rights to employees who have worked for the employer for at least twelve months and a total of 1,250 hours.

Although the FMLA gives workers the right to take leave, it is important to note that this leave is unpaid. Workers also may be required by their employers to use accrued paid vacation, personal, medical, or sick leave toward any part of the leave provided by the FMLA. If the leave is for the birth, adoption, or placement of a foster child, it must be taken within the first twelve months of the event. Unless the leave is not foreseeable, employees must give thirty days' notice of a leave request.

A "serious health condition" for which leave may be requested is an illness, injury, impairment, or physical or mental condition that requires inpatient care or continuing medical treatment. Its purpose is to provide leave for the more exceptional and presumably time-consuming events. Leave is also allowed for intermittent health episodes that make an employee unable to work. The care given to another includes psychological as well as physical care.

The benefit provided by the FMLA is that after taking the leave and returning to work, employees must be given back their previous positions. If this is not possible, the employer must put them in an equivalent job in terms of pay, benefits, and the other terms and conditions of employment. However, the employee must be able to perform the essential functions of the previous job without accommodation.

COURT CASE

FACTS: Employed as a registered nurse at Chicago-Read Mental Health Center run by the Illinois Department of Human Services (DHS), Elizabeth de la Rama called in sick beginning July 19. She sporadically submitted notes from physicians stating she was ill. The notes did not state her condition nor describe its severity. Although de la Rama had exhausted her sick leave, she continued to call in sick without explaining the nature of her illness. On August 11, she spoke with a human resources specialist, who told her that to request a medical leave she needed to submit a completed "CMS 95" form. On October 4, she submitted a completed CMS 95 form, which explained that she suffered from fibromyalgia and a herniated disk. Chicago-Read retroactively granted her FMLA leave to the date of her last sick day, September 2. De la Rama returned to work on January 3. Her absences in July and August were treated as unauthorized absences (UAs). Eight months later, she sued DHS, alleging that it had violated the FMLA by refusing to allow her to take leave in July and August for a serious medical condition.

OUTCOME: Although an employee is not required to refer to the FMLA in order to give notice of an intention to take FMLA leave, a notice must alert the employer of the seriousness of the health condition. The court said that calling in sick without providing additional information did not provide sufficient notice of such a condition.

—*de la Rama v. Illinois Dept. of Human Services*, 541 F.3d 681 (7th Cir.)

28-4b PLANT CLOSING NOTIFICATION

Under the provisions of the federal Worker Adjustment and Retraining Notification Act (WARN), a business that employs 100 or more employees must give sixty days' written notice of a plant closing resulting in an "employment loss" for fifty or more employees. Notice must also be given of a mass layoff which is a decrease in the workforce at a single site of employment that results in an "employment loss" during a thirty-day period for:

1. Thirty-three percent of the full-time employees (at a minimum of fifty employees)
2. At least 500 full-time employees

An employment loss is a termination that is not a discharge for a cause, a voluntary departure, or a retirement.

The written notice must be given to workers expected to experience some loss of employment, or their union representative, and to specified government officials. Workers in this instance include managers and supervisors. WARN does not require the full sixty days' notice if the plant closing or mass layoff occurs as a result of an unforeseeable business event (called the *faltering company exception*), a natural disaster, a labor dispute (a lockout or permanent replacement of strikers), the completion of a project by employees who knew the employment was temporary, or certain relocations when employees are offered transfers.

COURT CASE

FACTS: DHL Express Inc. (USA) (DHL) announced the closure of five Chicago-area facilities. The International Brotherhood of Teamsters that represented drivers and clerical workers there reached an agreement with DHL that included a number of severance packages. Some workers had only two days in which to consider the packages. Each worker who accepted any of the packages signed a release of DHL and the union of all claims from employment and termination by DHL and acknowledged that the worker was giving up employment with DHL. Ultimately, 506 workers signed a release and resigned employment in exchange for severance pay and benefits. Workers who did not participate in any severance agreement sued DHL, alleging violation of WARN because they had not gotten the required sixty days' notice.

OUTCOME: The court said that the fact that some decisions had to be made very quickly did not make the decisions involuntary. Since enough employees had resigned, the WARN Act did not apply.

—Ellis v. DHL Exp. Inc. (USA),
633 F.3d 522 (7th Cir.)

In case of a violation of WARN, an employee may sue the employer for back pay for each day of violation as well as benefits under the employer's employee benefit plan. Courts have the discretion to allow the successful party in such lawsuits to recover their reasonable attorneys' fees.

28-4c SMOKING

The disclosure of the damaging effects of breathing secondhand smoke has resulted in a desire by many nonsmoking employees to work in smoke-free environments. The right of employees to be protected from secondhand cigarette smoke is protected in a variety of ways.

Some employers have taken the initiative by prohibiting or restricting smoking at their workplaces. In addition, a number of states and municipalities have enacted restrictive smoking legislation. This legislation varies greatly. No state law totally bans smoking at all job sites. Some laws merely require employers to formulate and publicize a written policy about smoking in the workplace. Others require employers to designate smoking and nonsmoking areas. Nearly all of the laws have exceptions to the smoking ban that allow smoking in private offices. In spite of these exceptions, a very large percentage of employers have some kind of smoking restrictions in effect.

28-5 Other Sources of Rights

There are many other rights granted to employees, particularly through federal laws, which apply to large numbers of workers. These laws include the Rehabilitation Act and the Pregnancy Discrimination Act. The rights granted by these two laws are similar to those granted by statutes mentioned in this chapter.

QUESTIONS

1. How does federal law seek to create bargaining equality between employers and employees?
2. What does the National Labor Relations Board do?
3. To whom does Title VII of the Civil Rights Act of 1964 apply?
4. When does a hostile work environment exist?
5. What remedy are successful plaintiffs in Title VII cases entitled to?
6. What does the ADA prohibit?
7. Who is excluded from the definition of *employee* under the ADEA?
8. In what ways does the EPPA limit an employer's use of a polygraph test with respect to employees?
9. How do courts determine whether AIDS testing is reasonable under the Fourth Amendment?
10. Are any employees whose jobs do not involve public safety subject to discharge for refusal to take drug tests?
11. For what reasons does the FMLA allow an employee to take an unpaid leave?
12. When is it that WARN does not require the full sixty days' notice of a plant closing or mass layoff?

CASE PROBLEMS

LO ③ 1. After working as the manager of Piedmont Commons branch of Washington Mutual Bank (Washington), Dave Cummings was transferred to another branch. The new manager of Piedmont discovered $58,000 was missing from cash dispenser machines to which Cummings had had access. Bank investigators found security photos showing Cummings violating bank policy requiring two persons to be present when cash was handled. Employees told them he had frequently violated the policy. The investigators asked him to take a polygraph test and he refused. Washington fired him telling him it was because he violated the policy. Cummings sued Washington alleging it had violated the EPPA. Had it?

LO ② 2. A full-time sales associate for Kohl's Department Stores, Inc., Pamela Manning worked predictable shifts starting no earlier than 9 A.M. and lasting no later than 7 P.M. Kohl's carried out a nationwide staff restructuring which cut the hours for Manning's department. She kept her hours by working in other departments as needed. Her schedule became unpredictable and she had to work some swing shifts—a night shift, then an early shift the next day. She told Michelle Barnes, her supervisor, that working variable shifts aggravated her diabetes, threatening her health. Her doctor wrote Tricia Carr, the store manager, asking that Manning be assigned "a predictable day shift." Carr found out swing shifts could be eliminated, but Manning would have to work some nights. Manning met with Barnes and Carr, who told her the "higher ups" said she could not work only days. Manning said she had no choice but to quit since she would go into ketoacidosis or a coma with erratic hours. She put down her store keys, walked out, and slammed the door. Carr asked her to reconsider and consider other accommodations. Manning said, "Well, you just told me Corporate wouldn't do anything for me." She did not discuss other accommodations, but cleaned out her locker and left. Carr phoned her ten days later. She asked Manning to reconsider quitting and other accommodations saying she would ask the corporate office about accommodations. Not hearing anything from Manning, Kohl's terminated her. Manning filed an ADA discrimination claim. Should she recover?

LO ① 3. World Color operated a printing plant. A written policy stated: "Baseball caps are prohibited except for [World Color] baseball caps." The policy permitted employees to accessorize their uniforms "in good taste and in accordance with all safety rules." The Graphic Communications Conference of the International Brotherhood of Teamsters filed an unfair labor practice charge with the NLRB claiming that the policy prohibited employees from wearing union insignia at work. It said World Color was interfering with its employees' "right to self-organization, to form, join, or assist labor organizations, . . . and to engage in other concerted activities for the purpose of collective bargaining" as guaranteed by federal law. The NLRB agreed and World Color appealed. Was the baseball cap policy an unfair labor practice?

LO ④ 4. Alan Macfarlan worked as a maintenance director at a rehabilitation and nursing facility. On January 24 he had a stroke, so he took leave beginning January 29 under the FMLA. In April, his doctor said he could return to work May 1 for four hours a day as long as he did not move loads heavier than 20 pounds. The facility's administrator told him part-time work was unavailable. Then the doctor cleared him for full-time work with the load restriction. The facility fired him on April 20 and told him he would not be re-hired with load restrictions. From the time he was fired until July, when he was cleared to work without restrictions, Macfarlan received disability benefits from his insurer. He later sued the facility, claiming that by refusing to allow him to return to work in April, when he was cleared for full-time but restricted work, the facility had denied him his right under the FMLA to be restored to his previous or an equivalent position. The facility argued that since he received disability benefits based on his claims, with supporting medical documentation, he was unable to perform the duties of his regular occupation and therefore that it had not violated the FMLA and that the court should rule for it. Should it?

LO ③ 5. The Forest Service of the Department of Agriculture operated residential Job Corps (Corps) Civilian Conservation Centers (CCCs) for at-risk youth. The Corps had a zero-tolerance policy for drugs. All Corps employees were responsible for demonstrating and monitoring acceptable workplace behavior and maintaining the zero-tolerance policy. The Forest Service told the union representing its

CASE PROBLEMS (CONTINUED)

employees that all Corps staff would be subject to random drug testing. The union sued, alleging that such a policy violated the employees' Fourth Amendment rights. It offered evidence that there was no staff drug problem requiring random testing, and that different job categories at the CCCs had different levels of responsibility, or none, for maintaining the zero-tolerance policy, ensuring student safety, and transporting students. Should the court uphold the random drug testing?

6. Monika Samper, a neonatal intensive care unit (NICU) nurse at Providence St. Vincent Medical Center (Providence) had a condition that limited her sleep and caused her chronic pain. She never worked full-time but still had more unplanned absences than Providence allowed for full-time employees. Providence allowed Samper to call in when having a bad day and to move her shift to another day in the week. Even though NICU nurses require special training, thus limiting the pool of nurses who can be called in at the last minute, it did not require her to find a replacement. Since NICU nurses' absences can jeopardize patient care, Providence scheduled Samper's two shifts per week on non-consecutive days. At the end of the year, she received a warning because her absences were still excessive. Each year, she also had extended leaves that did not count against the unplanned absence limit. Providence ultimately fired her. She sued the hospital, claiming violation of the ADA because of Providence's failure to accommodate. Samper argued that regular attendance was not an essential function of a NICU nurse's job. What should the court rule? **LO ②**

7. Dunlop Sports Group Americas Inc. operated a golf ball manufacturing plant employing 350 people. On October 31, Dunlop's employees came to work and discovered that Dunlop had ceased operations. Dunlop notified all employees in writing that it was selling the factory. Their employment would continue until the earlier of December 31 or the date they accepted a position working for the successor company that intended to run the plant. Employees did not have to report for work, but they would continue to receive wages for forty hours per week and be eligible for benefits as long as they remained employed by Dunlop. In November, the successor company hired twenty-two Dunlop employees who had worked at the plant until October 31. In early December, Dunlop stopped paying wages and benefits to those twenty-two employees because they were employed full-time by the successor company. They sued, claiming that Dunlop should have continued to pay them wages and benefits until December 31 because it did not comply with the notice requirements of the WARN Act. Had Dunlop conformed to the WARN Act? **LO ④**

8. For years, Addie Stover, an African American female, worked as secretary to the associate superintendent and head of the personnel department of the superintendent of the Hattiesburg Public School District. She held a bachelor's degree in English with a minor in paralegal studies. She attended board meetings to take minutes and did not create agenda items, but typed and organized information that was provided to her. A high-level administrator for the district who held a doctoral degree resigned, and Stover assumed a few of his duties. Two years later, the district filled the opening without advertising the position by hiring Alan Oubre, a white male, as central office administrative coordinator. Oubre held a bachelor's degree in secondary-school English and a master's degree in educational administration and was paid $25,000 more than Stover. Stover argued that Oubre and she were administrative assistants who performed substantially equal work, and, therefore, that they should be paid the same. The superintendent said she was not qualified for Oubre's position. Stover filed suit, alleging race and sex discrimination under Title VII. Had the district discriminated against Stover? **LO ②**

9. Employee Daniel Worden called SunTrust bank claiming two men had kidnapped him in order to rob the bank. Worden asked a coworker to open the vault, but the coworker refused and told another employee to call the police. Worden told police he was held in his home overnight at gunpoint by two men who wanted to use him to rob the bank and threatened to kill him. He claimed the kidnappers had abandoned him when they realized their plan had failed. The police told Worden they suspected he was behind the attempted robbery. He agreed to take a polygraph examination. The **LO ③**

CASE PROBLEMS (CONTINUED)

police told Kevin Brock, a SunTrust manager, of their suspicions and Worden's agreement to the test. The polygraph examiner announced that Worden had failed the exam. The FBI gave a second test to which Worden consented. No one from SunTrust requested, participated in, or was present during either polygraph exam. The FBI told Worden the results indicated "deception," and he was a suspect. Worden told Brock he failed the second polygraph. The police told Brock that Worden was their prime suspect and that he would likely be charged with the crime. Telling him that SunTrust had concerns based on law enforcement's belief he had been involved in the attempted robbery, Worden was fired. The polygraphs were not mentioned. SunTrust had discharged another employee under virtually identical circumstances, except there had been no polygraph. Worden sued SunTrust, alleging that SunTrust had violated the EPPA by basing its decision to fire him on the polygraphs. Should Worden succeed?

 10. Burlington Resources Oil and Gas Company employed Paul Pippin as a senior engineer when Burlington began a reduction in force (RIF). Burlington sought to retain employees whose past performance reports and skill sets matched Burlington's future needs. Burlington fired Pippin, who was fifty-one years old. Fourteen out of nineteen employees fired in the RIF were over age forty. Each year, Burlington ranked its employees and, in the ranking before his firing, Pippin was last among thirteen senior engineers. In previous rankings, he was in or near the bottom half of his peers. Pippin sued Burlington, claiming age discrimination. Was this age discrimination?

ETHICS IN PRACTICE

Although employers are legally prohibited from hiring, promoting, and firing employees for reasons based on race, creed, color, national origin, or sex, and they may not discriminate against people over the age of forty or with a disability, there are still a number of grounds on which employers may discriminate against employees. For example, they could legally discriminate on the basis of height, weight (as long as it were not held to be a disability), attractiveness, or right- or left-handedness. Although employers may legally discriminate on such a basis, do you think it is ethical for them do to so?

PART 6 SUMMARY CASES

AGENCY AND EMPLOYMENT

1. Flex Frac Logistics, L.L.C., a nonunion company, delivered frac sand to oil and gas well locations. The rates it charged were confidential, so it required employees to sign a nondisclosure clause prohibiting employees from sharing confidential information outside the company. The information included "our financial information, including costs [and] prices." After Flex Frac fired Kathy Lopez, she filed an unfair labor practice complaint with the NLRB, alleging the clause prohibited employees from discussing employee wages. Were employees free to discuss terms and conditions of employment outside the company? [*Flex Frac Logistics, L.L.C. v. N.L.R.B.*, 746 F.3d 205 (5th Cir.)]

2. The City Board (Board) of Decherd, TN, passed a resolution covering employment of police officers that recited that it repealed any other resolution that conflicted with it. It further said, "[D]iscipline shall be for cause and shall follow the basic concepts of due process" and an employee had to be given written notice of "the exact offense violated." The Board fired the police chief, Terry Freeze, at a meeting without giving grounds for his termination other than "the betterment of the city." He had not been given written notice his termination would be considered and it was not on the agenda. He was not given a chance to present witnesses or other evidence and his request for a hearing was denied. He sued the city, alleging the resolution created a contract that changed his employment from at-will and required he could be fired only for good cause. Did it? [*Freeze v. City of Dechert, Tenn.*, 753 F.3d 661 (6th Cir.)]

3. James Pierce approached Terrance Wright of Wright Group Architects–Planners, P.L.L.C. about providing architectural and design services for a proposed eight-story condominium. Wright sent a contract in the form of a two-page letter addressed to "Mr. Jim Pierce, President, GHTM Inc." The letter referred to the parties as "Wright Group" and "Owner." At the bottom was the word "Accepted" and below it, Pierce's signature. Wright Group was not paid for its services, so it sued Pierce personally. Pierce claimed he had signed the contract as agent for Galveston Hidden Treasure Management Inc. Should Pierce be personally liable? [*Wright Group Architects-Planners, P.L.L.C. v. Pierce*, 343 S.W.3d 196 (Tex. Ct. App.)]

4. Thurman Mooneyham left Hugh Dancy Company Inc.'s (Dancy) employment but a year later, the office manager asked him to help clean out the construction shop. He spent four days per week there but was not put on the payroll, had no set schedule, and reported to no one. He received four checks from Dancy, for "reimbursement," "services rendered," "parts reimbursed," and "shop help." He suffered an injury while on the premises and filed a workers' compensation claim alleging that his injury was work-related. Was Mooneyham an employee eligible for workers' compensation? [*Hugh Dancy Co. Inc. v. Mooneyham*, 68 So.3d 76 (Miss. Ct. App.)]

5. In August, Carbonic System Inc. hired service department manager Robert Curren on a one-year contract. During his second year, Curren received a new employee handbook stating that employment was at-will. He subsequently received raises at times other than in August. Several years later, Scott Casey, the distribution manager, told his wife, Kathy, the president of Carbonic, that he had seen Curren loading a Carbonic computer into his vehicle. After Kathy determined that Curren did not have permission to take a computer, she called him. The parties disputed what happened during the call, but agreed it was tense and involved shouting and foul language. The next workday, Scott gave Curren a termination letter from Kathy, which gave the reason as his "continuing lack of organizational skills and inability to work well with other departments within the company." Curren sued Carbonic and the Caseys for interfering with his employment contract. Did Curren have an employment contract? [*Curren v. Carbonic Systems Inc.*, 872 N.Y.S.2d 240 (N.Y. App. Div.)]

6. After Marilyn Cappaert died, her accountant, Todd Boolos, asked Harris Barnes to provide legal services for the estate. BancorpSouth was the executor of the estate, and for eleven months Barnes provided the bank with monthly statements. He also filed five petitions and other legal documents with the court on behalf of BancorpSouth that were signed by the bank's trustee. BancorpSouth continued to allow Barnes to provide legal representation and made no objection to his representation until he was terminated. The estate then refused to pay Barnes's legal fees, so his law firm sued the estate. Had BancorpSouth ratified the apparent agency of Boolos in hiring Barnes? [*Barnes, Broom, Dallas and McLeod, PLLC v. Estate of Cappaert*, 991 So.2d 1209 (Miss.)]

7. Jose Mendoza contracted with John Rast as a commission merchant to market Mendoza's pomegranate crop. He harvested and delivered the crop to Rast. When Mendoza got information and documents reporting grades, quality, weights, sales, receipts, and expenses, he noticed that some sales were significantly below market price. He alleged that Rast had pretended to sell the pomegranates but really reconsigned the product to subagents, who had accepted the fruit without setting a designated price. Rast had then used false and misleading documents to hide the amount due Mendoza. Mendoza sued, alleging violation of fiduciary duty by Rast and the subagents. Did Mendoza allege a violation of duties owed him by the subagents? [*Mendoza v. Rast Produce Co. Inc.*, 45 Cal. Rptr. 3d 525 (Cal. Ct. App.)]

8. After creating a supermarket promotional game, Leo Weber & Associates contracted to implement it with four Winn Dixie (W/D) stores. The contract stated that each party was an independent contractor. Weber asked George Vickerman to do artwork and other materials for the game. Vickerman hired Process Posters Inc. (PPI) to manufacture some game materials and told PPI to bill Weber. Weber was the main contact with W/D. Vickerman's contact with W/D was pursuant to the contract between Weber and W/D. After completion of the game, W/D paid Weber, who paid Vickerman and gave PPI checks totaling $149,000. Several months later, PPI tried to cash the checks, but Weber's account had been closed. PPI sued W/D for payment, alleging that Vickerman was W/D's agent; therefore, W/D was liable when PPI, hired by Vickerman, was not paid. Was Vickerman W/D's agent? [*Process Posters Inc. v. Winn Dixie Stores Inc.*, 587 S.E.2d 211 (Ga. Ct. App.)]

9. Police officer Lori Ann Molloy heard an officer, Robert Sabetta, complain about being suspended for improper use of force. He said he should have killed, or should kill, the people who had complained. A month later, he shot and killed three teenage boys and wounded another. Some of the victims had filed the brutality complaints. The Rhode Island state police asked Molloy some general questions about Sabetta, and she did not volunteer what he had said. During his murder trial, the state police received a "tip" that Molloy had relevant information. When questioned, she disclosed his comments, but the police believed she knew more. They told Molloy's chief, Wesley Blanchard, that she was refusing to cooperate. She insisted she had disclosed everything, but Blanchard suspended her. He did not give her the hearing she requested under the Officers' Bill of Rights. In about twelve cases against male officers, Blanchard had granted such rights. He had not even suspended some of the male officers suspected of highly questionable behavior. Molloy sued Blanchard and the town for sex discrimination. Who should win and why? [*Molloy v. Blanchard*, 115 F.3d 86 (1st Cir.)]

10. The Aroostook County Regional Ophthalmology Center (ACROC) had an office policy manual, which at the end of a discussion of patient confidentiality stated, "No office business is a matter for discussion with spouses, families, or friends." It also stated, "It is totally unacceptable for an employee to discuss any grievances within earshot of patients." Four ACROC employees, within earshot of patients, expressed dissatisfaction and exasperation over the inconvenience caused by sudden changes in work schedules and complained that work schedules were often changed. They were fired. They filed a complaint, alleging that enforcing the policies was an unfair labor practice. Was it? [*Aroostook County Regional Ophthalmology Center v. NLRB*, 81 F.3d 209 (D.C. Cir.)]

Business Organization

Businesses come in all sizes, from small businesses like local restaurants, hair salons, dry cleaners, and others, to franchises and corporations. This part covers these types of businesses and the legal details for their organizational structures. You can also find more information on the websites of your state governments. The state of Illinois provides information on necessary form and fees for LLCs at its website www.cyberdriveillinois.com/publications/business_services/llc.html.

29 Introduction to Business Organizations

30 Creation and Operation of a Partnership

31 Dissolution of a Partnership

32 Nature of a Corporation

33 Ownership of a Corporation

34 Management and Dissolution of a Corporation

Introduction to Business Organization

LEARNING OBJECTIVES

① Discuss the nature of a sole proprietorship, including its main advantages and disadvantages.

② Explain the purposes of a partnership and various types of partnerships and partners.

③ Give two reasons why the limited liability company is an important form of business organization.

PREVIEW CASE

John Bankston was a sole proprietor doing business under the fictitious name Aarohn Construction. John obtained a construction license and submitted a bid to Pierce County for a public works project. Each bidder was required to hold a valid construction license. Pierce County informed John that he would be awarded the contract, as the lowest bidder, but shortly after the announcement, John's construction license was suspended. John's son, Richard Bankston, proceeded to form a sole proprietorship and applied for a separate construction license. Richard Bankston's small proprietorship was also called Aarohn Construction. Based on John's bid, Pierce County executed a written contract with Aarohn Construction. John signed his name on the signature page, but wrote Richard's construction license number on the contract. John stated that the contractor was a sole proprietor and that the business owner was "R.J. Bankston." A dispute arose, and Richard sued Pierce County for breach of contract. With whom did Pierce County contract? Was Aarohn Construction one business or two separate businesses? What is the nature of a sole proprietorship?

An individual who is contemplating starting a business has a choice of several common types of business organizations. The number of owners, the formality in setting up the business, and the potential for personal liability are important factors that help distinguish widely used types of business organization: sole proprietorship, partnership, limited liability company, and corporations. Corporations are discussed in Chapters 32 through 34.

29-1 Sole Proprietorship

A **sole proprietorship** is a business owned and carried on by one person, called the **proprietor**. A sole proprietorship, the simplest and most common form of business, has a nature different from other businesses. It also has significant advantages and disadvantages as a result of the fact that one individual owns and runs it.

29-1a NATURE

The proprietor directly owns the business. This means that the proprietor owns every asset of the business, including the equipment, inventory, and real estate, just as personal assets are owned. Although owned and run by one person, the business may have any number of employees and agents. However, the proprietor has ultimate responsibility for business decisions.

To start a sole proprietorship, an individual need only begin doing business. The law does not require any formalities to begin and operate this form of business. A license may be needed for the particular type of business undertaken. However, the type of business imposes this requirement, not the form of business organization. (See Illustration 29-1 for a sample Application for Employer Identification Number form.)

It is equally easy to end a sole proprietorship. The proprietor simply stops doing business. Because the proprietor directly owns all the business assets, the proprietor need not dispose of them in order to go out of business. A sole proprietorship normally ends at the death of the proprietor. Such a business may be willed to another, but the proprietor has no assurance the business will be continued.

29-1b ADVANTAGES

The sole proprietorship form of business has two major advantages:

1. Flexible management
2. Ease of organization

Flexible Management. As the sole owner, the proprietor has significant flexibility in managing the business. Other people do not have to be consulted before business decisions may be made. The proprietor has full control and the freedom to operate the business in any way desired.

Ease of Organization. Because an individual need do nothing but start doing business, the sole proprietorship is the simplest type of business to organize. The law imposes no notice, permission, agreement, or understanding for its existence. If the proprietor intends to operate the business under an assumed name, a state law will normally require registration of the name with the appropriate state official. These laws are called **fictitious name registration statutes**. In registering a fictitious name, the business must disclose the names and addresses of the owners of the business and the business's purpose. This allows anyone who wishes to sue the business to know whom to sue. A business that is operated under the proprietor's name, and that does not imply additional owners, does not have to be registered.

29-1c DISADVANTAGES

The most significant disadvantage of the sole proprietorship form of business is the unlimited liability of the owner for the debts of the business. **Unlimited liability** means that business debts are payable from personal, as well as business, assets. If

sole proprietorship
business owned and carried on by one person

proprietor
owner of sole proprietorship

LO ①
Nature of sole proprietorship

fictitious name registration statutes
laws requiring operator of business under assumed name to register with state

unlimited liability
business debts payable from personal assets

ILLUSTRATION 29-1   Application for Employer Identification Number U.S. Internal Revenue Service

Form **SS-4**	**Application for Employer Identification Number**	OMB No. 1545-0003
(Rev. January 2010) Department of the Treasury Internal Revenue Service	**(For use by employers, corporations, partnerships, trusts, estates, churches, government agencies, Indian tribal entities, certain individuals, and others.)** ▶ **See separate instructions for each line.** ▶ **Keep a copy for your records.**	EIN

Type or print clearly.		
1	Legal name of entity (or individual) for whom the EIN is being requested	
2	Trade name of business (if different from name on line 1)	**3** Executor, administrator, trustee, "care of" name
4a	Mailing address (room, apt., suite no. and street, or P.O. box)	**5a** Street address (if different) (Do not enter a P.O. box.)
4b	City, state, and ZIP code (if foreign, see instructions)	**5b** City, state, and ZIP code (if foreign, see instructions)
6	County and state where principal business is located	
7a	Name of responsible party	**7b** SSN, ITIN, or EIN

8a Is this application for a limited liability company (LLC) (or a foreign equivalent)? . . . . ☐ **Yes** ☐ **No**   **8b** If 8a is "Yes," enter the number of LLC members . . . . ▶

8c If 8a is "Yes," was the LLC organized in the United States? . . . . ☐ **Yes** ☐ **No**

9a **Type of entity** (check only one box). **Caution.** If 8a is "Yes," see the instructions for the correct box to check.

☐ Sole proprietor (SSN) _____
☐ Partnership
☐ Corporation (enter form number to be filed) ▶_____
☐ Personal service corporation
☐ Church or church-controlled organization
☐ Other nonprofit organization (specify) ▶_____
☐ Other (specify) ▶

☐ Estate (SSN of decedent) _____
☐ Plan administrator (TIN) _____
☐ Trust (TIN of grantor) _____
☐ National Guard   ☐ State/local government
☐ Farmers' cooperative   ☐ Federal government/military
☐ REMIC   ☐ Indian tribal governments/enterprises
Group Exemption Number (GEN) if any ▶

9b If a corporation, name the state or foreign country (if applicable) where incorporated | State | Foreign country |

10 **Reason for applying** (check only one box)

☐ Started new business (specify type) ▶ _____
_____
☐ Hired employees (Check the box and see line 13.)
☐ Compliance with IRS withholding regulations
☐ Other (specify) ▶

☐ Banking purpose (specify purpose) ▶ _____
☐ Changed type of organization (specify new type) ▶ _____
☐ Purchased going business
☐ Created a trust (specify type) ▶ _____
☐ Created a pension plan (specify type) ▶ _____

11 Date business started or acquired (month, day, year). See instructions. | **12** Closing month of accounting year

13 Highest number of employees expected in the next 12 months (enter -0- if none).

If no employees expected, skip line 14.

Agricultural	Household	Other

14 If you expect your employment tax liability to be $1,000 or less in a full calendar year **and** want to file Form 944 annually instead of Forms 941 quarterly, check here. (Your employment tax liability generally will be $1,000 or less if you expect to pay $4,000 or less in total wages.) If you do not check this box, you must file Form 941 for every quarter. ☐

15 First date wages or annuities were paid (month, day, year). **Note.** If applicant is a withholding agent, enter date income will first be paid to nonresident alien (month, day, year) . . . . ▶

16 Check **one** box that best describes the principal activity of your business.
☐ Construction ☐ Rental & leasing ☐ Transportation & warehousing   ☐ Health care & social assistance ☐ Wholesale-agent/broker
☐ Real estate ☐ Manufacturing ☐ Finance & insurance   ☐ Accommodation & food service ☐ Wholesale-other ☐ Retail
  ☐ Other (specify)

17 Indicate principal line of merchandise sold, specific construction work done, products produced, or services provided.

18 Has the applicant entity shown on line 1 ever applied for and received an EIN? ☐ **Yes** ☐ **No**
If "Yes," write previous EIN here ▶

Third Party Designee	Complete this section **only** if you want to authorize the named individual to receive the entity's EIN and answer questions about the completion of this form.	
	Designee's name	Designee's telephone number (include area code) ( )
	Address and ZIP code	Designee's fax number (include area code) ( )

Under penalties of perjury, I declare that I have examined this application, and to the best of my knowledge and belief, it is true, correct, and complete. | Applicant's telephone number (include area code)
( )

Name and title (type or print clearly) ▶

Signature ▶   Date ▶ | Applicant's fax number (include area code)
( )

For Privacy Act and Paperwork Reduction Act Notice, see separate instructions.   Cat. No. 16055N   Form **SS-4** (Rev. 1-2010)

the business does not have enough assets to pay business debts, business creditors may also take the proprietor's personal assets. The sole proprietor's financial risk cannot be limited to the investment in the business.

In addition to unlimited liability, a sole proprietorship has additional disadvantages of limited management ability and capital. Because only one person runs a sole proprietorship, the management ability of the proprietor limits the business. The business also has only whatever capital the proprietor has or can raise. This may limit the size of the business.

A sole proprietor has liability for the activities of the business because the proprietor is the sole manager of the business. The proprietor is in a sense the business. The responsibility for all business decisions rests with the proprietor. A sole proprietor may be liable not only in damages for torts committed by the business but also liable for crimes.

PREVIEW CASE REVISITED

FACTS: John Bankston was a sole proprietor doing business under the fictitious name Aarohn Construction. John obtained a construction license and submitted a bid to Pierce County for a public works project. Each bidder was required to hold a valid construction license. Pierce County informed John that he would be awarded the contract, as the lowest bidder, but shortly after the announcement, John's construction license was suspended. John's son, Richard Bankston, proceeded to form a sole proprietorship and applied for a separate construction license. Richard Bankston's small proprietorship was also called Aarohn Construction. Based on John's bid, Pierce County executed a written contract with Aarohn Construction. John signed his name on the signature page, but wrote Richard's construction license number on the contract. John stated that the contractor was a sole proprietor and that the business owner was "R.J. Bankston." A dispute arose and Richard sued Pierce County for breach of contract.

OUTCOME: The court stated that John and Richard were two individuals and, because the individual and the sole proprietor are legally indistinguishable, the fictitious name Aarohn Construction referred to two separate sole proprietorships. The contract was declared void, because Richard had not participated in the competitive bidding process as required by law.

—*Bankston v. Pierce County*, 301 P.3d 495 (Wash. App.)

29-2 Partnership

A **partnership** is a voluntary association of two or more people who have combined their money, property, or labor and skill, or a combination of these, for the purpose of carrying on as co-owners some lawful business for profit. The agreement of individuals to organize a partnership and run a business forms this type of organization. The individuals who have formed a partnership and constitute its members are called **partners**. They act as agents for the partnership.

The partnership must be formed for the purpose of operating a lawful business. The attempt to form a partnership to operate an unlawful business does not result in a partnership. Furthermore, a partnership may not be formed for the purpose of conducting a lawful business in an illegal manner.

A hunting club, a sewing circle, a trade union, a chamber of commerce, or any other nonprofit association cannot be treated as a partnership because the purpose of a partnership must be to conduct a trade, business, or profession for profit.

LO ② Purposes of partnerships

partnership association of two or more people to carry on a business for profit

partner member of a partnership

29-2a CLASSIFICATION

Several different kinds of partnerships exist, depending on the liabilities of the partners and the business carried out. Partnerships may be classified as follows:

1. Ordinary or general partnerships
2. Limited partnerships
3. Trading and nontrading partnerships

ordinary or general partnership
partnership with no limitation on rights and duties of partners

Ordinary or General Partnerships. An ordinary or general partnership forms when two or more people voluntarily contract to pool their capital and skill to conduct some business undertaking for profit. An ordinary partnership results in no limitations on a partner's rights, duties, or liabilities. The Uniform Partnership Act governs this type of business organization in most states.[1] This act aims to bring about uniformity in the partnership laws of the states.

limited partnership
partnership with partner whose liability is limited to capital contribution

Limited Partnership. A limited partnership is one in which one or more partners have their liability for the firm's debts limited to the amount of their investment. This type of partnership cannot operate under either the common law or the Uniform Partnership Act. However, all states now permit limited partnerships. Most do so because of passage of the Uniform Limited Partnership Act or the Revised Uniform Limited Partnership Act. A limited partnership cannot be formed without a specific state statute prescribing the conditions under which it can operate. If the limited partnership does not comply strictly with the enabling statute, courts hold it to be an ordinary partnership with resulting liability on the partners.

trading partnership
one engaged in buying and selling

nontrading partnership
one devoted to professional services

Trading and Nontrading Partnerships. A trading partnership is one engaged in buying and selling merchandise. A nontrading partnership is one devoted to providing services, such as accounting, medicine, law, and similar professional services. The distinction matters because the members of a nontrading partnership usually have considerably less apparent authority than the partners in a trading partnership. For example, one partner in a nontrading partnership cannot borrow money in the name of the firm and bind the firm. One dealing with a nontrading partnership must exercise more responsibility in ascertaining the actual authority of the partners to bind the firm than a person dealing with a trading partnership.

Who May Be Partners? As a contractually based entity, any person competent to make a contract has the competence to be a partner. A minor may become a partner to the same extent to which the minor may make a contract about any other matter. The law holds such contracts voidable, but a minor acting as the agent of the other partner or partners can bind the partnership on contracts within the scope of the partnership business. A minor partner also incurs the liabilities of the partnership. The states disagree as to whether a minor who withdraws from a partnership can withdraw the entire contribution originally made or whether a proportion of any losses must be deducted first.

ETHICAL POINT

Do you think it would be ethical for a minor to be able to withdraw the entire contribution originally made, or should losses first be deducted?

---

[1] The Uniform Partnership Act has been adopted in all states except Louisiana.

29-2b KINDS OF PARTNERS

The members of a partnership may be classified as follows:

1. General partner

2. Silent partner

3. Secret partner

4. Dormant partner

5. Nominal partner

General Partner. A **general partner** is one actively and openly engaged in the business and held out to everyone as a partner. Such a partner has unlimited liability in respect to the partnership debts. A general partner appears to the public as a full-fledged partner, assumes all the risks of the partnership, and does not have any limitations of rights. This is the usual type of partner. A limited partner can be held to the liability of a general partner but normally only when the limited partner exercises the rights of a general partner by managing the partnership.

general partner
partner actively and openly engaged in business

COURT CASE

FACTS: A group of 239 people invested $30 million as limited partners with Michael Vogelbacher in a project known as the Washington Supermall Project. Construction on the mall could not be completed with the original construction loan. Wells Fargo was asked to provide financing to complete the construction. It entered into an agreement by which it became a limited partner. However, certain debts, liens, obligations, selling of assets, or the entering into mergers could not occur without Wells Fargo's approval. Vogelbacher tried to sell the project, with the ultimate result that Wells Fargo received $4.9 million. But eventually, Glimcher Supermall Venture, LLC foreclosed on the project and the original investors lost their $30 million. They sued,

claiming Vogelbacher established the scheme for the supermall to defraud investors and that Wells Fargo elevated its status from limited partner to general partner by virtue of its extraordinary power over certain partnership actions.

OUTCOME: The court said that in spite of the power that the partnership agreement gave Wells Fargo, a court could not presume that it had exercised such power. Without having exercised the power, it had not acted as a general partner.

—*Asshauer v. Wells Fargo Foothill*, 263 S.W.3d 468 (Tex. Ct. App.)

Silent Partner. A **silent partner** is one who, although possibly known to the public as a partner, takes no active part in the management of the business. In return for investing in the partnership capital, such a partner has a right as a partner only to share in the profits in the ratio agreed on. Why would a person invest money but take no active part in the management? A person would do this because such a partner gains limited liability and no share of the losses beyond the capital contribution. People frequently refer to this type of partner as a **limited partner** when known to the public as a partner.

silent partner
partner who takes no part in firm

limited partner
partner who takes no active part in management and whom the public knows as a partner

secret partner
partner active but unknown to public

Secret Partner. An active partner who attempts to conceal that fact from the public is a secret partner. Such a partner tries to escape the unlimited liability of a general partner but at the same time takes an active part in the management of the business. Should the public learn of such a partner's relationship to the firm, however, unlimited liability cannot be escaped. Secret partners differ from silent partners in that secret partners: (1) are unknown to the public, and (2) take an active part in the management of the business. Secret partners may feign the status of employees or may work elsewhere, but they meet frequently with the other partners to discuss management problems.

dormant or sleeping partner
partner unknown to public with no part in management

Dormant Partner. A dormant partner (sometimes referred to as a sleeping partner) usually combines the characteristics of both the secret and the silent partner. A dormant partner is usually unknown to the public as a partner and takes no part in the management of the business of the firm. When known to the public as a partner, a dormant partner has liability for the debts of the firm to the same extent as a general partner. In return for limited liability so far as the other partners can provide it, a dormant partner forgoes the right to participate in the management of the firm. In addition, such a partner may agree to limit income to a reasonable return on investment, as no services are contributed.

nominal partner
person who pretends to be a partner

Nominal Partner. Nominal partners hold themselves out as partners or permit others to do so. In fact, however, they are not partners, as they do not share in the management of the business or in the profits, but in some instances, they may be held liable as partners.

29-2c ADVANTAGES OF THE PARTNERSHIP

By the operation of a partnership instead of a proprietorship, capital and skill may be increased, labor may be made more efficient, the ratio of expenses per dollar of business may be reduced, and management may be improved. Not all of these advantages will accrue to every partnership, but the prospect of greater profits by reason of them leads to the formation of a partnership.

29-2d DISADVANTAGES OF THE PARTNERSHIP

A partnership has the following disadvantages:

1. The unlimited personal liability of each partner for the debts of the partnership
2. The relative instability of the business because of the danger of dissolution by reason of the death or withdrawal of one of the partners
3. The divided authority among the partners, which may lead to disharmony

29-2e ORGANIZATIONS SIMILAR TO PARTNERSHIPS

Some business organizations resemble partnerships. However, they differ from them. These include joint-stock companies, joint ventures, and limited liability companies.

joint-stock company
entity that issues shares of stock, but investors have unlimited liability

Joint-Stock Companies. A joint-stock company resembles a partnership, but shares of stock, as in a corporation, indicate ownership. The ownership of these shares may be transferred without dissolving the association. Thus, one of the chief disadvantages of the general partnership is overcome. Shareholders in a joint-stock company do not have the authority to act for the firm. The joint stock-holders have liability, jointly and severally, for the debts of the firm while members.

For this reason, joint-stock companies do not offer the safeguards of a corporation. Some states permit joint-stock companies to operate by special statutes authorizing them, or in some states, without statute, as common-law associations.

Joint Ventures. A joint venture is a business relationship in which two or more people combine their labor or property for a single undertaking and share profits and losses equally or as otherwise agreed. For example, two friends enter into an agreement to get the rights to cut timber from a certain area and market the lumber. A joint venture resembles a partnership in that the parties exercise joint or mutual control over the undertaking and are jointly and severally liable. The primary difference is that a joint venture exists for a single transaction, although its completion may take several years. A partnership generally constitutes a continuing business.

joint venture
business relationship similar to partnership, except existing for single transaction only

COURT CASE

FACTS: Sheila Arthur and David Magiera entered an informal agreement with Jose Hernandez and John Willison to purchase an airplane. The plane was owned in Arthur's name, but Hernandez made payments toward it. Willison piloted the plane in return for a future ownership interest in it. All parties took turns using the plane for their individual business and personal purposes, and all agreed that there was no intent to operate the plane for profit or "for charter." Several days after the purchase, Willison and Hernandez used the plane to fly Dennis Ott and Janet Lyn Grimmett, who were friends of Hernandez. During the flight, the plane ran out of fuel and crashed, causing severe injuries to Grimmett.

Grimmett sued Arthur, Magiera, Willison, and a business owned by Magiera and Hernandez, alleging a joint venture existed between the defendants and all were jointly and severally liable for Grimmett's injuries. Arthur denied the existence of a joint venture and liability for Grimmett's injuries.

OUTCOME: The court held that there was no joint venture, because the plane was not owned for profit purposes, and no evidence existed to show the parties agreed to share losses. Arthur was not liable for Grimmett's injuries.

—*Arthur v. Grimmett*, 319 S.W.3d 711 (Tex. Ct. App.)

Limited Liability Partnerships. Many states have enacted laws that allow individuals to run a business but avoid normal partnership liability by forming a limited liability partnership or LLP. To form an LLP, the partnership must register with the appropriate state office. Like a partnership, the members of an LLP take an active role in managing the business, but like shareholders in a corporation, they do not have unlimited liability for business debts and normally no liability for other partners' misconduct or negligence. Unlike a limited partnership, in which one partner must be a general partner and is exposed to unlimited liability, all partners of an LLP may have limited liability. The limited liability partnership laws vary considerably among the states.

limited liability partnership (LLP)
registered partnership whose members run business but have limited liability

Limited Liability Companies. A limited liability company or LLC is a type of business organization that combines the management features of a partnership with the limited liability afforded to shareholders of a corporation. The owners or investors of an LLC are called members. An LLC can be a member-managed or manager-managed business entity. Member-managed LLCs closely resemble the management structure of a general partnership, because the owners are directly managing the company. In a manager-managed LLC, the members appoint one or more managers to direct the LLC's operations. The managers often form a board of directors, which looks more like a corporate management structure.

LO ③
Limited liability companies

limited liability company (LLC)
partnership-type organization but with limited liability

29-2f FORMATION OF THE LLC

The LLC is a legal entity distinct from its members. As such, the LLC may enter into contracts, hold property and be sued in its own name, separately from the members. LLCs are created by filing articles of organization with the appropriate state office. Many states also require the members to sign an operating agreement, which describes the rights and duties of the members and managers.

29-2g IMPORTANT FEATURES OF THE LLC

The LLC is an increasingly popular form of business organization due in part to two important features:

1. Members may elect how the LLC will be classified for income tax purposes
2. Limited liability for members

Tax Classification. Many business people favor the LLC, because the LLC offers flexibility in choosing how the business will be classified for income tax purposes. Since the LLC is created under state statutes, the federal government has not established a tax classification for the LLC. Instead, the LLC may elect to be taxed as a partnership, a corporation, or a sole proprietorship, depending on the number of members. For LLCs with two or more members, the default tax classification is that of a partnership. Being taxed as a partnership is advantageous to members, because the LLC's profits and losses pass through the company to the members. Members thus avoid the double taxation that a corporation incurs when the corporation pays taxes on profits, and the shareholders pay taxes on dividends received.

limited liability
capital contribution is
maximum loss

Limited Liability. Another valuable feature of the LLC is limited liability, the limitation of personal liability for the members. The personal assets of the members are shielded from contractual and tortious liabilities incurred by the LLC, and generally, the members' losses are limited to the amount they invested in the LLC. The limited liability feature of an LLC is especially attractive when compared to the unlimited personal liability risked by partners or sole proprietors for business debts.

COURT CASE

FACTS: Charming Charlie, Inc. agreed to rent space in a shopping mall from Perkins Rowe Associates, L.L.C. As managing member of Perkins Rowe, Joseph Spinosa signed the lease agreement, which provided for a reimbursement of $682,500 for a construction allowance to Charming Charlie. When Perkins Rowe failed to pay for the construction allowance, Charming Charlie sued Perkins Rowe Associates and Spinosa, individually. Charming Charlie argued that Spinosa was liable because he had a significant ownership interest in Perkins Rowe and managed the company.

OUTCOME: The court stated that the member of a limited liability company is not personally liable for the debts of the company to third parties, except in rare circumstances where the member ignores corporate formalities and treats the company as himself. Because Charming Charlie failed to give specific examples of Spinosa mixing his personal affairs with those of Perkins Rowe, the Court held that Spinosa was not personally liable.

—*Charming Charlie, Inc. v. Perkins Rowe Associates, L.L.C.*, 97 So.3d 595 (La. App.)

Piercing the Corporate Veil of the LLC. In rare instances, courts will disregard the LLC as a separate entity and will hold a member liable as if there were no LLC at all. In these instances, the court is said to be **piercing the corporate veil**. This occurs when members fail to follow formalities that distinguish the LLC as a separate entity and use the LLC as a shield to avoid liability for their own bad behavior. Examples of such breach of formality include members: comingling LLC assets with their personal assets, treating the LLC's assets as their own, undercapitalizing the LLC and failing to maintain an arm's length relationship with related entities. Members who mix their personal affairs with those of the LLC can be held personally liable for the LLC's debts and lose the important advantage of unlimited liability.

piercing the corporate veil
ignoring the corporate entity

COURT CASE

COURT CASEFACTS: Dean Freeman was the member-manager of Tradewinds, LLC, a company whose main asset was an airplane. Tradewinds hired Robert Martin to build a hangar and, during the course of construction, sued Martin for breaching the construction agreement. The court entered judgment in favor of Martin and awarded him damages against Tradewinds. While litigation was pending, Tradewinds sold the airplane and gave the proceeds to Freeman to pay for the LLC's legal expenses. Freeman commingled LLC assets with his personal assets and disregarded corporate formalities such as adequate record-keeping. Freeman also undercapitalized the LLC. Martin sued Freeman personally for the judgment liability, since the LLC was without any assets.

OUTCOME: The court held that Freeman was personally liable for the debt, because he had treated the LLC as a shell company, commingled funds and had not kept adequate records to distinguish the LLC's business from Freeman's personal affairs.

—Martin v. Freeman, 272 P.3d 1182 (Co. Ct. App.)

Dissolution. The LLC can generally be dissolved with the written consent of all members or upon majority votes of remaining members as provided in the operating agreement. The articles of organization can also decree that dissolution will occur upon the happening of a specific event or after the elapse of a specific period of time.

QUESTIONS

1. What is the purpose of fictitious name registration statutes?
2. What are the advantages and the most serious disadvantage of a sole proprietorship?
3. Since a sole proprietorship is owned and run by one individual, does this mean only one person can participate in the business? Explain.
4. Can a limited partnership be formed just as easily as a sole proprietorship or ordinary partnership?
5. Explain the difference between a general partner and a limited partner.
6. For what purposes may a partnership be formed?

QUESTIONS (CONTINUED)

7. What is a limited liability partnership?
8. How might a limited liability company be classified for income tax purposes?
9. What is the difference between a member and a manager of a limited liability company?
10. When will a court pierce the corporate veil of a limited liability company?

CASE PROBLEMS

LO ②

1. Greene County entered into an agreement with United Consulting Engineers Inc. and DLZ Indiana, LLC, jointly and in collaboration, collectively referred to as "the Firm," to provide professional architectural services for the design, renovation and remodeling of the county courthouse. DLZ was to provide certain design and engineering services, but United would act as the principal and have full responsibility and liability for all services provided. DLZ would be liable to the county, as a third-party beneficiary, for the services it provided. DLZ and United entered into a subcontract that labeled United as "the Architect" and DLZ as "the Consultant" on the project. It provided that DLZ was an independent contractor and would not be responsible for United's acts or omissions. United was to compensate DLZ by hourly rates established in a schedule of the contract. DLZ's fees were "not to exceed" $527,763. DLZ received payments directly from United. The county filed a complaint against DLZ and United for breach of contract, breach of warranty, and negligence, alleging DLZ and United were liable as joint venturers. Were they?

LO ②

2. Ernest Burns, Orlando Summemour, and Randy Hatcher formed SWI Partners, a general partnership. J. T. Turner Construction Company obtained a judgment against SWI Partners and Burns for breach of contract and negligent construction. As a judgment creditor, J. T. Turner then filed a lawsuit against Summemour and Hatcher, alleging that they were jointly and severally liable for the judgment against SWI Partners. Summemour and Hatcher responded that they could not be held liable for the judgment against SWI Partners until they "had their day in court." Were Summemour and Hatcher liable?

LO ①

3. Stanley Goessl was a plumber doing business as a sole proprietor under the fictitious name S&K Plumbing. Goessl entered into a long-term business relationship with AP Daino and Plumbing Inc. as a subcontractor. Goessl established his own hourly rate for projects and invoiced AP Daino on behalf of S&K Plumbing. Goessl also carried his own liability insurance, as requested by AP Daino. During one project, while Goessl was doing plumbing work for AP Daino, a fire broke out and damaged the premises. AP Daino's insurer refused coverage, stating that Goessl was not an employee of AP Daino. Whereas Goessl's insurer argued that it was not liable, because Goessl was working the project as an employee of AP Daino. Was Goessl an employee of AP Daino?

LO ③

4. Jackie Lora was the member of WDJ Realty V, LLC, a company that owned and managed apartment buildings. Lora later transferred her membership in the company to Nicole Pignone. Lora and Pignone did not own or manage the apartment building in an individual capacity, and the company affairs were maintained separately. Letitia Palmer and her infant son, Andrew Matias, were residents in one of the buildings owned by WDJ Realty. Palmer sued WDJ Realty, Lora, and Pignone on her son's behalf, alleging that the child had sustained injuries from exposure to lead paint and dust in the building. Should the court pierce the corporate veil and find Lora and Pignone personally liable?

LO ②

5. G&G Cement Contractors was a general partnership owned by two brothers, Dagoberto and Jose Gonzales. William Andrews was injured in a car accident with an employee of G&G Cement. Andrews sued G&G Cement, the employee, Dagoberto Gonzalez, and the estate of Jose Gonzales, who had died after the accident. Dagoberto was sued based on the theory of *respondeat superior*, which

CASE PROBLEMS (CONTINUED)

holds employers liable for the conduct of their employees in specific circumstances. A jury found that the employee and G&G Cement were liable for Andrews's injuries and awarded damages to the plaintiff. After Andrews was unable to collect on the judgment against G&G Cement, he filed a second action against Dagoberto Gonzalez as a general partner of the company. Dagoberto responded that the matter had already been litigated and he was not liable, because a judgment had been issued in his favor. Was Dagoberto correct?

6. Susan Breen was a bookkeeper for Patriot Truck Equipment, LLC. Breen obtained a judgment against Patriot to recover the money that she had personally loaned Patriot to keep the company in business. Craig Judge was the managing member of Patriot and owned 50 percent of the company. Breen sued Judge to hold him personally liable for the judgment against Patriot. Patriot followed corporate formalities, such as maintaining separate books, filing separate tax returns, and maintaining proper registration to do business in the state. When Patriot was dissolved, the company filed appropriate articles of dissolution with the state. Should Judge be liable for the judgment against Patriot?

CHAPTER 30

Creation and Operation of a Partnership

LEARNING OBJECTIVES

1. Describe how a partnership is created.
2. Specify the duties the law imposes on partners.
3. Identify the rights and liabilities every partner has.
4. Explain how partnership profits and losses are shared.

PREVIEW CASE

Larry Oehlert purchased residential real estate and titled the property solely in his name. About a year later, Oehlert resumed a relationship with his former girlfriend, Joyce Via, who sold her mobile home and moved into the residence owned by Oehlert. Over a period of years, while the parties cohabited, each contributed to the improvement of the property. Via's improvements included the purchase of drapes, wallpaper, plumbing, and electrical components. She also helped to install a woodworking shed, a patio, and landscaping around the home's exterior. Oehlert made payments on the mortgage while Via paid utility bills. But the parties maintained separate bank accounts and never jointly owned any property. When the relationship broke down, Via remained in the house without paying rent and received offers to buy the property, which Oehlert declined. Via file suit to dissolve what she claimed was a partnership between Oehlert and her and to obtain an accounting and distribution of the alleged partnership's assets. Did Oehlert and Via form a partnership? Was the home a partnership asset? Did Via have the right to a portion of the property?

A partnership is formed as a result of a contract, written or oral, express or implied, just as all other business commitments result from a contract. The parties to the contract must give the utmost fidelity in all relationships with the other partners. If any partner fails in this duty, the other partners have several legal remedies to redress the wrong.

30-1 Partnership Agreements

The partnership agreement must meet the five requirements of a valid contract as set out in Chapter 5. A partnership also may be created when two or more parties who do not have a written agreement, or even an intention to form a partnership, act in such a way as to lead third parties to believe that a partnership exists.

30-1a WRITTEN AGREEMENT

The partners ordinarily need not have a written agreement providing for the formation of a partnership. However, having an agreement in writing might help avoid some disputes over rights and duties. If the parties choose to put their agreement in writing, in the absence of a statute to the contrary, the writing need not be in a particular form. The written partnership agreement is commonly known as the **articles of partnership**. Articles of partnership vary according to the needs of the particular situation, but ordinarily they should contain the following:

1. Date
2. Names of the partners
3. Nature and duration of the business
4. Name and location of the business
5. Individual contributions of the partners
6. Sharing of profits, losses, and responsibilities
7. Keeping of accounts
8. Duties of the partners
9. Amounts of withdrawals of money
10. Unusual restraints on the partners
11. Provisions for dissolution and division of assets
12. Signatures of partners

30-1b IMPLIED AGREEMENT

A partnership arises whenever the people in question enter into an agreement that satisfies the definition of a partnership. Thus, three people who agree to contribute property and money to the running of a business as co-owners for the purpose of making a profit, even though they do not in fact call themselves partners, have formed a partnership. Conversely, the mere fact that people say, "We are partners now" does not establish a partnership if the elements of the definition of a partnership are not satisfied.

LO ①

How partnership is created

articles of partnership
written partnership agreement

PREVIEW CASE REVISITED

FACTS: Larry Oehlert purchased residential real estate and titled the property solely in his name. About a year later, Oehlert resumed a relationship with his former girlfriend, Joyce Via, who sold her mobile home and moved into the residence owned by Oehlert. Over a period of years, while the parties cohabited, each contributed to the improvement of the property. Via's improvements included the purchase of drapes, wallpaper, plumbing, and electrical components. She also helped to install a woodworking shed, a patio, and landscaping around the home's exterior. Oehlert made payments on the mortgage while Via paid utility bills. But the parties maintained separate bank accounts and never jointly owned any property. When the relationship broke down, Via remained in the house without paying rent and received offers to buy the property, which Oehlert declined. Via filed suit to dissolve what she claimed was a partnership between Oehlert and her and to obtain an accounting and distribution of the alleged partnership's assets.

OUTCOME: The court held that a partnership did not exist between Via and Oehlert, because the parties had not purchased and improved the property for the purpose of making a profit. The combination of their efforts was not a business undertaking.

—Via v. Oehlert, 347 S.W.3d 224 (Tenn. Ct. App.)

In many instances, the death of witnesses or the destruction of records makes proof of exactly what happened impossible. Because of this, the Uniform Partnership Act provides that proof that a person received a share of profits is *prima facie* evidence of a partnership. This means that in the absence of other evidence, it should be held that a partnership existed. This *prima facie* evidence can be overcome, and the conclusion then reached that no partnership existed, by showing that the share of profits received represented wages or payment of a debt, interest on a loan, rent, the purchase price of a business or goods, or some other justifiable payment.

prima facie
on the face of it

prima facie evidence
evidence sufficient on its
face, if uncontradicted

30-1c PARTNERSHIP BY *ESTOPPEL*

The conduct of people who in fact are not partners could be such as to mislead other people into thinking they are partners. The situation resembles that in which a person misleads others into thinking that someone is an authorized agent. In a case of a false impression of a partnership, the law will frequently hold that the apparent partners are estopped from denying that a partnership exists; otherwise, third persons will be harmed by their conduct.

COURT CASE

FACTS: Guy and Peggy Lyberger contracted with Mike Anderson d/b/a Great Western Homes to build a house. During construction, the funding bank called a meeting with Anderson and the Lybergers to determine the status of the construction and financing. Mike Reagan was asked to attend the meeting because he had information about Anderson's billing records. Reagan handled the bookkeeping for Great Western by tracking checks and receipts going through Anderson's account and had allowed him to use his credit card to buy appliances for a home built by Great Western. The Lybergers dealt solely with Reagan about financial matters. Anderson referred to Reagan as his partner. Reagan attempted to negotiate about items on the house that needed completion.

Anderson told Peggy he could not authorize the completion of a retaining wall because Reagan said they needed to get the money for it first. After the house was vandalized, Peggy's parents were at the house trying to repair damage when Reagan told them he was Anderson's partner. After criminal charges were brought against Anderson, the Lybergers sued him and Reagan as partners.

OUTCOME: Since Reagan was actively participating in the home building business with Anderson and had at least some control over the financial aspects of the business, the court found they were partners.

—*Reagan v. Lyberger*, 156 S.W.3d 925 (Tex. Ct. App.)

30-2 Partnership Firm Name

The law does not require a firm name for a partnership, but it makes identification convenient. The firm may adopt any name that does not violate the rights of others or the law. The partnership name may be changed at will by agreement. In some states, the name of a person not a member of the firm, or the words *and Company*, unless the term indicates an additional partner(s), may not be used. Many states permit the use of fictitious or trade names but require the firm to register under fictitious name registration statutes (see Chapter 29).

A partnership may sue or be sued either in the firm name or in the names of the partners. Under the Uniform Partnership Act, any partnership property, whether real or personal, may be owned either in the names of the partners or in the name of the firm. To hold partnership property in the names of the partners, the owner should convey the property to the partners d/b/a (doing business as) the partnership.

30-3 Partner's Interest in Partnership Property

In a **tenancy in partnership** (also called **owner in partnership**), each partner owns and can sell only a *pro rata* interest in the partnership as an entity. The purchaser of one partner's share cannot demand acceptance as a partner by the other partners. The purchaser acquires only the right to receive the share of profits the partner would have received. A surviving partner does not get full ownership on the death of the other partner, as is the case in joint tenancy. One partner may not freely sell an interest in partnership property. The personal creditors of one partner cannot force the sale of specific pieces of partnership property to satisfy personal debts, nor can they force the sale of a fractional part of specific assets. The personal creditors of one partner can ask a court to order that payments due the debtor partner from the partnership be made to the creditors. They also can force the sale of a debtor partner's interest in the partnership.

tenancy or owner in partnership
ownership of partner in partnership property

30-4 Duties of Partners

Five common duties that one partner owes to the others include:

LO ②
Partner's duties

1. Duty to exercise loyalty and good faith
2. Duty to work for the partnership
3. Duty to abide by majority vote
4. Duty to keep records
5. Duty to inform

30-4a EXERCISE LOYALTY AND GOOD FAITH

Partners owe each other and the firm the utmost loyalty and good faith. As an agent of the firm, each partner has a fiduciary duty to the firm, so strict fidelity to the interests of the firm must be observed at all times. No partner may take advantage of the copartners. Any personal profits earned directly as a result of one's connection with the partnership must be considered profits of the firm. If the personal interest or advantage of the partner conflicts with the advantage of the partnership, the partner has a duty to put the firm's interest above personal advantage. This duty lasts as long as the enterprise exists.

The partnership contract must be observed scrupulously. Each partner has the power to do irreparable damage to the copartners by betraying their trust. For this reason, the law holds each partner to the utmost fidelity to the partnership agreement. Any violation of this agreement gives the other partners at least two rights: First, they can sue the offending partner for any loss resulting from the failure to

ETHICAL POINT
How does the principle of business ethics influence the duties that a partner owes the partnership and other partners?

abide by the partnership agreement; second, they may elect also to ask a court to decree dissolution of the partnership. A trivial breach of the partnership agreement will not justify dissolution.

COURT CASE

FACTS: Chris Andersen and Stephen Weinroth were equity partners of Andersen, Weinroth & Co., LP (AWLP). Andersen and Weinroth each paid the same initial capital contributions to AWLP and agreed that all future capital contributions would be made equally. Weinroth managed and controlled all of AWLP's finances. Weinroth would notify Andersen when AWLP's capital accounts became low and would request a capital contribution from Andersen. Over the course of three years, Andersen's capital contributions exceeded Weinroth's by $1,385,000. During this time, Weinroth made false entries in the capital accounts to reflect that he had contributed $1,300,000. At one point, Weinroth faxed Andersen a note claiming he had made a capital contribution of $53,000, which Andersen then matched. Moreover,

in one of AWLP's business investments, Weinroth misrepresented his contribution to the investment as an equal share. Weinroth then divided the profits from the investment equally between the partners. Andersen sued Weinroth for breach of fiduciary duty owed to a partner.

OUTCOME: The court held that Weinroth's concealment of the true condition of the capital accounts and his misrepresentation related to the business investment breached a "sensitive and inflexible" duty of fidelity that he owed to his partner. Weinroth was liable to Anderson for the loss.

—*Andersen v. Weinroth*, 849 N.Y.S.2d 210
(N.Y. App. Div.)

30-4b WORK FOR THE PARTNERSHIP

Unless provided otherwise in the partnership agreement, each partner has a duty to work on behalf of the partnership. In working for the partnership, partners must use reasonable care and skill in conducting the firm's business. Each partner has liability for partnership debts, but a partner must reimburse any loss resulting to the firm because of the partner's failure to use adequate care and skill in transacting business. If the partnership supplies expert services, such as accounting or engineering services, then each partner must perform these services in a manner that will free the firm from liability for damages for improper services. However, honest mistakes and errors of judgment do not render a partner liable individually, nor the partnership liable collectively.

30-4c ABIDE BY MAJORITY VOTE

A partnership operates on the basis of a majority vote. Unless the partnership agreement provides otherwise, the majority of the partners bind the firm on any ordinary matters in the scope of the partnership business. A decision involving a basic change in the character of the enterprise or the partnership agreement requires the unanimous consent of the partners. Therefore, the majority rule does not apply to such actions as an assignment for the benefit of creditors, disposition of the firm's goodwill, actions that would make carrying on the firm's business impossible, confession of a judgment, or the submission of a firm claim to arbitration.

30-4d KEEP RECORDS

Each partner must keep such records of partnership transactions as required for an adequate accounting. If the partnership agreement provides for the type of records to be kept, a partner fulfills this duty when such records are kept, even though they may not be fully adequate. Because each partner must account to the partnership for all business transactions, including purchases, sales, commission payments, and receipts, this accounting should be based on written records.

30-4e INFORM

Each partner has the duty to inform the other partners about matters relating to the partnership. On demand, true and full information of all things affecting the partnership must be rendered to any partner or the legal representative of any deceased partner or partner under legal disability.

COURT CASE

FACTS: Brothers Kerwin and Perry Elting, along with their sons, Carl and Knud Elting, were four managing partners in a family farming partnership. The Partnership Agreement required the approval of a majority of the managing partners before any of them could contract on the partnership's behalf. The partnership had longstanding contracts to sell the partnership's anticipated corn production to Cargill Inc. Unknown to Perry and Knud Elting and without approval from the majority of managing partners, Kerwin Elting amended the contracts with Cargill so that the contracted price per bushel of corn was permitted to "float" with the market, based on fluctuations in market demand over a period of time. The amended contracts caused the partnership to lose $2,144,350 from the originally contracted price. Kerwin did not inform Perry and Knud Elting of the loss. After dissolving the partnership and taking steps to set up a new farming business, Perry and Knud Elting became aware of the loss. They sued Kerwin for damages, stating that Kerwin did not have authority to amend the contracts.

OUTCOME: Because Kerwin failed to inform two of the managing partners of the contract amendment and did not obtain majority approval, he did not have authority to enter the contract. He was liable to Perry and Knud for damages.

—*Elting v. Elting*, 849 N.W.2d 444 (Neb.)

30-5 Rights of Partners

Every partner, in the absence of an agreement to the contrary, has the following five well-defined rights:

1. Right to participate in management
2. Right to inspect the books at all times
3. Right of contribution
4. Right to withdraw advances
5. Right to withdraw profits

LO
Rights and liabilities of partners

30-5a PARTICIPATE IN MANAGEMENT

In the absence of a contract limiting these rights, each partner has the right by law to participate equally with the others in the management of the partnership business. The exercise of this right often leads to disharmony. It is a prime advantage, however, because the investor maintains control over the investment. The right of each partner to a voice in management does not mean a dominant voice. With respect to most management decisions, regardless of importance, the majority vote of the individual partners is controlling.

COURT CASE

FACTS: Saverio Pugliese and Ben Mondello entered into an oral partnership to buy, train, and race a horse named Marco's Tale. The horse sustained a fracture to a bone in his foot, and after consulting with Mondello, Pugliese directed the horse's trainer to place Marco's Tale in a claiming race. The horse was claimed and sold for $50,000. A dispute arose between the two partners over the payment and litigation ensued in which each partner alleged various claims against the other. Mondello claimed that Marco's Tale was worth $250,000 and that Pugliese's management decision to place the horse in the claiming race had caused Mondello significant monetary loss.

OUTCOME: The court held that as a partner, Pugliese had authority to place Marco's Tale in the claiming race and the decision was made to further a legitimate business interest.

—*Pugliese v. Mondello*, 871 N.Y.S.2d 315 (N.Y. App. Div.)

30-5b INSPECT THE BOOKS

Each partner must keep a clear record of all transactions performed for the firm. The firm's books must be available to all partners, and each partner must explain, on request, the significance of any record made that is not clear. All checks written must show the purpose for which they are written. There may be no business secrets among the partners, and as a result, partners are entitled to a financial accounting.

COURT CASE

FACTS: Kerry King and Kevin Bullard orally formed K & K Logging, a partnership in which they were equal partners. King provided capital, and Bullard performed almost all the labor. King maintained the partnership checking account but gave Bullard checks each day. They sometimes used cash to pay business expenses, but Bullard had very few receipts for cash expenditures. King did not keep partnership money and his own money separate. Neither partner kept books of account. The partnership's records consisted mainly of bank account statements, deposit slips, and cancelled checks. Both made deposits to the partnership checking account from proceeds of the logging operations; cash was withheld from deposits made by both; and personal expenses of both were paid from partnership funds. Bullard closed the partnership checking account and withdrew the balance. King sued for an accounting, claiming that Bullard refused to account for the money taken by him.

OUTCOME: While there were substantial challenges in rendering an accounting, each partner had a right to an accounting, so the court ordered that an accounting be made.

—*King v. Bullard*, 257 S.W.3d 175 (Mo. Ct. App.)

30-5c CONTRIBUTION

A partner who pays a firm debt or liability from personal funds has a right to contribution from each of the other partners.

The Uniform Partnership Act states that "the partnership must indemnify every partner in respect of payments made and personal liabilities reasonably incurred by him in the ordinary and proper conduct of its business or for the preservation of its business or property." The partner has no right, however, to indemnity or reimbursement when (1) acting in bad faith, (2) negligently causing the necessity for payment, or (3) previously agreeing to bear the expense alone.

30-5d WITHDRAW ADVANCES

A partner has no right to withdraw any part of the original investment without the consent of the other partners. One partner, however, who makes additional advances in the form of a loan, has a right to withdraw this loan at any time after the due date. A partner also has a right to interest on a loan unless there is an agreement to the contrary. A partner has no right to interest on the capital account. Therefore, the firm should keep each partner's capital account separate from that partner's loan account.

30-5e WITHDRAW PROFITS

Each partner has the right to withdraw a share of the profits from the partnership at such time as specified by the partnership agreement. Withdrawal of profits could be by express authorization of the majority of the partners in the absence of a controlling provision in the partnership agreement.

30-6 Liabilities of Partners

A partner's liabilities include the following:

1. Liability for contracts
2. Liability for torts
3. Liability for crimes

30-6a CONTRACTS

Every member of a general partnership has individual personal liability for all the enforceable debts of the firm. A partner who incurs a liability in the name of the firm but acted beyond both actual and apparent authority has personal liability for that debt. The firm has no liability for such unauthorized acts. The firm also has no liability for illegal contracts made by any member of the firm, since everyone is charged with knowledge of what is illegal. Thus, if a partner in a wholesale liquor firm were to contract to sell an individual a case of whiskey, the contract would not be binding on the firm in a state where individual sales are illegal for wholesalers.

30-6b TORTS

A partnership has liability for the torts committed by a partner in the course of partnership business and in furtherance of partnership interests. When such liability occurs, the responsible partner has liability for indemnifying the partnership for any loss it sustains. The partnership does not have liability for deeds committed by one partner outside the course of partnership business and for the acting partner's own purposes unless the deeds have been authorized or ratified by the partnership.

In addition to the partnership's liability, a partner has liability for the torts of another partner committed in the course of partnership business. This rule applies to negligent as well as intentional acts, such as embezzlement of funds, even if the innocent partner has no knowledge of the acts.

30-6c CRIMES

Courts will not imply criminal liability. In order to be guilty of a crime, an individual partner must somehow have agreed to or participated in the crime. Individual partners cannot be punished if they are free of personal guilt. However, the partnership has liability for any penalty incurred by the act of a partner in the ordinary course of business. **In the ordinary course of business** means while the partner acts as a partner in the business and in the promotion of partnership interests. The partnership has liability to the same extent as the acting partner. Thus, the criminal acts of one partner can justify a fine levied on partnership assets. The partnership can be guilty of a crime even if no individual is convicted of the crime.

in the ordinary course of business
while the partner acts as a partner in the business and in the promotion of partnership interests

---

COURT CASE

FACTS: Injured in an auto accident, David Goodman hired the law partnership Holmes & McLaurin (H&M), composed of Edward Holmes and Edward McLaurin. McLaurin had primary responsibility and filed a complaint. He dismissed it without Goodman's knowledge, and when he failed to refile, the statute of limitations barred Goodman's claims. McLaurin told Goodman the tortfeasors' insurer was St. David's Trust, of Barcelona, Spain. It did not exist. He told Goodman he was negotiating with St. David's and faxed purported "settlement offers." Goodman accepted a $200,000 offer. McLaurin sent Goodman a memo allegedly from St. David's, showing how the settlement would be paid over two years. H&M's trust account transferred $25,000 to Goodman. McLaurin told him this represented "interim payments" by St. David's. For two years McLaurin assured Goodman he was still "dealing with" St. David's. McLaurin had Goodman execute a verification of a purported complaint against St. David's for breach of the settlement agreement and told him the complaint had been filed. When Goodman pressed McLaurin about its status, McLaurin sent him a copy of an e-mail supposedly from a Spanish lawyer. Nine years after the accident, Goodman was in another auto accident and again hired H&M to represent him. Four years later, he learned of McLaurin's dismissal and failure to refile regarding the first accident and that McLaurin had not sued St. David's. Using another law firm, he sued H&M and Holmes for damages for McLaurin's fraudulent conduct.

OUTCOME: The court said that fraudulent conduct is not in the ordinary course of business of a law partnership; therefore, the claim against H&M and Holmes was dismissed.

—*Goodman v. Holmes & McLaurin Attorneys at Law*, 665 S.E.2d 526 (N.C. Ct. App.)

30-7 Nature of Partnership Liabilities

The partners have joint liability on all partnership contractual liabilities unless the contract stipulates otherwise. They are jointly and severally liable for all tort liabilities. For joint liabilities, the partners must be sued jointly. If the firm does not have adequate assets to pay the debts or liabilities of the firm, the general partners, of course, have individual liability for the full amount of debts or liabilities. If all the partners but one are insolvent, the remaining solvent partner must pay all the debts even though the judgment is against all of them. The partner who pays the debt has a right of contribution from the other partners but as a practical matter may be unable to collect from them.

Withdrawing partners have liability for all partnership debts incurred up to the time they withdraw unless creditors expressly release these partners from liability. Under the Uniform Partnership Act, incoming partners have liability for all debts as fully as if they had been partners when the debt was incurred, except that this liability for old debts is limited to their investment in the partnership. Withdrawing partners may contract with incoming partners to pay all old debts, but this agreement does not bind creditors.

COURT CASE

FACTS: The Doe Run Company was a general partnership that operated a lead smelter. During the process of converting lead ore concentrates into purified lead, the smelting plant emitted lead-containing dust into the surrounding community. The company's air emissions were at elevated levels for a sustained period of time. The partners knew of the elevated levels and the detrimental impact of such emissions, but continued to operate the smelter at such levels. Several area children developed health problems due to exposure to the lead dust emitted by the plant and sued the three general partners of the Doe Run Company partnership, claiming the three were liable for the partners' and the partnership's negligence that caused the children injury.

OUTCOME: The court held that negligence on behalf of the partners and the partnership caused the children injury and that the individual partners were liable for the tort.

—*Blanks v. Fluor Corp.*, 450 S.W.3d 308 (Mo. App.)

30-8 Authority of a Partner

A partner has authority expressly given by the partnership agreement, by the partnership, and by law. By virtue of the existence of the partnership, each partner has the authority to enter into binding contracts on behalf of the partnership, as long as they are within the scope of the partnership business. Thus, each partner can, and often does, act as an agent of the partnership. This right can be limited by agreement as long as notice of the limitation is given.

In addition, a partner has all powers that it is customary for partners to exercise in that kind of business in that particular community. As in the case of an agent, any limitation on the authority the partner would customarily possess does not bind a third person unless made known. The firm, however, has a right to indemnity from a partner who causes the firm loss through violation of the limitation placed on the partner's authority.

30-8a CUSTOMARY OR IMPLIED AUTHORITY

Each partner in an ordinary trading partnership has the following customary or implied authority:

1. To compromise and release a claim against a third party
2. To receive payments and give receipts in the name of the firm
3. To employ or to discharge agents and employees whose services are needed in the transaction of the partnership business
4. To draw and indorse checks, to make notes, and to accept drafts
5. To insure the property of the partnership, to cancel insurance policies, or to give proof of loss and to collect the proceeds
6. To buy goods on credit or to sell goods in the regular course of business

LO ④
Partnership profits and losses

30-9 Sharing of Profits and Losses

The partnership agreement usually specifies the basis on which the profits and the losses are to be shared. This proportion cannot be changed by a majority of the members of the firm. If the partnership agreement does not fix the ratio of sharing the profits and the losses, they will be shared equally, not in proportion to the contribution of capital. If designated partners fix the ratio, it must be done fairly and in good faith. In the absence of a provision in the partnership agreement to the contrary, the majority of the partners may order a division of the profits at any time.

QUESTIONS

1. Under what circumstances will the law prevent individuals who are not actually partners from denying a partnership exists?
2. Is it possible for two or more people to create a partnership unintentionally?
3. Under the Uniform Partnership Act, what constitutes *prima facie* evidence of a partnership?
4. Why must a partner keep diligent records of transactions related to the partnership?
5. Is it necessary for a partnership to have a firm name?
6. What can personal creditors of one partner do to try to collect the partner's debt from the partnership?
7. What must a partner do if personal interest or advantage conflicts with the advantage of the partnership?
8. How is each partner's right to participate in the management of partnership business an advantage to partners? How is this a disadvantage?
9. To what extent is a general partner liable for enforceable debts against the partnership?
10. How will partnership profits and losses be shared if the partnership agreement does not fix the ratio?

CASE PROBLEMS

1. James Carpenter contracted with Austin Estates LP to buy property in Travis County. Unable to raise the funds, he contacted Sandra McBeth and her husband, James Reynolds. Carpenter told them disputes had arisen with the city regarding water and wastewater services but misrepresented the status of discussions as well as the city's willingness to negotiate. McBeth, Reynolds, and Carpenter executed a written agreement stating that McBeth and Reynolds would supply the earnest money to

CASE PROBLEMS (CONTINUED)

hold the property purchase option, try to obtain a loan, and enter into a limited partnership with Carpenter to buy the property. They formed a limited partnership, StoneLake Ranch, L.P., with Carpenter as president of the general partner. McBeth and Reynolds deposited $300,000 in escrow for the land purchase and an additional $500,000 in $100,000 increments to obtain extensions on the purchase deadline. Unable to complete the sale, and without notifying McBeth or Reynolds, Carpenter had the money in escrow disbursed to Austin Estates. Subsequently, he secured other investors, and they purchased the property through an entity with which Carpenter was affiliated. The property was sold for a profit of $140,000. In the ensuing lawsuit, Carpenter argued that he had no duty to disclose information to McBeth and Reynolds. Did he?

2. **LO ①, ③** Travis Murrell signed an agreement with 1401 New York Avenue Inc. to lease office space for his law practice. Prior to signing the lease, Murrell and Brown practiced law together, referring to their firm as "Murrell and Brown" in paperwork filed in federal court. In one filing, Brown also attached a copy of his resume, which listed his title as a partner for Murrell and Brown. Their firm had stationary with Murrell and Brown letterhead, had a joint checking account from which both Murrell and Brown could issue checks, and had an office sign with the name Murrell and Brown. Moreover, Murrell signed the lease in Brown's presence as "Travis A. Murrell, Partner." There was no evidence that Murrell and Brown shared income or profits generated by the firm, but their accountant filed partnership tax returns on their behalf. When a dispute over the lease arose, 1401 New York Avenue filed suit against Brown, alleging that he was liable as a partner of Murrell and Brown. Brown denied that he and Murrell had formed a partnership at the time Murrell signed the lease and refused liability associated with the lease agreement. Should the court hold Brown liable?

3. **LO ①, ④** Kenneth Badon and Drew Ranier had a law partnership, Badon & Ranier. While sharing office space with the partnership for fourteen years, Michael Garber maintained a separate law practice and his own letterhead and phone line. He did not have a written agreement with the firm, but his name appeared on its letterhead, as did the names of other attorneys associated with the firm at various times. The partnership paid Garber an hourly rate based on invoices he submitted showing an hourly billing, or one-half if there was a flat fee. He sometimes received bonuses. When the partnership declined a case, Garber sometimes undertook it and collected the entire fee. He corresponded with such clients on his and the partnership's letterheads. He did not share fees from his practice with Badon and Ranier. Garber sued them and the firm, alleging that he was a special partner entitled to an accounting and fee participation in the firm's law suits, particularly the tobacco litigation, oil and gas royalties, Medicaid recovery, and asbestos remediation suits. Garber alleged that he left half his billable hours and half the flat fees earned on their cases with the partnership as his contribution to the firm for office expenses and costs. Should Garber recover?

4. **LO ③** As a general construction contractor, WDF Inc. contracted to renovate schools in New York City. WDF subcontracted with JLG Architectural Products, LLC to supply windows for the renovation. Under the subcontract, a company called East Coast Window Installers Inc. was designated to install the windows for the project. The subcontract provided that JLG Architectural Products and East Coast Window Installers would perform and complete the subcontract work together. The subcontract also specifically acknowledged that JLG Architectural Products proposed the work in partnership with East Coast Window Installers. After completion of the project, a dispute over payment and the quality of workmanship arose between the parties. WDF claimed that JLG Architectural Products and East Coast Window Installers should be jointly and severally liable for any liability found against either party, because the two were partners in the window installation project. Was WDF correct?

5. **LO ②** Shirley Lach and Lynwood Wiseman formed Man O' War Limited Partnership. Robert Miller and Wiseman were the general partners, and Lach was one of the limited partners. Miller discovered he was terminally ill. He asked Lach to agree to Wiseman, Jeffery Mullens, (brother-in-law of Robert Miller), and Jonathan Miller (son of Robert Miller) as the new general partners. Under the partnership

agreement, new general partners could not be added without the consent of all partners. Lach objected as the proposal would permit the Miller family, which owned less than Lach's individual interest, to manage and control the business. Miller and Wiseman restructured the business form of the partnership to eliminate the necessity of acquiring Lach's consent to the proposed management change. By forming Man O' War Limited Liability Company and transferring the partnership's interests and assets in the proportions of their previous partnership ownership, they set up an entity run by a majority vote of the owners. The initial managers were Wiseman, Jonathan Miller, and Mullens. They dissolved the partnership. Unless a partner signed the documents validating the restructuring, that partner would have no voting rights in the LLC. Lach refused to sign. Records of the partnership's attorney showed the restructuring was to avoid requiring Lach's consent to the management changes. Lach sued, alleging the general partners had breached their fiduciary duty to her and the partnership. Had they?

LO ③, ④

6. Nu-Day Partnership, LLLP was a limited partnership that owned and managed various properties. Lon Day and his three children, Lee, Don, and Nancy, were the limited partners of Nu-Day Partnership. The general partner was LLD Management, a company formed and initially managed by Lon Day. Some time later, Lon transferred all of his interest in LLD Management to his children, Don and Nancy, effectively making them the sole owners of the general partner of Nu-Day Partnership. Lon also transferred certain real estate located in Atlanta to Nu-Day Partnership. Five years later, Lon claimed that the transfer of his interest in the general partner to his children was beyond his power and that he actually still had an ownership interest in Nu-Day Partnership. Lon also attempted to unilaterally transfer the Atlanta property back to himself and then to his wife. The children filed suit to quiet title to the Atlanta property and claimed that the transfer of their father's ownership interest in the general partner of Nu-Day Partnership was within his power. How should the court rule?

LO ②

7. Gerald and Gary Carlson were brothers who formed a farming and ranching partnership. Land used for partnership business was held and titled individually by each brother. The purpose of the partnership was to pay expenses associated with the individually held land, such as mortgage payments, insurance, and taxes. The partnership also paid many personal and household expenses for each partner's family. After the partnership began to experience financial difficulty, the partners expressly agreed to limit expenses to mortgage payments, real estate taxes, utilities, life insurance premiums, vehicle payments, and property and vehicle insurance premiums. Two years later, Gerald Carlson, as managing partner, stopped paying the premiums for Gary Carlson's life insurance policy but continued to pay for his own policy with partnership funds. Gerald told his brother that he was still making payments for the policy. Gary Carlson's life insurance policy was terminated for failure to pay the premiums. Gary Carlson sued for breach of fiduciary duty. Should Gerald Carlson be liable?

LO ①, ③

8. Warren Cole was a partner and employee of MAK West 55th Street Associates (MAK West), a limited partnership. The Partnership Agreement specified that upon Cole's termination of employment from MAK West, Cole would sell his partnership interest to Henry Macklowe within 90 days of Cole's termination. Some time later, Cole was terminated from the company, but the sale transaction of his interest in the partnership never occurred. The remaining partners later sold the partnership's sole asset and excluded Cole from any distribution from the asset sale. Cole sued, alleging that he still owned an interest in the partnership and was entitled to a portion of the proceeds from the sale. Was he?

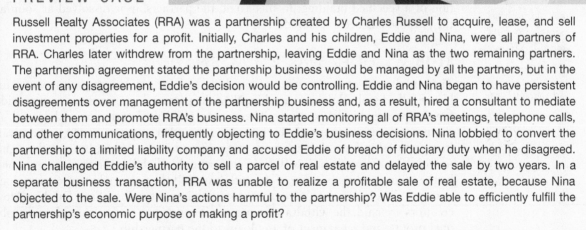

Dissolution of a Partnership

CHAPTER 31

LEARNING OBJECTIVES

1. List the methods the partners may use to dissolve a partnership.
2. Discuss the reasons why a court may order dissolution of a partnership.
3. Identify those events that result in dissolution of a partnership by operation of law.
4. Explain the activities that take place and should take place following dissolution.

PREVIEW CASE

Russell Realty Associates (RRA) was a partnership created by Charles Russell to acquire, lease, and sell investment properties for a profit. Initially, Charles and his children, Eddie and Nina, were all partners of RRA. Charles later withdrew from the partnership, leaving Eddie and Nina as the two remaining partners. The partnership agreement stated the partnership business would be managed by all the partners, but in the event of any disagreement, Eddie's decision would be controlling. Eddie and Nina began to have persistent disagreements over management of the partnership business and, as a result, hired a consultant to mediate between them and promote RRA's business. Nina started monitoring all of RRA's meetings, telephone calls, and other communications, frequently objecting to Eddie's business decisions. Nina lobbied to convert the partnership to a limited liability company and accused Eddie of breach of fiduciary duty when he disagreed. Nina challenged Eddie's authority to sell a parcel of real estate and delayed the sale by two years. In a separate business transaction, RRA was unable to realize a profitable sale of real estate, because Nina objected to the sale. Were Nina's actions harmful to the partnership? Was Eddie able to efficiently fulfill the partnership's economic purpose of making a profit?

The change in the relation of the partners caused by any partner's ceasing to be associated in the carrying on of the business is called **dissolution of a partnership**. The withdrawal of one member of a going partnership historically dissolved the partnership relation, and the partnership could not thereafter do any new business. The partnership continued to exist for the limited purpose of

dissolution of a partnership
change in relation of partners by elimination of one

winding up
taking care of outstanding
obligations and distributing
remaining assets

winding up or cleaning up its outstanding obligations and business affairs and distributing its remaining assets to creditors and partners. After the partnership completed this process, it was deemed terminated and went out of existence. However, if a partner wrongfully withdrew, the remaining partners could continue the business. The Revised Uniform Partnership Act somewhat modified these rules.

LO ①
Dissolution by partners

31-1 Dissolution by Acts of the Parties

Acts of the partners that dissolve a partnership include:

1. Agreement
2. Withdrawal or alienation
3. Expulsion

31-1a AGREEMENT

At the time they form the partnership agreement, the partners may fix the time when the partnership relation will cease. Unless they renew or amend the agreement, the partnership is dissolved on the agreed date. If no date for the dissolution is fixed at the time the partnership is formed, the partners may, by mutual agreement, dissolve the partnership at any time. Even when a definite date is fixed in the original agreement, the partners may dissolve the partnership prior to that time. In this case, the subsequent decision to dissolve the partnership does not bind the partnership unless all the partners consent to the dissolution.

Sometimes the parties do not fix a date for dissolving the partnership, but the agreement sets forth a particular purpose of the partnership, such as the construction of a specified building. In this event, the partnership is dissolved as soon as the purpose has been achieved.

31-1b WITHDRAWAL OR ALIENATION

The withdrawal of one partner at any time and for any reason unless wrongful historically dissolved the partnership. Now the partnership agreement may provide for the partnership to continue. There is no prescribed form for withdrawal. A partner can withdraw merely by informing the other partners of the withdrawal. In a partnership for a definite term, any partner has the power, but not the right, to withdraw at any time. A withdrawing partner has liability for any loss sustained by the other partners because of the withdrawal. If the partnership agreement does not set a dissolution date, a partner may withdraw at will without liability. After creditors are paid, the withdrawing partner is entitled to receive capital, undistributed profits, and repayment of any loans to the partnership.

If the partnership agreement or a subsequent agreement sets a dissolution date, the withdrawing partner breaches the contract by withdrawing prior to the agreed date. When a partner withdraws in violation of agreement, the withdrawal is wrongful and damages suffered by the firm may be deducted from that partner's distributive share of the assets of the partnership.

Similar to withdrawal, the sale of a partner's interest either by a voluntary sale or an involuntary sale to satisfy personal creditors does not of itself dissolve the partnership. But the purchaser does not become a partner by purchase, as the remaining partners cannot be compelled to accept as a partner anyone who might be *persona non grata* to them. The purchaser has a right to the capital and profits of the selling partner but not a right to participate in the management.

31-1c EXPULSION

The partnership agreement may, and should, contain a clause providing for the expulsion of a member, especially if the partnership has more than two members. This clause should spell out clearly the acts for which a member may be expelled and the method of settlement for such a partner's interest. A partnership may not expel a partner for self-gain. The partnership agreement should also set forth that the remaining partners agree to continue the business upon expulsion of a partner; otherwise, it might be necessary to wind up the partnership business and distribute all the assets to the creditors and partners, thereby terminating the partnership's existence.

COURT CASE

FACTS: Lois Fleck held 4 percent of JARL Investments, Limited Partnership, and was the general partner. Limited partners Janice Bioni and Daniel, Randall, and Lawrence Fleck each held 24 percent. Lawrence managed a restaurant that leased real estate owned by JARL. The restaurant stopped paying rent, and JARL paid many restaurant expenses. Janice, Daniel, and Randall, representing 72 percent of JARL, removed Lois as general partner of JARL and made themselves the general partners. The partnership agreement stated, "A Partner may be removed from the Partnership at any time upon the affirmative vote of all of the General Partners and a Majority in Interest (other than the Partner whose removal is proposed) of the Limited Partners." It also stated, "General Partners shall manage the affairs of the Partnership in a prudent and businesslike manner." Janice, Daniel, and Randall asked the court to confirm Lois's expulsion. Lois argued that "Partner whose removal is proposed" meant only a limited partner, so she could not be expelled without her consent.

OUTCOME: The court stated that Lois could be expelled. As the general partner, Lois owed a fiduciary responsibility to JARL. It would be absurd for her to be a fiduciary and required to operate "in a prudent and businesslike manner" yet not have the expulsion provision apply to her.

—*Jarl Investments, L.P. v. Fleck*, 937 A.2d 1113 (Pa. Super. Ct.)

31-2 Dissolution by Court Decree

Under certain circumstances, a court may issue a decree dissolving a partnership. The chief reasons justifying such a decree include:

LO ② Court-ordered dissolution

1. Insanity of a partner
2. Incapacity
3. Misconduct
4. Futility

31-2a INSANITY OF A PARTNER

A partner may obtain a decree of dissolution when a court declares another partner insane or of unsound mind.

31-2b INCAPACITY OF A PARTNER

If a partner develops an incapacity that makes it impossible for that partner to perform the services to the partnership that the partnership agreement contemplated, a petition may be filed to terminate the partnership on that ground. A member of an accounting firm who goes blind would probably be incapacitated to the extent of justifying dissolution. The court, not the partners, must be the judge in each case as to whether or not the partnership should be dissolved. As a rule, the incapacity must be permanent, not temporary, to justify a court decree dissolving the partnership. A temporary inability of one partner to perform duties constitutes one of the risks that the other partners assumed when they formed the partnership.

A question may arise as to whether an illness or other condition causing a partner's inability to perform duties is temporary or not. The safest procedure is for the remaining partners to seek a court order determining the matter.

31-2c MISCONDUCT

If one member of a partnership engages in misconduct prejudicial to the successful continuance of the business, the court may, on proper application, decree a dissolution of the partnership. Such misconduct includes habitual drunkenness, dishonesty, persistent violation of the partnership agreement, irreconcilable discord among the partners as to major matters, and abandonment of the business by a partner.

31-2d FUTILITY

All business partnerships are conducted for the purpose of making a profit. If this objective clearly cannot be achieved, the court may decree dissolution. One partner cannot compel the other members to assume continued losses after the success of the business becomes highly improbable, and further operation appears futile. A temporarily unprofitable operation does not justify dissolution. A court will issue a decree of dissolution only when the objective reasonably appears impossible to attain.

PREVIEW CASE REVISITED

FACTS: Russell Realty Associates (RRA) was a partnership created by Charles Russell to acquire, lease, and sell investment properties for a profit. Initially, Charles and his children, Eddie and Nina, were all partners of RRA. Charles later withdrew from the partnership, leaving Eddie and Nina as the two remaining partners. The partnership agreement stated the partnership business would be managed by all the partners, but in the event of any disagreement, Eddie's decision would be controlling. Eddie and Nina began to have persistent disagreements over management of the partnership business and, as a result, hired a consultant to mediate between them and promote RRA's business. Nina started monitoring all of RRA's meetings, telephone calls, and other communications, frequently objecting to Eddie's business decisions. Nina lobbied to convert the partnership to a limited liability company and accused Eddie of breach of fiduciary duty when he disagreed. Nina challenged Eddie's authority to sell a parcel of real estate and delayed the sale by two years. In a separate business transaction, RRA was unable to realize a profitable sale of real estate, because Nina objected to the sale. Eddie sued for dissolution of the partnership.

OUTCOME: The court issued a decree dissolving the partnership, because the economic purpose of the partnership was unreasonably frustrated by the partners' disruptive relationship.

—*Russell Realty Associates v. Russell*, 724 S.E.2d 690 (Va.)

The Revised Uniform Partnership Act modified this rule slightly. Under the revised law, a court may issue a dissolution decree when a partner has engaged in conduct that makes it not reasonably practicable to carry on the business with that partner or when the economic purpose of the partnership is unreasonably frustrated. A court may also issue a decree of dissolution when a partner's conduct makes it impractical to carry on business in conformity with the partnership agreement.

31-3 Dissolution by Operation of Law

LO ③
Events resulting in dissolution by operation of law

Under certain well-defined circumstances, a partnership will be dissolved by operation of law; that is to say, it will be dissolved immediately on the happening of the specified event. No decree of the court is necessary to dissolve the partnership.

The most common examples include:

1. Death
2. Bankruptcy
3. Illegality

31-3a DEATH

The death of one member of a partnership automatically dissolves the partnership unless the agreement provides it shall not be dissolved. A representative of the deceased may act to protect the interest of the heirs but cannot act as a partner. This is true even when the partnership agreement provides that the partnership is not to be dissolved by the death of a member. The representative receives the deceased partner's share of the partnership's profits.

The partnership agreement can provide for an orderly process of dissolution upon the death of a member. Thus, a provision that the surviving partners shall have twelve months in which to liquidate the firm and pay the deceased partner's share to the heirs is binding.

COURT CASE

FACTS: Marya Yee and Mary Donovan were partners in a law firm. The Partnership Agreement provided for the dissolution of the partnership upon the death of one of the partners, but contained a clause stating that the partnership could survive the death of a partner if a new partner was admitted within 90 days of the death. Yee died and within 90 days, Donovan, the surviving partner, admitted Andrea Calvaruso as a new partner. Yee's estate sued Donovan to obtain a judgment that the original partnership had been dissolved.

OUTCOME: The court held that the partnership was not dissolved, because the Partnership Agreement provided for continuation of the partnership if a new partner was hired.

—*Le Bel v. Donovan*, 117 A.D.3d 553 (N.Y. App. Div.)

31-3b BANKRUPTCY

People who have their debts discharged in bankruptcy no longer have responsibility for paying most of their debts, including those connected with the partnership. This destroys the unlimited liability of the partner that could otherwise exist, and the partner is not a good credit risk. Because of this, the law regards bankruptcy of a partner as automatically terminating the partnership. The trustee in bankruptcy has the right to assume control of the debtor partner's share of the partnership business, but the trustee does not become a partner. The trustee merely stands in the place of the partner to see that the creditors' interests are protected.

The bankruptcy of the partnership also terminates the partnership. The partnership cannot continue doing business, because its assets have been distributed in the course of the bankruptcy proceeding to pay its creditors.

31-3c ILLEGALITY

Some types of business are legal when undertaken, but because of a change in the law, they later become illegal. If a partnership is formed to conduct a lawful business and later this type of business becomes illegal, the partnership is automatically dissolved. A law restricting operating an insurance underwriting business to corporations dissolves a partnership formed for this purpose.

31-4 Effects of Dissolution

Historically, dissolution terminated the right of the partnership to exist unless there was an agreement to the contrary and had to be followed by the winding up of the business. Existing contracts could be performed. New contracts could not be made, except for minor contracts that were reasonably necessary for completion of existing contracts in a commercially reasonable manner. If part of the assets of the firm were goods in process, and additional raw materials had to be purchased before the goods in process could be converted into finished goods, these raw materials could be purchased.

The Revised Uniform Partnership Act mitigated these rules so that unless otherwise provided in the partnership agreement, a partnership may be continued when a partner departs if the remaining partners decide to buy out the departing partner's share. The power to buy out a departing partner does not even have to be expressly included in the partnership agreement. The remaining partners simply have to choose to buy out the departing partner.

After dissolution, a third person making a contract with the partnership stands in much the same position as a person dealing with an agent whose authority has been revoked by the principal. If the transaction relates to winding up the business, the transaction is authorized and binds the partnership and all partners just as though dissolution had not occurred. If the contract constitutes new business, it is not authorized, and the liability of the partnership and of the individual contracting partner depends on whether notice of dissolution has been properly given. Dissolution does not relieve the partners of their duties to each other. These duties remain until they wind up the business.

31-5 Notice of Dissolution

LO ④
Activities following dissolution

When a partnership is dissolved, creditors and other third parties who have done business with the old firm may not know of the change. For the protection of these third parties, the law requires that when dissolution is caused by an act of the parties, third persons who have done business with the firm must be given notice of the dissolution. If notice is not given, every member of the old firm may be held liable for the acts of the former partners that are committed within the scope of the business.

A partnership usually gives notice to customers and creditors by mail. It is sufficient to give the general public notice by publication, such as in a newspaper. When a new partnership or corporation has been organized to continue the business after dissolution and termination of the original partnership, the notice of dissolution will also set forth this information as a matter of advertising. If the name of the dissolved partnership included the name of a withdrawing partner, this name should be removed from the firm name on all stationery so that the firm will no longer be liable for the contracts or torts of that person.

Because a partnership exists as a result of the agreement of the parties to jointly operate a business, if one partner no longer agrees to operate the business, courts have held that dissolution of the partnership occurs. However, courts have required that the partner who no longer wishes to operate the business notify the other partners. Until such notice is given, the partnership will be held to continue.

Notice of dissolution is usually not deemed necessary in the following situations:

1. When the partnership was dissolved by the operation of law
2. When the partnership was dissolved by a judicial decree
3. When a dormant or a secret partner retires

31-6 Distribution of Assets

After the dissolution of a partnership, the partners share in the assets remaining after payment of the debts to creditors. The distribution of the remaining assets among the partners is usually made in the following order:

1. Partners who have advanced money to the firm or have incurred liabilities in its behalf are entitled to reimbursement.
2. Each partner is next entitled to the return of the capital that was contributed to the partnership.
3. Remaining assets are distributed equally, unless a provision in the partnership contract specifies an unequal distribution.

When a firm sustains a loss, the partners will share the loss equally, unless the partnership agreement provides otherwise.

QUESTIONS

1. Must all partnership activity cease after a partnership dissolves?
2. How are partnership assets distributed after dissolution?
3. If there is no dissolution date for the partnership, what rights does a withdrawing partner have?
4. Does the purchaser of a partner's interest in a partnership become a partner by the purchase? Explain.
5. What should the expulsion clause of a partnership agreement contain?
6. Does the temporary incapacity of a partner justify a court decree dissolving the partnership?

QUESTIONS (CONTINUED)

7. When is it unnecessary to give notice of dissolution to customers and creditors?

8. Why does the bankruptcy of a partner usually cause a partnership to automatically be terminated?

9. What is the potential liability if notice of dissolution is not given to third persons who have done business with the partnership?

10. How is a partnership dissolved when its primary business activity becomes illegal?

CASE PROBLEMS

LO ①, ④

1. Robert and James Matteson owned Matteson Communications, a partnership that sold and serviced two-way radios. James performed the service, installation, and repair work, and Robert handled customer service and sales. The business was conducted out of James's home. James owned 55 percent, and Robert owned 45 percent of the business. James told Robert he wanted to leave the business and retire, but they could not agree on dissolution. He sent Robert a notice of dissolution subject only to winding up, but he also said he did not want the business to shut down and offered a settlement. With James's approval, Robert transferred all the business property from his home and continued operation of the business as a limited liability company. James sent Robert a formal notice of dissolution demanding a wind-up of the partnership but died a month later. His estate sued Robert. What should the court order?

LO ③

2. Brothers Max and Robert Coleman were partners in a shipping business named Coleman Properties. After two decades of business, Robert committed suicide. Robert's widow, Debbie, attempted to recover her deceased husband's partnership interest. Debbie demanded that Max wind up the partnership's business and distribute the assets. Instead, Max changed the partnership name and continued to operate the business using partnership assets. Debbie sued Max for the "redemption value" or "buy-out value" of Robert's interest in the partnership. Max argued that Debbie was only a transferee of the partnership interest, not a partner, and was not entitled to the buy-out value of the partnership. Max claimed that Debbie was only entitled to the balance in Robert's capital account at the time of his death. What was Debbie entitled to receive?

LO ②

3. Clark Brevig and Joan McCormick executed a written partnership agreement reflecting their respective 75/25 percent interests in Brevig Land, Live & Lumber. McCormick worked as a landsperson and made financial contributions to the partnership. She also maintained the partnership's books and records. Brevig had responsibility for the day-to-day operation of the ranch. Brevig and McCormick made management decisions together. McCormick obtained an additional 25 percent interest in the partnership. Brevig and McCormick's relationship deteriorated as a result of disagreements about the management of the ranch, and particularly its debt load. Cooperation between Brevig and McCormick regarding the operation of the ranch and obtaining loans needed to fund the ranch ceased. McCormick sued Brevig and the partnership. Should the court order dissolution of the partnership?

LO ③

4. The Gast & Peters (G&P) partnership, composed of attorneys William Gast and Paul Peters, merged with Schmid, Mooney & Frederick (SM&F). The merger agreement required pending contingent fee cases to be valued by G&P and SM&F on the date of merger with percentages of the fees apportioned between the firms. The percentages of the fees would become "vested" in G&P and SM&F. When Gast and Peters left SM&F, two cases, Yager and Stenson, had not been concluded. Gast worked on Yager with his new firm, Gast, Ratz & Gutierrez (GR&G), and received a fee of $97,892. According to the merger agreement, 60 percent of the fee, or $58,735, was to go to G&P and 40 percent to SM&F. But Gast and GR&G paid only 24 percent, $23,494, to G&P. Peters kept the Stenson file when he left SM&F. G&P was entitled to 88.75 percent, or $74,032, of the Stenson fee, and SM&F

issued a check for that amount to G&P. Peters deposited the check in a G&P account and told Gast that since they each shared equally in G&P, he was taking 50 percent, or $37,016. Peters said he was withholding $17,620 from Gast's 50 percent share because Peters had been underpaid by that amount from the Yager fees. Gast sued, asserting that he was entitled to the $17,620. Peters alleged that dissolution of G&P had not relieved Gast of his obligation to properly account for profits of the firm, which he did not do when disbursing the Yager fees. Who is correct?

5. Beierling conceived a plan to develop educational software for teachers. After sharing her idea with Katie Urbain and Maureen Clinesmith, the three women formed a partnership. The partnership planned to stream online games into classrooms through paid subscriptions. Clinesmith initially loaned the partnership $10,000 and the three decided to receive equal portions of the profit, after the repayment of Clinesmith's loan. After several months, the partnership began to have problems. Clinesmith and Beierling told Urbain that she was no longer a partner and blocked her access to the partnership e-mail account. They dissolved the partnership, which never made a profit. While winding up the affairs of the partnership, Clinesmith assessed the value of partnership's limited assets and assumed ownership of the assets, since they were less than the $10,000 loan she made to the partnership. Urbain sued Clinesmith and Beierling, stating that the partnership was wrongfully dissolved and that she was entitled to damages. Was she correct?

LO ①, ④

6. Ronald Bendalin and Eldon Youngblood formed YB Partnership to provide loan preparation services to the mortgage banking industry. The partnership agreement contained a "service commitment" provision requiring Bendalin to provide his normal services to the partnership for ten years. The ten-year service commitment was required for Bendalin to receive his entire portion of the partnership's reserve fund. A separate paragraph of the partnership agreement stated that the partnership would continue until there was a bankruptcy and unanimous consent among the partners to dissolve the partnership. Bendalin withdrew from the partnership prior to fulfilling the ten-year service commitment. YB Partnership filed suit, claiming that Bendalin's withdrawal was wrongful, because it breached the ten year-term of the partnership. Did Bendalin wrongfully withdraw from the partnership?

LO ①

7. Brothers Rudy and Richard Corrales formed RC Electronics (RCE), a partnership that repaired and sold computer tape drives. They were the only partners of RCE. Rudy managed day-to-day business operations, while Richard helped secure financing and contributed business advice. After several lucrative years, Richard discovered that Rudy had formed a competing business that provided the exact same services as RCE. After Richard inquired about the other business, Rudy cut off all communications with Richard. Richard withdrew from the partnership and then sued Rudy and RCE for breach of fiduciary duty, misappropriation, and an accounting. Should the partnership be ordered to pay damages to Richard?

LO ①

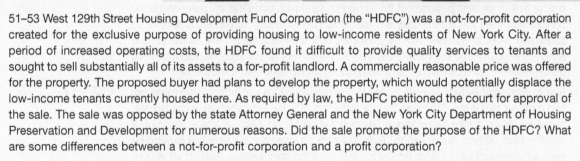

CHAPTER
32

Nature of a Corporation

LEARNING OBJECTIVES

1. List the different classifications and kinds of corporations.
2. Discuss how a corporation is formed and potential promoter liability.
3. Name the types of powers a corporation has and the significance of *ultra vires* contracts.

PREVIEW CASE

51–53 West 129th Street Housing Development Fund Corporation (the "HDFC") was a not-for-profit corporation created for the exclusive purpose of providing housing to low-income residents of New York City. After a period of increased operating costs, the HDFC found it difficult to provide quality services to tenants and sought to sell substantially all of its assets to a for-profit landlord. A commercially reasonable price was offered for the property. The proposed buyer had plans to develop the property, which would potentially displace the low-income tenants currently housed there. As required by law, the HDFC petitioned the court for approval of the sale. The sale was opposed by the state Attorney General and the New York City Department of Housing Preservation and Development for numerous reasons. Did the sale promote the purpose of the HDFC? What are some differences between a not-for-profit corporation and a profit corporation?

Corporations have become a widely used form of business organization. No matter what the size of a business, a corporation may be formed to run it. Because of the variety of uses to which corporations may be put, there are different types of corporations. They are also classified by the state of incorporation because, as an entity of the state, its laws of incorporation govern them.

32-1 Classification by Purpose

LO ①
Types of corporations

Corporations may be classified according to their purpose or function as public or private.

32-1a PUBLIC CORPORATIONS

A **public corporation** is one formed to carry out some governmental function. Examples of public corporations include a city, a state university, and a public hospital. The powers and functions of public corporations may be much greater than those of private corporations conducted for profit. Public corporations may, for example, have the power to levy taxes, impose fines, and condemn property. Public corporations are created by the state primarily for the purpose of facilitating the administration of governmental functions.

Some public bodies, such as school boards, boards of county commissioners, and similar bodies, are not true public corporations but have many similar powers. Such powers include the right to sue and be sued; the power to own, buy, and sell property; and the power to sign other contracts as an entity. These bodies are called **quasi-public corporations**, *quasi* meaning "as if" or "in the nature of."

public corporation
one formed for governmental function

quasi-public corporation
public body with powers similar to corporations

32-1b PRIVATE CORPORATIONS

Private corporations are those formed by private individuals to perform some nongovernmental function. They, in turn, include:

1. Not-for-profit corporations
2. Profit corporations

private corporation
one formed to do nongovernmental function

Not-for-Profit Corporations. A **not-for-profit corporation** is one formed by private individuals for some charitable, educational, religious, social, or fraternal purpose. Because this type of corporation is not organized for profit, it does not distribute income or profits to members, officers, or directors, and it usually does not issue stock. As a legal entity like any other corporation, it can sue and be sued as a corporation, buy and sell property, and otherwise operate as any other corporation. A person acquires membership in a not-for-profit corporation by agreement between the charter members in the beginning and between the present members and new members thereafter.

not-for-profit corporation
one formed by private individuals for a charitable, educational, religious, social, or fraternal purpose

PREVIEW CASE REVISITED

FACTS: 51–53 West 129th Street Housing Development Fund Corporation (the "HDFC") was a not-for-profit corporation created for the exclusive purpose of providing housing to low-income residents of New York City. After a period of increased operating costs, the HDFC found it difficult to provide quality services to tenants and sought to sell substantially all of its assets to a for-profit landlord. A commercially reasonable price was offered for the property. The proposed buyer had plans to develop the property, which would potentially displace the low-income tenants currently housed there. As required by law, the HDFC petitioned the court for approval of the sale. The sale was opposed by the state Attorney General and the New York City Department of Housing Preservation and Development for numerous reasons.

OUTCOME: The court held that the purpose of the not-for-profit corporation would be better served by denying the petition to sell the property.

—*51–53 West 129th Street HDFC v. Attorney General*, 95 A.D.3d 674 (N.Y. App. Div.)

for-profit corporation
one organized to run a business and earn money

stock corporation
one in which ownership is represented by stock

shares of stock
certificates representing ownership in a stock corporation

close or closely held corporation
one with a very small number of shareholders

Profit Corporations. A **for-profit corporation** is one organized to run a business and earn money. In terms of number and importance, **stock corporations** organized for profit constitute the chief type. Certificates called **shares of stock** represent ownership in a stock corporation. The number of shares of stock owned and the charter and the bylaws of the corporation determine the extent of one's rights and liabilities.

A for-profit corporation that has a very small number of people who own stock in it is called a **close corporation** or a **closely held corporation**. Because of the small number of stockholders, they normally expect to be (and are) active in the management of the business.

Many close corporations that meet the federal requirements, including a limitation on the number of stockholders, choose to be designated Subchapter S corporations for federal income tax purposes. Unlike other corporations, a Subchapter S corporation files only an information tax return. It does not pay corporate income tax. The owners report the profit of the corporation as income on their personal income tax returns. This results in tax savings. The corporation's profits are not taxed twice—once when shown on a corporate tax return, and a second time when shown as income from the corporation to the owners on their personal tax returns.

32-2 Classification by State of Incorporation

domestic corporation
one chartered in the state

foreign corporation
one chartered in another state

alien corporation
one chartered in another country

Corporations may be classified depending on where they were incorporated. A corporation is a **domestic corporation** in the state where it received its initial charter; it is a **foreign corporation** in all other states. If incorporated in another country, a corporation may be referred to as an **alien corporation**. The corporation can operate as a foreign corporation in any other state it chooses as long as it complies with the registration or other requirements of the other state.

32-3 Formation of a Corporation

LO ②
Formation of corporation and liability

promoter
one who takes initial steps to form corporation

One who acts as the **promoter** usually takes the initial steps of forming a corporation. A corporation can be organized in any state the promoter chooses. A lot of preliminary work must be done before the corporation comes into existence. The incorporation papers must be prepared, a registration statement may need to be drawn up and filed with the Securities and Exchange Commission (SEC) and the appropriate state officials, the stock must be sold, and many contracts must be entered into for the benefit of the proposed corporation. Filing with the SEC is not required in the case of smaller corporations.

Minor defects in the formation of a corporation may generally be ignored. In some instances, however, the defect is of a sufficiently serious character that the attorney general of the state that approved the articles of incorporation of the corporation may obtain the cancellation or revocation of such articles. In other cases, the formation of the corporation is so defective that the existence of a corporation is ignored, and the people organizing the corporation are held liable as partners or joint venturers.

32-4 Liability on Promoter's Contracts and Expenses

The corporation does not automatically become a party to contracts made by the promoter. After it is incorporated, a corporation will ordinarily approve or adopt the contracts made by the promoter. The approval may be either express or by the corporation's conduct. Once approved, such contracts bind the corporation, and it may sue on them.

The promoter may avoid personal liability on contracts made for the benefit of the corporation by including a provision in the contract that the promoter incurs no personal liability if the corporation does or does not adopt the contract. In the absence of such a provision, the promoter may have liability. Courts look at whether the other contracting party knew the corporation was not yet in existence. The wording of the contract is also very significant in determining whether it binds the promoter either pending the formation of the corporation or after it has come into existence.

COURT CASE

FACTS: Ideal Image Development Corp. (Ideal) franchised retail centers that performed cosmetic treatments. On March 30, Randy Hetrick and his wife, Cindy, respectively, as president and secretary of CIRA Corp., signed a franchise agreement with Ideal. CIRA was not incorporated until April 2. The Hetricks signed additional documents warranting that CIRA was buying the franchise. They spent hundreds of thousands of dollars to develop and sustain an Ideal franchise through CIRA. A year later, the Hetricks sold CIRA to another corporation, which failed. The Hetricks sued Ideal in their individual capacities, alleging that it had misrepresented the cost of the franchise and its profitability.

OUTCOME: The court held that CIRA by implication adopted the pre-incorporation agreement the Hetricks had signed as promoters. Thus, it was CIRA who had the right to sue on the agreement, not the Hetricks individually.

—*Hetrick v. Ideal Image Development Corp.*, 372 Fed. Appx. 985 (11th Cir.)

Along with the adoption of the promoter's contracts, the corporation may or may not pay the expenses of the promoter in organization of the corporation. After the corporation comes into existence, it customarily reimburses the promoter for all necessary expenses in forming the corporation. This may be done by a resolution passed by the board of directors.

ETHICAL POINT
Regardless of the law on the subject, do you think it is ethical for a promoter to be able to be relieved of liability on contracts made for the benefit of the corporation?

32-5 Issuance of Stock

When a new corporation is about to be formed, written agreements to buy its stock will generally be made in advance of the actual incorporation. Such agreements

subscription agreement
written agreement to buy stock

subscriber
one who agrees to buy stock in proposed corporation

are called **subscription agreements**. In such a case, the subscription agreement by a prospective stockholder or investor, called a **subscriber**, constitutes merely an offer to buy. In most jurisdictions, this offer may be revoked any time prior to acceptance. As the offeree, the corporation cannot accept the subscription until the state issues its charter. If an existing corporation sells stock, it can accept all subscriptions immediately and make them binding contracts. If the promoter is to be paid by means of a stock option, the corporation can make such a contract with the promoter before any services are performed. Most state laws provide that a minimum amount of stock must be sold and paid for before the corporation can begin operations.

Once a valid subscription agreement is signed, the subscriber has rights in the corporation even if the stock certificates have not been received or issued. If stock is fully paid for, even without an agreement, the purchaser becomes a shareholder.

COURT CASE

FACTS: Stock certificates indicated Melissa Hanks held twelve shares of Diabetes Self Management Center Inc. (DSMC). Rebecca Abel, Deborah Hotard, and Hanks ran DSMC and represented themselves in corporate documents as shareholders with Abel and Hotard each owning 48 shares, and Hanks owning 12, even though no payment had been made for any stock. Abel called a shareholder meeting for June 22. Hotard objected, saying that no stock had been issued, and no par value set for it, so there were no shareholders. She appeared at the meeting only to object. Hanks was elected a board member, and Abel, as president of DSMC, terminated Hotard's employment. Hanks and Abel sold their interest in the corporation to Louisiana Health Care Group Inc. On March 6, the board set the par value of the stock at $1,000 with a deadline for payment. Louisiana Health Care paid for its shares by the deadline. Hotard did not. At a shareholder's meeting on

March 12, the shareholders ratified the June 22 and March 6 actions. Hotard sued to have the June 22 shareholders' meeting declared invalid and the court recognize her status as a subscriber.

OUTCOME: Although there was no evidence Hanks, Abel, or Hotard had subscribed for stock, the court said that once the shares of DSMC had a value assigned, and payment was received, they could be considered fully paid and properly issued without a subscription agreement. Since there were shareholders at the meeting of June 22, and the shareholders present constituted a quorum, the appointment of Hanks to the board of directors, and the actions taken by the board that included Hanks were valid.

—*Hotard v. Diabetes Self Management Center Inc.*,
838 So.2d 94 (La. Ct. App.)

32-6 Articles of Incorporation

articles of incorporation
document stating facts about corporation required by law

The written document setting forth the facts prescribed by law for issuance of a certificate of incorporation or a charter and asserting that the corporation has complied with legal requirements is the **articles of incorporation**. Once approved by the state, the articles determine the authority of the corporation. This document constitutes a contract between the corporation and the state. So long as the corporation complies with the terms of the contract, the state cannot alter the articles in any material way without obtaining the consent of the stockholders. The articles include such information as the name of the corporation, the names of the people forming the corporation (the **incorporators**), and the amount and types of stock the corporation has authorization to issue. The incorporators elect a board of directors and begin business, which constitutes acceptance of the charter and binds all parties.

incorporators
people initially forming a corporation

32-7 Powers of a Corporation

A corporation has three types of powers: express, incidental, and implied.

LO ③
Types of corporate powers

32-7a EXPRESS POWERS

The statute or code under which a corporation is formed and, to a lesser degree, the corporation's articles of incorporation determine its express powers. In a few instances, the state constitution sets forth the powers of a corporation. The statutes limit a corporation's powers to what they grant, and a corporation may not do what statutes prohibit.

32-7b INCIDENTAL POWERS

Certain powers always incidental to a corporation's express powers or essential to its existence as a corporation include but are not limited to:

1. Having a corporate name
2. Having a continuous existence
3. Having property rights
4. Making bylaws and regulations
5. Engaging in legal actions
6. Having a corporate seal

Corporate Name. A corporation must have a corporate name. The members may select any name they wish, provided that it does not violate the statutes or that another firm or corporation within the state does not use it. Many of the states have statutes regulating corporate names. For example, statutes frequently require the name to end with *Corporation* or to be followed by the word *Incorporated*, an abbreviation thereof, or other indication of corporate status.

Continuous Existence. The existence of the corporation continues for the period for which the state grants the charter. This period can be perpetual, and this feature of a corporation makes this form of organization valuable. The death of a stockholder does not dissolve the organization. Sometimes people refer to this characteristic as *perpetual*, or *continuous, succession*.

Property Rights. A corporation has the right to buy, sell, and hold property necessary in its functioning as a corporation and not foreign to its purpose.

Bylaws and Regulations. The organization needs rules and regulations to govern it and to determine its future conduct. They must conform to the statutes and must not be contrary to public policy. The corporation's board of directors adopts these rules, called the corporation's **bylaws**.

bylaws
rules enacted by directors to govern corporation's conduct

Legal Actions. Long considered incidental to corporate existence is the corporation's power to sue in its own name. Because a corporation may be composed of hundreds or thousands of stockholders, it would be a cumbersome, if not impossible, task to secure the consent of all the stockholders each time a corporation needed to bring a suit. A corporation may likewise be sued in the corporate name. In some states, a corporation may represent itself in low-level trial courts by an officer/shareholder who is not an attorney, just as a person who is not an attorney may represent himself or herself.

Corporate Seal. A corporation has the incidental power to have and to own a seal. Normally, a corporation need not use a seal except (1) in executing written instruments that require the use of a seal when executed by natural individuals, or (2) in carrying out transactions for which special statutory requirements require the use of the seal.

32-7c IMPLIED POWERS

In addition to incidental or express powers conferred on all corporations, a corporation has the implied power to do all acts reasonably necessary for carrying out the purpose for which the corporation was formed. A corporation may borrow money and contract debts if such acts are necessary for the transaction of the corporate business. It may make, indorse, and accept negotiable instruments. It has the power to acquire and convey property and to mortgage or lease its property in case such transactions are necessary for carrying on its business. Corporation codes, as a rule, expressly list various implied powers so that they constitute express powers.

32-8 *Ultra Vires* Contracts

ultra vires **contract**
contract exceeding
corporation's powers

Any contract entered into by a corporation that goes beyond its powers is called an *ultra vires* **contract**. As between the parties to the contract, the corporation and the third person, the contract generally binds them. However, a stockholder may bring an action to prevent the corporation from entering into such a contract or to recover damages from the directors or officers who have caused loss to the corporation by such contracts. In extreme cases, the attorney general of a state may obtain a court order revoking the articles of incorporation of the corporation for frequent or serious improper acts that make it proper to impose such an extreme penalty.

COURT CASE

FACTS: West Daniels Land Association was incorporated to hold, own, and manage grazing land for the livestock owned by its shareholders. In order to generate revenue for the association, the board of directors voted to advertise the property for lease to the highest bidder. It leased all the association's land to a nonshareholder. Ray Okelberry, a shareholder, sued.

OUTCOME: The court said that by leasing all its land to a nonshareholder, the association acted contrary to the limited purpose for which it was incorporated, as expressed in the articles of incorporation.

—*Okelberry v. West Daniels Land Ass'n,*
120 P.3d 34 (Utah)

QUESTIONS

1. Explain the difference between public and private corporations.

2. How is a tax savings achieved when a corporation is designated a Subchapter S corporation?

3. Is a corporation automatically a party to contracts made by promoters?

4. When does a subscription agreement become binding upon a corporation and a subscriber?

5. What does the law frequently require to be included in a corporation's name?

6. What is a corporation's articles of incorporation, and what is their importance?

7. How may a shareholder respond to an *ultra vires* contract entered into by the corporation?

8. What powers does a corporation have in addition to incidental or express powers?

CASE PROBLEMS

1. Acacia Country Club Co. (the club), a nonprofit golf club corporation, decided to sell some real estate. Acacia Development Co., Ltd. (ADC) agreed to buy 17.9 acres. The club shareholders had authorized the sale of 16 acres. After the sale, a club member was upset and brought a lawsuit. In the suit, ADC claimed that the lack of shareholder authority for the sale was a cloud on title to the land and thus that the sale was beyond the power of the club. Assuming the sale did breach the regulations by which the club operated, was this a valid argument for ADC against the club? **LO ③**

2. The Resource Center was formed to serve mentally handicapped persons in Chautauqua County. The next year, it affiliated as a chapter with and agreed to be bound by the rules of NYSARC Inc., a not-for-profit corporation. Fifty years later, The Resource Center wanted to disaffiliate from NYSARC and keep its assets. It asked a court to determine that it had done so. NYSARC's bylaws stated that all property owned by one of its chapters was held in trust for NYSARC. Should the court allow disaffiliation of The Resource Center and allow it to keep its property? **LO ①**

3. On November 1, Joseph Mastroianni who owned an unimproved lot leased it to Domenic D'Attilo and Tony Dilorio doing business as Fairfield County Paving & Construction Inc. D'Attilo and Dilorio both signed the lease above their names. The initial term was for one year, with an option to renew. The lease required the lessee to "clear, properly grade, pave, and secure by fencing, the perimeter of the lot with a gate at the entrance" and "use the property in compliance with the zoning regulations." At the time the lease was signed, Fairfield County Paving & Construction Inc. was not in existence. The following November 19, the lessees sent Mastroianni notice of renewal. Mastroianni had sent the lessees a notice to quit. A lawsuit ensued in which Mastroianni alleged the property had not been properly tended as required by the lease and that D'Attilo and Dilorio were personally liable. Were they? **LO ②**

4. Brookhaven Academy Inc.'s articles of incorporation stated several purposes, including: to own and operate schools; to purchase, lease, and sell property; and "to have and to exercise all powers conferred by the laws of the State of Mississippi upon corporations." Brookhaven Academy formed Brookhaven Academy Educational Foundation Inc. (the "Foundation") and transferred assets via a lease to the Foundation for educational activities. As a shareholder, Dudley Keene filed suit against Brookhaven Academy. Keene argued that Brookhaven Academy was a specific-purpose corporation, created to provide education to youth, and that the formation of the Foundation and lease of property was *ultra vires*. Was Keene correct? **LO ③**

5. Luvena Miegs was a manicurist who wanted to open her own salon. She drew up a business plan and found a building to lease but was unable to secure a loan for the start-up costs. Madge Mobley, the grandmother of Miegs's husband, agreed to loan Miegs $50,000. Miegs opened a bank account **LO ②**

CASE PROBLEMS (CONTINUED)

and listed the owner of the account as "Luvena Miegs dba Allure Studio Inc." Mobley sent a check to Miegs and then wired funds to the bank account set up for the business. The outgoing wire-transfer referred to the beneficiary account as "Luvena K. Miegs." Two days later, Allure Studio Inc. filed its articles of incorporation, listing Miegs as the promoter. Miegs was the sole shareholder, and she and her husband were named as the two corporate directors. The entire $50,000 loan proceeds were spent on Allure Studio Inc.'s start-up costs, and Miegs made payments on the loan balance with checks bearing the name Allure Studio Inc. After Mobley's death, Miegs defaulted on the loan. Mobley's estate filed suit against Miegs individually to recover the outstanding loan balance. Miegs claimed that the loan was made to Allure Studio Inc. and that she was not personally liable as the promoter. Should Miegs be liable?

 6. Willie Ann Madison incorporated Cherokee Children & Family Services Inc. (CCFS) as a nonprofit public benefit corporation and was its executive director. CCFS was to provide childcare brokerage services to low-income families. The corporation had no members. Its income was almost exclusively state and federal grants. CCFS paid for travel to Hawaii, personal travel the next year, and a trip to London—all by Madison and several of her relatives. Madison was regularly paid bonuses of 50 percent of her salary. She bought a building and leased it to CCFS (signing on behalf of CCFS) for five years at an annual rent of $49,932. During the first year, the lease was renegotiated at a retroactive annual rent of $72,000. Prior to expiration, the lease was renegotiated again to reflect leasing 20,000 square feet, although the building had only 9,700 square feet, at an annual rent of $210,000. The next year, three members of the board of directors approved the payment of "prorated back rent" for the contract period. This was $210,000 rent times five, minus what CCFS had paid in rent to Madison. This amounted to $437,000 and was paid to Madison's company. The state attorney general sued to dissolve CCFS, saying it had abandoned its public purpose and had become devoted to private gain. Should it be dissolved?

 7. Universal Real Estate Solution Inc. was a closely held corporation with two shareholders, Randy Snowden and William Wendell, each of whom owned 50 percent of the corporation's shares. Universal bought, sold, and rented real estate properties. Snowden maintained properties owned by the corporation and negotiated the purchase of new real estate. Wendell funded the corporation. In one business transaction, Snowden located a group of houses for Universal to purchase, but Wendell felt the properties were in poor condition and did not want the corporation to purchase the properties. Snowden then purchased the properties himself and less than a year later resold the properties to Universal at a significant markup. Snowden then sold his shares in Universal to Wendell for $1 and Wendell assumed the corporation's debt. Universal filed suit against Snowden, alleging among other things, that Snowden breached his fiduciary duty to Universal by withholding material information. Snowden argued that he owed a fiduciary duty to the other shareholder of the closely held corporation but not to the corporation itself. Was he correct?

 8. Robert Hayden entered into an oral agreement with P. Zarkadas that provided he would be paid one-third of the legal fees recovered by Zarkadas in any personal injury cases upon which Hayden performed work. After entering into the agreement, Zarkadas created a professional corporation, P. Zarkadas, P.C., and the corporation adopted the agreement. When Hayden was not paid according to the agreement, he sued Zarkadas and the corporation, alleging she was personally liable because the corporation did not exist at the time of the agreement. Is she personally liable?

Ownership of a Corporation

CHAPTER 33

LEARNING OBJECTIVES

1. Define capital stock.
2. List the various types of stock and stock rights.
3. Explain what dividends are and how they may be paid.
4. Name the various laws regulating the sale of securities, exchanges, and brokers.

PREVIEW CASE

E-Smart Technologies Inc. was a publicly traded company that developed and manufactured biometric "smart" cards through the use of fingerprint identification technology. Despite promising research results, E-Smart Technologies had difficulty raising revenue necessary to continue operations. The company's CEO, Mary Grace, sought to encourage investment by issuing e-mails and press releases about new business growth. One such press release announced that Samsung had made an "irrevocable" purchase order for 20 million cards and that E-Smart Technologies estimated the order would generate profits of at least $100 million. The press release also stated that this was likely to be the first in a series of such contracts. In reality, Samsung had simply signed a supply agreement with E-Smart Technologies, giving Samsung the option to purchase cards if it wanted to. Samsung had not actually submitted a purchase order for any cards. The SEC sued E-Smart Technologies and Grace, alleging that they misrepresented material facts to investors in connection with the sale of securities. Why is it important that investors have accurate information regarding a company's contracts?

LO 1
Capital stock

capital stock
declared value of outstanding stocks

share
unit of stock

The **capital stock** of the corporation is the declared money value of its outstanding stock. The owners subscribe and pay for this stock. Generally, not all the stock that a corporation may issue need be subscribed and paid for before the corporation begins operation. After a corporation is formed, the board of directors authorizes the sale of stock. The amount of capital stock authorized in the charter cannot be altered without the consent of the state and a majority of the stockholders. The capital stock is divided into units called **shares**.

33-1 Ownership

A person achieves ownership in a stock corporation by acquiring title to one or more shares of stock. Owners are known as **shareholders** or **stockholders**. A person may obtain shares of stock by subscription either before or after organization of the corporation, or shares may be obtained in other ways, such as by gift or purchase from another shareholder.

33-2 Stock Certificate

The amount of ownership (the number of shares owned) may, but need not, be evidenced by a stock certificate. A certificate is not the actual stock, just written evidence of ownership of stock. If there is a certificate, it shows on its face the number of shares represented, the face value of each share if any, and the signatures of the officers. The fact that a person is named on the certificate, either by issuance or endorsement, and has possession of it is *prima facie* evidence that the person is the owner of the certificate. If ownership is not evidenced by a stock certificate, ownership is shown on the corporation's corporate record book.

COURT CASE

FACTS: When Bertha Vicknair formed Albany Wrought Iron Manufacturing Inc., two stock certificates, each for 250 shares, were issued—one to Vicknair, and the other to her daughter, Deborah. Vicknair later consulted with her lawyer about transferring her stock to Deborah. Vicknair endorsed her stock certificate before a witness and gave it to her lawyer, and the secretary recorded the alleged transfer on the corporate ledger for the lawyer. After a court declared Vicknair incompetent and appointed another daughter, Diana, to care for her affairs, Deborah alleged that she owned Vicknair's shares.

OUTCOME: Because Deborah never had possession of the endorsed certificate, she was not the owner of the stock.

—*In re Interdiction of Vicknair*, 822 So.2d 46 (La. App.)

33-3 Transfer of Stock

A stock certificate indicates the manner in which the stock may be transferred to another party. The owner may use a blank form on the back of the certificate in making a transfer. The signature of the previous owner gives the new holder full possession and the right to exchange the certificate for another made out by the corporation to the new owner. Whenever an owner transfers stock, the new owner should have the certificate exchanged for a new one showing the correct name so that the corporation's books will show the correct stockholders' names. Stockholders who are not registered do not have the rights and privileges of stockholders and will not receive any profits of the corporation.

If a broker holds the stock, and certificates have not been issued, the broker may transfer the stock at the written direction of the owner. Under the Uniform Stock Transfer Act, the unregistered holder of stock has a right to the distribution that represents a return of capital. As under common law, the unregistered holder has no right to any distribution that represents a share of the profits.

It is very common, particularly in the case of corporations with few shareholders, that there are restrictions on the sale of the corporation's stock. This allows the current shareholders to control the management of the corporation. Such restrictions frequently require a shareholder to offer the stock for purchase to the corporation or other shareholders on the same terms as a third party is willing to purchase them. While not favored by courts, such restrictions on sale are binding on stockholders.

33-4 Classes of Stock

LO ②
Types of stock and rights

Stock is divided into many classes. The articles of incorporation and the laws under which the corporation is organized determine the classes. The two principal classes of stock are:

1. Common stock
2. Preferred stock

33-4a COMMON STOCK

Common stock is the simplest form of stock and the normal type of stock issued. The owners of common stock control the corporation because they may vote for members of the board of directors. The board, in turn, hires the individuals who manage and operate the corporation. Unless selected as a director or appointed as an officer, a stockholder has no voice in the running of the corporation beyond the annual vote for the board of directors. Common stockholders have the right to a proportionate share of the assets of a corporation on dissolution.

common stock
stock that entitles owner to vote

33-4b PREFERRED STOCK

Preferred stock differs from common stock in that the holder of this stock has some sort of special advantage or preference. In return for a preference, the preferred stockholders usually give up two rights that common stockholders retain—the right to vote in stockholders' meetings and the right to participate in profits beyond the percentage fixed in the stock certificate.

preferred stock
stock giving special advantage

The preference granted may pertain to the division of dividends, to the division of assets on dissolution, or to both of these. Most often, the preference relates both to dividends and assets. Calling particular stock "preferred" does not tell what preference the holder has. The stock certificate will indicate the type of preference, although the certificate of incorporation governs the exact rights of preferred shareholders. Preferred stock may be:

1. Preferred as to assets
2. Preferred as to dividends
3. Participating
4. Nonparticipating

Preferred as to Assets. Stock preferred as to assets gives the holder an advantage only in the event of liquidation. Preferred stockholders receive their proportionate share of the corporation's assets prior to any share going to common shareholders.

Preferred as to Dividends. Stock preferred as to dividends means the preferred stockholders receive a dividend before any common stockholders receive one. Preferred stock usually states the percentage it receives. Once this percentage has been paid to preferred stockholders, any money remaining may be paid as a dividend to holders of common stock. This right to preference as to dividends may be cumulative or noncumulative.

cumulative preferred stock
stock on which all dividends must be paid before common dividends

Cumulative preferred stock is preferred stock on which all dividends must be paid before the common stock receives any dividend. These dividends on cumulative preferred stock must be paid even for years in which the corporation did not earn an adequate profit to pay the stated dividend.

noncumulative preferred stock
stock on which current dividends must be paid before common dividends

Noncumulative preferred stock is preferred stock on which dividends have to be paid only for the current year before common stock dividends are paid. Thus, dividends do not have to be paid for years in which the corporation does not make a profit or even for years in which the directors simply do not declare a dividend.

The difference between cumulative and noncumulative preferred stock can be significant if the corporation operates at a loss in any given year or group of years. For example, a corporation that has $1 million outstanding common stock and $1 million outstanding 7 percent preferred stock operates at a loss for two years and then earns 21 percent net profit the third year. Noncumulative preferred stock would be entitled to only one dividend of 7 percent. The common stock is entitled to the remaining 14 percent. Cumulative preferred stock would be entitled to three preferences of 7 percent, or 21 percent in all, before the common stock is entitled to any dividend. If the company were to earn a net profit each year equal to only 7 percent on the preferred stock, and the preferred stock were noncumulative, the directors could pass the dividend the first year and declare a 7 percent dividend on both the common and the preferred stocks for the second year. Because the common stockholders elect the directors, the common stockholders could easily elect directors who would act in ways to help them as much as possible. For that reason, the law provides that preferred stock be cumulative unless specifically stated to be noncumulative. All of this can occur, however, only when the corporation earns a profit but fails to declare a dividend. Unless the stock certificate expressly states that it is cumulative, the preference does not cumulate in the years during which the corporation operated at a loss.

participating preferred stock
stock that shares with common stock in extra dividends

Participating. Shareholders with **participating preferred stock** are entitled to share equally with the common shareholders in any further distribution of dividends made after the common shareholders have received dividends equal to those that the preferred shareholders have received by virtue of their stated preference. Thus, 7 percent participating preferred stock may pay considerably more than 7 percent annually. If the preferred stock is to participate, this right must be expressly stated on the stock certificate and in the articles of incorporation. It can participate only according to the terms of the articles of incorporation. The articles may provide that the preferred stock shall participate equally with the common stock. Conversely, the articles may provide, for example, that the preferred stock be entitled to an additional 1 percent for each additional 5 percent the common stock receives.

nonparticipating preferred stock
stock on which maximum dividend is stated percentage

Nonparticipating. **Nonparticipating preferred stock** is stock on which the maximum dividend is the percentage stated on the stock. If it is 7 percent nonparticipating preferred, for example, 7 percent annually would be the maximum to which the preferred stockholders would be entitled, no matter how much the corporation earned. The law presumes that stock is nonparticipating in the absence of a provision to the contrary in the articles of incorporation.

33-5 Kinds of Stock

In addition to the two classes of stock, stock comes in several different kinds. These include par-value stock, no-par-value stock, treasury stock, and watered stock.

33-5a PAR-VALUE STOCK

Stock to which a face value, such as $25, $50, or $100, has been assigned and that has this value printed on the stock is **par-value stock**. Preferred stock usually has a par value. The law requires that when a corporation issues par-value stock in return for payment in money, property, or services, the par value of the stock must be equal in value to the money, property, or services. This relates only to the price at which the corporation may issue the stock to an original subscriber. It has no effect on the price paid between a shareholder and a buyer thereafter. The price a buyer pays a shareholder ordinarily equals the market price, which may be more or less than the par value. If a corporation sells par-value stock at a discount, the purchaser incurs liability to subsequent creditors of the corporation for the discount.

par-value stock
stock with assigned face value

33-5b NO-PAR-VALUE STOCK

Stock to which no face value has been assigned is **no-par-value stock**. A corporation may issue no-par-value stock at any price, although some states do set a minimum price, such as $5, for which it can be issued. Common stock may be either par-value or no-par-value stock.

no-par-value stock
stock without face value

33-5c TREASURY STOCK

If a corporation purchases stock that it has sold, this reacquired stock is referred to as **treasury stock**. When a corporation first offers stock for sale, less sales resistance may be encountered if the prospective purchaser can be assured that the corporation will repurchase the stock on request. Treasury stock also may be reacquired by gift. The directors fix the price at which reacquired stock may be sold, and it need not be at par value. Until the corporation resells it, no dividends can be paid on it, nor can it be voted.

treasury stock
stock reacquired by a corporation

COURT CASE

FACTS: Wilson Lake Country Club (WLCC) was a for-profit corporation that operated a golf course. It was authorized to issue common stock having a par value of $10 per share. WLCC could issue stock only to members, and it could not issue more than one share of stock to any one person. WLCC's board of directors approved the transfer of 715 shares of its treasury stock to the Wilson Lake Members Corporation (WLMC), which comprised some dues-paying members of WLCC. WLCC did not receive any money in exchange for this stock transfer. The effect of the transfer was to shift control of WLCC from its shareholders to WLMC and its board. Some WLCC members sued, asking the court to declare the stock transfer void because no consideration was received for it.

OUTCOME: The court stated that since WLCC did not receive any payment or benefit in return for the transfer of the treasury stock, it was invalid.

—*Morison v. Wilson Lake Country Club*, 874 A.2d 885 (Me.)

33-5d WATERED STOCK

watered stock
stock paid for with property
of inflated value

Stock issued as fully paid up, but paid with property of inflated values, is said to be **watered stock**. If someone conveys real estate actually worth $40,000 for stock having a par value of $100,000, the stock is watered to the extent of $60,000. Watering stock may be prohibited outright, but in any case it cannot be used to defraud creditors. In the event of insolvency, the creditors may sue the original recipients of watered stock for the difference between the par value and the actual purchase price. This may not be true, of course, if the creditors knew the stock was watered. Although creditors are allowed these rights, most state statutes do not prohibit the watering of stock by corporations other than public utility companies.

If a person pays for stock with overvalued real estate, the extent of the watering should be determinable with reasonable accuracy. However, if a person pays in the form of patents, trademarks, blueprints, or other similar assets, the extent of the watering may be difficult to determine because the value of such assets might be extremely difficult to determine.

33-6 Stock Options

stock option
right to purchase shares
from corporation at set price

A **stock option** is a contract entered into between a corporation and an individual. The contract gives the individual the option for a stated period of time to purchase a prescribed number of shares of stock in the corporation at a given price. If a new corporation sells stock to the public at $2 a share, the individual having the option must also pay $2 but may be given two, five, or even ten years in which to exercise the option. If the corporation succeeds, and the price of the stock goes up, the individual will, of course, want to exercise the option and buy at the low option price and then resell at the higher market price. If the corporation fails, the option does not have to be exercised. Existing corporations may give officials of the corporation an option to purchase a given number of shares of stock in lieu of a salary increase. If the market price of the stock rises, an official may make a capital gain by buying the stock, holding it for the required time, and selling it. The income tax on a capital gain may be considerably less than that on other income. This type of compensation may be more attractive to top management officials than a straight increase in salary, enabling a corporation to retain their services at a lower cost than with a salary increase. If the corporation makes stock available to all the corporation's employees, the option price may be less than the fair market value.

33-7 Dividends

LO ③
Dividends and how they
may be paid

dividend
profits of a corporation
allocated to stockholders

The profits of a corporation belong to the corporation until the directors set them aside for distribution to the stockholders by declaring a **dividend**. Dividends may be paid in cash, stock, or other property.

A cash dividend usually can be paid only out of retained earnings with two exceptions. A cash dividend may be paid out of donated or paid-in surplus. Also, for corporations with depleting assets, such as coal mines, oil companies, lumber companies, and similar industries, cash dividends may be paid out of capital.

Stock dividends may be in the corporation's own stock or in stock the corporation owns in another corporation. When in the corporation's own stock, they are usually declared out of retained earnings, but they can be paid out of other surplus accounts. A stock dividend of the corporation's own stock cannot be declared if the corporation has no surplus of any kind. Dividends also may be paid in the form of property that the corporation manufactures, but this seldom happens.

The declaration of a dividend on either common or preferred stock depends almost entirely on the discretion of the directors. The directors, however, must act reasonably and in good faith. This means minority stockholders can ask the court to require a corporation to declare a dividend out of surplus profits only when they clearly have a right to a dividend.

COURT CASE

FACTS: Marilyn Holt-Smith and Kristin Yates formed Holt–Smith & Yates Advisors Inc. (HSYA), each owning 50 percent. They were both officers and directors. In addition to salaries, they each received identical year-end payments based on the profitability of the business. After Yates missed 25 to 30 percent of work, Holt-Smith offered to buy her out. After months of negotiations and several confrontations, Yates's employment at HSYA was suspended and then terminated. At a December meeting of the board of directors, which Yates did not attend, no vote was held on whether to make the normal year-end profitability payment. As a result, HSYA had

$1.7 million cash on hand. Yates sued, alleging that the year-end payment was a constructive dividend and that failure to declare it was a breach of Holt-Smith's fiduciary duty.

OUTCOME: The court held that Holt-Smith wanted to pressure Yates to sell her interest in the company on Hold-Smith's terms. Therefore, Holt-Smith had acted in bad faith with respect to the failure to declare the constructive dividend.

—*Yates v. Holt-Smith,* 768 N.W.2d 213
(Wis. Ct. App.)

Once the directors declare a cash dividend, it cannot later be rescinded. It becomes a liability of the corporation the minute the directors declare it. A stock dividend, in contrast, may be rescinded at any time prior to the issuance and delivery of the stock.

33-8 Laws Regulating Stock Sales

In order to protect investors in corporations, a number of laws have been enacted. These laws seek to prevent fraudulent activities and protect investors from loss as a result of stockbrokers becoming insolvent.

LO ④
Laws regulating securities sales, exchanges, brokers

33-8a BLUE-SKY LAWS

The purpose of so-called **blue-sky laws** is to prevent fraud through the sale of worthless stocks and bonds. State blue-sky laws apply only to intrastate transactions.

blue-sky laws
state laws to prevent sale of worthless stock

These security laws vary from state to state. Some prescribe criminal penalties for engaging in prohibited transactions. Others require that dealers be licensed and that a state commission approve sales of securities before a corporation offers them to the public.

33-8b SECURITIES ACT OF 1933

prospectus
document giving specified information about a corporation

Because the state blue-sky laws apply only to intrastate sales of securities, in 1933 Congress passed the federal Securities Act to regulate the sale of securities in interstate commerce. Anyone offering a new issue of securities for sale to the public must register it with the SEC and issue a **prospectus**, which is a document containing specified information about the stock offering and the corporation, including the information contained in the registration statement. An issuer includes a person in control of a corporation, such as an officer, director, or controlling shareholder. The SEC may exempt securities if it is not necessary to protect investors because of the small amount involved; however, every issuance of securities of more than $5 million must be registered. The act does not regulate the sale or purchase of securities after the corporation has properly issued them.

In addition to filing the registration statement with the SEC, a corporation must furnish a prospectus to each purchaser of the securities. Full information must be given relative to the financial structure of the corporation. This information must include the types of stock to be issued; types of securities outstanding, if any; the terms of the sale; bonus and profit-sharing arrangements; options to be created in regard to the securities; and any other data the SEC may require.

The company, its principal officers, and a majority of the board of directors must sign the registration statement. If either the registration statement or the prospectus contains misstatements or omissions, the SEC will not permit the corporation to offer the securities for sale. If the corporation sells them before the SEC ascertains the falsity of the information, an investor may rescind the contract and sue for damages any individual who signed the registration statement. Any failure to comply with the law also subjects the responsible corporate officials to criminal prosecution.

33-8c SECURITIES EXCHANGE ACT OF 1934

The security exchanges and over-the-counter markets constitute the chief markets for the sale of securities after the initial offerings. In 1934, Congress passed the Securities Exchange Act to regulate such transactions. The act requires the registration of stock exchanges, brokers, and dealers of securities traded in interstate commerce and SEC-regulated, publicly held corporations. The law also requires regulated corporations to make periodic disclosure statements regarding corporate organization and financial structure.

Under rule-making authority of the Securities Exchange Act, the SEC has declared it unlawful for any broker, dealer, or exchange to use the mails, interstate commerce, or any exchange facility to knowingly make an untrue statement of a material fact or to engage in any other act that would defraud or deceive a person in the purchase or sale of any security. This provision applies to sellers as well as buyers.

PREVIEW CASE REVISITED

FACTS: E-Smart Technologies Inc. was a publicly traded company that developed and manufactured biometric "smart" cards through the use of fingerprint identification technology. Despite promising research results, E-Smart Technologies had difficulty raising revenue necessary to continue operations. The company's CEO, Mary Grace, sought to encourage investment by issuing emails and press releases about new business growth. One such press release announced that Samsung had made an "irrevocable" purchase order for 20 million cards and that E-Smart Technologies estimated the order would generate profits of at least $100 million. The press release also stated that this was likely to be the first in a series of such contracts. In reality, Samsung had simply signed a supply agreement with E-Smart Technologies, giving Samsung the option to purchase cards if it wanted to. Samsung had not actually submitted a purchase order for any cards. The SEC sued E-Smart Technologies and Grace, alleging that they misrepresented material facts to investors in connection with the sale of securities.

OUTCOME: The court held that Grace misrepresented material facts and misled investors.

—SEC v. E-Smart Technologies Inc., 74 F.Supp.3d 306 (D.D.C.)

The act requires certain disclosures of trading by **insiders**—officers, directors, and owners of more than 10 percent of any class of securities of the corporation. The corporation or its stockholders suing on behalf of the corporation may recover any profits made by an insider in connection with the purchase and sale of the corporation's securities within a six-month period. Such profits are called **short-swing profits**. A group of individuals, each of whom owns less than 10 percent but who together own more than 10 percent of a corporation's stock and act together to acquire, hold, vote, or dispose of stock, is also subject to the short-swing profits rule.

A 1975 amendment to this act attempts to foster competition among securities brokers by reducing regulation of the brokerage industry.

insider
officer, director, or owner of more than 10 percent of stock in a corporation

short-swing profits
profits made by insider buying and selling corporation's stock in six months

33-8d SECURITIES INVESTOR PROTECTION ACT OF 1970

In order to protect investors when the stockbroker or investment house with which they do business has severe financial difficulty that threatens financial loss to the customers, Congress passed the Securities Investor Protection Act of 1970. This federal law requires generally that all registered brokers and dealers and the members of a national securities exchange contribute a portion of their gross revenue from the securities business to a fund regulated by the Securities Investor Protection Corporation (SIPC).

The SIPC is a not-for-profit corporation whose members are the contributors to the fund. If the SIPC determines that any of its members has failed or is in danger of failing to meet its obligations to its customers and finds any one of five other specified indications of its being in financial difficulty, the SIPC may apply to the appropriate court for a decree adjudicating the customers of such member in need of the protection provided by the act. If the court finds the requisite financial problems, it will appoint a trustee for liquidation of the SIPC member. The SIPC fund may be used to pay certain customers' claims, up to $500,000 for each customer.

QUESTIONS

1. How may an individual obtain shares of stock in a company?

2. If a corporation does not issue certificates of stock, how is ownership of stock shown?

3. What preference might be granted to preferred stockholders?

4. Why do corporations with a small number of stockholders frequently have restrictions on the transfer of its stock?

5. What does it mean if stock is 7 percent nonparticipating?

6. Must a purchaser of par-value stock always pay a price in money, property, or services equal to the par value of the stock?

7. How does treasury stock differ from other kinds of stock?

8. Why would management officials of a corporation find stock options to be attractive?

9. In what different forms may dividends be issued to shareholders?

10. Why must insiders of a corporation disclose their trading?

CASE PROBLEMS

LO ①

1. Robert Cook was a stockholder in Puritas Metal Products Inc. (PMP). Sale of the stock was restricted so that before a transfer of stock could take place, the stock had to be offered for sale to the corporation and the other shareholders on the same terms. Later, the PMP cancelled Cook's stock and reissued it to his trust, of which he and his wife, Barbara, were trustees. Under the terms of the trust, at Cook's death, the PMP shares were to be retained by the trustees of the trust to be "held" as a Marital Trust. After Cook's death, Barbara alleged that no transfer of PMP stock took place and that she should be allowed to administer the shares and vote them at shareholder meetings. Did Cook's death result in a transfer of the stock so that the corporation and other shareholders should be permitted to purchase it?

LO ②

2. Trados Inc. developed software to translate documents into foreign languages. After several years of growth, the company sought to raise venture capital in order to transition to a publicly held company. Several venture capitalists invested in Trados, and in exchange for their investment, they were given shares of preferred stock in Trados. The preferred stock gave the venture capitalists a payment preference in the event the company was liquidated and allowed the preferred stockholders to appoint directors of Trados. The preferred stock also paid a cumulative dividend each year, with any unpaid dividends resulting in an increased liquidation preference. Trados's revenues grew steadily, but the company remained unprofitable. Trados was unable to generate enough returns to pay the common shareholders any dividends. The board of directors approved a merger of Trados with SDL, whereby SDL paid $60 million in cash and stock for Trados. Trados's certificate of incorporation classified such merger as a liquidation and thus the preferred stockholders received the vast majority of the proceeds. Common shareholders received nothing from the sale. Marc Christen, a common shareholder, sued the directors. Christen claimed that the directors had a fiduciary duty to continue operating Trados independently to try to yield returns for the common stock. Did the board breach its fiduciary duty by approving a sale that yielded nothing to common shareholders?

LO ④

3. Investment funds managed by Alan Patricof Associates (APA) and Stuart and David Epstein were stockholders of Xpedite Systems Inc. Xpedite wanted to provide an exit strategy for investors, including APA and the Epsteins. Robert Chefitz, a representative from APA, and David Epstein, both board members, were on a committee evaluating strategies. Premiere Technologies Inc. proposed a

CASE PROBLEMS (CONTINUED)

stock-for-stock merger and acquisition. Although APA and the Epsteins were sophisticated investors, they failed to analyze Premiere or its assets meaningfully. Xpedite's board agreed to the merger and unanimously voted to recommend it. Premiere required APA and the Epsteins to execute agreements granting irrevocable proxies to Premiere to vote their stock in favor of the merger. Two months later, Premiere's registration statement for the merger became effective, and the merger was approved. Three months later, Premiere announced that it would have a shortfall in its revenues. This was not mentioned in the registration statement. The price of Premiere stock dropped 69 percent from the merger price. APA and the Epsteins sued Premier, its officers, and its directors, saying the decline in stock price was the result of material defects in the registration statement in violation of securities law. Should they succeed?

4. Henry Reget owned 19 of the 1,811 outstanding shares of Astronautics Corp. of America. He filed suit asking the court to order payment of dividends. The company had never paid a dividend. The corporation acquired significant profits, but the board of directors decided that it would be better off reinvesting its profits in research, development, acquisition of other companies and their assets, and profit sharing for its employees. Can Reget compel payment of a dividend? **LO ③**

5. Bank of America (BoA) sold numerous mortgage-backed securities to American International Group Inc. (AIG). After an economic downturn, Bank of America was exposed to significant litigation risk resulting from a high mortgage default rate. In its Annual Report, BoA noted that it "face[d] substantial potential legal liability and significant regulatory action, which could have a material adverse effect on [its] cash flows, financial condition, and results of operations." BoA's Annual Report also noted the difficulty in predicting litigation costs, but gave a detailed explanation of its method of accruing reserves to cover such costs. There was a considerable amount of information in the public domain about AIG's mortgage-backed securities and what portion of that portfolio had been purchased from BoA. Several national newspapers reported that AIG intended to sue BoA and gave detailed figures of AIG's claims. After AIG filed suit against BoA for claims related to the sale of mortgage-backed securities, several institutional stockholders of BoA sued the bank. The stockholders claimed that BoA had misled investors by failing to disclose the imminence and amount of a potential AIG lawsuit. Did BoA mislead investors? **LO ④**

6. Richard Rosso died owning shares of Strata Real Estate Corp. The actual certificates and other documents relating to Strata had been destroyed in a flood, and Richard had thrown all his papers out. His wife, Sandra, said the shares were owned by Richard and her jointly and therefore were not part of his estate. Linda, Richard's daughter from a previous marriage, sued, alleging that the shares had been owned by Richard alone. Under his will, she was entitled to one-sixth of his estate. She argued that even if the shares had been owned jointly and destroyed, Richard's disposal of them destroyed that joint ownership. Did Richard's disposal of the certificates alter the ownership of the stock? **LO ①**

Management and Dissolution of a Corporation

LEARNING OBJECTIVES

① Discuss how a corporation is managed and controlled by the stockholders.
② Identify the rights of stockholders.
③ Specify the responsibilities and powers of directors and officers.
④ Describe how a corporation is combined or dissolved.

PREVIEW CASE

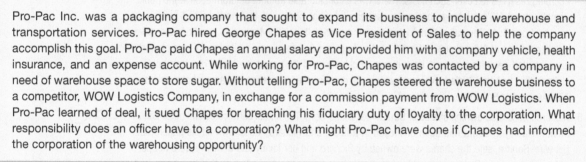

Pro-Pac Inc. was a packaging company that sought to expand its business to include warehouse and transportation services. Pro-Pac hired George Chapes as Vice President of Sales to help the company accomplish this goal. Pro-Pac paid Chapes an annual salary and provided him with a company vehicle, health insurance, and an expense account. While working for Pro-Pac, Chapes was contacted by a company in need of warehouse space to store sugar. Without telling Pro-Pac, Chapes steered the warehouse business to a competitor, WOW Logistics Company, in exchange for a commission payment from WOW Logistics. When Pro-Pac learned of deal, it sued Chapes for breaching his fiduciary duty of loyalty to the corporation. What responsibility does an officer have to a corporation? What might Pro-Pac have done if Chapes had informed the corporation of the warehousing opportunity?

LO ①
Management and control of corporations

As an artificial being, existing only in contemplation of law, a corporation can perform business transactions only through actual people, acting as agents. The directors as a group act as both fiduciaries and agents. To the corporation, they are trustees and have responsibility for breaches of trust. To third parties, directors as a group constitute agents of the corporation.

The board of directors controls the corporation by selecting the chief agents of the corporation, such as the president, the vice president, the treasurer, and other officers, who in turn perform the managerial functions. The board of directors also is the primary policy-making body of the corporation. The chief executives in turn appoint subagents for all the administrative functions of the corporation. These subagents constitute agents of the corporation, however, not of the appointing executives.

The directors and officers manage the corporation. Because the stockholders elect the board of directors, they indirectly control it. However, neither an individual director nor a stockholder, merely by reason of membership in the corporation, can act as an agent or exercise any managerial function.

Even a stockholder who owns 49 percent of the common stock of a corporation has no more right to work for, or take a direct part in running, the corporation than another stockholder or even a stranger would have. In contrast, a person who owns even 1 percent of a partnership has just as much right to work for the partnership and to participate in its management as any other partner.

34-1 Stockholders' Meetings

In order to make the will of the majority binding, the stockholders must act at a duly convened and properly conducted stockholders' meeting.

A corporation usually holds a regular meeting such as its annual meeting at the place and time specified in the articles of incorporation or in the bylaws; notice of the meeting is ordinarily not required (see Illustration 34-1). The directors of the corporation or, in some instances, a particular officer or a specified number

---

ILLUSTRATION 34-1 Notice of a Stockholders' Meeting

WATERS, MELLEN AND COMPANY
900 West Lake Avenue
Cincinnati, Ohio 45227

NOTICE OF ANNUAL MEETING OF STOCKHOLDERS
August 22, 20–

The Annual Meeting of Stockholders of Waters, Mellen and Company, a Delaware corporation, will be held in the Auditorium. Building C, at the headquarters of the Company, 900 West Lake Avenue, Cincinnati, Ohio on Wednesday, August 22, 20–at 10.00 A.M. for the following purposes:

1. To elect a Board of thirteen Directors of the Company;

2. To consider and vote upon the ratification of the appointment of Arthur Andrews & Co. as independent public accountants for the Company for the fiscal year May 1, 20–through April 30, 20– and

3. To transact such other business as may properly come before the meeting or any adjournment thereof.

The Accompanying Proxy Statement provides additional information relating to the above matters.

The Board of Directors has fixed the close of business on Friday, July 6, 20– as the record date for the determination of stockholders entitled to notice of and to vote at this meeting or any adjournment thereof. The stock transfer books will not be closed.

Please sign and mail the accompanying proxy in the envelope provided. If you attend this meeting and vote in person, the proxy will not be used.

By order of the Board of Directors.

RICHARD P. ROBERTS
Secretary

July 18, 20–

IMPORTANT—You can help in the preparation for the meeting by mailing your proxy promptly.

of stockholders, may call a special meeting. The corporation must give notice specifying the subjects to be discussed for a special meeting.

Meetings of the stockholders theoretically act as a check on the board of directors. Corporations must have one annually. If the directors do not carry out the will of the stockholders, they can seek to elect a new board that will carry out their wishes. In the absence of fraud or bad faith on the part of the directors, this procedure constitutes the only legal means by which the investors can exercise any control over their investment.

34-1a QUORUM

quorum
minimum number of shares required to be represented to transact shareholder business

A stockholders' meeting, in order to be valid, requires the presence of a **quorum**, or a minimum number of shares that must be represented in order that business may be lawfully transacted. At common law, a quorum consists of the stockholders actually assembled at a properly convened meeting. A majority of the votes cast by those present expresses the will of the stockholders. Statutes, bylaws, or the articles of incorporation now ordinarily require that a majority of the outstanding stock be represented at the stockholders' meeting in order to constitute a quorum. This representation may be either in person or by proxy.

COURT CASE

FACTS: A court ordered that an annual meeting of Stan Lee Media Inc. (Stan) be held and appointed a "special master" to conduct the meeting. A number of proxies were submitted, including ones signed by Stephen Gordon. While Gordon had signed the proxies, he had not indicated on them whether he was in favor of or against the matters being voted on. Because he had not indicated a vote, the master held the proxies invalid, and as a result, there was not a quorum of shareholders present for the meeting. Another shareholder argued

the proxy was valid therefore there were enough shareholders "present" to hold an election of the board of directors.

OUTCOME: The court held that there was no requirement that in order to be represented at a meeting a share be voted. Gordon's proxy should not have been rejected.

—P.F.P. Family Holdings, L.P. v. Stan Lee Media Inc.,
252 P.3d 1 (Co. Ct. App.)

LO ②
Stockholders' rights

34-1b VOTING

The right of a stockholder to vote is the most important right, because only in this way can the stockholder exercise any control over investment in the corporation. Only stockholders shown by the stockholders' record book have a right to vote. A person who purchases stock from an individual does not have the right to vote until the corporation makes the transfer on its books. Subscribers who have not fully paid for their stock, as a rule, may not vote. State corporation laws control the right to vote. Voting and nonvoting common stock may be issued if the law permits.

Two major classes of elections are held during stockholders' meetings in which the stockholders vote. They include the annual election of directors and the elections to approve or disapprove some corporate acts that only the stockholders can authorize. Examples of some of these acts are consolidating with another corporation, dissolving, increasing the capital stock, and changing the number of directors.

Giving Minority Stockholders a Voice. Each stockholder normally has one vote for each share of common stock owned. In the election of a board of directors, the candidates receiving a majority of the votes of stock actually voting win. In corporations with 500,000 stockholders, control of 10 percent of the stock often suffices to control the election. In all cases, the owners of 51 percent of the stock can elect all the directors. This leaves the minority stockholders without any representation on the board of directors. To alleviate this situation, two legal devices exist that may give the minority stockholders a voice, but not a controlling voice, on the board of directors. These devices are:

1. Cumulative voting

2. Voting trusts

Some state statutes provide that in the election of directors, a stockholder may cast as many votes in the aggregate for any one or more directors as is equal to the number of shares owned multiplied by the number of directors to be elected. This method of voting is called **cumulative voting**. Thus, if a stockholder owns ten shares, and ten directors are to be elected, 100 votes may be cast. All 100 votes may be cast for one director. As a result, under this plan of voting, the minority stockholders may have some representation on the board of directors, although still a minority.

cumulative voting
stockholder has votes equal to shares owned times number of directors to be elected

Under a voting trust, stockholders give up their voting privileges by transferring their stock to a trustee and receiving in return **voting trust** certificates. This is not primarily a device to give the minority stockholders a voice on the board of directors; but it does do that, and often in large corporations it gives them a controlling voice. Twenty percent of the stock always voted as a unit has more effect than individual voting. State laws frequently impose limitations on voting trusts, as by limiting the number of years that they may run.

voting trust
device whereby stock is transferred to trustee to vote it

Absentee Voting. Under the common law, only stockholders who were present in person were permitted to vote. Under the statutory law, the articles of incorporation, or the bylaws, stockholders who do not wish to attend a meeting and vote in person may authorize another to vote their stock for them. The person authorized to vote for another is known as a **proxy**. The written authorization to vote is also called a proxy (see Illustration 34-2). Corporations send proxy forms to shareholders; the law does not require any special form for a proxy.

proxy
person authorized to vote for another; written authorization to vote for another

As a rule, a stockholder may revoke a proxy at any time. If a stockholder should sign more than one proxy for the same stockholders' meeting, the proxy having the later date would be effective. A proxy may be good in some states for only a limited period of time. If the stockholder attends the stockholders' meeting in person, this acts as a revocation of the proxy.

The management of a corporation may legally solicit proxies for candidates selected by the board of directors. However, the incumbent board must disclose the proposals fairly by disclosing all material facts. A fact is material if there is a substantial likelihood a reasonable shareholder would find it important in deciding how to vote. Proxies secured by means of misleading or fraudulent representations to stockholders will be disqualified.

ILLUSTRATION 34-2 Proxy

WATERS, MELLEN AND COMPANY

PROXY
ANNUAL MEETING AUGUST 22, 20–

KNOW ALL MEN BY THESE PRESENTS, That the undersigned shareholder of WATERS, MELLEN AND COMPANY hereby constitutes and appoints O. W. PRESCOTT, A. B. BROWN, and GEORGE CONNARS, and each of them, the true and lawful proxies of the undersigned, with several power of substitution and revocation, for and in the name of the undersigned, to attend the annual meeting of shareholders of said Company, to be held at the Main Office of the Company, 900 West Lake Avenue, Cincinnati, Ohio, on Thursday, August 22, 20–, at 10.00 o'clock A.M., Standard Time, and any and all adjournments of said meeting, receipt of the notice of which meeting, starting the purposes thereof, together with Proxy Statement, being hereby acknowledged by the undersigned, and to vote for the election of a Board of thirteen directors for the Company, to vote upon the ratification of the appointment of Arthur Andrews & Co. as independent public accountants for the fiscal year May 1, 20–through April 30, 20– and to vote as they or he may deem proper upon all other matters that may lawfully come before said meeting or any adjournment thereof.

Signed the _____ 1st _____ day of March, 20–

_____ Wanda Klimecki _____

COURT CASE

FACTS: The Diasti Family Limited Partnership (DFLP) owned 67 percent of Coast Dental Services Inc.'s outstanding common stock. In order to control all the shares, DFLP formed Intelident Solutions Inc. and bid $9.25 for each share of Coast. The board of directors approved the offer, and the company scheduled the stockholders' vote for July 11. No one informed the minority stockholders about the offer until mailing the proxy statement on July 1. Because July 1 fell on a Friday, and because Monday, July 4, was a national holiday, the minority stockholders had a four-business-day window during which to receive and analyze the material and possibly notify Coast of a decision to seek appraisal of the stock. On July 11, DFLP voted its shares in favor of the merger. The minority stockholders were cashed out at $9.25 per share, and Intelident ended up owning 100 percent of DFLP. Stephen Berger, a former minority stockholder of Coast, sued DFLP and Intelident.

OUTCOME: The court said the timing of the proxy process precluded the minority stockholders from enjoying any realistic opportunity to exercise their statutory rights to an appraisal of the value of the stock, so a breach of the duty of disclosure occurred.

—*Berger v. Solutions Inc.*, 911 A.2d 1164 (Del. Ch.)

34-1c PROXY WARS

Stockholders dissatisfied with the policies of the present board of directors can try to elect a new board. Electing a new board is often a difficult or impossible task. If one or even several people own a majority of the voting stock, the objecting stockholders cannot obtain a majority of the voting stock to ensure success. If the voting stock is widely held, and no group owns a majority of the voting stock, then the objecting stockholders at least have a chance to elect a new board. To do this, this dissatisfied group must control a majority of the stock represented at a stockholders' meeting.

To ensure success, the leaders of the group will obtain proxies from stockholders who cannot attend the stockholders' meeting in person. The current board members will also attempt to secure proxies. This is known as a **proxy war**. The present board of directors may in most instances pay the cost of this solicitation from corporate funds. The "outsiders" generally must bear the cost of the proxy war out of their personal funds. If there are one million shareholders, the cost of soliciting their proxies is enormous. For this reason, proxy wars seldom happen.

proxy war
attempt by competing sides to secure majority of stockholders' votes

34-2 Rights of Stockholders

The stockholders of a corporation enjoy several important rights and privileges. Three of these rights that have already been discussed include the following:

1. A stockholder has the right to receive a properly executed certificate as evidence of ownership of shares of stock.
2. A stockholder has the right to attend corporate meetings and to vote unless this right is denied by express agreement, the articles of incorporation, or statutory provisions.
3. A stockholder has the right to receive a proportionate share of the profits when profits are distributed as dividends.

In addition, each stockholder has the following rights:

4. The right to sell and transfer shares of stock.
5. The right, when the corporation issues new stock, to subscribe for new shares in proportion to the shares the stockholder owns. For example, a stockholder who owns 10 percent of the original capital stock has a right to buy 10 percent of the shares added to the stock. If this were not true, stockholders could be deprived of their proportionate share in the accumulated surplus of the company. This is known as a **preemptive right**. Only stockholders have the right to vote to increase the capital stock.
6. The right to inspect the corporate books and to have the corporate books inspected by an attorney or an accountant. This right is not absolute, as most states have laws restricting the right. These laws tend to be drawn to protect the corporation from indiscriminate inspection, not to hamper a stockholder who has a proper purpose for the inspection.

preemptive right
right to purchase new shares in proportion to shares owned

COURT CASE

FACTS: David Lang and others were members of a nonprofit corporation, Western Provider's Physician Organization Inc. (WPPO). During an investment review, they requested WPPO corporate documents from the secretary of state. They discovered that WPPO had not filed annual reports and was not in good standing as a corporation. They requested an inspection of WPPO's books and records. WPPO turned over some requested documents but resisted an unlimited inspection. Lang asked the court to compel WPPO to allow a review of all corporate documents. WPPO contended that Lang had not met his burden of proving a "proper purpose" for an inspection.

OUTCOME: The court held that members must disclose their purpose for inspecting corporate books, but this purpose is presumed proper. The inspection was allowed.

—*Lang v. Western Providers Physician Organization Inc.*, 688 N.W.2d 403 (S.D.)

7. The right, when the corporation is dissolved, to share pro rata in the assets that remain after all the obligations of the company have been paid. In the case of certain preferred stock, the shareholders may have a preference in the distribution of the corporate assets on liquidation.

34-3 Directors

LO ③
Responsibilities and powers of directors and officers

A board of directors elected by the stockholders manages every corporation. Laws normally require every board to consist of at least three members; but if the number exceeds three, the articles of incorporation and the bylaws of the corporation fix the number, together with qualifications and manner of election.

The directors, unlike the stockholders, cannot vote by proxy, nor can they make corporate decisions as individual directors. All decisions must be made collectively and in a called meeting of the board.

The functions of the directors can be classified as:

1. Powers
2. Duties

34-3a POWERS

Law, the articles of incorporation, and the bylaws limit the powers of the board of directors. The directors have the power to manage and direct the corporation. They may do any legal act reasonably necessary to achieve the purpose of the corporation so long as this power is not expressly limited. They may elect and appoint officers and agents to act for the corporation, or they may delegate authority to any number of its members to so act. If a director obtains knowledge of something while acting in the course of employment and in the scope of authority with the corporation, the corporation is charged with this knowledge.

34-3b DUTIES

The directors have the duty of establishing policies that will achieve the purpose of the corporation, selecting executives to carry out these policies, and supervising these executives to see that they efficiently execute the policies. They must act in person in exercising all discretionary power. The directors may delegate ministerial and routine duties to subagents, but the duty of determining all major corporate policies, except those reserved to the stockholders, must be assumed by the board of directors.

34-4 Officers

In addition to selecting and removing the officers of a corporation, the board of directors authorizes them to act on behalf of the corporation in carrying out the board's policies. As agents of the corporation, the principles of agency apply to the officers' relationship with the corporation and define many of their rights and obligations.

State statutes may specify a few of the officers that corporations must have. The corporation's bylaws will specify what additional officers the corporation must have and the duties of each officer. A corporation commonly has a president, vice president, secretary, and treasurer. In small corporations, some of these offices may be combined. Additional officers may be assistant secretaries or treasurers, additional vice presidents, and a chief executive officer (CEO). The CEO is frequently the president or the chairperson of the board of directors. The board of directors creates or deletes some positions.

34-5 Liabilities of Directors and Officers

Although directors and officers of all corporations have potential liability for actions taken as a result of their positions with the corporation, directors and officers of publicly held corporations are subject to additional potential liabilities. This is because such individuals have a responsibility to perhaps hundreds of thousands of investors, both small and large. If the actions of directors or officers lead to the financial collapse of huge corporations, there can be a serious impact on enormous numbers of people. The responsibility for protecting investors in publicly held corporations has led to laws providing serious penalties for officers, directors, and even employees or those under contract with corporations who misuse corporate funds or mislead the public about the financial condition of the corporation. The most recent legislation relating to this is the Sarbanes–Oxley Act. Directors and officers of a corporation face the potential of personal liability for actions taken on behalf of the corporation as well as actions taken for personal gain. They can be liable if the corporation suffers losses or simply if the action is wrongful.

PREVIEW CASE REVISITED

FACTS: Pro-Pac Inc. was a packaging company that sought to expand its business to include warehouse and transportation services. Pro-Pac hired George Chapes as Vice President of Sales to help the company accomplish this goal. Pro-Pac paid Chapes an annual salary and provided him with a company vehicle, health insurance, and an expense account. While working for Pro-Pac, Chapes was contacted by a company in need of warehouse space to store sugar. Without telling Pro-Pac, Chapes steered the warehouse business to a competitor, WOW Logistics Company, in exchange for a commission payment from WOW Logistics. When Pro-Pac learned of deal, it sued Chapes for breaching his fiduciary duty of loyalty to the corporation.

OUTCOME: The court held that Pro-Pac could have made use of the warehouse business if Chapes had informed the corporation of the opportunity. Chapes breached his fiduciary duty of loyalty by diverting the business to a competitor.

—*Chapes v. Pro-Pac Inc.*, 473 B.R. 295 (E.D. Wis.)

34-5a DIRECTOR LIABILITY

Corporate Losses. As fiduciaries of the corporation, directors incur liability for losses when they are caused by bad faith and by negligence. They do not normally incur liability for losses when they act with due diligence and reasonably sound judgment. Directors make countless errors of judgment annually in operating a complex business organization. Only when losses are caused by errors resulting from negligence or a breach of good faith can a director be held personally liable.

The test of whether the directors failed to exercise due care depends on whether they exercised the care that a reasonably prudent person would have exercised under the circumstances. If they did that, they were not negligent and do not incur liability for the loss that follows.

The test of whether directors acted in bad faith is whether they acted in a way that conflicted with the interests of the corporation. The corporate directors have a duty of loyalty to the corporation similar to the duty of loyalty an agent has to a principal, or a partner has to the partnership and the other partners.

Wrongful Actions. Directors may be held liable for some acts without evidence of negligence or bad faith, either because the act is illegal or bad faith is presumed. Paying dividends out of capital and *ultra vires* acts constitute illegal acts. Loaning corporate funds to officers and directors constitutes an act to which the court will impute bad faith.

The members of the board of directors incur civil and criminal liability for their corporate actions. This means that a director does not get any immunity or protection from the legal consequences of actions taken. Because of this, individual directors who do not agree with action taken by the other directors must be careful to protect themselves by having the minutes of the meeting of the directors show that they dissented from the board's action. Otherwise stated, every director present at a board meeting is conclusively presumed to have assented to the action taken unless the director takes positive action to overcome this presumption. If the directors present who dissent have a record of their dissent entered in the minutes of the meeting, then they cannot be held liable for the acts of the majority.

34-5b OFFICER LIABILITY

A corporate officer or agent who commits a tort or crime incurs personal liability even when the act was done for the corporation in a corporate capacity. In this case, both the corporation and the individual could be jointly liable. Only personal liability is imposed when the acts are detrimental to the corporation and outside the scope of the officer's authority. Thus, an officer has liability when actions are improper or unjustified, such as when based on spite toward the injured party. Federal law even imposes liability on officers and agents for aiding and abetting lower-ranking employees in the commission of crimes. Specific statutes may impose liability on officers if they have a duty to ensure that violations do not occur and to seek out and remedy violations that do occur. Corporate officers and agents are not personally liable for acts they do not participate in, authorize, consent to, or direct.

Sarbanes–Oxley. The financial collapse of corporations such as Enron and WorldCom led to the demand for stronger federal laws imposing liability on corporate officers and directors. The Sarbanes–Oxley Act does so by requiring greater financial disclosure and by putting the responsibility for that disclosure on the CEOs and chief financial officers (CFOs) of corporations. It also requires attorneys and accountants to report evidence of certain law violations to the corporation's chief in-house lawyer or CEO. If they do not respond appropriately, the matter must be reported to the corporation's board of directors or audit board.

The law penalizes individuals who alter, destroy, or conceal records to obstruct an investigation and increases the penalties for certifying reports that do not comply with legal requirements.

The law also makes protection for informants stronger. People who expose wrongdoing in an organization are called **whistleblowers**. Often, corporate whistleblowers may face loss of their jobs. Sarbanes–Oxley penalizes anyone who takes action harmful to a person who truthfully reports information about the commission or possible commission of a federal crime to a law enforcement officer.

whistleblower
person who exposes
wrongdoing in an
organization

34-6 Corporate Combinations

When two corporations wish to combine, they frequently do so by means of a merger or a consolidation. A **merger** of two corporations occurs when they combine so that one survives and the other ceases to exist. One absorbs the other, and the surviving corporation assumes the absorbed corporation's liabilities. A **consolidation** occurs when two corporations combine to form a new corporation. Both of the two previous corporations disappear.

It has become a rather common practice recently for a corporation to try to take over another corporation. The acquiring corporation can do this by making a formal tender offer, an offer to buy stock in the target corporation at a set price. Because attempts at takeovers usually cause the price of the stock of the target company to rise, the acquiring corporation may try to obtain the amount of stock it wants in its target through the purchase of large blocks of the target's stock. The purchase of a large amount of stock cannot be kept quiet for long, however, because the Securities Exchange Act requires any person who acquires 5 percent of any class of stock to file a schedule reporting the acquisition within ten days.

LO ④
Combination and
dissolution

merger
one corporation absorbed by
another

consolidation
combining two corporations
to form a new one

34-7 Dissolution

A corporation may terminate its existence by paying all its debts, distributing all remaining assets to the stockholders, and surrendering its articles of incorporation. The corporation then ceases to exist and completes its dissolution. This action may be voluntary on the part of the stockholders, or it may be involuntary by action of the court or state. The state may ask for dissolution for any one of the following reasons:

1. Forfeiture or abuse of the corporate charter

2. Violation of the state laws

3. Fraud in the procurement of the charter

4. In some states, failure to pay specified taxes for a specified number of years

A foreign corporation that has been granted authority to do business in a state may have its authority revoked for similar reasons.

When a corporation dissolves, its existence is terminated for all purposes except to wind up its business. It cannot sue, transfer property, or form contracts except for the purpose of converting its assets into cash and distributing the cash to creditors and stockholders. Similarly, a foreign corporation whose authority to do business in the state has been revoked may not sue, transfer property, or form contracts until its authority has been reinstated.

In the event that assets cannot cover the corporation's debts, the stockholders do not incur personal liability. This is one of the chief advantages to business owners of a corporation over a sole proprietorship or partnership. It is an advantage from the stockholders' standpoint, but a disadvantage from the creditors' standpoint.

QUESTIONS

1. Explain how a corporation can perform business transactions as an artificial being.

2. How do directors directly control a corporation?

3. What is normally a quorum, and how is it determined?

4. In what way do stockholders' meetings act as a check on the board of directors?

5. What is a stockholder's most important right, and why is it the most important right?

6. Explain how a voting trust works.

7. May the management of a corporation legally solicit proxies for candidates selected by the board of directors? Explain.

8. How does the Sarbanes–Oxley Act expand the liability of corporate officers?

9. Under what circumstances may a director be held liable for an act when there is no evidence of bad faith or negligence?

10. How does a corporation complete its dissolution?

CASE PROBLEMS

LO ①

1. At a meeting of the Big Woods Springs Improvement Association Inc. (BWSIA), the president of the board of directors was handed a letter from Big Woods Land Development Inc. (BWLD). The letter stated BWLD had sold 288 lots to "new buyers," who allegedly took possession two days previously. The list of these buyers showed that 174 lots, only 20 of which were platted, were purportedly sold to Michael Nelson. The letter alleged that each "new buyer" had paid 1/12 of the annual BWSIA dues of $180. Hall was given a check for $4,320 ($15 × 288) and asked that all new members be allowed to vote. The letter was the only evidence that the "new members" had purchased lots. Following a motion for adjournment, second, and vote, the meeting was adjourned. After the existing members left, Nelson conducted a meeting of the "new members" at which he was elected president and a board member. BWSIA sued Nelson asking the court to prevent him from holding himself out as a director or officer and from exercising control of BWSIA assets. The BWSIA bylaws stated that a member must first pay the full annual assessment fee in order to vote. They also required a person to submit an application for membership in the association to the board of directors before obtaining ownership of any lot. Should the "new members" have been allowed to vote at the meeting?

LO ④

2. Vincent Meli was president of Flint Cold Storage (Flint) corporation, and his wife, Pauline, was secretary. Flint bought a life insurance policy on Vincent from Metropolitan Life Insurance Company (MetLife). Sometime later, Flint was dissolved. Twenty-five years after the dissolution, MetLife converted from a mutual insurance company owned by its policyholders, to a stock insurance company. As a result, MetLife had $188,000 payable to Flint, which it sent to the state unclaimed property office. Vincent died three years later. Pauline learned of the unclaimed $188,000 and tried to claim it in her capacity as an officer of a dissolved corporation. The state denied Pauline's claim, so she sued on behalf of Flint, alleging that although it had been dissolved 32 years previously, it had retained the right to sue. Did Flint have the right to sue for the funds?

LO ③

3. Hilb, Rogal & Hamilton Company of Atlanta (HRH) bought Hugh Holley's independent insurance brokerage and made him a vice president of HRH. Holley earned a salary and bonuses for selling professional liability insurance to clients needing specialized policies. He resigned from HRH and began working for a competing brokerage the next business day. Without HRH's knowledge, two months

CASE PROBLEMS (CONTINUED)

before he resigned from HRH, Holley had gotten approval from an existing client to appoint him as the client's contact at the competing brokerage. He had established an e-mail account and telephone number at the competitor and had printed conference invitations listing him as an employee of the competitor. He provided price benchmarking information to the competitor, offered to share techniques to reduce premiums for clients, and offered information to the competitor about a potential broker acquisition prospect. HRH sued Holley for breach of fiduciary duty. Had he breached his fiduciary duty?

4. Paul Nielsen was the founder and sole shareholder of Clever Innovations Inc. His wife, Gwen, was elected vice president and treasurer. The couple operated the business from their home, with Gwen handling the financial affairs. Sometime later, the Nielsens issued 100 shares of stock to Christopher Dooley, thereby giving him ownership of 50 percent of the company. Dooley was not formally elected as an officer or director but participated in the ongoing business operations of the company. After Paul Nielsen's death, Gwen became the administrator of her husband's estate, which included his stock in Clever Innovations. Relations between Gwen and Dooley quickly soured. The two reached a temporary arrangement whereby Dooley would run the business and inform Gwen of financial considerations. In the meantime, the two agreed to work toward a sale of the estate's half interest in the corporation to Dooley. However, a short time later, Dooley opened up a new bank account for the corporation and funded it with $280,000 from existing customers. Dooley redirected mail to be sent to his home and ignored Gwen's communications related to the sale of the estate's stock in the company. Gwen sued on behalf of the estate, alleging that Dooley's actions were oppressive to the other shareholder. Gwen sought dissolution of the corporation and a mandatory buy-out of the estate's shares for a fair market price. Should the court order dissolution? **LO ④**

5. After Lanier Carson retired from Kelley Manufacturing Company (KMC), James Martin became CEO and a member of the board. Timothy Maxwell became president, and he and Martin became the trustees of KMC's Employees Stock Ownership Plan (ESOP). The ESOP owned all the stock of KMC. Statements of account issued to employees who were ESOP participants reflected that the accounts were measured in "shares" vested in each participant. ESOP participants were referred to as shareholders. Martin and Maxwell got in a dispute with Carson. A few months later, Maxwell and Martin were fired by KMC, based on Carson's vote of 135 employees' proxies and powers of attorney. Also, both were removed as trustees of the ESOP, and Carson was voted the sole trustee of the ESOP and chairman of the board of KMC. Martin and Maxwell still had interests in the ESOP, with Martin's ESOP account being the largest single owner of an interest in KMC. When KMC did not allow them to inspect the proxies/powers of attorney and the list of shareholders at the time they were fired, they sued. Should they be allowed to inspect those corporate records? **LO ②**

6. Cooperative Bank was a commercial bank with deposits insured by the Federal Deposit Insurance Corporation (FDIC). The bank was routinely examined by the FDIC and independent auditors to ensure good underwriting and credit practices. The FDIC gave a "satisfactory" rating for the directors' management of the bank and the quality of assets held by the bank. An independent audit found that Cooperative Bank's loans were "well documented with credit memoranda that adequately articulated the credit decision process." After a period of economic turmoil, many of the loans approved by the bank were not repaid by borrowers. Cooperative Bank was declared insolvent and the FDIC was named as the bank's receiver. The FDIC sued the former directors of Cooperative Bank, alleging that the directors breached their fiduciary duty to shareholders by approving 86 loans that turned out to be bad credit decisions. Was the FDIC correct? **LO ③**

7. When TVG Network entered into a license agreement with Youbet.com, TVG received the right to purchase enough Youbet common stock to own 51 percent. Youbet was required "to use its best efforts" to allow TVG to designate directors to Youbet's board based on TVG's stock ownership. Youbet agreed **LO ②**

CASE PROBLEMS (CONTINUED)

not to "avoid or seek to avoid the observance or performance of any of the terms … hereunder … or take any act which is inconsistent with the rights granted to" TVG. Youbet hired a consulting firm to help develop a strategy regarding TVG's potential 51 percent ownership. In numerous meetings and documents, a strategy to discourage TVG from purchasing 51 percent by staggering the terms of the board and requiring a super majority of stockholders to change the bylaws was discussed. The Youbet board set an annual meeting to make these changes to the bylaws. It sent out proxy notices. These notices stated that the changes were to promote continuity and stability. They did not mention TVG or its potential 51 percent ownership. TVG sued, alleging that the proxy notices were misleading and that the board had breached its duty to disclose material information fully and fairly to the stockholders. Did TVG state a good case?

ETHICS IN PRACTICE

Suppose that an employee of a business finds some papers in a newspaper left on the subway. Miraculously, the papers are a report written by an employee of a competitor with some really helpful ideas for a report the employee has been asked to write. Would it be ethical for the employee to "borrow" the ideas in the found report and use them? Would it make any difference if the person who had written the report had intended to discard it?

PART 7 SUMMARY CASES

BUSINESS ORGANIZATION

1. Manual Moses, a new lawyer, put an ad in a law journal requesting a mentorship opportunity with an experienced lawyer so he could get trial experience. Laurence Savedoff responded to the ad. Moses referred two cases to Savedoff's office, conducted some depositions in Savedoff's cases, and drafted some documents for Savedoff. Moses received some payments from Savedoff. Four years later, after the payments ceased, Moses sued Savedoff, alleging Savedoff had proposed they work as partners in a law practice and share equally in the profits from the cases they worked on together. Moses claimed they had an oral partnership agreement. Savedoff alleged that since there was no evidence they shared earnings equally, that Moses shared in law firm losses or expenses, or that Moses contributed capital, there was no evidence of a partnership. What should the court hold? [*Moses v. Savedoff*, 947 N.Y.S.2d 419 (N.Y. App. Div.)]

2. Archon Corp. issued preferred stock called Exchangeable Preferred Stock (EPS). The certificate stated EPS would have a liquidation preference of $2.14 per share plus accrued and unpaid dividends. The dividends were to be paid twice yearly and be cumulative at the initial rate of 8 percent of $2.14 plus accrued but unpaid dividends. For the first three years Archon could pay dividends in EPS shares instead of cash. Beginning in the fifth year, the dividend rate was to increase to 11 percent and additionally increase 0.5 percent each six months to a maximum of 16 percent. For the first three years, dividend payments were in EPS shares. After that the dividends accrued and were not paid in cash. The EPS shares were redeemable by Archon at any time, and thirteen years after issuing them, Archon notified the holders it would redeem them for $5.241 per share, saying that included all accrued dividends. That number reflected the correct percentage dividend, but only on $2.14, not on the unpaid dividends. A group of holders of EPS shares sued Archon, saying that because the shares were cumulative, and the dividend accrued on unpaid dividends, the percentage each dividend payment period should be multiplied by $2.14 PLUS the accrued, unpaid dividends. Figuring that way, total accrued and unpaid dividends were $6.55 per share, so they alleged the redemption price should be $2.14 plus $6.55 or $8.69 per share. Should dividends be figured on only $2.14 for each payment period, or should they be figured on $2.14 plus accrued, unpaid dividends? [D.E. *Shaw Laminar Portfolios, LLC v. Archon Corp.*, 755 F.Supp.2d 1122 (D. Nev.)]

3. The Central Laborers Pension Fund (CLPF) sued News Corporation (News) to compel it to produce books and records related to its acquisition of Shine Group Ltd. (Shine). CLPF wanted to investigate potential breaches of fiduciary duty in connection with that transaction. CLPF's demand for inspection did not include evidence of its ownership of News' stock. Should CLPF's demand for inspection be granted? [*Central Laborers Pension Fund v. News Corp.*, 45 A.3d 139 (Del.)]

4. James Leach founded and was the majority shareholder of IDA Morehead Corporation, a company that manufactured electronic communications equipment. IDA Marketing Corporation purchased Leach's shares of stock in IDA Morehead through a capital debenture and agreed to pay Leach in monthly installments for the value of his stock. In the event of a missed payment, the purchase agreement required Leach to give IDA Marketing ninety days' notice and an attempt to make the required payment before the full amount of the stock price would be due to Leach. Leach and Reed Danuser were both shareholders and directors of IDA Marketing. Danuser eventually became the majority shareholder and president of IDA Marketing. After IDA Marketing missed monthly payments to Leach, Leach demanded payment of the full amount without giving the company ninety days' notice as required. Danuser told Leach that the company could not afford to repay the entire amount. Leach called a meeting of directors and led them to fire Danuser as president of IDA Marketing and to replace Danuser with himself. Leach also convinced the board to let him reclaim his IDA Morehead stock. As a result, all of the debenture payments that IDA Marketing had made to Leach were forfeited. The directors then authorized Leach to broker a sale of IDA Marketing. Because of Leach's actions, Danuser received nothing from the sale. Danuser sued Leach, claiming that Leach breached his fiduciary duty to Danuser by wrongfully terminating Danuser and by freezing him out of the company's governance and share of proceeds from the sale. Was Danuser correct? [*Danuser v. IDA Marketing Corp.*, 838 N.W.2d 488 (N.D.)]

5. Brothers Don and Harley Shoemaker signed a written partnership agreement for D & H Real Estate, in which each had a 50 percent interest. The agreement provided that in the event of the withdrawal of a partner, the remaining partner(s) would have the right to continue the business of the partnership. Twelve years later, Harley sent Don a letter saying he was withdrawing from the partnership in ninety days. The parties could not agree on a valuation of Harley's partnership interest, and eventually Harley sued. Did Harley's withdrawal dissolve the partnership? [*Shoemaker v. Shoemaker*, 745 N.W.2d 299 (Neb.)]

6. East Park Limited Partnership signed a $9 million note. Before the note was due, Joseph Della Ratta, the general partner issued a "capital call" to try to squeeze out some of the limited partners. He informed them East Park could not pay the note, so they would have to pay their proportionate shares of the balance. He said he would try to refinance the note but did not. Some partners said they were withdrawing from East Park before the loan due date. Della Ratta responded that they would forfeit their interests in East Park if they did not pay and accelerated the capital call to a date prior to the limited partners' withdrawal date. The withdrawing partners sued. Must they pay the capital call or lose their interests in East Park? [*Della Ratta v. Larkin*, 856 A.2d 643 (Md.)]

7. Morgan Joseph Holdings Inc. was organized to do investment banking and secured much of its initial funding from the sale of preferred shares of stock. The rights of the preferred stockholders were specified in Morgan Joseph Holding's certificate of incorporation. The certificate required Morgan Joseph to automatically redeem the Series A Preferred Stock if certain events, such as the merger of the company, occurred. The redemption value was to be $100 per share in such event. Moreover, the information material used to market the Series A Preferred Stock to investors supported the understanding that a redemption of Series A Preferred Stock would occur under certain circumstances. Almost ten years after its founding, Morgan Joseph Holdings merged with another investment bank. The newly created entity issued new Series A Preferred Stock and sought to exchange the new stock for Morgan Joseph's old Series A Preferred Stock. The preferred stockholders sued, claiming that the automatic redemption provision in the certificate of incorporation should be considered when appraising the value of their old Series A Preferred Stock. Should the court consider the language of the certificate of incorporation when appraising the value of the Series A Preferred Stock? [*Shiftan v. Morgan Joseph Holding Inc.*, 57 A.3d 928 (Del. Ch.)]

8. The owner of Central Plains, Joe Skeith, suggested to David Tate of C.J. Tate & Sons that Tate work with Central Plains on a job and they would share the profits. They both supplied equipment at the site: Tate provided the bonding, hired the workers, and did all the payroll paperwork; Skeith supervised on the job, set the working hours, and arranged for housing and transportation. Both obtained workers' compensation insurance. Tate hired Dennis Hickson, who usually worked for Central. One day after being paid, Hickson and his coworker roommate, L, went to dinner and then a club. L got aggressive toward other patrons, so Skeith asked Hickson and another to take L to his motel room. When Hickson later returned, L and a woman were in the room. L and the woman left. Hickson went to sleep but let L in when he returned. The next thing Hickson remembered was waking to find L attacking him. Hickson was stabbed. Hickson filed a workers' compensation claim against Central, and Central moved to add Tate, alleging Tate was Hickson's employer. Tate alleged Hickson was an employee of a joint venture of Central and Tate. Who was Hickson's employer? [*Central Plains Const. v. Hickson*, 959 P.2d 998 (Okla. Ct. App.)]

9. The board of directors of Dime Bancorp, Inc., solicited proxies in favor of five sitting directors prior to the annual meeting. North Fork Bancorporation Inc., a shareholder, solicited proxies against them. Both sets of proxy cards contained a general authorization of the holder to vote all the shares held and then allowed stockholders to vote "for" the election of the five candidates or vote to "withhold authority" for the election of them. The votes were 23,800,000 in favor and 55,200,000 withheld. The bylaws required the affirmative vote of a majority of the voting power present at the meeting. Dime claimed the proxies marked "withhold authority" did not give voting power at all so they did not count as "voting power present." By this reasoning, the five had been elected, basically unanimously. North Fork claimed that the shareholders who marked "withhold authority" gave instructions to the proxy holders to take action, so these proxies should be counted as "voting power present." Should the proxies be counted as "voting power present?" [*North Fork Bancorp., Inc. v. Toal*, 825 A.2d 860 (Del. Ch.)]

10. Gary Beach and Paul Touradji formed a limited partnership called Playa Oil and Gas, LP for the purpose of exploring oil and gas prospects. Touradji's company, DeepRock Venture Partners, LP held an 80 percent ownership interest in the partnership and contributed the start-up capital. Beach controlled the remaining 20 percent through two different entities, and contributed his rights to titles and interests in certain gas and oil leases and exploration opportunities to the partnership. After an unsuccessful drilling

attempt, each partner began to feel the other was missing good business opportunities and withholding information. As their business relationship fell apart, Beach proposed making a distribution to all partners, which DeepRock opposed. Despite this, Beach took approximately half of Playa Oil and Gas's cash on hand and distributed it to the partners. The distribution made it difficult for Playa Oil and Gas to meet its financial obligations and effectively made the company insolvent. DeepRock sued Beach on behalf of Playa Oil and Gas, alleging among other things, that Beach breached his fiduciary duty to the partnership. Did Beach act in the best interest of the partnership by making the distribution? [*Beach Capital Partnership, LP v. DeepRock Venture Partners, LP*, 442 S.W.3d 609 (Tex. App.)]

35 Principles of Insurance

36 Types of Insurance

37 Security Devices

38 Bankruptcy

Risk-Bearing Devices

Both the federal and state governments regulate insurance companies. Although some state laws apply to bankruptcy, the actual procedure is a federally regulated one. All of these issues are covered in the following chapters. State websites are excellent resources for specific information on state insurance, bankruptcy, and other related laws. Some state sites, such as Tennessee's, have easy ways to get to insurance information, whereas others will require a search through a list of state agencies. Try out Tennessee's website at www.tn.gov/commerce/section/insurance.

Principles of Insurance

LEARNING OBJECTIVES

(1) Identify important terms used in insurance.

(2) Explain who may obtain insurance.

(3) List the five aspects of the law of contracts that have special significance for insurance contracts.

PREVIEW CASE

Before obtaining malpractice insurance from Executive Risk Indemnity Inc. (Executive), the law firm Pepper Hamilton LLP (Pepper) learned that a client, Student Finance Corporation (SFC), had been involved in securities fraud. Prior to joining Pepper, attorney Roderick Gagne had assisted in setting up the company and its selling of pooled loans. Lawsuits were filed against SFC. Gagne thought that he and Pepper could be sued. Pepper did not include information concerning SFC to Executive. Executive's policy excluded any act occurring before the date of the policy which Pepper could reasonably foresee could be the basis for a claim. When Pepper was sued for malpractice, Executive denied coverage. Did Pepper know that it might be sued before obtaining the insurance? Would that fact be relevant to the amount charged for insurance?

insurance
contract that transfers risk of financial loss for a fee

Insurance provides a fund of money to a specified person when a loss covered by the insurance policy occurs. Life is full of unfavorable financial contingencies. Not every financial peril in life can be shifted by insurance, but many of the most common perils can. **Insurance** is a contract whereby a party transfers a risk of financial loss to the risk bearer, the insurance company, for a fee.

Every insurance contract specifies the particular risk being transferred. The name that identifies the policy does not control either the coverage or the protection provided by the policy. For example, a particular contract might carry the name "Personal Accident Insurance Policy," but this name might not clearly indicate the risk being assumed by the insurance company. A reading of the contract might reveal that the company will pay only if an accident occurs, for example, while the insured is actually attending a public school. In such a case, in spite of the broad title of the policy, the premium paid does not cover the loss due to any accident. The contract determines the risk covered, and it binds the parties.

35-1 Terms Used in Insurance

The company agreeing to compensate a person for a certain loss is known as the **insurer**, or sometimes as the **underwriter**. The person protected against the loss is known as the **insured**, or the **policyholder**. In life insurance, the person who will receive the benefits or the proceeds of the policy is known as the **beneficiary**. In most states, the insured may make anyone the beneficiary.

Whenever a person purchases any kind of insurance, a contract is formed with the insurance company. The written contract is commonly called a **policy**. The maximum amount that the insurer agrees to pay in case of a loss is known as the **face** of the policy, and the consideration the insured pays for the protection is called the **premium**.

The danger of a loss of, or injury to, property, life, or anything else, is called a **risk** or **peril**; when the danger may be covered by insurance, it is known as the **insurable risk**. Factors such as fire, floods, and sleet, which contribute to the uncertainty, are called **hazards**.

An insurance company assumes the risks caused by normal hazards. The insured must not do anything to increase the risk. Negligence by the insured constitutes a normal hazard. Gross negligence indicating a criminal intent does not. With regard to the risk, when a loss occurs, the insured must use all due diligence to minimize it. However, the insured has no responsibility for an increased risk over which the insured has no control or knowledge. For example, the insured must remove household effects from a burning building or keep a car involved in an accident from being vandalized if it can be done safely.

LO ①
Important terms

insurer or underwriter
company writing insurance

insured or policyholder
person protected against loss

beneficiary
person who receives proceeds of life insurance

policy
written contract of insurance

face
maximum insurer pays for loss

premium
consideration paid by insured

risk or peril
danger of loss

insurable risk
danger covered by insurance

hazards
factors that contribute to uncertainty

COURT CASE

FACTS: The Mellin's leased their condo to a tenant. After the tenant moved out due to an unpleasant odor, the Mellins' moved in. They, too, noticed the unpleasant odor. It was coming up from the downstairs unit via an open plumbing chase servicing the kitchen. The Mellins' were ordered by a health inspector to move out. Their homeowner's insurance policy insured "against risk of direct loss to property . . . if that loss is a physical loss to property," but excluded loss caused by "discharge, dispersal, seepage, migration, release or escape of pollutants." Was the Mellins' loss covered by the insurance policy?

OUTCOME: The court confirmed that resolving the issue required careful examination of the exact language of the policy. In this case, a reasonable person would not have thought that odors from a common household pet would be covered by the pollution exclusion clause.

—*Mellin v. Northern Security Insurance Company, Inc.*, 2015 WL 1869572 (N.H.)

A **rider** on an insurance policy is a clause or even a whole contract added to another contract to modify, extend, or limit the base contract. A rider must be clearly incorporated in, attached to, or referred to in the policy so that there is no doubt the parties wanted it to become a part of the policy.

Frequently, an individual needs insurance coverage immediately, or before an insurer can issue a formal policy. Insurance agents customarily have the authority to issue a **binder**, or a temporary contract of insurance, until the company investigates the risk and issues a formal policy.

rider
addition to insurance policy that modifies, extends, or limits base contract

binder
temporary contract of insurance

35-2 Types of Insurance Companies

There are two major types of insurance companies:

1. Stock companies
2. Mutual companies

35-2a STOCK COMPANIES

stock insurance company
corporation of stockholder investors

A **stock insurance company** is a corporation for which the original investment was made by stockholders and whose board of directors conducts its business. As in all other corporations, the stockholders elect the board of directors and receive the profits as dividends. Unlike other corporations, insurance companies must place a major portion of their original capital in a reserve account, so claims can be paid. As business volume increases, companies must increase the reserve by setting aside part of the premiums into this account.

35-2b MUTUAL COMPANIES

mutual insurance company
company of policyholder investors

assessment mutual company
mutual insurance company in which losses are shared by policyholders

In a **mutual insurance company**, the policyholders are the members and owners and correspond to the stockholders in a stock company. In these companies, the policyholders are both the insurer and the insured, but the corporation constitutes a separate legal entity. A person who purchases a $10,000 fire insurance policy in a mutual company that has $10 million of insurance in force owns 1/1000 of the company and is entitled to share the profits in this ratio. Losses also may have to be shared in the same ratio in an **assessment mutual company**. A policyholder is not subject to assessment where the policy makes no provision for it. In a stock company, policyholders never share the losses.

Insureds

35-3 Who May Be Insured

To be an insured and to contract for a policy of insurance, an individual must be competent to contract. Insurance does not constitute a necessary; thus, a minor who wishes to disaffirm is not bound on insurance contracts. A minor who disaffirms a contract may demand the return of any money. Because insurance contracts provide protection only, this cannot be returned. Some states hold that because of this, a minor can demand only the unearned premium for the unexpired portion of the policy. A few states have passed laws preventing minors from disaffirming some insurance contracts by reason of minority.

insurable interest
interest in nonoccurrence of risk insured against

To become a policyholder, one must have an insurable interest. An **insurable interest** means that the policyholder has an interest in the nonoccurrence of the risk insured against, usually because there would be financial loss. The insurance contract is in its entirety an agreement to assume a specified risk. If the insured has no interest to protect, there can be no assumption of risk, and hence no insurance. The law covering insurable interest is different for life insurance and for property insurance.

35-3a LIFE INSURANCE

The insured has an insurable interest in his or her life. When people insure another's life, however, and make themselves or someone else the beneficiary, they must have an insurable interest in the life of the insured at the time the policy is taken out. That interest normally does not need to exist at the time of the death of the insured. However, if a court finds that there is no longer an insurable interest, and that the interest of the beneficiary is adverse to that of the insured, the policy could be invalidated.

A person has an insurable interest in the life of another when such a relationship exists between them that a reasonable expectation of benefit will be derived from the continued existence of the other person. The relationships most frequently giving rise to an insurable interest are those between parents and children, husband and wife, partner and copartner, and a creditor in the life of the debtor to the extent of the debt. There are numerous other relationships that give rise to an insurable interest. With the exception of a creditor, if the insurable interest exists, the amount of insurance is irrelevant.

COURT CASE

FACTS: Johnson leased and farmed land owned by Minnick and his sister. Johnson and Minnick also entered into a written agreement such that Johnson would purchase Minnick's land at a specified price upon Minnick's death. Johnson purchased life insurance on Minnick's life in order to have liquidity to fund the purchase. Did Johnson have an insurable interest in Minnick's life?

OUTCOME: The court did not find an insurable interest in the landlord-tenant relationship or purchase agreement.

—*Johnson v. Nelson*, 290 Neb. 703

35-3b PROPERTY INSURANCE

One must have an insurable interest in the property at the time the policy is issued and at the time of the loss to be able to collect on a property insurance policy. Ownership is, of course, the clearest type of insurable interest, but there are many other types of insurable interest. Insurable interest occurs when the insured would suffer a monetary loss by the destruction of the property. Common types of insurable interest other than ownership include:

1. The mortgagee has an insurable interest in the property mortgaged, to the extent of the mortgage.

2. The seller has an insurable interest in property sold on the installment plan when the seller retains a security interest in it as security for the unpaid purchase price.

3. A bailee has an insurable interest in the property bailed to the extent of possible loss. The bailee has a potential loss from two sources. First, compensation as provided for in the contract of bailment might be lost. Second, the bailee may be held legally liable to the owner if the bailee's negligence or the negligence of the bailee's employees causes the loss.

4. A partner has an insurable interest in the property owned by the firm to the extent of the possible loss.

5. A tenant has an insurable interest in property to the extent of the loss that would be suffered by damage to, or destruction of, the property.

A change in title or possession of the insured property may destroy the insurable interest, which in turn may void the contract, because insurable interest must exist at the time of the loss.

COURT CASE

FACTS: William Balentine and Luke Gianetta jointly purchased a warehouse. When Balentine was in bankruptcy, they transferred the property for $1 to Gianetta, who let Balentine use the building. Gianetta executed a power of attorney to Balentine so he could take care of all incidents of ownership, including paying taxes, insurance premiums, and utilities. New Jersey Insurance Underwriting Association (NJIUA) issued an insurance policy on the building and the named insured was Luke Gianetta, c/o William Balentine. Gianetta did not personally pay the taxes, utilities, or other charges on the building; he was not involved in its management; he did not receive rental

income; and he had not claimed depreciation or tax deductions for the property. Someone broke into the building and vandalized it. NJIUA alleged that Gianetta did not have an insurable interest in the building.

OUTCOME: The court held that as the title holder, if a person were injured by a dangerous condition in the building, Gianetta would face potential liability. In the absence of insurance, he would be subject to financial loss, so he had an insurable interest.

—*Balentine v. New Jersey Ins. Underwriting Ass'n*,
966 A.2d 1098 (N.J. Super. Ct. App. Div.)

35-4 Some Legal Aspects of the Insurance Contract

LO ③
Contract law especially applicable to insurance

The laws applicable to contracts in general apply to insurance contracts. Five aspects of the law, however, have special significance for insurance contracts:

1. Concealment
2. Representation
3. Warranty
4. Subrogation
5. *Estoppel*

35-4a CONCEALMENT

concealment
willful failure to disclose pertinent information

An insurer must rely on the information supplied by the insured. This places the responsibility of supplying all information pertinent to the risk on the insured. A willful failure to disclose this pertinent information is known as **concealment**. To affect the contract, the concealed facts must be material; this means they must relate to matters that would affect the insurer's decision to insure the insured and the determination of the premium rate. Also, the concealment must be willful. The willful concealment of a material fact in most states renders the contract voidable.

PREVIEW CASE REVISITED

FACTS: Before obtaining malpractice insurance from Executive Risk Indemnity Inc. (Executive), the law firm Pepper Hamilton LLP (Pepper), learned that a client, Student Finance Corporation (SFC), had been involved in securities fraud. Prior to joining Pepper, attorney Roderick Gagne had assisted in setting up the company and its selling of pooled loans. Lawsuits were filed against SFC. Gagne thought he and Pepper could be sued. Pepper did not include information concerning SFC to Executive. Executive's policy excluded any act occurring before the date of the policy which Pepper could reasonably foresee could be the basis for a claim. When Pepper was sued for malpractice, Executive denied coverage.

OUTCOME: The court held that Pepper had an obligation to inform Executive of the potential for litigation. Since Pepper had not done so, Executive could deny coverage.

—Executive Risk Indem. Inc. v. Pepper Hamilton LLC, 891 N.Y.S.2d 1 (N.Y.)

The rule of concealment does not apply with equal stringency to all types of insurance contracts. In the case of property insurance, where the agent has an opportunity to inspect the property, the insurance company waives the right to void the contract. Concealment arises in ocean marine insurance whenever the insured withholds pertinent information, even if there is no intent to defraud.

35-4b REPRESENTATION

An oral or written misstatement of a material fact by the insured prior to the finalization of the contract is called a **false representation**. If the insured makes a false representation, the insurer may avoid the contract of insurance. This results whether the insured made the misstatement purposely or not.

false representation
misstatement of material fact

Some insurance applications require the applicant to state that the answers to questions in the application are made "to the best of the applicant's knowledge and belief" or in similar language. If the policy uses such language, and the applicant has answered truthfully, the fact that the applicant is unaware of the truth will not invalidate the contract.

COURT CASE

FACTS: In its application for commercial general liability insurance with Rutgers Casualty Insurance Co., Kiss Construction NY Inc. declared that its business was, "PAINTING–100%–100% INTERIOR." The declaration page of the policy described Kiss as a painting contractor, and the extension of declarations included the description, "PAINTING INTERIOR BUILDINGS–NO TANKS." Kiss later filed a claim under the policy for injuries occurring during construction of a three-family building, when Kiss was the general contractor. Rutgers did not write policies for such construction work and denied coverage based on

material misrepresentation in the application. Kiss asked the court to declare Rutgers liable under the policy to defend and indemnify it from the injury claim.

OUTCOME: The court said that since Rutgers did not write policies for heavy construction work, the misrepresentation made by Kiss in the application for insurance was material and Rutgers could deny coverage.

—Kiss Const. NY Inc. v. Rutgers Cas. Ins. Co., 877 N.Y.S.2d 253 (N.Y. App. Div.)

Insurance policies now usually provide that if the age of the insured is misstated, the policy will not be voided; however, the face amount paid on the policy "shall be that sum which the premium paid would have provided for had the age been correctly stated."

35-4c WARRANTY

warranty
statement of insured that relates to risk and appears in contract

A **warranty** is a statement or promise of the insured that relates to the risk and appears in the contract or another document incorporated in the contract. Untrue statements or unfulfilled promises permit the insurer to declare the policy void.

Warranties differ from representations in several ways. The insurance company includes warranties in the actual contract of insurance or incorporates them in it by reference. Representations are merely collateral or independent, such as oral statements or written statements appearing in the application for insurance or other writing separate from the actual contract of insurance.

Also, in order to void the contract of insurance, the false representations must concern a material fact, whereas the warranties may concern any fact or be any promise. A representation need only be substantially correct, whereas a warranty must be absolutely true or strictly performed.

Several states have enacted legislation that eliminates any distinction between warranties and representations and does not require a showing of materiality for a warranty or that the insured intended to defraud. In these states, a breached warranty does not void the policy. Even in states without such statutes, courts are reluctant to find policies invalid and will construe warranties as representations whenever possible and interpret warranties strictly against the insurer so as to favor the insured.

35-4d SUBROGATION

subrogation
right of insurer to assume rights of insured

In insurance, **subrogation** is the right of the insurer under certain circumstances to assume the legal rights of, or to "step into the shoes" of, the insured. Subrogation particularly applies to some types of automobile insurance. If the insurer pays a claim to the insured, under the law of subrogation the insurer has a right to any claims that the insured had because of the loss. For example, A has a collision insurance policy on a car. B negligently damages the car. The insurance company will pay A but then has the right to sue B to be repaid.

35-4e *ESTOPPEL*

estoppel
one party leads the second to a false conclusion the second party relies on; the second party would be harmed if the first party were later allowed to show the conclusion to be false

Neither party to an insurance contract may claim the benefit of a violation of the contract by the other party. Each party is estopped, or prevented, from claiming the benefit of such violation. An *estoppel* can arise whenever a party, by statements or actions, leads the second party to a conclusion, even if false, on which the second party relies. If the second party would be harmed if the first party were later allowed to show that the conclusion was not true, there is an *estoppel*. For example, if an insurer gives the insured a premium receipt, the insurance company would lead the insured to the conclusion that the premium had been paid. The insurer would be estopped from later asserting that the insured had not paid the premium in accordance with the terms of the policy.

COURT CASE

FACTS: Statements for Keith Matheny's U.S. Bank mortgage payments were generated when the bank got a payment. Matheny made his December payment in October. With his January statement was an offer of free $3,000 accidental death and dismemberment (AD&D) insurance from Unum Life Insurance Company of America. It stated: "All you have to do to receive this insurance is complete the enrollment form below and return it with your mortgage payment." It offered $250,000 additional coverage saying: "Premiums for the additional coverage . . . will be included with your monthly mortgage payment." On the back was, "Coverage is contingent upon our receipt of the first premium prior to the due date and during the insured's lifetime. Your coverage is effective on the first, regular billing date following acceptance of your application . . . provided your first month's premium has been paid." At the bottom, under "IMPORTANT," appeared: "Mail your completed form. DO NOT SEND ANY PREMIUM PAYMENT." Matheny chose additional insurance with his son, Rodrick, as beneficiary and in November received a "welcome packet," including a certificate of insurance. No document repeated that coverage depended on receipt of the first premium before the due date and during his lifetime. On January 6, the bank received Matheny's January mortgage payment equal in amount to the January statement generated before he chose optional insurance, so it did not include the $27.50 premium. The bank generated a February statement showing a mortgage payment and $27.50 insurance premium. Included was a "Notice of Non-Payment of Optional Insurance," stating: "The payment . . . of your loan has been applied without optional insurance premiums of 27.50. Please return your remittance . . . to keep your insurance in force." The bank mailed these to Matheny on January 7. On January 10, Matheny died before making additional payments. In February, Rodrick paid a mortgage payment plus $27.50 to U.S. Bank. Unum told Rodrick that additional benefits were not payable because it had not received Matheny's first premium prior to the due date and during his lifetime. Rodrick sued, alleging promissory estoppel.

OUTCOME: The court said that the solicitation materials told Matheny that all he had to do to receive coverage was return the enrollment form, and the additional documents gave the impression his coverage was in force. Since Matheny reasonably relied on those statements, and Roderick was injured because of his father's reliance, all three elements of estoppel were shown.

—*Matheny v. Unumprovident Corp.*, 594 F.Supp.2d 1212 (E.D. Wash.)

QUESTIONS

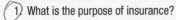

1. What is the purpose of insurance?

2. Identify the parties to an insurance contract.

3. Is the insured responsible for all increased risk when a loss occurs? Explain.

4. Why must a person have an insurable interest in order to be a policyholder?

5. a. Name three relationships giving rise to an insurable interest for life insurance.

   b. Name three types of insurable interest for property insurance.

6. Does the rule rendering an insurance contract voidable as a result of concealment apply with equal force to all types of property insurance?

7. Under what circumstances will a misstatement of a material fact by an insured prior to the finalization of an insurance contract not invalidate the contract?

QUESTIONS (CONTINUED)

8. How does a warranty differ from a representation?

9. When does the principle of subrogation apply?

10. When can an estoppel arise?

CASE PROBLEMS

LO ③

1. Kentucky Speedway, LLC (Speedway) purchased general liability insurance from Virginia Surety Company, Inc. (Surety). Cynthia Bivens and John Marsh, along with several others, attended an event at the Speedway at which food and alcoholic beverages were served. Bivens was killed when a vehicle driven by Marsh was involved in an accident leaving the Speedway. Bivens' estate sued Speedway for its negligence in serving alcohol to an already intoxicated Marsh. The Speedway reached a settlement with Bivens' estate, but sued Surety for its failure to defend and indemnify Speedway pursuant to the liability policy. Surety relied on the policy's liquor liability exclusion, which provided, in part, an exclusion for coverage for liability arising out of the sale of alcoholic beverages if the insured was "in the business of manufacturing, distributing, selling, serving or furnishing alcoholic beverages." Was Surety on the hook to cover Speedway's claim?

LO ②

2. McAdam was the largest owner and managing member of McAdam's Fish, LLC (LLC). The LLC owned several fishing boats on which McAdam purchased insurance. In the course of fishing operations, two of the boats sustained losses, and McAdam made a claim. The insurance company refused to pay on the grounds that McAdam had no insurable interest in the boats. Was the insurance company correct in denying the claim?

LO ②

3. Rick Muse mortgaged a house and five months later deeded it to Columbia Hills Management Company, Inc. (CHMC, Inc.). Three years later, the lender foreclosed on the house. Allstate Property and Casualty Insurance Company (Allstate) had issued a homeowner's insurance policy on the house, naming Ali Muhammad and Rick Muse as the insureds. After the foreclosure, Allstate notified Muhammad that it was going to cancel the policy since he no longer had an insurable interest. Allstate cancelled the policy. Muhammad and the corporation he owned, CHMC, Inc., sued, alleging the cancellation was improper. Did Allstate have the right to cancel the policy?

LO ③

4. Luis and Rosaura Mora contracted with Tower Hill Prime Insurance Company for homeowners insurance on their home. Part of the application included the question "Do you have any knowledge of any prior repairs made to any structures on the insured location for cracking damage?" The Moras answered "No." However, on the home inspection report the Moras procured as part of the purchase, notations were made regarding "cracks in drywall at ceiling," "nook drywall cracks," and "fix cracks" under three windows. Was the Moras' failure to list these cracks on the application a misrepresentation sufficient to void the homeowners policy?

LO ③

5. Superior Dispatch, Inc. (Superior) transported goods over short distances. Its application for insurance stated that it hauled produce, food goods and canned foods, beer/wine, textiles, and paper products. It gave the percentage of each item, which totaled 100 percent. Insurance Corporation of New York (Inscorp) issued an insurance policy covering damage to cargo in transit. A provision of the policy stated that it was void if the insured misrepresented any material fact. While Superior hauled a dump truck, the cab of the truck struck an overpass and was damaged. Superior filed a claim for the value of the truck with Inscorp, which denied the claim. Superior sued. Inscorp claimed that superior's failure to list motor vehicles as a commodity hauled was a material misrepresentation. Was it?

CASE PROBLEMS (CONTINUED)

6. Lawrence and Susan Pope applied for a homeowner's insurance policy with Mercury Indemnity **LO** ②
Company of Georgia. The Popes indicated that they had a swimming pool and a diving board. Mrs.
Pope wrote a check for the premium, and Mercury issued a policy. A month later, Mercury notified
their independent insurance agent, Gerald Woodworth, that it was cancelling the policy because
of the diving board. It mailed cancellation notices to Woodworth and the Popes and refunded the
premium. Woodworth spoke with the Mercury underwriter, who agreed that Mercury would reinstate the policy upon receipt of a photograph of the Pope's swimming pool with the diving board
removed. Lawrence Pope took down the diving board, took a picture of his swimming pool with the
diving board removed, and provided the picture, together with the premium-refund check, to Woodworth, who forwarded them to Mercury. Mercury then reinstated a policy. Sometime after providing the picture of the swimming pool with the diving board removed, Lawrence Pope reinstalled the
board. About a year later, the Popes' property sustained significant tornado damage. They made a
claim under the policy for that damage, so Mercury sent a claims adjuster to their residence. The
adjuster took pictures of the damage, one of which showed the swimming pool with the diving board
reinstalled. Mercury sued to rescind the homeowners' policy, alleging that the Popes had made a
material misrepresentation that they had permanently removed their diving board. Should the court
rescind the policy?

7. David Hilliard and Timothy Jacobs created Advance Marketing Technology, LLC (AMT). The business **LO** ③
became successful. They executed an agreement in which they each agreed to purchase term life
insurance policies on the other in the amount of $2,000,000 so that in the event of the death of
either, the other would be able to buy out the deceased member's shares of AMT. Eventually, AMT's
assets were sold to a third party, and AMT was dissolved. Hilliard asked Jacobs whether he wanted
to trade the life insurance policies that they held on each other's life. Jacobs declined and continued
to pay the premiums on the policies he held on Hilliard's life. Hilliard sued to require Jacobs to convey the life insurance policies to him or cancel the policies. The trial court ordered Jacobs to terminate the policies, and while Jacobs's appeal was pending, Hilliard died. Should Jacobs be required to
terminate the policies?

8. While employed to handle the refinancing of two mortgages for Credit Union Central Falls (CUCF), **LO** ③
attorney Lawrence Groff embezzled more than $200,000. CUCF provided funds to Goff. Goff would
get title insurance for the refinanced loan from Mortgage Guarantee & Title Insurance Company and
pay the difference between the prior loan and the CUCF loan to the mortgagors. He was to pay off
the prior loans, but he kept the money instead. CUCF filed claims on the title insurance policies and
Mortgage Guarantee paid $223,410 to pay off the prior loans. Mortgage Guarantee then alleged it
was subrogated to CUCF's claims in accordance with the terms of the title insurance policies. However, Doris Riendeau had obtained a judgment of $85,476.41 against Groff for misappropriation in
another matter and also claimed any funds that Groff had left. Should Mortgage Guarantee now
"stand in the shoes" of CUCF?

Types of Insurance

36

1. Explain the nature of life insurance and its normal limitations.
2. Define property insurance.
3. Identify the types of coverage afforded by automobile insurance.

PREVIEW CASE

Michael purchased a life insurance policy and designated his wife, Gail, as beneficiary. They later divorced, and Michael changed the beneficiary to his sister, Mary Ellen. Michael then married Evanisa, but unfortunately died from a work-related incident three months later. Evanisa sued the insurance company for the proceeds, arguing that the act of marriage created a presumptive right to the spouse's life insurance benefits. To whom should the insurance company pay the proceeds? Do Mary Ellen and Evanisa each have legitimate claims? What about Gail?

Insurance companies provide many types of policies to help people protect against financial loss. Three types of policies that most people purchase include:

1. Life insurance
2. Property insurance
3. Automobile insurance

36-1 Life Insurance

LO ①
Nature of life insurance

life insurance
contract of insurer to pay money on death of insured

Life insurance is a contract by which the insurer agrees to pay a specified sum or sums of money to a beneficiary upon the death of the insured. An insured generally obtains life insurance to protect the beneficiary from financial hardship resulting from the death of the insured.

36-1a TYPES OF LIFE INSURANCE CONTRACTS

The most important types of life insurance policies include:

1. Term insurance
2. Endowment insurance
3. Whole life insurance
4. Combinations

36-1b TERM INSURANCE

Term insurance contracts are those whereby the company assumes, for a specified period of time, the risk of the death of the insured. The term may be for only one year; or it may be for five, ten, or even fifty years. The term must be stated in the policy.

Many variations of term policies exist. In short-term policies, such as five years, the insured might have the option to renew it for another equal term without a physical examination. This is called **renewable term insurance**. The cost is higher for each renewal period. In nonrenewable term insurance, the insured does not have the right to renew unless the company consents.

Term policies also may be either level term or decreasing term. In level-term contracts, the face of the policy is written in units of $1,000. The face amount remains the same during the entire term of the policy. In decreasing-term contracts, the length of time the proceeds are collected or the face amount decreases over the life of the policy. The policy may be written in multiples of an amount of monthly income. For example, a person age 20 could purchase a decreasing-term policy of 50 units, or $500 a month, covering a period of 600 months, or 50 years. If the insured dies the first month after purchasing the policy, the beneficiary would draw $500 a month for 600 months or $300,000 ultimately. If the insured dies at the end of 25 years, the beneficiary would draw $500 a month for 300 months or $150,000 ultimately. Some decreasing-term insurance is paid in a lump sum rather than periodically.

All term policies have one thing in common—they are pure life insurance. They shift the specific risk of loss as a result of death and nothing more.

term insurance
contract whereby insurer assumes risk of death of insured for specified time

renewable term insurance
term insurance renewable without physical examination

36-1c ENDOWMENT INSURANCE

An **endowment insurance** policy is decreasing-term insurance plus a savings account. Part of the premium pays for the insurance, and the remainder earns interest so that at the end of the term, the savings will equal the face amount of the policy. If the insured dies during the term of the policy, the beneficiary will collect the face. If the insured is still living at the end of the term, the insurance company will pay the face to the insured or a designated beneficiary.

endowment insurance
decreasing-term insurance plus savings account

36-1d WHOLE LIFE INSURANCE

All life insurance contracts are either term insurance or endowment insurance. A whole life insurance policy is one that continues, assuming the premium is paid, until age 100 or death, whichever occurs first. If the insured is still living at age 100, the face of the policy is collected as an endowment. A whole life policy might correctly be defined as endowment insurance at age 100.

36-1e COMBINATIONS

The three basic life insurance contracts—term, endowment, and whole life—can be combined in an almost endless variety of combinations to create slightly different contracts. In the case of universal life insurance, any premiums paid that exceed the current cost of term insurance are put into a fund and earn interest. The fund can be withdrawn by the owner or paid to the beneficiary at the death of the insured. The family income policy, for example, is merely a straight life policy with a twenty-year decreasing-term policy attached as a rider.

Insurers frequently add several other riders to life insurance policies for an added premium. The disability income rider may be attached to any policy and pays an income to an insured who becomes disabled. A rider requiring the insurer to make a greater payment, customarily twice the ordinary amount when death is caused by accidental means, is called a **double indemnity rider**.

double indemnity rider
policy requiring insurer to pay twice ordinary face amount if death is accidental

36-1f LIMITATION ON RISKS IN LIFE INSURANCE CONTRACTS

Two common limitations on the risk covered by life insurance include: (1) suicide, and (2) death from war activity.

36-1g SUICIDE

Life insurance policies commonly refuse payment when death occurs from suicide. Other suicide clauses stipulate that the company will not pay if the suicide occurs within two years from the date of the policy.

COURT CASE

FACTS: Terry Riggs purchased life insurance through his employer's group plan. He also suffered from depression, and for 18 years had been prescribed antidepressants. His doctor later changed his prescription to an antipsychotic, but because the drug caused Riggs to feel "too lethargic," it was changed to a different antipsychotic. One week after the change in prescription, and 1 year and 50 weeks after his employer's current life insurance took effect, Riggs committed suicide. The insurance company declined to pay under the suicide clause, which prohibited payments for suicides committed within 2 years from the date the life insurance took effect. Riggs' wife claimed that because of the drugs, Riggs lacked the intent and motivation to commit suicide. Was the insurance company obligated to pay the death benefit to Riggs' wife?

OUTCOME: No. The court found that the physical act of taking one's own life was sufficient to fall under the definition of suicide.

—*Riggs v. Metropolitan Life Ins. Co.*, 940 F.Supp.2d 172 (D.N.J.)

36-1h DEATH FROM WAR ACTIVITY

A so-called war clause provides that if the insured dies as a consequence of war activity, the company will not pay. If a member of the armed forces dies a natural death, the company must pay. In order to refuse payment, the insurance company has the burden of proving that war activity caused the death.

36-1i PAYMENT OF PREMIUMS

If the premiums are not paid when due, and the policy so provides, it either will lapse automatically or may be declared forfeited at the option of the insurer. The policy or a statute of the state may provide that after a certain number of premiums have been paid, an unpaid premium results in the issuance of a smaller, paid-up policy for the same term. By the payment of an additional premium, the insured may generally obtain a policy containing a waiver of premiums that becomes effective if the insured becomes disabled. When disability occurs, the insured does not have to pay premiums for the period of time during which the disability exists.

36-1j GRACE PERIOD

The law requires life insurance companies to provide a **grace period** of thirty or thirty-one days in every life insurance policy. This grace period gives the insured thirty or thirty-one days from the due date of the premium in which to pay it without the policy lapsing. Without this provision, if the insured paid the premium one day late, the policy either might lapse or be forfeited by the insured. The insured might be able to obtain a reinstatement of the policy but might be required to pass a new physical examination. To buy a new policy, the insured might have to pass a physical examination and would have to pay a higher rate for the current age.

grace period
thirty- or thirty-one-day period in which late premium may be paid without policy lapsing

36-1k INCONTESTABILITY

Life insurance policies are incontestable after a certain period of time, usually one or two years. After that time, the insurance company usually cannot contest the validity of a claim on any ground except nonpayment of premiums.

36-1l CHANGE OF BENEFICIARY

Life insurance policies ordinarily reserve to the insured the right to change the beneficiary at will. Policies also permit the insured to name successive beneficiaries so that if the first beneficiary should die before the insured, the proceeds would pass to the second named or contingent beneficiary.

Courts uphold divorce decrees or separation agreements fixing beneficiaries of insurance policies. Later attempts by the insured to change a beneficiary required by a court order do not succeed.

PREVIEW CASE REVISITED

FACTS: Michael purchased a life insurance policy and designated his wife, Gail, as beneficiary. They later divorced, and Michael changed the beneficiary to his sister, Mary Ellen. Michael then married Evanisa, but unfortunately died from a work-related incident three months later. Evanisa sued the insurance company for the proceeds, arguing that the act of marriage created a presumptive right to the spouse's life insurance benefits. To whom should the insurance company pay the proceeds? Do Mary Ellen and Evanisa each have legitimate claims? What about Gail?

OUTCOME: The proceeds should be paid to the named beneficiary, Mary Ellen. No one else has a legitimate claim.

—*Fox v. Lincoln Financial Group*, 109 A.3d 221 (N.J.)

36-1m ASSIGNMENT OF THE POLICY

The policy of insurance may be assigned (or the rights in the policy may be transferred to another) by the insured. The assignment may be either absolute or as collateral security for a loan that the insured obtains from the assignee, such as a bank.

A beneficiary also may make an assignment; however, the assignee of the beneficiary is subject to the disadvantage that the insured may change beneficiaries. If the assignment is made after the insured has died, the assignment is an ordinary assignment of an existing money claim.

36-1n ANNUITY INSURANCE

annuity insurance
contract that pays monthly income to insured while alive

An **annuity insurance** contract pays the insured a monthly income from a specified age, generally age 65, until death. It is a risk entirely unrelated to the risk assumed in a life insurance contract, even though life insurance companies sell both contracts. Life insurance has been defined as shifting the risk of dying too soon, and annuity insurance as shifting the risk of living too long, or outliving one's savings. An individual age 65 who has $50,000 and a life expectancy of 72 years could use up the $50,000 over the expected seven additional years of life by using approximately $600 per month for living expenses. However, if the individual lives for more than seven years, there would be no money left. An annuity insurance policy could be purchased for $50,000, and the monthly income would be guaranteed no matter how long the insured lives. If the annuity contract calls for the monthly payments to continue until the second of two insureds dies, it is called a **joint and survivor annuity**. Couples who wish to extend their savings as long as either one is still living frequently use this type of annuity.

joint and survivor annuity
annuity paid until second of two people dies

36-2 Property Insurance

LO ②
Property insurance

property insurance
contract by which insurer pays for damage to property

Property insurance is a contract whereby the insurer, in return for a premium, agrees to reimburse the insured for loss or damage to specified property caused by the hazard covered. A contract of property insurance is one of indemnity or compensation for loss that protects the policyholder from actual loss.

If a building actually worth $40,000 is insured for $45,000, the extra premiums that were paid for the last $5,000 worth of coverage do not provide any benefit for the insured. The actual value, $40,000, is the maximum that can be collected in case of total loss. However, if a building is insured for only $20,000 and is totally destroyed, the insurance company has to pay only $20,000. The maximum amount paid for total loss of property is the lesser of the face of the policy or the value of the property.

36-2a LOSSES RELATED TO FIRE

hostile fire
fire out of its normal place

friendly fire
fire contained where intended

Normally, fire insurance covers damage to property caused only by hostile fires. A **hostile fire** is defined as one out of its normal place, whereas a **friendly fire** is one contained in the place where it is intended to be. Scorching, searing, singeing, smoke, and similar damages from a friendly fire are not covered under a fire policy. For a fire policy to cover damage, normally an actual fire must occur.

The policy does not cover loss caused by heat without fire. However, in one case the court held that soybeans were damaged by fire when there were hot spots in the beans that "glowed like charcoal and were orange" and there was an odor of smoke.

Fire insurance also does not cover economic loss that results from a fire. A hostile fire may cause many losses other than to the property insured, yet the fire policy on the building and contents alone will not cover these losses. One example is the loss of profits while the building is being restored. This loss can be covered by a special policy called **business interruption insurance**. If one leases property on a long-term, favorable lease, and the lease is cancelled because of fire damage to the building, the tenant may have to pay a higher rent in new quarters. This increased rent loss can be covered by a **leasehold interest insurance** policy but not by a fire policy.

The typical fire policy may also cover the risks of loss by windstorm, explosion, smoke damage from a friendly fire, falling aircraft, water damage, riot and civil commotion, and many others. Each of these additional risks must be added to the fire policy by means of riders. This is commonly known as extended coverage.

business interruption insurance
insurance covering loss of profits while business building is repaired

leasehold interest insurance
covers cost of higher rent when leased building is damaged

36-2b THE PROPERTY INSURANCE POLICY

The property insurance policy will state a maximum amount that will be paid by the insurer. When only a maximum is stated, the policy is called an **open policy**, and in the event of partial or total loss, the insured must prove the actual loss that has been sustained. The policy may be a **valued policy**, in which case, instead of stating a maximum amount, it fixes values for the insured items of property. Once a policyholder shows a covered total destruction of the property, the insurer pays the total value. If only a partial loss occurs, the insured under a valued policy must still prove the amount of loss, which amount cannot exceed the stated value of the property.

Insurance policies also may be *specific*, *blanket*, or *floating*. A specific policy applies to one item only, such as one house. A blanket policy covers many items of the same kind in different places, or different kinds of property in the same place, such as a building, fixtures, and merchandise in a single location. **Floating policies** are used for trucks, theatrical costumes, circus paraphernalia, and similar items that are not kept in a fixed location. A floating policy is also desirable for items that may be sent out for cleaning, such as rugs or clothes, and articles of jewelry and clothes that may be worn while traveling. An insurance policy on household effects covers for loss only at the named location. The purpose of the floating policy is to cover the loss no matter where the property is located at the time of the loss.

Most people who own their homes obtain a **homeowners policy** that normally protects the house and its contents from large numbers of perils. A homeowners policy can be an all-risk or named peril policy. An **all-risk policy** insures against all risks except those that are specifically excluded in the policy. In such a case, if a peril is not excluded, it is covered. A **named peril policy** only covers specifically listed perils, such as fire, wind, lightning, hail, theft, and liability of the homeowner in case someone suffers injury on the property. The actual terms of the policy determine what is covered and what is not covered. A tenant can obtain similar insurance that protects the tenant's personal property but not the building itself.

open policy
policy that requires insured to prove loss sustained

valued policy
policy that fixes values for insured items

floating policy
coverage no matter where property is located

homeowners policy
coverage of many perils for owners living in their houses

all-risk policy
policy covering all perils except those specifically excluded

named peril policy
policy covering only listed perils

FACTS: While hanging drywall to remodel a bathroom in Bernard and Gail Freedman's home, a contractor drove a nail entirely through a pipe. Five years later, corrosion around the nail caused a leak that resulted in extensive water damage. The Freedmans had an all-risk homeowners policy that excluded losses caused by and "regardless of whether the event occurs suddenly or gradually, . . . water damage, meaning . . . continuous or repeated . . . leakage of water . . . from a . . . plumbing system." The policy also excluded third-party negligence whenever it interacted with an excluded peril. After the Freedmans' homeowners insurer, State Farm Insurance Company, denied their claim, they sued, alleging that negligence was the cause of the loss.

OUTCOME: The Freedmans' loss was not covered. The court said the policy excluded third-party negligence when it interacted with an excluded peril, and continuous leakage of water was an excluded peril.

—*Freedman v. State Farm Insurance Co.*, 93 Cal.Rptr.3d 296 (Cal. Ct. App.)

Another type of insurance policy of particular interest to merchants is the **reporting form for merchandise inventory**. This policy permits the merchant to report periodically, usually once a month, the amount of inventory on hand. This enables the merchant to carry full coverage at all times and still not be grossly overinsured during periods when inventory is low.

reporting form for merchandise inventory
policy allowing periodic reporting of inventory on hand to vary coverage amount

36-3 Description of the Property

All property and its location must be described with reasonable accuracy in order to identify the property and to inform the insurer of the nature of the risk involved. It is not accurate to describe a house with asphalt brick siding as brick. Personal property should be so described that in the event of loss, its value can be determined. The general description "living room furniture" may make it difficult to establish the value and the number of items. A complete inventory should be kept. If this is done, such description as "household furniture" in the policy is adequate.

Because the location of the property affects the risk, it must be specified. If personal property used in a brick house on a broad paved street is moved to a frame house on an out-of-the-way dirt road, the risk from fire may be increased considerably. To retain coverage, express permission must always be obtained from the insurer when property is moved, except under a floating policy. Most homeowners policies sold today continue coverage at a new location for several days, together with coverage during the moving trip. If a loss occurs during the specified period, the company must pay, even though it received no notice of the changed location.

36-4 Coinsurance

coinsurance
insured recovers in ratio of insurance to amount of insurance required

Under the principle of **coinsurance**, the insured recovers on a loss in the same ratio as the insurance bears to the amount of insurance that the company requires. Many policies contain an 80 percent coinsurance clause. This clause means the insured may carry any amount of insurance up to the value of the property, but the company will not pay the full amount of a partial loss unless insurance is carried for at least 80 percent of the value of the property. If a building is worth $50,000, and the insured buys a policy for $20,000, the company under the 80 percent coinsurance clause will pay only half of the damage and never more than $20,000. Only half of the damage to the building can be collected because only half of 80 percent of the value of the building is the amount of insurance carried. The 80 percent clause requires the insured to carry $40,000, or 80 percent of $50,000, to be fully protected from a partial loss.

The coinsurance clause may be some percentage other than 80 percent. In burglary insurance, it may be as low as 5 or 10 percent. On rare occasions, it is as high as 100 percent in fire insurance.

36-5 Repairs and Replacements

Most insurance contracts give the insurer the option of paying the amount of loss or repairing or replacing the property. The amount the insurance company will pay for a loss will vary, depending on whether market value or replacement cost is used to measure the amount of loss. If market value is used, the insurance company will pay whatever the value of the property was immediately before the loss. If the property has been used for several years, the market value could be much less than the cost to replace the property. If replacement value is used, the insurance company will pay what the cost is to procure another item as identical to the insured item as possible. Even if the item is older and shows wear and tear, it will be replaced with a new one. For example, suppose fire damages Alphonse's fifteen-year-old furniture, for which he paid $5,000. Alphonse has raised four children, so the furniture has seen a lot of use and has not always had the best treatment. The market value of his much-used, fifteen-year-old furniture would probably be very little, say $500. If Alphonse has an insurance policy that pays only market value, he would recover only $500. If the policy pays replacement cost, it could easily cost $5,000 or more to replace the furniture. The amount paid by the insurance company can thus vary dramatically, depending on whether market value or replacement cost is the measure. Which measure is used will depend on the policy.

When the property is repaired or replaced, materials of like kind and quality must be used. The work must be completed within a reasonable time. When the insurance company has the choice of repair or replacement, the insurer seldom exercises the option to replace. The insurer also may have the option of taking the property at an agreed valuation and then paying the insured the full value of the damaged property.

36-6 Defense and Notice of Lawsuits

Under a **defense clause** found in property insurance policies that protect the insured from liability to others injured on the property or by the property, the insurer agrees to defend the insured against any claim for damages. This means that if the insured is sued, the insurance company supplies a lawyer to defend the suit. For example, under a normal homeowners policy, the homeowner is protected not only against damage to the property but also from liability to anyone injured on the property. If someone who slips on ice at the door sues the homeowner, the insurance company will supply a lawyer to defend the suit. This saves the insured the cost of hiring an attorney.

defense clause policy clause in which insurer agrees to defend insured against damage claims

In the event of an injury to a third party or an accident in the case of automobile insurance, the policyholder has the duty to give the insurer written notice and proof of loss regarding the damages. The notice must identify the insured and give such information as the names and addresses of injured people; the owner of any damaged property; witnesses; and the time, place, and detailed circumstances of the incident. This notice must be given within a reasonable time.

If a claim or a suit is brought against the insured, every demand, notice, or summons received must immediately be forwarded to the insurance company. The insured must give the fullest cooperation to the insurer, who normally has the right to settle out of court any claims or lawsuits as it deems best.

COURT CASE

FACTS: Christina Chera sustained injuries on property allegedly controlled and maintained by the Board of Hudson River–Black River Regulation District. Three months later, the board received notice of a claim for personal injuries relating to the incident but did not notify or send the claim to Praetorian Insurance Co., its liability insurer. A year later, the board was sued. The board then forwarded the complaint to its insurance broker, who promptly forwarded it to Praetorian. It refused coverage because it was not notified "as soon as practicable" of the occurrence, and the board did not "immediately" send Praetorian

notice of the claim as the policy required. The board asked the court to compel Praetorian to defend the suit and indemnify it.

OUTCOME: The court said that in the absence of a reasonable excuse, the board's one-year delay in notifying Praetorian of the occurrence was unreasonable. Praetorian did not have to defend the suit.

—Board of Hudson River–Black River Regulating Dist. v. Praetorian Ins. Co., 867 N.Y.S.2d 256 (N.Y. App. Div.)

LO ③
Auto insurance coverage

automobile insurance
insurance that the insured obtains to cover a car and possible injuries

physical damage insurance
insurance for damage to car itself

36-7 Automobile Insurance

Automobile insurance is a special type of property insurance and includes two major classes of insurance: physical damage insurance (including fire, theft, and collision) and public liability insurance (including bodily injury and property damage). To understand the law, one must know what specific risk the insurance carrier assumes and the terms of the policy covering that specific risk. **Automobile insurance** refers to insurance that the insured obtains to cover a car and the injuries that the insured and other members of the family may sustain. The term also refers to liability insurance, which protects the insured from claims that third persons may make for injuries to them or damage to their property caused by the insured.

36-7a PHYSICAL DAMAGE INSURANCE

As the name implies, **physical damage insurance** covers the risks of injury or damage to the car itself. It includes:

1. Fire insurance
2. Theft insurance

3. Collision insurance

4. Comprehensive coverage

36-7b FIRE INSURANCE

Much of the law of property insurance discussed in the preceding pages applies to automobile insurance. The fire policy covers loss to a car damaged or destroyed by the burning of any conveyance on which the car is being transported, such as a barge, boat, or train. Fire insurance can be obtained separately but is normally included in comprehensive coverage.

36-7c THEFT INSURANCE

Theft is taking another's property without the owner's consent, with the intent to wrongfully deprive the owner of the property. Automobile theft insurance, either by law or by contract, normally covers a wide range of losses. Obtaining possession of a car and converting it to one's own use to the exclusion of, or inconsistent with, the rights of the owner is known as **conversion**. Taking another's car by force or threat of force is known as **robbery**. In some states, the automobile theft policy must cover all these losses. The policy itself may define theft broadly enough to cover theft, conversion, and robbery. Unless the policy is broadened either by law or by the wording of the policy, a theft policy covers only the wrongful deprivation of the car without claim of right.

theft
taking another's property without consent

conversion
obtaining possession of property and converting it to own use

robbery
taking property by force

COURT CASE

FACTS: Government Employees Ins. Co. (GEICO) insured Janet Duddy's car, which was used by her son. He decided to sell the car and advertised it on Craigslist. George Gibson examined the car and agreed to buy it for $15,000. Gibson said he would return to pay for the car and pick it up. Duddy notified GEICO that the car was to be dropped from the policy, and a replacement added. Gibson returned as promised and gave Duddy $2,000 in cash and a cashier's check for $13,000. She gave him the keys and title and deposited the check in her bank account. She later learned the check was fraudulent. The car was not found. Duddy notified GEICO, which denied coverage, saying she had sold the car. She sued GEICO.

OUTCOME: The court said that since Duddy did not receive the bargained-for consideration, there was no sale of the car. As a result, the transaction was a theft and covered by the policy.

—*Duddy v. Government Employees Ins. Co.*, 23 A.3d 436 (N.J. Super. Ct. App. Div.)

Automobile theft insurance usually covers pilferage of any parts of the car but not articles or clothes left in the car. It also covers any damage done to the car either by theft or attempted theft. It does not cover loss of use of the car unless the policy specifically provides for this loss.

36-7d COLLISION INSURANCE

The standard collision policy covers all damage to the car caused by a collision or upset. A collision occurs whenever an object strikes the insured car, or the car strikes an object. The object need not be an automobile nor be moving. Frequently, collision policies require the collision to be "accidental." A court held that a rolling rock that crashed into a parked car constituted a collision. Likewise, there was a collision when a horse kicked the door of the insured automobile. However, no collision occurs when the colliding object consists of a natural phenomenon, such as rain or hail. If the language of an insurance policy can be given two different, reasonable interpretations, the interpretation most helpful to the insured is used.

Practically all collision policies void or suspend coverage if a car hauls a trailer unless insurance of the same kind carried on the car is placed on the trailer. The question of interpretation then arises as to what constitutes a "trailer." A small boat trailer and a small two-wheel trailer generally are not considered trailers, but horse or cattle trailers are.

If a car has collision insurance but not fire insurance, the policy will, in most states, pay both the fire loss and the collision loss occurring in the same wreck so long as the fire ensues after collision and is a direct result of it.

deductible clause
insurance provision whereby insured pays damage up to specified amount; company pays excess up to policy limits

Most collision insurance policies have a **deductible clause**. A deductible clause provides that the insurance company will pay for damages to the car in excess of a specified amount. The specified amount, called the deductible, is usually $100 to $500. The insured must pay this amount. Suppose a collision results in $850 in damages to a car covered by $250 deductible collision insurance. The insured must pay the first $250, and the insurance company pays the remainder—$600. Policies without any deductible clause have extremely high rates. It is much cheaper for the insured to assume some of the risk.

An insurance company may pay the insured a claim for collision damage caused by someone else's negligence. If so, under the law of subrogation the company has the right to sue this other party to the collision for the damages.

36-7e COMPREHENSIVE COVERAGE

Insurance companies will write automobile insurance covering almost every conceivable risk to a car, such as windstorm, earthquake, flood, strike, spray from trees, malicious mischief, submersion in water, acid from the battery, riot, glass breakage, hail, and falling aircraft. A comprehensive policy may include all of these risks plus fire and theft. A **comprehensive policy** covers only the hazards enumerated in the policy, and collision is normally excluded.

comprehensive policy
insurance covering large number of miscellaneous risks

36-7f PUBLIC LIABILITY INSURANCE

The second major division of automobile insurance, **public liability insurance**, protects third persons from bodily injury and property damage.

public liability insurance
insurance designed to protect third persons from bodily injury and property damage

36-7g BODILY INJURY INSURANCE

Bodily injury insurance covers the risk of bodily injury to the insured's passengers, pedestrians, or the occupants of another car. The insurance company obligates itself to pay any sum not exceeding the limit fixed in the policy for which the insured may be personally liable. If the insured has no liability for damages, the insurance company has no liability except the duty of defending the insured in court actions brought by injured persons. This type of insurance does not cover any injury to the person or the property of the insured. State law requires drivers to carry this kind of liability insurance. The coverage required varies significantly.

Coverage under an automobile liability policy is usually written as 25/50/10, 50/100/20, 100/300/25, or similar combinations. The first number indicates that the company will pay $10,000, $25,000, or $100,000, respectively, to any person for bodily injury in any one accident. The middle number fixes the maximum amount the company will pay, in thousands, for bodily injury to more than one person in any one accident. The third figure sets the limit the company will pay, in thousands, for property damage. This usually is the damage to the other person's car but may include damage to any property belonging to someone other than the insured.

A bodily injury insurance policy does not cover accidents occurring while an underage person drives the car. It might not cover accidents occurring while the car is rented or leased unless specifically covered, while the car is used to carry passengers for a consideration, while the car is used for any purpose other than that named in the policy, or while it is used outside the United States and Canada. Some policies exclude accidents while the car is being used for towing a trailer or any other vehicle used as a trailer. These are the ordinary exclusions. Policies may have additional exclusions of various kinds.

The insured may not settle claims or incur expenses other than those for immediate medical help. As in the case of property insurance, the insurer has a duty to defend any lawsuits and the insured must give prompt notice of any claims or suits. In the event that the insurance company pays a loss, it is subrogated to any rights that the insured has against others because of such losses.

36-7h PROPERTY DAMAGE INSURANCE

In automobile property damage insurance, the insurer agrees to pay, on behalf of the insured, all sums the insured may be legally obligated to pay for damages arising out of the ownership, maintenance, or use of the automobile. The liability of the insurer, however, is limited as stated in the policy.

The policy usually provides that the insurer will not be liable in the event that the car is being operated, maintained, or used by any person in violation of any state or federal law as to age or occupation. The insurer has no liability for damage to property owned by, leased to, transported by, or in charge of the insured.

36-7i MEDICAL PAYMENTS AND UNINSURED/ UNDERINSURED MOTORIST INSURANCE

In addition to physical damage and public liability insurance, there is insurance that covers injury to the insured or passengers in the insured's car. Medical payments cover bodily injury and are paid regardless of other insurance. Uninsured motorist coverage protects the insured when injury results from the negligence of another driver who does not have liability insurance. Underinsured motorist coverage allows insureds to recover from their own insurance companies if the driver responsible for an accident does not have enough insurance coverage to pay for all the damages. In some states, car owners must carry uninsured or underinsured motorist coverage.

COURT CASE

FACTS: Anitra Lakes drove a car with her mother and sister, Hannah, as passengers. James Issacs ran a stop sign and hit the Lakes's car, injuring them and his passenger, Dustin Gavin. Issacs had insurance with bodily injury limits of $25,000 per person and $50,000 per accident. The policy limit of $50,000 was divided among the injured persons. Hannah received $5,100, which did not cover her injuries. Anitra had underinsured motorist (UIM) insurance of $50,000 per person and per accident with Grange Mutual Casualty Co. (Grange). Hannah sued Grange for UIM coverage. Grange argued that Issacs' vehicle was not underinsured, since the per-accident limit

of Issacs's policy equaled the UIM limit of Anitra's policy. The UIM law defined an underinsured vehicle as a vehicle whose insurance "limits of coverage available for payment" are less than the limits of the insured's UIM coverage.

OUTCOME: The court stated that whether a vehicle is underinsured depends on whether the amount received from the tortfeasor's policy is less than the per-person limits of UIM coverage. Since Hannah received less, the UIM coverage was appropriate.

—*Lakes v. Grange Mut. Cas. Co.*, 964 N.E.2d 796 (Ind.)

36-7j RECOVERY EVEN WHEN AT FAULT

Normally, the injured party must prove the driver of the insured car was negligent or at fault before the insurer becomes liable. Frequently, both drivers are negligent. Formerly, if the driver who sues negligently contributed even slightly to the accident, no recovery could be had. This harsh rule has been replaced in most states by the **last clear chance rule**. This rule states that if one driver is negligent, but the other driver had one last clear chance to avoid hitting the negligent driver and did not take it, the driver who had the last clear chance is liable.

last clear chance rule negligent driver recovers if other driver had one last clear chance to avoid injury

In a number of states, **comparative negligence** statutes also have modified the harshness of the common-law rule as to contributory negligence. These statutes provide that the contributory negligence of the plaintiff reduces the recovery but does not completely bar recovery from a negligent defendant. That means the court balances the negligence of each party against that of the other. Suppose that Roemer and Griffero had an automobile accident, and both were negligent. It is determined that the damage to Roemer's car was caused 60 percent by Griffero and 40 percent by Roemer's own negligence. If the total damage to Roemer's car is $2,500, Griffero will have to pay 60 percent, or $1,500.

comparative negligence contributory negligence that reduces but does not bar recovery

Some states have established **no-fault insurance**. Under this plan, insurance companies pay for injuries suffered by their insureds, no matter who has responsibility for negligence. States use this no-fault plan for a limited amount of damages. Above this amount, the fault rules apply. The purpose of no-fault insurance is to make sure that injured parties are compensated promptly and to reduce the number of lawsuits. It is assumed that it is faster and easier to collect from your own insurance company than from the insurance company of the other driver.

no-fault insurance insurance companies pay for their insureds' injuries regardless of fault

36-7k REQUIRED INSURANCE

People with poor driving records might find it difficult or impossible to obtain mandatory automobile insurance. When the law requires a person to carry insurance in order to be permitted to drive, but no insurance company will sell a policy, a state agency will assign this driver to an insurance company. The company must issue the policy under the "assigned risk" rule. States require all insurance companies to accept the drivers assigned in this manner.

QUESTIONS

1. What is the difference between level-term and decreasing-term life insurance?

2. What are two common limitations on risks covered by life insurance?

3. Why is it desirable for the insured to have a grace period in a life insurance policy?

4. What is the maximum amount an insured can recover for total loss of property?

5. What risk does a fire insurance policy normally cover?

6. Why must property and its location be described accurately?

7. What does an 80 percent coinsurance clause in an insurance policy mean?

8. What kinds of losses does an auto theft policy cover?

9. What does automobile bodily injury insurance cover?

10. What is a no-fault insurance plan?

CASE PROBLEMS

1. Smarr purchased a family automobile insurance policy on his pickup truck from American National Property and Casualty Company (ANPAC). The policy excluded coverage for liability sustained "while any vehicle is used to carry persons or property for a charge." The truck was primarily used for farm work, but Smarr also ran a tree cutting and trimming business. One day the truck was used to transport logs from the tree cutting business to a local sawmill, when it was struck from behind, and the driver of the other vehicle was killed. ANPAC denied coverage on the basis of its exclusion clause. Was Smarr entitled to coverage? **LO** ③

2. Advocate Networks, LLC, received a copy of a lawsuit against it by Marketing on Hold Inc. on March 23. Networks retained counsel to represent it in connection with the lawsuit on March 26 but failed to provide Hartford Fire Insurance Company, which had issued two liability insurance policies to Networks, with any notice of the event that prompted the lawsuit, the underlying claim, or the lawsuit itself until July 25. The policies required Networks to notify Hartford of any claim or lawsuit "as soon as practicable" and to "immediately" send it copies of any legal papers in connection with any claim or lawsuit. Hartford asked the court to declare that Networks was not covered under the policies with respect to the lawsuit or the underlying claim. Networks said it had thought the dispute was a misunderstanding it could resolve by e-mail. It argued that no potential liability was indicated, so it did not have a duty to provide Hartford prompt notice. Is Networks covered? **LO** ②

3. Fatima Costello purchased a life insurance policy that included an incontestability provision so long as the policy "has been in force during the lifetime of the Insured for two years from the date of issue." Costello did not disclose the fact that she was taking medication for hypertension and elevated lipids and had a history of chronic obstructive pulmonary disease. Costello died twenty-one months after the policy was issued, and her husband made a claim on the policy within two weeks. United of Omaha Life Insurance Company (United) denied the claim four months later, twenty-five months after the policy was issued, on the basis of the contestability clause and the undisclosed medical information. The husband sued, claiming that the contestability clause meant that United had to contest the policy within the two-year period. Did United wait too long to contest the policy? **LO** ①

CASE PROBLEMS (CONTINUED)

LO ②   4. Coast Converters, Inc. (Coast) manufactured plastic bags. It carried a commercial all-risk insurance policy from Federal Insurance Company (Federal), including both property damage and business interruption. As a result of electrical modifications made to Coast's manufacturing facility, certain voltage fluctuations occurred causing the production of a larger-than-normal number of defective bags. In many cases, that stock actually was sold, and Coast only learned of the defects through returns of defective bags. Coast filed a claim with Federal to recover costs of damaged machinery and the increased number of scrap bags. Federal claimed that a significant portion of the losses were not covered under "property damage" because Coast was not in the business of producing defective bags. Was Coast covered for its costs in producing the defective bags?

LO ③   5. Thomas Hasselle injured his wife, Shirley, when he accidentally hit her with their car. They were both named insureds under their Alfa Insurance Corporation (Alfa) automobile policy. The policy excluded liability coverage for "any bodily injury to any covered person." "Covered person" included any named insured. Alfa denied liability coverage for Shirley's injuries. Should Alfa be allowed to deny liability coverage?

LO ①   6. Chase Insurance Life & Annuity Company issued a one-million-dollar life insurance policy to Theresa Officer effective on February 11. Her husband, Dean Officer, was the beneficiary. Two years of premiums were paid, but one year, ten months, and twenty-four days after the policy became effective, Theresa committed suicide. Dean made a claim under the insurance policy, and Chase sent him $540, the amount of the premiums that had been paid. The policy stated that Chase would limit the "proceeds" paid under the policy if the insured committed suicide "within 2 years from the Date of Issue; and after 2 years from the Date of Issue, but within 2 years from the effective date of the last reinstatement of this policy." The "limited amount" was the premiums paid. Should the court limit Dean's recovery to $540?

LO ③   7. As Jonathan Adrabi drove out of a parking lot, he stopped behind another car at a stop sign. The people from the car ahead of him got out and assaulted him. They hit him with the barrel of a shotgun, forced him into his car trunk, and drove at high rates of speed, occasionally slamming on the brakes, which banged him against the trunk interior. Adrabi made a claim for his injuries under his Allstate Insurance Co. (Allstate) uninsured motorist (UM) coverage. The UM provision provided payment for bodily injuries the insured was entitled to recover "from the owner or operator of an uninsured auto. Injury must be caused by accident and arise out of the ownership, maintenance or use of an uninsured … auto." An uninsured auto under the policy was one that had "no bodily injury insurance policy in effect at the time of the accident." Allstate denied coverage and Adrabi sued, alleging that once under the control of the assailants, his car was uninsured. Should he recover?

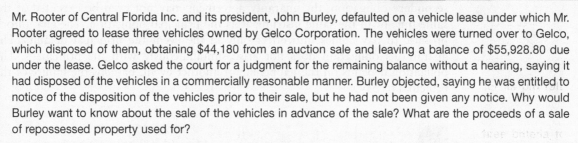

Security Devices

LEARNING OBJECTIVES

1. State the general nature of contracts of guaranty or suretyship.
2. Identify ways contracts of guaranty and suretyship are discharged.
3. Discuss the rights of the parties in a secured credit sale.
4. Discuss the rights of the seller and buyer in a secured credit sale.

PREVIEW CASE

Mr. Rooter of Central Florida Inc. and its president, John Burley, defaulted on a vehicle lease under which Mr. Rooter agreed to lease three vehicles owned by Gelco Corporation. The vehicles were turned over to Gelco, which disposed of them, obtaining $44,180 from an auction sale and leaving a balance of $55,928.80 due under the lease. Gelco asked the court for a judgment for the remaining balance without a hearing, saying it had disposed of the vehicles in a commercially reasonable manner. Burley objected, saying he was entitled to notice of the disposition of the vehicles prior to their sale, but he had not been given any notice. Why would Burley want to know about the sale of the vehicles in advance of the sale? What are the proceeds of a sale of repossessed property used for?

This chapter discusses two types of security devices: (1) guaranty and suretyship contracts, and (2) secured credit sales.

37-1 Guaranty and Suretyship

A contract of guaranty or suretyship is an agreement whereby one party promises to be responsible for the debt, default, or obligation of another. Such contracts generally arise when one person assumes responsibility for the extension of credit to another, as in buying merchandise on credit or in borrowing money from a bank, or when someone is responsible for another person's money.

A person entrusted with the money of another, such as a cashier, a bank teller, or a county treasurer, may be required to have someone guarantee the faithful performance of the duties. This contract of suretyship is commonly referred to as a **fidelity bond**.

LO 1
Nature of guaranty and suretyship

fidelity bond
suretyship for someone who handles another's money

bonding company
paid surety

Bonding companies have taken over most of the business of guaranteeing the employer against losses caused by dishonest employees. These bonding companies are paid sureties, which mean they receive money for entering into the suretyship. The bonding company's obligation arises from its written contract with the employer. This contract of indemnity details the conditions under which the surety will be liable.

37-1a PARTIES

guarantor or surety
party who agrees to be responsible for obligation of another

creditor
party who receives guaranty

A contract of guaranty or of suretyship involves three parties. The party who undertakes to be responsible for another is the **guarantor**, or the **surety**; the party to whom the guaranty is given is the **creditor**; and the party who has primary liability is the principal debtor, or simply the **principal**. Because these three parties are distinct and have differing rights and obligations, it is important to identify exactly what role a party has in a guaranty or suretyship arrangement.

principal
party primarily liable

37-1b DISTINCTIONS

The words *surety* and *guarantor* are often used interchangeably, and they have many similarities. Some states have abolished any distinction between them. However, in other states, their legal usages differ. In states in which they differ, a surety has liability coextensive with that of the principal debtor. The surety has direct and primary responsibility for the debt or obligation just like the primary debtor. The surety's obligation, then, is identical with the debtor's.

A guarantor's obligation is secondary to that of the principal debtor. As a secondary obligation, the guaranty agreement may not even be executed at the same time or in the same instrument as the principal obligation. The guarantor's promise to pay comes into effect only in the event the principal defaults. The guarantor's obligation does not arise simultaneously with the principal's. The obligation depends on the happening of another event, namely, the failure of the principal to pay.

COURT CASE

FACTS: Alerus Financial, N.A. (Alerus) loaned KRE, LLC (KRE) $2.6 million to buy real estate and obtained a first mortgage on the property. The Marcil Group Inc. (TMGI), Michael J. Marcil, and Arthur S. Rosenberg individually executed separate documents stating that each "absolutely and unconditionally . . . guaranty to you the payment and performance of each and every Debt, of every type . . . that the Borrower . . . may now or at any time in the future owe you." They also stated, "I am unconditionally liable under this Guaranty, regardless of whether or not you pursue any of your remedies against the Borrower." KRE defaulted on the note, and Alerus got a judgment in foreclosure. KRE filed for bankruptcy before the sheriff could sell the property, but Alerus sued TMGI, Marcil, and Rosenberg. They alleged the documents they signed were surety contracts not guaranties.

OUTCOME: The court held that the defendants' obligations were not triggered, creating a secondary liability, until KRE defaulted; therefore, they were guaranty contracts.

—*Alerus Financial, N.A. v. Marcil Group Inc.,* 806 N.W.2d 160 (N.D.)

For the most part, the law of suretyship applies with equal force to both paid sureties and accommodation sureties. A bail bondsman is a paid surety. An accommodation surety agrees to be a surety as a favor to the principal. A parent who cosigns a note for a teenager constitutes an accommodation surety. In some instances, the contract of a paid surety will be interpreted strictly. Thus, in the case of acts claimed to discharge the surety, courts sometimes require paid sureties to prove that they have actually been harmed by the conduct of the principal before allowing recovery.

37-1c IMPORTANCE OF MAKING A DISTINCTION

In states that recognize a difference between guarantors and sureties, the distinctions involve three aspects:

1. Form
2. Notice of default
3. Remedy

Form. All the essential elements of a contract must be present in both contracts of guaranty and contracts of suretyship. However, a contract of guaranty must be in writing (see Illustration 37-1), whereas most contracts of suretyship may normally be oral.

ILLUSTRATION 37-1 A Letter of Guaranty

WATERS, MELLEN AND COMPANY

900 West Lake Avenue

Cincinnati, Ohio 45227

May 16, 20–

Ms. Norma Rae

201 E. Fifth Street

Campton, KY 41301

Dear Ms. Rae

In consideration of the letting of the premises located at 861 South Street, this city, to Mr. William H. Prost for a period of two years from date, I hereby guarantee the punctual payment of the rent and the faithful performance of the covenants of the lease.

Very truly yours

Orvinne L. Meyer

Vice-President, Personnel

The Uniform Commercial Code (UCC) provides: "The promise to answer for the debt, default, or obligation of another must be in writing and be signed by the party to be charged or by his authorized agent." This provision should apply to a promise that creates a secondary obligation, which means an obligation of guaranty, not to a promise that creates a primary obligation or suretyship.

Notice of Default. A creditor need not notify sureties—parties primarily liable for the debt—if the principal defaults. Conversely, the creditor must notify guarantors. In some states, failure to give notice does not itself discharge the guarantyship. A guarantor damaged by the failure to receive notice may offset the amount of the damage against the claim of the creditor.

Remedy. In the case of suretyship, the surety assumes an original obligation. The surety must pay. Sureties have liability as fully and under the same conditions as if the debt were theirs from the beginning. The rule is different in many contracts of guaranty. In a conditional guaranty, the guarantor has liability only if the other party cannot pay.

For example, Arnold writes, "Let Brewer have a suit; if he cannot pay you, I will." This guaranty depends on Brewer's ability to pay. Therefore, the seller must make all reasonable efforts to collect from Brewer before collecting from Arnold. If Arnold had written, "Let Brewer have this suit, and I will pay you," an original obligation would have been created for which Arnold would have been personally liable. Therefore, Arnold would be deemed a surety if the understanding was that Arnold was to pay for the suit.

37-1d RIGHTS OF THE SURETY AND THE GUARANTOR

A guarantor and a surety have the following rights:

1. Indemnity
2. Subrogation
3. Contribution
4. Exoneration

indemnity
right of guarantor to be reimbursed by principal

Indemnity. A guarantor or surety who pays the debt or the obligation of the principal has the right to be reimbursed by the principal, known as the right of **indemnity**. The guarantor or the surety may be induced to pay the debt when it becomes due, to avoid the accumulation of interest and other costs on the debt.

Subrogation. When the guarantor or the surety pays the debt of the principal, the law automatically assigns the claim of the creditor to the guarantor or surety. The payment also entitles the guarantor or surety to all properties, liens, or securities that were held by the creditor to secure the payment of the debt. This right of subrogation does not arise until the creditor has been paid in full, but it does arise if the surety or the guarantor has paid a part of the debt, and the principal has paid the remainder.

coguarantors or cosureties
two or more people jointly liable for another's obligation

contribution
right of coguarantor to recover excess of proportionate share of debt from other coguarantor(s)

Contribution. Two or more people jointly liable for the debt, default, or obligation of a certain person are **coguarantors** or **cosureties**. Guarantors or sureties who have paid more than their proportionate share of the debt are entitled to recover from the other guarantors or sureties the amount in excess of their *pro rata* share of the loss. This is the right of **contribution**. It does not arise until the surety or the guarantor has paid the debts of the principal in full or has otherwise settled the debt.

COURT CASE

FACTS: Titan Framing Company (Titan) purchased general commercial liability insurance from Navigators Specialty Insurance Company (Navigators) and business auto insurance from Nationwide Mutual Insurance Company (Nationwide). After a company picnic, one of Titan's employees, Ivan Aquino, caused an accident while driving home, killing himself and the driver of another car. The family of the other driver sued Titan, and Titan informed Navigators. Navigators informed Nationwide of the claims, and invited Nationwide to participate in the defense and settlement meetings. Ultimately, Nationwide did not participate, and Navigators settled the claims.

Navigators then sued Nationwide for its pro rata contribution to the settlement.

OUTCOME: The court looked at three criteria to determine whether or not the right of contribution existed: (1) if the insurers insured the same risk; (2) if either was the primary insurer; and (3) if the loss was created by a covered risk. In this case, Navigators and Nationwide insured different risks, so Nationwide did not have to contribute to the settlement payment.

—*Navigators Specialty Ins. Co. v. Nationwide Mutual Ins. Co.*, 50 F.Supp.3d 1186 (D. Ariz.)

Exoneration. A surety or guarantor may call on the creditor to proceed to compel the payment of the debt; otherwise, the surety or guarantor will be released. This is the right of **exoneration.** The creditor may delay in pressing the debtor to pay because of the security of the suretyship. A creditor who fails to compel payment when due releases the surety in cases in which the debtor can pay. The surety then has no uncertainty concerning potential liability.

exoneration
guarantor's right to have creditor compel payment of debt

37-1e DISCHARGE OF A SURETY OR A GUARANTOR

The usual methods of discharging any obligation, including performance, voluntary agreement, and bankruptcy of the surety or guarantor, discharge both a surety and a guarantor. However, some additional acts that will discharge the surety or the guarantor include:

LO ②
Discharge of guaranty or suretyship

1. Extension of time
2. Alteration of the terms of the contract
3. Loss or return of collateral by the creditor

Extension of Time. If the creditor extends the time of the debt without the consent of the surety or the guarantor and for a consideration, the surety or the guarantor is discharged from further liability.

Alteration of the Terms of the Contract. A material alteration of the contract by the creditor without the surety's or guarantor's consent discharges the surety or guarantor. In most states, the change must be prejudicial to the surety or the guarantor. A reduction in the interest rate has been held not to discharge the surety, whereas a change in the place of payment has been held to be an act justifying a discharge of the surety. A material change in a contract constitutes substituting a new contract for the old. The surety guaranteed the payment of the old contract, not the new one.

COURT CASE

FACTS: Dotson 10s, LLC (Dotson) borrowed $550,677.53 from Vision Bank (Vision) secured by a mortgage on real estate. Fred and Nancy Eagerton executed guaranties for this loan, #78476 and any "extensions, renewals or replacements thereof." A year later, Dotson obtained a second loan from Vision, but the Eagertons were not guarantors of it. Four months later, both loans were in default. Dotson filed a petition for reorganization under Chapter 11 of the Bankruptcy Code. A confirmed plan consolidated the two loans with a maturity date a year after the maturity date of the first loan. Three months later, Dotson defaulted. The proceeds of foreclosure did not pay off the consolidated loan. Vision alleged that the consolidated loan was a "replacement" note and that the Eagertons were liable for 71.07 percent of the unpaid amount because the original loan was 71.07 percent of the consolidated loan. The Eagertons argued that they should pay nothing because there was a material alteration, without their consent, of the note they guaranteed.

OUTCOME: The court held that the consolidated loan was a new indebtedness that discharged the Eagertons from their guaranty.

—*Eagerton v. Vision Bank*, 2012 WL 1139148 (Ala.)

Creditor's Loss or Return of Collateral. If the creditor, through negligence, loses or damages collateral security given to secure the debt, a surety or a guarantor is discharged. The return of any collateral security to the debtor also discharges a surety or guarantor. Collateral must be held for the benefit of the surety until the debtor pays the debt in full.

37-2 Secured Credit Sales

When someone other than the buyer finances goods (a credit purchase is made), one convenient way to protect creditors from loss is to allow them to have an interest in the goods. When sellers retain the right to repossess the items sold if the buyers breach the sales contracts, the transactions are **secured credit sales**. In such cases, the buyers obtain possession of the items, and the risk of loss passes to them. Article 9 of the UCC governs secured credit sales. A security interest cannot attach or become enforceable until the buyer and seller agree it shall attach, the seller gives value, and the buyer has the right to possess or use the item.

secured credit sale
sale in which seller retains right to repossess goods upon default

37-2a SECURITY AGREEMENT

A creditor may not enforce a security interest unless the buyer has signed a security agreement. The **security agreement** is a written agreement, signed by the buyer, that describes the collateral, or the item sold, and usually contains the terms of payment and names of the parties.

security agreement
written agreement signed by buyer that creditor has a security interest in collateral

COURT CASE

FACTS: Matthew Hintze delivered a promissory note to Christopher James in the principal amount of $375,000. The note included a recital of security for payment of the principal "in all of Maker's assets." When Hintze later declared bankruptcy, James claimed certain of Hintze's personal property to repay the debt. Hintze claimed that the language of the note was too vague to create a security interest.

OUTCOME: The UCC requires that a description of the collateral be "reasonably specific" so that the identity of the collateral is "objectively determinable." That was not the case here, and the court found that a security interest had not been created.

—*In re Hintze*, 525 B.R. 780 (N.D. Fla.)

37-2b RIGHTS OF THE SELLER

The rights of the seller, referred to as the *secured party* under the security agreement, may be transferred to a third person by assignment. In any sale, the buyer may have claims or defenses against the seller. In the case of consumer sales, the Federal Trade Commission requires the seller to include in the agreement a notice that any holder of the agreement is subject to all claims and defenses that the buyer could assert against the seller. Thus, an assignee would be subject to any claims or defenses. This protection for the buyer applies only to consumer transactions.

37-2c RIGHTS OF THE BUYER

The buyer, also called the *debtor*, has the right to transfer the collateral and require a determination of the amount owed.

Transfer of Collateral. Even though there is a security interest in the collateral, the debtor may transfer the collateral to others. Such a transfer will usually be subject to the security interest.

Determination of Amount Owed. A buyer who wishes may sign a statement indicating the amount of unpaid indebtedness believed to be owed as of a specified date and send it to the seller with the request that the statement be approved or corrected and returned.

37-2d PERFECTION OF SECURITY INTEREST

When the rights of the seller to the collateral are superior to those of third persons, the seller has a **perfected security interest**. The use to which the buyer puts collateral at the time of perfection of the security interest determines how the creditor perfects a security interest.

Inventory and Equipment. Articles purchased with the intention of reselling or leasing them are called **inventory**. **Equipment** consists of goods used or purchased for use in a business, including farming or a profession. In order to have a perfected security interest in inventory or equipment, the seller must usually file a

LO ④
Rights of seller and buyer

perfected security interest
seller's right to collateral that is superior to third party's right

inventory
articles purchased with intention of reselling or leasing

equipment
goods for use in business

financing statement in the appropriate public office. However, filing need not be made when the law requires a security interest to be noted on the document of title to the goods, such as in the case of noting a lien on a title to a motor vehicle. Buyers of inventory sold in the regular course of business and for value acquire title free of the security interest. For example, any time a customer goes into a store and buys and pays for a TV, the customer obtains the TV free of any security interest. Any time an item subject to a security interest is sold at the direction of the secured party, the buyer takes it free of the security interest.

A **financing statement** is a writing signed by the debtor and the secured party that contains the address of the secured party, the mailing address of the debtor, and a statement indicating the types of or describing the collateral. A copy of the security agreement may serve as a financing statement if it contains the required items.

financing statement
writing with signatures and addresses of debtor and secured party and description of collateral

Fixtures.
Personal property attached to buildings or real estate is called a **fixture**. A creditor perfects a security interest in fixtures by filing the financing statement in the office where a mortgage on the real estate involved would be filed or recorded. This is normally the recorder's office in the county where the real estate is located.

fixture
personal property attached to real estate

Consumer Goods.
Consumer goods are items used or bought primarily for personal, family, or household purposes. A security interest in consumer goods is perfected as soon as it attaches and without filing in most cases. It is not perfected, however, against a buyer who purchases the item without the knowledge of the security interest, for value and for the buyer's own personal, family, or household use. The secured party can be protected against such a buyer only by filing a financing statement. However, as in the case of inventory and equipment, listing the secured party as the lienholder on a motor vehicle certificate of title is the way a security interest in a motor vehicle used for personal, family, or household purposes is perfected.

consumer goods
items purchased for personal, family, or household purposes

COURT CASE

FACTS: To finance the purchase of a compact utility tractor and front loader, Joseph Palmer executed a retail installment contract-lien contract-security agreement with Suburban Tractor Company. Suburban transferred its interests to Deere & Company. The security agreement stated that Palmer was borrowing as an individual. The first page read, "Unless I otherwise certify below, this is a consumer credit transaction and the Goods will be used primarily for personal, family or household purposes." The agreement had a commercial purpose affidavit that was blank and unsigned. No financing statement was filed. Palmer filed for bankruptcy protection. The trustee in bankruptcy alleged that Deere had an unperfected security interest because Palmer used the equipment in his dog training business, and as business property a financing statement had to be filed for perfection of a security interest.

OUTCOME: The court said the classification of collateral is fixed at the time the security interest is created. When the security agreement was signed, Palmer affirmatively represented that the goods were for personal, family, or household use. Since a purchase-money security interest in consumer goods is perfected upon attachment, and attachment occurs upon execution of the security agreement, Deere's interest was perfected.

—*In re Palmer*, 365 B.R. 816 (S.D. Ohio)

Duration of Filing. Perfection of a security interest by filing a financing statement lasts for five years. However, creditors may file a continuation statement that continues the effectiveness of the filing for five more years. Succeeding continuation statements may be filed, each of which lasts five years.

If a continuation statement is not filed, the effectiveness of a filing statement lapses at the end of five years. The security interest is then unperfected even against a purchaser of the goods before the lapse.

37-3 Effect of Default

Under the UCC, the seller has certain rights if the buyer fails to pay according to the terms of the security agreement or otherwise breaches the contract. These rights include repossession and resale. The buyer has the rights to redemption and an accounting.

Repossession. When the buyer has the right to possession of the collateral before making full payment, and the buyer breaches the purchase contract, the seller may repossess, or take back, the collateral. If it can be done without a breach of the peace, the repossession may be made without any judicial proceedings. In any case, judicial action may be sought. The seller may retain the collateral in satisfaction of the debt unless the debtor, after being notified, objects. Any personal property in the repossessed collateral must be returned to the debtor.

Resale. After default, the seller may sell the collateral. A public or private sale may be used, and any manner, time, place, and terms may be used as long as the disposition is commercially reasonable and done in good faith. Advance notice of the sale must be given to the debtor unless the goods are perishable. If the buyer has paid 60 percent or more of the cash price of the goods, the seller must resell the goods within 90 days after possession of them unless the buyer, after default, has signed a statement waiving the right to require resale. The purpose of this requirement is to cause a sale before the goods decline in value.

PREVIEW CASE REVISITED

FACTS: Mr. Rooter of Central Florida Inc. and its president, John Burley, defaulted on a vehicle lease under which Mr. Rooter agreed to lease three vehicles owned by Gelco Corporation. The vehicles were turned over to Gelco, which disposed of them, obtaining $44,180 from an auction sale and leaving a balance of $55,928.80 due under the lease. Gelco asked the court for a judgment for the remaining balance without a hearing, saying it had disposed of the vehicles in a commercially reasonable manner. Burley objected, saying he was entitled to notice of the disposition of the vehicles prior to their sale, but he had not been given any notice. Had he received notice, Burley argued, he would either have objected to the proposed sale or gone to the sale and bought the vehicles himself because their sale price was less than one-third the market price.

OUTCOME: Because Burley had not received the required notice, the court could not award judgment to Gelco without determining whether the vehicle sale had been in a commercially reasonable manner.

—*Burley v. Gelco Corp.*, 976 So.2d 97 (Fla. Dist. Ct. App.)

Redemption. At any time prior to the sale or the contracting to sell the collateral, the buyer may redeem it by paying the amount owed and the expenses reasonably incurred by the seller in retaking and holding the collateral and preparing for the sale. This includes, if provided in the agreement, reasonable attorney's fees and legal expenses.

Accounting. After the sale of the collateral, the creditor must apply payments in the following order: the expenses of retaking and selling the collateral, the amount owed on the security interest, and all amounts owed on any subordinate security interests. The seller must pay any surplus remaining to the buyer. If sale of the collateral does not cover the amount of the debt, the buyer is liable for any deficiency, and the creditor may obtain a judgment for that amount.

QUESTIONS

1. What is the difference between a paid surety and an accommodation surety?

2. What is the difference between a guaranty and suretyship in those states that retain a distinction between them?

3. What remedy does a guarantor damaged by the failure to receive notice of default of the principal have?

4. When does the right of contribution arise?

5. Why would a surety want to exercise the right of exoneration?

6. Under what circumstances will the creditor's extension of the time of the debt discharge a surety or guarantor?

7. How long must collateral be held for the benefit of a surety?

8. How may a buyer (debtor) who wants to determine the amount owed get such a determination from the seller (creditor)?

9. How is a security interest perfected in: (a) inventory and equipment, (b) fixtures, and (c) consumer goods?

10. When a seller repossesses collateral after a default, what may the seller do with it?

CASE PROBLEMS

LO ③, ④

1. Farm Credit Services of America, PCA (Farm Credit) made a loan to Bryan Stec which was secured by Stec's corn crop. Farm Credit filed the appropriate statement with the applicable authority to perfect its interest. Stec had a contract to deliver the corn to Cargill, Inc. (Cargill). Stec delivered a portion of the crop to Cargill, but then filed for bankruptcy. Farm Credit, as secured creditor, sold Stec's remaining crop, but not for enough to repay the loan plus costs. Farm Credit sued Cargill for return of the corn. Did Farm Credit have the right to repossess the corn?

LO ②

2. Brown's Roofing, Inc. (Brown) entered into surety bond agreements with International Fidelity Insurance Company (IFIC) to guarantee Brown's contributions to trust funds operated by the Local Union No. 30 of the United Union of Roofers, Waterproofers and Allied Workers (Union), pursuant to a collective bargaining agreement (CBA) between Brown and Union. The bond agreements provided that the Union was to notify IFIC within one year of Brown's default in payment. IFIC would then pay the amounts due under the CBA. Brown became delinquent on its payments, and the Union sued Brown for payment. After a few months, Brown and the Union entered into a settlement agreement, whereby

CASE PROBLEMS (CONTINUED)

Brown was required to pay the then-amount of the delinquency under the CBA. IFIC received no notice from the Union of any of the proceedings. Approximately one year later, Brown failed to make payments under the settlement agreement. This time, more than a year after the Union sued Brown, the Union notified IFIC that it was making a claim on the surety bond. Was IFIC still liable for payment under the terms of the surety bond?

3. In order to secure $1.5 million in loans from Fifth Third Bank (Fifth), Odle, McGuire & Shook (OMS) signed a security agreement giving Fifth a security interest in all its assets, including any deposit accounts it had with Fifth. Fifth perfected its security interest by filing a financing statement with the secretary of state. OMS defaulted on its loans but continued to conduct business, and Fifth honored checks that OMS drew on its account with Fifth. OMS also defaulted on a lease with People's National Bank (PNB), so PNB sued and obtained a judgment for over $60,000. To collect its judgment, PNB tried to attach any funds of OMS in accounts at Fifth. Fifth alleged that since it had perfected its security interest in OMS's accounts before PNB got a judgment against OMS, Fifth's security interest had priority over PNB's judgment lien. Did it? **LO ③, ④**

4. In December, Lil' River Grill, Inc. (LRG) entered into a five-year lease with Lawrenceville Properties. One part of the lease said its term lasted from the previous April. Another part, initialed by both parties, said it began the following May to June, and Lil' River had an option to terminate if not put in possession by then. It required the parties, after Lil' River gained possession, to execute a recordable document reciting the exact commencement date. Timothy Brown signed an unconditional guarantee of Lil' River's obligations under the lease. Four months after taking possession, Lil' River assigned the lease to LRG Group, and Brown signed as the "Personal Guarantor" of the assignor's obligations. The assignment stated that Lawrenceville and LRG could change or modify the lease in any way. The parties signed an amendment to the lease with new requirements by the lessee. Brown signed the amendment, which stated he would continue to guarantee the lease personally. Almost three years later, LRG defaulted on the lease. Lawrenceville sued Brown. He argued that the changes to the lease invalidated his guaranty. Did they? **LO ①**

5. Valley Bank and Trust Company provided financing to an automobile dealership to purchase cars. Valley had a security interest in the dealership's motor vehicle inventory and its proceeds. Valley perfected this interest by filing a financing statement with the secretary of state. Holyoke Community Federal Credit Union provided funding for three vehicles to customers of the dealership and filed security agreements to perfect its security interest in the vehicles. Valley discovered that the dealership sold those vehicles without remitting the proceeds to it. A lawsuit between Valley and Holyoke ensued. Whose security interest was superior? **LO ④**

6. As president of Leroy Arts and Products, Inc., Wioletta Plociennik signed a two-year building lease with O'Brien Brothers' Partnership, LLP. It contained no provision for extension or renewal and stated, "This lease contains the entire agreement between the parties." It stated the commencement date and that it ended two years later. Plociennik also signed a separate document that was a personal guaranty to pay O'Brien "the monthly terms as agreed to in an executed lease dated [the lease's date] between [Leroy] (Lessee) and O'Brien Brothers Partnership (Lessor), the terms and conditions as set forth in said lease." Two years later, they executed a two-year lease agreement that increased the space rented and set new rent and common area maintenance payments. Two years after that, they signed a third two-year lease of the same space but with increased rent. After Leroy began missing rent payments, Plociennik said she was no longer obligated on the guaranty, so O'Brien sued her. Did the guaranty cover the third lease? **LO ②**

7. To buy a car, Rubena Session signed a forty-eight-month retail installment sales contract with National Auto Sales, Inc. Shameka Grandberry signed as cosigner. National then assigned the contract **LO ③, ④**

CASE PROBLEMS (CONTINUED)

to Jefferson Loan Co., Inc. Sessions defaulted after two payments. Jefferson repossessed the car. Although Jefferson sold the credit life and credit disability insurance required by the forty-eight-month contract, Jefferson failed to save the unearned premiums by cancelling the policies even though the contract provided an assignment of "unearned premiums" to its holder. Jefferson sent a notice to Session and Grandberry at Session's address, stating that it had repossessed the car. It said, "[T]o redeem your vehicle, you will have to pay the entire amount owed . . . You may purchase your vehicle back . . . before it is sold. Information on the sale date will be supplied to you upon request." Jefferson returned the car to National, which was to make the remaining payments. When the last payment was made, Jefferson would assign the title to National, which could then resell the car. National made only five payments. Although Jefferson knew that National had stopped making payments, it never attempted to retrieve the car. National fraudulently obtained a duplicate motor vehicle title, sold the car, and kept the money. Jefferson learned that the car had been unlawfully sold by National five years later, when it received copies of the car's title documents from Grandberry during litigation. Jefferson eventually sued Session unsuccessfully, so four years after Grandberry cosigned the contract, it sued her. The complaint did not state that Jefferson had repossessed the car. Grandberry alleged Jefferson had not disposed of the car in a commercially reasonable manner. Had it?

Bankruptcy

LEARNING OBJECTIVES

1. Identify the purposes for bankruptcy and who may file for it.
2. Describe the procedures in a bankruptcy case.
3. Explain the effect of a discharge of indebtedness.

PREVIEW CASE

William Huszti, his wife, Anna Huszti, and BAM Investment Group, LLC (BAM) were awarded a judgment of $500,000 jointly and severally against Michael and HeChung Huszti. The William Husztis had originally asked for a judgment of $540,000 and BAM for $114,691. After the judgment, William, Anna and BAM filed an involuntary bankruptcy petition against Michael and HeChung. Michael and HeChung asked the court to dismiss the petition because, although the petition was brought by three entities, William, Anna, and BAM, the three counted as one since they jointly held one claim to a $500,000 debt. Does this case give any indication of how $500,000 was arrived at as a judgment? Why do you think the law requires three creditors in order to force a debtor into bankruptcy?

Bankruptcy is a judicial declaration as to a person's (the debtor's) financial condition. The federal bankruptcy law has two very definite purposes: to give the debtor a new start, and to give creditors an equal chance in the collection of their claims.

An honest debtor, hopelessly insolvent, may be tempted to cease trying even to earn a living. By permitting an insolvent debtor to give up all assets (with a few exceptions) and thereby get forgiveness of the debts, at least a new start can be made. The court determines what it deems an equitable settlement under the circumstances; and when these conditions are fully met, the debtor may resume full control of any business.

It is unfair to permit some unsecured creditors to get paid in full by an insolvent person while others receive nothing. By appointing a trustee to take over the debtor's property and pay each creditor in proportion to a claim, the trustee seeks to achieve a more equitable settlement. This arrangement promotes equity, wastes fewer assets, and costs less money than for each creditor to sue the debtor separately.

LO ①
Bankruptcy purposes and eligibility

38-1 Who Can File a Petition of Bankruptcy?

Today, any person who lives in, or has a residence, place of business, or property in the United States can be a debtor under the Bankruptcy Code except banks, insurance companies, savings and loan associations, and some municipalities. Rehabilitation proceedings may be instituted against all of these exempted institutions except municipalities, but the proceedings may not be filed under the Bankruptcy Code.

There are several chapters under the code, and only specified people may be debtors under the various chapters. They have different impacts on debtors as to what property is taken, how long the bankruptcy supervision lasts, and who runs the debtor's business. Also, Chapter 7, providing for liquidation, applies to any person; Chapter 9 applies to municipalities; Chapter 11, providing for reorganization, applies to any person; Chapter 12 applies to farmers; and Chapter 13 applies to individuals with regular income.

38-2 Kinds of Debtors

There are two kinds of debtors:

1. Voluntary
2. Involuntary

38-2a VOLUNTARY DEBTORS

Anyone, except the institutions listed previously, may file a voluntary petition with the bankruptcy court under one of the four chapters of the code. A husband and wife may file a petition for a joint case.

38-2b INVOLUNTARY DEBTORS

Under certain conditions, one may be forced into involuntary bankruptcy. Generally, if a debtor has twelve or more creditors, three must join the petition for involuntary bankruptcy. The requirement of three creditors is to prevent potential abuse of one creditor forcing a debtor into bankruptcy. If a debtor has fewer than twelve creditors, one may petition. The creditors who petition must have aggregate claims amounting to $14,425 in excess of any collateral held as security. The claims may not be contingent or subject to a valid dispute.

PREVIEW CASE REVISITED

FACTS: William Huszti, his wife, Anna Huszti, and BAM Investment Group, LLC (BAM) were awarded a judgment of $500,000 jointly and severally against Michael and HeChung Huszti. The William Husztis had originally asked for a judgment of $540,000 and BAM for $114,691. After the judgment, William, Anna and BAM filed an involuntary bankruptcy petition against Michael and HeChung. Michael and HeChung asked the court to dismiss the petition because, although the petition was brought by three entities, William, Anna, and BAM, the three counted as one since they jointly held one claim to a $500,000 debt.

OUTCOME: The court held that William, Anna, and BAM did not hold separate claims against Michael and HeChung. The judgment for a single amount could not be broken down and apportioned among them. Since three or more creditors did not file the involuntary petition, it was dismissed.

—*Huszti v. Huszti*, 451 B.R. 717 (Bankr. E.D. Mich.)

Involuntary petitions may not be filed under Chapters 9 or 13 or against farmers or charitable corporations. However, the court can, without the debtor's agreement, convert a voluntary filing to a filing under another section of the bankruptcy law that could not be filed involuntarily.

A court will enter an order for relief on the filing of an involuntary bankruptcy petition if either of the following two situations exists:

1. The debtor does not pay debts as they become due.
2. A custodian of the debtor's assets was established within 120 days preceding the filing of the involuntary petition.

Bankruptcy law uses the same procedure in liquidating the estate whether under a voluntary bankruptcy proceeding or an involuntary one. The filing of a petition automatically stays, or prevents, the filing or continuation of proceedings against the debtor that could have been begun or were to recover a claim against the debtor that arose before the bankruptcy petition. It also prevents a creditor from exercising control over property in the debtor's estate.

38-3 Required Counseling

LO ②
Procedures in bankruptcy cases

Before debtors may file for bankruptcy, they must complete a ninety-minute credit counseling session in the six months prior to filing. The counseling must be done by a credit counselor approved by the U.S. trustee's office. The U.S. trustee administers the bankruptcy procedures and enforces bankruptcy laws.

The counseling is to help debtors understand whether bankruptcy is necessary or whether a repayment plan is workable. Debtors do not have to agree with repayment plans proposed by credit counselors. However, any proposed plan must be submitted to the bankruptcy court in addition to a certificate attesting to completion of the counseling if a debtor wants to go ahead and file for bankruptcy.

In addition to prefiling credit counseling, after the bankruptcy case is done, a debtor must receive additional counseling on personal financial management. Debtors must provide proof of this counseling in order to get their debts excused.

38-4 Procedure in a Chapter 7 Case

After filing a petition in bankruptcy, creditors must be notified, and a meeting of them called. These creditors elect a trustee who takes over all [illegible] of the debtor. The trustee also steps into the shoes of the debtor and [illegible] due from the debtor, preserves all physical assets, sues all deli[illegible] estate, and finally distributes all money realized from these [illegible] definite priority that will be discussed later in this chapter. T[illegible] only property that the law exempts from liquidation.

38-5 Nonliquidation Plans

The bankruptcy laws provide special arrangements that do not result [in] liquidation and distribution of the debtor's assets. These are business reorganization and Chapter 13 plans.

38-5a BUSINESS REORGANIZATION

Bankruptcy proceedings under Chapter 7 result in the liquidation and distribution of the assets of an enterprise. Under Chapter 11, the Bankruptcy Code provides a special rehabilitation system designed for businesses so that they may be reorganized rather than liquidated. Although designed for businesses, the language of Chapter 11 allows individuals not engaged in business to request relief.

Reorganization proceedings may be voluntary or involuntary. Normally, the debtor will be allowed to continue to run the business; however, a disinterested trustee may be appointed to run the business in cases of mismanagement or in the interest of creditors. The debtor running its business has the first right, for 120 days, to propose a rehabilitation plan indicating how and how much creditors will be paid. The court will confirm a plan that does not discriminate; that is fair, equitable, and feasible; that is proposed and accepted in good faith; and by which all the payments made or proposed are found to be reasonable.

The court can impose a reorganization plan even if a class of creditors objects to the plan. This is called a **cram down**. A cram down cannot be imposed if dissenting unsecured creditors are not paid in full or the holder of a claim with less priority receives some property on account of a claim or interest. If no acceptable plan of reorganization can be worked out, the business may have to be liquidated under Chapter 7.

cram down
reorganization plan imposed by court in spite of creditors' objections

38-5b CHAPTER 13 PLANS

If the debtor is an individual, a Chapter 13 plan may be worked out. This chapter attempts to achieve for an individual an alternative to liquidation, just as Chapter 11 does not liquidate businesses. Any individual, even if self-employed or running an unincorporated business, who has unsecured debts of less than $360,475 and secured debts of less than $1,081,400 may in good faith file a petition under Chapter 13. This chapter is voluntary for the debtor.

Under Chapter 13, the debtor is put under a plan lasting up to five years, under which all disposable income is used to make payments on the debtor's debts. Not all debts may be fully paid, and a majority of creditors can impose a settlement plan upon a dissenting minority. The debtor is as fully released from debts as under Chapter 7 of the Bankruptcy Code. These arrangements help prevent the hardship of an immediate liquidation of all the debtor's assets. These plans benefit the creditors because they are likely, in the long run, to receive a greater percentage of the money owed them. The plan may not pay unsecured creditors less than the amount they would receive under a Chapter 7 liquidation.

38-6 Eligibility Restrictions for Chapter 7

In order to file under Chapter 7, debtors must compare what the law defines as their "current monthly income" to the median income of families of their size in their state. However, the law defines "current monthly income" to be a debtor's average income over the previous six months before filing. Thus, if a debtor has recently lost a job, "current monthly income" could be much more than actual income by the time of filing for bankruptcy.

If "current monthly income" is the same as or less than the median income, a debtor may file under Chapter 7. If "current monthly income" is greater than the median, a debtor must pass a means test, which can be somewhat complicated, in order to file under Chapter 7.

Debtors are allowed to prove that they face "special circumstances" by which they were forced into bankruptcy by a crisis beyond their control. For example, the U.S. trustee has classified a major hurricane as a "special circumstance," making its victims more likely to be allowed to file under Chapter 7.

38-7 Exempt Property

The federal bankruptcy law lists property that will not be used to pay debts. In addition, each state has laws exempting property from seizure for the payment of debts. Only individual debtors may retain property under an exemption, but the debtor has a choice between federal or state exemptions unless state law specifies that state exemptions must be used. The debtor must have lived in a state for two years before filing in order to use that state's exemptions. Otherwise, the exemptions of the state where the debtor previously lived must be used.

The most common types of excluded property include a limited interest in a residence and vehicle, household effects, tools of the trade, such as a carpenter's tools or a dentist's equipment, and similar items within reasonable limits. The debtor also may exclude unmatured life insurance contracts owned other than credit life insurance. Most states specifically exempt all necessary wearing apparel for the debtor and members of the family, such items as the family Bible, and all pictures of the members of the family even though some of these may be portraits of some value. Many of the federal exemptions set a limit on the value of items that may be excluded.

38-8 Included Property

The law includes some property acquired by the debtor after the bankruptcy proceedings have been instituted in the debtor's estate and uses it for the payment of creditors. This includes property acquired by inheritance or divorce or as a beneficiary of life insurance within 180 days after the date of filing.

If the debtor transfers property, normally within 90 days preceding the filing of the bankruptcy petition, to one creditor with the intent to prefer one creditor over another, and the debtor is insolvent, the transfer may be set aside, and the property included in the debtor's estate. Such a transfer that is disallowed is called a **preference**. If the creditor is a relative, a transfer made up to a year before the filing can be a preference.

preference
disallowed transfer to a creditor

COURT CASE

FACTS: Jeremy Alcede operated a gun store and shooting range through his limited liability company, CTLI, LLC (CTLI), under the business name "Tactical Firearms". He sold 30 percent of CTLI to Steven Coe Wilson and used the proceeds to expand, creating the "finest indoor firing range in the country." Over time, Wilson began to suspect Alcede of diverting cash from the corporation, and sued in state court. CTLI then defaulted on several loans, and Alcede caused CTLI to file Chapter 11 bankruptcy. Wilson submitted a plan, which was confirmed by the court, by which Wilson became the sole owner of the reorganized CTLI. Alcede refused to turn over the passwords to CTLI's Facebook and Twitter accounts, claiming that they belonged to him personally, and

it would be impossible to share control over the accounts with the reorganized CTLI without violating his privacy.

OUTCOME: The court recognized a social media account as a property interest, and then found the account was property of the business because (1) the title of the page was the same as the name of the business, (2) the page included a direct link to the Tactical Firearms website, (3) Alcede used the page to post status updates on behalf of Tactical Firearms, and (4) Alcede gave an employee access to the page to post status updates.

—*In re CTLI, LLC*, 528 B.R. 359 (S.D. Tex.)

38-9 Debtor's Duties during Bankruptcy

The debtor must cooperate fully with the trustee. When requested, the debtor must attend creditors' meetings and must furnish all relevant evidence about debts due. The debtor must file with the trustee a schedule of all assets and all liabilities. This schedule must be in sufficient detail so that the trustee can list the secured creditors, the partially secured creditors, and the unsecured creditors. Failure of the debtor to cooperate with the trustee and to obey all orders of the trustee not only may prevent discharge from bankruptcy but also may subject the debtor to criminal prosecution for contempt of court.

38-10 Proof of Claims

All unsecured creditors must present proof of their claims to the court. The court sets a deadline for filing proof of claims, but they generally must be filed within 90 days after the date for the first meeting of creditors.

COURT CASE

FACTS: Billy J. Harris and Dorothy E. Harris filed a Chapter 13 petition. About a month before the deadline, Three Rivers Federal Credit Union filed a proof of claim. Because of a secretarial error, the claim was prepared with the caption (heading) of a case Billy had filed that had been dismissed a month before the current case was filed. The claim was then electronically filed under the incorrect case number. Nine months later, the credit union realized its error and filed a proof of claim in the proper case. It asked the court to treat the claim as if it had been originally filed in the proper case.

OUTCOME: The court held that it did not have the power to allow a late-filed claim outside of narrow exceptions that did not apply in this case.

—*In re Harris*, 341 B.R. 660 (Ind.)

38-11 Reclamations

Frequently, at the time that the court discharges debts, the debtor has possession of property owned by others. This property takes the form of consigned or bailed goods, or property held as security for a loan. The true owner of the property is not technically a creditor of the debtor in bankruptcy. The owner should file a reclamation claim for the specific property so that it may be returned.

A person in possession of a check drawn by the debtor may or may not be able to get it paid, depending on the circumstances. If the check is an uncertified check, the holder is a mere creditor of the debtor and cannot have it cashed. This occurs because a check is not an assignment of the money on deposit, and the creditor merely holds the unpaid claim the debtor intended the check to discharge. If the check has been certified, the creditor has the obligation of the drawee bank on the check, which may be asserted in preference to proceeding upon the claim against the drawer of the check.

38-12 Types of Claims

Claims of a debtor in bankruptcy may be classified as fully secured claims, partially secured claims, and unsecured claims.

Fully secured creditors may have their claims satisfied in full from the proceeds of the assets that were used for security. If these assets sell for more than enough to satisfy the secured debts, the remainder of the proceeds must be surrendered to the trustee in bankruptcy of the debtor.

Partially secured creditors have a lien on some assets but not enough to satisfy the debts in full. The proceeds of the security held by a partially secured creditor are used to pay that claim; and, to the extent any portion of a debt remains unpaid, the creditor has a claim as an unsecured creditor for the balance.

Unsecured claims are those for which creditors have no lien on specific assets.

38-13 Priority of Claims

The claim with the highest priority is that for the administrative expenses of the bankruptcy proceedings (such as filing fees paid by creditors in involuntary proceedings and expenses of creditors in recovering property transferred or concealed by the debtor). Additional priority claims include debts incurred after the filing of an involuntary petition and before an order of relief or appointment of a trustee; wage claims, but there are limits to the amounts for each wage earner and the time period in which the wages were earned; fringe benefits for employees; claims by individuals who have deposited money with the debtor for undelivered personal, family, or household goods (up to certain limits); and tax claims.

38-14 Discharge of Indebtedness

If the debtor cooperates fully with the court and the trustee in bankruptcy and meets all other requirements for discharge of indebtedness, the discharge will be granted. To be discharged, the debtor must not hide any assets or attempt to wrongfully transfer them out of the reach of creditors. A discharge voids any liability of the debtor on discharged debts and prevents legal action for collection of such debts.

COURT CASE

FACTS: After Brandon Maxfield sued him, Bruce Jennings met with a bankruptcy lawyer. He bought property containing a house and adjacent hangar for $925,000 and spent $84,000 remodeling the house. On March 31, he contracted with Frank Baker for hangar expansion at $202,000. The contract stated "construction expenses will be paid in increments of Fifty Thousand Dollars ($50,000) and a complete accounting of those funds will be presented before any additional capital will be funded." Jennings paid $5,000 on the first $50,000 increment. On April 21, he was found liable to Maxfield. Site preparation work for the hangar expansion had not been done. Baker said Jennings had not given him money to begin. On May 5, Jennings gave Baker $130,000. Baker had spent less than $700 on the project. On

May 7, Maxwell got a verdict of $21 million against Jennings. On May 14, Jennings voluntarily filed a Chapter 11 petition. Maxfield asked the court to deny Jennings a discharge because the $130,000 transfer to Baker was made with the intent to hinder, delay, or defraud creditors. Jennings said he and Baker negotiated the amount so they could save money and move the project forward, but Baker contradicted this explanation.

OUTCOME: The court held that Jennings had transferred the $130,000 to Baker Builders with actual intent to hinder, delay, or defraud his creditors and denied the discharge.

—*In re Jennings*, 533 F.3d 1333 (11th Cir.)

38-15 Debts Not Discharged

Certain obligations cannot be avoided by bankruptcy. The most important of these claims include:

1. Claims for alimony and child support
2. Taxes incurred within three years
3. Debts owed by reason of embezzlement
4. Debts due on a judgment for intentional injury to others, such as a judgment obtained for assault and battery
5. Amounts owed due to the debtor's causing personal injury when operating a motor vehicle under the influence of alcohol or other drugs
6. Debts incurred by means of fraud
7. Educational loans

Under some other circumstances, bankruptcy does not discharge certain debts, but this list includes the most common ones.

QUESTIONS

1. Why is a trustee appointed in a bankruptcy case?
2. What are the different impacts on debtors that the various chapters of the bankruptcy code have?
3. Who may file a voluntary petition with the bankruptcy court?
4. What automatically happens when a bankruptcy petition is filed?
5. What are the two bases for entering an order for relief on an involuntary basis?
6. After a Chapter 7 case is filed, what must the creditors do?
7. Name three types of property that are exempt from being used to pay debts.
8. If the debtor holds bailed property, must this property be included in the debtor's estate to pay creditors?
9. How are partially secured claims handled?
10. What is the effect of a discharge of indebtedness?

CASE PROBLEMS

LO ① 1. Sylvia Castillo bought a pickup truck from Three Aces Auto Sales (TAAS) such that TAAS had a security interest in the truck. Her husband used the truck in his work as a cabinet maker. Sylvia defaulted on the payments, so TAAS repossessed the truck. Four days later, the Castillos filed a voluntary bankruptcy petition. TAAS refused to return the truck to the Castillos until it had proof of the bankruptcy filing and insurance coverage. The Castillos asked the bankruptcy court to compel TAAS to turn the truck over to them. TAAS said it would turn the truck over upon proof of insurance. The court ordered TAAS to turn the truck over. The Castillos finally got the truck. Did TAAS do anything wrong?

LO ② 2. Fred A. Topous, Jr., engaged Clarence Kenyon Gomery and Gomery's law firm to represent Topous in several business matters, including forming an LLC to purchase a golf course. Gomery fraudulently inserted himself as a 50 percent member of the LLC in the operating agreement, Topous sued

CASE PROBLEMS (CONTINUED)

for damages, and received a large verdict. When Gomery realized he was unable to post the bond required to stay the judgment pending appeal, Gomery filed for Chapter 13 bankruptcy. Prior to the first hearing on Gomery's proposed Chapter 13 plan, Gomery was also arrested and charged with solicitation of the murder of Topous's new counsel. Topous filed objections to the plan on the ground it was not offered in good faith, alleging Gomery failed to disclose significant and valuable assets (when later confronted with his tax returns claiming ownership of the assets, Gomery claimed the tax returns had been filed in error). Should the court find a lack of good faith? Should the court take into consideration Gomery's arrest and charge, but not (yet?) conviction?

3. Pedro and Alicia Diaz filed for Chapter 7 relief, listing Heavy Action Recovery, Inc. (Action), as an unsecured creditor. A copy of the discharge was mailed to Action. Action then sold or assigned the debt to ARA, Inc. (ARA). ARA mailed the Diazes a demand letter for over $10,000. Alicia immediately called ARA and informed ARA of the discharge, but ARA continued to send letters and left twenty-three collection messages on the Diazes' phones. Did either of Action or ARA have any right to continue to try to collect on the debt? **LO ③**

4. An involuntary Chapter 7 bankruptcy petition was filed against Michael Letourneau. The names of three petitioning creditors Letourneau owed a "partnership debt" were listed. Although a summons must be issued to a debtor in an involuntary case, none was issued, and there was no activity on the case for a month. The court set a hearing date, and notice of it was sent to the creditors and Letourneau. Meanwhile, American Chartered Bank moved to modify the automatic stay, so it could complete foreclosure on Letourneau's house. Before the filing of the petition, the house had been sold, and the sale approved by a state court. The bank reported that Letourneau had paid the filing fee for the bankruptcy petition. It turned out that the "creditors" whose names appeared on the petition were real people, but were not Letourneau's creditors and had not signed the petition. The court concluded that Letourneau had filed the involuntary petition himself. Was this proper? **LO ①**

5. Quay Corporation, Inc. engaged in lengthy litigation with Mexican Cheese Producers, Inc. (MCP) before and after a Chapter 11 case was filed by Quay. To save fees, costs, and time, the parties reached a settlement and asked the bankruptcy court to approve it. It provided full payment with interest, over a five-year period, of MCP's and the allowed claims of other unsecured creditors. It provided MCP with a lien and security interest in all of Quay's assets. If MCP foreclosed on its lien and acquired Quay's assets through foreclosure, MCP would pay the balances due to the other unsecured creditors. If MCP foreclosed and someone else bought Quay's assets, MCP would share the proceeds pro rata with the other unsecured creditors. While MCP's claim was unpaid, it would have a right of first refusal to buy Quay's assets if it sold any of them outside the ordinary course of its business. An unsecured creditor, the Wisconsin Cheese Group, objected to the Chapter 11 plan and settlement, contending that it unfairly distinguished in favor of MCP and against Wisconsin Cheese. Did the plan unfairly favor MCP? **LO ②**

6. Abbott and Deborah Estrin performed employment recruiting services for Twin City Fire Insurance Company (Twin City). Twin City filed suit against the Estrins in California, alleging conspiracy and fraud in their employment. The Estrins then filed under Chapter 7 in South Carolina, listing Twin City as a creditor. Twin City contacted the Estrins' attorney several times requesting settlement or lifting the stay long enough to transfer the California case to South Carolina, but the Estrins refused. Twin City moved in the South Carolina bankruptcy case to extend the deadline to object to discharge to allow it time to transfer its case. Was Twin Cities entitled to delay the Estrins' discharge? **LO ③**

7. While they were married, Dana Kostelnik's ex-husband executed a mortgage on real estate in favor of ABN AMRO Mortgage Group, Inc. Kostelnik did not sign the mortgage. Two years later, Kostelnik signed a "loan modification agreement." The modification did not change the identification of the **LO ②**

CASE PROBLEMS (CONTINUED)

borrower in the mortgage, who was Kostelnik's ex-husband and the only person in that document to have granted ABN a mortgage. The modification did not grant a mortgage and was not filed with the proper authorities, or perfected, until within 90 days prior to the commencement of a Chapter 7 proceeding in which Kostelnik was the debtor. The trustee asked the court to determine that ABN did not have any lien or property interest in Kostelnik's undivided interest in the real estate. Did ABN have any interest in Kostelnik's interest in the property?

ETHICS IN PRACTICE

The normal rule is that life insurance policies are incontestable after a specified period of time, usually one or two years. This means that the insurance company cannot contest the validity of the policy for any reason except nonpayment of premiums. Is this a rule that encourages people to take out insurance policies and hide facts from the insurance company until the policies are incontestable? Although hiding a fact that would otherwise invalidate an insurance policy might not end up invalidating the policy, is it ethical? What is the reason for this rule?

PART 8 SUMMARY CASES

RISK-BEARING DEVICES

1. Robert Baker owned several rental properties which he insured with Nationwide Mutual Insurance Company (Nationwide). The policy excluded coverage for property which had been "vacant for more than 60 consecutive days", but defined buildings under construction or renovation as not vacant. After water pipes burst in an unoccupied, multiunit property, Baker decided not only to repair the damage, but perform additional repairs to the property. During this period of making repairs, thieves broke in and stole copper plumbing and fixtures. Baker made a claim on the policy for the stolen copper, but Nationwide denied it because Baker did not make the repairs within 60 days of the theft. Should Baker have been covered? [*Baker v. Nationwide Mutual Insurance Company*, 2013 WL 1905334]

2. James Carlson founded PRACS Institute, Ltd. (PRACS) as a medical research facility. Sterling Development Group Three, LLC (Sterling), leased a building to PRACS, and Carlson signed a personal guaranty. Subsequently, Carlson sold PRACS to Contract Research Solutions, Inc. (Solutions). Sterling consented to this change in control under the lease. Solutions and Sterling entered into several modifications of the lease agreement concerning the provision of janitorial services, tax payments, and the contractual method for calculating base rent. When Solutions later filed for bankruptcy and stopped paying rent, Sterling sued Carlson on the guaranty. Carlson defended that the lease modifications were made without his knowledge or consent. Were these modifications sufficiently material to release Carlson from his guaranty? [*Sterling Development Group Three, LLC v. Carlson*, 859 N.W.2d 414 (N.D.)]

3. Thomas Montgomery, Kenneth Henning, and attorney Gary Derer formed HLM Assurance Group, LLC, to sell insurance to Derer's clients. Henning and Derer funneled money due HLM and/or Montgomery to other entities that Henning and/or Derer controlled. They did not allow Montgomery access to HLM's financial information or information related to the disbursement of commissions. They demanded that Montgomery return his key to HLM's office. Derer fraudulently transferred to Jordan Massad $165,000 in policy commissions that Montgomery had earned. When he filed a voluntary petition for relief under Chapter 7, Derer did not list an interest in HLM on his schedule of assets. In answer to a question on the bankruptcy forms requiring him to list all his business interests, he only listed his law firm. Montgomery objected to Derer's discharge. Should Derer be discharged? [*In re Derer*, 400 B.R. 97 (E.D. Tex.)]

4. A&J Hometown Oil, Inc. (A&J) took loans from Catskill Hudson Bank (Bank) and gave Bank a security interest in A&J's assets. Bank timely filed all appropriate documents to perfect its security interest. A&J later entered into a purchase agreement to sell many of its business assets to Morgan Fuel & Heating Company, Inc. (Morgan). Under the purchase agreement, Morgan

was to pay a lump-sum upon sale, followed by monthly installment payments for a three-year period. Bank agreed to release its lien on A&J's assets in exchange for the right to receive a lump-sum payment at the sale and certain fees and accounts receivable. The agreement also provided that A&J would not change the terms of the purchase agreement without the Bank's consent. Shortly after closing the sale, Morgan and A&J discovered that the purchase price had been incorrectly calculated, such that Morgan overpaid on the lump sum. Without the Bank's knowledge, Morgan and A&J executed an amendment to the purchase agreement allowing Morgan to keep certain accounts receivable as reimbursement for the overpayment. When Bank did not receive the accounts receivable from A&J, the Bank sued. Was the Bank's security interest still valid? [*Catskill Hudson Bank v. A&J Hometown Oil, Inc.*, 115 A.D.3d 1090 (N.Y. A.D.)]

5. Teresa McCurdy owned a house as rental property. Her husband, Robert McCurdy, contacted Hanover Fire & Casualty Insurance Co. (Hanover) about fire insurance. Hanover's employee assisted Robert in completing the application over the phone. The completed application listed "none" after a question requesting a list of all losses incurred by fire in the last five years. Three months later, the house was destroyed by fire. Hanover refused to pay the claim when its investigation revealed that McCurdy had had two prior fire losses and a theft claim in the past five years. Was the answer "none" on the application a representation or a warranty, and what difference would that make? [*McCurdy v. Hanover Fire & Casualty Insurance Co.*, 964 F.Supp.2d 863 (N.D. Ohio)]

6. Philip Markham's foot and ankle were run over and injured by a truck owned by Michael Roberts and insured by Mercury Insurance Company of Florida (Mercury). Markham sued Roberts and Mercury. Mercury rescinded the policy, returned Roberts' premium, and refused to defend the lawsuit. The insurance application Roberts signed asked, "Is any vehicle . . . modified [or] altered?" The application indicated a "yes" answer would mean a policy would not issue. Although Roberts had installed larger, wider tires, tinted windows, a stereo, and a lift kit on the truck, he answered, "no." In his courtroom testimony, Roberts stated the truck "had been altered in many ways." Mercury alleged that Roberts answer on the application was a material misrepresentation. Was it? [*Mercury Ins. Co. of Florida v. Markham*, 36 So.3d 730 (Fla. Dist. Ct. App.)]

7. In one year, Oral F. Sekendur filed two Chapter 13 petitions within days of adverse decisions in nonbankruptcy cases. They were dismissed because Sekendur failed to report all his assets. He was ordered to pay one opposing party's attorney's fees, and minutes before a hearing to consider sanctions for his failure to comply with that order, he filed another Chapter 13 petition. He never paid the filing fee. Sekendur admitted he had no income, and there was no change in circumstances following dismissal of his earlier Chapter 13 cases. He was warned that his Chapter 13 case might be dismissed for having been filed in bad faith, so he moved to convert his case to a Chapter 7 case. On its own motion, the court moved to consider dismissal for Sekendur's failure to pay filing fees. Sekendur did not show up at the hearing. The court dismissed the case for unreasonable delay prejudicial to creditors—that the case was filed in bad faith. Did Sekendur file in bad faith? [*In re Sekendur*, 334 B.R. 609 (Ill.)]

8. Beckon, Inc. (Beckon) leased a building for its business and made significant improvements to it. It obtained an insurance policy from AMCO Insurance Co., (AMCO) covering damage to the building and its contents—Beckon's business personal property. Separate premiums were charged for the building and the personal property, and the policy limits for each were different. After six years, sparks from a welder caused a fire that damaged the work area of the building and damaged much of the contents. Beckon had to move to another building for which it paid $10,000 a month rent for two years. AMCO investigated Beckon's ownership interest in the building. Since Beckon did not own it, AMCO added the owner and lessor as additional insureds. It charged a higher premium for this change, which Beckon paid. Four months later, a wind storm blew off the roof of the building, causing $35,000 in damage. AMCO then denied Beckon's claims for damage to the building, saying Beckon did not have an insurable interest in it. However, it did pay $532,810 under the separate coverage Beckon had bought for business personal property damaged by the fire. Beckon sued AMCO. Did Beckon have an insurable interest in the building? [*Beckon, Inc. v. AMCO Ins. Co.*, 616 F.3d 812 (8th Cir.)]

9. When Helga and Gene Hohertz divorced, the decree required Gene to pay alimony until he or Helga died and to name Helga as beneficiary of $100,000 of life insurance to secure his alimony obligation. Gene was also ordered to pay Helga $100 a month for every month the required insurance was not in effect. Gene remarried and sometime later changed the beneficiaries of his $200,000 life insurance policy to provide $100,000 to Helga and the remainder to his new wife, Vetta. Years later Gene was diagnosed with lung cancer and changed the beneficiary on his life insurance completely to Vetta. He paid an additional $100 in alimony to Helga and died within the month. When he died he had paid Helga $100,075 in alimony and was current in his payments. Helga asked the court to declare she was entitled to $100,000 of the insurance proceeds. Was she? [*Hohertz v. Estate of Hohertz*, 802 N.W.2d 141 (Neb. Ct. App.)]

10. Central Bank made a car loan to Lorraine Turner. Central was acquired by Mercantile Bank, which was acquired by Firstar Bank, NA. Turner then received the title to her car along with written confirmation that her loan was paid. Ten days later, Turner discovered that her car was missing. The police informed her that Shamrock Recovery Service, Inc., acting on orders of Firstar, had seized her car. Turner went to Shamrock and displayed the documents confirming payment of her loan and release of Firstar's lien. Shamrock said Firstar claimed she still owed $300. Turner's attorney ultimately succeeded in convincing Firstar to release her car. Turner had to go to Shamrock's impound lot but found her laptop computer, discs containing computer software, and a digital camera that she had left in the car were missing. For two years, Turner's lawyer attempted to secure their return. Firstar made no substantive response to Turner's inquiries and demand, so she sued. Is Firstar liable for an illegal repossession? [*Turner v. Firstar Bank, N.A.*, 845 N.E.2d 816 (Ill. App. Ct.)]

Real Property

This section on real property includes not only real estate—land, buildings, and houses—but also wills and trusts. Laws about these issues can be very complex. Transferring, buying, and selling real property involves the legalities of contracts, mortgages, deeds, titles, and many other items. Even being a landlord or tenant carries legal responsibilities. In addition, the transfer of real property to your heirs can be a complicated matter involving many legal issues, as discussed in Chapter 43.

39 Nature of Real Property

40 Transfer of Real Property

41 Real Estate Mortgages

42 Landlord and Tenant

43 Wills, Inheritances, and Trusts

Nature of Real Property

LEARNING OBJECTIVES

1. Define real property, and explain the rules about vegetation, running water, and fixtures.
2. Name the types of multiple ownership of property.
3. List the estates and other interests in real property.
4. Identify methods of acquisition exclusive to real property.

PREVIEW CASE

Frank bought a house and properly filed with the state for the homestead exemption from real property taxes. He later married Mary Jane, and conveyed the property by deed to himself and Mary Jane as tenants by the entireties. The two lived on the property for the duration of their marriage, when it ended upon Frank's death twenty-one years later. Mary Jane did not notify the Appraiser of Frank's death or apply for a separate homestead exemption for the property. The state claimed that Frank's death created a change in ownership, and the homestead exemption for which only Frank had filed was no longer applicable. As a result, Mary Jane was notified of a six-figure tax lien on her home. Mary Jane paid the lien under protest and sued for a refund. What does it mean to be a tenant by the entireties? Is the death of one tenant a change in ownership?

LO ①
Real property rules

real property
land and permanent attachments to land

Real property consists of land, including the actual soil, and all permanent attachments to the land, such as fences, walls, other additions and improvements, timber, and other growing things. It also includes minerals under the soil and the waters on it.

39-1 Distinguishing Real Property

Through court interpretations, a definite set of rules to guide in identifying real property and distinguishing it from personal property has accumulated. The most important of these rules pertains to the following specific items of property:

1. Vegetation—trees and perennial crops
2. Waters—rivers and streams
3. Fixtures

39-1a TREES AND PERENNIAL CROPS

Vegetation may be real or personal property. Trees growing on the land; orchards; vineyards; and perennial crops, such as clovers, grasses, and others not planted annually and cultivated, are classified as real property until severed from the land. Annual crops, such as corn or soybeans, and severed vegetation are personal property. When a person sells land, questions sometimes arise as to whether or not a particular item belongs to the land or constitutes personal property. The parties should agree on how to classify each item before completing the sale.

39-1b RIVERS AND STREAMS

If a non-navigable river flows through property, the person who owns the property owns the riverbed but not the water that flows over it. The water cannot be impounded or diverted to the property owner's own use in such a way as to deprive any neighbors of its use. If the river or the stream forms the boundary line, then the owner on each side of the river owns the land to the middle of the riverbed.

In most states where navigable rivers form the boundary, the owner of the adjoining land owns the land only to the low-water mark.

39-1c FIXTURES

Personal property attached to land or a building that becomes a part of the land is known as a **fixture**. To determine whether personal property has become real estate or not, a court may ask one or more of the following questions:

fixture
personal property so securely attached to real estate that it becomes part of the real estate

1. How securely is it attached? If the personal property has become a part of the real estate and lost its identity, such as the boards or bricks making up a house wall, it constitutes a fixture. If it is so securely attached that it cannot be removed without damaging the real property to which it is attached, such as windows or light switches, then it also ceases to be personal property.

2. What was the intention of the one installing the personal property? No matter what one's intention, the personal property becomes real property if it cannot be removed without damaging the property. However, if it is loosely attached, and the person installing the fixture indicates the intention to make the fixture real property, this intention controls. Refrigerators have been held to be real property when apartments were rented unfurnished but contained refrigerators. In determining intention, courts frequently consider the purpose of the attachment and who did the attaching.

   a. What is the purpose of attachment? The purpose for which the fixture is to be used may show the intention of the one annexing it.

   b. Who attached the item? If the owner of a building installs personal property to the building, this usually indicates the intention to make it a permanent addition to the real property. If a tenant makes the same improvements, the court presumes that the tenant intended to keep the fixture as personal property unless a contrary intention can be shown.

COURT CASE

FACTS: Upen and Avanti Patel purchased land from which they intended to remove the existing house in order to construct a new one. They allowed the local fire department to conduct live fire-training exercises on the house, during which it was destroyed. On their income tax return for that year, they claimed a noncash charitable contribution of the house to the local fire department. IRS rules do not allow a charitable deduction for a partial interest in property. The IRS disallowed the deduction, claiming that the right to conduct training exercises and burn down a building is not the entire interest in the property. The house was so attached to the land as to become part of it, and the Patels retained substantial interest in the land and what remained of the house. Should they have gotten the deduction?

OUTCOME: The charitable deduction was denied. The house was conveyed to the Patels as part of the land when they purchased it. The court noted that none of the documentation signed by the Patels or the fire department purported to convey title to the house, property, or any ownership therein to the fire department.

—*Patel v. CIR*, 138 TC No. 23 (U.S. Tax Ct.)

39-2 Multiple Ownership

One person can own property, or more than one person can own property. When more than one person owns land, each person has the right to use and possess it.

The most common ways real property can be owned by more than one person include:

1. Tenancy in common
2. Joint tenancy
3. Tenancy by the entirety
4. Community property

39-2a TENANCY IN COMMON

tenancy in common
multiple ownership in which, at death of one, that share passes to remaining owners

A **tenancy in common** occurs when two or more people own property such that when one owner dies, that owner's interest in the property passes to a person named in the deceased's will or, if no will exists, to the deceased's heirs. In this type of ownership, the other owner or owners have no automatic right to the deceased's share of the property. Each owner determines who gets the share of the property at his or her death. A tenant in common has the right not only to determine who becomes the owner of the fractional share on death but also to convey the property while alive. The property may be given away or sold. The new owner then becomes a tenant in common with the remaining owner or owners.

The owners of property held as a tenancy in common each own an undivided fractional share of the property. For example, if two people equally own a piece of land, each tenant owns an undivided one-half interest in the land. Three people who own land equally each own an undivided one-third interest in the land. This means they do not own a specific portion of the land but own a one-third interest in the entire piece of land. They thus have an interest in the entire property but only to the extent of their percentage interest.

The property does not have to be owned equally. Two people could own a piece of property as tenants in common, and one could own a one-third interest, and the other could own a two-thirds interest.

When more than one person takes title to property, the law presumes that they hold the property as tenants in common. Thus, when the type of ownership is not clearly spelled out, it will be held to be a tenancy in common.

39-2b JOINT TENANCY

In most states, a **joint tenancy** exists when two or more people own property and on the death of one, the remaining owner(s) own the entire property free of any interest of the deceased. This means that a joint owner does not have the power to determine who owns the property at death. The remaining joint owner or owners automatically own the entire property. This automatic ownership of the entire property by the surviving owners is called the **right of survivorship**. In a minority of states the right of survivorship must be specified even in a joint tenancy.

joint tenancy
multiple ownership in which, at death of one, that share passes to remaining owners

right of survivorship
automatic ownership of property by survivors

COURT CASE

FACTS: During their marriage, Anthony and Karen Hayes owned several rental properties as joint tenants with right of survivorship. Karen incurred a debt of $85,000, and her creditor obtained a lien on her interest in the rental properties to satisfy the debt. Subsequently, Anthony and Karen obtained an agreed divorce, through which Anthony received the rental properties and Karen received an automobile valued at $1,200. Karen deeded the property to Anthony and died a few months later. Anthony sued to stop the creditor from forcing a sale of the rental properties. He claimed that as a joint tenant, he succeeded to the entire interest in the rental property on Karen's death.

OUTCOME: The court noted that Karen, as a joint tenant, conveyed her interest in the property to Anthony. This conveyance defeated the right of survivorship but was subject to the creditor's lien. As a result, Anthony received Karen's interest subject to the lien.

—*Hayes v. Southern New Hampshire Medical Center*, 34 A.3d 1215 (N.H.)

As in the case of a tenancy in common, each joint owner owns an undivided interest in the property. No joint owner owns a specific portion of the property.

The law does not favor the creation of a joint tenancy, so there must be a clear intention to create one. The language normally used conveys the property "to X and Y as joint tenants with right of survivorship."

COURT CASE

·FACTS: Harold Norsworthy and his sister, Betty Bolding, each signed the bottom of a signature card for a bank account. The account was only in Norsworthy's name. There was no evidence that Bolding contributed to or paid taxes on the account. When Norsworthy died, Bolding claimed ownership of the account as a joint tenant with right of survivorship.

OUTCOME: The court said that a mere signature on the bottom of the signature card was insufficient to create a joint tenancy with right of survivorship. Bolding had no right to the account on Norsworthy's death.

—*Bolding v. Norsworthy*, 270 S.W.3d 394
(Ark. Ct. App.)

A joint tenancy can be destroyed by one joint tenant selling or giving that tenant's interest to another person. The new owner becomes a tenant in common of the interest conveyed. If there are three or more joint tenants and one sells his or her interest, the new owner is a tenant in common and the remaining, original joint tenants remain joint tenants as between themselves.

partition
suit to divide joint tenancy

A joint tenancy also can be destroyed by one joint tenant suing for a division of the property, called a suit for **partition**. Any joint tenant may sue for partition.

Because a joint tenant's interest in the property disappears at the joint tenant's death, a joint tenant cannot dispose of such an interest by will. If a joint tenant purports to dispose of an interest in jointly held property by will, the will has no effect with regard to such property.

39-2c TENANCY BY THE ENTIRETY

tenancy by the entirety
co-ownership by husband and wife with right of survivorship

Similar to a joint tenancy, a **tenancy by the entirety** can exist only between a husband and wife. At the death of one, the other becomes the sole owner of the property. Almost half of the states recognize this form of ownership. This type of tenancy is popular with married couples because most want the survivor to have title to the property and to get it without any court proceedings. Many couples also like this type of ownership because the creditors of just the husband or just the wife cannot claim the property. To have a claim against the property, a creditor must be a creditor of both spouses.

PREVIEW CASE REVISITED

FACTS: Frank bought a house and properly filed with the state for the homestead exemption from real property taxes. He later married Mary Jane, and conveyed the property by deed to himself and Mary Jane as tenants by the entireties. The two lived on the property for the duration of their marriage, when it ended upon Frank's death twenty-one years later. Mary Jane did not notify the Appraiser of Frank's death or apply for a separate homestead exemption for the property. The state claimed that Frank's death created a change in ownership, and the homestead exemption for which only Frank had filed was no longer applicable. As a result, Mary Jane was notified of a six-figure tax lien on her home. Mary Jane paid the lien under protest and sued for a refund.

OUTCOME: The state was ordered to reinstate the homestead exemption. In a tenancy by the entireties, the husband and wife own the property as one person, and the surviving tenant receives no greater or less than that already possessed.

—*Kelly v. Spain*, 2015 WL 774658 (Fla.)

A joint tenancy differs in other ways from a tenancy by the entirety. In the case of property held as a tenancy by the entirety, neither the husband nor the wife alone may sell or otherwise dispose of it. Both the husband and the wife must join in any conveyance of the property. A divorce changes the ownership of property of a husband and wife from tenants by the entirety to tenants in common.

39-2d COMMUNITY PROPERTY

Nine states, mostly in the West, recognize a form of ownership called **community property**. Community property is a type of ownership reserved for married couples such that both spouses own a separate and equal share of the property, no matter how titled. In these states, unless the parties agree that it shall be separate property, property acquired by a husband and wife during their marriage constitutes community property. This is normally important if a couple divorces. In that case, each owns one-half of the property acquired during the marriage. Property owned by one spouse prior to the marriage normally is that spouse's separate property and not community property.

ETHICAL POINT

Is it really ethical for a married couple to own property in a tenancy by the entirety if the creditors of just one of the spouses cannot claim the property? What competing interest is present here?

community property
property acquired during marriage owned separately and equally by both spouses

COURT CASE

FACTS: Before Linda Thomas and Paul Pace married, Thomas owned an A.G. Edwards investment account (172 account). Because they lived in a community property state, 23 days after they married, Thomas instructed A.G. Edwards to "sweep" all dividends, interest, and income from the 172 account monthly and place the income in a new account (204 account). Three years later, Thomas set up the Linda Ruth Thomas Management Trust as the donor, trustee, and sole beneficiary to segregate her separate property. The 172 account was transferred into the Management Trust, and A.G. Edwards continued to "sweep" all dividends, interest, and income from that account into the 204 account. After Thomas filed for divorce, Pace claimed that the Management Trust was community property.

OUTCOME: The court said that income earned during the marriage from the 172 account and, later, the Management Trust was community property; however, that income was never commingled with Thomas's separate property. The Management Trust was not community property.

—*Pace v. Pace*, 160 S.W.3d 706 (Tex. Ct. App.)

39-3 Estates in Property

An **estate** is the nature and extent of interest that a person has in real or personal property. The estate that a person has in property may be:

1. A fee simple estate, or
2. A life estate

39-3a FEE SIMPLE ESTATE

A **fee simple estate** is the largest and most complete right that one may possess in property. A fee simple owner of property, whether real or personal, has the right to possess the property forever. The owner of a fee simple estate may also sell, lease, or otherwise dispose of the property permanently or temporarily. At the

LO ③
Interests in property

estate
interest in property

fee simple estate
largest, most complete right in property

death of such an owner, the property will pass to the people provided for in the owner's will or, if no will exists, to the heirs at law.

A fee simple owner of land has the right to the surface of the land, the air above the land "all the way to heaven," and the subsoil beneath the surface all the way to the center of the earth. The courts have held, however, that the right to the air above the land is not absolute. An individual cannot prevent an airplane from flying over the land unless it flies too low. It is possible for a person to own the surface of the land only and not the minerals, oil, gas, and other valuable property under the topsoil. A person also may own the soil but not the timber.

39-3b LIFE ESTATE

life estate
estate for duration of a person's life

life tenant
person owning property for a lifetime

reversion
interest of grantor in life estate that returns to grantor on death of life tenant

remainder
interest in life estate that goes to someone other than grantor on death of life tenant

easement
an interest in land for nonexclusive or intermittent use

One may have an estate in property by which the property is owned for a lifetime, known as a **life estate**. The person owning for the lifetime is called a life tenant. At the death of the **life tenant**, the title passes as directed by the original owner. The title may revert, or go back, to the grantor, the one who conveyed the life estate to the deceased. In this case, the interest of the grantor is called a **reversion**. Alternatively, the property may go to someone other than the grantor. Such an interest is called a **remainder**.

The life tenant has the exclusive right to use the property and may exclude the holder of the reversion or remainder during the life tenant's lifetime. However, although the life tenant has exclusive use of the property, there is a duty on the part of the life tenant to exercise ordinary care to preserve the property and commit no acts that would harm the remainder interest permanently.

39-4 Other Interests in Real Property

Although not classified as estates, other interests a person may have in real property exist. Two common ones are easements and licenses.

An **easement** is a right to use land, such as a right-of-way across another's land or the use of another's driveway. An easement does not give an exclusive right to possession, but a right of permanent, intermittent use. It is classified as an interest in land and created by deed or by adverse use for a period of time set by statute. An easement that is not transferable may be granted; that is, only the specific person to whom it is granted can use it. Another type of easement transfers to any subsequent owner of the real estate to which the easement is granted. Such an easement is said to "run with the land."

COURT CASE

FACTS: Gloria and Willie Cater owned a parcel of land with no frontage on any street. The parcel was created in an 1899 deed, which included a "right of way" to reach a nearby road. No specific description of the location of the easement was given. The Caters filed suit to confirm the existence of the easement and establish its precise location. Owners of property between the Caters' parcel and the closest road claimed that any easement that might have existed had been extinguished from non-use.

OUTCOME: The court held that non-use alone was insufficient to extinguish the easement. Because no specific location had been designated on the deed, and there was room on the adjacent property for a reasonable right of way, the Caters' easement continued.

—*Cater v. Bednarek*, 969 N.E.2d 705 (Mass.)

A **license** is a right to do certain acts on the land but not a right to stay in possession of the land. It constitutes a personal right to use property for a specific purpose. A licensor normally may terminate a license at will.

license
right to do certain acts on land

COURT CASE

FACTS: The City of Waukegan sued several defendants for environmental contamination of a harbor. Defendant LaFarge had entered into an agreement with the Port District to construct and operate conveyors on a fifty-foot strip of land leading to the docks; for LaFarge employees to cross that strip; and for nonexclusive use of the harbor dock with forty-eight hours notice. LaFarge had no duty to maintain the dock and did not actually lease the land.

OUTCOME: The court said that because LaFarge only had permission to act and not possess any estate or interest in land, it was a licensee. Because a licensee is not an "owner" for purposes of environmental contamination and cleanup, the owner claim against LaFarge was dismissed.

—City of Waukegan, Illinois v. National Gypsum Co.,
587 F.Supp.2d 997 (N.D. Ill.)

39-5 Acquiring Real Property

Real property may be acquired in many of the same ways as personal property (see Chapter 14). However, some ways exist in which real property, but not personal property, can be acquired. These include accretion and adverse possession.

LO ④
Acquiring real property

39-5a ACCRETION

Accretion is the addition to land as a result of the gradual deposit by water of solids. It takes place most commonly when a stream, river, lake, or ocean constitutes the boundary line of property. Dirt deposited along the boundary is added to the property. In the case of a navigable river, if one's land extends to the low-water mark, title to some land may be acquired by the river's shifting its flow. This occurs slowly by the deposit of silt. Also, the accretion may be the result of dredging or channeling of the river. If the silt and sand are thrown up on the riverbank, thereby increasing the acreage of the land contiguous to the river, the added acreage belongs to the owner of the contiguous land.

accretion
addition to land by gradual water deposits

39-5b ADVERSE POSSESSION

An individual may acquire title to real property by occupying the land owned by another for a period fixed by statute. This is known as **adverse possession** and basically means the original owner may no longer object to a trespass. The statutory period required varies from seven years in some states to twenty-one in others. Occupancy must be continuous, open, hostile, visible, actual, and exclusive. It must be apparent enough to give the owner notice of trespass. In colonial times, this was known as "squatter's rights." To get title by adverse possession, one had to go one step further than the "squatter" did; this meant the adverse possession had to continue for the statutory period.

adverse possession
acquiring title to land by occupying it for fixed period

COURT CASE

FACTS: Woodstock Community Trust, Inc. (WCT) purchased land which had been previously owned and used by a church. Several owners of adjacent property brought a claim of adverse possession against portions of WCT's land. Vermont law recognizes a charitable use exception, such that any time property is owned for charitable purposes, it cannot be adversely possessed. The adjacent property owners' claim for adverse possession began while the property was owned by the church.

OUTCOME: An element of an adverse possession claim is a continuous period of time. Since the time the property was owned by the church could not be included, the time period element had not been satisfied.

—*Roy v. Woodstock Community Trust, Inc.,*
94 A.3d 530 (Vt.)

color of title
one's apparent title

Possession for the statutory period then gave clear title to all of the land one's color of title described. **Color of title** is a person's apparent title. It usually arises, but does not have to, from some defective document purporting to be a deed or a will or even a gift.

QUESTIONS

1. Give three examples of real property.

2. What types of vegetation are normally considered real property?

3. What is the difference in ownership rights of a person whose property borders a non-navigable river and a person whose property borders a navigable river?

4. What are the different ways in which multiple people may own one piece of real property?

5. What specific portion of a property does any single tenant in common own?

6. a. Which types of multiple ownership of property give the owners the right of survivorship?

   b. What does the right of survivorship mean?

7. In states that recognize community property, what specific language or actions are required for a married couple's property acquired during the marriage to be considered community property?

8. What is accretion?

9. Does a license give a person the right to possess land? Explain.

10. Is it possible for a trespasser to acquire title to the property on which the trespass is made?

CASE PROBLEMS

LO 1. The Jejers acquired real estate in 1950. Their parents owned the property next door. The Jejers improved the property with a driveway and barn. Parts of the driveway and barn overlapped onto the parents' property. The parents neither consented nor objected to the Jejers' use of the property. The Jejers exclusively used the driveway and barn, except when they leased part of the land to a third party. Both properties were subsequently sold. Theodore Mulle purchased the Jejers' property, and

CASE PROBLEMS (CONTINUED)

after a survey discovered that part of his driveway and barn were on the other parcel of land. Does Mulle own the entire driveway, or only half the barn?

2. Martin, DeWitt, and Prieto were tenants in common of a single family home in Wyoming, in which only Martin lived. DeWitt and Prieto asked Martin either to move out or pay them rent. Martin changed the locks, and refused to allow DeWitt and Prieto entry. DeWitt and Prieto sued Martin for rent payments. Must Martin pay rent to live in a home of which she is co-owner? If so, how much rent? **LO ②**

3. Richard Flowers's will left his wife a life estate in their marital home. The following year, Mrs. Flowers claimed a personal residence exemption from property taxes, but the state of Michigan denied the exemption on the grounds that Mrs. Flowers was not the owner. Was Mrs. Flowers an owner of the property when she only held a life estate? **LO ③**

4. Oxford's job required extensive travel between California, Texas, and Georgia. She purchased a membership in an R.V. Park (Park) in California and placed a fifth-wheel trailer on a lot at the Park. Utilities, including electricity, water, and sewer, which serviced the trailer were provided by the Park as part of the membership fee. Park rules required Oxford to move her trailer to a different lot within the Park every six months. After a few years, Oxford contracted with a builder to construct a house on a completely separate piece of property. When the house was finished, Oxford moved in and began using it as her residence. On Oxford's federal income tax return for the year of the move, she claimed a First-Time Homebuyer Credit. The IRS denied the First-Time Homebuyer Credit on the basis of Oxford's ownership of the trailer prior to building the house. Was the trailer personal property, as Oxford claimed? **LO ①**

5. Bankruptcy debtor Paul Titus arranged for his employer to directly deposit his paychecks into a checking account he owned jointly with his wife as tenants by the entireties. The bankruptcy trustee sued to get the money back out of the joint account. Could the bankruptcy trustee of only one spouse reach money that had been placed in a tenancy-by-the entireties account? **LO ②**

6. The town of Windham condemned real property owned by ATC Partnership. ATC claimed that located in the premises taken through the condemnation proceeding was personal property that Windham failed, neglected, and refused to return, and prevented ATC from removing it from the real estate. The property consisted of machinery and equipment previously used in the operation of a textile mill, the bulk of which was bolted to the realty. ATC conceded that at the time the pieces were installed, the mill owner intended them to be permanent accessions to the realty. ATC acquired the machinery by means of the deed by which it acquired the real property. The court had to decide whether the machinery was part of the real estate or personal property. What was it? **LO ①**

7. Carol Severance owned rental property on Galveston Island's West Beach. No public easement existed on her property, but there was a public easement for beach access on property seaward of the Severance property. Five months after Severance purchased her property, Hurricane Rita blew through Galveston Island, devastating the property seaward of Severance and pushing the vegetation line back past Severance's rental property. As a result, the State of Texas claimed that a portion of the rental house interfered with the public easement for beach access. When Texas attempted to enforce a public easement, Severance sued. Did Hurricane Rita move the public easement for beach access onto Severance's property? **LO ③**

Transfer of Real Property

LEARNING OBJECTIVES

(1) Describe the means by which title to real estate is transferred.

(2) Explain the provisions normally contained in a deed.

(3) Summarize the steps taken to transfer title safely and effectively to real property after a deed is signed.

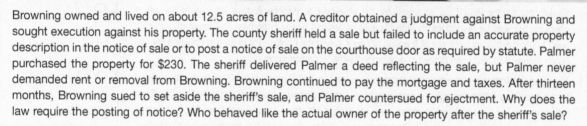

PREVIEW CASE

Browning owned and lived on about 12.5 acres of land. A creditor obtained a judgment against Browning and sought execution against his property. The county sheriff held a sale but failed to include an accurate property description in the notice of sale or to post a notice of sale on the courthouse door as required by statute. Palmer purchased the property for $230. The sheriff delivered Palmer a deed reflecting the sale, but Palmer never demanded rent or removal from Browning. Browning continued to pay the mortgage and taxes. After thirteen months, Browning sued to set aside the sheriff's sale, and Palmer countersued for ejectment. Why does the law require the posting of notice? Who behaved like the actual owner of the property after the sheriff's sale?

LO (1)
Means of transferring real estate

deed
writing conveying title to real property

A sale constitutes the most common reason for transferring title to real estate. In the ordinary case, the parties sign a contract of sale, but the title is not transferred until the seller delivers a deed to the buyer. A **deed** is a writing, signed by the owner, conveying title to real property. One may, by means of a lease, transfer a leasehold title giving the rights to the use and possession of land for a limited period. The provisions of the deed or the lease determine the extent of the interest transferred.

Even when the owner makes a gift of real property, the transfer must be evidenced by a deed. As soon as the owner executes and delivers a deed, title vests fully in the donee. Acceptance by the donee is presumed.

grantor
person conveying property

grantee
person receiving title to property

40-1 Deeds

The law sets forth the form that the deed must have, and this form must be observed. The parties to the deed include the **grantor**, or original owner, and the **grantee**, or recipient.

The two principal types of deeds are:

1. Quitclaim deeds

2. Warranty deeds

40-1a QUITCLAIM DEEDS

A **quitclaim deed** is just what the name implies. The grantor gives up whatever interest he or she may have in the real property. However, the grantor makes no warranty that he or she has any claim to the property.

quitclaim deed
deed that transfers whatever interest grantor has in property

COURT CASE

FACTS: Terry Layne purchased a townhome with his father, Joe Layne, and his father's wife, Nancy Layne. Joe and Nancy owned their undivided one-half interest as husband and wife, Terry owned the remaining undivided one-half interest, and they all owned as joint tenants with right of survivorship. After Joe and Nancy's divorce, Terry executed a quitclaim deed conveying his interest in the townhome to Joe and Nancy as tenants in common. Upon Joe's death, Nancy claimed that Joe's interest in the property passed only to her and Joe's daughter. Nancy claimed that the quitclaim deed prevented Terry from inheriting part of Joe's interest in the townhome. What did the quitclaim deed convey?

OUTCOME: Since a quitclaim deed transfers the grantor's full and complete interest at the time of the deed, the court held that Terry had no interest in Joe's property while Joe was living. However, after Joe's death, Terry and his sister were entitled to Joe's share of the townhome as beneficiaries of Joe's estate.

—*Layne v. Layne*, 74 So.3d 161 (Fla. Dist. Ct. App.)

In the absence of a statute or an agreement between the parties requiring a warranty deed, a quitclaim deed may be used in making all conveyances of real property. A quitclaim deed transfers the grantor's full and complete interest as effectively as a warranty deed. When buying real property, however, one does not always want to buy merely the interest that the grantor has. A buyer wants to buy a perfect and complete interest so that the title cannot be questioned by anyone. A quitclaim deed conveys only the interest of the grantor and no more. It contains no warranty that the grantor has good title. In most real estate transactions, therefore, a quitclaim deed cannot be used, because the contract will specify that a warranty deed must be delivered.

40-1b WARRANTY DEED

A **warranty deed** not only conveys the grantor's interest in the real property but also makes certain warranties or guarantees. The exact nature of the warranty or guarantee depends on whether the deed is a general warranty or a special warranty deed. A **general warranty deed** (see Illustration 40-1) not only warrants that the grantor has good title to the real property but further warrants that the grantor will defend the grantee against all claims by third parties. This warranty, then, warrants that all prior grantors had good title and that no defects exist in any prior grantor's title. The grantee does not have to assume any risks as the new owner of the property.

warranty deed
deed with guarantees

general warranty deed
warrants good title free from all claims

ILLUSTRATION 40-1 General Warranty Deed

WARRANTY DEED

Know All Men by These Presents:

That **Donald C. Coson and Millicent M. Coson, his wife**

of **Butler** *Country,* **Ohio**

in consideration of the sum of Forty-five Thousand Dollars ($45,000) to them *in hand paid by* Eugene F.Acknor, the grantee, the receipt of which is hereby acknowledged,

do hereby Grant, Bargain, Sell and Convey

to the said Eugene F. Acknor

h is *heirs*

and assigns forever, the following described Real Estate *situated in the* City *of* Hamilton *in the Country of* Butler *and State of* Ohio

Lot No. 10, Section 14, Range 62, Randall Subdivision, being a portion of the estate of Horace E. Cresswell and Alice B. Cresswell *and all the* Estate, Right, Title and Interest *of the said grantors in and to said premises;* To habe and to hold *the same, with all the privileges and appurtenances thereunto belonging, to said grantee,* his *heirs and assigns forever. And the Said* Donald C. Coson and Millient M. Coson *do hereby* Covenant and Warrant *that the title so conveyed is* Clear, Free and Unencumberred, *and that* they *will* Defend *the same against all lawful claims of all persons whomsoever.*

In Witness Whereof, *the said grantors have hereunto set* their *hands, this* first *day of* December *in the year A.D. two-thousand and-*

Signed and acknowledged in presence of us:

Michael R. Wisex	Donald C. Coson
Antonia C. Patricelle	*Millicent M. Coson*

State of Ohio. Butler County, ss-

on this first *day of* December A.D. 20 *.before me, a* Notary Public *in and for County, personally came* Donald C. Coson and Millicent M. coson *the grantor in the foregoing deed, and acknowledged the signing thereof to be* their *voluntary act and deed.*

Witness *my official signature and seal on the day last mentioned.*

Sarah M.Evans

Sarah M. Evans
Notary Public, State of Ohio
My commision expires June 1,20-

A **special warranty deed** warrants that the grantor has the right to sell the real property. The grantor makes no warranties of the genuineness of any prior grantor's title. Trustees and sheriffs who sell land at foreclosure sales use this

special warranty deed warrants grantor has right to convey property

type of deed. Executors and administrators also use such a deed. These officials should not warrant anything other than that they have the legal right to sell whatever interest the owner has.

When a builder sells a new house, most courts now impose an implied warranty of fitness not found in the deed. The warranty amounts to a promise that the builder designed and constructed the house in a workmanlike manner, suitable for habitation by the buyer.

40-2 Provisions in a Deed

LO ②
Deed provisions

Unless statutes provide otherwise, a deed usually has the following provisions:

1. Parties
2. Consideration
3. Covenants
4. Description
5. Signature
6. Acknowledgment

40-2a PARTIES

The grantor and the grantee must be identified, usually by name, in the deed, and the grantee must be a living or legal person. If the grantor is married, the grantor's name and that of a spouse should be written in the deed. If the grantor is unmarried, the word *single* or the phrase "a single person" should be used to indicate that status.

40-2b CONSIDERATION

The amount paid to the grantor for the property is the consideration. The payment may be in money or in money's worth. A deed usually includes a statement of the consideration, although the amount specified does not need to be the actual price paid. Some localities have a practice of indicating a nominal amount, such as $10, although a much larger sum was actually paid. The parties state a nominal amount as the consideration to keep the sale price from being a matter of public record.

40-2c COVENANTS

A **covenant** is a promise contained in a deed. There may be as many covenants as the grantor and the grantee wish to include. **Affirmative covenants** obligate the grantee to do something, such as agreeing to maintain a driveway used in common with adjoining property. In **negative covenants**, the grantee agrees to refrain from doing something. Such covenants frequently appear in deeds for urban residential developments. The more common ones prohibit the grantee from using the property for business purposes and set forth the types of homes that can or cannot be built on the property. Most covenants are said to "run with the land," which means they basically attach to the property and thereby bind all future owners.

covenant
promise in a deed

affirmative covenant
promise by grantee to do an act

negative covenant
agreement by grantee not to do an act

COURT CASE

FACTS: Wilson and Misita owned adjacent farms. Wilson deeded approximately three acres adjacent to Misita's land to Misita. The deed included a provision that "no structures are to be erected on the property." Wilson sold the remainder of his property to Conn. Subsequently, Misita informed Conn of his intention to build a "sign," consisting of a three-sided structure with a floor, corrugated metal roof, a door, window, and air conditioning, and display it on the three acres. Could Conn force Misita to remove the "sign" from Misita's own land?

OUTCOME: Yes. The deed included a negative covenant whereby Misita agreed not to construct a structure, which the "sign" certainly was.

—*Misita v. Conn*, 138 So.3d 138 (Miss.)

40-2d DESCRIPTION

The property to be conveyed must be correctly described. Unless the law provides otherwise, any description that will clearly identify the property suffices. Ordinarily, however, the description used in the deed by which the present owner acquired the title should be used if correct. The description may be by lots and blocks if the property is in a city; or it may be by metes and bounds or section, range, and township if the property is in a rural area. If the description is indefinite, the grantor retains title.

COURT CASE

FACTS: Two brothers, Bernard and Frederick Rice, owned five pieces of property as tenants in common. As the years passed, the brothers had many discussions about how to divide up the properties between their families for estate planning purposes. At one such meeting, the Rices signed four blank warranty deeds. There was no information on any of the deeds concerning the date of execution, the identity and address of the grantor, the identity and address of the grantee, the consideration paid, or a description of the property. Frederick later filled in this information on two of the deeds and filed them in the Recorder's office. Bernard sued for cancellation of the deeds.

OUTCOME: The court determined that the blank deeds had no legal effect. Further, when Frederick later filled in the missing information, there were no new grantor signatures and no new acknowledgements. The deeds were void.

—*Rice v. Rice*, 499 F.Supp.2d 1245 (M.D. Fla.)

40-2e SIGNATURE

The grantor should sign the deed in the place provided for the signature. A married grantor must have the spouse also sign for the purpose of giving up the statutory right of the spouse. In some states, a witness or witnesses must attest the signatures.

If the grantor cannot sign the deed, an agent, the grantor with assistance, or the grantor making a mark, may execute it as:

Maria Smith		His
Witness of the mark of	Henry	X Finn
Henry Finn		Mark

40-2f ACKNOWLEDGMENT

The statutes normally require that the deed be formally acknowledged before a notary public or other officer authorized to take acknowledgments. The acknowledgment allows the deed to be recorded. After a deed has been recorded, it may be used as evidence in a court without further proof of its authenticity. Recording does not make a deed valid, but it helps give security of the title to the grantee.

The **acknowledgment** is a declaration made by the properly authorized officer, in the form provided for that purpose, that the grantor has acknowledged signing the instrument as a free act and deed. In some states, the grantor also must understand the nature and effect of the deed or be personally known to the acknowledging officer. The officer attests to these facts and affixes an official seal. The certificate provides evidence of these actions.

acknowledgment
declaration grantor has stated execution of instrument is free act

40-3 Delivery

A deed has no effect on the transfer of an interest in real property until it has been delivered. **Delivery** consists of the grantor intending to give up title, possession, and control over the property. So long as the grantor maintains control over the deed and reserves the right to demand its return before delivery of the deed to the grantee, there has been no legal delivery. If the grantor executes a deed and leaves it with an attorney to deliver to the grantee, there has been no delivery until the attorney delivers the deed to the grantee. Because the attorney is the agent of the grantor, the grantor has the right to demand that the agent return the deed. If the grantor, however, delivers the deed to the grantee's attorney or agent, then there has been an effective delivery because releasing control constitutes evidence of intent that title pass. Once the grantor makes delivery, title passes.

LO ③
Steps taken after deed signed

delivery
giving up possession and control

PREVIEW CASE REVISITED

FACTS: Browning owned and lived on about 12.5 acres. A creditor received a judgment against Browning and sought execution against his property. The county sheriff held a sale for the judgment but failed to include an accurate property description in the notice or to post notice of sale on the courthouse door as required by statute. Palmer purchased the property for $230. The sheriff delivered Palmer a deed reflecting the sale, but Palmer never demanded rent or removal from Browning. Browning continued to pay the mortgage and taxes. After thirteen months, Browning sued to set aside the sheriff's sale, and Palmer countersued for ejectment.

OUTCOME: The court determined that the procedural irregularities, Palmer's continuing to allow Browning to reside on the property, pay the mortgage and taxes, along with the extremely low sales price, amounted to a mistake and surprise and justified setting aside the sale. Browning could keep his house.

—*Browning v. Palmer*, 2008 WL 747934 (Ala. Civ. App.)

40-4 Recording

To record a deed, grantees must file their deeds with a public official in the county in which the land lies. Other instruments affecting title to real property in the county also can be filed. These public records of land transactions give notice of title transfers to all, particularly potential subsequent purchasers.

A deed need not be recorded in order to complete one's title. Title passes on delivery of the deed. Recording the deed protects the grantee against a second sale by the grantor and against any liens that may attach to the property while still recorded in the grantor's name. Recording also raises the presumption of delivery of the deed.

When the recording official receives a deed for recording, the law ordinarily requires that the deed be stamped with the exact date and time the grantee leaves the deed for recording.

40-5 Abstract of Title

abstract of title
history of real estate

Before one buys real estate, an abstract of title may be prepared. An abstract company normally does this, but an attorney may also do it. The **abstract of title** gives a complete history of the real estate. It also shows whether or not there are any unpaid taxes and assessments, outstanding mortgages, unpaid judgments, or other unsatisfied liens of any type against the property. Once an abstracting company makes the abstract, an attorney normally examines the abstract to see whether it reveals any flaws in the title.

40-6 Title Insurance

Some defects in the title to real estate cannot be detected by an abstract. Some of the most common of these defects are forgery of signatures in prior conveyances; claims by adverse possession; incompetency to contract by any prior party; fraud; duress; undue influence; defective wills; loss of real property by accretion; and errors by title examiners, tax officials, surveyors, and many other public officials. The owner of real estate can obtain a title insurance policy that will cover these defects. The policy may expressly exclude any possible defects that the insurance company does not wish to be covered by the policy. The insured pays one premium for coverage as long as the property is owned. The policy does not benefit a subsequent purchaser or a mortgagee.

QUESTIONS

1. When is title to real estate transferred?
2. What is the inherent risk in accepting a quitclaim deed for property?
3. What is the difference between a general warranty deed and a special warranty deed?
4. What are six necessary elements in a deed?
5. Why might a deed not cite the actual consideration paid?
6. What is the difference between affirmative and negative covenants?
7. How is a deed delivered?

QUESTIONS (CONTINUED)

8. What is the purpose of recording a deed?

9. What does an abstract of title show?

10. How may an owner of real property be protected against defects in title?

CASE PROBLEMS

1. A.B., Alma, and Mike owned a home as tenants in common. As part of a swap transaction, they deeded their interest to Troy. Troy was not present when the deed was executed, but Mike brought the deed to Troy's house in an envelope. Mike said that he had recorded the deed, when in fact it had not been recorded. Mike handed the envelope to A.B., who placed it in the trunk of his car. A.B. told Troy he would leave Troy the car when A.B. died, and the deed would be right there in the trunk with the important papers. Mike subsequently deeded his one-third interest to his sisters, who did in fact record those deeds. Upon A.B.'s death, Troy retrieved his deed from the trunk of the car and discovered that it had not been recorded. Troy filed suit to set aside the subsequent recorded deeds. Did the deed left in the trunk of A.B.'s car effectively transfer the home to Troy? **LO ③**

2. Guyton entered into a contract to buy a homesite on which she moved her mobile home. The purchase price was to be paid as a down payment and 180 monthly payments. The seller executed a deed, but one of terms of the sale was that the deed would not be recorded until six monthly payments were timely made. Guyton made payments for about eight years, but only five were made on time. As a result, the seller had not recorded the deed by the time Guyton filed for bankruptcy. Who was the legal owner of the homesite? **LO ①**

3. Harvey Foster executed a deed for his home to his daughter, Jean Burbage, as trustee. Foster later was hospitalized and lived in an assisted living facility for a year. During this time, Burbage handled his finances. When he recovered, Foster asked a court to void the deed, saying he had signed it without reading it because he trusted his daughter. Foster had never executed any written trust declaration. He alleged that the deed was void because it named a grantee who did not exist. Is the deed valid? **LO ②**

4. Alma Goddard jointly owned with her adult son Carl a residence situated less than 1,000 feet from a school. Alma conveyed her interest to Carl in exchange for his agreement to care for her for the remainder of her life and allow her to reside in the home. Subsequently, Carl informed his mother that he was required to move from the home because he was a sex offender. Alma hired an attorney to prepare a quitclaim deed from Carl to her. Carl executed the deed, and Alma gave him money to record it. Carl informed Alma that he had recorded the deed. When Alma attempted to return home after a hospital stay, she learned that instead of recording the deed, Carl had transferred the property to a third party. What happened to Alma's home? **LO ③**

5. Woods purchased property which was subject to an express easement in favor of a neighboring property owner (Shannon) for ingress and egress. At the time of the purchase, the neighboring property had no other access to a road. Subsequently, a road was built on the opposite side of Shannon's land, so Shannon decided to use the easement for running his ATV. Woods filed for an injunction against Shannon's use of the easement, citing the fact that there was now a public road Shannon could use for ingress and egress. Did Shannon have a right to drive his ATV over the easement property? **LO ①**

6. Weaver and J. E. Jordan executed a warranty deed of 50 acres to Daniel and Pearline Dallinga. The deed contained restrictive covenants prohibiting commercial enterprise or enterprise of any kind on the property and was signed by Weaver and Jordan, but not by the Dallingas. There were several subsequent conveyances of the property until Jeremiah 29:11 Inc. became the owner. None of these conveyances referenced the restrictions of the Jordans' deed. Jeremiah used the property as **LO ②**

CASE PROBLEMS (CONTINUED)

a leadership-training center for pastors and leaders of nonprofit corporations and as a Boy Scout camp. Ernest Douglas and Leslie Seifert owned adjacent property formerly owned by the Jordans and alleged that Jeremiah's use violated the commercial enterprise restriction. Jeremiah alleged that it was not limited by the Jordans' restrictions because they had not signed the original deed, and the restrictions were not in subsequent deeds. Did the restrictive covenants apply to Jeremiah?

LO

7. Goodell was injured while doing carpentry work for Cathell Custom Homes. Rosetti was the developer of the property. For the purpose of securing financing for construction costs, Cathell would execute a deed for a particular lot to Rosetti, which would be held in escrow until the actual sale of the property to the buyer. Goodell sued Rosetti as record owner of the property. Rosetti claimed that as there was no intention actually to transfer ownership of the land, he did not own the property. Was the deed effective to transfer title to Rosetti?

Real Estate Mortgages

LEARNING OBJECTIVES

1. Define and discuss the effect of a mortgage.
2. List the duties and rights of a mortgagor.
3. Explain the rights of parties on foreclosure, sale, and assignment of the mortgage.

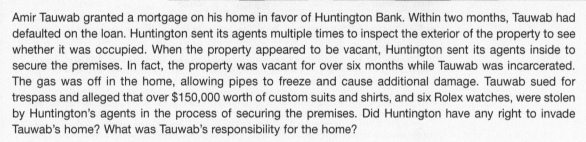

PREVIEW CASE

Amir Tauwab granted a mortgage on his home in favor of Huntington Bank. Within two months, Tauwab had defaulted on the loan. Huntington sent its agents multiple times to inspect the exterior of the property to see whether it was occupied. When the property appeared to be vacant, Huntington sent its agents inside to secure the premises. In fact, the property was vacant for over six months while Tauwab was incarcerated. The gas was off in the home, allowing pipes to freeze and cause additional damage. Tauwab sued for trespass and alleged that over $150,000 worth of custom suits and shirts, and six Rolex watches, were stolen by Huntington's agents in the process of securing the premises. Did Huntington have any right to invade Tauwab's home? What was Tauwab's responsibility for the home?

LO ①
Effect of mortgage

mortgage
interest in real estate given to secure debt

mortgagor
person who gives mortgage

mortgagee
person who holds mortgage

A **mortgage** is an interest in real estate given to secure the payment of a debt. The mortgage does not constitute the debt itself but the security for the debt. If the debt is not paid, the property may be sold to pay the debt. Land or any interest in land may be mortgaged. Land may be mortgaged separately from the improvements, or the improvements may be mortgaged apart from the land. A person who gives a mortgage as a security for a debt is a **mortgagor**. A person who holds a mortgage as security for a debt is a **mortgagee**.

The mortgagor normally retains possession of the property. In order for the mortgagee to obtain the benefit of the security, the mortgagee must take possession of the premises on default or sell the mortgaged property at a foreclosure sale. In some states, the mortgagee may not take possession of the property on default but may obtain the appointment of a receiver to collect the rents and income. If the sale of the property brings more than the debt and the costs, the mortgagor must be paid the balance.

41-1 The Mortgage Contract

A mortgage must be in writing. The contract, as a rule, must have the same form as a deed, which means it must be acknowledged. The mortgage, like all other contracts, sets forth the rights and the duties of the contracting parties (see Illustration 41-1). As a type of contract, mortgages are interpreted according to contract law rules.

ILLUSTRATION 41-1   Mortgage Contract

MORTGAGE
WITH POWER OF SALE (Realty)

KNOW ALL MEN BY THESE PRESENTS:

THAT _____Walter A. Righetti_____ and _____Susan L. Righetti_____ husband and wife, GRANTORS, for and in consideration of the sum of One Dollar ($1.00), to GRANTORS in hand paid, the receipt of which is hereby acknowledged, and in consideration of the premises hereinafter set forth, do hereby grant, bargain, sell and convey unto ___Third National Bank of Russellville__, GRANTEE, (Whether one or more) and unto GRANTEE'S heirs (Successors) and assigns forever, the following property, situated in ____Pope____ County, Arkansas:

Lot 37 in GREENE HEIGHTS SUBDIVISION

TO HAVE AND TO HOLD the same unto the said GRANTEE, and unto GRANTEE's heirs (successors) and assigns forever, with all appurtenances thereunto belonging; and all rents, income, and profits therefrom after any default herein.

We [I] hereby covenant with the said GRANTEE, GRANTEE's heirs (successors) and assigns, that said lands are free and clear of all encumbrances and liens, and will forever warrant and defend the title to said property against all lawful claims. And, we, GRANTORS, ____Walter A. Righetti and Susan L. Righetti____, for the consideration aforesaid do hereby release unto the said GRANTEE and unto GRANTEE's heirs (successors) and assigns forever, all our rights and possibility of dower, curtesy and homestead in and to the said lands.

The sale is on the condition, that whereas, GRANTORS are justly indebted unto said GRANTEE in the sum of Sixty Thousand and ⁰⁰/100 Dollars ($ 60,000.00), evidenced by ___their___ promissory note_____ dated ___October 17, 20—_, in the sum of $ 60,000.00 bearing interest from date until due at the rate of _10_% per annum and thereafter until paid at the rate of _10_% per annum, payable as follows: $ 545 per month, due and payable on the first day of the month, beginning November 1, 20— and continuing for 25 years.

This mortgage shall also be security for any other indebtedness of whatsoever kind that the GRANTEE or the holders or owners of this mortgage may hold against GRANTORS by reason of future advances made hereunder, by purchase or otherwise, to the time of the satisfaction of this mortgage.

In the event of default of payment of any part of said sum, with interest, or upon failure of GRANTORS to perform the agreements contained herein, the GRANTEE, GRANTEE's heirs (successors) and assigns, shall have the right to declare the entire debt to due and payable; and

GRANTORS hereby covenant that they will keep all improvements insured against fire, with all other full coverage insurance, loss payable clause to holder and owner of this mortgage; that said improvements will be kept in a good state of repair, and waste will neither be permitted nor committed; that all taxes of whatever nature, as well as assessments for improvements will be paid when due, and if not paid GRANTEE may pay same and shall have a prior lien upon said property for repayment, with interest at the rate of 10% per annum; now,

THEREFORE, if GRANTORS shall pay all indebtedness secured hereby, with interest, at the times and in the manner aforesaid, and perform the agreements herein contained, then this conveyance shall be void. In case of nonpayment or failure to perform the agreements herein contained, the said GRANTEE, GRANTEE's heirs (successors) and assigns, shall have the right and power to take possession of the property herein conveyed and expel any occupant therefrom without process of law; to collect rents and profits and apply same on unpaid indebtedness; and with or without possession to sell said property at public sale, to the highest bidder for cash, (or _____), at _____the county courthouse_____ of _____Pope_____ County, Arkansas, public notice of the time, terms and place of sale having first been given twenty days by advertising in some newspaper published in said County, by at least three insertions, or by notices posted in five public places in the County, at which sale any of the parties hereto, their heirs (successors), or assigns may bid and purchase as any third person might do; and GRANTORS hereby authorize the said GRANTEE, GRANTEE's heirs (successors), or assigns to convey said property to anyone purchasing at said sale, and to convey an absolute title thereto, and the recitals of such conveyance shall be taken as *prima facie* true. The proceeds of said sale shall be applied, first to the payment of all costs and expenses attending said sale; second to the payment of all indebtedness secured hereby, with interest; and the remainder, if any, shall be paid to said GRANTORS. GRANTORS hereby waive any and all rights of appraisement, sale, redemption, and homestead under the laws of the State of Arkansas, and especially under the Act approved May 8, 1899, and acts amendatory thereof.

WITNESS _our_ hand _s_ and seal _s_ this _17th_ day of ___October___, 20 —

Walter A. Righetti (seal)

Susan L. Righetti (seal)

(ACKNOWLEDGEMENT BEFORE NOTARY FOLLOWS)

COURT CASE

FACTS: Kevin Dorner executed a note and mortgage on a residence in favor of CitiMortgage. Two years later he executed another mortgage and note on the same residence in favor of OneWest Bank. Dorner failed to keep up the payments and OneWest Bank filed for foreclosure. CitiMortgage intervened, stating that its first-in-time mortgage should be paid first. OneWest Bank asked the court to find the CitiMortgage mortgage invalid, even though it had been recorded, because it had not been acknowledged. Was an acknowledgement necessary for CitiMortgage to have priority?

OUTCOME: The court held that an acknowledgement was necessary for the mortgage to be valid, just as it is necessary for a valid deed. The CitiMortgage mortgage was invalid.

—*OneWest Bank, FSB v. Dorner*, 953 N.E.2d 892 (Ohio Com. Pl.)

A mortgagor normally gives a mortgage to raise money for the purchase price of real estate, but it may be given for other reasons. One may borrow money for any reason and secure the loan by a mortgage. One may assume a contingent liability for another, such as becoming a surety, and receive a mortgage as security.

The effect of a mortgage is to be a lien against the mortgaged property. A **lien** is an encumbrance or claim against property. The lien of the mortgage attaches to the property described in the mortgage. A mortgage generally also provides that the lien attaches to additions thereafter made to the described property; for example, the lien of the mortgage attaches to personal property which thereafter becomes a fixture. A clause purporting to make the security clause of a mortgage cover future debts will be valid if the parties intended it to cover future debts.

lien
encumbrance or claim against property

41-2 Recording

Depending on the law of the state in which the land lies, the mortgage gives the mortgagee either a lien on the land or title to the land. The mortgagor's payment of the debt divests or destroys this title or lien. Recording the mortgage protects

COURT CASE

FACTS: The Coffelts used their interest in four lots to secure a $540,000 debt to M&I Bank. The bank filed the documents with the county register of deeds along with $108 in filing fees. However, the bank failed to pay a mortgage registration fee equal to 0.26 percent of the principal debt (approximately $1,404). In the Coffelts' subsequent bankruptcy, the bankruptcy trustee sought to sell the properties free of the bank's alleged lien.

OUTCOME: The court found that recording without payment of the appropriate fee was not proper. It said, "Those seeking protection of the notice system must pay for it." Because the bank did not pay, its mortgage was not perfected, and the court would not enforce a lien on the property.

—*In re Coffelt*, 395 B.R. 133 (Bankr. D. Kan.)

the mortgagee against subsequent creditors because the public record normally constitutes notice to the whole world as to the mortgagee's rights. There may be both a first mortgage and subsequent, or junior, mortgages. The mortgage recorded first normally has preference. This is not true when actual notice of a prior mortgage exists. However, a purchase money mortgage has preference over other claims arising through the mortgagor. The mortgage is also recorded to notify subsequent purchasers that as much of the purchase price as is necessary to pay off the mortgage must be paid to the mortgagee. Recording must be proper; otherwise the purpose of the mortgagee providing notice to others cannot be accomplished.

LO ②

Duties and rights of mortgagor

41-3 Duties of the Mortgagor

The mortgagor assumes three definite duties and liabilities when placing a mortgage on real estate. These pertain to:

1. Interest and principal
2. Taxes, assessments, and insurance premiums
3. Security of the mortgagee

41-3a INTEREST AND PRINCIPAL

The mortgagor must make all payments of interest and principal as they become due. Most mortgages call for periodic payments, such as monthly, semiannually, or annually. These payments are used to pay all accrued interest to the date of payment, and the mortgagee applies the balance on the principal. Other mortgages call for periodic payment of interest and for the payment of the entire principal at one time. In either case, a failure to pay either the periodic payments of interest and principal or of interest only constitutes a default. A default gives the mortgagee the right to foreclose. Most mortgages contain a provision that if the mortgagor does not make an interest or principal payment when due or within a specified time after due, the mortgagee may declare the entire principal immediately due. This is known as an **acceleration clause**.

acceleration clause
clause allowing entire principal to be due

If the mortgagor wishes to pay off the mortgage debt before the due date so as to save interest, the right must be reserved at the time the mortgage is given.

41-3b TAXES, ASSESSMENTS, AND INSURANCE PREMIUMS

The mortgagor, who is the owner of the land regardless of the form of the mortgage, must continue to make such payments as would be expected of an owner of land. The mortgagor must pay taxes and assessments. If the mortgagor does not pay the taxes and assessments, the mortgagee may pay them and compel a reimbursement from the mortgagor. If the mortgage contract requires the mortgagor to pay these charges, a failure to pay them becomes a default.

The law does not require the mortgagor to keep the property insured or to insure it for the benefit of the mortgagee. This duty can be imposed on the mortgagor by the mortgage contract. Both the mortgagor and the mortgagee have an insurable interest in the property to the extent of each one's interest or maximum loss.

41-3c SECURITY OF THE MORTGAGEE

The mortgagor must do no act that will materially impair the security of the mortgagee. Cutting timber, tearing down buildings, and all acts that waste the assets impair the security and give the mortgagee the right to seek legal protection. Some state statutes provide that any of these acts constitutes a default. This gives the mortgagee the right to foreclose. Other statutes provide only that the mortgagee may obtain an injunction in a court of equity enjoining any further impairment. Some states provide for the appointment of a receiver to prevent waste. Many state laws also make it a criminal offense to impair willfully the security of mortgaged property.

PREVIEW CASE REVISITED

FACTS: Amir Tauwab granted a mortgage on his home in favor of Huntington Bank. Within two months, Tauwab had defaulted on the loan. Huntington sent its agents multiple times to inspect the exterior of the property to see whether it was occupied. When the property appeared to be vacant, Huntington sent its agents inside to secure the premises. In fact, the property was vacant for over six months while Tauwab was incarcerated. The gas was off in the home, allowing pipes to freeze and cause additional damage. Tauwab sued for trespass and alleged that over $150,000 worth of custom suits and shirts, and six Rolex watches, were stolen by Huntington's agents in the process of securing the premises. Did Huntington have any right to invade Tauwab's home?

OUTCOME: Yes. Tauwab was clearly in default of his mortgage. Securing the premises was a proper exercise of authority under the property protection provision in the mortgage.

—*Tauwab v. Huntington Bank*, 2012 WL 760563 (Ohio Ct. App.)

41-4 Rights of the Mortgagor

The mortgagor has several rights, including:

1. Possession of the property
2. Rents and profits
3. Cancellation of lien
4. Redemption
5. Sale of the property

41-4a POSSESSION OF THE PROPERTY

As the owner of the property, the mortgagor usually has the right to retain possession of the mortgaged property. On default, the mortgagee usually may take possession to collect rents and profits and apply them to the mortgage debt in compliance with a duty as a fiduciary to the mortgagor. In some states, possession may not be taken, but the appointment of a receiver to collect rents and profits may be obtained.

COURT CASE

FACTS: After Thomas Tacon defaulted on his mortgage, Equity One Inc., the mortgagee, began foreclosure proceedings. The mortgage allowed Equity to enter to make repairs on default. Equity asked REO National to get a price for the property from a realtor. REO hired Century 21 to assess the exterior and verify the house was vacant. Debbie Muldoon, a Century 21 agent, took exterior photographs. She looked in the windows and found that the house contained junk and debris but no beds or couches, the electric meter was not running, and the house appeared unoccupied. Equity authorized Muldoon to rekey the locks and enter to "winterize" the pipes and inspect the interior to determine its value. Muldoon found that the house had been rekeyed, but the back door was open, and the electricity on. She did not think anyone was living in the house that had no heat. Concerned about vandals, she had four items of furniture removed and relocked the door. She put the furniture into storage and notified Tacon that the property appeared to have been "ransacked." He got inside and discovered several items missing. He sued, claiming Equity had not been entitled to enter the property to secure it.

OUTCOME: The court held that Equity was entitled to enter the house to secure the premises and protect its interest in the property.

—*Tacon v. Equity One Inc.*, 633 S.E.2d 599
(Ga. Ct. App.)

41-4b RENTS AND PROFITS

The mortgagor, as the owner of the property, has the right to rents and profits from the property. In the absence of an express agreement to the contrary, the mortgagor has the right to all rents and profits obtained from the mortgaged property. The mortgagor may retain the profits. This rule or any other rule may, of course, be superseded by a contract providing otherwise.

41-4c CANCELLATION OF LIEN

The mortgagor has the right to have the lien cancelled on final payment. As soon as the mortgagee receives the mortgage, it becomes a lien on the mortgaged real estate. The clerk in the recorder's office cancels a mortgage lien by entering a notation, usually on the margin, certifying that the debt has been paid and that the lien is cancelled. The mortgagee, not the mortgagor, must have this done. If the mortgagee does not, the mortgagor may institute court action to have this cloud removed from the title so that there may be a clear title.

41-4d REDEMPTION

redemption
right to free property from lien of mortgage

The mortgagor has the right to free the mortgaged property from the lien of the mortgage after default, known as the right of **redemption**. Statutes in most states prescribe a specific time after the foreclosure and sale when this right may be exercised. In order to redeem the property, the mortgagor must pay the amount of the mortgage, the costs of the sale, and any amounts paid to protect the purchaser's interest in the property, such as taxes or insurance.

Usually, only a person whose interests will be affected by foreclosure may exercise the right of redemption. This includes the executor or administrator and heirs of the mortgagor, and frequently a second mortgagee or junior lienholder.

41-4e SALE OF THE PROPERTY

The mortgagor has a right to sell the property on which a mortgage exists. The purchaser may agree to "assume the mortgage," which means to be primarily liable for its payment. "Assuming" the mortgage differs from buying the property "subject to the mortgage." In the first case, the buyer agrees to be liable for the mortgage obligation as fully as the original mortgagor. If the buyer takes the property "subject to the mortgage" and default occurs, the property may be lost, but no more.

A sale of the mortgaged property does not automatically release the original mortgagor whether the purchaser assumed the mortgage or bought it subject to the mortgage. The mortgagor remains fully liable in both cases.

To excuse the mortgagor from liability under a mortgage, a novation must take place. This can occur if the parties involved sign a written agreement releasing the mortgagor. Courts also have found novations if the mortgagee extends the time of payment for the purchaser of the property without the mortgagor's consent. Accepting an interest payment after the principal of the mortgage has become due constitutes an extension of the mortgage. If the mortgagee does this without the mortgagor's consent, a novation results and releases the mortgagor from all liability under the mortgage. However, the action of the mortgagee must amount to an extension of time of payment.

41-5 Foreclosure

If the mortgagor fails to pay the debt secured by the mortgage when it becomes due, or fails to perform any of the other terms set forth in the mortgage, the mortgagee has the right to foreclose for the purpose of collecting the debt. **Foreclosure** usually consists of a sale of the mortgaged property. Generally, an officer of the court makes the sale under an order of a court. The mortgagor must be properly notified of the foreclosure proceedings.

LO ③
Foreclosure and assignment of right

foreclosure
sale of mortgaged property to pay debt

COURT CASE

FACTS: The Ausburns originally purchased their home in 1976, and over the next 35 years, made payments on and refinanced the mortgage. Pursuant to the terms of the mortgage documents, the Ausburns waived their statutory right of redemption in the event of foreclosure. They then took out a second mortgage on the home. Eventually payments were missed, and the first lender began foreclosure proceedings. The court order gave the Ausburns ten (10) days in which to pay the balance due. After twenty (20) days, the Ausburns filed bankruptcy in an attempt to keep their home.

OUTCOME: The redemption period had expired. The Ausburns waived any statutory period in the mortgage documents, and they made no payments during the ten (10) days given them in the court order.

—*In re Ausburn*, 524 B.R. 816 (E.D. Ark.)

Foreclosure literally means "a legal proceeding to shut out all other claims." A first mortgage may not necessarily constitute a first claim on the proceeds of the sale. The cost of foreclosure and taxes always takes precedence over the first mortgage. People who furnish materials for the construction of a house and workers who work on it have a claim under what is known as a **mechanic's lien**.

mechanic's lien
lien of people who have furnished materials or labor on property

A mechanic's lien takes precedence over unrecorded mortgages. The law varies somewhat among the states, but normally a mortgage recorded before a mechanic's lien attaches has priority. The foreclosure proceedings establish the existence of all prior claims and the order of their priority. Foreclosure proceedings are fixed by statute and therefore the specific steps to be taken vary in different states.

If the proceeds of the sale of mortgaged property exceed the amount of the debt and the expenses of foreclosure, the surplus must be used to pay off any other liens such as second mortgages. Any money remaining belongs to the mortgagor.

If a deficiency results, however, the mortgagee may secure a deficiency judgment for this amount. In that case, the unpaid balance of the debt will be a claim against the mortgagor personally until it is paid.

When the mortgagor has given a mortgage for the purpose of purchasing the property, some states limit the amount of a deficiency judgment. The deficiency cannot be greater than the amount by which the debt exceeds either the fair market value or the selling price, whichever amount is smaller. This gives protection to the mortgagor from the mortgagee buying the property at foreclosure for a very low price. For example, suppose A mortgages property to B for $50,000, and the value of the property declines to $40,000. A defaults and B forecloses. B buys the property at foreclosure for $30,000.

	Fair Market Value	Selling Price
Amount of debt	$50,000	$50,000
Less amount received	40,000	30,000
Deficiency	$10,000	$20,000

B may obtain a deficiency judgment of $10,000 because it is the lesser of the two amounts.

41-6 Assignment of the Mortgage

The rights of the mortgagee under the mortgage agreement may be assigned. The assignee, the purchaser, obtains no greater rights than the assignor had. To be protected, the assignee should require the assignor to produce an *estoppel* certificate signed by the mortgagor. This certificate should acknowledge that the mortgagor has no claims of any kind in connection with the mortgage. This would bar the mortgagor from subsequently claiming the right of offset.

The assignee of a mortgage should have this assignment recorded. In the event that the mortgagee assigns the mortgage to more than one party, the one who records an assignment first has preference. This can be important when the proceeds are not adequate to pay both assignees.

41-7 Deed of Trust

deed of trust
deed that transfers property to trustee for benefit of creditor

trustee
one who holds title to property for another

In a number of states, parties commonly use a deed of trust instead of a mortgage for securing a debt with real estate. A mortgage involves two parties: a debtor and a creditor. A **deed of trust** involves three parties and conveys title to the property to a disinterested party, called a **trustee**. The trustee holds the property in trust for the benefit of the creditor. Most courts treat a deed of trust like a mortgage. If a default in payment occurs, the trustee forecloses on the property and applies the proceeds to the payment of the debt. The right to redeem under a deed of trust, when it exists, is similar to the right of redemption under a mortgage.

The advantage to the creditor in using a deed of trust instead of a mortgage is in the power held by the trustee. In the event that a mortgagor defaults on the payments, the mortgagee who holds an ordinary mortgage can foreclose. In most states, however, the mortgagee must go into court and have a judicial foreclosure in order to have the mortgaged property sold to satisfy the debt. A trustee of a deed of trust may sell the mortgaged property at public auction if the debtor defaults. No time-consuming court foreclosure proceedings are necessary. Hence, the property can be sold more quickly at a trustee's sale.

41-8 Mortgage Insurance

Private companies and several agencies of the federal government insure or guarantee mortgages against default by the mortgagor. The insurance lasts for the term of the mortgage. The government agrees to pay in case of default by the mortgagor in order to make it easier for some people to obtain a mortgage. The most frequently used government programs are those administered by the Federal Housing Administration (FHA) and the U.S. Department of Veterans Affairs (VA).

FHA-insured mortgages require a smaller down payment than conventional mortgages. Anyone who meets the financial qualifications may obtain an FHA loan. Because FHA mortgages are insured, the interest rate is slightly less than for a conventional mortgage. The FHA sets a maximum amount that may be mortgaged. The FHA bases this amount on the average sale price in the area for a home. The mortgagor pays premiums for this mortgage insurance.

The VA guarantees mortgages for people who have served on active duty in the armed forces for a minimum period of time. The mortgage must be on owner-occupied property. The VA charges the mortgagor a percentage of the loan amount for its guarantee. It sets the interest rate charged. As a benefit to veterans, it sets this rate less than the market rate for conventional loans. A VA mortgage may be for up to 100 percent of the value of the real estate. This means that no down payment is required. The maximum loan amount is determined by a formula that takes into consideration the value of other homes in the county.

QUESTIONS

1. How is a mortgage different from a debt?

2. What formalities are necessary for a mortgage?

3. For what reasons may a person secure a loan by a mortgage?

4. What duties does a mortgagor assume?

5. If two mortgages are executed on the same land, which has priority?

6. What rights does a mortgagor retain?

7. How may a mortgagor redeem property after it has been sold under a foreclosure sale?

8. What does it mean to "assume a mortgage"?

9. What is a mechanic's lien?

10. What government programs are available to assist people in obtaining a mortgage?

CASE PROBLEMS

LO ③

1. Bierwirth executed a note and deed of trust to purchase a residence. The note and deed of trust were subsequently assigned to BAC Home Loans Servicing, LP (BAC). Bierwirth ceased making payments, and BAC instituted non-judicial foreclosure proceedings pursuant to the deed of trust. Bierwirth attempted to stop the foreclosure proceedings by filing suit. Was BAC permitted to foreclose on the deed of trust without suing under the original note?

LO ②

2. Wilhelmina McEwan purchased a home on which she granted Ely Place, Ltd., a mortgage, which was recorded in a timely fashion. Ten years later, she leased the home to Catherine Lavery. The lease was not recorded. Ely Place thereafter assigned the mortgage to EiA Properties, LLC (EiA), and the assignment was recorded. Ultimately, McEwan defaulted on the payments, and EiA began court proceedings to foreclose on the mortgage. EiA was the high bidder at the court sale, but Lavery opposed EiA's motion for possession, alleging that EiA was bound by the terms of the lease to allow Lavery to continue to live in the home. Could EiA remove Lavery from the property?

LO ①

3. Arthur and Bobbie Ten Hove faced bankruptcy and foreclosure on their home. Christopher Johns, a real estate agent, would arrange for Allen Banks, a house "flipper," to purchase homes on the brink of foreclosure at an inflated price. The homeowners would execute a second mortgage in favor of Banks amounting to the difference between the purchase price and the amount owed. Immediately after the sale the seller would repay the second mortgage given to Banks. Banks used this money to rehabilitate the house and then sell it for its then (much higher) market value. The sellers would lose any equity that had been built up in the home but would avoid the black mark of foreclosure on their credit records. The Ten Hoves had already begun the bankruptcy process; therefore, any sale of their home needed to be approved by the bankruptcy trustee. The trustee smelled something fishy in the proposed transaction and, after investigation, Banks and Johns were charged with and convicted of criminal fraud. Johns argued that the second mortgage by which Banks received the excess purchase funds was a valid document, duly recorded and binding on the sellers. Was Johns correct?

LO ③

4. John Ball executed a deed of trust on property he owned in favor of Washington Mutual Bank to secure a $52,000 loan. Some years later, he executed a second deed of trust to Washington Mutual Bank to secure a home equity line of credit for $154,000. After financial difficulty, Ball defaulted on the first loan, and the trustee sold the property. Washington Mutual Bank was the highest bidder. Ball claimed that since the same bank held both loans and purchased the property at foreclosure sale, only the first loan should be paid off, and Ball should receive any remaining funds. Was Ball entitled to the excess?

LO ②

5. Allan and Deborah Cormier found themselves underwater on a mortgage. Fair market value of the property was estimated at $75,000, but a mortgage of $94,000 was owed to American Home Mortgage Service (American). The Cormiers asked the court to force American to acknowledge the Cormiers' surrender of the property and allow "them to deduct from their . . . payment, on account of administrative expenses, the actual amounts they [were] incurring to insure and preserve that property." The Cormiers wanted American to take over the expenses of the property so they could devote that money to other expenses. Once the Cormiers decided to abandon the property, was American responsible to pick up the tab immediately?

LO ①

6. Carl and Martha Traxler sold their 94-acre farm to Keith and Chastity Samuel for development of a residential subdivision. The Traxlers provided financing secured by a deed of trust. As the Samuels obtained buyers for various tracts of land, they requested partial releases from the deed of trust so that property could be transferred to buyers free and clear. The Traxlers generally cooperated. With respect to the sale of a tract to Darrel and Mellony Melson, no one asked the Traxlers for a partial release. Years later the Samuels fell behind on their payments. Four years after their purchase, the Melsons discovered that the deed of trust held by the Traxlers had not been released from their property. The Melsons asked the Traxlers for a partial release and were denied. Do the Melsons have a right to demand their tract be released from the Traxlers deed of trust?

CASE PROBLEMS (CONTINUED)

7. Wanda Williams purchased a residence that was financed by SunTrust Bank. After she failed to make the monthly payments, the bank began foreclosure proceedings. After required notices were given, the bank purchased the property at the foreclosure sale on October 2. On October 11, Williams filed a petition in bankruptcy and sought to set aside the foreclosure sale. Did she still have any interest in the property? Was there sufficient interest for the court to set aside the sale? **LO** ②

8. Denaro owned property appraised at $750,000, which secured a loan of approximately $500,000. After Denaro filed for bankruptcy, the bank foreclosed. At a sheriff's sale with multiple parties bidding, the bank purchased the property for a bid of $401,000. Denaro filed a motion in court arguing that based on the appraisal report showing a fair market value of $750,000, the bank was satisfied in full. Discuss the rights of the parties depending on whether the state has a law regarding the sufficiency of the sale price at a foreclosure. **LO** ③

Landlord and Tenant

LEARNING OBJECTIVES

1. Explain the nature and formation of the landlord–tenant relationship.
2. Name the various types of tenancies.
3. List the rights and duties of tenants and landlords.
4. Explain how a lease may be terminated.

PREVIEW CASE

Brewster Park, LLC, leased certain property to Aaron Hochman pursuant to a residential rental agreement. Fred Berger was an employee of Hochman who used the rental property throughout the term of the agreement, from August through February. Berger did not sign the lease as a lessee, but did sign his name at the bottom of the lease paragraph dealing with the damages and costs due from a tenant who held over. No rent was ever paid by Hochman, and in November Brewster Park caused a notice to quit to be served on Berger. The ensuing eviction process was finally completed when Berger moved out in July. Was Brewster Park entitled to damages from Berger?

LO ①
Nature and formation of relationship

landlord or lessor
owner of leased property

tenant or lessee
possessor of leased property

lease
contract between landlord and tenant

rent
amount paid landlord for possession of property

A contract whereby one person agrees to lease land or a building to another creates the relationship of landlord and tenant. Such an agreement does not require special words or acts for creation unless the lease lasts for more than a year, in which case it must be in writing. The tenant's temporary possession of the premises and payment of rent for its use constitute the chief characteristics that determine the relationship of landlord and tenant. The landlord may retake possession of the property at the end of the lease period.

The owner of the leased property is known as the **landlord**, or **lessor**. The person given possession of the leased property is the **tenant**, or **lessee**. The contract or agreement between the landlord and tenant is called a **lease** (see Illustration 42-1). The amount that the tenant agrees to pay the landlord for the possession of the leased property is called the **rent**.

A tenant differs from a lodger or roomer in that the former has the exclusive legal possession of the property, whereas the latter has merely the right to use the premises subject to the control and supervision of the owner.

42-1 The Lease

The lease may be oral or written, express or implied, formal or simple, subject, however, to the general statutory requirement that a lease of land for a term longer than one year must be in writing to be enforceable. If a dispute arises between the tenant and the landlord over their rights and duties, the court will look to the terms of the lease and the general body of landlord and tenant law to determine the decision.

ILLUSTRATION 42-1 Lease

RENTAL AGREEMENT

1. Parties:
___Richard T. Mowbray, Cincinnati, OH_____(Owner) and _____Edward J. and Doris L. Caldwell,
Cincinnati, OH_____(Tenant) hereby agree as follows:

2. Premises:
Owner rents to Tenant and Tenant rents from Owner for residential use only, the premises located at:
___2669 Russell Road, Cincinnati, OH 45299 together with the following furnishings, appliances, and fixtures:
___stove, refrigerator, dishwasher, washer, and dryer on the following terms:

3. Term:
This agreement shall begin on__May 1, 2015_____ and shall continue from that date
___A) on a month-to-month basis. This agreement will continue for successive terms of one month each until either owner or tenant terminate the tenancy by giving the other thirty (30) days written notice of an intention to terminate the tenancy. In the event such notice is given, tenant agrees to pay all rent up to and including the notice period.
X B) for a period of ___12___ months, expiring on _April 30, 2016___.

4. Rent:
Tenant shall pay Owner rent of __$775__ per month. Rent for each month is payable in advance on or before the first day of the month for which the rent is due. Rent shall be paid by personal check, money order, or cashier's check only, to the order of __Mowbray Apartments_____ (Cash shall not be accepted).

5. Security Deposit:
Tenant shall deposit __$400_____ with Owner as security. Owner may use all or any part of this security deposit to remedy defaults in the payment of rent, to repair damage to the premises, to clean the premises, or for any other purpose allowed by law. This deposit shall be refunded to Tenant within three weeks (21 days) after vacating said apartment, if the following conditions have been satisfied:
a) Proper notice of termination has been given;
b) There is no default in the payment of rent and/or late charges;
c) The premises are left in clean, orderly condition, including the cleaning of carpets, refrigerator, stove, oven, etc.
d) There has been no damage to premises, equipment, or furnishings; and
e) All other terms and conditions of this agreement have been satisfied.
In the event Owner incurs expenses to remedy any default in this agreement, including but not limited to the above conditions, the cost may be deducted from the Security Deposit. If Owners' expenses exceed said deposit, Tenant shall be liable for excesses.

6. Utilities:
Tenant shall pay all utility charges related to his/her occupancy of the premises except _trash collection services._

7. Late Charges:
Tenant shall pay Owner a late charge of __$100__ if rent is not received by Owner by 5:00 p.m. on the fifth day of the month for which it is due.

8. Habitability:
Tenant has examined the entire interior and exterior of the premises and acknowledges that the entire premises are in good, clean condition. Tenant, to the best of his/her ability, has examined all furnishings, appliances, and

ILLUSTRATION 42-1   Lease (*continued*)

fixtures on the premises including plumbing, heating and electrical appliances, and fixtures and acknowledges that these items are in good working order with the following exceptions:

_____ Tenant shall immediately give Owner written notice upon discovery of any damage, defects, or dangerous conditions on or about the premises, including plumbing, heating and electrical appliances, and fixtures.

9. Disturbances:
Tenant shall not use the premises for any unlawful purpose, violate any law or ordinance, commit waste, or create a nuisance on or about the premises or permit such acts to occur. It shall be presumed that three disturbance complaints from other tenants in the building or occupants of nearby buildings during any consecutive sixty-day period shall constitute an irremediable breach of this agreement and Owner shall have the right to immediately terminate the tenancy.

10. Right of Entry:
Upon reasonable notice, Owner may enter the premises during reasonable hours for the purpose of making repairs, alterations, decorations or improvements, to supply services, to show the premises to others, or for any other purpose allowed by law. In an emergency, Owner may enter the premises at any time without prior notice to Tenant for the purpose of taking such action as is necessary to alleviate the emergency.

11. Smoke Detectors:
The premises are equipped with a smoke detection device(s), and Tenant shall be responsible for reporting any problems, maintenance, or repairs to Owner. Replacing batteries is the responsibility of the Tenant.

12. Termination of Tenancy:
A thirty-day notice of termination may be given by either Tenant or Owner at any time during the month and tenancy does not have to terminate at the end of the calendar month. Rent shall be due and payable up to and including the date of termination. When the thirty-day notice is given by Tenant, it may not be revoked or modified without written approval of the Owner. As a condition for the full refund of all of the security deposit Tenant shall do the following: a) completely vacate the premises, including any storage or other areas of the general premises which Tenant may be occupying or in which Tenant may have personal property stored; b) deliver all keys and other personal property furnished to Tenant during the term of this Agreement; c) and leave Tenant's forwarding address. Tenant shall cooperate in allowing the Manager to show Tenant's apartment at any reasonable time during this thirty-day period.

Tenant's and Co-Signer's Certificate and Acknowledgement of Receipt:

I hereby certify that I have read all provisions of this agreement, that I understand them, that I agree to abide by them, and that I acknowledge receipt of a copy of this agreement and all attachment to it.

April 18, 2015	_Edward J. Caldwell_
Date	Tenant
April 18, 2015	_Doris L. Caldwell_
Date	Tenant
April 18, 2015	_Richard J. Mowbray_
Date	Owner/Agent

In order to avoid disputes, a lease should be in writing and should cover all terms of the contract. The parties should include such items as a clear identification of the property, the time and place of payment of rent, the notice required to vacate, the duration or the nature of the tenancy, and any specific provision desired by either party, such as the right of the landlord to show the property to prospective purchasers or an agreement requiring the landlord to redecorate.

COURT CASE

FACTS: On September 3, Hinton gave her landlord, Sealander, "thirty days' notice" that she was leaving. On September 26, Sealander learned from a neighbor that the house was vacant and unsecured. While inspecting, Sealander discovered broken windows, doors torn off hinges, and such disarray of personal property that it appeared to have been ransacked. All locks and deadbolts had been removed. The lease contained a clause allowing "Landlord . . . access to the premises at any reasonable time for the purpose of inspection or repair." Three days later, Sealander installed new locks and offered to allow Hinton access to retrieve her personal property at any reasonable time. Hinton sued, claiming she was entitled to her own set of keys and unrestricted, unaccompanied access to the property during the remainder of the lease.

OUTCOME: The court found that having paid rent through September 30, Hinton was entitled to unrestricted access, and Sealander was liable for such damages Hinton could show due to the two-day eviction from the property.

—*Hinton v. Sealander Brokerage, Co.,*
917 A.2d 95 (D.C.)

42-2 Types of Tenancies

LO ②
Tenancy types

Four separate and distinct classes of tenancies exist, each of which has some rule of law governing it that does not apply to any other type of tenancy. The four classes of tenancies are:

1. Tenancy for years
2. Tenancy from year to year
3. Tenancy at will
4. Tenancy at sufferance

42-2a TENANCY FOR YEARS

A **tenancy for years** is a tenancy for a definite period of time, whether it is one month, one year, or 99 years. The lease fixes the termination date. However, most states limit the length of time a lease may last by law. A lease for a time greater than the statutory limit is void. The payment of the rent may be by the month even when a tenancy for a specified number of years exists. No notice to terminate the tenancy need be given by either party when the lease fixes the termination date. Most leases provide that they will continue to run on a year-to-year basis after the termination date, unless the tenant gives notice to the landlord not less than a specified number of days before the termination date that the tenant intends to leave on that date.

tenancy for years
tenancy for any definite period

42-2b TENANCY FROM YEAR TO YEAR

A tenancy for an indefinite period of time with rent set at a yearly amount is known as a **tenancy from year to year**. Under such a tenancy, a tenant merely pays the rent periodically, and the lease lasts until proper notice of termination has been given. A tenancy of this kind also may be by the month or any other period

tenancy from year to year
tenancy for indefinite period with yearly rent

tenancy from month to month
tenancy for flexible period with monthly rent

agreed on. If by the month, it is called a **tenancy from month to month**. The length of the tenancy is usually determined by the nature of the rent stated or paid, although there could be a tenancy from year to year with the rent paid quarterly or monthly.

Notice to terminate this type of tenancy must exactly follow the state law governing it. Notice must normally be in writing. In a tenancy from month to month, the law usually requires notice thirty days before a rent due date.

42-2c TENANCY AT WILL

tenancy at will
tenancy for uncertain period

A **tenancy at will** exists when the tenant has possession of the property for an uncertain period. Either the tenant or the landlord can terminate the tenancy at will, because both must agree to the tenancy. This tenancy, unlike any of the others, automatically terminates on the death of the tenant or the landlord, if the tenant attempts to assign the tenancy, or if the landlord sells the property.

42-2d TENANCY AT SUFFERANCE

tenancy at sufferance
holdover tenant without landlord's permission

When a tenant holds over the tenancy after the expiration of the lease without permission of the landlord, a **tenancy at sufferance** exists until the landlord elects to treat the tenant as a trespasser or as a tenant. The landlord may treat the tenant as a trespasser, sue for damages, and have the tenant removed by legal proceedings. If the landlord prefers, payment of the rent due for another period may be accepted, and thus the tenant's possession may be recognized as rightful.

PREVIEW CASE REVISITED

FACTS: Brewster Park, LLC leased certain property to Aaron Hochman pursuant to a residential rental agreement. Fred Berger was an employee of Hochman who used the rental property throughout the term of the agreement, from August through February. Berger did not sign the lease as a lessee but did sign his name at the bottom of the lease paragraph dealing with the damages and costs due from a tenant who held over. No rent was ever paid by Hochman, and in November Brewster Park caused a notice to quit to be served on Berger. The ensuing eviction process was finally completed when Berger moved out in July. Brewster Park sued Berger for damages.

OUTCOME: The court said that the fact that Berger had not signed the lease did not entitle him to live in the property rent-free for nearly nine months after being put on notice to quit possession. The measure of damages was the fair market value for use of the property.

—*Brewster Park, LLC, v. Berger*, 14 A.3d 334 (Conn. App. Ct.)

LO ③
Tenant and landlord rights and duties

42-3 Rights of the Tenant

A lease gives the tenant certain rights, as follows:

1. Right to possession
2. Right to use the premises
3. Right to assign or sublease

42-3a RIGHT TO POSSESSION

By signing the lease, the landlord warrants the right to lease the premises and that the tenant shall have possession during the period of the lease. During the term of the lease, tenants have the same right to exclusive possession of the premises as if they owned the property. If someone questions the owner's right to lease the property, the landlord must defend the tenant's right to exclusive possession. Failure of the landlord to give possession on time or to protect the tenant's rights subjects the landlord to liability for damages.

A nuisance that disturbs the tenant's quiet enjoyment of the property often causes disputes between landlords and tenants. Courts have held that failure to remove dead rats from the wall, failure to stop disorderly conduct on the part of other tenants, and frequent and unnecessary entrances on the property by the landlord or agents constitute acts that destroy the tenant's right to quiet enjoyment and constitute a breach of warranty on the part of the landlord.

If the nuisance existed at the time the tenant leased the property and the tenant knew of its existence, the right to complain would be deemed to have been waived. Also, if the landlord has no control over the nuisance, the tenant cannot avoid the contract even though the nuisance arose subsequent to the signing of the lease. If the landlord fails or refuses to **abate**, or reduce the effects of, a nuisance over which the landlord has control, the tenant not only may terminate the lease but also may sue for damages. In other cases, the tenant may seek an injunction compelling the landlord to abate a nuisance.

abate
to end or put to end

42-3b RIGHT TO USE THE PREMISES

Unless the lease expressly restricts this right, the tenant has the right to use the premises in any way consistent with the nature of the property. A dwelling cannot be converted into a machine shop, nor can a clothing store be converted into a restaurant. Damage to leased property, other than that which results from ordinary wear and tear, is not permissible. In the case of farming land, the tenant may cut wood for personal use but not to sell.

42-3c RIGHT TO ASSIGN OR SUBLEASE

If the tenant transfers all interest in the lease to another party who agrees to comply with its terms, including the payment of the rent to the landlord, there is an **assignment**. In an assignment, the assignee pays the rent directly to the landlord. An assignment must include the entire premises. In a **sublease**, the tenant transfers the premises for a period less than the term of the lease or transfers only a part of the premises. The tenant usually collects the rent from the subtenant and pays the landlord. Ordinarily, a written lease prohibits assigning or subleasing the premises unless the lessor gives written consent thereto first. Residential leases commonly restrict the use of the premises to the tenant and the immediate family or to a certain number of people. Unless the lease expressly prohibits both assignment and subleasing, either may be done. If the lease prohibits only subleasing, then the lease may be assigned.

assignment
transfer to another of tenant's rights

sublease
transfer of less than a tenant's full rights under a lease

Joint occupancy closely relates to subleasing. A provision in the lease prohibiting subleasing does not forbid a contract for a joint occupancy. In joint occupancy, the tenant does not give up exclusive control of any part of the premises. The tenant merely permits another party to occupy jointly all or a part of the premises.

42-4 Duties of the Tenant

The lease imposes certain duties upon the tenant:

1. To pay rent
2. To protect and preserve the premises

42-4a TO PAY RENT

The tenant's primary duty is to pay the rent. This payment must be made in money unless the contract provides otherwise, such as a share of the crops. The rent may be a specific dollar amount or, as is increasingly common in commercial situations, a percentage of gross sales or profits subject to a minimum dollar amount. The rent is not due until the end of the term, but leases almost universally provide for rent in advance.

Landlords commonly appoint an agent for the purpose of collecting the rent. The death of the principal automatically terminates such a principal–agent relationship. Any rent paid to the agent after this termination and not remitted to the proper party must be paid again.

If the tenant fails to pay rent on time, the landlord may terminate the lease and order the tenant to vacate, or the landlord may permit the tenant to continue occupancy and sue for the rent. However, even if the landlord forces the tenant to vacate the property, the tenant is still liable for the agreed rent. Under the common law, the landlord could seize and hold any personal property found on the premises. This right has been either curtailed or abolished by statute.

42-4b TO PROTECT AND PRESERVE THE PREMISES

Traditionally, a tenant had to make repairs on the premises. This was because a tenant had a duty to keep the leased property in as good condition as the landlord had it when the lease began. Some states have enacted statutes requiring the landlord to make repairs. Other states find a warranty of habitability, which makes the landlord responsible for keeping the premises livable. Some statutes even give tenants

COURT CASE

FACTS: Palatine Associates was the owner of a shopping center. All American was a tenant of two spaces in the shopping center, the first for "approximately 7500 square feet" and the second for "approximately 2500 square feet." All American paid a fixed base rent plus a pro-rata share of real estate taxes and common area maintenance charges. The lease spelled out All American's proportionate shares as 4.49 percent (7,500 out of 500,000 sq. ft.) and 1.50 percent (2,500 out of 167,142 sq. ft.). Partial rent payments were made, but two years into the lease Palatine served All American with a notice of termination, including a demand for past-due rental. All American claimed that the leases overstated the actual square footage of the premises such that it had actually overpaid its rent. It also alleged that it was entitled to reduce its rent payments based on a reduction in square footage.

OUTCOME: The court held that by their very terms the leases approximated the square footage. All American was not entitled to pay a lesser amount simply because actual square footage differed from the approximations in the leases.

—Village of Palatine v. Palatine Associates, LLC,
966 N.E.2d 1174 (Ill. App. Ct.)

a form of self-help. The tenant must notify the landlord of needed repairs. If the landlord does not make the repairs, the tenant may fix things and deduct the cost from the rent. Tenants, however, must repair damage caused by their negligence. In states in which statutes have not altered the traditional responsibility, tenants must repair damage except reasonable wear and tear and damage by the elements.

42-5 Rights of the Landlord

The landlord has three definite rights under the lease:

1. To regain possession
2. To enter on the property to preserve it
3. To assign rights

42-5a TO REGAIN POSSESSION

On termination of the lease, the landlord has the right to regain peaceable possession of the premises. If the tenant refuses this possession, the most common remedy is to bring an **action of ejectment** in a court of law. On the successful completion of this suit, the sheriff will forcibly remove the tenant and any property.

action of ejectment action to have sheriff remove tenant

When the landlord repossesses leased property, all permanent improvements and fixtures may be retained. Courts determine whether the improvements have become a part of the real estate or not. If they have, they cannot be removed.

42-5b TO ENTER ON THE PROPERTY TO PRESERVE IT

The landlord has a right to enter on the property to preserve it. Extensive renovations that interfere with the tenant's peaceable occupancy cannot be made. If the roof blows off or becomes leaky, the landlord may repair it or put on a new one. This occasion cannot be used to add another story. A landlord who enters the property without permission may be treated as a stranger. A landlord has no right to enter the premises to show the property to prospective purchasers or tenants unless the lease reserves this right.

42-5c TO ASSIGN RIGHTS

The landlord has the right to assign the rights under the lease to a third party. The tenant cannot avoid any duties and obligations by reason of the assignment of the lease. Like all other assignments, the assignment does not release the assignor from the contract without the consent of the tenant. If, for example, the tenant suffers injury because of a concealed but defective water main cover, and the landlord knew of this condition, the landlord has liability even though rights under the lease were assigned before the injury.

42-6 Duties of the Landlord

The lease imposes certain duties on the landlord:

1. To pay taxes and assessments
2. To protect the tenant from concealed defects
3. To mitigate damages on abandonment by the tenant

42-6a TO PAY TAXES AND ASSESSMENTS

Although the tenant occupies and uses the premises, the landlord must pay all taxes and special assessments. Sometimes the lease provides that the tenant shall pay the taxes. In such event, the tenant has no liability for special assessments for sidewalks, street paving, and other improvements.

42-6b TO PROTECT THE TENANT FROM CONCEALED DEFECTS

The landlord has liability to the tenant if the tenant suffers injury by concealed defects that were known, or should have been reasonably known, to the landlord at the time of giving the tenant possession of the premises. Such defects might be contamination from contagious germs; concealed, unfilled wells; and rotten timbers in the dwelling. The tenant bears the risk of injury caused by apparent defects or defects reasonably discoverable on inspection at the time that the tenant enters into possession. Most cities and many states have tenement laws that require the landlord to keep all rental property habitable and provided with adequate fire escapes. The question of the habitability of the property relates to major defects in the structure. Any damage caused by a failure to observe these laws may subject the landlord to liability for damages.

42-6c TO MITIGATE DAMAGES UPON ABANDONMENT BY THE TENANT

Unless the landlord accepts the abandonment, a tenant who abandons leased property before the end of the lease term still has an obligation to pay the rent due through the end of the term. Under the common law, the landlord could do nothing and sue the tenant for the unpaid rent. However, in most states the landlord now has a duty to take reasonable steps to mitigate the tenant's damages by attempting to secure a new tenant. If a new tenant occupies the premises, the landlord's damage from the first tenant abandoning the property equals the difference between the rent the original tenant had to pay and the rent the new tenant pays. In this way, the original tenant's obligation amounts to less than the original rent called for by the lease, and the new tenant's payments mitigate the landlord's damage due from the original tenant.

COURT CASE

FACTS: Flawlace, LLC (Flawlace), leased unfinished commercial space from Francis Lin, intending to operate a beauty salon. City ordinance required suitable fire protection before the beauty salon could be operated. The terms of the lease were silent on who would pay for improvements for fire protection, but Lin voluntarily undertook to provide it. Flawlace concurrently began building out the space for purposes of its salon. By the time the city approved the fire protection system over a year later, Flawlace gave up on the beauty salon in that location, and abandoned the premises. After three months, Lin found another tenant, and sued Flawlace for the missed three months' rent.

OUTCOME: Because the lease was silent as to fire protection, the court did not find a duty in the landlord to provide suitable fire protection for the tenant's specific use. As a result, the tenant was liable for rent until the replacement tenant could be found.

—*Tri-Lin Holdings, LLC v. Flawlace, LLC,*
2014 WL 1101577

42-7 Termination of the Lease

A lease for a fixed time automatically terminates on the expiration of that period. The death of either party does not ordinarily affect the lease. If the leased property consists of rooms or apartments in a building and fire or any other accidental cause destroys them, the lease terminates without liability on the part of the tenant. In the case of leases of entire buildings, serious problems arise if fire, tornado, or any other cause destroys the property. Under the common law, the tenant had to continue to pay rent even though the property was destroyed. Some states retain this rule; other states have modified it. A landlord who has a ten-year lease on a $100,000 building destroyed by fire one year after signing the lease would not be inclined to rebuild if fully covered by fire insurance. The landlord would find it more profitable to invest the $100,000 and continue to collect the rent. To prevent this, statutes may provide that if the landlord refuses to restore the property, the lease terminates. The lease itself may contain a cancellation clause. If it does not, the tenant can carry fire insurance for the amount of possible loss. Even when the lease will thus terminate, the tenant will probably wish to carry fire insurance for personal property and, if the premises are used for a business purpose, may carry insurance to indemnify for business interruption or loss of business income.

The landlord may agree to the voluntary surrender of the possession of the premises before the lease expires. This terminates the lease. However, an abandonment of the premises without the consent of the landlord does not constitute a termination of the lease, but a breach of contract.

If the lease runs from year to year or from month to month, the party wishing to terminate it must generally give the other party a written notice of this intention (see Illustrations 42-2 and 42-3). Statutes prescribe the time and the manner

ILLUSTRATION 42-2 Landlord's Notice to Leave the Premises

NOTICE TO LEAVE THE PREMISES

_____

To Mr. C. Harold Whitmore_____

  You will please take notice that I *want you to leave the premises you now occupy, and which you have rented of* me *, situated and described as follows:*
_____Suite 4_____
_____Lakeview Apartment_____
_____Lake Shore Drive at Overview street_____
_____
_____

in Cleveland *County of* Cuyahoga *and State of* Ohio
  Your compliance with this Notice July 31_____

will prevent legal measures being taken by me *to obtain possession of the same, agreeably to law.*

                    Yours respectfully,
                    H. L. Simpson
                    _____
                    May 1   20–

ILLUSTRATION 42-3 Tenant's Notice That the Tenant Is Leaving the Premises

January 2, 20-

Mr. George A. HardWick
1719 Glenview Road
St. Louis, Missouri 65337

Dear Mr. Hardwick

This is to notify you that on March 31, 20-, I intend to vacate the premises now leased from you and located at 1292 Clarendon Road, St. Louis, Missouri. In accordance with the terms of our written lease, this letter constitutes notice of the termination of said lease as of March 31, 20–.

Sincerely,

John N. Richter

JOHN N. RICHTER

of giving notice; they also may specify other particulars, such as the grounds for a termination of the tenancy.

If either party fails to give proper notice, the other party may continue the tenancy for another period.

42-7a EVICTION

Tenants sometimes refuse to give up possession of the property after the expiration of the lease or fail to comply with requirements of the lease or laws. In such a case, a landlord may seek an **eviction** of the tenant. Eviction is the expulsion of the tenant from the leased property. The laws of the states vary, but all have some form of summary eviction law. The summary action brought by the landlord is called a **forcible entry and detainer action**. The tenant has a right to written notice and a court hearing. However, the court will set an early date, usually seven to fifteen days after notification of the tenant, for the trial. If the landlord wins, law enforcement officers may enforce the eviction in a few days. The proceedings permit quick recovery of real property by the one legally entitled to it.

eviction
expulsion of tenant from leased property

forcible entry and detainer action
summary action by landlord to regain possession

42-8 Improvements

Tenants frequently make improvements during the life of the lease. Many disputes arise as to the tenant's right to take these improvements after the lease is terminated. Courts must determine whether an improvement has become a fixture, which must be left on the land, or whether it remains personal property. If the improvements are **trade fixtures**, or fixtures used in business, and can be removed without substantial injury to the leased property, the tenant may remove them. If a farm tenant builds a fence in the normal way, the fence is a fixture, and the tenant has no right to remove it on leaving. A poultry house built in the usual way is a fixture and cannot be removed. In a similar case, a tenant built the poultry house on sledlike runners. When ready to leave, the tenant had the poultry house hauled away and took it when vacating. The court held that the shed had not become a fixture but remained personal property.

> **trade fixtures**
> fixtures used in business

Unless prohibited by law, one may freely contract away rights or may waive them, so the parties may agree as to how to treat fixtures. In one case, a tenant built a permanent frame house on leased property with the landlord's agreement that the house could be moved at the end of the lease. The landlord was bound by this contract.

42-9 Discrimination

Federal law prohibits landlords from discriminating against tenants or proposed tenants because of race, color, religion, sex, familial status, or national origin. The term **familial status** refers to whether the tenant has children. Additionally, some states and even municipalities prohibit discrimination based on such aspects as physical or mental handicaps, age, or marital status.

> **familial status**
> whether or not tenant has children

QUESTIONS

1. What formalities are required to create a lease?
2. What is the difference between a tenant and a lodger or roomer?
3. What guidance is available to courts attempting to resolve a dispute between a landlord and a tenant?
4. Does a lease without a definite, set time period last forever?
5. What are a landlord's options when a tenant holds over?
6. What is the difference between an assignment of lease and a sublease?
7. Explain the primary duty of a tenant.
8. From what kinds of defects must a landlord protect a tenant?
9. How may a lease be terminated?
10. What must a tenant remove from the property at the end of a lease?

CASE PROBLEMS

LO ④ 1. James Hayes leased the family farm from his mother, Elma Hayes, for five dollars an acre for twenty-five (25) years, which was well below market price. Elma wanted the land to continue as a family farm, so the lease expressly prohibited assignment, subletting, or transfer of the lease. The lease immediately terminated if James stopped farming the land. When Elma passed away, her will distributed separate tracts of the farm to each of her four children. James then sold his land to a third party. When his siblings learned of the sale, they declared that the lease had been terminated, and rented to another party at market rates. Did James's sale terminate the entire lease?

LO ① 2. Katharine Gasparich moved her family from California to New York to be closer to the children's grandfather. The grandfather offered the family an apartment free of rent in a building owned by 247 East 32nd LLC, which was principally owned by the grandfather. Apparently, the grandfather failed to communicate this offer to the company, because 247 East 32nd brought an eviction action against Gasparich and her family. Could Gasparich enforce the oral agreement with the grandfather?

LO ③ 3. Brennan Associates owned a shopping center, and leased a unit to Physicians for Women's Health, LLC. The terms of the lease permitted an assignment to a new lessee, with the lessor's permission. After an initial five-year lease term, the parties renewed for another five years. After only two more years, Physicians vacated and moved to another location, and attempted to find a replacement tenant. Brennan wanted Physicians to find another medical services tenant. For the first two years, Physicians continued to pay the rent. Finally Physicians found a tanning salon as a prospective tenant. Brennan entered into negotiations with the tanning salon, which offered slightly different terms from the lease with Physicians, but was never able to come to an agreement. Physicians stopped paying rent, and Brennan sued. Was Brennan required to come to terms with the tanning salon in order to mitigate its damages?

LO ① 4. Coinmach Corp. (Coinmach) entered into a lease with the Brittany Sobery Family Ltd. Partnership (Sobery) to operate a coin-operated laundry facility in an apartment complex owned by Sobery. The lease was for a term of ten years, with right of first refusal in Coinmach to match any future lease offers from third parties. After ten years passed, Coinmach continued in possession and continued to pay the same amount of rent on a monthly basis for several years. Ultimately, Sobery executed a new lease with a third party for provision of laundry services, and demanded Coinmach vacate the premises. Coinmach responded that it was exercising its right of first refusal on the lease. Did Sobery have the right to rent to a new tenant?

LO ② 5. Restorations Inc. and Cantarella Realty entered into a five-year lease for commercial property owned by Cantarella. The lease included a flat monthly rental for the first three years, with increases in the fourth and fifth years. It also granted Restorations an option to extend the lease up to five years on written notice two months prior to the expiration of the original term. Restorations occupied the property six and one-half years, paying the original rental price each month without the scheduled increases or formally extending the lease. At the beginning of the sixth year, Cantarella made a demand for the rent differential for lease years four and five and for market rental value during Restorations' holdover period. Restorations admitted that it had become a tenant at sufferance on the expiration of the original lease, but claimed that the payment and Cantarella's acceptance of continued rent payments created a tenancy at will for the original monthly rental price. Cantarella claimed that neither party was aware of the rent increases, and that both sides had mistakenly believed that they were proceeding in accordance with the lease terms. Does this mistake prevent Cantarella from collecting the increased rent?

LO ③ 6. King hired a laboratory to inspect and report on the mold levels in her apartment. Six different types of mold and bacteria were found, at "typical levels." None was toxic. The landlord had the tub recalked and installed an air filter. A second testing again showed "typical" levels of mold. King withheld rent, arguing that the mold condition constituted a breach of the implied warranty of habitability. Did the presence of mold entitle King to live there rent-free?

Wills, Inheritances, and Trusts

CHAPTER 43

LEARNING OBJECTIVES

① Describe a will, its characteristics, and the limitations on disposition of property.

② Explain the normal formalities required for executing the various types of wills.

③ Name the ways in which a will may be changed or revoked.

④ Discuss the requirements for probate and administration.

⑤ Recognize a trust and the parties to a trust.

PREVIEW CASE

Spouses Earl and Harriet Clemetson each had children from prior relationships, but no children together. When Earl died in January, he left a life estate in most of his property to Harriet, with the remainder passing to his daughter. In addition, some property passed directly to his daughter. Upon Harriet's death in October, her grandson, Kenneth Evanson, was unable to find a will and asked the court to be appointed personal representative. After the court agreed, Earl's grandson, Kevin Sprague, produced an undated, unsigned document, purporting to be a copy of Harriet's will, leaving her property in equal shares to all her grandchildren and step-grandchildren. How should the court treat this photocopy of a will?

Title to all property, both real and personal, may be transferred by a will. A **will** is an instrument prepared in the form prescribed by law that provides for the disposition of a person's property and takes effect after death. The property left by a person who has died is called the **estate**.

The person making the will is called a **testator** (**testatrix** if a woman). Testators do not have to meet as high a standard of capacity to make a will as a person does in order to make a contract. They must have the mental capability at the time of making the will to know the natural objects of their bounty, understand the nature and extent of their property, understand that they are making a will, and have the ability to dispose of their property by means of a plan they have formulated. Even if they do not have the mental capacity to carry on a business, or if they make unusual provisions in the will, this does not necessarily mean that they

LO ①
Will characteristics

will
document providing disposition of property after death

estate
property left by a deceased

testator or testatrix
person making a will

do not have the capacity to make a will. An insane person lacks sufficient capacity; however, an insane person who has intervals of sanity has capacity during sane intervals to make a will. Any person, other than a minor, of sound mind ordinarily has the competence to make a will. In a few states, under limited circumstances, minors can make a will.

COURT CASE

FACTS: In December, Leonard Brener died aged 85, without a wife or children. He had a close relationship with a niece, Lois Rosen, and her husband, acting as their financial advisor, spending holidays at their home and vacationing with them in the summer. During his last year, the Rosens were very involved in assisting Brener with doctor's visits, assisting with transportation, and advocating for his medical care. In March, Brener executed documents leaving the bulk of his $8 million estate to four charities. About five weeks before his death, Brener told his executor that he had given one of the charities "enough." He had just given it $338,000. He said he wanted to give the residue of his estate to the Rosens "for the love and affection that they had shown him and in appreciation of all of the attention and assistance that they had given him during his illness." After his lawyer read through the amendments, and Brener

made minor changes, he amended his estate-planning documents naming the Rosens as sole recipients of the entire residue of his estate. He made several, smaller, immediate cash and stock gifts to the charities. The charities sued, alleging Brener's lack of mental capacity and undue influence of the Rosens.

OUTCOME: The court found the standard for testamentary capacity to be understanding the nature and situation of the property and the relation to people who would have some claim to remembrance. The deliberation and judgment that Brener had used to rework his estate plan in October proved his capacity, so the amendment was upheld.

—*Maimonides School v. Coles*, 881 N.E.2d 778
(Mass. App. Ct.)

43-1 Limitations on Disposition of Property

The law places few restrictions on the right to dispose of property by will. However, some restrictions include:

1. A spouse may elect to take that share of property that would have been received had the deceased died without leaving a will, or the share provided by statute, if the spouse's will does not leave as large a share, called the **right to take against the will**.

right to take against the will
spouse's right to share of estate provided by statute if will leaves smaller share

Most state laws now provide that when an individual dies without leaving a will, a spouse has the right to a set portion of all the property the deceased spouse owned at the time of death. The spouse's portion varies depending on the number of children or other heirs who survive. The surviving spouse in some states also may claim an interest in property conveyed by the deceased spouse during the marriage without the consent of the surviving spouse.

The right to take against the will can be barred by actions of the surviving spouse. If the surviving spouse commits acts that would have justified the deceased in securing a divorce, the surviving spouse generally cannot elect to take against the will.

Except for the cases of a surviving spouse electing to take against the will, and in some cases of a subsequent marriage, birth, or adoption, the testator may exclude or disinherit any person from receiving any portion of the estate. If the testator gives the entire estate to someone else, all people who would inherit in the absence of a will are excluded. The testator does not even have to mention in a will those people disinherited except for disinherited children, who must be mentioned to prove the testator did not forget them. A nominal sum does not have to be left to those disinherited.

2. In some states, one cannot control by will the distribution of property in perpetuity (for all time). The common law rule against perpetuities requires that an interest in property must vest within twenty-one years after the death of people living on the date the owner of the property creates the interest. When the interest is created by will, the date of death of the owner constitutes the date of creation. A number of states have abolished this common law rule.

43-2 Terms Common to Wills

A number of terms may refer to individuals named or gifts given in a will. The one receiving a gift of real estate (the beneficiary) is called the **devisee**; the beneficiary of personal property is a **legatee**. A **devise** is real property given by will. A **bequest**, or a **legacy**, is a gift by will of personal property. The person named in a will as the one to administer the estate is an **executor** or **personal representative**. One who dies without having made a will is said to die **intestate**. A person appointed by a court to settle the affairs of an intestate is an **administrator** (man) or an **administratrix** (woman) or the **personal representative**.

devisee
one receiving realty by will

legatee
one receiving personal property by will

devise
realty left by will

bequest or legacy
personal property left by will

executor or personal representative
person named in will to administer estate

intestate
one who dies without a will

administrator, administratrix, or personal representative
person appointed by court to administer estate of intestate

43-3 Distinguishing Characteristics of a Will

A will has the following outstanding characteristics that distinguish it from many other legal instruments:

1. The courts construe a will with less technical strictness than a deed or any other kind of written document.
2. A will devising real property must be executed in conformity with the law of the state in which the property is situated. The law of the state in which the testator was domiciled (had permanent residence) at the time of death governs a will bequeathing personal property.
3. A will may be revoked at any time during the life of the testator.

43-4 Formalities

LO ②
Will formalities

All states prescribe formalities for wills. These formalities must be strictly followed. A will almost always must be in writing and signed by the testator.

A will written in the testator's own handwriting and dated need not be witnessed in a number of states. In almost all states, the will must be witnessed by at least two, and in some states three, disinterested witnesses regardless of how it is written. Usually, the witnesses and the testator must sign in the presence of each other. Many states also require the testator to inform the witnesses that the instrument being signed is the testator's will. This is called **publication**.

publication
testator's informing witnesses that document is will

When the law requires subscribing witnesses, they must be available at the time of probate of the will to identify their signatures and the signature of the testator and to state that they were present when the testator signed the will. If the witnesses cannot be found, two people must normally identify the signature of the testator on the will. They base their opinion regarding the testator's signature on their experience through prior correspondence or business records involving the testator's signature. A will executed in another jurisdiction is valid if correctly executed in the other jurisdiction. If a person's will is not drawn according to the legal requirements, the court may disregard it and the testator's estate may be disposed of in a manner entirely foreign to the testator's wishes.

PREVIEW CASE REVISITED

FACTS: Spouses Earl and Harriet Clemetson each had children from prior relationships but no children together. When Earl died in January, he left a life estate in most of his property to Harriet, with the remainder passing to his daughter. In addition, some property passed directly to his daughter. Upon Harriet's death in October, her grandson, Kenneth Evanson, was unable to find a will and asked the court to be appointed personal representative. After the court agreed, Earl's grandson, Kevin Sprague, produced an undated, unsigned document, purporting to be a copy of Harriet's will, leaving her property in equal shares to all her grandchildren and step-grandchildren. Sprague alleged it was a valid will.

OUTCOME: The court pointed out that it is the duty of one proposing a will to show its validity. This is normally done by showing that proper formalities have been followed. That could not be done in this case; therefore, the photocopy was not admitted to probate.

—In re Estate of Clemetson, 81 N.W.2d 388 (N.D.)

43-5 Special Types of Wills

Under special circumstances, testators can make valid wills that are less formal than usual. Three special types of wills include:

1. Holographic wills
2. Nuncupative wills
3. Soldiers' and sailors' wills

43-5a HOLOGRAPHIC WILLS

holographic will
will written out by testator

Holographic wills are written entirely in longhand by the testator. Some states make no distinction between holographic and other wills. In other states, variations of the general law of wills exist for holographic wills. In still other states, holographic wills may not be recognized.

COURT CASE

FACTS: After Mark Lambert died in Montana, his mother, Charlotte Lambert, found a will in his papers completely handwritten and signed by Mark. He had titled the document "Last Will and Testament," and in it he had declared the "instrument as and for my Last Will and Testament hereby expressly revoking any and all wills and codicils . . . heretofore made by me." In eleven pages, Mark detailed the distribution of his estate. The will named Charlotte executrix, and she offered it for probate in Montana. To be valid in Montana, a holographic will's material provisions had to be written and signed by the testator and the testator must have had testamentary intent— he must have intended that the document would dispose of his property after death. Joshua Lambert, Mark's son, alleged that the handwritten will was invalid in Montana.

OUTCOME: The court found that the document was a valid holographic will.

—*In re Estate of Lambert*, 333 Mont. 444 (Mont.)

43-5b NUNCUPATIVE WILLS

Nuncupative wills are oral wills declared by the testator in the presence of witnesses. Usually, such a will can only be made during the testator's last illness. A nuncupative will only applies to personal property, and sometimes only a limited value of personal property may be so disposed. The witnesses frequently must reduce the will to writing within a specified number of days, and they must agree as to how the deceased disposed of the property.

nuncupative will
oral will made during last illness

43-5c SOLDIERS' AND SAILORS' WILLS

Most states make special provision for members of the armed forces. They are allowed to make oral or written wills of personal property without complying with the formalities required of other wills. These wills are in force even after the testator returns to civilian life. They must be revoked in the same manner as other wills.

43-6 The Wording of a Will

Any words that convey the intention of the testator suffice (see Illustration 43-1). No matter how rough and ungrammatical the language may be, if the intention of the testator can be ascertained, the court will order that the provisions of the will be carried out. Because the court will order the terms of a will to be carried out exactly, the wording of the will should express the exact wishes of the testator.

43-7 Codicils

A **codicil** is a separate writing that modifies a will. Except for the part modified, the original will remains the same. A codicil must be executed with all the formalities of the original will.

codicil
writing that modifies a will

ILLUSTRATION 43-1 Will

WILL OF FRANK JOSEPH ROSE

I, Frank Joseph Rose, of the City of Chicago and State of Illinois, revoke all prior wills and codicils and declare that this is my will.

FIRST: If she survives me, I give to my beloved daughter, Anna Rose, now residing in Crestwood, Illinois, that certain piece of real estate, with all improvements thereon, situated at 341 Hudson Avenue, Crestwood, Illinois. If my daughter predeceases me, I give this real estate to my brother, James Earl Rose, now residing in Crestwood, Illinois.

SECOND: All the remainder and residue of my property I give to my beloved wife, Mary Ellen Rose, if, she survives me. If my wife predeceases me, I give the remainder and residue of my property to my daughter, Anna. If both my wife and my daughter predecease me, I give the remainder and residue of my property to my brother, James.

THIRD: I hereby nominate and appoint my wife, Mary Ellen Rose, executrix of this will. If my wife is unable or unwilling to act as executrix, I nominate and appoint my daughter, Anna, executrix. I direct that neither Mary Ellen nor Anna be required to give bond or security for the performance of duties as executrix.

IN WITNESS WHEREOF, I have subscribed my name this tenth day of October, in the year two thousand-.

Frank Joseph Rose
Frank Joseph Rose

We, the undersigned, certify that the foregoing instrument was, on the tenth day of October, signed and declared by Frank Joseph Rose to be his will, in the presence of us who, in his presence and in the presence of each other, have, at his request, hereunto signed our names as witnesses of the execution thereof, this tenth day of October, 20-.

Constance O. Moore	4316 Cottage Grove Avenue residing at Chicago, Illinois 60600
Sarah J. King	1313 East 63 Street residing at Chicago, Illinois 60600
Stewart S. Samuels	2611 Elm Street residing at Chicago, Illinois 60400

LO ③
Will revocation and change

43-8 Revocation

A will may be revoked at any time prior to the death of the testator. The revocation may take any of several forms.

43-8a DESTRUCTION OR ALTERATION

If the testator deliberately destroys a will, this constitutes a revocation. If the testator merely alters the will, this may or may not revoke it, depending on the nature and the extent of the alteration. If the testator merely obliterates a part of the will, in most states this does not revoke the will.

43-8b MARRIAGE AND DIVORCE

If a single person makes a will and later marries, the marriage may revoke the will in whole or in part, or the court may presume it is revoked unless made in contemplation of the marriage or unless it made provision for a future spouse. In some states, a marriage will not revoke a will completely, but only so that the spouse will get the estate that would have been received in the absence of a will. A divorce automatically revokes a will to the extent of the property left to the divorced spouse if the court orders a division of property; otherwise, a divorce usually in no way affects the will.

COURT CASE

FACTS: Terry Nelson and Anita Moi met and lived together but did not marry until five years later. Moi drafted a will about a year after she met Nelson, giving him $100,000, but leaving the bulk of her $7 million estate to her six stepchildren from a previous marriage. Again, before marrying Nelson, Moi met with her attorney to draft a codicil to her will (which would not have changed the gift to Nelson) and a prenuptial agreement. However, neither the codicil nor the agreement was signed when she married Nelson two years later. Less than a month after the wedding, Moi died unexpectedly, and Nelson sued her estate, claiming to be an omitted spouse.

OUTCOME: The will specifically mentioned Nelson by name, and the bequest to him was not nominal. Therefore, Nelson was provided for in the will.

—*In re Estate of Moi*, 135 (Wash. App. 1029)

43-8c EXECUTION OF A LATER WILL

The execution of a later will automatically revokes a prior will if the terms of the second conflict with the first will. If the second will merely changes a few provisions in the first will and leaves the bulk of it intact, then a second revokes the first will only to the extent of such inconsistency.

43-8d AFTER-BORN CHILD

A child may be born or adopted after a person makes a will. If the original will does not provide for subsequent children or the testator makes no codicil to provide for the child, this revokes or partially revokes the will.

43-9 Abatement and Ademption

An **abatement** occurs when a testator makes bequests of money in the will and the estate does not have enough money to pay the bequests. The legatees will receive a proportionate share of the bequests.

An **ademption** occurs when a testator makes a bequest of specific property and the estate does not have the property at death. In that case, the legatee gets nothing.

abatement
proportionate reduction in monetary bequest because of insufficient funds

ademption
failure of bequest because property not in estate

If a testator leaves $20,000 to his son John, $10,000 to his sister Mary, and a painting to his brother Adam, there could be both an abatement and an ademption. If the estate has only $15,000 in cash left after paying all debts, the cash gifts to John and Mary will abate. Each will receive a proportionate share, in this case 50 percent, or $10,000 and $5,000, respectively. If the testator had sold the painting, given it away, or if someone had stolen, destroyed, or lost the painting before the death of the testator, Adam would get nothing. The bequest to him would be adeemed because the property would not be in the estate at the testator's death. He would have no right to its cash value or any other substitute item of property.

COURT CASE

FACTS: Charles Stanford never married nor had children. His will directed that "all stock in Redfields Inc. left to [him] by [his] father" devise to the children of his two sisters, excluding the children of his two brothers. About five years after executing his will, Stanford, his brothers, and his sisters, who were the only shareholders of Redfields Inc., dissolved the company and distributed the assets equally among themselves. Later that month, the five siblings formed the partnership "Redfields" to carry on the business formerly conducted by Redfields Inc. Each sibling contributed the assets distributed to him from Redfields Inc. to the partnership Redfields. Upon Charles's death, the partnership

Redfields property was distributed to the sisters' children. The brothers' children complained. Had the "stock in Redfields Inc. left" by his father been adeemed?

OUTCOME: No. A specific legacy could be adeemed if it were lost, destroyed, disposed of, or so changed in substance or form that it no longer remained when the will took effect. Here, the specific legacy had been changed from stock to a partnership. The court found this to be in identical form and, therefore, not adeemed.

—*Stanford v. Paris*, 703 S.E.2d 488 (N.C. Ct. App.)

LO ④
Requirements for administration

probate
court procedure to determine validity of a will

43-10 Probate of a Will

When a testator dies leaving a will, the will must be probated. **Probate** is the court procedure that determines the validity of a will. The will normally names an executor to preserve and handle the estate during probate and distribute it to the rightful individuals. An executor has liability to legatees, creditors, and heirs for loss to the estate as a result of negligence, bad faith, or breach of trust and must comply with any instructions in the will. A will may expressly direct the executor to continue a business owned by the deceased. If the will does not so provide, an executor frequently can obtain permission of the appropriate court to continue the business. With but few exceptions, anyone may be appointed executor. The testator may excuse the executor from furnishing a bond that would be an expense to the estate. If the will does not name an executor, then on petition of one of the beneficiaries, the court will appoint an administrator.

If a person contests the will, the court must hear the contest to determine the validity of the will. A contest of the will differs from litigation over the meaning or interpretation to be given the will. If the contest alleges and proves fraud, undue influence, improper witnessing, mental incapacity of the testator, revocation of the will, or any other infirmity in the will affecting its legality, the court will find the will nullified. It will then distribute the property of the testator according to the law of descent described later in this chapter.

43-11 When Administration Is Unnecessary

Of course, if an individual does not own any property at the time of death, no need for administration exists. Also, all property jointly owned with someone else who acquires the interest by right of survivorship does not require administration.

Some states have special statutes allowing the administration procedures to be shortened for very small estates. In many states, all of the people interested in the estate, relatives and creditors, can agree on the share each one is to receive and can divide the estate without formal court proceedings.

43-12 Title by Descent

When a person dies intestate, the property is distributed in accordance with the state law of descent. Every state has such a law. Although these laws vary slightly, on the whole they provide as follows: The property of the intestate goes to any children, subject to the rights of the surviving spouse. If no spouse, children, or grandchildren survive, the father and mother, as the next of kin, receive the property. If no parents survive, the brothers and sisters become the next of kin, followed by grandparents, aunts and uncles, and so on. Some statutes permit any person related by blood to inherit when no nearer relative exists. Other statutes do not permit those beyond first cousins to inherit. In any case, if no proper person to inherit survives, the property passes to the state.

The administrator conveys title to real estate by means of an administrator's deed. When approved by the court, the grantee obtains good title to the property.

43-13 *Per Capita* and *Per Stirpes* Distribution

The lineal descendants of a decedent include the children and grandchildren. If all of the children were living at the time of an intestate's death, and the spouse was dead, the property would be distributed ***per capita***, meaning per head, or equally to the children (see Illustration 43-2). If one child predeceased the intestate and left two surviving grandchildren, then the property would be divided into equal

per capita
per head

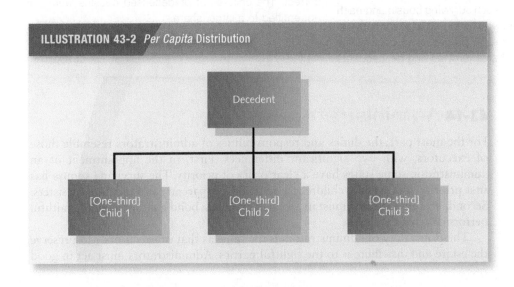

ILLUSTRATION 43-2 *Per Capita* Distribution

Decedent

[One-third]
Child 1

[One-third]
Child 2

[One-third]
Child 3

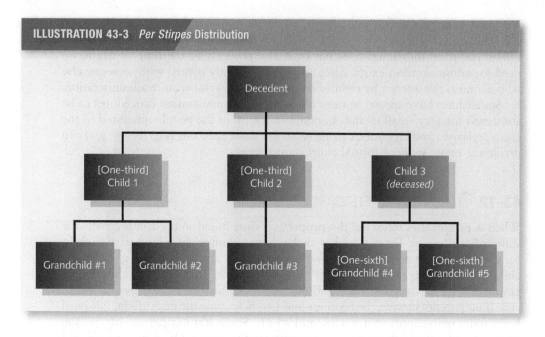

ILLUSTRATION 43-3 *Per Stirpes* Distribution

---

per stirpes
distribution among heirs
according to relationship to
deceased

parts on the basis of the number of children the intestate had. The dead child's part would then be divided into two equal parts with one of these parts going to each of the grandchildren. This divides the property (see ***per stirpes*** Illustration 43-3).

If the deceased child left no children or other lineal descendants, then the surviving children of the intestate would take the deceased child's share.

COURT CASE

FACTS: Marjorie Cann, a retired schoolteacher who never married or had children, died without a will. Her parents, aunts, uncles, and several first cousins predeceased her. Her estate was divided into equal shares for each surviving cousin and each predeceased cousin who had living descendants (*per capita*). The share of each predeceased cousin was divided into equal shares for the living descendants

(*per stirpes*). Some of the children of predeceased cousins sued for a larger share of the estate.

OUTCOME: The original division of the estate was correct. The children of predeceased cousins were not entitled to a larger share.

—*Stokan v. Estate of Cann*, 266 S.W.3d 210
(Ark. Ct. App.)

43-14 Administrators

For the most part, the duties and responsibilities of administrators resemble those of executors, with two significant differences. First, in the appointment of an administrator, some states have a clear order of priority. The surviving spouse has first priority, followed by children, grandchildren, parents, and brothers or sisters. Second, an administrator must in all cases execute a bond guaranteeing the faithful performance of the duties.

The prime duty of administrators is the same as that of executors—to preserve the estate and distribute it to the rightful parties. Administrators must act in good faith, with prudence, and within the powers conferred on them by law. If any part of the estate is a going business, with only a few exceptions the business must be liquidated. However, the administrator may obtain leave of court to continue the business for either a limited time or an indefinite time, depending largely on the wishes of those entitled to receive the estate. Third parties dealing with administrators, as well as executors, must know of limitations on their authority.

43-15 Trusts

A **trust** is a form of contract by which one person or entity agrees to hold property for the benefit of another. Chapter 39, "Nature of Real Property," examined one way in which ownership of property may be divided between two owners. That chapter discussed the difference between a life estate, or income interest, and a remainder interest in property. This division in ownership separates the total ownership, or the fee simple estate, over time. The life tenant is the first owner, and the holder of the reversion or remainder is the second after the death of the life tenant.

LO ⑤
Trust and its parties

trust
contract by which one holds property for another

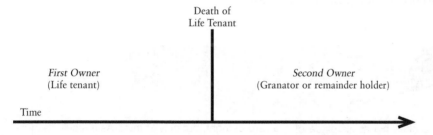

Ownership of property in trust can be described as a division at the same time of two ownership interests—the legal ownership and the beneficial ownership. The legal owner of trust property is the person or entity who holds title to the property and who has the authority to control, or administer, the way in which the property is used. The legal owner of trust property is usually referred to as the **trustee**. If no trustee is specified, a court will appoint one because there must be a person with title to the property.

The beneficial owner of trust property is entitled to the income, enjoyment, or benefits of the trust property. The beneficial owner is usually referred to as the trust **beneficiary**. The benefits of the property usually include income generated by property and the right to inhabit or use the property. In older documents, you might encounter the Latin words *cestui que trust*, meaning *beneficiary*. Both the trustee and the beneficiary have ownership interests in the property at the same time.

trustee
legal owner of trust property for another

beneficiary
person entitled to income or enjoyment of trust property

Owner 1 (Trustee—holds legal title)

Time ⟶

Owner 2 (Beneficiary—enjoys use of property)

43-15a CREATION OF A TRUST

Because a trust is a specific form of contract, the law of contracts generally applies to trusts. Since a contract may be oral or written, a trust may also be oral or written, subject to the Statute of Frauds. Of course, the more valuable the property subject to the trust contract, the more important it is that the trust be written. It is easier both to remember and to enforce the terms of a written trust than those of an oral trust.

grantor, settlor, or trustor
creator of trust

The person who creates a trust is known as the **grantor**. Other words used to describe the grantor include **settlor** and **trustor**. A grantor must have the legal capacity to enter into a contract in order to create a trust. Normally, the grantor gives the trust property to the trustee and instructs the trustee regarding how the property is to be used to benefit the beneficiary.

It is not necessary that the grantor, trustee, and beneficiary all be different people or entities. However, they cannot all be the same person. That is, property may be given to the grantor, as trustee, to hold for another beneficiary. Or a grantor may give property to another, as trustee, to hold for the benefit of the grantor. The legal and beneficial ownership must be separate; therefore, the trustee and beneficiary must be separate and distinct entities. Otherwise, the grantor has simply given the property to the trustee/beneficiary in fee simple.

Because a trust is based on the law of contracts, the grantor has almost limitless ability to place restrictions on, or grant options to, the trustee and beneficiary as to the use of the trust property. Nonetheless, the trustee must have some identifiable purpose for administering the trust.

COURT CASE

FACTS: After sustaining a broken hip at his place of employment, Jesus Arellano received two workers' compensation awards. One, for just over $72,000, was paid as a Medicare "set aside," to be used for future treatment for Arellano's injuries. Some years later, Arellano filed for bankruptcy. The bankruptcy trustee wanted to include what remained of the $72,000 award as debtor's assets subject to distribution by the trustee. Arellano claimed that he did not own the Medicare

award outright, but only in trust. As a result, the funds would not constitute part of the bankruptcy estate.

OUTCOME: The court found that the elements for creating a valid trust had been satisfied: property (the $72,000) was given to Arellano to be held for the benefit of his medical providers.

—*In re Arellano*, 524 B.R. 615 (M.D. Pa.)

43-15b SPECIFIC TYPES OF TRUSTS

Several types of trusts are frequently used. These include:

1. Express trust
2. Resulting trust
3. Constructive trust
4. Blind trust
5. Testamentary trust

express trust
trust clearly established as a trust

Express Trust. A trust that is created by a grantor clearly establishing a trust, whether oral or written, is sometimes referred to as an **express trust**. This designation helps distinguish express trusts from other types of trusts, some of which may be implied. However, no specific words are required to create an express trust. It only must be clear that the grantor intended to create a trust.

Resulting Trust. A **resulting trust** occurs when one person supplies the purchase price for property but has title issued in another person's name. This is sometimes called a **purchase money trust**. The theory of this type of trust is that unless the purchaser intended to make a gift, the one who pays for property should be the one to enjoy it and receive the benefits from it.

resulting or purchase money trust
resulting trust created when person buys property but takes title in another's name

Constructive Trust. A **constructive trust** arises by operation of law when one acquires title to property to which he or she cannot in good conscience retain the beneficial interest. A constructive trust is most often declared by a court in cases of fraud but also arises in cases of bad faith, duress, coercion, undue influence, mistake, wrongdoing, or any other form of unconscionable conduct. Under these circumstances, a court will declare a constructive trust to prevent a wrongdoer from continuing to take advantage of the other party.

constructive trust
trust created by court to correct a wrong

COURT CASE

FACTS: Betty Lou Bradshaw inherited from her parents a fractional share of a royalty interest in the mineral and gas production of most of a nearly 2,000 acre parcel of land. The terms entitled her to receive a portion of any lease income, but no portion of any bonuses. Another interest holder, Gary Humphreys, had the right to negotiate the lease terms with a developer. Two potential developers approached Humphreys with plans to extract the minerals. One plan involved a straight lease payment. Another included a lower base lease payment but provided for bonus payments if certain benchmarks were met. Humphreys leased the property under the lower lease but potential bonus structure. Bradshaw sued under a constructive trust theory, claiming that Humphreys couldn't negotiate a structure that excluded her from payments when another contract was available.

OUTCOME: There are three criteria for a constructive trust: (1) breach of a special fiduciary relationship; (2) unjust enrichment of the wrongdoer; and (3) identifiable trust property. In this case, Humphreys had no special duty to Bradshaw, so no constructive trust was found.

—*KCM Financial LLC v. Bradshaw*, 2015 WL 1029652 (Tex.)

Blind Trust. A **blind trust** is most commonly used when the grantor, for some reason, does not want to know exactly what is in the trust, but wants to retain the benefit of the property. For example, a government official with authority to regulate a certain industry may give management of property to a trustee so that there will be no conflict between the official's personal financial interests and official government duties. Wealthy members of Congress frequently use blind trusts so they will not know exactly what securities they own. Then, when they vote on legislation, they cannot know whether their vote helps the companies in which they have a personal financial interest.

blind trust
assets and administration of trust hidden from grantor

Testamentary Trust. A **testamentary trust** is a special form of express trust created by the will of a testator. Even though the trust will not actually be created until the death of the testator, it will become a valid trust at that time. The trustee may, but need not, be the same person or entity as the executor of the will. A trust created by a will is subject to the same rules as other trusts.

testamentary trust
trust created in will

Consider, as an example, the will of Heinrich Heine, the famous nineteenth-century German poet. His will included the following provision for his wife: "I leave all my estate to my wife on the express condition that she remarry. I want at least one person to sincerely grieve my death." Does this language have the effect of placing the entire estate into a trust? Heine died in France, but if his will had been probated in the present-day United States, it is highly unlikely a court would enforce this provision because of the requirement that Heine's widow remarry. Instead, the property would most likely be distributed directly to Heine's widow, outright and free from trust.

QUESTIONS

1. What capacity must people have in order to make valid wills?

2. What are two common restrictions on the right to dispose of property by will?

3. What characteristics distinguish a will from other legal instruments?

4. What is the difference between ademption and abatement?

5. What is probate?

6. What if no beneficiary survives to inherit an estate?

7. a. What is the difference between distributing property *per capita* and *per stirpes*?

   b. When would a *per stirpes* distribution be required?

8. What are two ways in which the duties of an administrator differ from those of an executor?

9. Must the grantor, trustee, and beneficiary of a trust all be different people?

10. What formalities must be followed to create a testamentary trust?

CASE PROBLEMS

LO ②   1. Louisiana law required that a will be signed on each page as well as at the end of the will. Arthur Simonson signed each page except page 6. Simonson's will followed all other formalities and there was no evidence of fraud. When the two beneficiaries filed the will for probate, the district court found the will invalid since it was not signed on page 6. Should the entire will be invalid? Should page 6 be left out, but the rest of the will be probated?

LO ①   2. Duskin died a few weeks after executing a will, in which he left his two daughters each 10 percent of the Mahalia Jackson Family Corporation (MJFC). A few years later, Lott presented the court with a document entitled, "Irrevocable Last Will and Testament," and dated ten years prior to the probated will. The "Irrevocable Will" was signed by both Duskin and Edison Lazard, as president and vice president of the MJFC, and purporting to bequeath all rights to MJFC. Was the second will valid? Was the first will irrevocable? Was it even a will?

LO ⑤   3. Eric Faulkner, Duncan Faure, Alan Longmuir, Derek Longmuir, Leslie McKeown, and Stuart Wood were members of the 1970s rock band the Bay City Rollers (Rollers). Worldwide record sales have been estimated at between $70 million and $100 million. Despite having various contractual agreements to receive royalties from their record label, Arista Records LLC, the Rollers filed suit seeking, among other things, the imposition of a constructive trust for their failure to receive royalties for over twenty-five years. Arista did not deny its failure to pay, but defended, among other assertions, that the statute of limitations barred breach of contract claims and that no constructive trust could exist because no fiduciary relationship existed. Can a fiduciary relationship sufficient to impose a

CASE PROBLEMS (CONTINUED)

constructive trust exist between two for-profit entities? Can one party to a contract, who has failed to take action under the contract within the time prescribed by the statute of limitations, seek the equitable remedy of a constructive trust?

4. Jack and his parents purchased a piece of land, with Jack tendering the down payment, and his parents taking out a mortgage for the remaining purchase price. The deed showed only Jack's parents' names, but Jack testified that they verbally agreed to split the property in half. In fact, Jack built a house, resided on, and maintained "his" half of the land for over forty years. An issue arose after first Jack's father, then mother, died. The mother left a will devising the property to Jack's brother, Charles. Charles's wife then asked Jack to sign a lease in order to remain on the property. Jack sued, alleging a constructive trust had been established at the time of the purchase. Had it? **LO ⑤**

5. John and his wife, Christine, had four biological children, and then decided to adopt "Emily" from China. John made provisions for his children in his will, which included any children who had been legally adopted by the date of his death. Emily's adoption was finalized and a fifth biological child was born to John and Christine after the date of John's last will. One year later, John died from cancer. Emily was found to have special medical and educational needs, and after several years, Christine asked her attorneys about finding someone to "re-adopt" Emily. Fortunately for Emily, new adoptive parents were found. Some years later, Emily's second adoptive parents discovered that John's estate was worth in excess of $250,000,000. Was Emily entitled to a share of her first adoptive father's estate? **LO ④**

6. William Melton executed a formal will consisting of two forms which Melton and three witnesses signed. Some years later, he handwrote a letter to a close friend, which read: **LO ③**

   "I am on the way home from Mom's funeral. Mom died from an auto accident so I thought I had better leave something in writing so that you Alberta Kelleher will receive my entire estate. I do not want my brother Larry J. Melton or Vicki Palm or any of my other relatives to have *one penny* of my estate." [his italics]

   The letter was dated and signed by Melton, but Kelleher predeceased Melton. Assume the jurisdiction recognized holographic wills. Is this letter a valid will, or codicil? What would you argue on behalf of William's only child, Vicki Palm?

7. Shirley Webb was survived by her three sons, Roger, Mark, and Danny. For many years, Danny had been working in the family business, Webb's Water Truck Service, and assisting his mother in her home. Shirley left the business and all its assets to Danny because he "continued to work for and directly assist . . . in the equity and value." The remainder of her estate, her personal assets, were to be split among Roger, Mark, and Danny. Danny was appointed personal representative. After nine months, Roger and Mark filed an application for Danny's removal. No inventory had been filed, Danny had removed some items from Shirley's home, claiming they were part of the business, and Danny was preparing to sell Shirley's home to his son. Was there sufficient cause to remove Danny? **LO ④**

8. Anderson lived to the age of 98 in her own home with the assistance and support of her grandsons who lived with her. At her death, the grandsons offered a will for probate, naming them personal representatives and sole beneficiaries of the estate. Anderson's daughter disputed the will on the grounds of undue influence. The grandsons had not only assisted Anderson in daily living, such as buying groceries and paying bills, but also had held Anderson's power of attorney, made appointments for her with her attorney, and taken her to the attorney's office. Testimony from a state worker who made surprise visits to the home declared Anderson to be well cared for and "very alert to be a ninety-eight-year-old woman." Anderson's life-long friend, Mary, testified that Anderson told her she did not want her son-in-law "to get his hands on any of her property." In addition, the power of attorney was never used, and no substantive changes were made to Anderson's will. Should it be admitted to probate? **LO ①**

ETHICS IN PRACTICE

Having learned that real property is conveyed by deed and that property that is owned by two people as joint tenants with right of survivorship passes automatically to the survivor at the death of one owner, consider the following scenario:

After her husband dies, Rose Markovitz lives with her daughter, Sandy Olsen, and her family in Markovitz's house, and Olsen pays the real estate taxes for Markovitz. In order to permit Olsen to deduct the real estate taxes on her income tax return, Markovitz executes a quitclaim deed to the house to herself and Olsen as joint tenants with right of survivorship. Markovitz tells her five other children that she is quitclaiming the house to Olsen as joint tenant only to enable Olsen to deduct the taxes that she pays for Markovitz. After Markovitz dies, Olsen claims that the house belongs to her alone by right of survivorship. Discuss the ethical considerations involved in this situation.

PART 9 SUMMARY CASES

PROPERTY

1. Stehlik lived next door to her aunt, Czerwinski, in the other half of Czerwinski's duplex. Czerwinski put Stehlik on her bank account as a joint tenant. Stehlik never contributed any money to the account. Stehlik drove Czerwinski to appointments, the grocery store, and handled some banking transactions for Czerwinski until Czerwinski's death. Did Czerwinski intend to make a gift of the funds to Stehlik upon Czerwinski's death, or was this account for convenience only?

2. Irv Groat filed a five-line document as a codicil to the will of Frank Halgas. It read,

   January 21, 20--

   Upon my death I will transfer all of my stock to Irv Groat for the sum of $10,000.00.

   A copy of the check should be furnished to MicroLambda to initiate the transfer.

   Frank Halgas   _____(signed)_____

   Irv Groat   _____(signed)_____

       (another signature)

   Should the court admit the document to probate?

3. A vacant and neglected building sat on Beardstown Street, and the City sought to impose fines on its owner to encourage him to clean up his property. The last filed deed in the recorder's office showed Mitchell to be the owner. After being served with a citation, Mitchell claimed he had already conveyed the property to Swan by quitclaim deed. The City noted that the deed to Swan purported to convey property on Beardstown *Road* instead of Beardstown *Street*, the recited $500 consideration had not been paid by Swan, and the notary public's acknowledgment was dated one day prior to the signature dates. Was the deed effective to convey the property?

4. Prior to their marriage, Robert and Eve Schneberger executed a prenuptial agreement granting Eve a life estate in Robert's home should he predecease her. Eve could occupy the home but not rent it out. Robert died still married to Eve. Subsequently, the home was damaged by a hurricane, and a dispute arose over responsibility to pay for the damages between Eve and her stepson, who was both the remainder beneficiary and trustee of Robert's trust. Eve argued that she did not have a true life estate because she could not deal with the property as her own by, for instance, renting it for income to pay the costs, and thus she should not have the obligations of a normal life tenant. Who was responsible for the hurricane damage? [*Schneberger v. Schneberger*, 979 So.2d 981 (Fla. Dist. Ct. App.)]

5. Perrin Blank purchased a dental practice, including a lease of professional office space, equipment, and patient records. At the expiration of the lease term, Blank entered into his own five-year lease with the landlord. The lease was renewed three times. The offices were then sold to a new landlord, who notified the tenants that he planned to demolish the building. Blank found another property and sued the landlord for damages for

> lost profits; injury to business; loss of good will; lost earnings; lost earning capacity; lost lease value; relocation costs and expenses (including new office plan, design and build-out; cost of non-movable equipment and fixtures; moving expenses of movable equipment and computers; new cabinetry; new telephone and speaker systems; new advertising/promotion/signage/stationary; rent differentials); water, electric and other utility expenses; higher premiums for new insurance; borrowing/financing costs and expenses; tax liabilities; consultant and broker fees; and attorneys' fees.

State law allowed a wrongfully evicted tenant to recover the difference between the value of the leasehold and the rent payable, lost profits that could be reasonably determined, and damages "for losses that are the natural, direct and necessary consequences of the breach . . . such as should reasonably have been contemplated by the parties." Did the new landlord owe Blank anything? If so, was he responsible for all the different types of damages Blank claimed? [*WSG Palm Beach Development, LLC v. Blank*, 990 So.2d 708 (Fla. Dist. Ct. App.)]

6. Alma Rodowicz leased property to United Social and Mental Health Services Inc. for ten years. The written lease allowed United to renew it only by notifying Rodowicz within six months of the expiration of the lease or any extension of it. Three days before the expiration, Rodowicz's attorney wrote United that the parties had come to an agreement that United could continue as a tenant at a reduced rent. United never responded but referred to the new lease as a month-to-month tenancy and paid the reduced rent for five years. United then notified Rodowicz that it planned to renew the lease for five more years. Rodowicz demanded United vacate and pay an increased monthly rental until it vacated. United protested but paid the increased rent and sued for enforcement of the lease. Had United renewed or extended the lease? [*United Social and Mental Health Services Inc. v. Rodowicz*, 899 A.2d 85 (Conn. App. Ct.)]

7. Adolph Liebig owned several parcels of real property. As part of an estate plan, Adolph recorded a Deed of Trust purporting to create 100 "Certificates of Beneficial Interest" for ease of distribution. By its terms, the trust would terminate in 25 years, and the assets were to be distributed to the holders of the 100 shares. Adolph distributed 50 shares to his wife, Valeria, and 50 shares were divided among Valeria and their three sons. The following year, Adolph died. Over time, Valeria gave her 50 shares equally to the three sons. No shares were ever given to the couple's three daughters. At the end of 25 years, Valeria and her son, who then were trustees of the trust, filed an accounting, received court approval, and wound up the trust. The real estate was deeded to the three sons as tenants in common. A few years later, one of the daughters sued to set aside the trust and quiet title in the six siblings equally. The daughter claimed that the trust was defective and void, so that upon Adolph's death the property should have passed to his heirs at law when he died. Were the daughters entitled to inherit anything? [*Newman v. Liebig*, 810 N.W.2d 408 (Neb.)]

Table of Cases

51–53 West 129th Street HDFC v. Attorney General, 95 A.D.3d 674 (N.Y. App. Div.), *393*

A

Acorne Productions, LLC v. Tjeknavorian, 33 F.Supp.3d 175 (E.D.N.Y.), *15*

Agri-Sales Associates Inc. v. McConnell, 75 UCC Rep.Serv.2d 24 (Tenn.), *186*

Alerus Financial, N.A. v. Marcil Group Inc., 806 N.W.2d 160 (N.D.), *456*

Allegiance Hillview, L.P. v. Range Texas Production LLC, 347 S.W.3d 855 (Tex. Ct. App.), *138*

Alqasim v. Capitol City Hotel Investors, 989 So.2d 488 (Miss. Ct. App), *121*

American Seamount Corp. v. Science and Engineering Assocs. Inc., 812 P.2d 505 (Wash. Ct. App.), *319*

Andersen v. Weinroth, 849 N.Y.S.2d 210 (N.Y. App. Div.), *374*

Anderson v. Burson, 9 A.3d 870 (Md. Ct. Spec. App.), *286*

Aprigliano v. American Honda Motor Co., Inc., 979 F.Supp.2d 1331 (S.D. Fla.), *213*

Aroostook County Regional Ophthalmology Center v. NLRB, 81 F.3d 209 (D.C. Cir.), *355*

Arrington v. Liz Claiborne Inc., 688 N.Y.S.2d 544 (N.Y. App. Div.), *22*

Arthur v. Grimmett, 319 S.W.3d 711 (Tex. Ct. App.), *365*

Arthur Glick Leasing, Inc. v. William J. Petzold, Inc., 858 N.Y.S.2d 405 (N.Y. App. Div.), *222*

Asshauer v. Wells Fargo Foothill, 263 S.W.3d 468 (Tex. Ct. App.), *363*

Audio Visual Associates Inc. v. Sharp Electronics Corp., 210 F.3d 254 (4th Cir.), *60*

Auringer v. Department of Bldgs. of City of New York, 805 N.Y.S.2d 344 (N.Y.), *6*

Austin v. Countrywide Home Loans, 261 S.W.3d 68 (Tex. Ct. App.), *242*

A.V. ex rel. Vanderhye v. iParadigms, LLC, 562 F.3d 630 (4th Cir.), *70*

B

Baker v. Nationwide Mutual Insurance Company, 2013 WL 1905334, *477*

Balentine v. New Jersey Ins. Underwriting Ass'n, 966 A.2d 1098 (N.J. Super. Ct. App. Div.), *434*

Ballantyne v. C.I.R., 99 T.C. Memo. 2010-125 (T.C.), *304*

Bankston v. Pierce County, 301 P.3d 495 (Wash. App.), *361*

Barnes, Broom, Dallas and McLeod, PLLC v. Estate of Cappaert, 991 So.2d 1209 (Miss.), *354*

Barton v. Sclafani Investments Inc., 320 S.W.3d 453 (Tex. Ct. App.), *81*

Beach Capital Partnership, LP v. DeepRock Venture Partners, LP, 442 S.W.3d 609 (Tex. App.), *427–428*

Beckon Inc. v. AMCO Ins. Co., 616 F.3d 812 (8th Cir.), *479*

Bengal Motor Company, Ltd. v. Cuello, 121 So.3d 57 (Fla. App), *227*

Bennett v. Broderick, 858 N.E.2d 1044 (Ind. Ct. App.), *254*

Berg v. Traylor, 56 Cal. Rptr. 3d 140 (Cal. App.), *69*

Berger v. Solutions Inc., 911 A.2d 1164 (Del. Ch.), *416*

Beverick v. Koch Power Inc., 186 S.W.3d 145 (Tex. Ct. App.), *146*

Blanks v. Fluor Corp., 450 S.W.3d 308 (Mo. App.), *379*

Board of Hudson River–Black River Regulating Dist. v. Praetorian Ins. Co., 867 N.Y.S.2d 256 (N.Y. App. Div.), *448*

Bock v. Hansen, 170 Cal.Rptr.3d 293 (Cal. Ct. App.), *316*

Bolding v. Norsworthy, 270 S.W.3d 394 (Ark. Ct. App.), *486*

Bono v. McCutcheon, 824 N.E.2d 1013 (Ohio Ct. App.), *78*

Borley Storage and Transfer Co. Inc. v. Whitted, 710 N.W.2d 71 (Neb.), *258*

Boroian v. Mueller, 616 F.3d 60 (1st Cir.), *345*

Brackin v. Brackin, 894 N.E.2d 206 (Ind. Ct. App.), *152*

Brewster Park, LLC v. Berger, 14 A.3d 334 (Conn. App. Ct.), *516*

Brooklyn Union Gas Co. v. Diggs, 2003 WL 42106 (N.Y. City Civ. Ct), *54*

Brown Development Corp. v. Hemond, 956 A.2d 104 (Me.), *117*

Browning v. Palmer, 2008 WL 747934 (Ala. Civ. App.), *497*

Burley v. Gelco Corp., 976 So.2d 97 (Fla. Dist. Ct. App.), *463*

Burton v. Arkansas Secretary of State, 737 F.3d 1219 (8th Cir.), *338*

C

C&J Vantage Leasing Co. v. Wolfe, 795 N.W.2d 65 (Iowa), *103*

Cash v. Granite Springs Retreat Ass'n Inc., 248 P.3d 614 (Wyo.), *112*

Cater v. Bednarek, 969 N.E.2d 705 (Mass.), *488*

Catskill Hudson Bank v. A&J Hometown Oil, Inc., 115 A.D.3d 1090 (N.Y.A.D.), *478*

Central Laborers Pension Fund v. News Corp., 45 A.3d 139 (Del.), *425*

Central Plains Const. v. Hickson, 959 P.2d 998 (Okla. Ct. App.), *427*

Chapes v. Pro-Pac Inc., 473 B.R. 295 (E.D. Wis.), *419*

Charming Charlie, Inc. v. Perkins Rowe Associates, L.L.C., 97 So.3d 595 (La. App.), *366*

Chartier v. Farm Family Life Insurance Company, 113 A.3d 234 (Me.), *276*

Cheap Escape Co. Inc. v. Haddox LLC, 900 NE.2d 601 (Ohio), *12*

Chesler v. City of Derby, 899 A.2d 624 (Conn. App. Ct.), *327*

Chicago Bridge and Iron Co. NV v. F.T.C., 534 F.3d 410 (5th Cir.), *42*

Cincinnati Ins. Co. v. Leighton, 403 F.3d 879 (7th Cir.), *122*

City of Alexandria v. Brown, 740 F.3d 339 (5th Cir.), *128*

City of Waukegan, Illinois v. National Gypsum Co., 587 F.Supp. 997 (N.D. Ill.), *489*

City Rentals Inc. v. Kesler, 946 N.E.2d 785 (Ohio Ct. App.), *296*

Cloud Corp. v. Hasbro Inc., 314 F.3d 289 (7th Cir.), *194*

Coastal Agricultural Supply, Inc. v. JP Morgan Chase Bank, N.A., 759 F.3d 498 (5th Cir.), *295*

Columbia Ass'n Inc. v. Poteet, 23 A.3d 308 (Md. Ct. Spec. App.), *52*

Conference America Inc. v. Conexant Systems Inc., 508 F.Supp.2d 1005 (M.D. Ala.), *62*

Conner v. City of Dillon, 270 P.3d 75 (Mont.), *51*

Cook Tractor Co. Inc. v. Director of Revenue, 187 S.W.3d 870 (Mo.), *164*

Crystal Colony Condominium Ass'n Inc. v. Aspen Specialty Ins. Co., 6 F.Supp.3d 1295 (S.D. Fla.), *81*

Curren v. Carbonic Systems Inc., 872 N.Y.S.2d 240 (N.Y. App. Div.), *354*

Curtis v. Anderson, 106 S.W.3d 251 (Tex. App.), *115*

D

DaimlerChrysler Corp. v. Smelser, 375 Ark. 216 (Ark.), *58*

Danuser v. IDA Marketing Corp., 838 N.W.2d 488 (N.D.), *426*

Daugherty v. Allee's Sports Bar & Grill, 260 S.W.3d 869 (Mo. Ct. App.), *218*

de la Rama v. Illinois Dept. of Human Services, 541 F.3d 681 (7th Cir.), *347*

Del Lago Partners Inc. v. Smith, 206 S.W.3d 146 (Tex. Ct. App.), *173*

Della Ratta v. Larkin, 856 A.2d 643 (Md.), *426*

DeMott v. Old Town Trolley Tours of Savannah Inc., 760 S.E.2d 703 (Ga. App.), *178*

D.E. Shaw Laminar Portfolios, LLC v. Archon Corp., 755 F.Supp.2d 1122 (D. Nev.), *425*

DiMaio v. Com., 636 S.E.2d 456 (Va.), *31*

Dimension Funding, LLC v. D.K. Associates Inc., 191 P.3d 923 (Wash. Ct. App.), *207*

Drake v. Sagbolt, LLC, 112 A.D.3d 1132 (N.Y.A.D.), *172*

Driscoll v. Standard Hardware Inc., 785 N.W.2d 804 (Minn. Ct. App.), *233*

Drury v. Assisted Living Concepts Inc., 262 P.3d 1162 (Or. Ct. App.), *63*

Duddy v. Government Employees Ins. Co., 23 A.3d 436 (N.J. Super. Ct. App. Div.), *449*

Dumont Telephone Company v. Power & Telephone Supply Company, 962 F.Supp.2d 1064 (N.D. Iowa), *192*

E

Eagerton v. Vision Bank, 2012 WL 1139148 (Ala.), *460*

EA Management v. JP Morgan Chase Bank, N.A., 655 F.3d 573 (6th Cir.), *266*

E&G Food Corporation v. Cumberland Farms, Inc., 2011 Mass. App. Div. 204, *291*

Easterling v. Russell, 2015 WL 1198651 (Miss. Ct. App.), *147*

Eggl v. Letvin Equipment Co., 632 N.W.2d 435 (N.D.), *217*

Ellis v. DHL Exp. Inc. (USA), 633 F.3d 522 (7th Cir.), *348*

Elting v. Elting, 849 N.W.2d 444 (Neb.), *375*

Environmental Staffing Acquisition Corp. v. B&R Const. Management Inc., 725 S.E.2d 550 (Va.), *145*

Executive Risk Indem. Inc. v. Pepper Hamilton LLC, 891 N.Y.S.2d 1 (N.Y.), *435*

F

Farmers Ins. Exch. v. Crutchfield, 113 P.3d 972 (Or. Ct. App.), *183*

FCI Group Inc. v. City of New York, 862 N.Y.S.2d 352 (N.Y. App. Div.), *145*

Federal Ins. Co. v. Winters, 354 S.W.3d 286 (Tenn.), *124*

Ferris v. Fetters, 26 N.E.3d 1016 (Ind. Ct. App.), *71*

First Act Inc. v. Brook Mays Music Co., 429 F.Supp.2d 429 (D. Mass.), *25*

Flex Frac Logistics, L.L.C. v. N.L.R.B., 746 F.3d 205 (5th Cir.), *353*

Fostveit v. Poplin, 301 P.3d 915 (Or. App), *134*

Fox v. Lincoln Financial Group, 109 A.3d 221 (N.J.), *443*

Freedman v. State Farm Insurance Co., 93 Cal. Rept.3d 296 (Cal. Ct. App.), *446*

Freeze v. City of Dechert, Tenn., 753 F.3d 661 (6th Cir.), *353*

Froug v. Carnival Leisure Industries, Ltd., 627 So.2d 538 (Fla. Ct. App.), *101*

F.T.C. v. Publishers Business Services Inc., 821 F.Supp.2d 1205 (D. Nevada), *225*

G

Gajovski v. Estate of Philabaun, 950 N.E.2d 595 (Ohio Ct. App.), *145*

Gallwitz v. Novel, 2011 Ohio 297 (Ohio Ct. App.), *252*

Gardner v. Quicken Loans, Inc., 567 Fed. Appx. 362 (6th Cir.), *251*

Garofoli v. Whiskey Island Partners, Ltd., 25 N.E.3d 400 (Ohio App.), *158*

General Motors Acceptance Corp. v. Honest Air Conditioning and Heating Inc., 933 So.2d 34 (Fla. Dist. Ct. App.), *250*

Gen. Tire Inc. v. Mehlfeldt, 691 N.E.2d 1132 (Ohio Ct. App.), *147*

GGNSC Springfield LLC v. N.L.R.B., 721 F.3d 403 (6th Cir.), *335*

Golden v. Citibank, N.A., 853 N.Y.S.2d 261 (N.Y. App. Div.), *263*

Goodman v. Holmes & McLaurin Attorneys at Law, 665 S.E.2d 526 (N.C. Ct. App.), *378*

Grassi Design Group Inc. v. Bank of America, N.A., 908 N.E.2d 393 (Mass. App. Ct.), *297*

Great American Insurance Company v. Nextday Network Hardware Corporation, 2014 WL 7365805 (D. Md.), *207*

Grebing v. 24 Hour Fitness USA, Inc., 184 Cal. Rptr.3d 155 (Cal. App.), *184*

Greer v. Arroz, 330 S.W.3d 763 (Ky. Ct. App.), *179*

Grover v. Smarte Carte Inc., 836 F.Supp.2d 860 (D. Minn.), *340*

H

Hall v. Bean, 582 S.W.2d 263 (Tex. Civ. App.), *61*

Hall v. Hall, 27 N.E.3d 281 (Ind. Ct. App.), *146*

Hansen v. Fincantieri Marine Group, LLC, 763 F.3d 832 (7th Cir.), *346*

Hayes v. Southern New Hampshire Medical Center, 34 A.3d 1215 (N.H.), *485*

Hester v. District of Columbia, 505 F.3d 1283 (D.C. Cir.), *136*

Hetrick v. Ideal Image Development Corp., 372 Fed. Appx. 985 (11th Cir.), *395*

Hinton v. Sealander Brokerage, Co., 917 A.2d 95 (D.C.), *515*

HLT Existing Franchise Holding, LLC v. Worcester Hospitality Group, LLC, 994 F.Supp.2d 520 (S.D.N.Y), *140*

Hohertz v. Estate of Hohertz, 802 N.W.2d 141 (Neb. Ct. App.), *479*

Hotard v. Diabetes Self Management Center Inc., 838 So.2d 94 (La. Ct. App.), *396*

House Hasson Hardware Co., Inc. v. Lawson's Home Center, Inc., 772 S.E.2d 389 (Ga. App.), *116*

Hugh Dancy Co. Inc. v. Mooneyham, 68 So.3d 76 (Miss. Ct. App.), *353*

Hunt v. NationsCredit Financial Services Corp., 902 So.2d 75 (Ala. Civ. App.), *297*

Huszti v. Huszti, 451 B.R. 717 (Bankr. E.D. Mich.), *468*

I

Ingram v. State, 261 S.W.3d 749 (Tex. Ct. App.), *155*

In re Agriprocessors, Inc., 490 B.R. 852 (Bkrtcy. N.D. Iowa), *282*

In re American Remanufacturers Inc., 451 B.R. 349 (Bankr. D. Delaware), *199*

In re Arellano, 524 B.R. 615 (M.D. Pa.), *536*

In re Ausburn, 524 B.R. 816 (E.D. Ark.), *507*

In re Black Diamond Min. Co., LLC, 596 Fed. Appx. 477 (6th Cir.), *126*

In re Carmichael, 443 B.R. 698 (Bankr. E.D. Pennsylvania), *288*

In re Coffelt, 395 B.R. 133 (Bankr. D. Kan.), *503*

In re CTLI, LLC, 528 B.R. 359 (S.D. Tex.), *471*

In re Derer, 400 B.R. 97 (E.D. Tex.), *477*

In re Estate of Clemetson, 81 N.W.2d 388 (N.D.), *528*

In re Estate of Hollett, 834 A.2d 348 (N.H.), *94*

In re Estate of Lambert, 333 Mont. 444 (Mont.), *529*

In re Estate of McKenney, 953 A.2d 336 (D.C.), *91*

In re Estate of Miller, 446 S.W.3d 445 (Tex. Ct. App.), *312*

In re Estate of Moi, 135 (Wash. App. 1029), *531*

In re Estate of Robinson, 140 S.W.3d 782 (Tex. Ct. App.), *146*

In re Estate of Schmidt, 723 N.W.2d 454 (Iowa Ct. App.), *82*

In re Estate of Sheppard, 789 N.W.2d 616 (Wis. Ct. App.), *137*

In re Harris, 341 B.R. 660 (Ind.), *472*

In re HighSide Pork, L.L.C., 450 B.R. 173 (N.D. Iowa), *201*

In re Hintze, 525 B.R. 780 (N.D. Fla.), *461*

In re Hussain, 508 B.R. 417 (9th Cir. BAP.), *243*

In re Interdiction of Vicknair, 822 So.2d 46 (La. App.), *402*

In re Jennings, 533 F.3d 1333 (11th Cir.), *473*

In re Johnson, 371 B.R. 336 (Bankr. C.D. Ill.), *264*

In re Miller, 666 F.3d 1255 (10th Cir.), *240*

In re Palmer, 365 B.R. 816 (S.D. Ohio), *462*

In re Payless Cashways, 306 B.R. 243 (Bankr. 8th Cir.), *202*

In re Redondo Construction Corp., 411 B.R. 114 (Bankr. D. Puerto Rico), *273*

In re RLS Legal Solutions, LLC, 156 S.W.3d 160 (Tex. App.), *93*

In re Sekendur, 334 B.R. 609 (Ill.), *478*

In re Smith Trust, 731 N.W.2d 810 (Mich. Ct. App.), *62*

In re St. Felix, 436 B.R. 786 (E.D. Pennsylvania), *317*

In re Sunbelt Grain WKS, LLC, 427 B.R. 896 (Kan.), *204*

In re Target Corp. Data Sec. Breach Litigation, 2014 WL 7192478 (D. Minn.), *156*

In re Wolverine Fire Apparatus Co. of Sherwood Michigan, 465 B.R. 808 (E.D. Wisc.), *157*

Isaac v. Deutsche Bank Nat. Trust Co., 74 So.3d 495 (Fla. Dist. Ct. App.), *296*

J

Janet Travis, Inc. v. Preka Holdings, LLC, 856 N.W.2d 206 (Mich. App.), *26*

Jarl Investments, L.P. v. Fleck, 937 A.2d 1113 (Pa. Super. Ct.), *385*

Jasphy v. Osinsky, 834 A.2d 426 (N.J. Super. Ct. App. Div.), *159*

Jenkins v. Wachovia Bank, Nat. Ass'n, 711 S.E.2d 80 (Ga. Ct. App.), *296*

Jensen v. Bailey, 76 So.3d 980 (Fla. App.), *92*

J.H. Renarde Inc. v. Sims, 711 A.2d 410 (N.J. Super. Ct. Ch. Div.), *123*

Johnson v. Nelson, 290 Neb. 703, *433*

K

Kawasaki Kisen Kaisha, Ltd. v. Plano Molding Co., 696 F.3d 647 (7th Cir.), *179*

Kawasaki Kisen Kaisha Ltd. v. Regal-Beloit Corporation, 130 S. Ct. 2433, *169*

KCM Financial LLC v. Bradshaw, 2015 WL 1029652 (Tex.), *537*

Kelly v. Spain, 2015 WL 774658 (Fla.), *486*

King v. Bullard, 257 S.W.3d 175 (Mo. Ct. App.), *376*

Kiss Const. NY Inc. v. Rutgers Cas. Ins. Co., 877 N.Y.S.2d 253 (N.Y. App. Div.), *435*

Kolodziej v. Mason, 774 F.3d 736 (11th Cir.), *59*

Koss Corporation v. American Express Corporation, 309 P.3d 898 (Ariz. App. Div.), *264*

Kulovany v. Cerco Products Inc., 809 N.Y.S.2d 48 (N.Y. App. Div.), *178*

L

Lakes v. Grange Mut. Cas. Co., 964 N.E.2d 796 (Ind.), *452*

Lane-Lott v. White, 126 So.3d 1016 (Miss. Ct. App.), *87*

Lang v. Western Providers Physician Organization Inc., 688 N.W.2d 403 (S.D.), *417*

Lawson v. Hale, 902 N.E.2d 267 (Ind. Ct. App.), *234*

Layne v. Layne, 74 So.3d 161 (Fla. Dist. Ct. App.), *493*

L.D.F. Family Farm, Inc. v. Charterbank, 756 S.E.2d 593 (Ga. App.), *253*

Le Bel v. Donovan, 117 A.D.3d 553 (N.Y. App. Div.), *387*

Lee v. Mercedes-Benz USA, LLC, 622 S.E.2d 361 (Ga. Ct. App.), *235*

Legacy Hall of Fame Inc. v. Transport Trailer Service Inc., 139 So.3d 105 (Miss. App.), *74*

Lerma v. Border Demolition & Environmental Inc., 459 S.W.3d 695 (Tex. Ct. App.), *65*

Lewis v. City of Shreveport, 985 So.2d 1249 (La. Ct. App.), *170*

Liberty Mutual Insurance Company v. Zurich Insurance Company, 402 Ill. App. 3d 37 (Ill. App. Ct.), *174*

M

Macy's Inc. v. Martha Stewart Living Omnimedia, Inc., 127 A.D.3d 48 (N.Y.A.D.), *24*

Maimonides School v. Coles, 881 N.E.2d 778 (Mass. App. Ct.), *526*

Manasquan Savings & Loan Assn. v. Mayer, 236 A.2d 407 (Super. Ct. of N.J.), *72*

Marquardt v. Perry, 200 P.3d 1126 (Co. Ct. App.), *83*

Martello v. Santana, 713 F.3d 309 (6th Cir.), *100*

Martin v. Freeman, 272 P.3d 1182 (Co. Ct. App.), *367*

Matheny v. Unumprovident Corp., 594 F.Supp.2d 1212 (E.D. Wash.), *437*

Matveychuk v. Deutsche Lufthansa, AG, 2010 WL 3540921 (E.D.N.Y.), *171*

Mays v. Porter, 398 S.W.3d 454 (Ky. App.), *95*

McCurdy v. Hanover Fire & Casualty Insurance Co., 964 F.Supp.2d 863 (N.D. Ohio), *478*

McEvoy v. Aerotek Inc., 34 P.3d 979 (Ariz. Ct. App.), *59*

McPeters v. LexisNexis, 11 F.Supp.3d 789 (S.D. Tex.), *147*

Mellin v. Northern Security Insurance Company, Inc., 2015 WL 1869572 (N.H.), *431*

Mendoza v. Rast Produce Co. Inc., 45 Cal. Rptr. 3d 525 (Cal. Ct. App.), *354*

Mercury Ins. Co. of Florida v. Markham, 36 So.3d 730 (Fla. Dist. Ct. App.), *478*

Meteor Motors Inc. v. Thompson Halbach & Associates, 914 So.2d 479 (Fla. App.), *104*

Metro-Goldwyn-Mayer Studios Inc. v. Grokster, Ltd., 545 U.S. 913, *154*

Michigan v. Bay Mills Indian Community, 134 S.Ct. 2024 (U.S.), *5*

Miller v. Dombek, 390 S.W.3d 204 (Mo. App.), *80*

Miner v. New York State Dept. of Correctional Servs., 479 N.Y.S.2d 703 (N.Y. Sup. Ct.), *301*

Misita v. Conn, 138 So.3d 138 (Miss.), *496*

Mitsch v. General Motors Corp., 833 N.E.2d 936 (Ill. Ct. App.), *220*

Molloy v. Blanchard, 115 F.3d 86 (1st Cir.), *355*

Morgan v. New York Life Ins. Co., 559 F.3d 425 (6th Cir.), *341*

Morison v. Wilson Lake Country Club, 874 A.2d 885 (Me.), *405*

Moses v. Savedoff, 947 N.Y.S.2d 419 (N.Y. App. Div.), *425*

MTW Inv. Co. v. Alcovy Properties Inc., 616 S.E.2d 166 (Ga. Ct. App.), *139*

Mueller v. Kerns, 873 N.E.2d 652 (Ind. Ct. App.), *146*

Munar v. State Farm Ins. Co., 972 So.2d 1273 (La. Ct. App.), *178*

N

National Liability & Fire Ins. Co. v. R&R Marine Inc., 756 F.3d 825 (5th Cir.), *178*

Navigators Specialty Ins. Co. v. Nationwide Mutual Ins. Co., 50 F.Supp.3d 1186 (D. Ariz.), *459*

Newman v. Liebig, 810 N.W.2d 408 (Neb.), *542*

New Randolph Halsted Currency Exchange, Inc. v. Regent Title Insurance Agency, LLC, 939 N.E.2d 1024 (Ill. App.), *296*

Nichols v. Estate of Tyler, 910 N.E.2d 221 (Ind. Ct. App.), *73*

Nichols v. Zurich American Ins. Co., 423 S.W.3d 698 (Ky.), *89*

North Fork Bancorp., Inc. v. Toal, 825 A.2d 860 (Del. Ch.), *427*

O

Okelberry v. West Daniels Land Ass'n, 120 P.3d 34 (Utah), *398*

Oldja v. Warm Beach Christian Camp and Conference Center, 793 F.Supp.2d 1208 (E.D. Wash.), *151*

OneWest Bank, FSB v. Dorner, 953 N.E.2d 892 (Ohio Com. Pl.), *503*

O'Rourke v. McIlvaine, 19 N.E.3d 714 (Ill. App. Ct.), *328*

Orton v. Masquerade Inc., 716 S.E.2nd 764 (Ga. Ct. App.), *308*

Oshkosh Storage Co. v. Kraze Trucking, LLC, 2014 WL 7011850 (E.D. Wisc.), *166*

P

Pace v. Pace, 160 S.W.3d 706 (Tex. Ct. App.), *487*

Parrish v. Jackson W. Jones, P.C., 629 S.E.2d 468 (Ga. Ct. App.), *191*

Parsons ex rel. Cabaniss v. American Family Ins. Co., 40 N.W.2d 399 (Wis. Ct. App.), *72*

Pastimes, LLC v. Clavin, 274 P.3d 714 (Mont.), *53*

Patel v. CIR, 138 TC No. 23 (U.S. Tax Ct.), *484*

People v. Terry, 54 Cal. Rptr. 2d 769 (Cal.), *7*

People v. Trejo, 199 Cal. App. 4th 646 (Cal. App.), *61*

P.F.P. Family Holdings, L.P. v. Stan Lee Media Inc., 252 P.3d 1 (Co. Ct. App.), *414*

Pintos v. Pacific Creditors Ass'n, 605 F.3d 665 (9th Cir.), *227*

Precision Drywall & Painting Inc. v. Woodrow Wilson Constr. Co. Inc., 843 So.2d 1286 (La. Ct. App.), *79*

Process Posters Inc. v. Winn Dixie Stores Inc., 587 S.E.2d 211 (Ga. Ct. App.), *354*

Pugliese v. Mondello, 871 N.Y.S.2d 315 (N.Y. App. Div.), *376*

Q

Quedado v. Boeing Co., 276 P.3d 365 (Wash. Ct. App.), *323*

R

Reagan v. Lyberger, 156 S.W.3d 925 (Tex. Ct. App.), *372*

Rebel Distributors Corp. v. Devos, Ltd., 376 Fed. Appx. 772 (9th Cir.), *179*

Reed v. City of Chicago, 263 F.Supp.2d 1123 (N.D. Ill.), *223*

Reed v. Triton Servs., Inc., 15 N.E.3d 936 (Ohio Ct. App.), *140*

Regions Bank v. Maroone Chevrolet, L.L.C., 118 So.3d 251 (Fla. App.), *295*

REL Development Inc. v. Branch Banking and Trust Co., 699 S.E.2d 779 (Ga. Ct. App.), *267*

ReMapp Intern. Corp. v. Comfort Keyboard Co. Inc., 560 F.3d 628 (7th Cir.), *193*

Rice v. Rice, 499 F.Supp.2d 1245 (M.D. Fla.), *496*

Riggs v. Metropolitan Life Ins. Co., 940 F.Supp.2d 172 (D.N.J.), *442*

Robins v. Zwirner, 713 F.Supp.2d 367 (S.D.N.Y.), *234*

Robinson v. National Autotech Inc., 117 S.W.3d 37 (Tex. Ct. App.), *158*

Rochester Equipment & Maintenance v. Roxbury Mountain Service Inc., 891 N.Y.S.2d 781 (N.Y. App. Div.), *215*

Roy v. Woodstock Community Trust, Inc., 94 A.3d 530 (Vt.), *490*

Russell Realty Associates v. Russell, 724 S.E.2d 690 (Va.), *386*

S

Sabia v. Mattituck Inlet Marina & Shipyard, 805 N.Y.S.2d 346 (N.Y. App. Div.), *187*

Schaeffer v. United Bank & Trust Co. of Maryland, 360 A.2d 461 (Md. Ct. Spec.App.), *290*

Schettler v. RalRon Capital Corporation, 275 P.3d 933 (Nev.), *295*

Schneberger v. Schneberger, 979 So.2d 981 (Fla.Dist. Ct. App.), *541*

Schuhardt Consulting Profit Sharing Plan v. Double Knobs Mountain Ranch, Inc., 2014 WL 7185081 (Tex. Ct. App.), *51*

Sclafani v. Brother Jimmy's BBQ Inc., 930 N.Y.S.2d 566 (N.Y. App. Div.), *24*

SEC v. E-Smart Technologies Inc., 74 F.Supp.3d 306 (D.D.C.), *409*

Seikaly & Stewart, P.C. v. Fairley, 18 F.Supp.3d 989 (D. Ariz.), *30*

Service Employees Intern. Union, Local 250 v. Colcord, 72 Cal. Rptr. 3d 763 (Cal. Ct. App.), *329*

Shiftan v. Morgan Joseph Holding Inc., 57 A.3d 928 (Del. Ch.), *426–427*

Shoemaker v. Shoemaker, 745 N.W.2d 299 (Neb.), *426*

Silvestri v. Optus Software Inc., 814 A.2d 602 (N.J.), *133*

Singletary, III v. P&A Investments, Inc., 712 S.E.2d 681 (N.C. App.), *234*

Six L's Packing Co., Inc. v. Beale, 524 Fed. Appx. 148 (6th Cir.), *185*

S.N.R. Management Corp. v. Danube Partners 141, LLC, 659 S.E.2d 442 (N.C. Ct. App.), *303*

Soults Farms Inc. v. Schafer, 797 N.W.2d 92 (Iowa), *249*

Springob v. University of South Carolina, 757 S.E.2d 384 (S.C.), *113*

Stanford v. Paris, 703 S.E.2d 488 (N.C. Ct. App.), *532*

State v. Benoit, 311 P.3d 874 (Or.), *8*

State v. Egan, 287 So.2d 1 (Fla.), *3*

State v. Guyer, 353 S.W.3d 458 (Mo. Ct. App.), *18*

State v. Paige, 40 A.3d 279 (Conn.), *28*

State v. Rynhart, 125 P.3d 938 (Utah), *155*

State ex rel. Stenberg v. Consumer's Choice Foods, Inc., 755 N.W.2d 583 (Neb.), *287*

Steinberger v. Steinberger, 676 N.Y.S.2d 210 (N.Y. App. Div.), *114*

Sterling Development Group Three, LLC v. Carlson, 859 N.W.2d 414 (N.D.), *477*

Stokan v. Estate of Cann, 266 S.W.3d 210 (Ark. Ct. App.), *534*

Structural Polymer Group, Ltd. v. Zoltek Corp., 543 F.3d 987 (8th Cir.), *78*

T

Tacon v. Equity One Inc., 633 S.E.2d 599 (Ga. Ct. App.), *506*

Tauwab v. Huntington Bank, 2012 WL 760563 (Ohio Ct. App.), *505*

Taylor v. State, 879 N.E.2d 1198 (Ind. Ct. App.), *29*

Texas Ass'n of Psychological Associates v. Texas State Bd. of Examiners of Psychologists, 439 S.W.3d 597 (Tex. App.), *41*

Thompson v. Estate of Maurice, 150 So.3d 1183 (Fla. Dist. App.), *64*

Tracy v. Morell, 948 N.E.2d 855 (Ind. Ct.App.), *234*

Transcontinental Holding Ltd. v. First Banks Inc., 299 S.W.3d 629 (Mo. Ct. App.), *284*

Tri-County Nat. Bank v. GreenPoint Credit, LLC, 190 S.W.3d 360 (Ky. Ct. App.), *297*

Triffin v. Liccardi Ford Inc., 10 A.3d 227 (N.J. Super. Ct. App. Div.), *296*

Tri-Lin Holdings, LLC v. Flawlace, LLC, 2014 WL 1101577, *533*

Trost v. Trost, 525 Fed. Appx. 335 (6th Cir.), *192*

Trumbull Corp. v. Boss Constr. Inc., 801 A.2d 1289 (Pa. Commw. Ct.), *114*

Turner v. Firstar Bank, N.A., 845 N.E.2d 816 (Ill. App. Ct.), *479*

U

Unami v. Roshan, 659 S.E.2d 724 (Ga. App.), *100*

United Social and Mental Health Services Inc. v. Rodowicz, 899 A.2d 85 (Conn. App. Ct.), *542*

United States v. Rothberg, 2002 WL 171963 (N.D. Ill.), *33*

United States v. Zen Magnets, LLC, 2015 WL 2265385 (D. Colo.), *224*

Unlimited Opportunity, Inc. v. Waadah, 290 Neb. 629 (Neb.), *105*

UPS Supply Chain Solutions, Inc. v. Megatrux Transport, Inc., 750 F.3d 1282 (11th Cir.), *167*

Ureneck v. Cui, 798 N.E.2d 305 (Mass. App. Ct.), *106*

U.S. v. Agosto-Vega, 617 F.3d 541 (1st Cir.), *43*

U.S. v. Aguilar, 783 F.Supp.2d 1108 (C.D. Cal.), *34*

U.S. v. Steele, 595 Fed. Appx. 208 (4th Cir.), *32*

U.S. Bank Nat'l Assn. v. Marcino, 908 N.E.2d 1032 (Ohio Ct. App.), *273*

V

Valentín-Almeyda v. Municipality of Aguadilla, 447 F.3d 85 (1st Cir.), *339*

Ventura v. The Cincinnati Enquirer, 396 F.3d 784 (6th Cir.), *107*

Via v. Oehlert, 347 S.W.3d 224 (Tenn. Ct. App.), *371*

VisionStream, Inc. v. Director of Revenue, 2015 WL 3978835 (Mo.), *233*

Vitt v. Apple Computer Inc., 469 Fed. Appx. 605 (9th Cir.), *233*

Vonada v. Long, 852 A.2d 331 (Pa. Super.), *88*

W

Ward v. Stanford, 443 S.W.3d 334 (Tex. App.), *259*

Ward v. Ward, 874 N.E.2d 433 (Mass. App. Ct), *90*

Waterton v. Linden Motor Inc., 810 N.Y.S.2d 319 (N.Y. Civ. Ct.), *179*

Webadviso v. Bank of America Corp., 448 Fed. Appx. 95 (2d Cir.), *27*

Williams v. Baptist Health Systems Inc., 857 So.2d 149 (Ala. Civ. App.), *70*

Willnerd v. First Nat. Nebraska Inc., 558 F.3d 770 (8th Cir.), *342*

Wilson v. Brawn of California Inc., 33 Cal. Rptr.3d 7618 (Cal. Ct. App.), *205*

Winship v. Gem City Bone and Joint, P.C., 185 P.3d 1252 (Wyo.), *125*

W.L. Lindeman Operating Company, Inc. v. Strange, 256 S.W.3d 766 (Tex. App.), *153*

World of Boxing, LLC v. King, 56 F.Supp.3d 507 (S.D.N.Y.), *146*

Worley v. Wyoming Bottling Co. Inc., 1 P.3d 615 (Wyo.), *146–147*

Wright Group Architects-Planners, P.L.L.C. v. Pierce, 343 S.W.3d 196 (Tex. Ct. App.), *353*

WSG Palm Beach Development, LLC v. Blank, 990 So.2d 708 (Fla.Dist. Ct. App.), *542*

Y

Yates v. Holt-Smith, 768 N.W.2d 213 (Wis. Ct. App.), *407*

Young v. Wardley Corp., 182 P.3d 412 (Utah Ct. App.), *314*

Z

Zatakia v. Ecoair Corp., 18 A.3d 604 (Conn. App. Ct.), *135*

Glossary

A

abandon Discard with no intention to reclaim

abate To end or put to end

abatement Proportionate reduction in monetary bequest because of insufficient funds

abstract of title History of real estate

acceleration clause Clause allowing entire principal to be due

acceptance 1. Assent of buyer to become owner of goods; 2. Assent to an offer resulting in a contract; 3. Drawee's signed agreement to pay draft

acceptor Person who agrees to pay a draft

accession Acquiring property by the addition of personal property of another

accretion Addition to land by gradual water deposits

acknowledgment Declaration grantor has stated execution of instrument is free act

action of ejectment Action to have sheriff remove tenant

active fraud Party engages in action that causes the fraud

ademption Failure of bequest because property not in estate

administrative agency Governmental board or commission with authority to regulate matters or implement laws

administrator, administratrix, or personal representative Person appointed by court to administer estate of intestate

adverse possession Acquiring title to land by occupying it for fixed period

affirmative covenant Promise by grantee to do an act

agency Contract by which one party is authorized to contract for another

agency by *estoppel* Agency arising when one person leads another to believe third party is agent

agency coupled with an interest Agency in which agent has financial stake in performance of agency because of having given consideration to principal

agent Person appointed to contract on behalf of another

alien corporation One chartered in another country

allonge Paper so firmly attached to instrument as to be part of it

all-risk policy Policy covering all perils except those specifically excluded

alteration Unauthorized change or completion of negotiable instrument to modify obligation of a party

annual percentage rate (APR) Amount charged for loan as percentage of loan

annuity insurance Contract that pays monthly income to insured while alive

answer or motion Response of defendant to a complaint

anticipatory breach One party announces intention not to perform prior to time to perform

antitrust law Statute that seeks to promote competition among businesses

apparent authority Authority an agent is believed to have because of principal's behavior

appellate court Court that reviews decision of another court

articles of incorporation Document stating facts about corporation required by law

articles of partnership Written partnership agreement

assessment mutual company Mutual insurance company in which losses are shared by policyholders

assignee Person to whom a contract right is assigned

assignment 1. Conveyance of rights in a contract to a person not a party; 2. Transfer to another of tenant's rights

assignor Person making an assignment

attorney in fact General agent appointed by written authorization

auction Sale of property to the highest bidder

automated teller machine (ATM) EFT terminal that performs routine banking services

automobile insurance Insurance that the insured obtains to cover a car and possible injuries

B

bad check Check the drawee bank refuses to pay

baggage Articles necessary for personal convenience while traveling

bailee Non-owner in possession of bailed property

bailment Transfer of possession of personal property from owner on condition that property will be returned

bailor Person who gives up possession of bailed property

balloon payment   Payment more than twice the normal one

bank draft or teller's check   Check drawn by one bank on another

bearer   Payee of instrument made payable to whomever is in possession

bearer paper   Commercial paper payable to bearer

beneficiary   1. Person entitled to income or enjoyment of trust property; 2. Person who receives proceeds of life insurance

bequest or legacy   Personal property left by will

bidder   Person who makes the offer at an auction

bilateral contract   Contract consisting of mutual exchange of promises

bill of exchange   Another name for a draft

bill of lading   Receipt and contract between a consignor and a carrier

Bill of Rights   First ten amendments to U.S. Constitution

bill of sale   Written evidence of title to tangible personal property

binder   Temporary contract of insurance

blank indorsement   Indorsement consisting of signature of indorser

blind trust   Assets and administration of trust hidden from grantor

blue-sky laws   State laws to prevent sale of worthless stock

boardinghouse keeper   Person in business to supply accommodations to permanent lodgers

bond   Sealed, written contract obligation with essentials of note

bonding company   Paid surety

breach of contract   Failure or refusal to perform contractual obligations

broker   Agent with job of bringing two contracting parties together

business crime   Crime against a business or committed by using a business

business interruption insurance   Insurance covering loss of profits while business building is repaired

business law   Rules of conduct for the performance of business transactions

business tort   Tort caused by or involving a business

bylaws   Rules enacted by directors to govern corporation's conduct

C

cancellation   Act that indicates intention to destroy validity of an instrument

capital stock   Declared value of outstanding stocks

carrier   Transporter of goods, people, or both

cashier's check   Check drawn by bank on its own funds

caveat emptor   Let the buyer beware

certificate of deposit (CD)   Acknowledgment by bank of receipt of money with engagement to repay it

certified check   Check accepted by bank's writing certified on it

check   Draft drawn on a bank and payable on demand

check truncation   Shortening a check's trip from payee to drawer

civil law   Law dealing with enforcement or protection of private rights

close or closely held corporation   One with a very small number of shareholders

code   Collection of laws, rules, or regulations

codicil   Writing that modifies a will

coguarantors or cosureties   Two or more people jointly liable for another's obligation

coinsurance   Insured recovers in ratio of insurance to amount of insurance required

collateral note   Note secured by personal property

collective bargaining   Process by which employer and union negotiate and agree on terms of employment

color of title   One's apparent title

commercial unit   Quantity regarded as separate unit

common carrier   One that undertakes to transport without discrimination for all who apply for service

common law   English custom recognized by courts as binding on parties to a dispute

common stock   Stock that entitles owner to vote

communication   Telling something to a third person

community property   Property acquired during marriage owned separately and equally by both spouses

comparative negligence   Contributory negligence that reduces but does not bar recovery

compensatory damages   Amount equal to the loss sustained

complaint or petition   Written request to a court to settle a dispute

composition of creditors   When all of multiple creditors settle in full for a fraction of the amount owed

comprehensive policy   Insurance covering large number of miscellaneous risks

computer crime   Crime that is committed with aid of computers or because computers are involved

computer trespass   Unauthorized use of, or access to, a computer

concealment   Willful failure to disclose pertinent information

confusion   Inseparable mixing of goods of different owners

confusion of source   Representing goods or services as those of another

consideration   What promisor requires as the price for a promise

consignee   One to whom goods are shipped

consignment   Transfer of possession of goods for purpose of sale

consignor   One who ships by common carrier

consolidation   Combining two corporations to form a new one

constitution   Document that contains fundamental principles of a government

constructive bailment   Bailment imposed when a person controls lost property

constructive notice   Information or knowledge imputed by law

constructive trust   Trust created by court to correct a wrong

consumer goods or services   Goods or services primarily for personal, family, or household use

contract   Legally enforceable agreement

contract to sell   Agreement to transfer title to goods for a price

contribution   Right of coguarantor to recover excess of proportionate share of debt from other coguarantor(s)

contributory negligence   Negligence of the injured party

conversion   Obtaining possession of property and exercising ownership rights without permission

convict   Person found guilty by court of a major criminal offense

copyrights   Exclusive rights given to author of songs, books, and compositions

corporation   Association of people created by law into an entity

counteroffer   Offeree's response that rejects offer by varying its terms

coupon bond   Bond with detachable individual coupons representing interest payments

court of original general jurisdiction   Court of record in which case is first tried

court of record   Court in which an official record of the proceedings is kept

covenant   Promise in a deed

cram down   Reorganization plan imposed by court in spite of creditors'objections

creation   Bringing property into being

creditor   Party who receives guaranty

creditor beneficiary   Person to whom promisee owes obligation, which is discharged if promisor performs

crime   Offense against society

criminal law   Law dealing with offenses against society

cumulative preferred stock   Stock on which all dividends must be paid before common dividends

cumulative voting   Stockholder has votes equal to shares owned times number of directors to be elected

customary authority   Authority an agent possesses by custom

D

damages   A sum of money a wrongdoer must pay to an injured party

debarment   Prohibition on doing business with government

debenture   Unsecured bond issued by a business

debt   Obligation to pay money

deductible clause   Insurance provision whereby insured pays damage up to specified amount; company pays excess up to policy limits

deed   Writing conveying title to real property

deed of trust   Deed that transfers property to trustee for benefit of creditor

default   Breach of contractual obligation other than money

defendant   Person against whom a case is filed

defense clause   Policy clause in which insurer agrees to defend insured against damage claims

delegation   Transfer of duties

delivery   Intentional transfer of possession and control of something

depository bank   Bank receiving check for deposit

destination contract   Seller liable until goods delivered to destination

devise   Realty left by will

devisee   One receiving realty by will

disaffirmance   Repudiation of a voidable contract

discovery   Means of obtaining information from other party before a trial

disgorgement of profits   Having to pay back profits received illegally

dishonor   Presentment made, but acceptance or payment not made

disparate impact   Fair policy disproportionately affecting protected class

disparate treatment   Intentional discrimination against a particular individual

dissolution   Termination of corporation's operation except activities needed for liquidation

dissolution of a partnership   Change in relation of partners by elimination of one

diversity jurisdiction   Federal jurisdiction based on parties being from different states

dividend   Profits of a corporation allocated to stockholders

document of title   Document that shows ownership

domestic corporation   One chartered in the state

domestic relations court　Court that handles divorce and related cases

donee　Person who receives a gift

donee beneficiary　Third-party beneficiary for whom performance is a gift

donor　Person who makes a gift

dormant or sleeping partner　Partner unknown to public with no part in management

double indemnity rider　Policy requiring insurer to pay twice ordinary face amount if death is accidental

draft or bill of exchange　Written order by one person directing another to pay a sum of money to a third person

drawee　Person ordered to pay a draft

drawer　Person who executes a draft

durable power of attorney　Appointment of agency that survives incapacity of principal

duress　Obtaining consent by means of a threat

E

easement　An interest in land for nonexclusive or intermittent use

electronic fund transfer (EFT)　Fund transfer initiated electronically, telephonically, or by computer

embezzlement　Fraudulent conversion of property lawfully possessed

employment at will　Employment terminable by employer or employee for any reason

endowment insurance　Decreasing term insurance plus savings account

equipment　Goods for use in business

equity　Justice system based on fairness; provides relief other than merely money damages

estate　1. Interest in property; 2. Property left by a deceased

estoppel　One party leads the second to a false conclusion the second party relies on; the second party would be harmed if the first party were later allowed to show the conclusion to be false

ethics　Principles that determine the morality of conduct, its motives, and its duties

eviction　Expulsion of tenant from leased property

executed contract　Fully performed contract

executor or personal representative　Person named in will to administer estate

executory contract　Contract not fully carried out

existing goods　Goods that are in being and owned by the seller

exoneration　Guarantor's right to have creditor compel payment of debt

express authority　Authority of agent stated in agreement creating agency

express contract　Contract with the terms of the agreement specified in words

express trust　Trust clearly established as a trust

express warranty　Statement of guarantee made by a seller

F

face　Maximum insurer pays for loss

factor or commission merchant　Bailee seeking to sell property on commission

factor *del credere*　Factor who sells on credit and guarantees price will be paid

false representation　Misstatement of material fact

familial status　Whether or not tenant has children

federal court of appeals　Court that hears appeals in federal court system

federal district court　Trial court of federal court system

fee simple estate　Largest, most complete right in property

fellow servant　Employee with same status and working with another worker

felony　A more serious crime

fictitious name registration statutes　Law requiring operator of business under assumed name to register with state

fidelity bond　Suretyship for someone who handles another's money

fiduciary　A person in relationship of trust and confidence

finance charge　Total amount paid for credit

financing statement　Writing with signatures and addresses of debtor and secured party and description of collateral

firm offer　A merchant's signed, written offer to sell or purchase goods, saying it will be held open

fixture　Personal property so securely attached to real estate that it becomes part of the real estate

floating policy　Coverage no matter where property is located

forbearance　Refraining from doing something

***force majeure* clause**　Contract provision excusing performance when extraordinary event occurs

forcible entry and detainer action　Summary action by landlord to regain possession

foreclosure　Sale of mortgaged property to pay debt

foreign corporation　One chartered in another state

formal contract　Contract with special form or manner of creation

for-profit corporation　One organized to run a business and earn money

fraud Inducing another to contract as a result of an intentionally or recklessly false statement of a material fact

fraud in the execution Defrauded party did not intend to enter into a contract Indication by adult that a contract made by a minor is binding

fraud in the inducement Defrauded party intended to make a contract

free on board (FOB) Designated point to which seller bears risk and expense

friendly fire Fire contained where intended

full warranty Warranty with unlimited duration of implied warranties

fungible goods Goods of a homogeneous nature sold by weight or measure

future goods Goods not both existing and identified

G

gambling contract Agreement in which parties win or lose by chance

general agent Agent authorized to carry out particular kind of business or all business at a place

general partner Partner actively and openly engaged in business

general warranty deed Warrants good title free from all claims

gift Transfer without consideration

goods Movable personal property

grace period Thirty- or thirty-one-day period in which late premium may be paid without policy lapsing

grantee Person receiving title to property

grantor, settlor, or trustor 1. Creator of trust; 2. Person conveying property

guarantor or surety Party who agrees to be responsible for obligation of another

guest Transient received by hotel for accommodations

H

hacker Unauthorized outsider who gains access to another's computer system

hazards Factors that contribute to uncertainty

holder Person in possession of instrument payable to bearer or that person

holder in due course 1. Holder for value and in good faith with no knowledge of dishonor, defenses, or claims, or that paper is overdue; 2. Person who acquires rights superior to original owner

holder through a holder in due course Holder subsequent to holder in due course

holographic will Will written out by testator

homeowners policy Coverage of many perils for owners living in their houses

hostile fire Fire out of its normal place

hostile work environment Alteration of terms or conditions of employment by harassment

hotelkeeper One engaged in business of offering lodging to transients

I

identified goods Goods picked to be delivered to the buyer

implied authority Agent's authority to do things in order to carry out express authority

implied contract or implied in fact contract Contract with major terms implied by the parties' conduct

implied warranty Warranty imposed by law

incidental beneficiary Person who unintentionally benefits from performance of contract

incorporators People initially forming a corporation

Incoterms International commercial terms

indemnity Right of guarantor to be reimbursed by principal

independent contractor One who contracts to do jobs and is controlled only by contract as to how performed

indorsee Named holder of indorsed negotiable instrument

indorsement Signature of holder on back of instrument with any directions or limitations

indorser Payee or holder who signs back of instrument

inferior court Trial court that hears only cases involving minor offenses and disputes

injunction Court's permanent order forbidding an action

injunctive powers Power to issue cease-and-desist orders

injurious falsehood, commercial disparagement, or trade libel False statement of fact that degrades quality of another's goods or services

inland draft Draft drawn

innocent misrepresentation False statement made in belief it is true

insider Officer, director, or owner of more than 10 percent of stock

insurable interest Interest in nonoccurrence of risk insured against

insurable risk Danger covered by insurance

insurance Contract that transfers risk of financial loss for a fee

insured or policyholder Person protected against loss

insurer or underwriter Company writing insurance

intangible personal property Evidences of ownership of personal property

intellectual property   Property produced by human innovation and creativity

intestate   One who dies without a will

in the ordinary course of business   While the partner acts as a partner in the business and in the promotion of partnership interests

inventory   Articles purchased with intention of reselling or leasing

issue   First delivery of negotiable instrument by maker or drawer to give rights to another and payable in the United States

J

joint and several contract   Two or more people bound jointly and individually

joint and survivor annuity   Annuity paid until second of two people dies

joint contract   Contract obligating or entitling two or more people together to performance

joint tenancy   Multiple ownership in which, at death of one, that share passes to remaining owners

joint venture   Business relationship similar to partnership, except existing for single transaction only

joint-stock company   Entity that issues shares of stock, but investors have unlimited liability

judge, justice of the peace, magistrate, or trial justice   Chief officer of a court

judicial admission   Fact acknowledged in the course of legal proceeding

jurisdiction   Authority of a court to hear a case

juvenile court   Court that handles delinquent, dependent, and neglected children

L

landlord or lessor   Owner of leased property

larceny   Taking and carrying away of property without consent

last clear chance rule   Negligent driver recovers if other driver had one last clear chance to avoid injury

law   Governmental rule prescribing conduct and carrying a penalty for violation

law merchant   Rules applied by courts set up by merchants in early England

lawyer or attorney   Person licensed to represent others in court

lease   Contract between landlord and tenant

leasehold interest insurance   Covers cost of higher rent when leased building is damaged

legal rate   Interest rate applied when no rate is specified

legal tender   Any form of lawful money

legatee   One receiving personal property by will

license   Right to do certain acts on land

lien   Encumbrance or claim against property

life estate   Estate for duration of a person's life

life insurance   Contract of insurer to pay money on death of insured

life tenant   Person owning property for a lifetime

limited defense   Defense that cannot be used against a holder in due course

limited liability   Capital contribution is maximum loss

limited liability company (LLC)   Partnership-type organization but with limited liability

limited liability partnership (LLP)   Registered partnership whose members run business but have limited liability

limited partner   Partner who takes no active part in management and whom the public knows as a partner

limited partnership   Partnership with partner whose liability is limited to capital contribution

limited warranty   Written warranty, not a full warranty

liquidated damages   Sum fixed by contract for breach where actual damages are difficult to measure

long-arm statutes   Laws allowing a state to have jurisdiction over nonresidents

lost property   Property unintentionally left, with no intention to discard

M

maker   Person who executes a note

malpractice   Failure to perform with ability and care normally exercised by people in a profession

marshal   Executive officer of federal court

maximum contract rate   Highest legal rate of interest

mechanic's lien   Lien of people who have furnished materials or labor on property

merchant   Person who deals in goods of the kind or by occupation and thus is considered to have particular knowledge or skill regarding goods involved

merger   One corporation absorbed by another

minor   Person under the legal age to contract

misdemeanor   A less serious crime

misrepresentation   False statement of a material fact

model   Replica of an article

money order   Instrument issued by business indicating that payee may receive indicated amount

mortgage   Interest in real estate given to secure debt

mortgagee   Person who holds mortgage

mortgagor   Person who gives mortgage

movable personal property   All physical items except real estate

mutual insurance company   Company of policyholder investors

mutual mistake   Mistake by both parties to a contract

N

named peril policy   Policy covering only listed perils

necessaries   Items required for living at a reasonable standard

negative covenant   Agreement by grantee not to do an act

negligence   Failure to exercise reasonable care

negotiable instrument or commercial paper   Writing drawn in special form that can be transferred as substitute for money or as instrument of credit

negotiability   Transferability

negotiation   Act of transferring ownership of negotiable instrument

no-fault insurance   Insurance companies pay for their insureds' injuries regardless of fault

no-par-value stock   Stock without face value

nominal damages   Small amount is awarded when there is technical breach but no injury

nominal partner   Person who pretends to be a partner

noncumulative preferred stock   Stock on which current dividends must be paid before common dividends

nonparticipating preferred stock   Stock on which maximum dividend is stated percentage

nonresellable goods   Specially made goods not easily resellable

nontrading partnership   One devoted to professional services

not-for-profit corporation   One formed by private individuals for a charitable, educational, religious, social, or fraternal purpose

notice and comment rule making   Enacting administrative rules by publishing the proposed rule and then the final rule without holding formal hearings

novation   Termination of a contract and substitution of a new one with same terms but a new party

nuncupative will   Oral will made during last illness

O

offer   A proposal to make a contract

offeree   A person to whom an offer is made

offeror   A person who makes an offer

open policy   Policy that requires insured to prove loss sustained

option   Binding promise to hold an offer open

oral contract   Contract with terms spoken

order bill of lading   Contract allowing delivery of shipped goods to bearer

order paper   Commercial paper payable to order

ordinance   Law enacted by cities

ordinary or general partnership   Partnership with no limitation on rights and duties of partners

P

parol evidence   Oral testimony

parol evidence rule   Complete, written contract may not be modified by oral testimony unless evidence of fraud, accident, or mistake exists

participating preferred stock   Stock that shares with common stock in extra dividends

partition   Suit to divide joint tenancy

partner   Member of a partnership

partnership   Association of two or more people to carry on a business for profit

par-value stock   Stock with assigned face value

passive fraud   Failure to disclose information when there is duty to do so

patent   Absolute title to invention for fourteen or twenty years

pawn   Tangible personal property left as security for a debt

payee   Party to whom instrument is payable

payor bank   The drawee bank of a check

per capita   Per head

per se violation   Activity that is illegal regardless of its effect

per stirpes   Distribution among heirs according to relationship to deceased

perfected security interest   Seller's right to collateral that is superior to third party's right

personal property   Movable property; interests less than complete ownership in land or rights to money

physical damage insurance   Insurance for damage to car itself

piercing the corporate veil   Ignoring the corporate entity

pirated software   Software copied illegally

plaintiff   Person who begins a civil lawsuit

pledge   Intangible property serving as security for a debt

point-of-sale system (POS)   EFTs begun at retailers when customers pay for goods or services

policy   Written contract of insurance

polygraph   Lie detector

postdated check   Check drawn before its date

power of attorney   Writing appointing an agent

preauthorized credit   Automatic deposit of funds to an account

preauthorized debit   Automatic deduction of bill payment from checking account

precedent   Court decision that determines the decision in a subsequent, similar case

preemptive right   Right to purchase new shares in proportion to shares owned

preference   Disallowed transfer to a creditor

preferred stock   Stock giving special advantage

premium   Consideration paid by insured

presentment   Demand for acceptance or payment

price   Consideration in a sales contract

prima facie   On the face of it

prima facie **evidence**   Evidence sufficient on its face, if uncontradicted

primary liability   Liability without conditions for commercial paper that is due

principal   1. Person who appoints another to contract with third parties; 2. Party primarily liable

private carrier   Carrier that transports under special arrangements for a fee

private corporation   One formed to do nongovernmental function

privity of contract   Relationship between contracting parties

probate   Court procedure to determine validity of a will

probate court   Court that handles estates

procedural law   Law specifying how actions are filed and what trial procedure to follow

promissory estoppel   Substitute for consideration when another acts in reliance on a promisor's promise

promissory note   Unconditional written promise to pay sum of money to another

promoter   One who takes initial steps to form corporation

property   Anything that may be owned

property insurance   Contract by which insurer pays for damage to property

proprietor   Owner of sole proprietorship

prosecutor or district attorney   Government employee who brings criminal actions

prospectus   Document giving specified information about a corporation

protected class   Group protected by antidiscrimination laws

protest   Certification of notice of dishonor by authorized official

proxy   Person authorized to vote for another; written authorization to vote for another

proxy war   Attempt by competing sides to secure majority of stockholders' votes

public corporation   One formed for governmental function

public liability insurance   Insurance designed to protect third persons from bodily injury and property damage

publication   Testator's informing witnesses that document is will

punitive damages   Amount paid to one party to punish the other

purchase   Ownership by payment

Q

qualified indorsement   Indorsement that limits liability of indorser

quasi-contract or implied in law contract   Imposition of rights and obligations by law without a contract

quasi-public corporation   Public body with powers similar to corporations

quitclaim deed   Deed that transfers whatever interest grantor has in property

quorum   Minimum number of shares required to be represented to transact business

R

ratification   1. Approval of unauthorized act; 2. Indication by adult that a contract made while a minor is binding

real estate mortgage note   Note secured by mortgage on real estate

real property   Land and things permanently attached to land

receipt   Taking possession of goods

recognizance   Obligation entered into before a court to do an act required by law

redemption   Right to free property from lien of mortgage

reformation   Judicial correction of a contract

registered bond   Bond payable to specific person, whose name is recorded by issuer

remainder   Interest in life estate that goes to someone other than grantor on death of life tenant

renewable term insurance   Term insurance renewable without physical examination

rent   Amount paid landlord for possession of property

renunciation   Unilateral act of holder giving up rights in the instrument or against a party to it

reporting form for merchandise inventory   Policy allowing periodic reporting of inventory on hand to vary coverage amount

rescind   Set aside or cancel something

respondeat superior   Theory imposing liability on employers for torts of employees

restraining order   Court's temporary order forbidding an action

restrictive indorsement   Indorsement that restricts use of instrument

resulting or purchase money trust   Resulting trust created when person buys property but takes title in another's name

reversion   Interest of grantor in life estate that returns to grantor on death of life tenant

rider   Addition to insurance policy that modifies, extends, or limits base contract

right of survivorship Automatic ownership of property by survivors

right to take against the will Spouse's right to share of estate provided by statute if will leaves smaller share

risk or peril Danger of loss

robbery Taking property by force

rogue program Set of software instructions that produces abnormal computer behavior; see www.copyright.gov

S

sale Transfer of title to goods for a price

sale on approval Sale that is not completed until buyer approves goods

sale or return Completed sale with right to return goods

sample Portion of whole mass of transaction

secondary boycott Attempt by employees to stop third party from dealing with employer

secondary liability Liability for a negotiable instrument that has been presented and dishonored, and for which notice of dishonor has been given

secondary meaning Special meaning of a mark that distinguishes goods

secret partner Partner active but unknown to public

secured credit sale Sale in which seller retains right to repossess goods upon default

security agreement Written agreement signed by buyer that creditor has a security interest in collateral

setoff A claim by the party being sued against the party suing

several contract Two or more people individually agree to perform obligation

share Unit of stock

shareholder or stockholder Person who owns stock

shelter principle Rule giving holder rights of holder in due course

sheriff Court of record executive officer

shipment contract Seller liable until goods delivered to carrier

shoplifting Taking unpurchased goods from a store

shop right Employer's right to use employee's invention without payment of a royalty

short-swing profits Profits made by insider buying and selling corporation's stock in six months

sight draft Draft payable on presentation by holder

silent partner Partner who takes no part in firm

simple contract Contract that is not formal

sole proprietorship Business owned and carried on by one person

special agent Agent authorized to transact specific act or acts

special federal court Federal trial court with limited jurisdiction

special indorsement Indorsement that designates a particular person to whom payment is to be made

special warranty deed Warrants grantor has right to convey property

specific performance Carrying out the terms of contract

stale check Check presented more than six months after its date

stare decisis Principle that a court decision controls the decision of a similar future case

state court of appeals Intermediate appellate court

state supreme court Highest court in most states

statute Law enacted by legislative bodies

Statute of Frauds Law requiring certain contracts to be in writing

statute of limitations Time within which the right to sue must be exercised or lost

stock corporation One in which ownership is represented by stock

stock insurance company Corporation of stockholder investors

stock option Right to purchase shares at set price

straight bill of lading Contract requiring delivery of shipped goods to consignee only

strict liability Manufacturer of product liable without proof of negligence for dangerous product

sublease Transfer of less than a tenant's full rights under a lease

subrogation Right of insurer to assume rights of insured

subscriber One who agrees to buy stock in proposed corporation

subscription agreement Written agreement to buy stock

summons or process Notice of suit

Supreme Court of the United States The highest court in the United States

T

tangible personal property Personal property

tenancy at sufferance Holdover tenant without landlord's permission that can be seen, touched, and possessed

tenancy at will Tenancy for uncertain period

tenancy by the entirety Co-ownership by husband and wife with right of survivorship

tenancy for years Tenancy for any definite period

tenancy from month to month Tenancy for flexible period with monthly rent

tenancy from year to year   Tenancy for indefinite period with yearly rent

tenancy in common   Multiple ownership in which, at death, one owner's share passes as will directs or to heirs

tenancy or owner in partnership   Ownership of partner in partnership property

tenant or lessee   Possessor of leased property

tender of payment   Offer and ability to pay money owed

tender of performance   Offer to perform in satisfaction of terms of contract

term insurance   Contract whereby insurer assumes risk of death of insured for specified time

testamentary trust   Trust created in will

testator or testatrix   Person making a will

theft   Taking another's property without consent

third-party beneficiary   Person not party to contract but whom parties intended to benefit

time draft   Draft payable specified number of days or months after date or presentation

title   1. Evidence of ownership of property; 2. Ownership

tort   Private wrong for which damages may be recovered

tortfeasor   Person whose action causes injury

trade acceptance   Draft drawn by seller on purchaser of goods

trade fixtures   Fixtures used in business

trade secrets   Secret, economically valuable information

trademark   Word, symbol, device, or combination of them used to identify and distinguish goods

trademark or trade name dilution   Lessening the capacity of a famous mark to identify and distinguish goods

trademark or trade name infringement   Unauthorized use or imitation of another's mark or name

trading partnership   One engaged in buying and selling

trailing edge   Left side of front of check

traveler's check   Instrument like cashier's check but requiring signature and countersignature by its purchaser

treasury stock   Stock reacquired by a corporation

trial court   Court that conducts original trial of a case

trust   Contract by which one holds property for another

trustee   1. Legal owner of trust property; 2. One who holds title to property for another

U

***ultra vires* contract**   Contract exceeding corporation's powers

uncured default   Not all payments on instrument fully made and not all made by due date

undue influence   Person in special relationship causes another's action contrary to free will

unenforceable contract   Agreement that is not currently binding

unfair competition   Total impression of product results in confusion as to its origin

unilateral contract   Contract calling for an act in consideration for a promise

unilateral mistake   Mistake by one party to a contract

unit pricing   Price stated per unit of measurement

universal defense   Defense against any holder

unjust enrichment   One party benefiting unfairly at another's expense

unlimited liability   Business debts payable from personal assets

usury   Charging higher rate of interest than the law allows

V

valid contract   Contract enforceable by law

valued policy   Policy that fixes values for insured items

venue   Location where a case is to be tried

verdict   Decision of a jury

violation or infraction   Offense less serious than a misdemeanor

void   Of no legal effect

voidable contract   Enforceable agreement that may be set aside by one party

voting trust   Device whereby stock is transferred to trustee to vote it

voucher check   Check with voucher attached

W

warehouse receipt   Document of title issued by storage company for goods stored

warranty   1. Assurance article conforms to a standard; 2. Statement of insured that relates to the risk and appears in insurance contract

warranty deed   Deed with guarantees

watered stock   Stock paid for with property of inflated value

whistleblower   Person who exposes wrongdoing in an organization

will Document providing disposition of property after death

winding up Taking care of outstanding obligations and distributing remaining assets

with reserve Auction goods may be withdrawn after bidding starts

without reserve Auction goods may not be withdrawn after bidding starts

wobbler An offense that can be either a felony or a misdemeanor

writ of *certiorari* Order to produce record of a case

written contract Contract with terms in writing

Index

A

Abandoned property, 155
Abate, 517
Abatement, 531
Abstracts of title, 498
Acceleration clauses, 252, 504
Acceptance
  contracts, 63–65
  defined, 63, 191, 260
  drafts, form of, 261
Acceptors, 241
Accession, 152
Accommodation sureties, 457
Accountings, 313, 374–376, 464
Accretion, 489
Acknowledgements, 497
ACPA (Anticybersquatting Consumer Protection Act), 27
Actions of ejectment, 519
Active fraud, 92
Acts of God, 165
ADA (Americans with Disabilities Act), 342–343
ADEA (Age Discrimination in Employment Act), 340–341
Ademption, 531
Administrative agencies, 6, 39–41
Administrative agency orders, 6, 105
Administrators, 114–115, 527, 534–535
Administratrix, 527
Admissions, 19, 261–262

Adverse possession, 489–490
Advertisements, 60, 225
Affirmative covenants, 495
After-born children, 531
Age Discrimination in Employment Act (ADEA), 340–341
Agency
  overview, 300
  creation of, 306–307
  importance of, 301
  parties involved, 300–302
  powers delegated in, 301
  termination, 316–319
  third persons, principals and, 316
Agency by *estoppel*, 307
Agents
  authority of, 304–305
  classification of, 302–304
  defined, 300
  duties to principals, 312–313
  employees compared, 308
  independent contractors compared, 308
  liability of, 283–284
  negotiable instruments, liability for, 283–284
  principal's duties to, 314–315
  third persons, liabilities to, 315–316
Agreements, contracts compared, 49
AIDS testing, 344
Alien corporations, 394
All-risk policies, 445

Allonges, 272
Alterations, 135, 291
Ambiguity in contracts, 116–117
Americans with Disabilities Act (ADA), 342–343
Annual percentage rates (APR), 226
Annuity insurance, 444
Answers, 18
Anticipatory breach, 138
Anticybersquatting Consumer Protection Act (ACPA), 27
Antitrust, 41–42
Apparent authority, 305
Appeals, 19–20
Appellate courts, 13, 17
Applications
  for Employer Identification Number, 359–360
APR (annual percentage rates), 226
Armed forces wills, 529
Articles of incorporation, 384, 396–397
Assault, 22
Assessment mutual companies, 432
Assessments, 504, 520
Assigned risk rule, 453
Assignees, 122
Assignment
  effect of, 125–126
  form of, 125
  generally, 122–123
  leases, 517, 519
  life insurance, 444
  mortgages, 508
  notice of, 124
  negotiable instruments, 243

technicalities of, 124–127
  warranties of assignor, 126-127
Assignors, 122
Assumption of mortgages, 507
Assumption-of-risk, 326
At-will employees, 323–324
Attorneys, 17
Attorneys in fact, 304
Auctions, 193, 202–203
Authority of agents, 304–305
Automated teller machines (ATM), 245
Automobile insurance, 448–453

B

Bad checks, 265
Baggage, 171
Bailees, 156
Bailments, 156–160, 206. *See also* Carriers; Hotelkeepers
Bailors, 156
Bank drafts, 263–264
Bankruptcy
  overview, 467
  agency and, 318
  assignment and, 124
  Chapter 7, 469–470
  Chapter 11, 470
  Chapter 13, 470
  contract termination and, 135
  counseling requirement, 469
  courts, 13
  debtor's duties, 472
  defined, 467
  discharge, 473–474
  exempt property, 471

included property, 471
negotiable instruments and, 290
partnerships and, 388
priority of claims, 473
proof of claims, 472
reclamations, 472
reviving debts after, 82
types of claims, 472–473
types of debtors, 468–469
who can file, 468
Banks, 265–268
Battery, 22
Bearer paper, 239–240, 276–277
Bearers, 242
Beneficiaries, 431, 443, 535
Bequests, 527
Betting contracts, 101–102
Bidders, 193
Bilateral contracts, 54
Bill of Rights, 4
Bills of exchange. *See* Drafts
Bills of lading, 164, 166–169
Bills of sale, 186–187
Binders, 431
Blank indorsements, 274
Blanket policies, 445
Blind trusts, 537
Blood testing, 344
Blue-sky laws, 407
Blurring, 27
Boardinghouse keepers, 171
Boards of directors, 412, 418–420
Bodily injury insurance, 450–451
Bona fide purchasers for value, 206–209
Bonding companies, 456
Bonds, 258–259
Bottom lines, ethics and, 9
Breach of contract, 48, 95–96, 138–141
Bribery, 34

Brokers, 304
Business contracts, minors, 70
Business crimes
overview, 27–28
computer crimes, 29–32
copyright infringement, 32
defined, 27
Foreign Corrupt Practices Act, 33–34
RICO, 29–30
theft, 28
Business ethics, 9–10
Business interruption insurance, 445
Business law, 2
Business names, 359, 372–373, 397–398
Business organization. *See* Corporations; Partnerships; Sole proprietorships
Business reorganization, 470
Business torts, 23–27
Bylaws, 397

C

Cancellation, 277
Capacity for wills, 525–526
Capacity to contract, 68–74
Capital stock, 401
Car insurance, 448–453
Carriers
overview, 163–165
common carriers, 164–165
defined, 163
of goods, 165–171
of people, 169–171
private carriers, 164
Cash on delivery (COD), 202
Cashier's checks, 263
Causation, 22
Caveat emptor, 220–221
Cease and desist orders, 225

CERCLA (Comprehensive Environmental Response, Compensation, and Liability Act), 44–45
Certificates of deposit (CD), 260
Certified checks, 263
Cestui que trusts, 535
CFR (Cost and Freight), 203
Chapter 7, 469–470
Chapter 11, 470
Chapter 13, 470
Charity, pledges to, 82
Check truncation, 244–245
Checks. *See also* Drafts
bank duties, 265–267
customer duties, 267–268
defined, 262
negotiability and, 252–253
types of, 263–265
Children. *See* Minors
CISG (United Nations Convention on Contracts for the International Sale of Goods), 188, 203
Civil action, procedures for, 18–20
Civil law, 6–8
Civil Rights Act of 1964, 337–339
Clayton Act, 42, 105
Clean Air Act, 43
Clean Water Act (CWA), 43
Close corporations, 394
Closely held corporations, 394
COD (cash on delivery), 202
Codes, 5
Codes of professional responsibility, 9
Codicils, 529
Coguarantors, 458
Coinsurance, 446–447
Collateral notes, 259

Collective bargaining, 335
Collision insurance, 450
Color of title, 490
Commerce Clause, 4
Commercial disparagement, 25
Commercial paper. *See* Negotiable instruments
Commercial units, 206
Commission merchants, 303
Commissions, 6, 39–41
Common carriers, 164–165. *See also* Carriers
Common consent, 153
Common law, 3
Common stock, 403
Communication, 25, 59
Community property, 487
Comparative negligence, 23, 452
Compensation, 314, 406
Compensatory damages, 139
Complaints, 18
Component parts, 223
Composition of creditors, 79
Comprehensive Environmental Response, Compensation, and Liability Act (CERCLA), 44–45
Comprehensive policies, 450
Computer crimes, 29–33
Computer Fraud and Abuse Act, 31–32
Computer trespass, 30–31
Concealed defects, 520
Concealment, 92, 434–435
Conditional delivery, 289
Confidential relationships. *See* Fiduciary relationships
Confidentiality, 328

Confusion about products, 25–27
Confusion of personal property, 152–153
Confusion of source, 25
Connecting carriers, 168
Consent orders, 225
Consequences, ethics and, 8–9
Consideration
  adequacy of, 78–82
  assignment and, 125–126
  deeds, 495
  defined, 77
  exceptions to requirement for, 82–83
  nature of, 77–78
Consignees, 164
Consignments, 157, 207
Consignors, 164
Consolidations, 421
Constitutions, 4
Construction contracts, 132–133
Constructive bailment, 156, 157
Constructive notice, 216
Constructive trusts, 537
Consumer credit contracts, 286
Consumer goods or services, 286, 462
Consumer loans, 103
Consumer paper, 286–287
Consumer Product Safety Commission (CPSC), 224
Consumer protection, 224–230
Consumer sales, 461
Continuous succession, 397
Contract offers
  defined, 57
  duration of, 61–63
  invitations to make, 60–61
  requirements for, 57–59
Contract termination
  acceptance of breach, 138

force majeure clauses, 138
  impossibility of performance, 136–138
  by operation of law, 134–135
  performance, 131–134
  remedies for breach, 138–141
  by voluntary agreement, 135–136
Contracts. See also Agency; Breach of contract; Contract offers; Contract termination; Unlawful contracts; Written contracts
  acceptance of, 63–65
  agreements compared, 49
  assignment, 122–127
  capacity to contract, 68–74
  classification of, 49–54
  consideration, 77–83
  cosignors, 72
  counteroffers, 64
  defined, 48
  delegation, 123–124
  duress, 93–94
  fraud and, 90–93
  joint and several contracts, 128
  joint contracts, 127
  memorandums and, 115–116
  minors, misrepresenting age, 72
  mistakes and, 86–90
  not to compete, 104–105
  novation, 121–122
  oral contracts, 110–111
  parol evidence rule, 116–117
  partnerships and liability, 377–378
  privity of contract, 221–222
  remedies for fraud, duress, undue influence, 95–96

requirements for, 49
  to sell, 183–184
  several contracts, 127
  Statute of Frauds and, 111–116
  third-party beneficiaries, 120–121
  ultra vires contracts, 398
  unconscionable contracts, 226–227
  undue influence, 94–95
  written contracts, 110–117
Contribution, 377, 458–459
Contributory negligence, 23, 325
Conversion, 449
Convicts, 74
Copyright infringement, 32, 154
Copyrights, 153–154
Corporate seals, 398
Corporations. See also Stock
  boards of directors, 412, 418–420
  classification of, 392–394
  combinations of, 421
  dissolution of, 318, 421
  dividends, 406–407
  formation of, 394–395
  management overview, 412–413
  officers, 418–421
  ownership of, 402
  powers of, 397–398
  promoters and, 395
  stockholder rights, 417–418
  stockholders' meetings, 413–417
  stock issuance, 395–396
  ultra vires contracts, 398
Cosignors, 72, 457
Cost and Freight (CFR), 203

Cosureties, 458
Counteroffers, 64
Coupon bonds, 258
Court of Appeals for the Federal Circuit, 14–15
Court of International Trade, 13–14
Court officers, 17
Courts
  classification of, 13–17
  courts of record, 18–20
  function of, 11
  jurisdiction of, 12–13
  of original jurisdiction, 17
  small claims court, 20
  state versus federal, 11
Covenants, 495–496
CPSC (Consumer Product Safety Commission), 224
Cram downs, 470
Creation, 153
Creditor beneficiaries, 121
Creditors, 456
Crimes, 7, 378. See also Business crimes
Criminal copyright infringement, 32
Criminal law, 7–8
Cumulative preferred stock, 404
Cumulative voting, 415
Current monthly income, 470
Customary authority, 305, 380
CWA (Clean Water Act), 43

D

Damages, 2, 138–141
Death
  agency and, 318
  assignment and, 125
  checks, payment after, 267
  contract termination and, 137
  partnerships and, 387
  Statute of Frauds and, 114

Debarment, 35
Debentures, 260
Debtors, 461
Debts
    defined, 113
    guaranty and surety-
        ship for, 455–460
    part payment as con-
        sideration, 79
    of record, 82
    reviving of, 82, 135
    Statute of Frauds and,
        113–115
Deductible clauses, 450
Deductibles, 450
Deeds, 492–497
Deeds of trust, 508–509
Default, 113. *See also*
    Breach of contract
Defective agreements
    duress, 93–94
    fraud, 90–93
    mistakes, 86–90
    undue influence,
        94–95
Defective goods, 214
Defendants, 18
Defense clauses, 447–448
Deficiency judgments,
    508
Delegation, 123–124
Delivery, 253–254, 289,
    497
Demand notes, 252
Depositions, 18
Depository banks,
    275–276
Descent, 152, 533–535
Destination contracts,
    202
Destruction of con-
    tract subject matter,
    136–137
Devisees, 527
Devises, 527
Diligence, 313
Dilution, 27
Directors, 412, 418–420
Disabilities, 343, 443
Disability income riders,
    442
Disability insurance
    benefits, 331

Disaffirmance, 71
Disclaimers of warran-
    ties, 219–221
Discovery, 18–19
Discrimination, 172,
    336–343, 523
Disgorgement of profits,
    35
Dishonor, 281–282
Disparate impact, 338
Disparate treatment, 337
Dissolution, 318, 367,
    383–389, 421
District attorneys, 7
Diversity jurisdiction,
    13, 15
Dividends, 406–407
Divisible contracts, 100
Divorce, 531
DNA testing, 345–346
Documents of title, 208
Domain names, 27
Domestic corporations,
    394
Domestic relations
    courts, 17
Donee beneficiaries, 121
Donees, 152
Donors, 152
Dormant partners, 364
Double indemnity riders,
    442
Double jeopardy, 7
Drafts, 240, 260–262.
    See also Checks
Drawees, 241
Drawers, 241
Drinks, warranties for,
    218
Drug testing, 344
Drug use, capacity to
    contract, 74
Duress, 93–96, 290

E

Easements, 488
Economic duress, 94
EEOC (Equal
    Employment
    Opportunity
    Commission), 339,
    341

Ejectment actions, 519
Elections, 415
Electronic
    Communications
    Privacy Act, 30
Electronic fund transfer
    (EFT), 244–245
Electronic Fund Transfer
    Act (EFTA), 244
Electronic Signatures in
    Global and National
    Commerce Act, 115
Embezzlement, 28
Emotional duress, 94
Employee handbooks,
    324
Employee Polygraph
    Protection Act (EPPA),
    343
Employees, 308
Employees' rights
    overview, 334–335
    discrimination and,
        336–343
    protections for,
        346–349
    testing, 343–346
    union representation,
        335–336
Employer and employee
    relationship
    common law and, 322
    creation of, 323–324
    employee duties to
        employer, 328–329
    employer defenses,
        325–326
    employer duties and
        liabilities, 324–325,
        328–329
Employment at will, 324
Employment contracts,
    noncompetition agree-
    ments, 104–105
Employment loss, 348
Endorsements. *See*
    Indorsements
Endowment insurance,
    441
English legal system, 3
Entrustees, 206–207
Environmental protec-
    tion, 43–45

EPPA (Employee
    Polygraph Protection
    Act), 343
Equal Employment
    Opportunity
    Commission (EEOC),
    339, 341
Equal Pay Act, 340
Equipment, 461–462
Equity, 3–4
Estates, 114–115, 525
Estoppel, 208, 307, 434,
    436
Ethics, 8–10
Eviction, 522
Executed contracts, 53
Executive officers, 17
Executors, 114–115, 527
Executory contracts, 53
Exemplary damages, 139
Exempt property, 471
Existing goods, 185
Exoneration, 459
Express authority, 304
Express contracts, 50
Express misrepresenta-
    tions, 92
Express powers of cor-
    porations, 397
Express trusts, 536
Express warranties,
    212–214
Expulsion, 385
Extended coverage, 445
Extraordinary bail-
    ments. *See* Carriers;
    Hotelkeepers

F

Face of policies, 431
Factorages, 303
Factors, 303
Factors *del credere*,
    303–304
Fair Credit Reporting
    Act (FCRA), 227–230
False imprisonment, 22
False representations,
    435–436
Faltering company
    exception, 348
Familial status, 523

Merchants, 217
Mergers, 421
Minimum contacts, 12
Minimum wages, 11
Minors
  agency and, 302
  capacity to contract, 69–72
  insurance and, 432
  negotiable instruments and, 290
  voidable contracts, 50
Mirror-image rule, 65
Misdemeanors, 7
Misrepresentations, 92
Mistakes, 86–90, 95–96
Mistakes of law, 90
Mitigation of damages, 520
Models, 216
Money orders, 262
Morality, 8
Mortgage insurance, 509
Mortgagees, 501
Mortgages
  overview, 501
  assignment, 508
  contracts for, 502–503
  deeds of trust instead, 508–509
  defined, 501
  foreclosure of, 507–508
  mortgagor duties, 504–505
  mortgagor rights, 505–507
  notes for, 259
  recording, 503–504
Mortgagors, 501
Motions, 18
Movable personal property, 182–183
Mutual-benefit bailments, 159
Mutual insurance companies, 432
Mutual mistakes, 86

N

Named peril policies, 445

Names for businesses, 359, 372–373, 397
National Labor Relations Board (NLRB), 335–336
Necessaries, minors and, 69–70
Necessity, agency by, 307
Negative covenants, 495
Negligence, 21
Negligence torts, 22–23
Negotiability, 249, 272–273
Negotiable instruments. *See also* Checks; Holders in due course; Indorsements
  assignment of, 243
  bearer paper and obligations of negotiators, 276–277
  classification of, 240–241
  date and place requirements, 254
  defenses to liability, 287–291
  defined, 52, 238
  discharge of, 277
  drafts, 240, 260–262
  electronic fund transfer and, 244–245
  face of the paper, liability for, 280–283
  history of, 238–239
  incomplete instruments, 254, 289
  indorsements, 239, 243, 272–273
  instruments of collection, 244
  instruments of credit, 244
  issue and delivery, 253–254
  multiple payees, 273–274
  negotiation of, 239, 243
  notes, 257–260
  order paper and bearer paper, 239–240
  parties to, 241–243

requirements for, 248–253
  Statute of Frauds and, 192
  warranties, liability for, 283
Negotiation, 239, 243
NLRB (National Labor Relations Board), 335–336
No-fault insurance, 452
No-par-value stock, 405
Nominal damages, 138–139
Nominal partners, 364
Noncumulative preferred stock, 404
Nonparticipating preferred stock, 404
Nonregulatory agencies, 40
Nonresellable goods, 193
Nontrading partnerships, 362
Not-for-profit corporations, 393
Notes, 257–260
Notes and memorandums, Statute of Frauds and, 115–117
Notice and comment rule making, 41
Notice of dishonor, 282
Novation, 121–122, 507
Nuisances, 517
Nuncupative wills, 529

O

Obamacare, 331
Obedience, 313
Obstructing administration of justice, 107
Occupational Safety and Health Administration (OSHA), 327
Offerees, 57
Offerors, 57
Offers
  defined, 57
  duration of, 61–63
  invitations to make, 60–61

requirements for, 57–59
Office of Foreign Assets Control (OFAC), 40
Officers, 418–421
Old-age benefits, 330
Open policies, 445
Opinions, 93, 213
Options, 61
Oral contracts, 53, 110, 191–194
Oral wills, 529
Order bills of lading, 169
Order paper, 239–240
Orders to pay, 250, 252–253
Ordinances, 4–5
Ordinary partnerships, 362
OSHA (Occupational Safety and Health Administration), 335
Owner in partnership, 373

P

Paid sureties, 457
Par-value stock, 405
Parodies, 27
Parol evidence, 116
Parol evidence rule, 116–118
Part payment as consideration, 79
Part performance, 111
Partially secured creditors, 473
Participating preferred stock, 404
Partners, 361
Partnerships
  overview, 361–367
  authority of partners, 379–380
  defined, 361
  dissolution of, 383–389
  distribution of assets, 389
  duties of partners, 373–375

joint-stock company compared, 364–365
joint ventures compared, 365
liabilities of partners, 377–378
LLCs compared, 365
LLPs compared, 365
notice of dissolution, 388–389
partner interest in property, 373
partnership agreements, 370–372
partnership liabilities, 378–379
profits and losses, sharing of, 380
rights of partners, 375–377
Passengers, 169–171
Passive fraud, 91, 92–93
Past performance as consideration, 81–82
Patent infringement, 217
Patents, 153, 329
Patient Protection and Affordable Care Act, 331
Pawns, 159
Payees, 241
Payor banks, 282
Payroll taxes (FICA), 331
Per capita, 533–534
Per se violations, 42
Per stirpes, 533–534
Perfection of security interests, 461–463
Performance, 131–133, 136–137
Peril or risk, 431
Perpetual succession, 397
Personal defenses, 287, 288–289
Personal jurisdiction, 12
Personal property. *See also* Bailments; Sales of goods
overview, 150–151
acquisition of, 151–155

defined, 150
distinguishing from real property, 482–483
trusts for, 535–538
Personal representatives, 527
Personal services, 122, 141
Petitions, 18
Physical damage insurance, 448–449
Physical duress, 94
Piercing the corporate veil, 367
Pirated software, 32
Plaintiffs, 18
Plant closings, 348
Pledges, 82, 159
Point-of-sale systems (POS), 245
Policies, 431
Policyholders, 431
Polygraph testing, 343–344
Postdated checks, 265
Powers of attorney, 306
Pre-incorporation, 395
Preauthorized credits, 245
Preauthorized debits, 245
Precedent, 5
Preemptive rights, 417
Preferences, 471
Preferred stock, 403–404
Premiums, 431
Prepayment clauses, 252
Presentment, 261, 281
Price-fixing, 105
Prices, sales of goods, 184–185
Prima facie, 372
Prima facie evidence, 372
Primary liability, 280
Principals, 300, 456
Private carriers, 164. *See also* Carriers
Private corporations, 393–394
Privity of contract, 221
Probate, 532
Probate courts, 17

Procedural law, 18–20
Process, 18
Product liability, 23, 221–222
Product safety standards, 224
Prohibition of unfair labor practices, 336
Promises as consideration, 77–78
Promises to pay, 250
Promissory estoppel, 83
Promissory notes, 240–241, 257–268
Promoters, 394, 395
Proof of claims, 472
Property. *See* Personal property; Real property
Property damage insurance, 451
Property insurance, 433–434, 444–446
Proprietors, 359
Prosecutors, 7
Prospectus, 408
Protected classes, 337
Proxies, 414, 415
Proximate cause, 23
Proxy wars, 416–417
Public corporations, 393
Public liability insurance, 450
Public policy, unlawful contracts and, 106–107
Public service, contracts injuring, 107
Publication, 528
Puffing, 213
Punitive damages, 139
Purchase money trusts, 537
Purchases, 151

Qualified acceptance, 261
Qualified indorsements, 275
Quasi contracts, 54
Quasi-public corpora-

tions, 393
Quiet enjoyment, 517
Quitclaim deeds, 493
Quorums, 414

R

Racketeer Influenced and Corrupt Organizations Act (RICO), 29, 30
Racketeering activity, 29
Railway Labor Act of 1947, 335
Random drug testing, 344
Ratification, 71, 72, 95, 307
Real estate mortgage notes, 259
Real property. *See also* Landlord and tenant; Mortgages
abandonment of, 155
acquisition of, 489–490
deeds to, 492–495
defined, 183, 482
distinguishing from personal property, 482–483
easements, 488
estates in, 487–488
fixtures, 462, 483
licenses, 489
multiple ownership, 484–487
specific performance, 141
Statute of Frauds and, 111–112
trusts for, 535–538
Reasonable accommodations, 343
Receipt, 191
Reclamations, 472
Recognizances, 52
Recording, 498, 503–504
Redemption, 464, 506
Reformation, 96
Registered bonds, 259
Registration statements, 408

Regulations. *See* Government regulations

Regulatory agencies, 39–40

Reimbursement of agents, 314–315

Reliance, *promissory estoppel*, 83

Remainders, 488

Renewable term insurance, 441

Rent, 512, 518

Rentals. *See* Landlord and tenant

Renunciation, 277, 318

Repairs, 518–519

Replacement value, 447

Reporting form for merchandise inventory, 446

Repossession, 463

Resale, 463

Rescission, 96, 140

Reservation of title, 205

Resource Conservation and Recovery Act, 44

Respondeat superior, 327

Restraining orders, 4

Restraint of trade, 104–105

Restrictive indorsements, 275

Resulting trusts, 537

Return rights, 205–206

Reversions, 488

Revised Uniform Partnership Act, 387, 388

Revocation, 62, 317, 530–531

RICO (Racketeer Influenced and Corrupt Organizations Act), 29, 30

Riders, 431

Right of survivorship, 485

Right to attorney, 7

Rights to take against the will, 526

Risk or peril, 431

Rivers, 483

Robbery, 449

Robinson-Patman Act, 42, 105

Rogue programs, 31

Rule against perpetuities, 527

Rule-making, 40–41

Rule of reason approach, 41–42

S

Safety, workplace, 325, 327

Sales of goods. *See also* Statute of Frauds; Warranties
  bills of sale, 186–187
  classification of, 200
  consumer protection issues, 224–230
  contracts for services compared, 184
  contracts to sell compared, 183–184
  damage to or destruction of, 203–205
  defined, 183
  existing goods, 185
  future goods, 185
  illegal sales, 187
  international sales contracts, 187–188
  issues possible with, 199–200
  ownership and risk of loss issues, 200–203
  price, 184–185
  property subject to, 182–183
  sales on approval, 205
  sales or returns, 205–206
  title, 183, 198
  title transfers, special rules for, 206–209

Sales on approval, 205

Sales or returns, 205–206

Samples, 206

Sarbanes–Oxley Act, 420–421

Satisfactory performance, 132–133

Seals, 51–52, 398

Search and seizure, 344

Secondary boycotts, 336

Secondary liability, 280–282

Secondary meanings, 26

Secondhand goods, 219

Secondhand smoke, 349

Secret partners, 364

Secured credit sales, 460–463

Secured parties, 461

Securities Act of 1933, 408

Securities and Exchange Commission (SEC), 394, 408

Securities Exchange Act of 1934, 408–409

Securities Investor Protection Act of 1970, 409

Securities Investor Protection Corporation (SIPC), 409

Security agreements, 460

Security devices
  guaranty and suretyship, 455–460
  secured credit sales, 460–463

Seller's opinions, 213

Serious health conditions, 347

Service marks, 27

Setoffs, 286

Settlors, 536

Several contracts, 127

Sexual harassment, 338–339

Shareholders, 402

Shares of stock, 394, 402. *See also* Stock

Shelter principle, 286

Sheriffs, 17

Sherman Antitrust Act, 41, 105

Shipment contracts, 202

Shop rights, 329

Shoplifting, 28

Short-swing profits, 409

Sight drafts, 252, 260

Signatures, 194–195, 249, 282–283, 496–497

Silence, 63–64, 92–93

Silent partners, 363

Simple contracts, 51–53

SIPC (Securities Investor Protection Corporation), 409

Sleeping partners, 364

Small claims court, 20

Smoking, 349

Social regulatory agencies, 40

Social Security Act, 329–331

Sole proprietorships, 359–361

Special agents, 302

Special courts, 17

Special federal courts, 13

Special indorsements, 274–275

Special warranty deeds, 494–495

Specific performance, 4, 140–141

Specific policies, 445

Squatter's rights, 489

Stale checks, 266

Standard of proof, 7

Stare decisis, 5

State agencies, 41

State constitutions, 4

State consumer protection agencies, 230

State courts, 16–17

State courts of appeals, 16, 17

Statute of Frauds, 111–115, 190–195

Statute of limitations, contract termination and, 134–135

Statutes, 4–5

Stock
  certificates, 402
  classes of, 403–404
  corporations, 394
  defined, 401
  dividends, 406–407

exchange trading, 102
issuance of, 395–396
kinds of, 405–406
options, 406
ownership and, 402
sales laws, 407–409
shares of stock, 394
transfer of, 402–403
Stock insurance companies, 432
Stockholders, 402
Stop-payment orders, 266–267
Straight bills of lading, 168–169
Streams, 483
Strict liability, 23
Subagents, 313
Subchapter S corporations, 394
Subject matter jurisdiction, 12
Subleases, 517
Subrogation, 436, 458
Subscribers, 395–396
Subscribing witnesses, 528
Subscription agreements, 395–396
Substantial performance, 133
Suicide, 442
Summons, 18
Sunday contracts, 102
Superfund, 44, 45
Supervisory employees, 335
Supreme Court, U.S., 4, 6, 14, 15, 16
Supreme courts, state, 4, 6, 17
Sureties, 456
Suretyship and guaranty, 455–460
Survivors' benefits, 330

T

Takeovers, 421
Tangible personal property, 151
Tarnishing, 27
Taxes, 331, 366, 504, 520

Teller's checks, 263–264
Tenancy at sufferance, 516
Tenancy at will, 516
Tenancy by the entirety, 486–487
Tenancy for years, 515
Tenancy from month to month, 515–516
Tenancy from year to year, 515
Tenancy in common, 484–485
Tenancy in partnership, 373
Tenants, 512
Tender of payment, 132
Tender of performance, 132
Tender offers, 421
Term insurance, 441
Termination. See Contract termination
Testamentary capacity, 525–526
Testamentary trusts, 537–538
Testators, 525
Testatrix, 525
Testing, 343–346
Theft, 28, 289, 449
Theft insurance, 449
Third-party beneficiaries, 120–121
Third persons. See also Agency; Agents
assignment, 122–127
breach of warranty, 223
delegation, 123–124
employer liability to, 327–328
joint and several contracts, 128
joint contracts, 127
malpractice and, 141
novation, 121–122
several contracts, 127
Statute of Frauds and, 114
third-party beneficiaries, 120–121
TILA (Truth in Lending Act), 226

Time drafts, 260
Time is of the essence clauses, 132
Title, 183, 198, 208–209, 492–498
Title insurance, 498
Title VII, 337–339
Tolling, 135
Tortfeasors, 22
Torts
overview, 21–22
business torts, 23–24
defined, 21
intentional, 22
minors, misrepresenting age, 72
negligence torts, 22–23
partnerships and liability, 377–378
Trade acceptance, 261
Trade fixtures, 523
Trade libel, 25
Trade name dilution, 27
Trade name infringement, 26
Trade secrets, 154
Trademark dilution, 27
Trademark infringement, 27, 217
Trademarks, 25–27, 154
Trading partnerships, 362
Trailing edges, 272
Transcripts, 19–20
Traveler's checks, 265
Treasury stock, 405
Trespass, 22, 30–31
Trial courts, 13
Trial justices, 17
Trial procedure, 19
Trustees, 508–509, 535
Trustors, 536
Trusts, 535–538
Truth in advertising, 225
Truth in Lending Act (TILA), 226

U

UCC. See Uniform Commercial Code (UCC)
Ultra vires contracts, 398

Unconscionable contracts, 226
Uncured defaults, 285
Underinsured motorist coverage, 451
Underwriters, 431
Undue influence, 94–95
Unemployment compensation, 330–331
Unenforceable contracts, 50
Unfair competition, 27, 105
Unfair labor practices, 336
Uniform Commercial Code (UCC). See also Statute of Frauds
acceptance, manner of, 65
allonges, 272
alterations, 291
breach of warranty, 223
carriers' liability, 166
certificates of deposit, 260
defined, 5
express warranties, 212–213
fixed amount of money, 251
guaranties, 458
issue, 253–254
leases, application to, 219
modification of sales contracts, 83
negotiable instruments, 239
offer definiteness, 58
presentment, 281
privity of contract not required, 221
reasonable promptness under, 268
sales of goods as governing, 182
seals and, 52
services not governed by, 184
unconscionable contracts, 226
warranties, 283

Uniform Disposition of Unclaimed Property Act, 155
Uniform Partnership Act. *See also* Revised Uniform Partnership Act
overview, 362
evidence of partnership, 372
indemnification, 377
partnership liabilities, 379
property, how held, 373
Uniform Stock Transfer Act, 402–403
Unilateral contracts, 53–54
Unilateral mistakes, 86
Uninsured motorist coverage, 451
Union representation, 335–336
NLRB, 335–336
unfair labor practices prohibition, 336
Unions, 324
Unit pricing, 225
United Nations Convention on Contracts for the International Sale of Goods (CISG), 187–188, 203
Universal defenses, 280, 289–290
Universal life insurance, 442
Unjust enrichment, 54, 111
Unlawful contracts
overview, 99–100
administrative agency orders and, 105
gambling, 101–102
illegality from change of law, 137
prohibited articles, sale of, 104
public policy and, 106–107

Sunday contracts, 102
unlicensed operators, 103
unreasonable restraint of trade, 104–105
usurious contracts, 102–103
Unlicensed operators, 103
Unlimited liability, sole proprietorships, 359, 361, 363
Unreasonable restraint of trade, 104–105
Unsecured creditors, 473
U.S. Constitution, 4
U.S. Court of Federal Claims, 13, 14, 15
U.S. Department of Veterans Affairs (VA), 509
U.S. Supreme Court, 4, 6, 14, 15–16
U.S. Tax Court, 13, 14
Usage of trade, 220
Used goods, 219
Usurious contracts, 102–103
Usury, 102, 226

V

VA (U.S. Department of Veterans Affairs), 509
Value, 284–285
Valued policies, 445
Vegetation, 483
Venue, 12–13
Verdicts, 19
Violations, 7
Viruses, 31
Void agreements, 50
Voidable contracts, 50
Voidable title, 208–209
Voluntary debtors, 468
Voluntary subscriptions, 82
Voting, 414–415, 416
Voting trusts, 415
Voucher checks, 264

W

Wages, 122
War, agency and, 319
Warehouse receipts, 200
WARN (Worker Adjustment and Retraining Notification Act), 348
Warranties
of all sellers, 214–216
assignment and, 126–127
of conformity, 216
defined, 212
against encumbrances, 216
exclusion or surrender of, 219–221
express warranties, 212–214
of fitness for a particular purpose, 216
full warranties, 214
implied warranties, 214
of indorsers, 276
against infringement, 217
insurance and, 436
limited warranties, 214
of merchantability, 217
of merchants, 217
negotiable instruments, 283
in particular sales, 218–219
product liability and, 221–222
of title, 214–215
Warranty deeds, 493–495
Wars, 319, 442
Water Pollution and Control Act, 43
Watered stock, 406
Whistleblowers, 421
Whole life insurance, 441
Williams–Steiger

Occupational Safety and Health Act, 327
Wills
abatement and ademption, 531–532
administrators for, 534–535
capacity for, 525–526
characteristics of, 527
codicils to, 529
defined, 525
descent laws, 533
formalities of, 527–528
limitations on disposition of property in, 526–527
probate of, 532
revocation of, 530–531
terminology, 527
to transfer title, 152
types of, 528–529
wording of, 529–530
Winding up, 383–384
With reserve, 194
Withdrawal of partners, 384
Without reserve, 194
Witnesses, 527–528
Wobblers, 7
Worker Adjustment and Retraining Notification Act (WARN), 348
Workers' compensation, 326–327
Workplace safety, 325, 327
Writ of *certiorari*, 15
Written contracts
alteration of, 135
defined, 53
notes and memorandums, 115–116
parol evidence rule, 116–117
reasons for, 110–111
state requirements, 115
Statute of Frauds and, 111–115